The Iconography Of Manhattan Island, 1498-1909

Compiled From Original Sources And Illustrated By Photo-Intaglio Reproductions Of Important Maps, Plans, Views, And Documents In Public And Private Collections

I. N. Phelps Stokes

Alpha Editions

This Edition Published in 2021

ISBN: 9789354484582

Design and Setting By
Alpha Editions
www.alphaedis.com
Email – info@alphaedis.com

THE ICONOGRAPHY OF MANHATTAN ISLAND

·1498 ✻ 1909·

·COMPILED·FROM·ORIGINAL·SOVRCES·
·AND·ILLVSTRATED·BY·PHOTO-INTAGLIO·
·REPRODVCTIONS·OF·IMPORTANT·
·MAPS·PLANS·VIEWS·AND·DOCVMENTS·
·IN·PVBLIC·AND·PRIVATE·COLLECTIONS·

BY
·I·N·PHELPS·STOKES·

NEW YORK
·ROBERT·H·DODD·
MDCCCCXV

TO

THE DEEP FEELING OF

LOVE AND VENERATION FOR HOME AND LIBERTY

AND TO THE EVER GROWING CONSCIOUSNESS

OF HIGH RESPONSIBILITY

WHICH WARMED THE HEARTS AND GUIDED THE ACTIONS OF

THE TRUE LEADERS

AMONG OUR DUTCH, ENGLISH, AND AMERICAN FORBEARS

THIS RECORD OF THEIR MATERIAL ACHIEVEMENTS

IS PROUDLY, YET HUMBLY, INSCRIBED

WITH THE HOPE AND BELIEF

THAT THE SAME SPIRIT WILL EVER CONTINUE

A CHIEF STRENGTH AND INSPIRATION

TO SUCCEEDING GENERATIONS OF

HAPPY SOJOURNERS UPON

MANHATTAN

ISLAND

PREFACE

PURPOSE AND METHOD

THE ICONOGRAPHY OF MANHATTAN ISLAND represents the result of a two-fold purpose: to collect, to condense, and to arrange systematically and in just proportion, within the confines of a single work, the facts and incidents which are of the greatest consequence and interest in the history of New York City, with special reference to its topographical features and to the physical development of the island; and to illustrate this material by the best reproductions obtainable of important and interesting contemporary maps, plans, views, and documents; in other words, to produce a book dealing with the physical rather than with the personal side of the city's history, which shall be at the same time useful and interesting to the student of history, the antiquarian, the collector, and the general public. It was originally hoped that this end could be accomplished within the compass of a single volume; but as the work progressed and its scope naturally broadened, the amount of available material of a quality to deserve inclusion proved to be so great that this ideal was reluctantly abandoned, as impossible of accomplishment. The general catalogue of the New York Public Library alone, under the heading of "New York City," was found to contain more than 10,000 titles, representing probably half that number of separate books dealing in one way or another with the city.

To have read, or even to have examined cursorily, this great mass of material would have been impossible; notwithstanding the encouragement offered by the conspicuous example of G. M. Asher, who tells us that, in the preparation of his *Essay on the Dutch Books and Pamphlets relating to New-Netherland,* in one single summer he bestowed "at least a searching glance" on seven thousand pamphlets in the Royal Library at The Hague, seven thousand in the Thysiana Library at Leyden, and eight thousand at Amsterdam, besides consulting many manuscript and printed authorities, and examining critically many hundred maps. Naturally, the greater part of these titles in the Public Library could be put aside at once as relating to subdivisions of the subject foreign to our particular field of investigation, or as being of too specialised a character to be immediately useful.

In addition to a careful examination of such well-known sources as *Records of New Amsterdam, Documentary History of New York, New York Colonial Documents, Ecclesiastical Records, Calendars of Historical Manuscripts* (*Dutch and English*), *Journals of the Assembly, Laws of New York,* and *Minutes of the Common Council,* and of such authorities as Brodhead, O'Callaghan, Mrs. Lamb, Mrs. Van Rensselaer, and Riker, every promising title was investigated, and several hundred works, both printed and manuscript, were read or carefully scrutinised. The most important of these, as well as a number of newly discovered sources, will be found described in the Bibliography and in the Cartography. These researches, beginning in the New York Public Library, were eventually extended to cover the principal libraries and collections of America, and included the New York Historical Society, the various city departments, the State Library at Albany, the office of the Secretary of State, the Library of Congress, the American Antiquarian Society, the Boston Public Library, the Massachusetts Historical Society, the Massachusetts Archives, the Connecticut Historical Society, the Rhode Island Historical Society, the John Carter Brown Library, the New Jersey Historical Society, the Newberry Library, of Chicago, the Library Company of Philadelphia, and the Historical Society of Pennsylvania.

Investigations were also undertaken abroad, personally, as well as through agents and by correspondence, more especially for the Cartography, in connection with which government archives and the principal libraries and private collections of Europe were investigated; and even in South America, where the Surinam records, at Paramaribo in Dutch

Guiana, were examined in the hope that they might add something to our knowledge of the early years of the Dutch occupation of New York. These researches have extended over a period of six years and have covered most of the known sources and repositories of information.

From the outset, the chief aim has been to secure accuracy and to give full references to all authorities quoted. Original sources have been used whenever available, and no effort has been spared to discover and to develop new sources of information. The disastrous fire which, in 1911, consumed the precious manuscripts and other treasures of the State Library, almost on the eve of their removal to the present fire-proof building of the State Education Department, destroyed many unique and invaluable records, especially of the Dutch and early English periods, which would have helped as nothing else ever can to complete our knowledge of those remote times. At first it seemed that this irreparable loss, which occurred when the present work was hardly fairly under way, must so seriously handicap its successful completion as to render the task hopeless. Fortunately, however, the loss, although appalling, proved less complete than had at first been supposed, and many manuscript records of the first importance finally emerged from the salvage, fire-scarred and water-stained, it is true, but still decipherable. It was the writer's fortune to be present during the second day of the fire and to assist the State Archivist, Mr. van Laer, in saving from the flames and recovering from the débris, the charred remains of many precious records. Through the kindness of the library authorities, who extended every facility for the examination of such records as were saved, as soon as they had been temporarily repaired, and thanks to the long familiarity of Mr. Paltsits, then State Historian, with the contents of the archives, it proved possible after all to secure much valuable information from this source. Fortunately, too, the author had himself examined many of the more important documents before the fire, and had secured photographs of some, alas too few, of those which were destroyed. He had also had prepared a brief list of the most important maps, plans, and views contained in the library's collections.

Although, as a rule, in selecting material for the ICONOGRAPHY, reliable documentary evidence has been insisted upon, it has seemed best not to ignore entirely the legends or myths, which are the poetry of history, and which often contain more truth than the demonstrable facts which have passed the test of higher criticism. Moreover, it cannot justly be denied that tradition, although frequently discredited by the modern historical scientist, often preserves the spirit if not the letter of truth. A conscientious and persevering attempt has, however, been made to trace such myths to their source, so that the reader may be in a position to judge intelligently for himself of their exact historical value or interest.

Where it has been impossible to reach definite conclusions, both sides of the case have usually been stated, and the reader has been left to draw his own conclusions; this despite the scathing remarks written many years ago by Mr. Henry Stevens on the "would be historians and 'narrative' writers of New York and Boston," who, he tells us, in his delightful little book of reminiscences of James Lenox, "are industriously picarooning and compiling 'history' by stringing together an ostentatious show of discordant authorities, relevant, irrelevant and contradictory, leaving the victimized reader to draw his own conclusions because, as historians, they either are not able to form a sound opinion, or dare not express it."

In its completed form, the present work aims to constitute a comprehensive history of the Island of Manhattan and of the City of New York, from the earliest times down to the Hudson-Fulton Celebration (1498-1909); and special efforts have been made to discover new information relating to the pre-Hudsonian explorations in the immediate vicinity of Manhattan Island, and to the period of the island's first settlement and early development.

Feeling that, perhaps, some readers may be interested to know why the work was undertaken, as well as how it was carried on, I shall state the facts briefly before describing the plan and scope of the ICONOGRAPHY.

I had long been interested, in a desultory sort of way, in historical prints, and especially in views of Old New York, and from time to time had yielded to the temptation to buy some old map or view which, because of its quaint or decorative qualities, made a particular appeal to my imagination. I well remember my first purchase—a fine copy of the Nicholas Visscher Map, bought from Richmond, I think in 1892—and I now reflect with sorrow upon the many neglected opportunities of the following years.

One afternoon in the early summer of 1908, an itinerant dealer brought to my office several early views, among them a fine impression of the Carolus Allard View with Ships, from the *Orbis Habitabilis*, which I bought for $15, and happening not to be very busy, indulged in a half hour's chat about early New York prints, as a result of which my dormant interest became keenly aroused. Shortly afterwards, my attention was attracted by a sign on Fourth Avenue, announcing an exhibition of Old New York City views. I went in, and an hour later emerged the proud and happy owner of a full dozen respectable, if not very valuable, prints. My enthusiasm now rapidly increased, and soon knew no bounds. I pored with delight over Mr. Andrews's *New Amsterdam New Orange New York*, studied Asher's *List of Maps and Charts*, and read everything else I could find on my chosen subject. I rushed from dealer to dealer, and spent every spare moment feverishly delving through portfolios and drawers of old stock, and in a few weeks had scraped together a very decent little collection of prints, at prices which to-day seem ridiculously small. I now began to correspond with out-of-town and foreign dealers, and by the end of the summer had secured some really good and rare pieces, and had begun to have some idea what prints of the city existed, and to understand something of their relative interest, rarity, and value.

As I look back now to the enthusiasm of those early days of collecting, I realise that I must have experienced much the same feelings—although hardly so well justified—that Mr. Henry Stevens suggests, in his reminiscences already referred to, when he paused to consider the result of his first fortnight's bibliographical hunt in London, in which he had "scooped" the market of American rarities.

There were at that time very few collectors of old New York prints. Mr. Ogden Goelet had died some years before, and the only other specialists in this field who had made collections worthy of the name were Mr. William Loring Andrews, Mr. Amos F. Eno, Mr. John D. Crimmins, Mr. William F. Havemeyer, Mr. Francis W. Ford, Mr. and Mrs. H. H. Neill, Mr. Edwin Babcock Holden, and Mr. R. T. Haines Halsey. Dr. Emmet's fine collection had already passed into the possession of the New York Public Library, and Mr. Augustin Daly's, the nucleus of which had been formed by Mr. Benjamin Millet Lander, was slumbering, almost forgotten, in the picture gallery of Mr. M. C. D. Borden.

Mr. Holden was almost the last to join this little band of pioneers, and he was the most enthusiastic of all, and collected with rare judgment and intelligence, not only New York prints, but historical prints generally.

He was a favourite with the dealers because of his genial personality and his willingness to pay a fair price for whatever he wanted. He, therefore, had the first offer of everything good that came into the market. His death, in 1906, while still in the vigour of youth, removed the most conspicuous figure in the field of Old New York collecting, and the man who, with the single exception of Mr. Andrews, has contributed the most to make the collecting of New York City material popular. The disposal, by auction in 1910, of Mr. Holden's splendid collection is the most important event which has taken place in this field, and from it dates the real beginning of popular interest in this fascinating subject. The sale is memorable, also, for having, with the Neill sale which preceded it by less than a month, set the high standard of values which in the case of the finer and rarer prints has since been maintained—indeed has even increased. Had Mr. Holden lived, he perhaps might have undertaken the preparation of a book somewhat along the lines of the present work, for his interest in the subject was far beyond that of the average collector. He loved his prints, not only for their picturesque qualities and for their rarity, but because of the tales they could tell of by-gone days and of life in the old city. His was the historian's—the antiquary's—interest, as well as the collector's. Indeed, in company with Mr. R. H. Lawrence and Mr. Halsey, he had already begun a systematic study of the prints in his own and other collections with a view to the ultimate preparation of a descriptive catalogue; and a file of cards prepared in this way by Mr. Lawrence, and forming the nucleus of such a catalogue, proved very helpful during the early stages of the present work.

It was at the house of Mr. Halsey, in the winter of 1908, that the idea first came into my mind of undertaking the preparation of an illustrated catalogue of the most important New York City prints, accompanied by historical notes. I had spent a delightful evening among his varied but exquisitely harmonious treasures of American art, and had followed with deep interest his description of some of the more important pieces. Naturally, my attention was chiefly engrossed by the historical prints, and particularly by those of New York City, and I remember that it was while examining the beautifully drawn and coloured pair of St. Mémin views that something in the aspect of the little group of houses clustering along the river bank at the foot of Mt. Pitt, combined with something in the attitude of the two figures in the foreground and in the appearance of the coach hurrying along the road in the middle distance, suggested to me the idea of writing a book on the history of New York prints.

By the following spring, this idea had assumed definite form, as the following extracts from a letter written to Mr. Halsey, on May 8, 1909, indicate:

* * *

I am whiling away some of the long hours of convalescence from typhoid in turning over in my mind a plan for the preparation and publication of a pictorial record of the development of New York from its origin until the present day, a subject which has long appealed to my imagination but which did not take definite form until after that delightful evening spent at your house early last winter.

The plan as it now presents itself to me is to reproduce, at a somewhat larger scale than in Mr. Andrews's book, and by the best photographic process (I presume photo-engraving on copper), about 80 maps, plans, and views very carefully selected from the best collections, private and public, here and abroad, and to supplement these by a few descriptive extracts from the best contemporary writers. The plan of the book would be somewhat as follows:

PREFACE

CHAPTER 1 New York on the earliest maps and sea charts, with extracts from the earliest voyages, etc.

CHAPTER 2 New York under Dutch Rule: 1609–1664. Plans, views, and contemporary descriptions.

CHAPTER 3 New York under English Rule: 1664–1765. Plans, views, and contemporary descriptions.

CHAPTER 4 New York during the Revolutionary Period: 1765–1783. Plans, views, and contemporary descriptions.

CHAPTER 5 New York under the Constitution, from the close of the Revolution to the end of the second war with Great Britain: 1783–1815. Plans, views, and contemporary descriptions.

CHAPTER 6 New York from the close of the second war with Great Britain until the close of the Civil War: 1815–1865. Plans, views, and contemporary descriptions.

CHAPTER 7 New York from the close of the Civil War to the present day: 1865–1909. Plans, views (contemporary descriptions?)

CHRONOLOGY

TABLE OF CENSUS REPORTS, STATISTICS, ETC.

TWO KEY MAPS:

(a) Showing growth of city from the earliest times to 1811 (Viele's map with Bridges's map superimposed), topography, important buildings, with dates of erection and demolition, points from which principal views shown in prints were taken, etc., etc.

(b) Showing growth of the city from 1811 to the present time (Bridges's map, with map of Manhattan from St. Louis World's Fair Greater New York map superimposed), topography, etc., etc.

List of Important Maps, Plans, and Views mentioned by early writers or advertised in early newspapers but of which no copy is now known.

(Note) In connection with prints, all known states to be enumerated and briefly described, and owner's name cited; cite also copies contained in public collections.

Index

Portraits (?)

Broadsides (?)

* * *

My ambition is to produce a book which, although probably supplying little or no new or original matter, will, from its character and from the manner of its arrangement, be of distinct interest and value to the collector as well as to that larger and growing class of intelligent book lovers who take an interest in all that relates to the early history of the city. In general form of presentation I would follow pretty closely Mr. Andrews's admirable book, while not expecting or even attempting to rival its matter and charm of expression. But I hope it might prove possible, by using a different paper, to increase somewhat the size of the page without adding materially to the weight of the book.

* * *

The plan and scope of the book, as here outlined, have been pretty closely adhered to, but I soon realised the importance of going to the original sources, as well as the desirability of undertaking original investigations, and the work has thereby been extended far beyond my early expectations.

Mr. Halsey's response to this letter was both encouraging and helpful, and I immediately set about the congenial task of collecting material, little suspecting that the work would occupy somewhat more than my leisure hours during over six years.

The most comprehensive available collection of New York prints, at that time, was that belonging to the New York Historical Society. Unfortunately, as the Society had only recently moved into its new building on Central Park, its prints had not yet been arranged for exhibition, being for the most part packed away in drawers and cases. However, I received from the President, Mr. Hoffman, and from the Librarian, Mr. Kelby, permission to examine and to photograph whatever was needed, and I spent a profitable week in listing, comparing, and describing the more important prints and drawings in this fine collection, the foundation of which was laid by John Pintard in 1807, and which is undoubtedly the oldest existing collection of New York City views and plans in existence.

I was fortunate from the start in obtaining the encouragement and co-operation of collectors, and of every public institution, as well as every national, state, and city department to which I appealed, both in this country and abroad; and I have to record only one refusal to allow a print, drawing, or document to be reproduced—that of Mr. Henry Harrisse, who replied to a request for a photograph of his so-called "Vingboons Survey" that he could supply no information regarding my inquiry. Notwithstanding this rather brusque refusal, he later relented and showed this treasure to a friend who called on him in Paris at my request. Although still unwilling that the plan should be photographed, saying that this would diminish its value, he told my friend that he soon should be dead, and that his legatee, the Library of Congress, could then do with this and the rest of his collection whatever it saw fit. Two years later, after Mr. Harrisse's death, I had the "Vingboons Survey" photographed in Paris, with the consent of his executors and heirs, and that of the French government.

Most of the subjects for illustrating the Iconography were chosen and photographed during the summer and autumn of 1909, some at the houses of their owners, and others in the gallery of The Metropolitan Museum of Art, a much-appreciated privilege, extended through the courtesy of Mr. Robert W. de Forest, then Secretary, and now President of the Museum. During the summer, I began to collect material for the Chronology, Bibliography, and Plate Descriptions. The work thus begun has been continued ever since; and, as it increased in diversity and volume, and grew beyond the powers of a single individual, it was divided up among several, each working along predetermined lines, guided by daily consultations, criticism, and advice, and each contributing his or her share to the accomplishment of the common task.

Much of the work of investigation had to be done by correspondence, and I find on looking through my personal files that they contain over twenty-five hundred communications; and, besides these, many letters have, of course, been written and received by my associates in the work.

In the summer of 1911, I went abroad, chiefly to see for myself the collections of the British Museum, the Admiralty, and the War Office, in London, those of the Bibliothèque Nationale and the Dépôt des Cartes de la Marine, in Paris, and the Rijksarchief at The Hague.

While in Holland, I made the personal acquaintance of Dr. F. C. Wieder, with whom I had long corresponded, and who later consented to undertake for the present work a study of the early Dutch maps and charts of the vicinity of Manhattan Island. This study was eventually extended to embrace the principal map collections of Europe and resulted in the Essay on Cartography, which is for the greater part his work, as is more particularly explained in the special introduction to that subject.

In 1912, a private study in the New York Public Library was put at my disposition by the kindness of the late Dr. John S. Billings, where, ever since, we have enjoyed the hospitality of the Trustees and the Director, and have benefited by the unequalled facilities for work of this description afforded especially by the noble collections of the Lenox Foundation, and by the efficient and cheerful help of the officials in all departments of the library.

PLAN AND SCOPE

The Iconography divides itself, chronologically as well as topographically, into two main parts. The first begins with the second voyage of Vespuccius, in 1498, on which, probably for the first time, the precincts of Manhattan Island were approached by Europeans,[1] and ends with the report and plan of the Commission of 1807, which sounded the death-knell of the old city. The second begins with the development of the new city in accordance with the Commission's plan, and ends with the Hudson-Fulton Celebration of 1909.

The first period is covered by Volumes I and II, the second volume being in the form of an appendix devoted almost exclusively to the cartography and to the early topography of the island. The third volume deals with the later period of the city's history. The fourth, which is modelled upon Prince's *Annals*, consists of a chronology and an index, the former composed of briefly stated facts, carefully selected from all available manuscript and printed sources, full references always being given, to enable the reader to refer readily for more detailed information to the sources quoted. Whereas the primary object in the Chronology has been to record the facts vividly and in strict chronological sequence, the more important and interesting events, sites, buildings, etc., have been

[1] The De la Cosa Map, of 1500, which probably records the observations made on this voyage, supplies the earliest pictorial representation of a shore line, which may possibly have been drawn from actual observations of that in the neighbourhood of Sandy Hook and Long Island.

treated also in brief monographs, under such heads as The Dutch Settlement of Manhattan; The Fort; The Stadt Huys; Seawant; Early Mills; Origin of the Postal System; The Leislerian Troubles; Colonial Laws; The Montgomerie Charter; Trinity Church; King's College; The Tammany Society; The Stock Exchange; The City Hall; The Fire Department; Central Park, etc.

In the Chronology, especially during the early period, and in connection with matters of topographical or antiquarian interest, considerable space has often been devoted to facts and occurrences which in themselves may sometimes seem of but little moment. It, however, not infrequently happens that these very insignificant trifles acquire interest and importance beyond themselves, through their association with people, events, or places which have since become famous. Mrs. Van Rensselaer has expressed this thought very happily in the preface of her admirable *History of New York in the Seventeenth Century*, where she says:

> . . . a special quality of interest pertains to the city of New York in its early years by reason of the preëminence it has since achieved; for it is with places as with men—the greater their importance in adult life the greater is the interest that attaches to their birth and antecedents, the incidents of their youth, and the influences that moulded their spirit and shaped their destinies.

As some months must elapse before the publication of the third and fourth volumes, it has seemed desirable to provide in the first volume an outline, or Table of Contents, covering the entire work. This will be found following the List of Plates. Here it is sufficient to comment briefly upon its principal features.

The Historical Summaries, which precede the Plate Descriptions in each chapter, have been prepared with the object of supplying, in the briefest readable form, an outline of the more interesting events, and a description of the more important sites and buildings, given in more detail in the Chronology. They are intended primarily for the information of the general reader and the collector who are interested in knowing something of the history contemporary with the illustrations, but who may not have the time or the inclination to consider the subject in detail.

Separate introductory notes have been prepared for the Cartography, the Manatus Maps, the Castello Plan, the Dutch Grants, and the Early Newspapers; and the reader is referred to these, as well as to the Plate

Descriptions, the Landmark Map, and the Bibliography, for more detailed information.

Perhaps no other city of equal age and importance—certainly no other city of the New World—possesses so complete and rich a pictorial record of its early years as is supplied by the Manatus Maps, the Prototype View, and the Castello Plan. These three wonderful documents, which are here reproduced and described for the first time, taken together, present an accurate and almost complete picture of the city and island during the Dutch period, and show clearly the development of New Amsterdam from a sparsely populated village community, in 1639, to a compact little city in 1661.

The Manatus Map, which can be positively dated at 1639, and which is known to us through two practically contemporary copies, is the earliest known survey of Manhattan Island, and shows the plantations, bouweries, roads, and buildings constructed during the first thirteen or fourteen years of occupation. It gives the names of more than forty of the earliest settlers on Manhattan, in the Bronx, and on the adjacent shores of New Jersey, Long Island, and Staten Island. A careful study of these maps in connection with contemporary records has brought to light many hitherto unknown facts relating to this interesting period.

The Castello Plan is the earliest plan of the city known to be extant, and the only one that has come down to us from Dutch times. This wonderful plan, or rather bird's-eye view, the reproduction and description of which constitute one of the most important features of the present work, depicts in minute detail virtually every topographical feature and every building which existed in the little town of New Amsterdam in the summer of the year 1660. By the aid, again, of contemporary records, and especially of the Nicasius de Sille manuscript street directory of the city belonging to this same year, it has proved possible to determine the owner or occupant of nearly every house, and to give much interesting information regarding each, as well as many new facts relating to the city itself just before it passed from Dutch to English rule.

The Dutch Grants, shown by a map and key, give the location and boundaries, with dimensions, of virtually every ground-brief or patent granted to the settlers in New Amsterdam by the Directors and Council in New Netherland. The key, after setting forth the date and description of each ground-brief, proceeds with the history of the title, its partitioning by transports (deeds of conveyance), etc., up to the close of Stuyvesant's administration (1664), and in some cases beyond this date.

The List of Early Newspapers consists of historical information and a check-list locating, in nearly one hundred American and European libraries, files and separate issues of the most important New York papers, covering collectively the period from the issue of the first newspaper, in 1725, to the end of the first period, 1811.

The Landmark Map and Key supply descriptive references to about one thousand of the most important and interesting localities, names, topographical features, streets, sites, and buildings, from the first settlement of the island to the present day.

The Bibliography describes and locates many hundreds of the most important manuscript and printed sources and the best primary and secondary authorities and reference books relating to the island and city, and includes, besides, an extended report on the documents preserved in the various New York City and County departments.

The plans and views have been selected and described with the double purpose of illustrating the physical development of the city and island, and of preserving in permanent form clear, accurate, and artistic reproductions of the rarer and more important drawings and prints, and those which best depict the ever changing aspect of the old city and of its principal streets and buildings.

The plates have been made by photography from originals in such public collections as those of the New York Historical Society, the New York Public Library, the Merchants' Association, the Library of Congress, the British Museum, the Bibliothèque Nationale, and the Rijksarchief, and in such private collections as those of Mr. William Loring Andrews, Mr. Amos F. Eno, Mr. John D. Crimmins, Mr. J. Clarence Davies, Mr. R. T. Haines Halsey, Mr. Harris D. Colt, Mr. Robert Goelet, Mr. Percy R. Pyne, 2d, and Mr. Edward W. C. Arnold.

The Plate Descriptions are divided into two parts; technical information intended primarily for the collector, such as medium employed, date depicted, date issued, dimensions, artist or author, engraver, provenance, other copies, states, etc., and information of general history, antiquarian, or topographical interest relating to the buildings or sites depicted.

The present time is perhaps the most auspicious that has existed or is likely to exist for the preparation of such a descriptive list of plans and views of our city as is given in the ICONOGRAPHY, for the recent stimulation of interest in Old New York, brought about largely by various exhibitions of New York City prints, of which the first was held by The Grolier Club in 1897, by the Neill and Holden sales of 1910, and by the Hudson-Fulton Celebration; and the high prices realised during the past few years by the rarer and more interesting views, have brought into the market many hitherto unknown or long forgotten prints, most of the more important of which have found their way into one or other of the above-mentioned collections; and these prints it has been possible to reproduce and describe here before they again become scattered or are lost sight of.

PRINTS AND PRINT COLLECTING

Print collecting has long been considered one of the most profitable and alluring of hobbies, as well as one admirably suited to the enthusiast of moderate means, who, if his fancy did not turn to Rembrandts and Dürers, could usually contrive to add to his collection any particularly coveted treasure which came his way, and who, moreover, had the satisfaction of knowing that, if his patience and enthusiasm did not wane, and he were favoured by a fair share of good luck, he could reasonably expect to gather, in time, a really good collection, and that without squandering a fortune.

The collecting of Old New York prints has, until the last five or six years, been no exception to this general rule, and has yielded a harvest of delight to those few collectors who so long enjoyed the field to themselves. Unfortunately, conditions have changed, and print collecting is no longer the poor man's hobby. But the serious collector, even of New York prints, will not despair. He knows that although the time is past, at least temporarily, for bargains in the shops and auction rooms, there is still an ample reward in store for his perseverance and his discriminating knowledge, along unbeaten paths, farther afield; and that the greater effort required to bag the elusive game only adds new zest and pleasure to the quest. Unquestionably, the last few years have been propitious times for those fortunate collectors who have had the courage of their convictions, and who could afford to keep pace with the ever-climbing prices demanded for really desirable prints.

In almost every form of collecting it is a wise rule to buy the best—when one knows enough to recognise it—and those who began to practise this rule a few years ago are to-day rejoicing in the possession of treasures which are rated at many times their cost, and are now unprocurable at any price. Whether present values will continue or not, no one can foretell. For my part, except in the case of the finer and rarer prints of the seventeenth, eighteenth, and first third of the nineteenth centuries, I am disposed to think that they will not.

When we compare, for example, the present values, or rather prices, of early New York and London prints, the disparity is striking, and a comparison of early New York prints with those of Boston and Philadelphia is almost equally illuminating and convincing. New York prints are more valuable, not because they are rarer or more interesting than those of other cities, but because there are more people who want them and can afford to pay the prices asked for them.

But even if it be true that the heyday of the average print collector has passed, we should glean some satisfaction from the thought that this may mean that in future the gathering of the rarer prints will be more closely confined to public institutions and to those individuals from whom the museums and libraries of our cities have a right to expect to receive them eventually.

The importance, as an educational factor, of maintaining cabinets of historical prints in connection with art galleries and libraries, and always readily accessible to the public, has long been recognised in European cities, and should be encouraged by our own. Such collections not only give pleasure to the eye and educate the mind, but stimulate patriotism and civic pride.

Mr. William Loring Andrews, to whom we owe so many charming books, a collector for nearly fifty years, and one of the first to appreciate and describe the earlier and rarer New York prints, tells us, in his preface to *The Bradford Map*, that "it is quite conceivable that the most ardent bibliophile might in time grow weary of gathering Aldines and Elzevirs" (some of us believe he might even have included Rembrandts and Dürers), but that "it is yet to be recorded of an antiquary born within sound of the bells of Trinity Church that he tired in his quest for memorials of the city he loved."

There is much of mysterious interest surrounding the cradle of most of our early American settlements. Boston, our sister city, exults in the proud recollection of a past which is even more stirring than our own; Philadelphia, for over a century, outstripped us in prosperity and consequence; but somehow there is a fascination and a charm bound up with the memory of the early struggles and triumphs of our little island which make its kaleidoscopic history—to us at least—more interesting than that of any other city of the New World. Even the skyscraper and the elevated railroad have failed to dispel this charm, in the eyes of the born New Yorker, although he sadly admits, at least to himself, that the city is not what it once was. There are spots, though, in the remote depths of Central Park, beyond Inwood, and especially one little wooded bay on the shores of the Hudson, in Fort Washington Park, still almost as wild and unspoiled as in the days of Hudson; but these are growing sadly few, and we can hardly hope that they can retain their seclusion and primitive beauty more than another decade. But even if the old haunts and the rural beauties of our island have gone forever, their memory remains—and a sweet and inspiring memory it is, especially to the intelligent print collector, to whose enchanted vision the book of the past is ever open, and for whom every by-way and corner of the old city has a thrill and an inspiration.

In most of the higher forms of collecting, beauty is the ideal towards which the collector strives, the one essential characteristic which guides his choice. Not so with the collecting of historical prints, which, for the most part, must be judged by a different standard. Few of the prints of Old New York can justly be called beautiful, but many possess other qualities which endear them to the heart of the intelligent collector, who regards them almost with reverence and awe as the frail documents of a by-gone age,—the silent bearers of many a half-read message, which perhaps his alert eye is destined to decipher. In themselves admittedly incomplete and unsatisfying, if judged by the standards of the average picture lover, as contemporary illustrations of successive steps in the physical growth of our great city, they render more real and vivid our written history, and become at once instructive and intensely interesting.

Until early in the nineteenth century, engraving upon copper continued to be the well-nigh universally employed medium of pictorial reproduction. Wood engraving existed, it is true, but in our chosen field it played so unimportant a part as to be nearly negligible. Engraving on steel never found favour among those masters of the art who sought the most sympathetic mediums of expression. The discovery of lithography, by introducing more freedom in the preparation of the "plate," gave promise of better things; but the artist soon tired of drawing with his own hand upon the stone, and turned over his sketch to a draughtsman to copy.

Mr. Stauffer tells us that the year 1825 marks about the beginning of what may be termed the commercial period. At this time engraving, and shortly afterward lithography, ceased for the most part to be undertaken by individual artists, signing their own names to their work, and were undertaken by companies. There were notable exceptions, of course, and such names as John Hill, J. W. Hill, William J. Bennett, Peter Maverick, Asher B. Durand, William S. Leney, John R. Smith, Samuel Imbert, James Smillie, H. Fossette, and Robert Havell, all of which are found attached to copperplate engravings or lithographs of New York produced during the second quarter of the nineteenth century, show that the decadence was neither complete nor abrupt. With the introduction of photography, in the early '50's, engraving by hand and lithography as an art virtually ceased, and, after the period of mechanical development which followed close upon the Civil War, there came the introduction of the various forms of photographic reproduction, known generally as process-work, and these soon completely supplanted original drawing and hand engraving, which latter had already become almost a lost art, although it is a pleasure to realise that, in the form of etching, it has recently been revived to some extent in our field by Pennell, Mielatz, Deville, Charles Henry White, B. J. Olsson-Nordfeldt, W. Sherwood, and several others.

Let us take courage and dare to hope that, in the not too distant future, the new beauty and charm of our city will again find some even more worthy form of permanent expression, and collectors have something better than process-work with which to fill their portfolios.

NEW YORK CITY'S CONTRIBUTION TO THE FOUNDING AND DEVELOPMENT OF THE NATION

Although New York, for a century, has enjoyed a position of unchallenged national pre-eminence, and during this period has put her stamp upon tens of millions of embryo citizens, it would be foolish to claim for her a greater share in the evolution and upbuilding of the United States than justly belongs to Boston and Philadelphia. And yet, from the beginning, she has borne a leading, and generally an honourable, part, for which she has not always received from historians a due share of credit —a part of increasing importance and influence in the Republic and in the world. Situated on a splendid harbour, capable of sheltering the commerce of the world; with a mighty river at her back, which provides easy access to the untold riches of the interior, the city has possessed from the beginning natural advantages destined to make her the chief city on the western shores of the Atlantic. Established by the enterprise of the people of the United Netherlands, she stood, in a sense, alone, with colonies of a hostile nation on either side. From an early day she excited the distrust and cupidity of these neighbours, not only because she possessed such great advantages of position, but because she separated the English colonies of New England from Virginia, and cut off from expansion westward the colonies of Connecticut and Massachusetts. The causes of this early distrust were largely removed when New Amsterdam and New Netherland passed into the hands of the English, in 1664, and were incorporated into a proprietary province subject to the Duke of York.

This event, however, did not remove all points of difference between New York and her neighbours. Long after the conquest, a considerable majority of her citizens continued to be of Dutch extraction. These combined with the incoming English and gave to New York's population an unusual character, more varied, and in many respects more interesting, than that of any other American colony. In succeeding years circumstances united to increase rather than diminish this composite character of the people, and not the least among these is the fact that, from early times, New York enjoyed a greater degree of religious liberty and political freedom than did most of the other colonies. Late in the seventeenth century came refugees from France, whom the intolerance of Louis XIV had driven from home. Germans from the Palatinate followed; in the eighteenth century, also, came settlers from England, Ireland, and Scotland, whom the final collapse of the Stuart cause drove to seek their fortunes in the New World. Many of these people eventually found homes beyond New York City; some, however, settled there and served to give to the town at an early date the cosmopolitan character which has been so marked in its more recent years.

New York has never ceased to be the principal gateway through which the blood of the Old World has poured to build up the sinews of the New. The stream of immigration increased greatly after the close of our second war with England; it rose to a flood in the years succeeding 1840, and continued, with a volume scarcely abated, until the outbreak of the present European war. In all these years the immigrant has derived his first impressions of America and of American ideals and opportunities from the city across whose threshold he entered the country. But New York has been more than a gateway for the influx of this endless procession. From the beginning, a very considerable number of the people arriving at her doors have been content to remain, and these have made the city permanently their home. In this sense New York has always remained a frontier town. To the city, this circumstance has been both a benefit and a disadvantage: a benefit, in that it has furnished her with young men of enterprise and vigour, who have helped to build up her varied industries and have provided her with an unlimited supply of labour; a disadvantage, in that the accumulation annually of hordes of poor and illiterate immigrants has vastly complicated her social and political problems, and has at times well-nigh overwhelmed her. But New York has not drawn her citizens from abroad only. From every section of America, men of enterprise and achievement have come, attracted by the opportunity for wider activity which the city offers. As a result, the development, or at least the domination, of a distinct type, such as early appeared in semi-ecclesiastical New England, was prevented.

Another element of interest attaches to the evolution of liberal institutions of government in New York. Unlike the people of New England, who came to the New World to escape political and religious conditions which seemed to them intolerable, the first settlers of New Amsterdam came as the employees of a commercial company which was seeking to establish the new settlement entirely for its own pecuniary advantage. One might expect that in such a community there would be no particular opportunity for the development of political liberty and of free institutions. Such, however, was not the case. The conditions of life in the new country stimulated a desire for political freedom in New Amsterdam no less than in New England. In Stuyvesant's administration this spirit became peculiarly noticeable. With the beginning of the English régime, the demand became even stronger, until there developed a continuous struggle between the governor, representing the king, and the assembly, representing the people. The most important incident in this long contest was the conflict between Zenger and Governor Cosby. To Zenger's success we owe largely the establishment of a free press and free speech in the land. Other controversies occurred over the right claimed by the king to billet troops upon the citizens, and over the control of the provincial judiciary. In the events leading up to the Revolution itself, New York took an active and honourable part. Perhaps this is the more remarkable since many of her citizens were of non-English descent, and differed from the people of New England and Pennsylvania in that they were struggling for rights to which they were not attached by the bonds of immemorial inheritance. In opposing the Stamp Act, the citizens were particularly active and successful, and, in 1770, it was found that of the colonies which had bound themselves not to trade with England New York alone was really observing the agreement. This was peculiarly remarkable in a colony whose prosperity rested primarily upon its commerce.

When actual war came, New York's exposed position forced her to bear the brunt of attack. For strategic reasons, England was particularly anxious to gain control of New York. The British forces attacked in overwhelming force, compelled Washington to withdraw, and held the city from the autumn of 1776 until the end of the war. No other city endured so long a period of occupation by the enemy. All patriots withdrew; Royalists from all parts of the country flocked to New York, and she became the centre of Tory activity. The city suffered miserably during this period. Two disastrous fires destroyed large numbers of buildings; and it is estimated that the population decreased from twenty thousand before the capture to ten thousand at the evacuation in 1783.

In the formation of the national government and the adoption of the federal constitution, New York did not take a leading part, but, in the persons of her distinguished representatives, Alexander Hamilton and John Jay, she contributed largely to the direction of public affairs in this formative period.

The great wave of immigration which began about 1840 came at a time when the government of the city was being reorganised on a more democratic basis by the removal of property qualifications for voters and by making city offices elective. These measures enabled corrupt politicians to use the votes of new citizens to acquire control of the government, and to manage municipal affairs for their own profit. Corruption was widespread; the police were unable to keep the peace, and riots between hostile political or religious factions were frequent. The most serious scene of disorder occurred some years later, during the Civil War, when unscrupulous politicians and mobs of foreigners persistently, and with force, resisted the draft law. After the close of the war political corruption continued, and it is only within recent years that its control over municipal affairs seems to have been broken.

New York's municipal government, while still far from perfect, has of late certainly been greatly improved, and the outlook for still better things is encouraging.

From the beginning, commercial activity has been a leading characteristic of New York and the chief source of her prosperity. Founded as a trading-post, she early became and has continued a centre to which commerce was naturally attracted. Her splendid harbour and the great river which bring to her markets both foreign and domestic commodities, have been the unceasing producers of wealth for her merchants. In years when conditions were unfavourable to trade, New York languished; when trade flourished, New York grew in wealth and in number of inhabitants. In 1790, her population surpassed that of Boston, and by 1820 had gone beyond that of Philadelphia. The completion of the Erie Canal, in 1825, gave her a monopoly of the trade of the states bordering upon the Great Lakes, and established her supremacy as the greatest commercial city in America. At a later date, railroads, converging here from all points, made New York the greatest distributing centre as well as the most important railway terminal of the continent.

The proximity of the great coal fields of Pennsylvania has long enabled New York to obtain an ample supply of cheap fuel. Immigration has furnished her with abundant labour. As a result of this combination, manufactures were early developed, and by the middle of the nineteenth century she had become the greatest manufacturing city in the New World. When New York became the industrial head of the country, she inevitably became its financial head also; and to-day the city dominates the industry and finance of the continent.

New York's claim to intellectual leadership is not so secure. At the beginning she seems to have lacked the impulse to intellectual development that was so characteristic of New England. Perhaps this is not to be wondered at. In New Amsterdam, the trading-post, there were few educated persons. To be sure, the clergy sent over by the Company were men of education, but they occupied a much less influential position in the community than the New England clergy; consequently, they were less able to cope with adverse conditions and to secure the establishment of schools of advanced learning. The Boston Latin School, for example, had been in existence for some years before a Latin school was established in New York. This early lack has been supplied in later years, and to-day New York is rich in schools of all classes. Yet even now her educational activities stand out less prominently in the public mind than would be the case, did not the city's industrial and commercial importance so overshadow all other activities.

Of her achievements in the making of books New York has no need to be ashamed. Jacob Steendam, one of the earliest of American poets, lived and wrote in New Amsterdam. William Smith, the eighteenth-century historian, did his chief work here. But it is upon the accomplishments of the "Knickerbocker" writers of the nineteenth century that New York bases her strongest claim to recognition. The first American work that deserves to be called literature came from the pens of Irving, Cooper, and their fellow-writers; and if for a time literary leadership passed to New England, it has since returned to its earlier home. In architecture, New York has perhaps contributed more than any other city of the world to the development of a modern style which expresses in a high degree her own individual needs. The magnitude of her buildings and bridges dwarfs those of the Old World cities, and compels the acceptance of new standards of municipal architecture. In the possession of ancient land-marks New York is lamentably poor in comparison with Boston and Philadelphia. Although this is largely the result of the many disastrous fires which occurred in the last quarter of the eighteenth, and in the first half of the nineteenth century, it is also due to the marked lack of veneration, or even appreciation, for the monuments of the past, which resulted from her rapid commercial expansion in the later half of the nineteenth century, when many fine and interesting old buildings were ruthlessly destroyed. But the civic pride of her citizens has at last been aroused, as was clearly shown in the well-nigh universal protest which, in 1909, followed the attempt to replace St. John's Chapel by a commercial structure; and this new-born enthusiasm has since saved the City Hall Park from further desecration, and bids fair to end in the removal of the County Court House and the main Post Office building, and the restoration of the Park to its original condition.

In the field of art New York has always led her sister cities. Even in the earliest days, as we know from wills and other contemporary records, the houses of many of the more well-to-do Dutch settlers contained pictures as well as silver plate, which the thrifty burghers had brought with them from the fatherland, not only on account of their appreciation of the beautiful, but because they had been accustomed to consider such things as a good form of investment for their savings.

It is interesting to note that the earliest reference to portrait painting in New York, if not the earliest in this country, is found in a statement made before the Burgomasters of New Amsterdam, on June 12, 1663, by the wife of Hendrick Cousterier, or Coutrie, who stated that the burgher-right had been given to her husband by Stuyvesant because he had painted "the portrait of his Honour and drawn pictures of his sons." It is not unreasonable to suppose that this portrait is the well known oil painting so long preserved in the Stuyvesant family, and recently given to the New York Historical Society.

Throughout the period of settlement and early development, there was but little opportunity for artistic expression, but even from those times more names of artists and engravers of New York have survived than of any other city; and when it comes to the close of the eighteenth century, the city assumes in this field a distinct leadership, which she has ever since maintained; until now, in the appreciation, production, collecting, and teaching of art, she is beginning to rank with the foremost cities of the world. She is also the chief centre of music and of the drama in America.

By the irony of fate, or perhaps in accordance with a wise dispensation of Providence, New York, which has become the unchallenged leader of America in finance, industry, and intellectual activity, has failed to become the political capital of the country. During the colonial period, she enjoyed for many years the distinction of being the capital of the province; for a time she was the capital of the state; and for a few months the seat of the federal government; but many years ago she lost all these positions of honour and influence. New York is not, and never can be, the metropolis of the United States in the same sense that London and Paris are the metropolitan capitals of England and France. In spite of this, she has already come to dominate the United States in a far greater degree than any other city. She has not yet become the distributor of a "communicating current of formative ideas and purposes which makes the different parts of the social body articulate, and which stamps the mass of its works with a kindred spirit and direction." No American city does this, and it may well be questioned whether American life has yet reached a degree of development when such centralised control is possible, although New York, more than any other city, is coming to be, in this sense, the American metropolis.

What New York's future is to be, and what part she is destined to play in the further development of the nation and of the world, one can only guess. On the whole, one inclines with Mr. Barrett Wendell to guess hopefully; for it is certainly true, as he remarks in his *Literary History of America*, that

> Beneath her bewildering material activity, there is a greater vitality, a greater alertness, and, in some respects, a greater wholesomeness of intelligence than one is apt to find elsewhere. The great wealth of New York, and its colossal material power . . . involve a social complexity greater than America has hitherto known.

Whether material advantages and great vitality will enable her to maintain and to improve her abundant opportunities for usefulness and true leadership is a question that only time can definitely determine.

I. N. Phelps Stokes

New York
October, 1915

ACKNOWLEDGMENTS

In the preparation of the Iconography, I am particularly fortunate in having had the advice and assistance of Mr. Victor Hugo Paltsits, lately New York State Historian, and at present Keeper of Manuscripts in the New York Public Library, who has spent the greater part of three years in special investigations for this work, to which he has contributed the Bibliography and the major portion of the historical material relating to the Dutch period. During the four years that we have been associated, Mr. Paltsits has been a veritable mentor, to whom I have turned on every occasion for advice and guidance, and with whom I have discussed every knotty question, sure of an attentive and sympathetic hearing, and of an intelligent interpretation based on wide knowledge and sound judgment. I am also greatly indebted to Miss Helen L. Young, Assistant Professor of History in Hunter College, who has contributed largely to the material and form of the Historical Summaries, especially to those dealing with the English and Revolutionary periods, and to Miss Emily Hickman, Associate Professor of History in Wells College, who is chiefly responsible for the List of Early New York Newspapers. In the difficult and almost unexplored field of cartography relating to the neighbourhood of Manhattan Island, I have had the co-operation of Dr. F. C. Wieder, Assistant Librarian of the University of Amsterdam, and a close student of cartography, who has prosecuted researches on behalf of this work in the principal collections of Europe, and has made discoveries of interest and importance. In this field, I am also indebted to M. Henri Tropé, of Paris, and to Mr. Henry N. Stevens, of London, who has also contributed to the preparation of the Plate Descriptions. In connection with the early Dutch grants and the topography generally, I am under obligation for very active and valuable help to Miss J. V. Macarthy, location expert and historian of the Title Guarantee and Trust Company, and to Mr. Clinton H. Macarthy, who has spent more than two years in unravelling some of the intricacies of this obscure and important subject.

I am also deeply beholden to Mr. Wilberforce Eames of the New York Public Library, whose unsurpassed knowledge of books relating to America has been of the greatest assistance in the preparation of this book, and whose generous help and advice, always cheerfully given, have contributed much to the enjoyment of the work. It is a pleasant duty also to express here my gratitude to Dr. Herbert Putnam, Librarian of Congress, whose general letter of introduction to foreign libraries was most helpful, and to Mr. P. Lee Phillips, Chief of the Division of Maps and Charts of the Library of Congress; to Dr. Austin Baxter Keep, Instructor in History in the College of the City of New York; Mr. A. J. F. van Laer, State Archivist; Mr. Robert H. Kelby, Librarian, and Mr. Alexander Wohlhagen, Assistant Librarian, of the New York Historical Society; Mr. Frank B. Bigelow, Librarian of the New York Society Library; Dr. Frank Weitenkampf, Curator of Prints of the New York Public Library; Dr. Edward Luther Stevenson, Director of the Hispanic Society of America; Mr. C. S. Brigham, Librarian of the American Antiquarian Society; and Mr. George Parker Winship, so long custodian of the treasures of the John Carter Brown Library and now in charge of the Widener Library at Harvard; and also to Dr. Johannes de Hullu, of the Dutch National Archives at The Hague; to Mr. Basil H. Soulsby, formerly head of the Map Room of the British Museum and now transferred to the South Kensington branch; and to the custodians of many other collections in America and Europe; as well as to the officials of national, state, and city departments who, one and all, have given ungrudgingly of their time and knowledge in answering my inquiries, and whose courtesy and help I deeply appreciate. I want also to record a word of special thanks to Mrs. Robert W. de Forest, who generously lent me the transcript and translation of the *De Forest Journal*, since printed in annotated form in her delightful book, *A Walloon Family in America*, and to the Hon. George McAneny, who, as President of the Borough of Manhattan, did much to facilitate the researches for this work in the city departments.

To my fellow-collectors, who have lent their treasures for study and reproduction, I have already expressed my thanks in person. It is a pleasure to record here my appreciation of their generous confidence, without which this book could not have been written. To my old friend, Mr. Joseph F. Sabin, and to Mr. Robert Fridenberg I gladly acknowledge my indebtedness for many courtesies and for much information.

Mr. Fridenberg's comprehensive card catalogue of New York prints, generously placed at my disposal, has proved very helpful, especially in connection with the supplementary list of prints.

To all of these, and to my secretary, Miss Zula Ziebach, and to Mr. Thomas W. Hotchkiss, both of whom have been associated long and intimately with the work, and whose zeal and devotion have been unflagging, as well as to Mr. Rawson W. Haddon and to the several others who at one time or another have laboured patiently at the common task, and have given cheerfully of their time and energy, I cannot easily express all that I feel of appreciation and gratitude. The completed work, such as it is, is theirs quite as much as mine, and there is satisfaction in the thought that we have shared alike in the toils and pleasures of its production. Mistakes have been made, no doubt—sins of omission as well as of commission—and I am painfully conscious of many shortcomings, both in matter and in form. The field to be covered is so wide, and the work of investigation has necessarily been divided among so many, that some contradictions, and numerous inconsistencies in form, have been unavoidable, and I trust these will be forgiven.

A few conspicuous contradictions between the Summary of the Dutch Period and the Cartography, Plate Descriptions, and Chronology, represent divergent interpretations of the usually meagre facts, made on the one hand by Mr. Paltsits, and on the other by the author who, while exercising an editorial supervision over the whole work, has preferred to allow such inconsistencies to remain rather than arbitrarily to unify statements of fact or theory in accordance with his own judgment.

The typography and make-up of the book are the work of Mr. Walter Gilliss, whose broad experience and wise judgment have been of the greatest value, and who has spared neither time nor pains to make it a worthy example of modern book-making. Most of the head-bands and tail-pieces were engraved, with rare skill, by Mr. Sidney L. Smith, from designs composed by the author.

These acknowledgments would be incomplete, indeed, without at least a word of grateful appreciation for what has been accomplished by the present administration towards the better housing and classification of the city's archives, especially in the Register's and Comptroller's offices and in the Department of Public Works; but, so far, only a beginning has been made, and there remains a vast amount still to be done before these invaluable records can be considered safe from fire, mould, and loss. Much has already been lost: to save and properly to preserve what remains, it is greatly to be hoped that in the near future an archives building will be constructed, designed in accordance with the best modern experience and theory, with ample accommodation for all of the city and county records, of perhaps twenty years standing, and which, therefore, are no longer required in the actual routine work of the various departments; and where complete indexes and calendars will be available to the public. Such a building is now being planned to house the federal archives, in Washington, and similar buildings should eventually be found in all of our cities. It is only by such a centralisation that the administrative business of a community, or group of communities, can be efficiently and economically administered, and the interest of historical study adequately forwarded. The various phases of this important subject are yearly receiving more serious and wide-spread consideration in our country, in pursuance of well-established principles, which obtain, already, in European countries, and for which the Public Archives Commission of the American Historical Association has laboured for somewhat over fifteen years.

TABLE OF CONTENTS

*The descriptions are divided into two parts: (*a*) technical information of special interest to collectors, such as medium employed, date depicted, date issued, dimensions, author or artist, engraver, provenance, other copies, states, etc.; (*b*) information of general history, antiquarian, or topographical interest relating to the buildings or sites depicted.

LIST OF PLATES

THE PRINTED OR CONTEMPORARY MANUSCRIPT TITLES OF ALL MAPS, PLANS AND VIEWS ARE GIVEN IN CAPITALS AND SMALL CAPITALS. THE NAMES BY WHICH THE PRINTS ARE KNOWN TO COLLECTORS ARE GIVEN IN BRACKETS IN CAPITALS AND SMALL LETTERS. WHEN THE REPRODUCTION IS BEFORE LETTERS, OR WHEN IT IS GIVEN IN TRANSLATED FORM THE TITLE IS SUPPLIED IN PARENTHESES. THE DIMENSIONS, UNLESS OTHERWISE NOTED, ARE TAKEN BETWEEN THE INSIDE BORDER LINES.

FOLLOWING CHAPTER II

FOLLOWING CHAPTER IV

TABLE OF CONTENTS OF THE COMPLETE WORK

TABLE OF CONTENTS OF THE COMPLETE WORK

VOLUME I

1498–1811

VOLUME II (APPENDIX)

HISTORICAL SUMMARY

CHAPTER I

THE PERIOD OF DISCOVERY
1524–1609

THE DUTCH PERIOD
1609–1664

CHAPTER I

THE PERIOD OF DISCOVERY

1524–1609

THE DUTCH PERIOD

1609–1664

THE explorer who was so closely associated with the discovery of the Hudson River that his name began to be applied to it almost immediately after his death, was not in reality the first European to discover and describe the confines of the bays and harbour of New York.[1] It is now an established fact that another had entered these waters eighty-five years before Henry Hudson's failure to find a north-east passage to the riches of the Orient had turned him towards the west and brought his ship along our shores.[2] In 1524, Giovanni da Verrazzano, an Italian explorer sailing in the interest of the King of France, coasted along the eastern shore of North America from North Carolina to Newfoundland and on the way "found a very agreeable situation located within two small prominent hills [the Narrows], in the midst of which flowed to the sea a very great river [the Hudson], which was deep within the mouth." His ship, the "Dauphine," a caravel of a hundred tons, was "anchored off the coast in good shelter." Not risking to enter

[1] For further details regarding early explorations in the neighbourhood of Manhattan Island, see Appendix, I, Essay on Cartography.

[2] See Cartography and Vol. III, Chronology.

in with her "without knowledge of the entrances," he used his smaller boat, "entering the said river to the land," which was "found much populated." The natives were "almost like the others" he had found to the southward, "clothed with the feathers of birds of various colours," and approached him and his party "joyfully, uttering very great exclamations of admiration." They showed him where he could "land with the boat more safely." He then "entered the said river, within the land, about half a league" and "saw it made a very beautiful lake with a circuit of about three leagues [the Upper Bay], through which they [the Indians] went, going from one and another part to the number of thirty of their little boats, with innumerable people," who, passing from one shore to the other, sought to get a sight of him and his men. An unfavourable gale arose and he was forced back to the "Dauphine." Weighing anchor, he now "sailed toward the east," as he found the land turned in that direction, and "travelled eighty leagues always in sight of it." Verrazzano never returned to this region and nothing resulted from this part of his discovery; yet he undoubtedly visited the lower and upper bays of New York.

About the beginning of May, 1525, Estevam Gomez, a Portuguese pilot in the service of Emperor Charles V, of Spain, having skirted the North Atlantic from Newfoundland to Cape May, was probably in the vicinity of New York. His explorations extended over a period of about ten months and had a great influence upon the map-makers for a long period thereafter, while they stimulated interest in the region of the North Atlantic.

The rest of the sixteenth century is a period of myth and mystery so far as the neighbourhood of Manhattan Island is concerned. It is probable that during this time a number of voyagers approached its precincts, but only one has left a record of his discoveries, Jehan Cossin, of Dieppe, whose curious and interesting map (C. Pl. 16), dated 1570, contains indications which prove that he explored the outer and inner bays. The really significant "discovery" of New York Bay was not made, however, until 1609—by Henry Hudson, an Englishman, sailing under the auspices of the Dutch East India Company. On September 2d of that year, he rounded Sandy Hook—if we may accept the usual interpretation of the log of Robert Juet, an officer of his ship—and on the eleventh passed through the Narrows into the Upper Bay. He "saw that it was a very good Harbour for all windes, and rode all night." On the afternoon of the twelfth he entered the Upper Bay "two leagues and Anchored," perhaps opposite the Battery. During the succeeding days Hudson ascended the stream to the end "of the River's Navigableness" and explored with his smaller boat as far as the present vicinity of Troy and the mouth of the Mohawk River. Becoming convinced that in this direction no passage was afforded to the Orient, he retraced his course and passed out of sight of Sandy Hook on October 4th.

Hudson's voyage had been undertaken in the interest of the Dutch East India Company, and his ship, "de Halve Maen" (Half Moon), was its property. His landfall at New York was a misdirection, when viewed in the light of his contract and the accompanying instructions. They specified a voyage to search "for a passage by the North, around by the North side of Nova Zembla," and to "continue thus along that parallel" until he should "be able to sail Southward to the latitude of sixty degrees." Furthermore, he was enjoined from going along any other routes or passages on this voyage. In conformity with these requirements, he had taken the course around the North Cape of Norway on his way to Nova Zembla. His progress, however, was blocked by dangerous icebergs, while the severe suffering occasioned by fogs, cold, and snow-storms precipitated dissensions between his Dutch and English sailors. Hudson then, "contrary to his instructions" (*tegens sijn instructie*), although perhaps in conformity with a preconceived plan (see Cartography), gave his crew the choice between going to America in forty degrees north latitude or searching for a north-west passage through Davis Strait.

The Dutch East India Company was limited by its charter of 1602 to the pursuit of the East Indian trade by way of the two known routes, namely, around the Cape of Good Hope and via the Strait of Magellan. The attempt to find a north-east passage, as entrusted to Hudson by his employers, was designed, no doubt, to secure to this company a like monopoly over the new route, if it were found to be passable. The Company took no steps to reap the benefits which might have been derived from his American discoveries, partly because its course was limited by charter and partly because the year 1609 marked the beginning of the truce with Spain. At this time the peace party of the Netherlands, headed by Oldenbarnevelt, to whose policies the Company adhered, was averse to interfering with the Spanish pretensions to the eastern coast of North America, which were derived from discoveries and the Papal bulls confirming these claims of Spain. This inaction was also in part due to the fact that Hudson on his return from his eventful third voyage was detained in England by the authorities, and was not permitted to communicate to his employers in Holland anything more than a brief summary of his discoveries. See Cartography.

There was a connection, however, between Hudson's discovery and the later Dutch activities in North America. In 1610 several merchants of Amsterdam sent a ship to the Hudson River, "called Manhattes from the savage nation that dwells at its mouth." This expedition may have been under the command of Hendrick Christiaensen, of Cleves, who, as the Dutch historian Wassenaer tells us, was the first after Hudson to sail to the river, and is known to have been a most active skipper associated in numerous voyages to the Hudson River between the years 1610 and 1616, in which latter year he was killed by an Indian at Fort Nassau on Castle Island, near Albany. During this period he entered into a partnership with Adriaen Block and the two visited the Hudson in a ship of which one Ryser was the skipper. By 1613 this partnership had apparently become established, but we know very little about it. Christiaensen was commander of the ship "Fortune" and Block had charge of the "Tiger." In the beginning of 1614, the "Tiger" was accidentally burned in New Netherland. Block spent the remainder of this winter in building a small yacht, named by him the "Onrust," [1] in which he subsequently passed through Hellgate and made important discoveries along the New England coast.

On March 27, 1614, the States General of the Netherlands issued a placard or proclamation to encourage the discovery of new "Passages, Havens, Countries, and Places," and offered to "all and every of the Inhabitants of the United Netherlands" a monopoly of trading in such newly discovered regions for four voyages. This proclamation resulted from a petition of traders asking for this exclusive privilege for six voyages. On October 11th of this year, the States General formally granted to a company of thirteen merchants of Amsterdam and Hoorn a trade-monopoly for four voyages to the lands lying between the 40th and 45th

[1] "Onrust" (Unrest, usually translated Restless). It has been asserted in numerous secondary histories that the "Tiger" was burned at or near Manhattan Island and that the "Onrust" was built in the same vicinity, but there is no evidence in support of such claims. On the other hand, there is strong circumstantial evidence in the works of Van Meteren, De Laet, and Wassenaer in support of the assumption that Block was in the vicinity of Albany during the experiences of this winter. There is also no evidence in favour of the view expressed by some writers, that Block and his party built huts near the southern point of Manhattan Island and that they were supplied with food by the Indians of that neighbourhood during this winter. One error has followed naturally upon another. See Chronology under 1614 for the argument. See also the Cartography.

degrees of north latitude. The voyages were to be made within three years and to begin with January, 1615, or earlier. This charter of the United New Netherland Company, which gives the earliest designation of New Netherland to the regions to be explored, records the names of the five ships owned by the merchants of Amsterdam and Hoorn who were members of this first Dutch mercantile company trading to these parts. It reveals that the petitioners had, during the year 1614, "after great expenses and damages by loss of ships and other dangers, . . . discovered and found with the . . . five ships certain New Lands" in the latitude described in the grant. Block's lost ship, the "Tiger," was one of these ships.

Several voyages were made in the next few years (see Cartography). The United New Netherland Company's grant expired in 1618, but its voyages were continued in a desultory manner until 1621, when the newly organised Dutch West India Company was granted a monopoly in supersession of all others in America. New Netherland, however, was not specifically named in its charter. In 1619, Captain Thomas Dermer, who was in the employ of Sir Ferdinando Gorges, of the Plymouth Company, sailed along the coast from the Kennebec to Virginia in search of a north-west passage, and probably passed through Long Island Sound, Hellgate, and the Narrows. On his return voyage, he met some of the Dutchmen "who had a trade in Hudsons river some yeares before that time, with whom he had conference about the state of that coast, and their proceedings with those people, whose answer gave him good content."

It has already been indicated that the peace party of the Netherlands controlled the Dutch East India Company. Its opponents, the war party (sometimes called the Belgians because it contained so many who had left the southern provinces when they yielded to Spain), was headed by the House of Orange and favoured fighting Spain at every point until Belgium should again be united to the northern provinces. Willem Usselinx was a prominent leader of this party. After several years of unsuccessful effort, he had persuaded the States General to charter the West India Company. This charter, granted on June 3, 1621, gave the Company not only exclusive privileges of trade, but also the right to plant colonies, to make alliances with natives, and to build forts to protect its property. The Company was governed by five local chambers of directors, the largest of which sat at Amsterdam, and the executive power was vested in a College of Nineteen, which was made up by proportional representation from the local chambers. The colonies to be planted by virtue of this charter were to be governed by a governor-general[1], appointed by the Company and accountable to it. His appointment, however, was subject to confirmation by the Lords of the States General and he and "all other vice-governors, commanders, and officers" were "obliged to take the oath of allegiance" to the States General and the Company. Any appeal from the governor-general's decisions went to the College of the Nineteen and thence to the Lords of the States General. The objects for which this company was formed were the weakening of Spain by war and by commercial repression.

The usual voyage from Holland to New Netherland was made in seven or eight weeks. Its course lay "towards the Canary Islands; thence to the savage islands [the Desertas], then towards the mainland of Virginia, steering across, in fourteen days, leaving the Bahamas on the left, and the Bermudas on the right hand." The first colony sent out by the Dutch West India Company left Holland "in the beginning of March," 1624, in the ship "Nieu Nederlandt," with Cornelis Jacobsen May as skipper and first director-general. This colony consisted of thirty families, mostly Walloons, and in the beginning of May, arrived at the mouth of the Hudson River, where a French ship was found and driven away. The colonists then proceeded up the river, where they built a fort which they named "Orange," on the site of the present city of Albany. There is no proof that any settlement was made at this time on Manhattan Island, nor is there any record of an earlier settlement, although it is possible that some rough huts or shelters were erected by traders for temporary occupation. (See Cartography.)

The birth of the Dutch Reformed Church in America took place at Fort Orange at this time under Bastiaen Jansz. Krol as comforter of the sick.[2] He was not an ordained minister. His principal duties were to read common prayers every morning and evening, as well before as after meals; faithfully to instruct and comfort all the sick; to speak in particular to those who desired or had need of exhortation in the Scriptures, and, at opportune times, according to his calling, to read chapters from the Scriptures or from books by authors of the Reformed religion, and even to read a sermon. He could not exercise functions allowed

[1] In the general practice in New Netherland this official was usually called "director-general" or simply "director."

[2] Termed "krankenbezoeker" (visitor of the sick) and "ziekentrooster" (comforter of the sick).

only to the ordained clergy, such as the administration of the sacraments. Krol's first residence at Fort Orange lasted only a short time. By the end of the year he had returned home and, on November 14, 1624, he appeared before a session of the church council of Amsterdam, where he reported that the colonists of New Netherland desired a regular clergyman, because children had been born in the colony and awaited baptism. The ecclesiastical council did not approve of sending an ordained minister, since there were so few families in the colony; whereupon Krol sought and obtained authority to baptise and marry in New Netherland, whither he returned a second time, no doubt with the second group of colonists, those who left Holland in April, 1625.

An agricultural colony without cattle was an impossibility; accordingly, to strengthen the colony begun at Fort Orange in 1624, a second contingent of forty-five colonists was sent thither in April, 1625, with an "extraordinary shipment" of domestic animals and all sorts of seeds and agricultural implements. The expedition was fitted out by the Amsterdam Chamber of the West India Company in three ships, accompanied by a fast-sailing yacht; but the yacht was captured on April 27th and taken to Dunkirk.[1] Two months later, the Amsterdam Chamber, probably to replace the losses suffered from this capture, sent over "a fly-boat" laden with "sheep, hogs, wagons, ploughs, and all other implements of husbandry." Director-General May was superseded by Willem Verhulst,[2] the *commis* or commissary of the expedition of 1625. With Verhulst came also Gerrit Fongersz. as *onder-commis* or deputy commissary, and Kryn Fredericksz. went along as engineer and surveyor. The cattle of the expedition under Verhulst were landed first, for "a day or two," on Nut (now Governors) Island; but as there was no pasturage there, they "were shipped in sloops and boats to the Manhates, right opposite the said island," where they remained until the middle of September, with loss of "full twenty" from eating "something bad from an uncultivated soil." They were then removed "to meadow grass, as good and as long as could be desired,"[3] which was without much doubt at Fort Orange, where the colonists had already shown good results in the fields the year before.

[1] The three ships were the "Paert" (Horse), "Koe" (Cow), and "Schaep" (Sheep). The yacht was named "Macreel" (Mackerel). [2] Also "vander Hulst."

[3] All we know about this matter is from Wassenaer (*vide* Jameson's *Nar. N. Neth.*, p. 83). In another passage (p. 82) he says, "The cattle carried thither were removed *upwards* to a convenient place abounding with grass and pasture." Apparently, whenever Wassenaer uses the direction "upwards," he means up the river to Fort Orange, and he distinguishes it from "northwards."

Peter Minuit, who had been appointed to supersede Verhulst as director-general, prepared to leave Holland on December 19, 1625, but did not get away before January 9, 1626, in the ship "Zeemeeuw" or "Meeuwken" (Sea-Mew), of which Adriaen Joris was skipper. Minuit arrived in New Netherland on May 4th, and, after apparently attempting a settlement on Nut Island,[1] began the first real settlement of Manhattan Island. Soon after he had established himself here, he ordered the outlying families and most of the men at Fort Orange (Albany) and Fort Nassau (Gloucester, N. J.) to concentrate at the Manhattan settlement. The "Wapen van Amsterdam," a ship which sailed from New Netherland on September 23, 1626, and arrived at Amsterdam on November 4th, carried to the Fatherland news of this plan and an account of the colony. The population of all New Netherland had "now increased to two hundred souls." During the summer Minuit had effected the purchase of Manhattan Island from the Indians by giving them trinkets valued at sixty guilders ($24). The validity of this transaction was disputed in 1632, during the diplomatic negotiations between the States General and Great Britain. Minuit and Isaack de Rasieres,[2] who came out as provincial secretary and chief commercial agent of the Company, lived together; while the others lived in "thirty ordinary houses on the east side of the river"—in fact, near the strand of the East River on the southern extremity of Manhattan Island, where they occupied mean hovels, huts made "of the bark of trees," and even holes, as we are told by Wassenaer and Michaëlius. Jan Lempou was *schout*, an officer who exercised a composite authority, combining the duties of an English sheriff and a public prosecutor.

Among the first buildings erected upon Manhattan Island after its settlement under Minuit was "the counting-house" of the West India Company, a "stone building, thatched with reed." It was the headquarters of the Company's stores and here its business was transacted under the supervision of the *koopman* or chief commercial agent. It did not survive long, and probably was burned in a general conflagration which destroyed other property of the Company, notably a mill.[3]

The status of the Manhattan settlement in the summer of 1626, as reported in Holland in November of that year, is recorded by the con-

[1] Governors Island.

[2] Isaack de Rasieres had arrived at the end of July in the "Wapen van Amsterdam."

[3] The counting-house may have been located near the strand of the East River and more definitely on the later Marckveldt (Whitehall), between Bridge and Pearl Streets. In 1638 its site could be determined only with difficulty.

temporary historian, Wassenaer, whose account furnishes virtually the only detailed information in print of the conditions on Manhattan at this time. He says:

"The colony is now established on the Manhates, where a fort has been staked out by Master Kryn Frederycks,[1] an engineer. It is planned to be of large dimensions. The ship[2] which has returned home this month brings samples of all sorts of produce growing there, the cargo being 7246 beaver skins, 675 otter skins, 48 mink, 36 wild cat, and various other sorts; many pieces of oak timber and hickory.[3]

"The counting-house there is kept in a stone building, thatched with reed; the other houses are of the bark of trees. Each has his own house. The Director and *Koopman*[4] live together[5]; there are thirty ordinary houses on the east side of the river, which runs nearly north and south. The Honorable Pieter Minuit[6] is Director there at present; Jan Lempou *schout;* Sebastiaen Jansz. Crol[7] and Jan Huych,[8] comforters of the sick, who, whilst awaiting a clergyman, read to the commonalty there, on Sundays, texts of Scripture and the commentaries. François Molemacker[9] is busy building a horse-mill,[10] over which shall be constructed a spacious room sufficient to accommodate a large congregation, and then a tower is to be erected where the bells brought from Porto Rico[11] will be hung." There is no further mention in the records of this tower, which probably was never built.

[1] The engineer and surveyor who came over with Verhulst in 1625.

[2] The "Wapen van Amsterdam," which had arrived in New Netherland on July 27th, was homeward bound from Manhattan on September 23d, and arrived at Amsterdam on November 4th. Wassenaer's annals are placed under November, 1626.

[3] These figures and statements are a quotation in part and a summary of Pieter Schaghen's letter of November 5th, addressed to the Lords of the States General at The Hague. A facsimile of Schaghen's letter (the authority for these facts and of the purchase of Manhattan Island by the Dutch) is given for the first time in Wilson's *Mem. Hist. N. Y.*, Vol. I, p. 160. (See also Chronology.)

[4] Isaack de Rasieres was chief commercial agent. [5] Minuit's wife had not come over with him.

[6] In all known autographs of Minuit he writes his prænomen "Peter."

[7] Properly Bastiaen Jansz. Krol, first comforter of the sick in New Netherland and Minuit's immediate successor in the directorship.

[8] Perhaps more correctly "Huygen," who was Minuit's brother-in-law.

[9] François, the millwright.

[10] It was a grist-mill, a fact borne out by every bit of very early evidence (see Chronology under 1626). Its site is nowhere indicated, but there is strong presumptive evidence that it was burned in a general conflagration some time prior to the arrival of Domine Michaëlius in 1628. In that case, it must have been located near the counting-house, at the strand of the East River. It is pertinent to remark that the first building solely devoted to worship was put up in this vicinity in 1633. Innes, who has called the mill a bark-mill for grinding bark for tan pits, has endeavoured to find a location on "the north side" of the lane "early called the Slyck Steegh, or 'muddy lane,' and upon a site now [1903-4] occupied by the buildings Nos. 32 and 34 South William street." There is no evidence that there was such a street before a couple of decades after 1626, and the later records which he cites as evidence furnish no connecting link, while a supposed building having a "conical roof," as he sees it in the so-called Danckers View, upon which so much of his theory is built, is evidently merely a hay-barrack.

[11] Captured at San Juan at the sacking by the Dutch fleet under Admiral Boudewyn Hendricksz., in October, 1625.

In the account by Wassenaer given above we have the earliest allusion to Christian worship on Manhattan Island. It is not known in what building the two comforters of the sick conducted religious services by reading to the people on Sundays. Manifestly, it was not in the horse-mill, which was only being built, and "over which" it was planned to construct "a spacious room" as a place of worship. Bastiaen Jansz. Krol was for a time the only comforter of the sick and lay reader in Minuit's Manhattan colony, for Jan Huygen, Minuit's brother-in-law, was yet in Amsterdam on April 2, 1626, and could not have reached Manhattan before July 27th, when the "Wapen van Amsterdam" arrived. But Krol was not long in this service at Manhattan after the arrival of Huygen. When the aforesaid ship sailed from Manhattan, on September 23d, Pieter Barentsz., hitherto commander at Fort Orange, returned to Holland, and Krol, appointed to fill the vacancy, went to his new post. It is not likely, therefore, that he was any longer a resident at Manhattan when the horse-mill loft was ready for religious services. If not, then Huygen was the only person serving there in the capacity of comforter of the sick and lay reader, and the first person to conduct a religious service in the first regularly established place of worship on Manhattan Island.

Wassenaer also informs us that "the council there administers in criminal matters as far as imposing fines, but not as far as corporal punishment. Should it happen that any one deserves that, he must be sent to Holland with his sentence." Of the occupations of the people, he says: "Everyone there who fills no public office is busy about his own affairs. Men work there as in Holland; one trades, upwards, southwards, and northwards; another builds houses, the third farms. Each farmer has his farm-stead on the land purchased by the Company, which also owns the cows; but the milk remains to the profit of the farmer; he sells it to those of the people who receive their wages for work every week. The houses of the Hollanders now stand outside the fort, but when that is completed, they will all repair within, so as to garrison it and be secure from sudden attack."

Kryn Fredericksz., the engineer and surveyor who came over with Verhulst in 1625, had received "particular instructions"[1] charging him with the construction of a fortification, as well as houses, in such suitable places as might be discovered by the council in New Netherland. Noth-

[1] Van Rappard Document E. For a brief summary of this document, see Cartography.

ing is known definitely of this engineer's work during the year 1625. After Minuit's arrival in 1626, as Wassenaer shows us, he was at Manhattan, where he "staked out" a fort, "planned to be of large dimensions." This idea was entertained prior to September 23, 1626, as it was then intended to house all of the people within its enclosure, instead of in houses outside, "so as to garrison it and be secure from sudden attack." But this plan of concentration within a large fort was never carried out. Instead, a poor sodded earthwork fort was constructed, so poor, indeed, that in less than two years' time "the ramparts crumbled away like sand" and Minuit, by 1628, had resolved to build a new fort at Manhattan, "having four bastions and faced outside entirely with stone." The population of Manhattan in that year consisted of two hundred and seventy souls—men, women, and children, who "remained as yet without the fort, in no fear" of the Indians, who lived peaceably in their midst. "The small fort, New Amsterdam," was now deemed necessary only as a protection against foreign invasion. Its construction proceeded at a snail's pace. Minuit was succeeded by Krol and he by Wouter van Twiller, in 1633; but the fort was yet incomplete. Thereafter, the Company's negro slaves—first introduced into New Netherland about 1626—were steadily employed "in building Fort Amsterdam, which was completed in the year 1635." The subsequent history of the fort proves that the plan of 1628, for facing it outside entirely with stone, was not executed.

Accounts of the physical conditions on Manhattan Island have come down to us in two letters written by Jonas Michaëlius,[1] the first minister, who arrived in April and at once established a church organisation, which continues to-day as the Collegiate Church of New York and is the oldest communion of the Reformed Church in America. Neither he nor any other contemporary tells us anything of the place or building where this first organisation took place. Michaëlius, in his letter of August 8, 1628, says that food was "scanty and poor" and that "fresh butter and milk" were obtained with difficulty "owing to the large number of people and the small number of cattle and farmers." The great need was a supply of "horses and cows, and industrious workers for the building of houses and fortresses, who later could be employed in farming." He wrote: "True, this island is the key and principal stronghold of the country, and needs to be settled first, as is already done; but it is some-

[1] See Chronology.

what less fertile than other spots, and causes more trouble on account of the multitude of roots of shrubs and trees. . . . The country produces many species of good things which greatly serve to ease life: fish, birds, game, and groves, oysters, tree-fruits, fruits from the earth, medicinal herbs, and others of all kinds. But all is as yet uncultivated, and remains in a wild state as long as no better regulations are made to have things arranged by people who understand the work and make it their business, which, apparently, will be gradually done. A new fortress is in course of construction, not so much for protection against the savages . . . as against enemies from abroad. They are meanwhile beginning to build new houses in place of the hovels and holes in which heretofore they huddled rather than dwelt. They are also cutting wood and erecting another mill for the purpose of exporting to the Fatherland whole cargoes of timber fit for building houses and ships. And for building purposes there is a greater lack of laborers than of materials. For besides many kinds of good timber, there is here clay for the making of bricks and tiles, though rather poor, but the quarry stones, not far away, are better for our use, and there are large quantities of oyster shells to burn for lime." Three days later (August 11th), Michaëlius wrote another letter from New Amsterdam, in which he said: "From the beginning we established the form of a church; and as Brother Bastiaen Crol very seldom comes down from Fort Orange, because the directorship of that fort and the trade there is committed to him, it has been thought best to choose two elders for my assistance and for the proper consideration of all such ecclesiastical matters as might occur, intending the coming year, if the Lord permit, to let one of them retire, and to choose another in his place from a double number first lawfully proposed to the congregation. One of those whom we have now chosen is the Honorable Director [Minuit] himself, and the other is the storekeeper of the Company, Jan Huygen, his brother-in-law, persons of very good character, as far as I have been able to learn, having both been formerly in office in the Church, the one as deacon, the other as elder in the Dutch and French churches, respectively, at Wesel.[1] At the first administration of the Lord's Supper which was observed, not without joy and comfort to many, we had fully fifty communicants—Walloons and Dutch; of whom a portion made their first confession of faith before us, and others exhibited their church certificates. Others had forgotten

[1] In the Rhine Province, Germany.

to bring their certificates with them, not thinking that a church would be formed and established here; and some who brought them, had lost them unfortunately in a general conflagration, but they were admitted upon the satisfactory testimony of others to whom they were known, and also upon their daily good deportment, since one cannot observe strictly all the usual formalities in making a beginning under such circumstances. . . . We are busy now in building a fort of good quarry stone, which is to be found not far from here in abundance. . . . There is good opportunity for making salt, for there are convenient places, the water is salt enough, and there is no want of heat in summer. Besides, what the waters yield, both of the sea and rivers, in all kinds of fish; and what the land possesses in all kinds of birds, game, and woods, with vegetables, fruits, roots, herbs, and plants, both for eating and medicinal purposes, and with which wonderful cures can be effected, it would take too long to tell, nor could I yet tell accurately."[1]

Secretary de Rasieres, not earlier than 1628 and not later than 1630, wrote an account of the agricultural conditions and a physical description of Manhattan Island, as follows [2]: "The island of the Manhatas extends in length along the Mauritse [Hudson] River, from the point where the Fort 'New Amsterdam' is building. It is about seven leagues in circumference, full of trees, and in the middle rocky to the extent of about two leagues in circuit. The north side has good land in two places, where two farmers, each with four horses, would have enough to do without much clearing at first. The grass is good in the forest and valleys, but when made into hay is not so nutritious for the cattle as here [Holland], in consequence of its wild state, but it yearly improves by cultivation. On the east side there rises a large level field, of from 70 to 80 morgens of land,[3] through which runs a very fine fresh stream; so that that land can be ploughed without much clearing. It appears to be good. The six farms [of the West India Company], four of which lie along the River Hellgate [East River], stretching to the south side of the island, have at least 60 morgens of land ready to be sown with winter seed, which at the most will have been ploughed eight times.[4] But as the greater part must have some manure, inasmuch as it is so exhausted by

[1] He also repeats, with some variation, the description of the country, the harvests, and general conditions, as already cited from his letter of August 8th.

[2] See also Chronology, 1626, for brief summary of an earlier letter, written by De Rasieres (Van Rappard Document F.) from Fort Amsterdam, September 23, 1626.

[3] From 140 to 160 acres.

[4] This ploughing "eight times" does not mean eight years.

the wild herbage, I am afraid that all will not be sown; and the more so, as the managers of the farms are hired men. The two hindermost farms, Nos. 1 and 2, are the best; the other farms have also good land, but not so much, and more sandy; so that they are best suited for rye and buckwheat. The small fort, New Amsterdam, commenced to be built, is situated on a point opposite Noten [now Governors] Island; [the channel between] is a gun-shot wide, and is full six or seven fathoms deep in the middle. This point might, with little trouble, be made a small island, by cutting a canal through Blommaert's valley,[1] so as to afford a haven winter and summer, for sloops and ships; and the whole of this little island ought, from its nature, to be made a superb fort, to be approached by land only on one side (since it is a triangle), thus protecting them both. The river marks out, naturally, three angles; the most northern faces and commands within the range of a cannon shot, the great Mauritse [Hudson] River and the land; the southernmost commands on the water level, the channel between Noten Island and the fort, together with the Hellegat; the third point, opposite to Blommaert's valley, commands the lowland; the middle part, which ought to be left as a market-place, is a hillock, higher than the surrounding land, and should always serve as a battery, which might command the three points, if the streets[2] should be arranged accordingly."

In 1629, the West India Company endeavoured to encourage colonisation by granting, on June 7th, a "Charter of Freedoms and Exemptions," to those who would establish colonies in New Netherland. This resulted in the foundation of patroonships under such men as Kiliaen van Rensselaer, Johannes de Laet, David Pietersz. de Vries, Michiel Pauw, Samuel Godyn, and Samuel Blommaert, all of whose names figured more or less in the early place-nomenclature of the province. In this charter the Company announced its intention of peopling the island of Manhattan first, and made it, provisionally, the staple port for all products and wares "found on the North River and lands thereabouts," except such as could not "without great loss to their owners be brought there," in which case measures were to be taken as required by circumstances. This meant that the trading ships were to unload at New Amsterdam or pay certain duties there for the benefit of the Company.

[1] A depression about on the line of the later canal or *gracht* and present Broad Street. The insular idea was not, of course, executed.

[2] This is the earliest mention of streets in connection with the laying out of New Amsterdam and tends to prove that a street-plan was not in existence when De Rasieres made the suggestion given above.

The year 1630 saw the building of the first large ship, named the "Nieu Nederlandt," on the upper Hudson below Albany.[1]

Farming had not yet succeeded very well, if we may accept the information which Symon Dircksz. Pos sent from Manhattan Island to Kiliaen van Rensselaer, on September 19, 1630. He wrote thus: "Concerning the occurrences [at] the Manathans [*sic*], there is much land ploughed everywhere daily by the peasantry. I have now great hope that the Hon. Lords Directors, after their long waiting, shall be released for once from the great charges, as well as to be able to deliver a number of lasts of rye and wheat, raised on land here, in order to meet their heavy expenses. Concerning the current year [1631], we shall need much seed, as we are clearing, harrowing, and ploughing much land."

In February or March, 1632, Bastiaen Jansz. Krol became director-general in place of Minuit, who had been recalled to answer for his acts. Krol served for a period of thirteen months, or until the arrival of Wouter van Twiller, who, upon his appointment in July, 1632, through the influence of Kiliaen van Rensselaer, his uncle, had sailed from Holland, and after a delay of eight months had arrived at New Amsterdam in March, 1633. Everardus Bogardus came over with Van Twiller as the second Dutch minister to preside over the ecclesiastical affairs of New Amsterdam.[2]

During Van Twiller's administration Fort Amsterdam was finished (1635). In the enclosure of the fort he had built a guard-house with lattice-work and a roof and a small house for the soldiers to live in, and had made other improvements, including the repair of his official residence. On the island, outside of the fort, he erected a new bakery, a small house for the midwife, a goat-house behind the five large stone houses of the Company, a church with a house and stable behind it, a large shed, where the ships were built, having a sailmaker's loft above; and completed and covered with pan-tiles the house of the smith, corporal, and cooper. On the Company's chief farm, No. 1, the improvements included a very good barn, dwelling-house, boat-house, and a brewery covered with tiles. Saw- and grist-mills were put in order or provided with necessary articles. Much work was done at the bouweries or farms of Jacobus van Curler and Johannes La Montagne. A house

[1] Numerous modern historians have, with varying degrees of elaboration, claimed that this ship was built on Manhattan Island, usually giving the year as 1631; but neither the place nor the year is tenable, for reasons shown in the Chronology, under 1630, where the subject is discussed at length.

[2] This was Bogardus's first charge after ordination, though he had served a time in Guinea as a comforter of the sick.

was set up on Van Twiller's plantation at Sapokanikan,[1] and houses were built for Tymen Jansen, the shipwright, and for Bogardus, the clergyman. In other parts of the province, also, various improvements were carried out under Van Twiller's directions. The church which Van Twiller caused to be built in 1633,[2] was the first building in New Netherland solely dedicated to religious uses and continued to be used as a church in 1642, when it was spoken of as a "mean barn."

The directors of the Amsterdam Chamber had been divided into two parties; one was in favour of promoting colonization and the other was opposed and favoured economy. The patroonships in New Netherland, which had grown out of this controversy, in turn gave rise to considerable dispute and bad feeling. The young colony at Manhattan suffered from strife and bickerings among the provincial and local authorities. No wonder that the West India Company had reverses in 1634. The Company's accounts, drawn up the next year, showed that $1,669 had been spent upon Fort Amsterdam and upwards of $165,000 for all New Netherland.

Director-General van Twiller issued ground-briefs or patents for land outside of Manhattan Island, but as this island was the property of the Company, occupation of farms or lots there continued to be by permission or lease and without formal ground-briefs. Leases were usually for six years and often carried with them the right of permanent tenure and conveyance, unless the land were needed by the Company at the time the lease expired. In 1636, Van Twiller permitted Roelof Jansen to occupy sixty-two acres. Jansen did not live long; his widow, having been married to Domine Bogardus, was subsequently confirmed in her possession by a formal instrument, and this farm-stead was known for many years thereafter as the "Anneke Jans farm." It was a part of the famous grant which Queen Anne made over to Trinity Church, and which was involved in long-standing legal controversies, echoing unto our day.

The earliest extant land records of Manhattan Island begin with the year 1638, after the arrival of the next director-general, Willem Kieft, and the earliest known private conveyances also date from this time. Perhaps the earliest outright ground-brief was one for two hundred acres in Harlem, dated July 20, 1638, to Andries Hudde, who had married the widow of Hendrick de Forest—a land occupation allowed to De

[1] Later Greenwich village.

[2] On what is now 39 Pearl Street. For the subsequent history of the church-lot, see Chronology, under this year.

Forest in 1637. Grants at Turtle Bay and in Harlem followed in 1639, and in the Smits Vly and in the neighbourhood of the Company's principal bouwery, No. 1, in 1640.

In the course of time grave objection to Van Twiller's administration had arisen and had been accentuated by the strife that raged in the alignment of the Directors at Amsterdam. He was superseded, on September 2, 1637, by Willem Kieft, who arrived at New Amsterdam on March 28, 1638, in the ship "de Harinck" (Herring). Kieft appointed as provincial secretary and bookkeeper of the monthly wages Cornelis van Tienhoven, for years thereafter an evil genius in the government and finally a suicide; and as provincial councillor the able and worthy Dr. Johannes Mousnier de la Montagne, son-in-law of Jesse de Forest. With Kieft came over Adam Roelantsen[1] as schoolmaster, reader, and precentor in New Amsterdam, who conducted the first school supported by the Company, which was begun in 1638.[2] Kieft found Fort Amsterdam "wholly in a ruinous condition; . . . people could go in and out . . . on all sides except alone at the stone bastion," and the cannon were dismantled. Five of the Company's bouweries were unoccupied and "fallen into decay," and they were without any live-stock, which had all been given over to other farms. The shipping was unserviceable, save a yacht, the "Prins Willem," and a new ship was on the stocks. "The whole of the house in the Fort" was "yet in need of repair, as well as the five stone houses, the wooden church, lodge, and smith's."

On April 15, 1638, Kieft promulgated the earliest city ordinance of which there is a record, in regard to port regulations, court days, immorality, and other matters. An ordinance of May 17th was directed against immoderate drinking and the harbouring of sailors. In this month occurred the earliest murder in New Amsterdam, so far as known, when Gerrit Jansen, a gunner, was stabbed to death in front of the gate of Fort Amsterdam during a brawl. Other ordinances of this year were directed against clandestine trade (June 7th); provided for the issuing of patents to freemen (June 24th); related to tobacco regulations and the validity of legal instruments (August 19th); and sought to prevent the Company's servants from departing from Manhattan (November 25th). During this year, on August 20th, the Company proposed to encourage

[1] Also called Adam Roelantsen Groen. He was from Dockum, in Friesland, and had been accepted by the Classis of Amsterdam on August 4, 1637. He is the first schoolmaster in New Netherland of whom we have a record. [2] Not 1633, as usually given through a misinterpretation.

immigration to New Netherland by opening the trade thither to all persons, provided that the merchandise were transported only in the Company's ships, and that an import tax of ten per cent and an export tax of fifteen per cent were paid on all goods going to or coming from the province; but this plan failed. In 1639 the fur trade with the Indians was "thrown free and open to everybody" in the province instead of being reserved to the Company, as formerly. This change stimulated immigration. The bouweries and plantations of Manhattan and its environs increased quickly in numbers, and "one hundred more" were "expected in a short time from the plantations which were taken up."[1] In August, 1639, George Holmes and seven other Englishmen, new settlers in the Dutch province, took the oath of fidelity to the States General, the stadtholder, and the provincial government, promising "to give instant notice of any treason and injury to the country," and "to assist, support, and protect, by all means" at their command, "the inhabitants against all public enemies." A month later Captain John Underhill and more English families were given permission to reside in New Netherland, if they would take the oath of allegiance. Probably a few English families settled under this offer, but Underhill did not come at this time.[2] On November 15th, Holmes and Thomas Hall secured from Kieft a grant of land for a tobacco plantation "from Deutel [Turtle] bay along the East river to the kill of Schepmoes," and from the river "directly into the woods," embracing the section between 47th and 52d Streets, and between the East River and Second Avenue. On September 13th, Kieft leased to three men, for three years, the Company's saw-mill and appurtenances on Nut (Governors) Island at an annual rental of five hundred merchantable or sound planks, one half pine and the other half oak; the lessees were required to keep the mill in repair at their expense and deliver it back in good order at the expiration of the leasehold.[3] It was probably the first saw-mill erected in the environs of New York City. On the same day, September 13th, Kieft granted to Burger Jorissen, a blacksmith who had come down recently from the colony of Rensselaerswyck, "the use of an anvil and bellows, with half of the

[1] The Manatus Map of this year (C. Pls. 41, 42) shows the following in operation or begun: on Manhattan Island, six bouweries of the Company and eight other bouweries and fourteen plantations; off the island but in its environs, eight bouweries and eighteen plantations.

[2] On June 6, 1641, a "considerable number of respectable Englishmen with their clergymen" were given like privileges for settling in the province.

[3] The Company reserved the right to "saw not less than sixty-five to the balk." Among the appurtenances of this saw-mill were twenty saws, forty clamps, two jack-screws, ten log irons, three large and two small sledges, log ropes, log hooks, files, clamp-irons, cranes, a boat-hook, and a cross-cut saw.

smith's house" of the Company, for four years, on the agreement that he should keep the house and tools in good order.

Kieft's bellicose attitude toward the natives began to manifest itself in various ways. On March 31, 1639, the sale of powder and lead to the Indians was prohibited by ordinance; and, on September 15th, he and his council resolved to exact from them a tribute in maize, furs, or wampum, and to enforce the demand if the Indians showed reluctance. Such measures aroused the resentment of the Indians and sowed the seeds of an Indian war, which broke out in 1643. Although Kieft later alleged that he had acted upon orders from Holland, the Directors at Amsterdam denied it altogether. Meanwhile, on July 28th, a mutiny had broken out among the garrison of Fort Amsterdam, in which nine soldiers refused to perform their allotted work. Various sentences were meted out, among them dishonourable discharge, deportation and the death sentence. On May 10, 1640, the earliest militia regulations were established by the provincial council. They required every male inhabitant "residing at and around Fort Amsterdam" to "provide himself with a good gun," keep it ready for use, and in times of danger to repair at once to the corporal to whom each man had been assigned. Fuel was added to the Indian council fire when Kieft, on July 16th, sent Secretary van Tienhoven with a force of soldiers and sailors to punish the Raritan Indians for depredations committed on Staten Island.

The negro quarter of the slaves of the West India Company was, in 1639,[1] on the East River shore, apparently just north of the Saw Kill, at about the present 75th Street. Several of these slaves, in January, 1641, were implicated in the murder of one of their race. It could not be determined which one had given the fatal blow, hence the court drew lots among them, to determine which negro should be hanged in expiation of the crime. The lot fell upon Manuel Gerrit, called the Giant, who accordingly was led to the gibbet. The hangman, also a negro, used two strong halters, turned off the ladder, and the ropes snapped; whereupon the spectators cried out for mercy, which was granted. Curiously enough, this negro was among the first lot of the Company's slaves to be emancipated on February 25, 1644. To them grants of land were allotted during the succeeding years.[2]

[1] This negro quarter is shown on the Manatus Map, but no mention of it is found in any records or printed works.

[2] These grants centred about the Fresh Water (Kolch) and the public wagon road, west of the Bowery and between Canal Street and Astor Place.

A tavern was opened in 1641 by Philip Geraerdy near the present corner of Whitehall and Stone Streets (now the site of the Produce Exchange), which bore the "sign of the Wooden Horse," an object of military punishment. An ordinance of this year prohibited the sale of liquors during divine service or after ten o'clock at night; and another established annual fairs for cattle and hogs on the open space before Fort Amsterdam, on October 15th and November 1st, respectively. On August 29th, the heads of families among the commonalty, whom Kieft had summoned to adopt means for punishing an Indian who had murdered a Dutchman at Turtle Bay, met at Fort Amsterdam and selected a board of twelve men as their representatives. This board, sometimes called the beginning of representative government in New York, had no judicial authority and few functions of importance. It was dissolved peremptorily by Kieft on February 8, 1642.

About the beginning of the year 1642, the Company's city tavern, called the "Stadt Herbergh,"[1] was completed and rented to Philip Gerritsen for six years, and a well and a brew-house were also erected behind it. In this year, also, a new stone church was begun in the south-east corner of the fort; it occupied almost one-fifth of the space within its walls.[2] Delegates from Connecticut met with Kieft and his council at Fort Amsterdam, on July 9th–10th, to negotiate terms for the surrender of Fort Hope (Hartford, Conn.). On June 26th, Andries Hudde was appointed surveyor of New Netherland, and on December 11th, George Baxter was chosen as English secretary of the province, because of "the great number of English" residents who had "numerous law suits." Fugitive servants came daily from New England and Virginia, wherefore an ordinance, of April 13th, forbade the harbouring of strangers for more than one night "without first notifying the Director and having their names recorded." Defendants in court cases were often in default and, on October 16th, fines were established to correct these abuses.

A party of armed Mahicans from the upper Hudson came down in February, 1643, and made war upon the Wickquasgecks, Tapaens, and near-by Indians, who fled for refuge to the Dutch. Some of these

[1] The City Tavern stood on what is now the north-west corner of Pearl Street and Coenties Alley, originally facing the East River with uninterrupted view. It became, in 1653, the "Stadt Huys" or City Hall. It was used by the city for a long time and remained its property until August 23, 1699, when the authorities sold it and the land belonging to it, to John Rodman. It was demolished in 1700 and replaced by another structure.

[2] See Chronology, under this year, for the contract and subsequent operations and history.

refugees encamped on Manhattan Island behind Corlear's Hook on the East River, and on the New Jersey side of the North River at Pavonia. On the twenty-fifth of this month, Kieft commissioned Maryn Adriaensen to attack the former and Sergeant Juriaen Rodolff to go against the latter. The attacks were made simultaneously, about midnight (25th to 26th). Some forty were massacred in their sleep at Corlear's Hook, and about eighty shared a like fate at Pavonia. When the affiliated Indians awoke to a realisation of this treachery to their people, they revenged themselves by killing many men on the farms and devastating the outlying districts by burning "houses, farms, barns, stacks of grain," in fact, everything they could lay waste.

Adriaensen and Kieft fell out over this outrageous affair and, on March 21st, Kieft's life was twice in jeopardy within less than two hours, first from murderous designs of Adriaensen and then from two shots fired at him by a servant of Adriaensen. In March, Kieft made peace with the Long Island Indians, and in April, with the Hackensacks and other Indians of the lower Hudson. The sale of intoxicants to Indians was a breeder of dangerous consequences and was interdicted, yet an illicit trade continued for many years despite all of the ordinances that were promulgated. An ineffectual peace concluded with the Indians in May, was broken by depredations along the Hudson River, begun during the summer by the Wappingers. Kieft summoned the commonalty to name representatives to advise with him in this crisis. On September 13th, they chose a Board of Eight Men, and two days later this board resolved to renew hostilities against all of the Indians except those of Long Island, who were encouraged as allies. Men were enlisted for the campaign; fifty Englishmen enrolled under the command of Captain John Underhill. On October 24th, the Eight Men appealed to the executive authority of the West India Company for succour, and said: "On the Island of Manachatas [*sic*], from the north even unto the Fresh Water, there are no more than five or six spots inhabited at this date. These are threatened by the Indians every night with fire, and by day with the slaughter of both people and cattle. . . . The Fort is defenceless and entirely out of order, and resembles . . . rather a molehill than a fort against an enemy. . . . [the Indians] threaten to attack the Fort with all their force, which now consists of about 1500 men; . . . all the outside places are mostly in their power. . . . The population is composed mainly of women and children; the freemen (exclusive of the English) are about 200 strong, who must protect by force their families now skulking in straw huts outside the Fort. . . . The most of the houses have been fired and destroyed, those still standing are in danger of being also burnt. . . . Cattle destroyed, houses burnt; the mouths of women and children must remain shut." In a memorial to the States General, on November 3d, the Eight Men reiterated their distresses. From that day until the early summer of the following year the Eight Men were not reassembled by Kieft, "though in that period many things occurred." In their complaint of October 28, 1644, to the Directors at Amsterdam, they made the first suggestion of reform by the creation of municipalities throughout the province, and at the same time accused Kieft of showing them scant respect as the representatives of the people. The bloody Indian war lasted until the general peace concluded at Fort Amsterdam on August 30, 1645.

The frequency of depredations by the Indians during the war induced Kieft and his council, on March 31, 1644, to decree the construction of "a Fence, Palisade, or Clearing, beginning from the Great Bouwery to Emanuel's plantation," as a common pasture for the cattle of those persons who aided in constructing the fencing thereof. About a month later (April 25th), he granted to Jan Jansen Damen a large tract of land, situate on both sides of Broadway, from Wall Street to Maiden Lane, and to the Smits Vly. To raise means for continuing the soldiers in service, he sought to lay an excise on liquors and beaver skins, against which the brewers protested in August of that year. The Indian war seriously embarrassed the Company, because its expenses were unusually heavy and, at the same time, those who were indebted to it were so impoverished as to be unable to pay their debts. Kieft had desired to continue the war until the Indians were exterminated, but he was overruled. In 1646, he was recalled to answer for his administration and defend himself against his accusers. He sailed in the ship "Princess"[1] and with others perished in her when she was lost on September 27, 1647. Meanwhile, on July 28, 1646, the authorities of the Company had appointed Petrus Stuyvesant as his successor, but his arrival at New Amsterdam was delayed until May 11, 1647.

In the last year of Kieft's administration (May, 1646), the first cargo of negro slaves, so far as known, to be sold in New Netherland, arrived at New Amsterdam from Tamandaré, a port on the coast of Brazil. On

[1] Also called the "Princess Amelia."

June 12th, a law declared invalid all legal instruments written by private individuals, which were not confirmed by oath before the court or other magistrates, and annulled all affidavits not written by the provincial secretary or other duly authorised person, "likewise Contracts, Testaments, Agreements, and other important documents."[1] During the years 1646 and 1647 a portion of the open space of the esplanade before Fort Amsterdam, situate in front of the five stone houses of the Company, was divided into five grant-lots. These lots faced the later Marckveldt (Whitehall Street) and covered the block from Brouwer (Stone) to Brugh (Bridge) Street, creating a narrow lane on the east called Winckel Straet. One of these grants was to Reverend Everardus Bogardus, Kieft's implacable enemy.

As already mentioned, Stuyvesant arrived on May 11, 1647. A few days later, on the twenty-seventh, he appointed Willem (called also Jelmer) Tomassen as naval commander and Paulus Leendertsen vander Grift as superintendent of naval equipments[2]; and on June 6th the latter was ordered to fit out a naval expedition against the Spaniards within the limits of the West India Company's charter. The earliest recorded ordinance of Stuyvesant's council, dated May 31st of this year, was designed to regulate the sale of intoxicants during certain hours on Sunday and to fix the hours of closing on week-days. On July 1st, the inhabitants throughout the province were commanded to fence their lands properly against damage by cattle and horses; cows and especially goats and hogs were to be herded or kept from doing harm, and the fiscal was instructed to erect a pound in which to detain animals until the damage they committed was made good. An ordinance of July 4th, for regulating shipping at New Amsterdam, defined the anchorage or roadstead on the East River for private vessels as "between Capske Point and the Guide-board near the City Tavern," and for larger ships from Capske Point to "the Second Guide Board . . . on the way down towards the Smith's valley."[3] Fort Amsterdam had fallen into decay and its walls were trodden down daily by men and cattle. Such a sorry spectacle could not fail to inspire contempt in the English, French, and Swedish neighbours, as well as among the Indians; while it presented a condition "most perilous and dangerous in time of attack." Stuyvesant and his

[1] Infractions of this law led to a renewal, on May 8, 1649, whereby illegal instruments were voided.

[2] Their commissions were signed by Stuyvesant, Kieft, Van Dincklagen, and La Montagne.

[3] From about Whitehall Street to Coenties Alley, in the first case; and, perhaps, to about Wall Street in the other case.

council, therefore, on July 4th, levied an excise on imported wines and spirituous liquors to raise funds for repairing the fort, completing the church, erecting a pier "for the convenience of the Merchants and Citizens," and constructing a sheet-piling along the East River. At the same time regulations against smuggling were promulgated and an export duty on furs was established. In the same month, the Reverend Johannes Cornelisz. Backer was chosen as a supply minister in place of Bogardus, who was sailing in the "Princess" for Holland;[1] and Lubbertus van Dincklagen, a member of the council, was raised to the presidency of the ordinary court, to be assisted by some of the principal officers of the Company; to Stuyvesant was reserved the prerogative of presiding in important cases. Councillor van Dincklagen, Naval Officer vander Grift, and Secretary van Tienhoven were appointed a board of city surveyors to prevent a continuance of irregularities in the building and erecting of houses, such as extending lots far beyond their boundaries, setting up nuisances on highways and streets, and neglecting to build on granted lots. They were empowered "to condemn and in future to stop all unsightly and irregular Buildings, Fences, Palisades, Posts, Rails, etc.," and no one was allowed to build without first obtaining from them a proper survey and permit.[2]

On September 25, 1647, Stuyvesant and his council designated a Board of Nine Men out of eighteen names submitted by the commonalty, to co-operate in promoting the public welfare. Three merchants, three burghers, and three farmers composed the first board. It was closely controlled by Stuyvesant, who appointed its president, authorised its meetings, and allowed consideration only of questions that he proposed. None the less, the board "constituted a permanent element in the governmental system" for prospective acquisition of popular rights—hence it was a step in the direction of representative government. Six members retired annually and their places were filled by men chosen by Stuyvesant and his council from a double number nominated by the full board on the last day of each calendar year. In November, Stuyvesant sought the advice of the Nine Men with respect to the best way of procuring means to restore Fort Amsterdam, now "entirely out of repair"; complete

[1] It is interesting to note that the ship "Princess," in which Kieft, Bogardus, and others left New Amsterdam for Holland, perishing in her when she was lost on September 27th, had aboard "very exact Maps" of New Netherland, probably copies of the original surveys, on which, a few years later, the first of the important Visscher series of maps was based (see Cartography).

[2] This committee combined, in some measure at least, the duties and prerogatives of the present Bureau of Buildings and the Art Commission.

the church in the fort; provide a new schoolhouse and a dwelling for the schoolmaster; and make proper provision in case of conflagrations, since most of the houses in New Amsterdam were built of wood and covered with thatch. Every male person from sixteen to sixty years of age was required, by an order of November 22d, to work at the fort twelve days in the year, or, finding it inconvenient to perform such labour, to be exempt on the payment of two guilders for each day's default.

A stirring event occurred in the province a few days after the first Board of Nine Men had been chosen. Andrew Forrester, a Scotchman acting as agent and attorney for Mary, the widow of Lord Stirling, came to New Amsterdam as a pretended governor of Long Island and places adjacent, and demanded to see Stuyvesant's commission and authority. Stuyvesant answered Forrester by clapping him into prison in the City Tavern and the council ordered him before them to examine him as to his own commission and authority. The inquisition resulted in his being sent a prisoner in the ship "Valckenier" (Falconer) to Holland, there to vindicate himself before the States General; but the ship was forced by bad weather into Spithead, England, where Forrester was released from his confinement by the captain of an English man-of-war.

During Kieft's administration the Company's effects had been lent liberally to the farmers and others; these were, on January 12, 1648, called in by the provincial authorities, who, at the same time ordered the Company's saw-mill on Nut (Governors) Island, now "wholly decayed and in ruin," to be dismantled, if possible—otherwise to be burned down in order to salvage the iron. It was the oldest saw-mill in the environs of Manhattan Island and antedated, perhaps, the founding of New Amsterdam in 1626. In August, the Company's flour-mill near Fort Amsterdam, hitherto rented at a loss, was taken over for the Company's profit and Abraham Pietersen was appointed as public miller on a salary.

To insure a proper entry and collection of the excise in New Amsterdam and the surrounding country, the council, on January 12th, prohibited the retail trade to brewers, but gave them the exclusive right of brewing. Flagrant infractions of the ordinance against the sale of intoxicants on Sunday troubled the government greatly; it declared that "this sort of business and the profit easily accruing therefrom" diverted many "from their original and primitive calling, occupation, and business to resort to Tavern-keeping, so that nearly the just fourth of the city of

New Amsterdam" consisted "of Brandy shops, Tobacco, or Beer houses," to the neglect of "more honorable Trades and occupations" and the debauching of "the Common people and the Company's servants," and "still worse, the Youth." On March 10th an ordinance was enacted, which provided that no "new Alehouses, Taverns, or Tippling places" were to be opened without consent of the director-general and council; those already in existence might continue "at least four consecutive years more, but, in the meantime, remain bound and obliged to supply themselves, like other decent trades, . . . with proper and respectable citizen houses for the embellishment and improvement" of the city. They were allowed to engage in another business; but could not sell their taverns or lease or sell house or dwelling to anyone else for such purpose without official permission. A few days later, the tavern-keepers promised to obey this ordinance. No doubt, Domine Backer was instrumental in forwarding this decree, as well as one of April 29th for holding a second or afternoon Sunday service and extending the operation of Sunday observance under a heavy penalty. In September, he wrote to the Classis at Amsterdam that his congregation numbered about one hundred and seventy members; that most of these were "very ignorant in regard to true religion, and very much given to drink." "To this," he added, "they are led by the seventeen tap-houses here." He hoped the Classis could prevail upon the Directors at Amsterdam to order the "closing of these places, except three or four"; for then "the source of much evil and great offense would be removed." On July 23d, a tavern was ordered closed because a murder had been committed there.

Another evil was the clandestine trade in liquors with the Indians, who were seen daily "running drunk along the Manhattans," ever likely to engender "new troubles and wars." A new ordinance, of May 13th, prescribed "an arbitrary corporal punishment" and fines upon offenders; and, on August 19th, the prohibition of the sale of firearms, etc., to Indians was reënacted. Drink was not the only thing that provoked the Indians to misdeeds. Inhabitants who employed Indians frequently dismissed them without pay, which injustice inspired a threat of summary vengeance. An order of September 28th sought to remedy this evil.

In his appeal, on September 2d, to the Classis at Amsterdam for a schoolmaster, Domine Backer wrote: "He should not only know how to read, write, and cipher, but should also be a man of pious life and decent habits. He should have a good knowledge of the principal points of our

Faith, and set a holy example to the children. In order to best help the church of God here, and resist a bad world, I think, we must begin with the children; for many of the older people are so far depraved, that they are now ashamed to learn anything good." On October 26th, Pieter vander Linde, an old resident, was appointed temporarily as lay reader (*voorleser*) and precentor of the church at New Amsterdam, in place of Jan Stevensen, the former schoolmaster, who had returned to Holland.

The danger of fire was constantly imminent in the city, where the houses were "for the most part built of Wood and thatched with Reed," and with some of the chimneys of wood.[1] Careless people neglected to keep their chimneys cleanly swept and failed to watch their hearths. Two houses had recently been burned from these causes; therefore, on January 23d, the government ordered that no more chimneys should be built "of wood or plaister in any houses between the Fort and the Fresh Water," in other words, within the town limits. Those already erected were allowed to remain "until further order and pleasure of the Fire-wardens." Four fire-wardens were now appointed by the council to inspect all of the chimneys within the prescribed territory and to levy "a fine of three Guilders for every flue found to be dirty, to be expended for Fire ladders, Hooks, and Buckets." Notwithstanding the reaffirmation of this ordinance from time to time, it was "obstinately neglected by many Inhabitants."

Orchards, gardens, and other improvements were damaged daily by hogs and goats running about the city, and so, on March 10th, the inhabitants were enjoined in future from pasturing or keeping hogs or goats within the precincts of the town unless they were kept within enclosures that were fenced high enough to prevent their leaping over them. Beyond the Fresh Water, goats were not to be pastured without a herdsman or keeper, on pain of forfeiture.

On March 10th, concessions were granted "to the Stranger and Inhabitant" of the town of "a Weekly Market-day, to wit Monday, and annually a Free Market for ten consecutive days," beginning on the first Monday after St. Bartholomew's day (September 2d, new style), and corresponding to the legal Amsterdam Fair in Holland. On these weekly and annual days "the Neighbor and Stranger, as well as the Inhabitant"

[1] Built up of small logs, notched together at the corners, and having the crevices filled in with clay or lime mortar.

were "allowed . . . to supply the purchaser from a Booth, by the ell, weight, or measure, wholesale or retail." An elaborate ordinance, of the same date, provided for the regulation of trade and navigation. It declared the East River from the Sound to the Bay open and free "to all persons of what quality or nation soever." It also regulated the retail and wholesale trade of New Amsterdam, prescribed Dutch weights and measures, limited trade on the Delaware and Hudson to burghers and inhabitants who possessed real estate to the value of from two to three thousand guilders, and allowed only those who owned real estate below the Fresh Water, or within the town limits, "to have built or to buy Yachts, Sloops, or Vessels." Some of the trade provisions were disapproved by the Directors at Amsterdam. By September of this year, the provincial government was obliged to issue an ordinance against traders who came over to New Netherland, undersold resident traders, and departed in the same year "without bestowing or conferring any benefit on the Country," while inhabitants who owned property had to bear the burdens of taxation. Those traders who came from Holland were now to take up their abode in the province for three consecutive years and, in addition, build a decent private dwelling. Objections from the Directors at Amsterdam greatly modified this law; but it bore fruit in 1657, when the great and small burgher-rights in New Amsterdam were promulgated.

The breaking up of winter had caused almost universal distress from inundations, floods, shipwrecks, sickness, and pestilence, whereby thousands met an untimely death in Europe and America. New Netherland suffered especially from heavy rains and high water. On April 16th, Stuyvesant and his council proclaimed a general day of fasting and prayer in an appeal to Heaven for alleviation.

On May 25th, the council resolved to furnish guns and to build a guard-house for the burgher corps or militia of New Amsterdam; and, on June 28th, the officer of the burgher-guard was ordered to fine such citizens as neglected to attend the guard in turn, or who behaved in a disorderly manner.

Many of the commonalty neglected to build decent houses on their granted lots; moreover, it was found that the lots had been laid out too large for practical needs, and other persons, who were now desirous of building, could not obtain convenient sites. The derelict were to be notified "once more for the last time to erect proper buildings" or, failing to comply, to have their grants disposed of to persons more inclined than they to build in the city, in which case the original owners were to be indemnified "at the discretion of the Street Surveyors." This order was issued on December 15th.

Among the public works recommended by Stuyvesant's council, on July 4, 1647, less than two months after his arrival in New Amsterdam, was the erection of "a Pier for the convenience of the Merchants and Citizens." This desire was reiterated in an ordinance of September 27th of that year. The outcome was "a wooden wharf" or dock built on the East River in 1648-49.[1] It continued to be the sole pier of New Amsterdam until a new and larger one, called the "Bridge," was built in 1659, near the foot of the present Moore Street.

The year 1649 was a stormy one in the annals of New Netherland. On May 8th, Stuyvesant went in person to the house of Domine Backer and ordered him not to read or allow others to read "from the pulpit or elsewhere in the church . . . any writing, petition, or proposal having relation to the municipal government," unless such writing bore his or the secretary's signature, or was by his order and that of the council. The prohibition did not apply to ecclesiastical affairs, but was intended to prevent publication by the representatives of the commonalty of a remonstrance against him. This remonstrance, formally drawn up on July 28th by Adriaen vander Donck and ten others as representatives of the commonalty—as well as a petition of the twenty-sixth—appealed to the States General for redress of their grievances against the incompetent administrations of Kieft and Stuyvesant and for the enactment of measures which would improve conditions in the province of New Netherland. It contained the first specific application for a municipal government for New Amsterdam. It recommended "a public school, provided with at least two good masters." It intimated favoritism and governmental corruption, and protested that Fort Amsterdam lay then like a mole-hill or a tottering wall, on which there was not one gun carriage or one piece of cannon in a suitable frame or on a good platform. It stated that the people had been asked for money for the public works, but they had excused themselves because they were poor, and from fear of Stuyvesant, lest with a strong fort he should become more cruel and severe; hence nothing was done. The Company's grist-mill near the fort, it declared, was so rotten from a leaky roof that it could not "go with more than two arms," which added to the shortage of bread. A scarcity of crops

[1] Undoubtedly the little wooden jetty built at the end of Schreyers Hoek and shown on the earliest views.

in this year caused a contingent scarcity of bread; and to alleviate this condition, on November 8th, the council prohibited malting or brewing of wheat and exportation from New Netherland of wheat, rye, or baked bread. An assize on bread, the first recorded for New Netherland, was established. At the same time, owing to frauds and smuggling in contravention of the excise, the brewers were forbidden to deliver their product without first obtaining a permit from the chief clerk of the provincial secretary. On July 19th, the old Amsterdam standard for weights and measures, used by wholesale and retail merchants, bakers, and others, was ordered to be put into effect on August 1st. In the meantime all weights and measures were to be tested at "the Company's warehouse in the Fort." On the same day, a council of the chiefs of the Indians from the neighbourhood of Manhattan was held with Stuyvesant and his council on behalf of the Minquas and other tribes.

The Directors in Holland, on January 27, 1649, complained to Stuyvesant against the erection of "a storehouse 100 feet long and 19 feet in width," the well-known "Pack Huys" of the West India Company,[1] a building designed to be a salesroom of the Company as well as a custom-house. In this they recognised one of the grievances of the remonstrance of the commonalty. At the same time the Directors estimated that Stuyvesant must have received since his arrival in 1647, "in values, money, and goods about 170 to 180 thousand florins,"[2] for which they demanded "a complete statement of the revenues and expenditures."

The treaty of peace between Spain and the Netherlands, called the Peace of Westphalia, whereby the independence of the United Provinces was recognised and the Thirty Years' War terminated, was observed in New Netherland on February 1st by a day of general fasting, prayer, and thanksgiving. In this year, the "Breeden-Raedt," the earliest separate publication dealing with affairs in New Netherland, was printed at Antwerp.

The farmers on Manhattan Island petitioned Stuyvesant and his council for a free pasturage or common "between the plantation of Schepmoes and the fence of the Great Bouwery No. 1," which was allowed them on March 4th, and it was agreed that no new plantations should be laid out within these boundaries. Tobacco was a staple grown in the province, but excessive export duties had been imposed. On April 21st, the duty was reduced by ordinance so as to equalise it with "tobacco coming from

[1] On the site of the present 33 Pearl Street. [2] Between sixty-eight and seventy-two thousand dollars.

the Caribean Islands," namely, forty-five stivers for the hundred. It was intended to offset in this way a tobacco monopoly that was carried on by the Swedes on the Delaware and to encourage farming and agriculture in New Netherland.

In August, Domine Backer, who had resolved to return to Holland, was succeeded by Domine Johannes Megapolensis, late of the colony of Rensselaerswyck, as minister of the church at New Amsterdam, where he served eminently until his death in January, 1670. In October, Stuyvesant, as elder of the church and on behalf of its Consistory, requested the Classis of Amsterdam for "a pious and diligent schoolmaster and precentor" to fill a vacancy that had existed for a year, to the deprivation and damage of the youth. In compliance with this appeal, Willem Vestius[1] sailed from Holland in April, 1650; he served until he was succeeded, in March, 1655, by Harmen van Hoboocken.

A report of April 11, 1650, made by a committee of the States General and entitled a "Provisional Order respecting the Government, Preservation, and Peopling of New Netherland," was designed to meet the complaint of the commonalty by a removal of the causes that had so greatly disturbed the conduct of affairs in the province oversea. Among other things, it recommended that there be granted "within the city of New Amsterdam a municipal government, consisting of one Sheriff (*schout*), two Burgomasters, and five Schepens," and that the Board of Nine Men, in the meantime, "continue three years longer, and have jurisdiction over small causes arising between Man and Man, to adjudicate definitely on suits not exceeding the sum of fifty guilders and on higher amounts under privilege of appeal." This was the foundation on which the municipal concessions of 1653 were built.

In this year (1650) the first flag for the use of the burgher-guard was brought over from Holland, but Stuyvesant would not allow it to be carried about the city. Numerous accessions were made to the population of Manhattan by persons who came over from Holland and, on July 24th, the Directors at Amsterdam instructed Stuyvesant to "allot to each according to his capacities and family sufficient quantities of land." They also advised him to "govern the people with the utmost caution and leniency." Clandestine abuses and frauds in the transfer of real estate had been practised "to the serious injury of Creditors," and so Stuyvesant and the council, on February 7th, ordered that no deeds should be passed

[1] Written also Vestensz. or Vestiens.

by the provincial secretary or his chief clerk before they had been "examined and approved by the Director and Council" on a regular court day. On May 23d, the provincial authorities passed an ordinance against the obstruction of streets, paths, and highways by the placing of stones in them, or the felling of trees, prescribing that the streets be kept in a condition fit for travel. Moreover, the inhabitants were warned, on June 27th, against keeping "Hogs, Sheep, Goats, Horses, or Cows" at large without a herder or driver anywhere between the fort, the Company's farm at the end of the Heeren Wegh (Broadway), and the house of Isaac Allerton (Peck Slip), except within their own fenced lots or farms. This ordinance was generally disobeyed and the ruinous conditions continued.

In September, 1650, Stuyvesant, accompanied by a suite, went to Hartford, and began negotiations with the commissioners of the United Colonies of New England for the settlement of existing differences. The matter was by agreement referred to a joint commission consisting of Simon Bradstreet, of Massachusetts Bay; Thomas Prence, of Plymouth Colony; and Thomas Willett and George Baxter, representing the interests of New Netherland. After a brief deliberation these commissioners presented their conclusions. The chief result was the signing of the treaty of Hartford, on the twenty-ninth, by which a provisional boundary between New Netherland and New England was fixed upon, which played an important rôle in all subsequent boundary negotiations.

The Directors at Amsterdam, who in February, 1650, had complained of the extravagant grants of land that had been made to Wouter van Twiller, took the matter in hand more particularly on March 21, 1651. These grants, as well as those to Cornelis Melyn and others, they claimed, were "without formality and without determination by survey, as if the Company and its officers had nothing to say about it and had been robbed or deprived of their prerogatives." They directed Stuyvesant not to grant land to anybody unless the grantee made proper acknowledgment of the authority of the West India Company and showed that he had the means "to populate, cultivate, and bring into a good state of tillage" such lands as he received. An interesting land transaction of this year was the conveyance by the Directors at Amsterdam, on March 12th, of the Company's "Great Bouwery" or Farm No. 1, to Stuyvesant for 6,400 guilders ($2,560). It extended from about the present 5th to 17th Street and from the East River to an irregular line coinciding approximately with Fourth Avenue. This was the farm which was known for a long time afterwards as Stuyvesant's Bouwery.

On November 15th, Stuyvesant wrote to the Nine Men that he had made "several fruitless representations to the late Board" for assistance in the repair of the fort; that he had himself "begun the highly necessary and urgent work with the few negroes and servants of the Company" and, during "the last two summers of 1650 and 51," had made "tolerable progress"; that he "would have enclosed the Fort all round and put it in good shape" for the Company's and the country's service, if "his and the Company's servants had not been obliged to go to the South [Delaware] river and remain there the greater part" of the summer of 1651, to build the new Fort Casimir. Meanwhile, "the newly erected work on Fort New Amsterdam" had been "destroyed and trampled down by horses, cows, and hogs." He had spoken several times to the Nine Men of the vexation and disgust he felt on seeing the results of his endeavours brought to ruin. He agreed that "the negligence and connivance" of Fiscal Hendrick van Dyck were to blame; for he had failed to enforce the proclamations of government. "We are . . . compelled," Stuyvesant added, "to leave the Fort, to our shame and the detriment of this place, as we found it, and to suspend all work on it or to execute and enforce our orders and proclamations, now already three or four times published . . . , namely, to impound" the cattle, etc., found on the fort and confiscate them to the benefit of the Company. Fiscal van Dyck, in his defence of September 16, 1652, declared that Stuyvesant's operations in 1651 consisted in having "the outside of the fort faced with flat sods by the Company's Negroes"; but, as the soil was sandy and the foundation weak, "the sods mostly sagged and fell to pieces so that the inhabitants' swine damaged the fort," and that Stuyvesant ordered the soldiers to shoot the hogs that were found there. This order for shooting hogs was mitigated the next year at the request of the Board of Nine Men.

Many people came over from Holland in the year 1652, because the transportation to New Netherland was cheapened for indigent passengers embarking in private freighters. The assurance of a more progressive government and greater privileges for the commonalty, resulting from the recent remonstrances to Holland, no doubt had its effect in an increased immigration. An export duty of eight per cent on New Netherland tobacco was abolished. On August 6th, the first suggestion for postal regulations in New Netherland was made to Stuyvesant by the

Directors at Amsterdam; but the first operation of a post office at New Amsterdam, in all of its ramifications, did not obtain before the year 1660. The City Tavern (Stadt Herbergh) was leased to Abram de la Noy on January 24th. In February, regulations were made in council for the proper conduct of the Company's wind-mill near the fort and for the appointment of a superintendent, at a yearly salary. The grain of the Company had precedence; after that the grain of those inhabitants who had "obtained a permit at the Office of the Store" of the Company, was to be ground on the basis of "first come, first served." The surgeons, on February 12th, petitioned for a monopoly of the tonsorial art. This was disallowed; but they were the only ones permitted to keep "a shop to do it in," while the ships' barbers were forbidden to "dress any wounds, bleed, or prescribe for any one on land," without the consent of the city's surgeons. Megapolensis was still the only clergyman in the city. His ecclesiastical duties had grown beyond his ability to fulfill them alone, and, in this year, the Reverend Samuel Drisius was appointed as the second minister, to assist him. In March, Hendrick van Dyck, the fiscal or prosecuting officer of the province, was removed from his office for uttering calumnies against Stuyvesant and for his "connivance, negligence, and general failing to do his duty." He was charged with calling Stuyvesant a "Scoundrel, Murderer, Tyrant, Hound, Baby, and other like names." He entered a general denial, demanded a copy of the proceedings accompanying his suspension, and, when he was given a copy of Stuyvesant's letter, retorted that it was a mere pasquil or lampoon. On April 29th, the Directors at Amsterdam ordered Stuyvesant to accommodate Marcus Hendrick Vogelsang, a ship carpenter, with space in a convenient locality on Manhattan Island for "erecting a shipyard and dock and a house."

To prevent accidents in the city, an ordinance was passed on June 27th by Stuyvesant and the council against fast driving. This also prohibited drivers from sitting or standing on their conveyances anywhere within the city limits, except on Broadway; in all other places they were to "walk by the Wagons, Carts, or Sleighs, and so take and lead the horses." Shooting partridges and other game was a daily diversion in the city and the "many guns" that were discharged endangered life and evoked complaints to the provincial authorities, who, on October 9th, issued an ordinance against the practice and prescribed a forfeiture of firearms and a fine for violations. If there were internal dangers, there were also external fears. On account of a break in the diplomatic relations between the States General and England and impending war, the Directors, on August 6th, warned the New Netherland officials to "arm all freemen, soldiers, and sailors and fit them for defence" under "proper officers" and to appoint "places of rendezvous"; also to "put the fortifications at New Amsterdam, Orange, and Casimir in a good state of defence," while keeping an eye on their New England neighbours.

The Directors at Amsterdam had often demanded of Stuyvesant an accounting of the prizes captured, ships sold, the proceeds from merchandise sent to New Netherland, etc., and had been met by the excuse that there was not a sufficient clerical force available to furnish a proper return. Therefore, on April 4th, they informed Stuyvesant that a bookkeeper had been sent from Holland and that "a special bureau for New-Netherland matters" had been established at Amsterdam. They also asked him to send over, at the earliest opportunity, "accurate registers of all lands, bouweries, and houses let out on lease by the Company, with the rents and conditions" under which they were rented. They referred to the charter of liberties and exemptions by which Manhattan Island was wholly reserved for the Company, and, since they suspected that some lands and lots on the island had been given to private individuals without their knowledge, they required of him a detailed report covering these matters. They mentioned by name examples of the fraudulent tenure of land that had come to their notice and ordered the vacating of "all such contracts of purchase made heretofore." Following upon these instructions, Stuyvesant and the council on July 1st passed an ordinance for regulating the purchase of Indian lands and vacating and annulling certain extravagant grants and purchases, including those of Wouter van Twiller, Brant Aertsen van Slichtenhorst, Lubbertus van Dincklagen, and Govert Loockermans. The whole subject of land occupation had been a *bête noire* in the administration of New Netherland for many years. On December 13th, the Directors said they had never intended that their consent given to immigrants for acquisition of land in New Netherland should mean that anyone could become the owner of from two to four hundred acres and then leave the land in an uncultivated state, so depriving others of obtaining convenient land, save at an enhanced price. They declared that the land must be actually occupied and ploughed within the space of three years and be settled by the number of people stipulated in the conditions with respect thereto, or revert for the benefit of the Company and the accommodation of other persons. The edicts that grew out of this decision, published "in front of the City Hall" on August 4, 1654, stipulated "that the quit-rent or annual payment of 12 stivers for each morgen" (two acres) should "become due a year after the land" had "first been ploughed or otherwise put to use."

The year 1653 was the banner year of New Amsterdam during the entire Dutch régime. Until this time its government was co-ordinate with that of the province, under the administration of a director-general, provincial council, and fiscal. We have seen that in April, 1650, a suggestion for municipal government in New Amsterdam was made in a report of a committee to the States General, but deferring its inception for several years; also that, on April 4, 1652, the Directors at Amsterdam informed Stuyvesant and his council that a municipal form of government, under a *schout*, two burgomasters, and five schepens, was granted to New Amsterdam; but the separate office of *schout* was not reposed in the city at this time.

On February 2, 1653, Stuyvesant and his council proclaimed the form of municipal government for New Amsterdam in a long instrument, the full text of which has been unknown hitherto to historians.[1] The substance of this text is as follows: The director-general and council of New Netherland "do by these presents declare, that their Honors the Directors of the Chartered West India Company of the Chamber of Amsterdam, Lords and Patroons of this Province, have thought well, under the superior administration of their director-general and council of New Netherland, to grant to this growing town of New Amsterdam and its inhabitants a bench of justice, to be framed, as far as possible and as the situation of the country permits, after the laudable customs of the city of Amsterdam, which gave her name to this first commenced town; but also that all sentences shall remain revocable and appealable to the director-general and council, in order to be definitely determined by them." This bench of justice was to consist of two burgomasters and five schepens who thenceforth were to be sworn in on the second of February (Candlemas), Sunday excepted. It was to be served by a secretary or clerk and a *boode* or messenger. Each year a certain number of the bench were to be changed, the others remaining in order to acquaint the incoming members with the former transactions of the court. The jurisdiction of the

[1] This text and its importance in the history of this city were discovered and recognised for the first time for this work by Victor Hugo Paltsits in the course of researches made in 1911. For the full particulars, see the Bibliography.

burgomasters was fixed as "between both rivers [Hudson and East Rivers] and as far as the Fresh Water." They were enjoined from making or publishing any new ordinances without the knowledge, approbation, and ratification of the director-general and council. In administrative matters they were given absolute authority to nominate persons to be weigh-masters, church-wardens, city surveyors, fire-inspectors, etc.; but the nominees were subject to election and confirmation by the director-general. The instrument provided that the bench of schepens should consist of the two burgomasters and five schepens—the oldest burgomaster to preside and the oldest schepen to be vice-president. The powers of this bench were to hear, examine, and determine by sentence or arbitration all civil cases moved and brought before them; also criminal dereliction of a middle degree. The methods and orders for appeal to the supreme bench were defined. The instrument prescribed also the form of oath to be taken by burgomasters and schepens and gave instructions to the secretary or clerk of this inferior bench of justice (*clyne banck van Justitie*).

Already on January 27th, Stuyvesant and the council had appointed Jacob Kip "to serve as Secretary or Clerk to the Burgomasters and Schepens of New Amsterdam," his term "to begin on the next first of February." His appointment, therefore, preceded the induction of the first board, which consisted of Arent van Hattem and Martin Cregier, burgomasters; and Paulus Leendertsen vander Grift, Maximilianus van Gheel, Allard Anthony, Willem Beeckman, and Pieter Wolphertsen van Couwenhoven, schepens. Cornelis van Tienhoven, the provincial fiscal, served this court as *schout* or prosecutor. The separation of this function did not repose in the city before the year 1660. The first sessions of the court were held at Fort Amsterdam. On February 6th, notice was given that regular sessions would be held "in the house hitherto called the City tavern,[1], henceforth the City Hall (*Stadt Huys*), on Monday mornings," where they began to sit on February 24th.

Among the first interests of the burgomasters and schepens was the care of widows and orphans. On February 10th, they recommended to Stuyvesant and the council the necessity of having in the city a court of orphan-masters, and were informed, on the twenty-sixth, that the proposal was praiseworthy but needed "appendages . . . before such an Orphans Court could be established, for which the weak state of this just beginning city" was not prepared. They were advised that the care of widows

[1] Pearl Street and Coenties Alley. The Directors at Amsterdam granted this building to the city in May, 1654.

and children could be left to the deacons of the church and, in particular cases, "special curators" could be appointed "for this or that widow and orphans or over their estates."[1] Another suggestion made by the city fathers to the provincial authorities, on February 10th, was the need of a weigh-house "for the convenience of everybody, to weigh all wares, none excepted," that were delivered in the city, and of provision for its administration and the standardisation of weights and measures. The establishment of a weigh-house and scales became a fact in the spring of 1654. The building, which originally probably stood near the little dock built at Schreyers Hoek by Stuyvesant in 1648-9, was later removed to a point near the head of the pier, built in 1659 opposite the end of the present Moore Street, where it is conspicuous on the so-called "Duke's Plan," as well as on the views of the period.

Early in this year, rumours of warlike preparations in New England reached New Amsterdam. The mother countries of these American neighbours were engaged in sanguinary conflict. On March 13th, a general meeting of the Dutch provincial and city authorities, held to discuss the evil forebodings, led to a plan for the defence of the city by establishing a burgher night watch, "to stand guard in full squads over night" at designated places, but beginning at once "at the City Tavern, now the City Hall." The plan provided, secondly, "that Fort Amsterdam be repaired and strengthened," and, thirdly, as the fort could not contain all of the inhabitants or "defend all the houses and dwellings in the City," it was determined "to surround the greater part of the City with a high stockade and a small breastwork," behind which in time of peril the inhabitants could be sheltered from attack and defend themselves and their possessions. As it was deemed impossible then, either by stockades or by other means, to protect the outlying villages with their scattered inhabitants, a concentration at New Amsterdam was planned "for the better protection of one place." Ways and means were discussed and a provisional list of contributions, amounting to over five thousand guilders, was fixed upon.[2] Skipper Jan Jansen Visscher was to be secretly instructed to make "ready with his ships, loaded with pieces of artillery, in case of emergency." On March 15th, the burgomasters and schepens chose Pieter Wolphertsen van Couwenhoven and Willem Beeckman to act with Johannes La Montagne, of the provincial council, in arranging

[1] On October 18, 1655, a new departure was made, and on February 25, 1656, an independent court, in the nature of a surrogate's court, was created.

[2] This list of names is the earliest assessment list of the kind for this city.

for the security of the city. They at once began to advertise proposals for the erection of the palisades; but their original specifications were not carried out, partly because there were no bidders at the low figure they named. On April 20th, at a meeting of the Council of New Netherland, it was resolved that "the citizens without exception" should begin "immediately digging a ditch from the East river to the North river, 4 to 5 feet deep and 11 to 12 feet wide at the top sloping in a little towards the bottom"; that the carpenters should "be urged to prepare jointly the stakes and rails"; that "the soldiers and other servants of the Company with the free negroes, no one excepted," should "complete the work on the Fort by making a parapet, and the farmers . . . be summoned to haul pieces of turf"; that the sawyers should "immediately begin to saw planks of four inches' thickness for gun carriages and platforms." The proposal of compulsory service was fixed at a joint meeting, on May 12th, by a law which provided for apportioning the physical labour on the inhabitants by rotation in four divisions of three-day shifts, until completed. It included "Burghers, Merchants, Mechanics, or crews of ships, sloops in harbor or to come." Those who could not work were allowed to provide a fit substitute at their own expense. The palisades, completed early in July, surrounded the land side on the line of the present Wall Street "and [extended] along the Strand of the East River," the present Pearl Street. Entrance from the north was past a guard-house and through a gate in the stockade at the present Wall and Pearl Streets. This gate came to be known as "the Water Gate."

In the spring of the year, Arent van Hattem, presiding burgomaster, and Cornelis van Tienhoven, provincial secretary, were despatched on an embassy to Virginia to promote a continuation of correspondence, peace, and commerce; but Richard Bennett, governor of Virginia, and his council felt themselves unauthorised, in this time of war between the mother countries, to enter into negotiations without the consent of their superiors in England. On December 16th, the Reverend Samuel Drisius was commissioned by Stuyvesant as diplomatic agent, to reiterate to the Virginia government the "former good intentions" of the New Netherlanders "and to learn their reply." The Directors at Amsterdam highly approved this act of Stuyvesant and the results were beneficial to New Netherland. On August 18th, the burgomasters and schepens voted to ask Stuyvesant to send "a personal embassy" to New England, "to see how much can be effected with them respecting the state." While the

Dutch of New Netherland were of this mind, "frivolous and false charges" were being spread in New England, which were magnified by the publication in London of what was termed by the Directors at Amsterdam "the most shameless and lying libel, which the devil in hell could not have produced, under the title 'The second Amboyna Tragedy or truthful Account, etc.,' . . . employed by that nation in order not only to irritate against us their own people, but also to bring down upon us the whole world."

On September 11th, a general assembly of deputies and delegates "of the respective Colonies and Courts of New Netherland" was convened by Stuyvesant in Fort Amsterdam to consider the general welfare, and "divers Ordinances and Regulations touching the great and excessive dearness of all sorts of Merchandizes, Provisions, Grain and Laborers' wages" were enacted. The Directors at Amsterdam, on March 12, 1654, expressed surprise at the action taken without their knowledge and consent, and ordered alterations or abrogations, particularly with respect to the fixing of prices, which they deemed to be "impracticable" and "highly injurious to the State."

English piracies in the neighbourhood of Flushing, L. I., led by Thomas Baxter, a former resident of New Amsterdam and a fugitive from justice, disturbed the populace in the late autumn of this year. Stuyvesant, therefore, summoned deputies to a provincial assembly to devise means for putting a stop to these incursions. They met at the City Hall, on November 26th, except the English delegates, who sent in a written protest against the provincial government and endeavoured to get the burgomasters and schepens "to enter into a firm alliance with them." The city fathers replied that they could not oppose the vested authority, yet wanted to be at peace with their English neighbours on Long Island. The English delegates then announced that "they would form a union on Long Island among each other," while the city's delegates counselled "it would be better to write about it" to the Directors at Amsterdam. It was agreed, thereupon, to hold another assembly on December 10th, to "remonstrate" to Holland; but Stuyvesant and his council, on December 3d, objected, saying that the conduct of the English delegates bordered on revolt, vilified the supreme authority, and contained calumnies; they also found fault with the proceedings of November 26th and 27th. On December 5th, the burgomasters and schepens went to Stuyvesant in a body and besought him to permit the proposed general meeting. The result was that a *land-dag*, or general assembly, consisting of ten Dutchmen and nine Englishmen, and representing New Amsterdam, Breuckelen, Vlissingen (Flushing), Middelburgh (Newtown), Heemstede, Amersfoort (Flatlands), Midwout (Flatbush), and Gravesend, met at the City Hall on the tenth. As a popular assembly it transcended any that had ever assembled in New Netherland. On the eleventh, the delegates signed a "Humble Remonstrance and Petition of the Colonies and Villages," which, having been drawn up in English by George Baxter, of Gravesend, was translated into Dutch and presented to Stuyvesant and his council, who, protesting and declaring the assembly illegal, ordered the "so-called delegates not to address either them or anybody else under such a name and title." On the thirteenth, the delegates again sought to have their assembly recognised and their requests answered; but Stuyvesant and the council rejoined that they were convoked illegally in a mere "conventicle," as a "self-created, unlawful gathering," and demanded that they disperse immediately or become liable to "arbitrary correction." In their remonstrance, they requested, among other things, a common council (*Vroetschap*) for the city, "to represent the body of the Commonalty." Stuyvesant, however, had no sympathy with popular rights and turned the matter off with the explanation of unrelated subjects. On December 24th, the burgomasters and schepens, in their long memorial sent to the Directors at Amsterdam, cited their restrictions; sought the right to fill the office of *schout* as an independent appointment; applied for a change in the excise revenues and for the right to levy new imposts, and to have the farming out of the Brooklyn ferry; asked for authority "to verify the execution of deeds and conveyances of houses and lots within this City, the fee simple of which is sold, as well as of mortgages according to the custom of the City of Amsterdam," and that, for this purpose, they might be allowed "a City seal different from the seal of the province." They requested a supply of firearms and petitioned for the ownership of the City Hall. In the answer of the Directors, on May 18th, communicated to the city authorities on July 21, 1654, they were warned against holding "private conventicles with the English or others," either to deliberate on matters of state or "attempt an alteration in the State and Government thereof." However, certain concessions were made to the city,[1] though a good deal was left for Stuyvesant's confirmation or inspection. An order was

[1] One empowered them to execute transports and deeds of conveyance for houses and lots within the limits of the city, but with certain reservations.

given in Holland "for making a City Seal"[1] and the former City Tavern was granted to the city as a city hall, on condition that no one should claim "any right to it individually, or alienate or mortgage it collectively."

The excise troubles of 1653 began on March 26th, when an additional excise was imposed on all wines and spirituous liquors consumed in or exported from the city, to provide funds for the provincial government. This act met with opposition from the inhabitants of New Amsterdam, who, in an assembly held on August 2d, declared they would contribute no more unless Stuyvesant and his council surrendered "the whole excise on wines and beer" to the city treasury. Stuyvesant demurred. On November 11th, another assembly of the commonalty met with the city fathers at the City Hall and received from Stuyvesant the cession of the excise to the city from November 1st, to be "employed for the public good." But Stuyvesant demurred again and excepted the revenue on exports "until the approbation of the Directors at Amsterdam had been obtained," with the further proviso that the city should also "support the two preachers, the schoolmaster, and secretary; which, being added together, amount to about thirty-two hundred guilders, annually." This was declared to be more than the excise would furnish. The burgomasters and schepens were wroth and decided "to go in a body to the Director General, and demand" of him to keep his promise or, in case of his refusal, to request their dismissal from office. Stuyvesant replied that he had no power to dismiss them and would consent to no alterations in the terms of the excise. The upshot of the controversy was, the city fathers, though much chagrined, remained in office, but protested that they would not be responsible if mischief arose from the negligence. They drew up a memorial on December 24th to the Directors at Amsterdam, as we have already observed, voiced their grievances, and sought the excise "without any limitation." The Directors, in their answer of May 18, 1654, said they considered it strange that the burgomasters and schepens should go so far "as not only to assist in organizing an independent Assembly without authority, but moreover to send in remonstrances." They denied them their request to be freed from paying the

[1] This "seal cut in silver" and also a "painted coat of arms of the City of New Amsterdam" were sent over from Holland in July, in the ship "De Pereboom" (Peartree) and were delivered at a joint meeting of Stuyvesant and the council with the burgomasters and schepens at Fort Amsterdam, on December 8, 1654, into the hands of Martin Cregier, the presiding burgomaster. See Chronology, December 28, 1630, for description of two contemporary drawings sold by Frederik Muller, in 1869, and described in the catalogue as proposed coats of arms for the city of New Amsterdam. Mr. Paltsits is of the opinion that the catalogue descriptions are erroneous and that these drawings were merely tentative designs for a coat of arms for New Netherland.

salaries of the ecclesiastical and civil servants, unless the commonalty allowed the levy of a "new small excise or impost," and obtained the consent of Stuyvesant and the council to the exemption; but they gave the city board additional authority for providing a revenue and made other concessions. All of this did not last long; for on May 26, 1655, the Directors at Amsterdam withdrew from the city the excise revenues and ordered them paid again "in the general treasury of the Company," on the ground that the city had misapplied the proceeds, and for other causes.

On October 4th, the Lutheran inhabitants petitioned Stuyvesant for permission to call a clergyman of their own persuasion and organise a Lutheran church. The Dutch clergy—Megapolensis and Drisius—supported by Stuyvesant, vigorously opposed this request as tending to "the diminution of hearers of the Word of God and the increase of dissensions," as well as paving "the way for other sects." Suffice it to say that no other religious denomination than the Dutch Reformed was permitted to erect a house of worship on Manhattan Island during the Dutch régime. The Lutherans obtained that concession from Governor Richard Nicolls on December 6, 1664.

Provincial ordinances of 1653 related to farm-servants and the brewing and malting of hard grain (February 18th). Most of the cultivation was limited to tobacco planting. Owing to an increase of population, a scarcity of breadstuffs was imminent; to avert a famine an ordinance of March 20th required the tobacco planters "to plant or sow as many hills with Maize, or as much land with Pease or other hard grain for Bread," as they planted with tobacco. Every first Wednesday of each month was set aside as a day of fasting and prayer, and April 9th, on account of the war, was named as a general day of fasting and prayer throughout the province.

On January 27, 1654, the first annual term of the first board of burgomasters and schepens was about to expire, and so the members of the bench asked Stuyvesant whether he desired them to nominate a double number of candidates for a new board, and how many of the old board should retire or remain in office. He informed them, on the following day, that no changes were contemplated, except the filling of two vacancies, "for the sake of peace and harmony." At the same time salaries of 350 florins to burgomasters and 250 florins to schepens were granted, to be paid out of the city treasury. The secretary or city clerk, Jacobus

Kip, was confirmed as "Receiver and Bookkeeper of the Revenues" of the city, on January 12th, his salary to begin from the previous November, when he began to exercise this new function in the administration. Teunis Kraey or Cray was the first "crier" of the city and Claes van Elslandt, Jr., was its first court messenger or "boode."

The ferry tavern at Brooklyn had been conducted by Cornelis Dircksen Hooglant; but on January 20th, the city granted the privilege "to keep a Tavern over at the Ferry . . . for the convenience of Travelers" to Simon Joosten.

Specified duties were proclaimed by a provincial ordinance, on January 28th, on imported Indian goods, brandy, wines, beer, and salt, which were to be paid henceforth "as the staple right" at New Amsterdam, in lieu of the standard one per cent duty imposed but "not hitherto collected" from merchants "from their cargoes and Merchandize." The export duties were unchanged. As certain merchants of the city had petitioned for exemption from the payment of new duties, a concession was made through a reduction of tariff on most of the articles enumerated, and salt, on account of its scarcity, was put upon the free list, on July 22d of this year. Moreover, on February 19th, the burgomasters and schepens had petitioned the provincial government for "a grant of authority provisionally to impose" certain duties on imported and exported goods, on ship tonnage, on beer and wines, etc., and to be allowed "to appoint two sworn Beer Carriers." They pleaded the necessity of this grant for the payment of debts incurred for the construction of public works, and were given the burgher excise, on the twenty-third, but the duty on imported and exported goods was denied them, on the ground that it was a provincial asset. On June 2d, Stuyvesant and the council had proposed an additional provincial revenue for the support of government, by a tax upon real estate and cattle; in July an edict from the Directors at Amsterdam was received and published, requiring a census of the cattle in each colony of New Netherland, it being the first general census of cattle here of which we have knowledge. The proposal for an additional revenue was enacted by ordinance, on August 28th. It was found that the collection of "the tenths" was impracticable, costing almost as much to gather as the receipts therefrom. It was decided, therefore, "not to demand and collect the tenth for some years to come, until the population shall have increased, levying instead a tax on cattle and land."[1]

[1] These taxes were approved by the Directors at Amsterdam in their letter of May 26, 1655, communicated to the city bench on August 17th of that year.

Every morgen of land owned by anyone by a patent was to be taxed twenty stivers once a year; upon every head of horned cattle, if above three years old—goats and sheep excepted—a tax of twenty stivers was fixed; and on houses and lots granted for building purposes in New Amsterdam, Beverwyck, "the neighborhood of the Ferry [Brooklyn], and elsewhere," a tax of "the hundredth penny of the real value" was to be "paid at the General office" of the Company in New Amsterdam. Two tax appraisers were to be chosen from the respective courts of the city and villages, to act with a commissioner from the supreme council, in order to fix upon the valuation and attend to the disposal of vacant lots upon which the present owners neglected to build.

Piracy and threatened invasion due to war brought consternation to the New Netherlanders in 1654. On February 9th, a joint meeting of the city fathers and the provincial authorities was held at the fort to discuss "in what manner the piracy of certain English pirates should be stopped." The city fathers thought the "best means" would be "to station a vessel with 20 to 30 men for a certain time at and about Minnewits [Manursing] Island" to keep a watch. The plan was accepted and, on the next day, the city bench proposed the apportionment of a tax levy, amounting to 1,600 florins per month, for the support of forty men. The provincial government, after some vexatious delay, agreed that the levy should be among the towns. On April 8th, Cornelis van Tienhoven and Captain Martin Cregier were commissioned by Stuyvesant as special envoys to Governor Theophilus Eaton, of the New Haven Colony, to negotiate in regard to the suppression of English piracies. They received their passports on the fourteenth and on the twenty-seventh delivered the journal of their proceedings to the council, by whom it was communicated to the city bench. On April 8th, a provincial edict was drawn up and published at the City Hall on the twenty-seventh, against "some Pirates and Vagabonds," said to be "Runaways and Transports from New England," who had been guilty of "frequenting Long Island and the Mainland" between the Dutch and New England, spying out even the city of New Amsterdam "under the color and guise of Travelers," and committing depredations "at the Flatlands," while receiving protection and covert in their nefarious acts from inhabitants of the English towns of the Dutch province. Communicating with, aiding, or abetting the freebooters in any manner was interdicted. It was required that prompt publication of their presence should be made to the nearest magistrate; failure to give an alarm subjected the derelict persons to confiscation of their property and banishment. In every village a night watch was to be maintained and a reward of one hundred "thalers" was promised "for every Pirate or Vagabond" who was "delivered into the hands" of the provincial authorities. A system of identifying strangers by passes, etc., was established. Guns were not to be discharged between sunset and sunrise, except when a raid was manifest, and then three shots were to be fired in quick succession by watches, as a signal to call together the burghers, "each under his competent Officer, at the appointed place of Rendezvous."

Several secret meetings were held on June 28th and 29th at Gravesend, L. I., by about fifty Englishmen, "among whom were some privateersmen from the North, the rest being English subjects . . . from the villages of Gravesend, Heemstede, and Middelburgh." Rumour said they were bent upon mischief against the Dutch. When the news reached New Amsterdam, it caused some of the recalcitrant English residents to "immediately remove and carry away their Movables, Furniture, Beavers, and other Valuables to the English Villages," thereby creating an increase of uneasiness and spreading disaffection among "the good and well disposed Citizens" of the city and "in the Rural districts also," and exposing the weakened state of the city to "Privateers and other threatening enemies" of the province. Stuyvesant and the council by an edict forbade any more removals, warning that forfeiture of goods, loss of citizenship, and banishment in twenty-four hours would be visited upon offenders.

Notwithstanding that peace negotiations between England and the States General were in progress, a number of ships had been sent over to New England to engage in a menacing expedition against the Dutch of Manhattan and other places in New Netherland. Information of the plan reached Stuyvesant, in May, from several Englishmen and particularly from Isaac Allerton. This rumour also added fuel to the imminent excitement among the Dutch. Meanwhile, the English ships had arrived at Boston, in May and June, and enlistments were secured among the New Englanders; but during the course of these preparatory stages, news of the peace, signed at Westminster in April, was received in New England, whereupon the colonists deserted and the design fell through, so far as the objective against the Dutch was concerned. It was during this crisis that Stuyvesant and the council, on June 2d, declared by resolutions that "all possible means must be used . . . first in the repairing of the fort and to provide it with proper gabions and palisades; for the completion of those begun at the Gracht,[1] then in endeavoring to enlist, as quickly as possible . . . at least 60 to 70 men"; but it was adjudged best not to enlist people from the English villages of New Netherland, lest to do so would be dragging "the Trojan horse" within the city walls. Another plan of fortification, suggested on the thirteenth, was to build a small earthwork and breastworks at the City Hall and to plant thereon two or three cannon. The work was proclaimed by ordinance and by June 16th it was set in motion.[2] News of the Treaty of Westminster was received and proclamation thereof was made to the commonalty at the City Hall on July 18th, and August 12th was appointed as a day of general thanksgiving throughout New Netherland to signalise the happy event. One of the items of the city's expenses for the celebration was fifty-eight florins "to pay for beer at the bonfire for the victory."

With peace restored, the city found its funds depleted and its obligations to the provincial government in abeyance. The necessity of devising ways and means had been urged repeatedly upon the burgomasters and schepens by Stuyvesant and the council, who, on August 4th, again reminded them that no "further dilatory exceptions" could be tolerated and demanded an answer by the following Monday, "together with an account of the receipt and expenditure of the Tapsters' Excise" collected by the city. The board appointed a committee to go over the records with the secretary, in order to show what expenditures were "incurred last year on the public works," and directed the Receiver to "briefly make out the balance of the Excise and then communicate the same" to Stuyvesant "and likewise verbally to propose some points." The estimate showed expenses on "the outer and inner works constructed this and last year" amounting "to about sixteen thousand guilders." They offered their quota, of "about three thousand guilders" if the council would vest them with authority "to lay a tax on real estate" under their jurisdiction, wherever they might find it. On August 31st, they offered "to support henceforth" at the city's charge one minister, a precentor, who should be at the same time a schoolmaster, one dog-whipper or beadle, a schout,

[1] The ditch or canal that ran along the present Broad Street. The sheet-piling here had "again fallen down" by August 24th, due to "the heavy rain and water." These storms also destroyed the "Waal" or bank of the East River in front of the City Hall and even endangered that structure, and so plans were laid in November for having it "properly protected with sheet-piles."

[2] What led up to these public works is seen in the records of March 23d and June 8th, with respect to the decay and dilapidation of the palisades, earthworks, and other defences that had been erected only a year earlier.

two burgomasters, five schepens, a secretary, a court messenger, and such others as they deemed necessary. They also offered to devise "some small subsidies" in case the revenue was insufficient; but opposed supporting the military, as a concern not of the city alone, but of the country in general. On September 16th, a reasonable concession of the real estate tax levy was granted to the city; but the city fathers were severely castigated for "deceitfully and perversely" misleading the director-general and council in not fulfilling their promises and agreements, and in misapplying the excise revenue. This quarrel continued throughout the year and led to the resumption of the tapsters' excise by the provincial government the following year.

Among the events of 1654, we find that, on February 25th, the two burgomasters and a majority of the schepens appeared before Stuyvesant and protested because he and his council, without consulting them, had "interdicted and forbidden certain farmers' servants to ride the goose on the feast of Bacchus at Shrove-tide." This interdict had been served by the court messenger of the supreme bench upon the servants on the day before the feast and had been disregarded. The members of the city court considered the interdict and the sentences that followed the misdemeanours as an invasion of their judicial authority; but Stuyvesant and his council rejoined that they were only an inferior court of justice and could "in no wise infringe on or diminish the power of the Director General and Council to enact any Ordinances . . . prevent more sins, scandals, debaucheries and crimes, and properly correct, fine and punish obstinate transgressors." The sport of plucking, pulling, or riding the goose consisted in smearing the neck and head of a goose with oil or soap and fastening the goose by a rope between two poles. The contestants on horseback rode at full gallop and attempted to seize the prize. He who bore off the goose was declared to be king of the festival. On this occasion several persons were fined and others were put in prison. The country people had, in other years, endeavoured to revive the orgy, which was characterised by excessive drinking, but had been prevented.

In the spring of 1654, the weigh-house and scales for the proper regulation of weighing and measuring in New Amsterdam, according to the standards of old Amsterdam, were finished at the expense of the Company, and, on August 10th, the provincial government established rules for the standardisation of all weights and measures in general use. All goods brought into or carried from the city were to be "weighed and measured by the sworn Weighmaster and Measurer" and established fees were to be "handed into and paid in current pay at the General Office" of the Company, until such time as the council had opportunity "to farm out the Weighhouse." Goods of or for the Company, the board of deacons, and other charitable bodies were exempt from fees. On September 22d, the burgomasters and schepens complained to the Directors at Amsterdam that they were deprived of the proceeds for the city treasury and requested a grant of this revenue. The ordinance of August 10th was renewed with amplifications on April 27th, 1656, when there were established at the weigh-house[1] regular office hours during which the regular weighing should be done, and extra pay for extra weighing out of hours was prescribed.

The city court decided, on July 24th, that extraordinary sessions should be paid for by the person at whose request the session was convened. On August 20th, there was passed by Stuyvesant and the council an ordinance for regulating the duties of the provost-marshal or jailer. He was their subordinate and under the immediate control of the fiscal. He received specified fees for arrests and certain fines for penalties, whether the prisoners were from the military or the commonalty. His residence was "in Fort New Amsterdam," where he was provided with the keys, locks, and chains of the prison, of which he was obliged to take good care, and "to lock up and feed the Prisoners in the manner . . . ordered by the Fiscal." He was to visit the prisoners in the morning and evening "and take particular care that no file, rope, ironwork, or anything sharp," should be left with any of them. On August 23d, Arent Jansen, of Vlieringen, was appointed and qualified for the post.

At this time (on August 22d), Jacob Barsimson, who had sailed from Holland in the "Pereboom" (Peartree) on July 8th, arrived in New Amsterdam, being the first Jew on record to settle in New Netherland. In September, twenty-three Jews—adults and children—arrived on the ship "St. Charles," of which Jacques de la Motthe was master. This was the first party of Jews to arrive here.

At a meeting "of the Burghers' Court Martial in the City Hall," on November 10th, the burgomasters and schepens, with Stuyvesant's approbation, proposed the establishment of "a Rattle Watch [Night Patrol] of 4 to 6 men" to guard the city by night, and advertised for applicants for the places. On the sixteenth, "the rules for the Rattle Watch were

[1] This weigh-house was probably on Pearl Street near the pier built on Schreyers Hoek in 1648-9; but there is no documentary evidence to prove its exact location.

made"; but at the appointed hour (11 A.M.) nobody had appeared to take up the night watch, and so "the meeting adjourned without anything having been done."

To increase the population in New Netherland and promote the cultivation of the soil, boys and girls from the almshouses of Amsterdam were sent over, arriving in the autumn. This was the first trial of the kind in New Netherland. Others were sent over in 1655 and in 1659. The idea had been considered by the Directors at Amsterdam as early as the year 1650, but it came to naught. It had been again contemplated in 1652 and all arrangements had been made, but its consummation had been prevented by the difficulties existing between the Dutch and the English at home.

On December 8th, Stuyvesant informed his council and the burgomasters and schepens, at a joint meeting held in the fort, of "the necessity of his voyage to Curaçao." At his suggestion two vacancies in the city board were filled, and on the same day he presented a painted coat of arms and a silver city seal to the presiding burgomaster. On the twelfth, the city fathers, in view of Stuyvesant's intended voyage, voted unanimously to "compliment him, before he take his gallant voyage," and that "for this purpose" there should be provided "a gay repast" at the noon hour of the sixteenth, which was a Wednesday. This feast was held "at the City Hall, in the Council Chamber." Stuyvesant sailed for Curaçao on the twenty-fourth with three ships, to establish trade in the West Indies. After an absence of nearly seven months, he returned to New Amsterdam in the ship "Liefde" (Love), on July 10, 1655, and, on July 14th, the council made record that he had submitted to them a report of his transactions in Curaçao and the Caribbean Islands. A few days prior to Stuyvesant's departure, namely, on December 17, 1654, Andries Hudde was appointed surveyor of the province.

The year 1655 began with a very severe winter. All the rivers about New Amsterdam were "frozen and the land and roads covered with snow." It was possible to cross "the East river on the ice at White Stone," L. I.

We have seen that the burgomasters and schepens, immediately after the first institution of city government in 1653, were allowed the use of the "Stadt Herbergh" or City Tavern as a "Stadt Huys" or City Hall and that the grant of this structure to the city was vested by the Directors at Amsterdam on May 18, 1654. The formal transfer was made by an order of the provincial council on March 2, 1655. It now passed irrevocably under the city's jurisdiction. On March 23d, Harmanus van Hoboocken was appointed by the council, with the consent of the Consistory of the church at New Amsterdam, "as Chorister and Schoolmaster" of the city. He succeeded Willem Vestius, and his services ended when Evert Pietersen was commissioned to replace him, on May 2, 1661. Fire-wardens had been created and fire regulations had been made by Stuyvesant and the council on January 23, 1648. This was before the organisation of an independent city government; but now, on April 13, 1655, the burgomasters and schepens nominated the fire-wardens of the city and the supreme council elected and confirmed these three: Hendrick Kip, Govert Loockermans, and Jan Paulusen Jacquet. On April 10th, the city court enacted an ordinance for governing the time of attendance of its members and its secretary "both in Ordinary and Extraordinary Sessions," namely, "to appear, on notification of the Court Messenger, at all ordinary sessions in the City Hall precisely at 9 o'clock on the ringing of the bell; or at extraordinary sessions at the hour appointed." A gradation of fines for absences and lateness was named; the court messenger kept the time record by means of a sand-box or hour-glass. In February, Dirck van Schelluyne had been appointed by the provincial council as "Concierge" (high constable or city marshal), with the function of maintaining justice and executing sentences in civil cases. In March, we find the earliest record of a Jew charged in the city court with violation of a Sunday ordinance, when Abraham de Lucena was accused of keeping a store open during sermon and selling at retail.

It is interesting to observe that the city's prisoners under bond were confined in the City Hall. On May 5th, Arent Jansen, the provost-marshal or city jailer, was allowed "to reside in the little side room of the City Hall in order to be able more conveniently to attend to the prisoners." In front of the City Hall certain public auctions were held in January and February by order of the city court. In March, we find the earliest record of a lottery held in New Netherland. Gysbert van Imbroeck was given permission, under the supervision of a joint lottery commission of the council and city bench, "to make a lottery of a certain quantity of Bibles, Testaments, and other books according to catalogue," with the proviso that the books be valued at one hundred per cent "over the Invoice" and that a third of the proceeds be devoted to the poor, the balance to come to him. A poor-farm had been bought some time before by "the Board of Overseers of the Poor of the city"; it was "situate on the other side of Hellgate" or in the present Borough of Queens, overlooking Berrian Island. Other revenues for the poor consisted of "alms collected among the people, and some fines and donations of the inhabitants."

Ten residents on the "Straet van de Graft," or street from the ditch,[1] offered "to pave the said street with round stone on the first favorable opportunity." It is the first mention of cobblestone pavement in the records of the city. In their petition of March 15th, they proposed that the work be authorised and executed by the city, for which they agreed "to furnish the stone, the raising and lowering necessary thereto, each to the extent of his house and lot, and further to follow the general rule relative to paving and expenses." This request was granted; but execution was delayed until 1658, and then the city did it by a pro rata assessment on the abutting owners. In June, 1655, a request was made to the council for enlarging the city gate at the East River, so as to permit the passage of a cart, and for repairing the road in that vicinity. In this month and the next the city fathers sought permission from the council to raise funds for the needs of the city by a tax for stamping and marking weights and measures; also that each tavern-keeper should be required to take out quarterly a license and pay six guilders for it. Nothing was done at this time; but when the request was renewed in January, 1656, it was granted.

During the summer of 1655, the first cargo of negro slaves imported directly into New Netherland from Africa arrived at New Amsterdam in the ship "Wittepaert" (White Horse). The negroes were "from the Bight of Guinea." Neither the Company nor the inhabitants derived any revenue from this direct introduction of slavery and, on this account, a provincial edict of August 6th levied thereafter a duty of ten per cent ad valorem on all negroes "carried or exported" from the province "elsewhere beyond the jurisdiction of New Netherland." In August, Stuyvesant was seized with illness during a general epidemic, which also attacked Councillor La Montagne. It was at the time that Captain Fredrick de Koninck was expected daily in the man-of-war "De Waagh" (Scales) and while preparations for an expedition against the Swedish settlements on the Delaware were being made. August 25th was set apart as a day of prayer, fasting, and thanksgiving, to invoke the divine

[1] Brouwer or Brewers', later Stone Street, running from Whitehall to Broad Street. It has been claimed that this was the first street paved in New Amsterdam, but that view seems not to be tenable.

blessing on the Dutch expedition, and all common business, work, sports, and drinking were inhibited. The expedition sailed on September 5th in seven ships, having on board some six to seven hundred men. Stuyvesant had recovered and personally commanded, accompanied by Vice-Director Nicasius de Sille and the clergyman Megapolensis. Of the successful operations of the expedition and the complete reduction of the Swedes we make only passing mention.

Stuyvesant returned to New Amsterdam on October 12th, under an urgent request for his presence; for during his absence and the depletion of the male population, an Indian invasion of Manhattan Island and its environs threw the people into a state of consternation. These Indians represented ten tribes, including the Mahicans, Esopuses, Hackensacks, and Tappans. It is said that they numbered nineteen hundred, of whom many were armed. Before the break of day on September 15th, they appeared in their canoes before New Amsterdam and, entering some houses under pretence, aroused the people. A parley took place in the fort between the principal officials and leading men of the commonalty and the chief sachems. The Indians were to retire before dusk to Noten (now Governors) Island, but broke their agreement. Injuries to some of the Dutch officials aroused the people, and the soldiers and burgher guard sallied forth from the fort in an attack upon the Indians, driving them to their canoes. The Indians laid waste Pavonia and Hoboken, desolated Staten Island, and in three days killed one hundred of the Dutch, captured one hundred and fifty—mostly women and children—ruined in estate three hundred, destroyed twenty-eight bouweries, burned twelve thousand schepels of grain, the total damage being estimated at two hundred thousand guilders ($80,000), a vast sum. When the troubles were rife, the resident councillors wrote to Stuyvesant, on September 17th, as follows: "Madame, your Honor's wife, with her whole family and all those, in whom your Honor and she are concerned, are well. As the citizens are unwilling to guard other people's houses far from the Manhattans, we have, with her advice, hired 10 Frenchmen, to protect your Honor's bouwery on the Manhattans, subject to your Honor's pleasure. We'll keep as good watch as possible, and expect your Honor's speedy return . . . all the country-people are flying, except those of Amersfoort [Flatlands], Midwout [Flatbush], Breukelen, and the English villages. There is a great deal of lamenting here, which we give your Honor to consider." In a letter of October 27th, Vice-Director de Sille wrote that sixty Indians had been killed, and that the remainder continued their depredations and were yet round about Manhattan. On the twenty-eighth, Stuyvesant, in a letter to the Directors at Amsterdam, laid the blame for the Indian massacres on the officials of New Netherland. He counselled peace as the best thing and proposed that the Indians be prevented from coming into any village or place with firearms; that they be obliged to deliver up the murderers to be punished; that drunken Indians be kept in prison; and that when animals were killed by them, payment be exacted for the damage. He said that the temper of the commonalty was for revenge. On November 7th, he wrote again that the Indians in New Netherland were stirred up by the Dutch themselves and that restoration of captives in their hands was being hindered. He mistrusted Councillor La Montagne as a bad instrument, "a snake harbored in the bosom of the colony." But on the tenth of this month, Stuyvesant submitted to the council propositions as to the expediency of declaring war against the Indians, raising funds for the support of the military, and the redemption of captives. Each councillor gave his opinion, which showed that only Cornelis van Tienhoven favoured war, and Stuyvesant held to the expediency of peace.

When the Indian incursions took place, the public works, constructed along the present line of Wall Street in 1653 and repaired in 1654, were again in need of reconstruction. On September 20th, two members of the provincial council met with the city fathers to consider "the present dangerous condition of the times." With unanimity the conference adjudged it "necessary that the works of this City be again repaired," and resolved "that the aforesaid erected works" should "be repaired with planks 5 @ 6 feet high, nailed to the sides of the Palisades," and the fence viewers of the city were commissioned "to contract for the said works at the smallest expense and quickest despatch." This work was completed by September 25th. Subsequently, an assessment on real estate was made to pay for this and other charges; but "not one third part" had been collected by the end of 1656, "through inability of the commonalty."

On February 23d, the provincial council had granted to the burgomasters the right "to demand for a Deed executed before them for Houses and Lots" situate within the jurisdiction of the city, one beaver or eight guilders ($3.20), to be paid as follows: three guilders for the seal; one and one-half guilders for two schepens who signed the deed, and three and one-half guilders as a fee for the clerk. The Indian massacres in September had brought numerous refugees and others to New Amsterdam, who were inclined to settle there, and who petitioned the city authorities for "small lots" on which each might "erect a house." The city board put the matter before Stuyvesant, "who answered that a proper survey must be first made." Application for a survey was presented to the council on November 10th and Councillor La Montagne and Burgomaster Anthony, together with the fence viewers or city surveyors, were appointed in council "to advance the desired survey," as they judged fit, "without any regard to persons, gardens, or places," in order that settlers might be served "at a reasonable price." Methods for condemnation were prescribed, subject to approval by the provincial body. This resulted in the making of a survey of the city, which "survey and plot map[1] of New Amsterdam," according to which the streets were staked out, were confirmed and approved by the council on February 25, 1656.

The year 1655 ended with an inhibition by provincial ordinance, on December 31st, upon the firing of guns, planting of Maypoles, beating of drums, and treating of intoxicants on New Year's or May day anywhere in the province, under a system of penalties for violations of the law.

The massacres during the Indian uprising of September, 1655, had shown that isolation of the country people was impracticable. On January 18, 1656, a provincial ordinance commanded the scattered inhabitants "to concentrate themselves, by next Spring, in the form of Towns, Villages, and Hamlets," and those who failed to comply were to suffer for their remissness and be fined.

The survey of the streets of the city of New Amsterdam, already alluded to as laid down on a plan or map, "according to which the Streets" were "set off and laid out with stakes," was confirmed on February 25th by Stuyvesant and the council. The carrying out of the city improvements was referred to the two burgomasters, who were authorised "first and foremost" to give public notice and fix a time within which everyone who had a claim against the city for being "damaged or injured by the said Survey," might present that claim and have it settled on the lowest terms and "for the benefit of the city." Disputed claims were to be referred "to two or three respectable persons conversant with the subject and not interested in the Survey," as arbitrators. After all

[1] This "plot map" is not known to be extant. For a particular account of this survey, see *infra*.

was done, the burgomasters were to "appraise the aforesaid lots according to the determined quota" and to distribute them among those who were prepared to build thereon, giving the preference to interested parties "to build on their own lots themselves, according to the Survey," if their circumstances allowed it, "and remain in the mean time possessors and owners of their Gardens and Lots falling without the line of the Streets, until payment shall have been made therefor"; but if there proved to be a dearth of vacant lots at the time of distribution, disposal was to be made to others. It was left to the burgomasters "to determine what Streets and Lots" should be first built on, "only that according to ancient usage the patents required therefor" should "be applied for and obtained from the Director General and Council." The burgomasters fixed the time for damage claims "within the period of eight days" after publication of the notice (February 26th). The plan of this most important survey is lost. It showed 120 houses and 1000 inhabitants in the city and was the first plotting of the city on a street plan that was at all systematic.

From a record of February 1st, it appears that the condition of "the bank on the East River, near the City Gate" (now Pearl and Wall Streets), was bad. The two burgomasters deemed it necessary that "a firm sheeting of thick plank or boards" be constructed, "to begin the same at the point of the old City Works," which lay thereby, "and again to raise up the fence; also a large and suitable gate [the Water Gate] according to the plan and design of Capt. Coninck [Fredrick de Koningh] and already begun to be fixed in the works"; also, "that the sheeting before the City Hall" should "be renewed with thick plank and boards, like the other work at the gate aforesaid according to the plan of Capt. Coninck." After considerable backing and filling by the abutting owners, who were charged with the execution of the work on the sheet-piling along the East River, from the present Broad to Wall Street, to replace that which had been destroyed by high water and storms, the work was finished at the end of this year. The land "before the City Hall" was filled in with earth taken "from the Hill" before the lot that adjoined the City Hall. The "church in the Fort" was "more and more out of repair" and neglected, so that in this year we find that Evert Duyckingh, the New Amsterdam glazier, put in the church glass panes, bearing painted coats of arms, for each of the members of the city court. A bell was hung in the City Hall.

Persons "of quality or of good name and character," who were arrested for debt, might be committed in "a decent tavern," if they paid their own expenses; they went "otherwise, to the City Hall" prison, like other persons under arrest. Mattheus de Vos, a city notary, who held the post of *castelynschap* or governor of the City Hall, was given the office of *concierge* (high constable, bailiff, or city marshal) on November 6th, in the place of Dirck van Schelluyne, resigned. An important criminal action had been before the city court for several months, in which Geert (Gertrude) Coerten and her husband, Guert, were accused of slandering the reputations of Cornelis Steenwyck and the wife of Willem Beeckman, one of the schepens. The gossips of New Netherland had a live subject, and Beeckman pursued the case relentlessly. But the court considered its authority "too limited" to pronounce judgment, a condition which inspired the city fathers to petition Stuyvesant and the council for an extension of authority, so as to be able to "judge and execute sentence in all criminal matters, capital cases excepted." On December 21st, the provincial body granted to the inferior court of justice the right "to judge all injuries and criminal delicts of a minor degree to branding and incarcerating," unless an appeal were taken by the defendant to them as a supreme court, within twenty-four hours after sentence had been pronounced. Final execution of judgment, in any case, was to repose in the city bench.

The multifarious duties of the burgomasters led them to ask for a release from the care of orphans, and, on February 25th, Paulus Leendertsen vander Grift and Pieter Wolphertsen van Couwenhoven were chosen as the first orphan-masters of the newly created independent court of that name, to administer the property of "orphans and minor children" who were resident within the jurisdiction of the city. This was the first independent exercise of surrogates' practice in the city. We find in this year, too, the first instance of the operation of the brokerage system in the city; also the first appointment of sworn butchers, "to serve in butchering and cutting up" animals for consumption by the people. In September, a Saturday market-day for the sale of country produce of all kinds was established by an ordinance which located the market "on the Strand near the house of Master Hans Kierstede," situate at the present Whitehall and Moore Streets.

On April 8th, the lot on Pearl Street, with the "Old Church" building erected in 1633, was sold by order of Stuyvesant and the council to the highest bidder. The purchaser was Jacob Wolphertsen van Couwenhoven, a brewer, who almost at once became involved in debt and was obliged to give the deed to the bailiff, to sell the house and lot, as security for his debts. The "voluntary sale" was fixed by the city court for August 19th, and at the sale the property was bought by Isaac de Foreest.

A suggestion had been made early in the year for the removal of the general burial-ground from Broadway to a spot behind the fort; but this was not acceptable. The Jews, who were averse to burying their dead "in the common burying ground" of the city, had petitioned Stuyvesant, on July 27, 1655, for permission "to purchase a burying place for their nation," and had been told that a grant would be made to them "when the need and occasion therefor arose" by deaths among their number. On February 22, 1656, they renewed their request, whereupon the council instructed Nicasius de Sille and Cornelis van Tienhoven "to point out to the petitioners a little hook of land situate outside of this city for a burial place." This cemetery has been placed at the New Bowery and Chatham Square, in which location a "Jews Buring [sic] Place" appears on a manuscript map of *c.* 1733 (Pl. 30). The right to worship in a synagogue was denied the Jews, but this did not preclude them from the exercise of their religion "in all quietness . . . within their houses." This limitation was deduced from an ordinance of February 7th, which permitted only the authorised services of the Dutch Church, according to the Synod of Dort, to be carried on publicly in the city. This year the Jews were also granted, by order of the Directors at Amsterdam, the right to own real property, which had hitherto been denied them. This and other concessions from Holland displeased Stuyvesant and his council, who told the Directors at Amsterdam that the grant of these concessions to the Jews was "abominable."

In June, Cornelis van Tienhoven, provincial fiscal and secretary of New Netherland, as well as city schout, who had been repeatedly accused of malefactions and misconduct in public and private life, was dismissed, by order of the Directors at Amsterdam, from all public offices held by him. Later he absconded and the council ordered the seizure and sealing of all books and papers belonging to him and their removal from his late residence. His real and personal property was put under arrest until an inventory thereof could be made. These circumstances materially disturbed the public business of the province, now turned over to Nicasius de Sille. In the meantime, Van Tienhoven committed suicide by drowning. The receipts from duties in New Netherland during the year were estimated by the Directors at Amsterdam, on December 19th, to amount to 51,400 florins ($20,560), which did not include "all the other revenues in the country." Nevertheless, all the revenues together were "hardly sufficient to pay the old debts," on account of gross defalcations that had taken place in the treasury through the misconduct of the brothers Adrian and Cornelis van Tienhoven.

The year 1657 is particularly interesting on account of the establishment of the great and small burgher-right or citizenship in New Amsterdam. The matter was proposed on January 8th at a conference or "Common Council," held at the City Hall, and attended by Stuyvesant, the city fathers, and seven of the principal merchants. The law enacted on February 2d granted the "Great Burgher-right" to all former as well as present provincial officials, burgomasters, schepens, Dutch clergymen, "and commissioned officers to the Ensign inclusive of the City regiment," and to the descendants of each in the male line, provided an established residence had not been forfeited by failure to keep "fire and light" through absence from the city. Public officials could be chosen from this class only. The "Common or Small Burgher-right" was granted to all male inhabitants who had "kept fire and light within the City one year and six weeks," and to all native born or those who had married or who thereafter married "native born daughters of Burghers." Other persons who kept a shop and carried on business in the city were required to secure the small burgher-right from the burgomasters and pay twenty guilders to the revenues of the city treasury. Between April 10th and May 3d the burghers were registered.

Excessive land grants had been made in former years to persons who had since failed to take advantage of them. Land lay yet "unimproved, yea, wild and waste." The timber lands were not fenced and some of the inhabitants who sought to earn an honest living by chopping timber were frequently prevented by those who claimed the land. It was ordered, therefore, that claimants of land should properly set off and fence in their grants, so that the boundaries would be visible and the land available for others distinguishable. Cutting timber was now permitted on unfenced land.[1]

It was discovered that "many burghers and inhabitants" were throwing "their rubbish, filth, ashes, dead animals, and such like things into

[1] This ordinance was published at New Amsterdam on January 22d.

the public streets," as well as into the graft or canal (Broad Street), and so a city ordinance was issued, on February 20th, for putting an end to the nuisance. It prescribed that "all such things" must be brought to the "most convenient of the following places, to wit, the Strand [of the East River], near the City Hall [Pearl Street and Coenties Alley], near the gallows [Pearl Street and Whitehall], near Hendrick [Willemsen] the baker [north-west corner of Bridge and Broad Streets], near Daniel Litsco [just outside of the city gate, Pearl near Wall Street], where tokens to that effect" were to be displayed. Moreover, "everybody" was required to "keep the streets clean before his house or lot." These regulations were carried out under a system of penalties for transgressions. A second survey of New Amsterdam was begun about April by Jacques Cortelyou.[1] It was completed by May 3d and, in some localities, altered the streets, lots, and fences considerably. On June 26th, the burgomasters appealed to Stuyvesant and the council for a loan to the city of ten to fifteen hundred florins, with which to repair "the City's works as well at the City Hall as the sheet piling at the Graft, etc.," and promised "to repay it from the City revenue" at the earliest opportunity. By December 3d, the work of excavating and sheeting the graft, so as to make it accessible for small boats, was "just commenced"; but it was found that the people or their servants were throwing filth, ashes, dead animals, etc., into the ditch and "again filling up" what had been excavated. The work on the *Heere Gracht* (Broad Canal) was completed in 1659 and cost 2792.19 florins, which amount was levied early in 1660 on the owners of lots on both sides of the canal.

From the beginning, the revenues of the city were not forthcoming and its debts remained more or less unliquidated. Funds had been secured from "private" individuals as a loan to the city on interest. The administration of the finances called for reform and, in March, the city was empowered each year to name its own treasurer, who was to be "the last retired Burgomaster."[2] The finances of the city were weak through the inability to respond of a people overburdened with taxation and impoverished by wars and Indian incursions; and there was a crying demand for reform in the conduct of the provincial treasury, which had suffered from bad management and peculations. On May 26th, the Directors

[1] Cortelyou had been appointed surveyor-general of New Netherland on January 23d of this year, at a yearly salary of 250 guilders and fees for surveys made for private parties or for the council or Company. The plan of this survey is lost.

[2] Oloff Stevensen van Cortlandt was the first person, under this provision, "to administer the city's income on orders signed by the Burgomasters . . . and not otherwise."

of the Company at Amsterdam drew up a new plan of financial administration for New Netherland, so that they might "for once . . . see well and correctly kept books." They appointed Johannes de Decker chief administrator and made him also a member of Stuyvesant's council, committing "the funds and books of the treasury to the care" of Cornelis van Ruyven, the provincial secretary. This plan worked satisfactorily. The Company in this year made the first attempt to introduce the silkworm culture into New Netherland.

On February 6th, we meet with the first detailed arrangements for the city jail, as administered by the city itself, when Anthony Lodewycksen Baeck was confirmed as city jailer in charge of the jail in the City Hall. He was required to receive "all prisoners . . . committed or delivered over to him by the Schout, Burgomasters, and Schepens, or Burgher Court Martial . . . or in their name," whether arrested in civil or criminal cases, and to "sleep every night in his ordinary chamber," even if there were no prisoners in the jail. Searching of capital prisoners, periodical inspection of the cells, and cleaning of the prison every week were but a part of his duties, for which full instructions were given to him. Prisoners who were permitted to "sit in the prison chamber" were allowed candle-light and fire; "but no fire nor light" was allowed "in the other rooms of the prison" at any time. That the jail was a necessity, we may not doubt. Daily there were "quarreling, fighting, beating, and smiting," provoked by "a mere word by some quarrelsome persons, because of the small fine imposed." In December, a new ordinance was promulgated, forbidding "Street broils or Quarrels, much less Beating or Striking one another," on pain of a penalty of 25 guilders ($10) "for a simple blow of a fist" and, "in case blood" flowed, "four times as much." If the act was committed "in the presence of the Officer, Burgomaster, or Schepen, a double fine" was to be applied. Excessive drinking, which had been the curse of New Amsterdam for years, notwithstanding the enactment of all kinds of laws to reduce the evil, was producing its brood of crimes. Complaints were made to the city court that many of the tapsters of the city were luring their patrons to linger unduly long in their taverns, taking from them not only their daily earnings, but receiving goods in pawn for drink, to the impoverishment of families, who became a burden to the deaconry and poor-masters of the city. On December 3d, the tavern-keepers were forbidden by ordinance "to receive in pawn any goods, of whatever nature . . . such as clothing, furniture, or the like, and to sell drinks therefor." Heavy penalties for infractions were established. On the same day, the surgeons were ordered, whenever they dressed a wound for a patient, to find out who had wounded him and report the facts to the schout.

Occasionally strangers were committed to prison. A singular instance occurring this year is worthy of segregation. On August 6th, a strange ship "approached the Fort, having no flag flying from the topmast, nor from any other place on the ship." It "fired no salute before the fort," as was customary on arrival. The master of the ship, coming ashore, paid no respects to Stuyvesant, "but stood still with his hat firm on his head, as if a goat." With difficulty Stuyvesant learned that the ship "had come from London" and at last discovered "that it was a ship with Quakers on board." She sailed away again on the next morning through Hellgate and apparently to Rhode Island, whereto, in the language of the Dutch clergymen, "all the cranks of New England retire." The Quakers left at New Amsterdam Mary Weatherhead and Dorothy Waugh, "two strong young women," who, "as soon as the ship had fairly departed . . . began to quake and go into a frenzy, and cry out loudly in the middle of the street, that men should repent, for the day of judgment was at hand." The inhabitants, "not knowing what was the matter, ran to and fro, while one cried 'Fire,' and another something else." The upshot of the matter was the arrest of the women by the fiscal and an assistant, who "seized them both by the head, and led them to prison." On the way the women "continued to cry out and pray according to their manner," and "from this circumstance" the Dutch clergymen perceived "that the devil is the same everywhere."

Something of the failure to Christianise the Indians is revealed in a letter of August 5th, sent to the Classis of Amsterdam by the Dutch clergymen of New Amsterdam, who wrote: "We have had an Indian here with us for about two years. He can read and write Dutch very well. We have instructed him in the fundamental principles of our religion, and he answers publicly in church, and can repeat the Commandments. We have given him a Bible, hoping he might do some good among the Indians, but it all resulted in nothing. He took to drinking brandy, he pawned the Bible, and turned into a regular beast, doing more harm than good among the Indians."

On March 8th, the two burgomasters resolved to "meet once a Week for the future in the City Hall" on Thursday mornings, at nine o'clock, to confer with respect to the business of the city. The burgomasters who introduced these administrative sessions were Allard Anthony and Paulus Leendertsen vander Grift, and administrative minutes of business transactions were kept separately from this time onward. The reasons which impelled them to this action were the daily occurrence of "divers matters" which concerned "only the Burgomasters; such as the repairs and construction of necessary works; finances, how to find means; and order, that everything proceed in order; also should anyone have to request or propose any thing relating to the City, to direct it for the public good." On December 15th, a fire ordinance was enacted by the provincial government. For the want of convenient stone, "many Wooden houses" had been built in the city, compactly located, and constantly exposed to the danger of a conflagration. This ordinance provided for a proportional tax on each householder in order to provide a fund for the purchase of "150 leather Fire-buckets . . . and Fire-hooks." A contract for the buckets was made, in August, 1658, with two of the shoemakers of the city, and when the buckets were delivered at the City Hall in January, 1659, it was ordered that they be distributed, fifty at the City Hall and the remainder in lots of a dozen or less in various houses. These buckets were numbered seriatim and the city arms were painted on them. Fire-ladders and fire-hooks were ordered in August, 1659. The funds for this object had not been fully paid in by August, 1661, through the dereliction of the property owners. The ordinance of December 15, 1657, also ordered the removal of "all Thatched roofs and Wooden chimneys, Hay-ricks, and Hay-stacks," as well as "Henhouses and Hog-pens," that were "found within the walls" of the city of New Amsterdam.

It has already been observed that the city faced a problem in finding suitable lots as sites for houses to accommodate new comers. The earlier ground-briefs had granted unduly large plots and so the new arrivals were now unable to find convenient sites to purchase because, notwithstanding former ordinances which sought to force building operations, "many spacious and large lots, even in the best and most convenient part of the City," were not built on, the owners holding them for a rise in value or using them as orchards and gardens. It appears that this state of affairs resulted from the ineffectiveness of the former ordinances, since no penalties or fines were enforced. On January 15, 1658, another law was made, which placed a yearly tax of "the 15th penny" on "several hundred" vacant city lots, following upon a close valuation under the direction of the burgomasters. This law also prohibited the erection of houses "near the City walls and gates" outside of the city enclosure, until "all the lots within the City" were properly built upon. In April, the burgomasters decided not to grant any more lots until "a map thereof be made" and asked Stuyvesant "to order the surveyor to draw as soon as possible a map of the lots" within the city. At the same time, the city schout was authorised "to tell everyone having vacant unfenced lots" to fence them within six weeks. On June 13th, they decided "to give an order to the [Court] Officer, to warn every one to settle their vacant lots as an ornament to the place" and "to direct the Court Messenger to go around and notify every one," who had "received lots from the City, or enquire" whether they intended to build or not; also to get "the plan" from Burgomaster vander Grift. Two months had elapsed since they had asked Stuyvesant to order the surveyor, Jacques Cortelyou, "to draw as soon as possible a map of the lots within this City." As he was dilatory, they now (June 13th) determined "to Notify the surveyor" themselves, "to make out a Map," and on July 11th agreed to instruct him "not to measure any lots except by foot wood-measure (*hout voet*); further, to request Stuyvesant that a map (*Platte Kaart*) be drawn of the lots measured within the City." When the burgomasters brought up the subject before the whole city bench, "nothing was done therein." The dilatoriness of Cortelyou nettled the burgomasters, who, on August 9th, remonstrated to Stuyvesant and the council "that they had repeatedly requested the surveyor to make a map," but could not get one from him, notwithstanding their interest in the matter. They besought the provincial authorities to order the surveyor to make the map with despatch, and the council issued such an order to Cortelyou on August 30th. The burgomasters, on October 4th, resolved to obtain from the Directors at Amsterdam the concession of the public sale of all real estate in the city through its secretary. On February 13, 1659, their request was granted, henceforth relieving the provincial secretary of "the office of auctioneer," and ordering that in future the treasury of the Company should receive from such sales "the 40th penny," paid one-half each by seller and purchaser, but on sales of execution, "the 80th penny by the purchaser alone, together with one-halt of a guilder to the Secretary besides his office fees."

It was on February 14, 1658, that Stuyvesant petitioned the provincial council of New Netherland and the burgomasters of New Amsterdam for a ground-brief or patent and a transport or deed for the lots on the East River (now Pearl Street), then at the foot of the present Whitehall Street, upon which he had erected a costly and handsome residence, known in later years as "The Whitehall." The right of giving ground-briefs resided in the director-general and council, while the issuing of transports rested with the burgomasters, since that right had been surrendered to the city. Stuyvesant could not, as director-general, give himself a valid grant, hence he proceeded according to the usual method. In his petition, he said he had "fenced, recovered, and raised up, at great cost and labor, out of the water and swamp, certain abandoned lots granted in the year 1647" by Kieft, which had been conveyed, subsequently, by the patentee "to one Thomas Baxter," who was "a bankrupt and fugitive from the Province."[1] These lots had been forfeited and reverted to the Company. Stuyvesant asked for the proper annulment of Kieft's ground-brief, which, however, could not be "found in the Register," and sought for a grant to himself and his heirs, so that they might "enjoy in peace the fruits of the great expense incurred and still [to be] incurred" on the property. The council allowed the ground-brief "after proper survey," and the burgomasters gave a "due conveyance thereof according to the survey," because the object was considered laudable.

By this year the sheet-piling along the East River extended north of the Ferry, at the present Fulton and Pearl Streets. On April 11th, the city schout was ordered "to notify all who lie along the North River to level their bank and lay it off according to the General's [Stuyvesant's] plan." On May 25th, the provincial government proposed the surrounding of the city with palisades, leaving two openings as gates, in order to prevent smuggling. This idea is reflected in records of a later date and received the approval of the Directors at Amsterdam in February, 1659. On November 9th, the city was given permission to construct a pier[2] and collect wharfage fees. The city court gave notice, on August 12th, to all persons in the city who had "placed thatched roofs on their houses" or had plastered chimneys, to remove them. The court officer reported, two weeks later, that he had gone the round and given the warning, but the people had only "made fun of him" when he communicated the message. In July, we find the earliest record relating to the establishment of guilds for the labouring classes in New Amsterdam.

[1] This was the pirate who caused so much annoyance some years before and of whom mention has been made in this chapter. [2] This pier was erected in 1659 and is discussed *infra*.

A street or lane running from Hoogh Straet (now Stone Street) to the East River (now Pearl Street), between the lots of Charles Bridges[1] and Solomon La Chair, was to remain open provisionally "for the use of the city until further order," according to the order of the burgomasters, on March 28th. This lane separated the original grants of 1645 to Thomas Willett[2] and Richard Smith,[3] and lay between the Stadt Huys Lane (now Coenties Alley) and the Burghers Path beyond. On August 8th, the burgomasters agreed "to propose" to Stuyvesant "the paving of the Winckel Straet, and to make one of the Burghers Overseer of the Ward (*Buirtmeester*) on behalf of the Company." This street, now closed, was east of and parallel to Whitehall Street and extended from the present Stone to Bridge Street. Its easterly side was occupied by the five large stone houses, or shops, of the West India Company, whence its name was derived. On the fifteenth of this month, the burgomasters resolved to include the grading of the Brugh Steegh or Bridge Lane, also no longer in existence, which was at first merely a short passage running from the present Stone Street to the rear of a lot of Abraham Planck or Verplanck, on Bridge Street, about midway between the present Whitehall and Broad Streets. Eventually, it was extended through the Planck lot to Bridge Street and had a more contracted outlet through the next block to the shore of the East River (Pearl Street), as a short cut to the dock and weigh-house. In November, 1658, the earliest mention in the records of *'t Maagde Paatje* or Maiden Lane is found, thus showing its Dutch origin. In July, the burgomasters proposed the making of "a public Well . . . in the Heere Straet" (Broadway). There is no certainty that the proposal was carried out; but it is known that there were several wells in the road-bed of Broadway at a later date.[4] A city ordinance, published on August 27th, ordered "the removal of privies on the street having their outlet level with the ground" and required them to be rebuilt in such places as would prevent them from becoming a public nuisance; moreover, as "the constant rooting of the hogs" of the city made the roads and streets "unfit for driving over in wagons and carts," the ordinance provided that all owners of hogs "in and about the City" should "put a ring through the noses of their hogs."

[1] During the Dutch period this Englishman was generally known as Carel van Brugge, a translation of his English names.

[2] In 1665 Willett was the first mayor of New York City, under the English system. This lane is shown on the Castello bird's-eye view or plan.

[3] Smith was the father of Richard Smith, founder of Smithtown, L. I.

[4] For example, as shown on Miller's plan of 1695.

In August, the city bench ordered all weights and measures to be marked, and established stamping fees for the benefit of the city treasury. Shopkeepers who failed to comply were fined for first and second offences; upon a third discovery of disobedience, the shop of the offender was to be closed. In September, the burgomasters and schepens memorialised the Directors at Amsterdam for the entire revenue of the weigh-scales, instead of only one fourth part, provisionally granted to them earlier in the year. They asked also for the income from the rental of the ferry to Brooklyn, in order that excessive old debts and the current expenses of the city could be met. They spoke of "the sober condition of the trade" and the "high price of goods." The merchants of the city desired permission to trade directly with those foreign countries that were within the limits of the Company's charter. On February 13, 1659, the Directors at Amsterdam granted greater liberty to the people of New Netherland with respect to the foreign trade.[1]

The inception of intercolonial trade between the Dutch at Manhattan and the French in Canada is interesting. In the autumn of 1657, Father Simon Le Moyne, the Jesuit missionary among the Mohawks, visited Manhattan. Upon his return to Canada he bore with him an expressed wish of the Dutch to open trade relations with the Canadians. On February 18, 1658, Louis d'Ailleboust de Coulonge, acting governor of Canada, wrote Father Le Moyne that as the Dutch and French were allies, he and the principal persons of Canada saw no reason why the Dutch should be denied permission to trade with Canada, and thereupon he gave them consent to "come when they please under the condition that they submit to the same customs as French vessels, forbidding trade with the savages and the public exercise on land of their religion." Father Le Moyne transmitted this letter to Stuyvesant and proposed intercourse. He wrote: "Dear friends of the Manhatans, draw your furrows through the sea to our Quebec and some time hereafter our Canadians will unexpectedly with God's guidance safely reach your shores." On July 2d, Jean de Pré,[2] aged twenty-three years, a native of Comines in Flanders, who had received the small burgher-right of New Amsterdam in April, 1657, petitioned the provincial council for

[1] As a result of this liberty, "several prominent burghers" of New Amsterdam freighted a flyboat, named "Moolen" or "Gulde Meulen," despatching her "directly to France." She carried lumber to be exchanged "for wine and other goods." This was "the first attempt" to establish direct commerce between France and New Netherland and nearly created a scandal on account of alleged smuggling.

[2] Also Jean Du Pré, Jan Peri, or Perier. His drowning recalls the fate, less than a decade later, of Arent van Curler, founder of Schenectady, in Lake Champlain, while on an intercolonial mission from Governor Nicolls to the governor of Canada.

remission of duties on a cargo of sugar and tobacco in the sloop "Jean Baptiste," which request was granted because his was the first trading voyage to Canada. His vessel was wrecked on the Island of Anticosti and he perished, leaving behind him heavy debts which involved his wife in court litigation and impoverished her.

In 1658, there were two companies of train-bands or city militia in New Amsterdam, one under the orange flag, the other under the blue flag. On September 23d, the city fathers requested "three new standards," because Stuyvesant intended "to divide the two Burgher Companies into three." On February 13, 1659, the Directors at Amsterdam wrote: "The three flags, the partisans, halberds, and drums, required for the train-bands, are sent herewith, also some drumskins, snares, and strings, to be used when necessary." On October 4th, the burgomasters decided "to establish a watch" in the city and engaged eight men, four of whom were required to watch each night. This was the establishment of the "Rattle Watch" or night police. On the twelfth, they prescribed the duties of the watch; among them, not to come on watch drunk, be insolent, or commit nuisances in going the rounds, or be "found asleep on the street." Regulations were made for the equable distribution of lock-up money, fines from prisoners, etc., among the watchmen. On going the rounds, they were required "to call out how late it is, at all the corners of the streets, from nine O'Clock in the evening until *reveille* beat in the morning," and were to have a captain over them. The first captain was Lodowyck Pos, who went from house to house every month to collect from each housekeeper fifteen stivers (30 cents) for the support of the Rattle Watch.

Earlier in this year, the city bench had directed the apportionment of all fines—one third to the schout, one third to the city, and one sixth, each, to the church and the poor of the city. It also changed its regular court days from Mondays to Tuesdays. On March 19th, the city jailer at the City Hall was privileged to "lay in beer for the prisoners, also wine and liquors, free of excise," on condition that he would not permit associated drinking. The provincial government renewed sundry ordinances in 1658, and the compilation thereof, made by Cornelis van Ruyven, the secretary of New Netherland, constitutes the earliest edition of revised laws affecting the province. In this year, also, an epidemic of fever seized the city, from which "many died." This increased materially the work of the court of orphan-masters in regulating decedent estates.

An ordinance of November 28th established "two Markets or Fairs" in the city, "one for Lean cattle, to commence on the first of May [1659] and to continue until the end of said month; the other for Fat cattle, to commence on the 20th of October and to terminate on the last of November of each year." Stalls were ordered erected for the cattle to be brought to market. The market for lean cattle was located "beside the Church Yard" on Broadway, near the fort. On April 18, 1659, the burgomasters determined "to erect the Meat-Market; further, to cover it with tiles" and have a "block therein."[1]

Stuyvesant was absent from New Amsterdam at least twice during 1658, once on a visit to the South (Delaware) River, and again to the Esopus (Kingston, N. Y.), where he went to allay the Indian troubles and to concentrate the settlers in a stockaded village, which came to be known as Wiltwyck. This concentration was important, as was also the founding of the village of Harlem on Manhattan Island. On March 4th, Stuyvesant and the council gave notice that for the promotion of agriculture, furthering the security of Manhattan and the cattle pasturing there, "as well as for the greater recreation and amusement" of the city, they had "resolved to form a New Village or Settlement at the end of the Island." This proved to be the beginning of the village of Harlem. Each settler was promised a land grant, free from the "tenths" for fifteen years, at the price of eight guilders per morgen, payable in instalments, and military protection[2] was vouchsafed to the settlers when required. As soon as twenty or more families were settled, "an Inferior Court of Justice" was to be erected, a clergyman provided, assistance given "with the Companies Negroes" in the construction of "a good wagon road" to the city, authorisation of "a Ferry and a suitable Scow near the aforesaid Village," and the favour of "a Cattle and Horse Market." On November 27th, formal notice was given to the grantees to take possession and make preparations within six weeks for fencing and planting their lands.

Salt as a commodity had been open to the trade of all, but on February 13, 1659, the Directors at Amsterdam proposed a special monopoly over the salt trade in New Netherland, for the benefit of the West India Company. They ordered that the stock "be stored in the Company's Warehouse [at New Amsterdam] and not be sold by anyone except by the Company at a fair and honest price." On July 23d, Stuyvesant and

[1] In July, 1660, "de Hall," or shambles, was located on Hoogh (now Stone) Straet, behind the City Hall lot, and it is shown there on the Castello bird's-eye view. (Appendix, III.)

[2] The council appointed military officers of Harlem on March 23, 1660.

the council drew up very strong animadversions to their superiors, in which they showed in detail that the execution of this mandate would be an infraction of the Company's own former regulations, and divert, or at least obstruct, the commerce of New Netherland, to the embarrassment of the province and the Company. These arguments were convincing and the Directors withdrew the demand.

New Amsterdam was again visited during the summer of 1659 by an epidemic of fever. On September 4th, Stuyvesant informed the Directors at Amsterdam that he had been ill "during the past four weeks with a sickness accompanied by a hot internal fever," perhaps typhoid fever, and indicated his convalescence under medical treatment, adding that he had been up "for two or three days," but remained "still very sick and weak." No doubt, it was this epidemic that inspired a request, on the seventeenth, for "some medicinal seeds and plants . . . from the Botanical Garden of Leyden" for cultivation in New Netherland.[1] It was during the hardships of this visitation that Indian depredations at the Esopus and in other parts of the province added to the trials of the sick director-general. A provincial notice was issued for military enlistments "to serve for the protection of the country and destruction of the Indians, whether on monthly wages or as Volunteers for plunder." The distresses were enhanced, moreover, because the Company sent over many "free people" at its expense, who, as Stuyvesant complained, were "mostly traders and hence persons unaccustomed to labor," who soon became "a charge of the Poormasters," while others, "more honest," entered the military service when the call was made. Stuyvesant said the country needed above all "farmers or farm laborers, foreigners and exiles, used to labor and poverty."

On September 12th, twenty of the principal men of New Amsterdam addressed a remonstrance to the burgomasters, who, they declared, were "sufficiently acquainted with the low condition" of the city, "through the constant complaints" of the burghers, of whom some had "fled from their lands and houses," turning to the city as a refuge in their poverty, in the hope of gaining a living there; others who had tried to help the stricken were themselves reduced to want, "so that the debts they . . . contracted from year to year among this poor Commonalty" were estimated to be "more than one hundred thousand guilders" ($40,000) above what they were able to repay; some had lost heavily in life and property

[1] Some were sent in the following year for the use of Dr. Alexander Carolus Curtius, for an herbarium.

during the Indian uprising in 1655, and now others had, through dread of a similar destruction, "left their lands and houses." The remonstrants said it was a matter of conscience to save the needy of the "Netherlands Nation," aiding them "by disbursement of money, provisions, or by new advances of goods"; but when this was done, it was certain the debts contracted could never be repaid. The burden fell upon the burghers who still had some means. It was a burden that worked injustice. They averred that they supported an "excessive heavy day and night watch; Yea, even every night," and also gave "voluntary services against enemies at divers times for the public service, from which public burthens all surrounding places" were exempt. They complained against "the Scots or traders" who went to and fro from their ships, taking "all the profit out of the country, selling everything for cash (for which the old inhabitants must wait) without having to bear any burthens." They asked the burgomasters to secure the following reforms or concessions from the provincial government, viz: (1) that the burgher-right should be established in all places in New Netherland under the Company's authority; (2) that a burgher of New Amsterdam, who departed out of or into the country for a year and six weeks, might retain his burgher-right, provided he kept at least a free room, fire, and light in the city; (3) "that no one coming first from Holland" should be allowed to "go to Fort Orange or other places with Cargoes to trade there with the Indians or Christians," unless he had first obtained his burgher-right in the city; (4) that no man should be a burgher of the city unless he promised to remain in the country three years, otherwise he should be obliged to pay one thousand guilders for his burgher-right, a sum they adjudged reasonable for those who came to New Netherland only with cargoes; (5) that the privileges allowed the merchants of the city "on the subject of foreign trade be forthwith published." These concessions the remonstrants believed would redound to prosperity and be serviceable alike to the province and the Fatherland. On November 5th, the presiding burgomaster transmitted the remonstrance to Stuyvesant and the council for favourable action, leaving to their discretion, however, the amount of the burgher-right tax upon traders, if it were considered too high. Stuyvesant and the council, by apostill of January 31, 1660, conceded virtually everything asked for, except the fourth item, which was disallowed, as it was contrary to the order of the Directors at Amsterdam and "prejudicial to this place." The disallowance of this heavy tax on traders vitiated in large measure the reforms desired, although some remedy was effected by a city ordinance of March 9, 1660, and a provincial edict of May 25th of that year, requiring the "newly arrived Traders, Scotch factors, and Merchants" to keep "an open store" in the city for a period of "at least six weeks" after securing their burgher-right. We have already seen how the great and small burgher-rights were inaugurated in 1657. On February 28, 1659, the burgomasters prepared a draft of a certificate for granting the burgher-right in the city and authorised the secretary to receive fees, as follows: "for the writing of a great Burgher certificate twenty stivers [40 cents], and for a small Burgher certificate twelve stivers." These certificates were issued by the presiding burgomaster, who affixed the seal of the city.[1] On January 11th, Evert Duyckingh had been ordered "to put the Arms of Amsterdam in New Netherland on the windows of the City Hall."

The city treasury was empty and long-standing loans remained unliquidated. A large sum, lent at various times by Cornelis Steenwyck for public works, a part thereof as old as 1653, was yet unpaid. These conditions fell to the lot of Allard Anthony when, as retiring burgomaster in 1657, he became the first regular treasurer of the city. On January 4, 1659, he reported to the burgomasters that there was "not a styver in the Treasury," and that he was unable to obtain any money. He was succeeded, on February 7th, by Paulus Leendertsen vander Grift, but Anthony was remiss in making up a return of the city's accounts during his administration, wherefore he was ordered peremptorily in June "to deliver in the account" by the thirtieth of that month, so that it could be sent to Holland in a ship then in harbour. However, he continued derelict, and it was only on January 31, 1660, that he made his return, which was two days before he again became a burgomaster of the city.

The Directors at Amsterdam, on April 25th, sent over for distribution among the burgomasters and schepens "twelve copies of a little book, called *Ordinances and Code of Procedure before the Courts of the City of Amsterdam*." They were sent to the city court of New Amsterdam to be put into practice by them. In an inventory of books found in the City Hall, in November, 1674, a folio volume of "Bye laws of Amsterdam" is mentioned; but no "little book" of the sort sent over in 1659 is found in this inventory of the first city court library.

[1] Impressions of this city seal are excessively rare. It is singular that only one of these burgher certificates with the seal is extant, namely, that conferring the small citizenship on Cornelis Jansen van Hoorn (see Chronology).

It is not unlikely that a Latin school was commenced in New Amsterdam in the summer of 1652, and continued for about two years.[1] The next Latin school had its origin in the repeated urging by Domine Drisius of the Directors at Amsterdam. He had asked them "to establish . . . a Latin school for the instruction and education of the young people, offering thereto his own services." The Directors, on May 20, 1658, said that they had "no objection to this project" and suggested that Stuyvesant and the council might "make an experiment by opening such a school." On September 19th, the burgomasters and schepens sent a memorial to the Directors at Amsterdam in which they stated that "the Burghers and inhabitants" were "inclined to have their children instructed in the most useful languages, the chief of which is the Latin tongue"; that no opportunity was afforded nearer than Boston, which was "a great distance" from New Amsterdam, "and many of the Burghers and inhabitants of this place and neighbourhood" had "neither the ability nor the means to send their children thither." Therefore they requested that "a suitable person" be sent over from Holland as "Master of a Latin School," in order that their children might "be instructed in, and study such language, not doubting but were such person here, many of the neighbouring places would send their children hither to be instructed in that tongue; hoping that, increasing from year to year, it may finally attain to an Academy [university], whereby this place arriving at great splendour your Hon^{rs} shall have the reward and praise next to God the Lord, who will grant His blessing to it." They, on their part, offered "to have constructed a suitable place or school." The Directors, on February 13, 1659, wrote that they had decided to make inquiry for a competent teacher, one who could write "a good hand, to teach the children also calligraphy" and that the teacher might be expected "by ships sailing from here [Amsterdam] during the spring." On April 10th, Alexander Carolus Curtius, late a professor in Lithuania, appeared before the Directors at Amsterdam and was engaged "as Latin schoolmaster in New Netherland at a yearly salary of 500 fl." and "a gratuity of 100 fl." in merchandise. Upon his arrival in New Netherland he was to receive "a piece of land convenient for a garden or orchard." He was also to "be allowed to give private instructions" as far as it could "be done without prejudice to the duties" for which he had been engaged. Curtius sailed on April 25th in the "Bever" and at

[1] According to Kilpatrick, *The Dutch Schools of New Netherland*, etc., p. 99. Next to nothing is known about it.

once upon arrival in New Amsterdam opened his school. On July 4th, he asked the burgomasters for more salary because "he had but few scholars," and said that when he should have as many as "twenty-five or thirty, he would be willing to serve for less salary." The burgomasters had allowed him two hundred florins "as a yearly present from the city," in addition to his regular grants from the Directors on behalf of the Company, and his request was for an increase of the perquisites from the city. His request was granted by a further allowance of fifty florins. The records reveal him as inclined to be mercenary, as he not only sought an increase in his allowances, but overcharged his pupils and practised medicine on the side. On February 25, 1661, the burgomasters reprimanded him for his overcharges and said that he did "not keep strict discipline over the boys in his school, who fight among themselves and tear the clothes from each others bodies, which he should prevent and punish." He defended himself against these charges, and said his hands were bound, because "some people do not wish to have their children punished," wherefore he requested the burgomasters to "make a rule or law for the school" and said it was also necessary that his schoolhouse "should be enlarged." His school, successful at first, declined, and, on July 21, 1661, he resigned. He was succeeded, in May 1662, by Ægidius Luyck, a young man aged twenty-one years. The school seems to have lapsed during the interim. Luyck remained until the English occupation and in May, 1665, accompanied Stuyvesant to Holland.[1]

Other interesting incidents of 1659 remain to be recorded. On March 7th, Resolved Waldron, the under schout of the city, was made superintendent of the *graght* or canal (present Broad Street), and he asked the burgomasters for written regulations with respect to his duties. He was given a commission which authorised him, "according to the Placard dated 3d Decembr 1657" and renewed on March 4, 1659, to take "good care and superintendence of the newly constructed *Graght*, that no filth be cast into it; also that boats, canoes, and skiffs be placed in regular order therein." The cost of the enlarged and deepened canal, now called in the records the *Heeren Graght*, or Broad Canal, was assessed on twenty-one abutting owners, on both sides of the canal. This levy caused considerable opposition and was met with some obstinacy, so that not all of the tax was paid in for a year. On July 11th, Joannes Nevius, the secretary of the city, was ordered to inform the skippers "lying in the road-

[1] He returned, however, as a minister and in 1671 assisted Drisius.

stead" before New Amsterdam, that the city had secured "authority to take from the traders and skippers, for the erection of a Pier, and for the benefit thereof, 8 stivers per last for loading and discharging at the aforesaid Pier [on Pearl Street at the head of the present Moore Street]; the smaller merchandize and goods in proportion," of which the skippers were to pay one-third and the owners or receivers two-thirds. These fees were exacted "on account of the accommodation received by them through the abovementioned Pier," built in this year. On November 25th, the burgomasters ordered the weigh-house porters "to keep the Bridge clean"; "to be found at the Beam" (or Crane), or, when they went from their post, "to leave word" where they might be found. The reference is to the weigh-house at the new pier. Notices of the fees fixed upon for service here were issued on December 12th and "affixed to the Beam." As certain persons had been fined for driving their carts along the strand of the East River (now Pearl Street) without dismounting, the city court, on December 16th, empowered the schout and his deputy to "seize the cart" whenever they found "any carters sitting riding on their carts along the streets." In the summer of this year masons were at work on the fort, and negroes of the Company were busily employed in quarrying and hauling stone, lime, and other materials for its walls. Stuyvesant and the council informed their superiors in Holland that if the same progress continued, they hoped "to have the fort completed" by the summer of 1660, when it would "be necessary to build new carriages for the guns," for which wheels would also be needed.

In January, 1660, Hendrick Jansen Claarbout van ter Goes, "commonly called the *Speck Coper*" (pork buyer), was indicted as a felon, for theft and abuse of the public officers. The case is important in the criminal jurisprudence of the city, because the members of the city court did "not find themselves qualified by their Instructions to sentence and execute capital punishment." They sought, therefore, for a "further and more ample qualification" from Stuyvesant and the council, who conceded to the city bench the authority desired; but with the proviso that, if they found "the offence of the aforesaid prisoner" to be one to "be adjudged by them to be capital in *majori gradu*, they demand the Director General and Council's approval thereof." By a plurality vote of the city court, the felon was condemned to "be brought to the place where justice is usually executed and, with the rope around his neck, be whipped, branded, and banished the country, and condemned in the costs and mises of justice." The supreme body gave its assent and likewise permitted the city to erect a half-gallows before the City Hall, "should that be necessary for carrying the judgment into effect." On the twenty-seventh of this month, Claarbout and his wife and children were ordered deported "to the Virginias." On February 20th, the city bench requested the supreme body for authority to demand the deposit of a certain sum from persons applying for the revision of any judgment of that court, which request was allowed. The numerous city ordinances that were in force had "not been renewed for many years" and were "unknown to many Burghers and inhabitants," who through ignorance failed to observe them. On this account, the schout was "ordered and charged" by the city court "yearly at proper seasons to renew such placards as occasion" demanded, so that observance might be assured and ignorance be no longer justly pleaded in extenuation of infractions.

The Directors at Amsterdam separated the office of schout of New Amsterdam from that of the Company's fiscal and, on April 9th, commissioned Pieter Tonneman for the new place, giving him particular instructions and the oath of office which he was to take. Almost from the beginning of the city government in 1653, the burgomasters and schepens had sought a separate prosecuting officer for the city. They had repeatedly solicited it from the Company and its provincial representatives, yet without avail. But now the Directors finally acquiesced, because they had come to believe "it would not only much gratify the burghers of the city, but also would promote the administration of justice and law." Tonneman came over from Amsterdam in the ship "Gulden Otter" and was sworn in by the provincial authorities on August 5th, as the first independent schout of New Amsterdam. His duties as schout were "to bring to trial all who break political, civil, and criminal laws, placats, and ordinances; to arrest all delinquents in the city and its jurisdiction" according to his instructions; "to fine, execute, and inflict the punishment, therein prescribed; to demand, that upon his direction and complaint all criminal matters and abuses be corrected and decided and all sentences speedily and without delay executed." He was also to "convoke the board of Burgomasters and Schepens and preside at their meetings, also move all matters coming up for deliberation, collect the votes, and decide by their plurality."

We have seen that one of the promises made to the new village at

Harlem in 1658, was the erection of an "Inferior Court of Justice." This was now, on August 16th, carried out by Stuyvesant and the council, who named three commissaries, before whom all minor actions were to be tried, and the senior commissary was empowered to represent the schout in all criminal actions. The right of appeal in actions exceeding fifty guilders lay to the supreme bench. The commissaries were also specifically commissioned to enact ordinances, so "that the arable Lands and Gardens" might "be carefully fenced, kept inclosed, and the broken fences properly repaired."

On February 9, 1660, Stuyvesant and the council renewed the provincial ordinance of January 18, 1656, regarding the forming of villages or hamlets as a protection against the Indians. The isolated farmers of the province were required, on pain of confiscation of their goods, and "without any distinction of persons, to remove their houses, goods, and cattle before the last of March, or at the latest the middle of April, and convey them to the Village or settlement, nearest and most convenient to them; or, with the previous knowledge and approval of the Director General and Council, to a favorably situated and defensible spot in a new palisaded Village to be hereafter formed," where suitable lots would be granted to all applicants. The people were slow in complying, hence another order was issued on April 12th, and a notice on May 18th, to cause their removal and concentration. Meanwhile, on May 3d, Thomas Hall and others, farmers and proprietors north of and adjoining the Fresh Water on Manhattan Island, petitioned Stuyvesant and the council to allow their houses there to stand, and to permit other interested persons to build near them, in order that a village might be formed. On the same day, a council order gave Wolphert Webber and Hall permission to let their houses stand, and also allowed a village or hamlet to be formed near the bouwery of Augustine Heerman, or near that of Director-General Stuyvesant. This appears to be the earliest official act suggesting the Bowery Village. On August 30th, Stuyvesant offered to pay 250 guilders annually toward the support of Reverend Henricus Selyns, provided he would preach the Sunday evening sermon at Stuyvesant's bouwery; and on the same day Selyns was appointed to be minister to Breuckelen and at Stuyvesant's bouwery, his formal induction at Breuckelen taking place on September 3d. Selyns preached in Breuckelen on Sunday mornings, "but at the Bouwery at the end of the catechetical sermon." On October 4th, he wrote to the Classis of Amsterdam:

"The Bouwery is a place of relaxation and pleasure, whither people go from the Manhattans, for the evening service. There are there forty negroes, from the region of the Negro Coast, beside the household families. There is here [at the Bouwery] as yet no Consistory, but the deacons from New Amsterdam provisionally receive the alms; and at least one deacon, if not an elder, ought to be chosen here."

The revenues of the city having been found to be insufficient for the payment of the ever-increasing expenses, the burgomasters, on July 1st, petitioned for permission "to impose some chimney tax" as a subsidy, from which they might "derive from each chimney or fireplace" as much as the director-general and council might deem proper, this tax "to be collected every three months by the Treasurer" of the city. A record of February 24th shows that it was customary to lead the cows to the common pasture upon a signal given by "the blowing of the horn." The sheet-piling of the river-banks, which had all along been a live subject of official consideration and, equally, of a dull remissness in the commonalty, cropped up again in this year. On February 27th, the burgomasters directed that an order be made, "instructing each one residing along the beach of the East River, to build up and raise their sheet piling higher within the space of six weeks," or suffer a fine of twenty-five guilders. On May 4th, the schout was directed "to warn and order for the last time those residing on the East and North Rivers" to "build up their sheet piling, within three weeks' time" and "to cite those in default to the City Hall" for prosecution. A similar order for the East River was made out on September 10th. Acting on a petition "of the neighbours on both sides of the Prince Graght" (Broad Street, between Beaver Street and Exchange Place), the burgomasters ordered "each and every one to pave his lot before his door as far as his lot extends," and to do it "this winter so far at least that it" could "be made use of a-foot." There was a vacant lot belonging to Jochem Beeckman, and here the burgomasters offered to make the way passable. On November 3d, they "agreed with Jan Jansen Hagenaar and his son Jeremias for the making of four rods of pier" as an addition "to the pier at the Weighscales." This was the custom-house bridge which had been built in 1659 at what is now Pearl and Moore Streets. The contract was for 225 guilders in wampum "and a half barrel of beer in addition." The father was drowned accidentally in the East River, on November 22d, perhaps in connection with this work, and Jeremias, who was twenty-two years of age, was ordered on January 7, 1661, "to proceed with the making and completing the undertaken Pier" and to get another to work with him "in the place of his dec^d father." In June, 1660, the first post office in New Netherland was inaugurated at the office of the provincial secretary in New Amsterdam.

On the seventh of this month, Jacques Cortelyou, surveyor-general of New Netherland, was directed by the provincial officials to survey and make a map of the lots within the city. This plan of the city was completed by October 6th, when Stuyvesant and the council transmitted it to the Directors at Amsterdam, saying: "After closing our letter the Burgomasters have shown us the plan of this city, which we did not think would be ready before the sailing of this ship. In case you should be inclined to have it engraved and publish it, we thought it advisable, to send you also a small sketch of the city, drawn in perspective by Sieur Augustin Heermans three or four years ago, or perhaps you will hang it up in some place or other there." This was perhaps the original from which the Montanus View (Pl. 6) was engraved. On December 24th, the Directors acknowledged the receipt of the plan and made the following criticisms: "We have been pleased to receive the map of the City of New Amsterdam: we noticed, that according to our opinion too great spaces are as yet without buildings, as for instance between Smee [William] Street and Princes Gracht [Broad Street above Exchange Place] or between Prince Street [Broad Street above Exchange Place] and Tuyn Street [Garden, now Exchange Place], also between Heeren Street [Broadway] and Bevers Gracht [Beaver Street], where the houses apparently are surrounded by excessively large plots and gardens; perhaps with the intention of cutting streets through them, when the population increases, although if standing closer together, a defence might be easier." This interesting plan is not known to be extant; but the original manuscript return of an important census of the houses in New Amsterdam, partly in the handwriting of Nicasius de Sille, and dated July 10th, 1660, is preserved in the New York Public Library. It perhaps accompanied the plan of the Cortelyou survey and without doubt depended upon it for the particulars which it gives of the number of houses on each street or in each quarter, enumerating altogether 342 houses in the city.[1]

A number of the more important provincial affairs occurring during 1660 remain to be mentioned. On February 25th, Nicholas Varlet or

[1] For the details of this census, see Appendix, III and Chronology.

Verlètt, Stuyvesant's brother-in-law, petitioned the provincial government for the use of the Company's yacht for a voyage to Virginia, and it was agreed to let the ship to him and to send along an officer to enlist soldiers in Virginia. Two days later, Varlet and Captain Brian Newton were commissioned as ambassadors to Virginia, to express on behalf of New Netherland condolence on account of the death of Governor Samuel Mathews; to propose a league, offensive and defensive, against the Indians; to conclude a commercial treaty; and to request permission to enlist men. They were given particular instructions on March 1st, and at the same time the council issued a proclamation, offering protection against all prosecutions for debt, for three or four years, to such fugitives from justice as would return from Virginia and Maryland to New Netherland. The envoys were well received in Virginia and negotiated an intercolonial treaty of amity and commerce. On May 18th, Sir William Berkeley and Theodore Bland, respectively governor and speaker of Virginia, wrote to Stuyvesant and the council, empowering Sir Henry Moody as special envoy to receive their signatures to the treaty concluded by the Dutch envoys in Virginia. Moody appeared before the Dutch provincial authorities on June 21st; the treaty was considered and presently was completed. It received the hearty assent of the Directors at Amsterdam. During the year, the Esopus Indians were again on the war-path. The Dutch proclaimed war against them on March 25th, and peace was concluded on July 15th. Another storm from New England threatened the Dutch province. On April 20th, Stuyvesant wrote to the general court of Massachusetts, vindicating the Dutch title to New Netherland and the Hudson River, in reply to a letter from Secretary Rawson, of November 12, 1659, in which Massachusetts claimed the Hudson River north of 42° 20′. A day later, Stuyvesant and the council informed the Directors at Amsterdam that owing to the "troublesome time," occasioned by the danger of an invasion by New Englanders, which compelled the maintenance at New Amsterdam of "more than 200 soldiers, the officers and trainmen not counted," and because of a depleted treasury, the Dutch provincial government was compelled to be economical. It is at this time that we meet with the first mention of Jacob Leisler, of Frankfort, Germany, in a roll of the soldiers sent to New Netherland.

It has already been shown how a limited foreign trade from New Netherland was begun in 1659. On May 3, 1660, Cornelis Steenwyck and other merchants of New Amsterdam requested the provincial government for permission to trade along the west coast of Africa, from Cape Verde to Cape Lopez de Gonsalvo, etc., and they were at once referred to the Directors at Amsterdam. It is not known whether these concessions were granted by the Company, but it is doubtful, in view of the difficulties experienced about this time by the Dutch on the African coast. None the less, the request has interest as showing the enterprise and vision of these New Amsterdam merchants.

We have seen how Pieter Tonneman was sworn in as the first independent city schout in 1660. His instructions did not make it clear whether he was entitled to preside over the city bench or cast a vote, and therefore a controversy developed on these points. On February 1, 1661, Tonneman arose in court and asked whether any member of the court had objection to his participation in making nominations for a new bench. The members of the court voted against his doing so, "inasmuch as it manifestly conflicted with the Instruction of the Schout and the laws and customs of the City of Amsterdam." Stuyvesant, who sat with the court on this occasion, interposed, deciding that the schout should have a vote, and "assuring them" that the matter would be "so concluded" by him and the council. The provincial body by a peremptory "Acte" sought to enforce its mandate; but the lower court declared that the document was "contrary to the Instruction" and deprived them of their authority. Then Stuyvesant read the schout's instructions and said he understood the "first rank remaining to the schout" to mean "the presidency." This the presiding burgomaster disputed, claiming that the presidency, "of which they were now deprived," had always pertained to the burgomasters. Stuyvesant rejoined, that, while this was true, it had been "connived at" by him and the council. This resulted in a suspension of action until the dispute could be referred for determination to the Directors at Amsterdam. Meanwhile, the schout was allowed to co-operate in the present nominations, if he desisted from any further voting, unless authorised thereto later by the Directors. Stuyvesant and Tonneman gave their assent to this compromise.

On April 15th, the burgomasters contracted with Jonas Bartelsen "for cases in the Council-chamber [of the City Hall], to place therein the City's papers, books, etc." This is the earliest record with respect to the care of the archives of the city.

Richard Bullock, a prisoner at the jail in the City Hall, made his escape; and Hans Vos, who, having been appointed deputy schout on

March 3d, had "his residence in the prison room," was on May 19th confined "on bread and water" by the court for allowing the prisoner to decamp, while Pieter Schaafbanck, the city jailer, was "reprimanded for not having fastened the doors of the prison better." The jailer pleaded in extenuation that he could not attend to the prisoners in confinement, because Vos resided in the prison room. Vos petitioned the court for his release from imprisonment, alleging his innocence. On the twenty-fourth, he was "reprimanded for his drunkenness and excused for this time," and Schaafbanck was required "to make good the loss." In a city court proceeding of June 25th, the operation of the third degree against a female prisoner is shown. The case was one about stolen stockings that had been disposed of. The woman, Annetje Minnes, was "placed on the rack, and threatened with torture," in order to elicit information from her.

Some of the householders of the city, among them being some of the watchmen, were unwilling to pay the tax for the support of the Rattle Watch, and so on February 25th, the burgomasters decided "that the members of the Rattlewatch" should be exempted on condition that they should call out the hours "outside of the gates, the Landgate as well as the Watergate," since the householders of these districts were also obliged to pay this tax. The reference is particularly interesting as proving the existence at this time of only two gates in the stockade along the line of the present Wall Street and as giving the local names by which they were known.[1] In a record of March 18th, Lodowyck Pos, the captain of the Rattle Watch, said that he understood his men were "not to go farther than the Maagde Paatje," or Maiden Lane; but the burgomasters replied "that this order referred to bad weather, at any other time they had to go as far as Tomas Hal's."[2] On July 8th, the burgomasters ordered the Rattle Watch "not to call before day break: *Rise up from bed, etc.*" This order was not adhered to and, on October 7th, the presiding burgomaster complained that this call was sounded as early as four o'clock in the morning, whereas the midnight cry was omitted altogether. This led to an order to the men to adhere to the prescribed rules; but they continued to disobey because, as their captain reported on the fourteenth, they did "not want to be ridiculed by other people and call in the day

[1] The Watergate was the original and earliest entrance and was situated at the East River, now Pearl Street; and the Landgate was the entrance recently made at the Heere Straet, or Broadway.

[2] Thomas Hall, one of the oldest English settlers on Manhattan Island, whose house was now in the vicinity of the Ferry, present Fulton Street.

time," or, as the drummer explained it, "when reveille is beaten it is day." The watchmen were therefore summoned before the burgomasters and asked if they would call "when the day breaks," whereupon they replied affirmatively.[1]

On June 23d, the fiscal made complaint to the provincial authorities that the merchants of the city were making false entries of their goods and, on the same day, Stuyvesant and the council passed an ordinance to prevent false entries being made at the custom-house, by demanding of "all Merchants, Factors, and Traders not to ship off or send away any Peltries, either in case or package, unless the same" were "first brought into the Hon[ble] Company's store, and there inspected and appraised," as well as "marked with the Company's mark." Hides and tobacco were to be dealt with similarly "and shipped off only from the Pier [present Pearl and Moore Streets] and from no other place." On July 29th, Joris Rapalje was appointed by the burgomasters to the post of harbour-master. He was one of the oldest settlers in New Netherland, first at Fort Orange (Albany) and afterwards as a pioneer of Brooklyn, and had been a member of the Board of Twelve Men in 1641. Following upon the aforesaid irregularities, we find Nicholas Varlet, the collector of export duties, operating on behalf of the Company a revenue cutter for the seizure of smugglers. A record of November 11th gives the information that the city of New Amsterdam was building a ship, called "the City's ship" or "the City's barge," and that the burgomasters had learned that the shipwrights were drawing "more than 1100 fl. in wampum from the Treasury for wages, at the rate of 16 fl. in beavers." On August 25, 1662, Pieter Jansen van de Langestraat was engaged to enter "the service of the City" and "sail as skipper of the City's ship." By renewals, he continued as the city's skipper during the rest of the Dutch régime. About the end of 1661, a basin or inclosed harbour was formed by the pier or custom-house bridge and an extension of the piling which protected the made land before Stuyvesant's residence, where he had built the little dock or pier in 1648–9. On January 19, 1662, the city court asked the provincial government for approval of the fees which it had been suggested should be paid by vessels unloading at the wharf and by

[1] It is shown in records of 1662, that persons who were not residents of New Amsterdam, but who were in the city for a time, were obliged to pay the Rattle Watch tax as long as they remained; also, that this tax was demanded of "everybody above 16 years old, without exception." In June, 1663, Lodowyck Pos was named "Marshall" of the three burgher companies or militia, and on July 10th the members of the Rattle Watch were informed by the burgomasters "that the Trainbands," or three burgher companies, had "taken the place" of the Rattle Watch, and these men entered the militia service.

sloops wintering in the recently constructed basin, which request was allowed.

The fire-wardens were ordered by the burgomasters, on January 7, 1661, "to go around . . . and inspect all the fireplaces and chimneys" in the city, to see if they were clean, so that conflagration from "large collections of soot" might be averted. This inspection was ordered to begin at the end of the month.

On March 25th, the city court established a new bread assize for the city and ordered each baker "to mark his baked bread with a particular mark" and bring to the office of the secretary of the city, within three days, the stamp with which he intended to mark his bread, so that it might be registered. Seven bakers were registered under this order. On October 13th, inspectors or "overseers of the bread" were appointed, who accepted their posts on the twenty-first. Their duties were to see that the bread was made of good materials, had the proper weight, and was well baked. A new bread assize of this time prohibited the baking of cakes (*Koeckjes*), cracknels, or sweet cakes. On November 4th, the schout was ordered "to direct the bakers . . . not to bake anything else, but coarse and white bread and always to keep coarse bread publicly for sale in their shops." The bakers protested against these limitations and obtained some modification of the law.

The provincial council resolved, on September 2d, to offer at public sale, on the public account, forty negroes, young and old, male and female, recently received from Curaçao, payment for them to be made in beavers, beef, pork, wheat, or peas. Conditions for the sale of a lot of negroes were issued by the council on November 7th, and three slaves were given to the city on December 8th as a gift.

As certain persons forestalled the city, to the detriment of the general interest, by securing what the Indians brought to sell, "such as venison, maize, and fish," the city court decided, on October 11th, to enforce a provincial ordinance of July 21, 1660, against runners in the woods and to provide that no Indian should "bring any articles to any places except such as" should be "ordered and appointed therefor." On the thirteenth, the provincial council authorised the burgomasters to adopt measures for preventing a monopoly, and, on the twenty-first, each burgomaster was asked to give his advice for putting an end to the "covetous engrossers" who intercepted the Indians on their way "to market" and then sold "at enhanced prices to the poor people." The burgomasters deliberated carefully and decided "that two trading houses should be established for this purpose and the savages be charged to sell their goods at no other places than these." It was also ordered that "one trading house for the Indians" should be erected "before the house" of Dr. Hans Kierstede, at the present Pearl and Whitehall Streets. The next step taken, so far as known from the records, was an interrogation of Adolph Pietersen by the burgomasters, on March 24, 1662, as to whether he could work eight or ten days for the city, in "putting up a little house for the Indians to offer their wares." If a second trading-house was erected, its location is nowhere stated.

At the request of the church wardens of the city, the burgomasters, on February 18, 1661, directed Secretary Joannes Nevius "to issue two orders, one for Claes van Elslandt the elder, the other for Jan Gellisen Koeck, about ringing the bell and burying the dead." On the twenty-fifth, an order was handed to Koeck, authorising him "to take care that the bell be tolled for the dead at the proper time; also to preserve the pall, collect the hire thereof for the church, as well as the fees for ringing the bell, the rent of the straps, benches, and boards; to keep a record of all who have died and are buried, without concerning himself with anything else in this regard." At the same time, the son[1] of Van Elslandt was directed to bring his father before the burgomasters, but he reported that his father was engaged with public business. Nevertheless, they directed Van Elslandt the elder "to take care only of the graves of the dead dug in the church and in the church yard; to look after the bier being fetched and brought back to the proper place; to invite, according to old custom, everybody to the funeral, walk decently before the corpse, and to demand and receive pay only for his services, without asking for more." This is the most circumstantial reference during the Dutch régime to the funeral arrangements for burial in New Amsterdam and shows that Christian interments were made in two places—the church in the fort, and the churchyard on the west side of Broadway, outside of the fort. On February 25th, the burgomasters ordered "that the vacant seats in the pews should be rented out or sold for the benefit of the Church" in the fort.

On June 11, 1661, the deacons of the church at New Amsterdam petitioned the provincial council that each of the adjacent villages be obliged to make weekly contributions for its own poor. They were led

[1] The younger Claes van Elslandt was messenger of the city court. His father held a like post under the provincial body.

to make this demand because of "the many applications and great trouble" which they experienced daily "from persons residing in the outlying villages, with whose characters and wants" they were wholly unacquainted, causing a depletion in their treasury to the disadvantage of the poor and needy of New Amsterdam. Stuyvesant and the council, therefore, passed on October 22d the first poor law applicable to the province, in order, as they said, "that the Lazy and the Vagabond" might "as much as possible be rebuked, and the really Poor [be] the more assisted and cared for." The deacons of New Amsterdam were not to give assistance to any persons not residents of the city, unless they brought a certificate showing "their character and poverty." Collections were ordered to be taken "in all Villages and Settlements" and to be "laid up for the Poor and Needy." This was to be done in every place, whether there was preaching there or not. In those places which had no preaching service, the local magistrates were required "to nominate and qualify two proper persons" to "go around every Sunday with a little bag among the congregation and collect the Alms for the support of the Poor of that place"; but, if they fell short in their needs, they might apply to the deacons of New Amsterdam in the manner specifically prescribed for such cases. This law did not solve the difficulty, and on December 28th, the presiding burgomaster proposed to the city court "to decree, whereas divers poor seek their support here from other towns, that the Deaconry of this City intend to permit a collection to be made every Sunday in each town from which the outside poor may be maintained—then inasmuch as such would tend rather to the prejudice than interest of this place—to resolve that such ought not to be undertaken before and until they communicate the same to the W: Court of this City, and to prefer acquainting the Honble Director General and to speak to his Honor thereupon, and that a collection be made by the Honble Director General and Council throughout the entire land for this object, so as thus to be freed from the trouble." On January 26, 1662, it was reported to the burgomasters that the Consistory of the church at New Amsterdam deemed it necessary, because many poor people came from the country, "to pass the plate for a general collection"; and, moreover, Stuyvesant had written that not only in the city, "but also outside of it a collection was demanded for the support of the poor coming from outside." But the burgomasters resolved "to send an order to the Deaconry" of the city, "directing them not to give assistance to anybody, except to the poor" of the city, and "to provide these poor with clothing, food, and a little money; also to make a note of to whom assistance is given." We have here an early demand for the home rule principle in this city.

An interesting anti-garnishee ordinance was passed on October 22, 1661, to protect the servants of the West India Company from "some self-interested persons" who got assignments "on the Company's books of account" against the servants for debts contracted for "trifles," for which they charged "over 50 ℔ cent more than the people could purchase them for Beaver."

On September 15th, Stuyvesant and the council by ordinance directed the inhabitants of certain towns and villages, among them those of Harlem, within three months, or at the latest by January 1, 1662, to have all lands claimed by them, whether cultivated or not, surveyed by the sworn surveyor "and set off or designated by proper marks, and on the exhibition of the Return of survey thereof, apply for and obtain a regular Patent as proof of property, on pain of being deprived of their right," so that the remaining land might be given to others.

Stuyvesant had been shown letters by Captain Thomas Willett that came "from London and Boston" and revealed "designs upon the Province of New Netherland." Willett had reported that not only was a rupture imminent between the mother countries, "but also the King [Charles II], the Duke of York, and Parliament" were "urgently asked for three or four frigates to take this capital [New Amsterdam] and whatever else belongs to the Company here," and that Charles II was urged "to grant this demand, by telling him that the W. I. Company" claimed and held New Netherland "by unlawful title, because in 1623 King James had granted to the Company only a watering place on Staten Island and nothing more." This alarm induced Stuyvesant and the council, on September 22d, to draw up proposals for fortifying the city and for strengthening the fort. Orders were given in October to the captains of yachts and sloops to bring cargoes of stone from Tappaen, to be used in surrounding the city "with a wall in course of time" and building proposed redoubts. This interesting record shows in embryo the English designs as carried out in 1664. The recently found "Description of the Towne of Mannadens in New Netherland, as it was in Sept: 1661," [1] shows that the anonymous author was familiar with the proposals of the

[1] Printed for the first time in Jameson's *Narratives of New Netherland* (New York, 1909), pp. 421-4, from the original manuscript in the Royal Society, London. See also Chronology.

Dutch government. In his description of the "half moon of stone" before the City Hall, on which were "mounted 3 smal bras guns, tho it be large enough to mount 8 guns on it," he adds, "They then [at the time of his observation] said, they would build 2 half moons more between y^{t} and the North-east gate." His account is found to be singularly correct when compared with the Dutch records and contains some particulars not otherwise revealed in them. The observations, so particular as to the topography and defences, offer strong presumptive evidence that this observer made his deductions for use by the English.[1]

In a petition to the city court, on March 21, 1662, the city schout requested that no more judgments pronounced by that court should be executed "until the successful party" obtained "a receipt from the Treasurer and paid the Schout his fees; and that the Bailiff be charged . . . not to execute any more judgments until, on notice given by the Court Messenger, the receipt is also produced." This was allowed because it had already been decreed by the provincial government. On November 16th, the schout was given permission by the provincial authorities to "agree and compound" with accused persons "for all civil and criminal cases up to one hundred guilders," on condition that he pay over to the church every month the share in the fines to which the church was entitled, as well as the shares that accrued to the city and the poor.

A prisoner who had been charged with the theft of a sack of grain, which he alleged "he had bought from a negro by the new Bridge," was "subjected to Torture" and pleaded guilty on four counts. He was condemned by the city court to be taken "to the place where justice is usually executed, and there to be tied to a stake, severely scourged, branded, and banished out of this City's jurisdiction for the term of ten years," as well as to pay "the costs and mises of justice." This punishment was inflicted on him on April 29th.

At a meeting of the burgomasters held at the City Hall on January 26, 1662, Jacques Cortelyou, the surveyor, appeared "on summons" and was "asked how he progresses with the map of the City." He replied that "as far as he is concerned, it is done" and has "already been

[1] In the heading of this manuscript as printed, the name of the town is given as "Mannadens"; but throughout the text it is spelled "Manados." The title of the enigmatical so-called Duke's Plan is almost a counterpart of the title of the manuscript narrative and the name of the town is given as "Mannados," while the plan also shows the town "as it was in September 1661." The two agree and are closely associated in time and basic origin. The plan is enigmatical because it shows English ships and the English ensign on the ships and on the fort, and has the year 1664 twice in the cartouche. Perhaps the most likely explanation is that the plan was copied in 1664 from an original made in 1661.

in the hands" of the draughtsman "for six weeks," or since the middle of December, 1661. He said the draughtsman promised "to have it ready this week,"[1] or not later than January 28th. The burgomasters allowed Jacob van de Water, on March 3d, "for making the map of this City, according to his bill for 96 fl. in beavers, the sum of 100 fl. in wampum," and on March 10th, they allowed Cortelyou "for making the map and other services for the City 100 fl. [$40] in heavy money," after Cortelyou had said that he would leave the valuation to them, but if made in Holland, "such a map would bring 100 ryksdaalders [$100]." The chief interest of this information lies in its probable association with the recently discovered Castello manuscript bird's eye view—reproduced and described in this volume (Appendix, III)—which is the most remarkable depiction of any town or city of the Western Hemisphere, north of Mexico, of so early a period.

Complaint was made at this time by the church wardens against Claas Mareschalk, with whom they had "agreed . . . to repair the glass in the Church" in the fort, because "he undertook" the work "for a reasonable price," yet rendered an unreasonably high bill. They exhibited his account for examination. The glazier defended himself by saying he had "calculated according to the Church work" and "had great trouble to set the lozenges in the arms in their proper places." The reference is to the family coats of arms that adorned the windows of the church.

On May 26th, the burgomasters resolved "to lay before the Director General and Council . . . the necessity of keeping up the Heere Gracht [now Broad Street] and for that purpose to ask permission" to compel persons who were unwilling "to pay their share of expenses," and to submit "at the same time the resolutions" of Stuyvesant "adopted at the meeting" of the burgomasters in the City Hall on June 23, 1660. The burgomasters decided "to have erected in the Heere Gracht at the East River [at what is now Broad and Pearl Streets] a convenient and durable lock, to keep said Gracht at all times full of water, so that in time of need because of fire . . . and at other occasions it may be used and that especially the great and unbearable stench may be suppressed, which arises daily when the water runs out." To carry out the project, they resolved, on June 2d, that "everybody dwelling on either side of said Gracht" should "pay, upon demand of the Treasurer or on his order, the share

[1] There is a discrepancy in the records as to the name of the draughtsman. On January 26th, he is called "van der Veen" and in the vote of record for services, on March 3d, his name is given as "Jacob van de Water," which is no doubt correct, as Van der Veen was a notary public whose record is well known in that capacity.

as imposed by the tax of February 13, 1660, even though these moneys were intended to pay expenses for the Gracht," and were now "to be used for erecting the aforesaid lock." A year later, Tryntie van Campen asked the burgomasters to appoint her husband as "lock-tender"; but they informed her that "there was no salary attached to it," because the city received "no revenue from the lock." At the same time (May 25, 1663), they mentioned in a resolution that the city had put the Heere Gracht "in good condition by making a good lock and repairing the old one," so that the canal would "retain the water" and "prevent unbearable stench at low water"; but now the canal was again "very foul and muddy," and the burgomasters therefore directed "every resident along the same to dig out and carry away two feet in depth of the mud," and "the overseers of the graft" were "ordered to have it done."

On March 3d, the city treasurer reported to the burgomasters that there were still "some houses with wooden and plastered chimneys," which might "cause great damage by fire," and cited certain cases, among them a house in the Marketfield Alley. This condition was a violation of an earlier ordinance, which had directed the removal of all chimneys of this character; therefore, the fire-wardens and the schout were ordered to make a tour of inspection and to condemn these chimneys forthwith. The city fire-wardens, having asked the burgomasters on March 24th "for written orders," were given formal instructions on April 21st. These directed them to see "that no more roofs" were "covered with reeds," nor the old roofs of this character repaired; that "no wooden nor plastered chimneys" were constructed on buildings, "and to condemn those which may have remained, and have them torn down in a prescribed time"; that when they found "any chimney foul," they might fine the householder; that they were to see "that the ladders and fire-buckets" were not used by the inhabitants; "to go to a fire with a black staff with three crosses"; "to make an inspection at least every three months," in order to note that the fire-buckets were in their proper places at the points designated for their deposit, and to have those which were damaged "brought to the City Hall," where they would be repaired by order of the burgomasters; to see "that the porters of the Weigh-house and the beer carriers, as well as the grainmeasurer," went to fires and remained there until the fire was out or as long as the fire-wardens deemed it advisable; to see "that no little fires" were "made outside of the houses, to cook by in summer," because these fires might "cause a conflagration"; and for the performance of these services they were to receive all of the fines provided for in their instructions. In a record of September 23d, it is shown that "4,000 bricks" had been "used for two chimneys of the guardhouse." These bricks had been delivered to the city by Rachel, the widow of Cornelis van Tienhoven.

On April 18th, the city court granted permission to Anna Claas Croesens, widow of Daniel Litschoe, a tavern-keeper, "to sell by the Bailiff some books" in her possession, which were the property of Sir Henry Moody, Bart., upon which she had a lien "for a considerable sum." This is the earliest record of a book auction in this city. A dispute arose between Mattheus de Vos, the concierge or bailiff, and Secretary Joannes Nevius "concerning the fees for selling goods at auction," each claiming the fees as his perquisite. These differences they submitted voluntarily to the burgomasters, on June 9th, who decided that the fees and the per diem charges of the concierge should be equally divided between them. On August 4th, Surgeon Jacob Huges produced a judgment against Lodowyck Pos, the captain of the Rattle Watch or night patrol. He requested the burgomasters to liquidate his tax for the support of the Rattle Watch by a garnishee of Pos's perquisites; but this they said could not be done "except with the consent of the debtor" and "City property" could not "be attached." A sick benefit fund for the porters at the weigh-house was supported by weekly contributions of eight stivers (16 cents), placed in a common fund. This system was devised by the burgomasters, on November 3d, at the request of the foreman of the porters.

On August 11th, the burgomasters resolved "that henceforth there shall be two market days in the week, to wit, Tuesday and Saturday, at which time the country people may offer for sale and sell their wares." They also raised the question whether a person who had married in New Amsterdam a burgher's daughter might enjoy the burgher-right himself without paying for it. "After some discussion," this concession was granted, but with the proviso that the claimant should give "notice of it within six weeks after marriage."

A general or provincial day of thanksgiving, fasting, and prayer was proclaimed on January 26, 1662, setting apart March 15th for its observance. The proclamation referred to the visitation in 1661 of "pestilence and hitherto unknown fevers and diseases"; also "sudden heavy rains and floods of water in the summer, by which the promising harvest was rendered unfruitful to the inhabitants; again by severe drought, by reason of which the fruits of the field were greatly injured and nearly cut off; and also by other trials," such as "prevailing rumors of new commotions and violence" from "foreign and domestic enemies." A change for the better had come, and the day was intended to signalise the gratitude of the Dutch for their deliverance.

Former edicts against the holding of conventicles were being violated, particularly by Quakers on Long Island; wherefore, on September 21st, a provincial ordinance on the subject, enlarging upon the earlier laws, was passed. It prohibited the public exercise of any other religion than "the Reformed worship and service" and prescribed that "no Conventicles or meetings shal[l] be kept in this province whether it be in houses, barnes, ships, barkes, nor in the Woods nor fields upon forfeiture of fifty guldens [$20] for the first time for every person w[h]ether man or woman or Child," found present, whether exhorting or teaching or having "lent his house barne or any place to that purpose." Larger fines and ultimately punishment were fixed upon for repetitions of the offence. Moreover, "the importation" of "seditious & erroneous" books, writings, and letters was interdicted, and "communicating or dispersing, receaving, hiding the same" was punished by a fine of one hundred guilders, "to be paid by the importers and distributers," and fifty guilders by the receivers thereof.

In this year, three negro women, slaves, sought their manumission, which was granted by the provincial council on December 28th, on condition that one of the three should come weekly to do Stuyvesant's housework. On April 19, 1663, an old and sickly negress, who had served as a slave since 1628, was manumitted by the council, and in December of the same year, the council issued a certificate conferring liberty upon certain negro slaves of the West India Company in New Amsterdam, and granted to a coloured orphan her freedom on the payment of three hundred guilders.

Although laws had been passed from time to time requiring the improvement of lands granted and ceded on Manhattan Island, Long Island, and elsewhere in the province, there yet remained "many tracts" in a "wild, waste, unoccupied, and unfenced" state. Stuyvesant and the council bewailed these conditions as a "serious damage to the Public," as well as effecting a "loss of the Honorable Company's long expected Tenths and other Revenues," that were to become due after the lands were occupied and improved. On April 26, 1663, therefore, the derelict parties were ordered to "fence in and improve, within the term of six months, the lands" to which they laid claim, or suffer their forfeiture and have them "disposed of for the public benefit." When the inhabitants of Harlem, on March 19th, requested the council for leave to pay for their lands in wampum, they were ordered to pay the "tenths."

City improvements in 1663 included work at the canal, street grading, and the construction of bulkheads along the water front. On March 9th, Abraham Jansen, a carpenter, was requested by the burgomasters "to make a model or plan for a sluice to be put in" at Jochim Beeckman's lot on the Heere Gracht or canal, now Broad Street. On April 20th, Adolph Pietersen and Aldert Coninck were appointed by the burgomasters as overseers (*buyrmeesters*), "to see that the High [now Stone] Street be properly made higher and passable," and "the people living on High Street" were "directed, each to raise and improve the street before his house and lot." On May 25th, these overseers were ordered "to do their duty in improving the street." Again, on April 20th, "the people living between the first bridge and the shore" along the Heere Gracht were directed by the burgomasters "not to put earth beyond the posts set and to improve the street, so that people may drive and walk over it." To expedite this work, Jacob Kip, Joannes Vervellen, and Coenraet ten Eyck were "appointed overseers." On August 31st, Hans Stein, Cornelis Jansen van Hoorn, Adolf Pietersen, Sibout Claesen, and Hendrick Jansen vander Vin were notified of the desirability of sheet-piling the strand (*wal*) "from the City Hall to the new bridge" (Pearl Street, then the East River shore, from Coenties Alley to Broad Street). Stein was exempted, but the others were required to pay 125 guilders. As some of the fire-ladders belonging to the city had been taken by persons who failed to return them, the burgomasters on June 8th issued an order to the fire-wardens, from which we learn that the "prescribed place" for the fire-ladders was "back of the City Hall," where they were to be locked up. From this place they could be rented to the inhabitants at six stivers (12 cents) for each use made thereof, the proceeds being designated as a repair fund.

When the burgomasters, on June 12th, ordered the wife of Hendrick Cousturier to purchase her burgher-right because she sold at retail, she replied that the burgher-right had been given by Stuyvesant to her husband, who had "painted the portrait of his Honour and drawn pictures of his sons." This hitherto unnoticed reference is the earliest mention of portrait painting in what is now the state of New York.[1]

Timothy Gabry, the vendue master, or public auctioneer, brought suit against the city clerk and the city marshal for interfering with his functions. On November 29th, judgment was given in his favour by the supreme court of the province, enjoining the city clerk and city marshal from selling a certain class of property by public auction and providing that the sale of all property surrendered for the benefit of creditors should be by the provincial secretary or his deputy.

Some of the inhabitants of Harlem had planted a May-pole decorated with rags before the door of a newly married couple and had assembled themselves around the house "horning," etc. This innocent prank caused Johannes la Montagne, the schout of Harlem, to lodge a complaint with the provincial authorities, on February 5th, charging the participants with riot.

On account of the Indian troubles that were rife and as a mark of identification for the Wickquaeskecks, who were friendly to the Dutch, the provincial council, on November 15th, gave these Indians permission to fish near Harlem and voted them sixteen impressions of the West India Company's seal on tickets for their protection.

In December, 1660, the Directors at Amsterdam had urged economy upon Stuyvesant and the council, and advised them to "begin with the military establishment," deeming it "utterly unnecessary to keep 250 soldiers in the service." What was done at that time is not certainly known; but on April 5, 1663, the provincial government determined to reduce both the military force and the number of persons employed as civil servants in New Netherland. This proved to be a serious handicap later when Indian uprisings and threatenings from New England were abroad. Stuyvesant and his council were troubled by the number of "Vagabonds, Quakers, and other Fugitives" that were brought daily to New Netherland without the previous knowledge or consent of the authorities, being smuggled in contrary to the prescribed forms of notice, identification, and subscription to the oath of fidelity required of "other Inhabitants." They made a law on May 17th, which directed "all Skippers, Sloop captains, and others . . . not to convey or bring, much less land" in the province, "any such Vagabonds, Quakers, and other Fugitives, whether Men or Women," unless they had first obtained the

[1] It is not unlikely that the portrait of Stuyvesant in the New York Historical Society is the one painted by Cousturier.

consent of the director-general and council. A fine of twenty pounds, Flemish, was laid up against "the Importers" for every infraction, "and in addition [it was ordered that they] be obliged to depart again" out of the province "with such persons." In this way the government sought to rid itself of uncongenial interlopers.

The Indian peace of 1660 was broken in June, 1663. About noon on the seventh of this month, the Esopus Indians entered "in bands through all the gates" of the village of Wiltwyck (now Kingston), scattering themselves "among all the houses and dwellings in a friendly manner," under the pretence of trading maize and beans to the unwary inhabitants. In this way they spied out the strength of the place in men, most of whom were at work in the fields. Presently, the Indians "plundered the houses and set the village on fire to windward, it blowing at the time from the South." Of the inhabitants of Wiltwyck and at the New Village twenty-one lost their lives, of whom some were women and children who were burned to death in or near their houses; and about forty-five persons, mostly women and children, were carried away into captivity. Twelve houses in Wiltwyck were destroyed. All that remained in the New Village after the sacking was "a new uncovered barn, a rick, and a little stack of reed." Reinforcements were sent from New Amsterdam to Wiltwyck.[1]

A campaign of extermination was waged against these Indians; their country was invaded, their forts destroyed, their chief slain, numbers killed or captured, and many of the Dutch captives recovered. It was not until May, 1664, that the last treaty of peace with the Esopus Indians and their confederates was signed at New Amsterdam. Now, because "most of the soldiers in garrison" at New Amsterdam had been sent to Wiltwyck, it was found necessary to provide a proper watch over the city; therefore, on June 14th, the burgomasters directed the captains and principal officers of the train-hands or militia to see to it "that henceforth every evening a non-commissioned officer with a sufficient number of men with hand and side arms" should "go on guard for the night at the Land gate" (Broadway and Wall Street), and that sentries should be posted, and the rounds made. On June 22d, they issued, through Lodowyck Pos, the marshal, fifty pounds of powder to each of the three burgher companies. The members of the Rattle Watch were absorbed

[1] The command was given to Burgomaster Martin Cregier as "Captain-Lieutenant." On June 26th, he took his leave of the city bench and delivered to Burgomaster van Cortlandt "the City Seal and the Key of the Chest of Deposits."

in the train-hands at this juncture. The inhabitants were warned by the provincial authorities not to travel on the public roads, save in parties of four or five persons "and provided with proper arms," and a provincial proclamation appointed July 4th, and the first Wednesday of each succeeding month, as days of fasting and prayer everywhere in New Netherland.

The unsettled boundaries between New Netherland and her neighbours, Massachusetts and Connecticut, now loomed up as disturbing factors to the Dutch provincials. In September, Stuyvesant went to Boston for the purpose of coming to some agreement, if possible, with the commissioners of the United Colonies with respect to the intercolonial boundaries. This was the last conference that Stuyvesant had with the commissioners and it ended unsatisfactorily. On October 13th, Cornelis van Ruyven, Oloff Stevensen van Cortlandt, and John Laurence were commissioned by the provincial body to proceed to Hartford, there to endeavour to procure a settlement of the boundary between that colony and New Netherland; but this move also ended unsatisfactorily for the Dutch. Funds were needed to prepare against aggression and attack, as well as to carry on the warfare with the hostile Indians. On October 11th, the provincial council voted to raise 4,000 guilders, in Holland currency, for public purposes, and was obliged to give as security for its note four brass cannon in Fort Amsterdam. Two days later, they made a contract with Cornelis Steenwyck, one of the wealthiest burghers, to advance 12,000 guilders in wampum on the above bill of exchange and security.

The Dutch province faced a critical juncture of affairs, "as well in regard to the perilous war with the barbarous Esopus nation and their allies, as the menacing anticipations and encroachments of neighbours, together with the already mutinous revolts of some English subjects" on Long Island. The city court, on October 22d, addressed to the provincial government a request, in which they said they represented "only one member and the danger" was a concern of "the Province in general." For this reason they adjudged it "to be very necessary and advantageous that some Delegates be convoked and called" together from New Amsterdam and the "other surrounding places and villages," as well as from Beverwyck (Albany) and the colony of Rensselaerswyck, "to deliberate and consult together," under the "direction and higher authority" of the provincial government, "for the good of the commonwealth."

They requested Stuyvesant to order the convoking of such an assembly "as early as possible." The provincial body declared the "request consistent with justice" and approved of the plan, save that they believed Beverwyck and Rensselaerswyck should not be included, on account of the lateness of the season, but should be apprised of the proceedings in writing by a courier, and their advice secured. On October 29th, the city court laid down the "points and articles necessary to be proposed for the good of this Province at the General Assembly," as follows: "to demand assistance against the savages"; to take up the matter of boundaries with the English; "to send Delegates to Fatherland," and to make their demands to the Directors at Amsterdam for assistance and, failing therein, "to address themselves to the Lords, the High and Mighty States General." The city appointed two delegates from the bench. On the same day a circular letter was despatched to the towns in the vicinity of New Amsterdam, requesting them to send delegates to the city on November 1st, to meet in general convention. This general meeting assembled on the prescribed day and continued to sit until the third. The delegates sent an address to Stuyvesant and the council, in which they recommended the appointment of agents in Holland, to procure a settlement of the boundary controversy and free trade with the neighbouring English colonies. On the second they drew up a remonstrance to the Directors at Amsterdam "in the name and on the behalf of all the inhabitants of this Province." In this they referred to the "distress arising from the depreciated value of returns," and the "excessive rise and dearness of wares imported," which had resulted in the removal "of several families" and the consequent "depreciation in houses and real estate." They chided the Directors for their neglect of the province and said they felt "the licentious, bloody, and impending ruinous effects thereof," from "the deplorable and tragical massacre and slaughter of the good people of the beautiful and fruitful country, Esopus," which resulted from a "reduction of the military force of the Province"; from "a powerful neighbor who keeps quarrelling with this State about the limits"; and from the "aggressions attempted on the part of the English Nation, our neighbours, on divers places under the jurisdiction of this Province." They said they seemed, "as it were upon glare ice," because they had been given "ground and lands," to which, according to the contention of their English neighbours, the Company had "no real right;" that "the total loss of this Province is infallibly to be expected and anticipated, such apprehension being indubitably very strong," and that if the Directors would not make speedy amends, the situation would be carried up to the "Supreme Sovereigns." This instrument was signed by the delegates from New Amsterdam, and the villages of Amersfoort, Breuckelen, Midwout, Haerlem, New Utrecht, Boswyck, and Bergen.

On December 22d, Stuyvesant, on behalf of the Amsterdam Chamber of the West India Company, and in compliance with their order of September 11th, ceded and conveyed to the burgomasters of the city of Amsterdam in Holland the "South [Delaware] River from the sea upwards to as far as the river reaches, on the east-side inland three leagues from the bank of the river, on the west-side as far as the territory reaches to the English Colony, with all streams, kils, creeks, ports, bays, and outlines belonging thereto."

We have now reached the closing year of the Dutch régime—a year of grave anxiety, of Indian massacres, of rebellion, of invasion and conquest. Before entering upon a narration of these momentous events, it is necessary to mention some of the lesser incidents that occurred before the English conquest. On January 10, 1664, the provincial council, at the request of the magistrates of the new village of Harlem, appointed Johannis la Montagne, Jr., as schoolmaster of that place, where he served acceptably until October, 1670. On January 24th, the Directors at Amsterdam voted to allow some Huguenot families to proceed in their own ships from La Rochelle and other parts of France to New Netherland, and upon their arrival to receive gratuitous grants of land there. Stuyvesant, apprised of this action and furnished with a copy of their resolution, was ordered to give every assistance to the immigrants when they landed in the province. In August, less than a month before he lost the province, Stuyvesant wrote to the Directors that "seven or eight persons," representing the French Huguenots of La Rochelle and St. Martin, had arrived "by the last ship, the *Eendracht*, to view the land" for a colony of refugees, and had been particularly pleased with Staten Island as a place for a settlement. The "few families" of French that were on Staten Island in this year were "very poor" and unable to contribute to the support of a preacher, and so Stuyvesant, at their request, allowed Domine Samuel Drisius "to go over there every two months to preach and administer the Lord's Supper."

Experience showed that an improper conveyance of real property had been carried on for some time in the Dutch villages of Amersfoort,

Breuckelen, Midwout, and New Utrecht—to such an extent that some lands were sold four or five times "without being duly recorded." This practice resulted from the inconvenience and expense attending a trip to the office of the provincial secretary at New Amsterdam. The magistrates of the respective villages joined in a petition to Stuyvesant and the council for a correction of this abuse, and on February 14th, were granted authority to have deeds, mortgages, and quitclaims for land in their jurisdictions executed before them, provided each village kept a correct and separate register of the records and annually delivered certified copies to the provincial secretary.

In the city court in April, Hendrick Jansen, the smith, was charged by the schout with furnishing drink, at his house on Stone Street, to twenty-one persons, in violation of the Sunday ordinance; and on May 27th, he was brought before the court charged with another violation of the law, was fined sixty-three guilders and reprimanded from the bench. Soon afterward he committed suicide by hanging himself "on the branch of a tree at the Kalck-hoeck on this [south] side of the Fresh Water." The schout, on July 16th, asked the court to declare his goods forfeited, and to order that "the corpse [be] drawn on a hurdle as an example and terror to others, and [be] brought to the place where it was found hanging and there shoved under the earth; further that a stake, pole, or post . . . be set there in token of an accursed deed." The city court, considering that Jansen had been "an old Burgher" concerning "whom no bad behaviour was ever heard," and because "his next neighbours, eight in number," had besought the court to grant him "a decent burial," decided "that the body" should "be interred in a corner of the Church yard[1] in the evening before the ringing of the nine o'clock bell." This decision brought the city court into conflict with the provincial authorities over the right of jurisdiction in such cases.

By direction of Stuyvesant and the council a number of negroes, male and female, were sold at New Amsterdam, on May 29th, to the highest bidder, and two days later the provincial authorities made a contract with Thomas Willett for a quantity of beef and pork, promising to pay the same in negroes. On August 14th, the ship "Gideon" landed at New Amsterdam, for the account of the West India Company, 290 negro slaves, of whom 137 were women. They were brought by way of Curaçao, from the coast of Guinea in Africa, and figured later in the con-

[1] The regular cemetery on the west side of Broadway near the fort.

troversy that arose over the effects of the West India Company, confiscated by the English governor of New York.

Broken-down fences "around some Bouweries on Manhattan Island" permitted cattle to wander into and damage the corn-fields of other people. Complaints were made to Stuyvesant and the council, who on June 23d passed an ordinance to prevent such conditions in future by appointing three persons as fence viewers for Manhattan Island. Heavy fines were imposed for dereliction and for damage caused by trespass, and one third of the fines was designated for "the maintenance of the Pound."

Joannes Nevius, the secretary of New Amsterdam, having discovered that Walewyn vander Veen, a notary, made copies of papers appertaining to suits in the city court, asked the bench whether "such copying by others" was permissible. The court answered that it was not, "and that the papers in the suit consisting of demand, answer, reply and rejoinder, which parties enter against each other, must be copied" by the secretary of the city. The notary was warned not to accept fees for what he had copied and was threatened with a disbarment for six weeks if he continued to trespass on the prerogatives and perquisites of the secretary.

In July, the question was raised, whether the inhabitants of New Amstel on the Delaware River were to be allowed to trade with strangers and Indians at Manhattan, while such trading was forbidden at New Amstel to the merchants of New Amsterdam. The provincial council decreed that traders from the Delaware could trade on Manhattan Island only after taking out the burgher-right of the city.

The States General of the United Netherlands, on January 23, 1664, confirmed the charter rights of 1621 to the West India Company, and declared that the Company had, pursuant to these rights and the "sincere intention" of the States General, "established their people and colonists on the coast of America, in the country called New Netherland." This action was taken, they declared, because "some persons," that is, the New Englanders and particularly Connecticut, were "evil disposed towards our State and the said Company" and endeavoured "to misrepresent Our good and honest meaning, as the same is contained in the said Charter, as if We had privileged the said Company only to trade within the said limits, and not to colonize or to plant settlements, or take possession of lands, calling the Company's right thereto in question."

On February 8th, Stuyvesant addressed a representation of ten items to the provincial councillors, city schout, and burgomasters in regard to the invasion of Long Island by the English and the possibility of an attack on New Amsterdam. On account of the "great importance" of the matter, the schout and burgomasters gave notice thereof to the schepens and to Oloff Stevensen van Cortlandt and Allard Anthony, both former burgomasters, asking them to co-operate in giving advice and "to deliberate" upon the representation, of which each was furnished a copy. This representation related to "summons and demand, first by letters from those of Hartford, subsequently by force of arms—first by one Jan Coo [John Coe] with a troop of about 80 @ 90 foot and horsemen in the English towns only on Long Island; afterwards and recently by one Jan Scott [John Scott] with a troop of about 80 horse and also as many foot not only in the English but also in the Dutch towns," on Long Island. Stuyvesant said that "no similar hostile proceeding" had "hitherto been made use of against these, but to prevent bloodshed and consequent greater mischiefs, efforts" had "been made by embassies and written protests to bring matters to an accommodation, at least to refer [the controversy] to the Lords Sovereigns" of the respective countries. Little was expected in the way of an agreement abroad. Meanwhile, opinions were divided in New Netherland, "some praising the forbearance" shown by the provincial government, others declaring "the non-resistance and non-opposition by force and violence to be cowardice, scandal and insult" for the Dutch nation.

The conferees advised resistance to any further invasion by John Scott, should he return in March, as he had threatened to do. They said that the Directors at Amsterdam should have used their profits from "duties both in Fatherland and here," obtained "now for so many years," in "enrolling and sending 2 @ 300 brave discharged soldiers" and "in fortifying this our City"; which measures would have prevented the revolt. They deemed it expedient "that every Burgher" of the city should defend his own house or estate, while "the military or soldiers of the Company" protected "outside and the country and villages round about" from the Indians and English. Stuyvesant had said that he thought the English were merely trying to pick a quarrel, ending in bloodshed, as a pretence to give up "the Dutch villages . . . to fire and sword" and to plunder New Amsterdam. With this opinion the conferees agreed, and dubbed the invaders "a ragged troop" ready for pillage. They declared that they would defend their "lives and fortunes" and acquit themselves as well in "defending the Company" as they had done "in the Year 1653, in the English War." Owing to the "openness" of the city "along the water side, both along the East and North Rivers," a situation acknowledged to be "notorious and manifest," Stuyvesant had asked them "in what manner" it was "best to fix and defend" the place, and whether they did not "think it practicable and necessary to set" the city "off," as expeditiously as possible, "with sufficient palisades against an unexpected attack." He desired "that an estimate be made for that purpose as to how many palisades each householder and each unmarried man, each according to quality, ought to" and was "able to furnish and within what time." They responded that the burghers were exhausted and unable to be burdened more; that the city's income was so meagre, that even the few works "heretofore begun for the City" could not be completed; that "the greater the revenue, the greater the expences," and for this reason they told Stuyvesant that he should "be pleased to lend the Company's Negroes to cut and haul palisades with the City's Negroes for two wings, one to be brought to the North, the other to the East River." Day and night watches for the city were discussed. The city conferees asserted that the solution of the difficulties arising from the English encroachment at "the Neuwesinghs," the reported recruiting of "every sixth man in the adjoining colonies" of New England, and the anticipated trouble in the Dutch and English towns on Long Island was a provincial obligation and beyond their jurisdiction.

On February 19th, the burgomasters entered into an agreement with Jan Boeckhout, Gerrit Jansen from Arnhem, and Jacob Keeren to make gabions, as follows: "thirty two 4½ feet high and wide, thirty two 3½ feet wide and 5 feet high, and twenty eight 6 feet high, and 4¼ wide," for which they were to receive thirty-five stivers each "and besides a barrel of good beer, on condition that they themselves cut the wood." The gabions were to be "strong and good" and the burgomasters agreed to pay for carting them.

On February 20th, the burgomasters resolved to submit to Stuyvesant and the council a request, in which they declared that experience had shown that "all wars and troubles caused" to the Dutch by their "neighbours of the English nation" were "based upon the desire" of plundering New Amsterdam and obtaining booty. They said New Amsterdam was a "capital" whose inhabitants were "mostly Dutchmen," who had "at their own expense built . . . many fine houses," surpassing "nearly every other place in these parts of North America." It had a "garrison of three complete companies of militia," and "should therefore be properly fortified in the manner" they recommended, for then the city would be "formidable to evilminded neighbours or the savages"; and they should "also considerably secure both rivers, East and North, making them safe for help to come, as a road to retreat or go to the assistance of so many villages, hundred of farms, with houses, grain, lands, cattle and nearly ten thousand souls, mostly Dutchmen and some Frenchmen, who in the course of years and with God's blessing" would "grow into a great people" in a province so favourably situated, "where thousands of acres of land" were yet "uninhabited and untilled." They dreamed that it might even be a refuge for the people of the Netherlands, if the mother country were "visited by cruel wars, civil or with outside nations," or become a "granary" for it in the event of the "failure of the Eastern crops or a prohibition of trade by the Northern kings and princes." They estimated "that in these troublous and dangerous times about eight thousand schepels of winter grain" were "in the ground, besides the large quantity of summer grain, rye, pease, oats, barley, buckwheat and others to be sown," from which they expected "an abundance of cereals," if peace reigned. They added: "We may even expect to become the staple of commerce for our Fatherland by the planting of tobacco, hemp, flax and other necessities." They adjudged that, "next to God, the only salvation of this country after the boundary question" was settled, lay "in the fortification" of New Amsterdam "by a bastion at the East River gate, palisades closely set through the water to the round bulwark before the City Hall, from there palisades to the Kapsken,[1] where a water battery should be built to protect from there the East and North Rivers and specially the City and the port, then again palisades to prevent a landing to about half way up the North River to a bastion, which is to protect the part as far as the North West bastion, to be built with a wing of closely set palisades, running down to the river and well protected against the floating ice; from there on the island a strong stone wall with two bastions as far as the East River gate, again with a wing into the river." They said that "to build these fortifications it would require a large sum of money," which they knew the provincial government could not now spare, because of the Indian war and the depletion of its treasury; nor could the inhabitants of the city be burdened with more taxes than were already being imposed. They added: "However, in this

[1] A point or reef of rocks at the southern extremity of Manhattan Island.

pressing necessity we promise to spend the whole of the City's income on the fortifications and to raise among the merchants and richest Burghers and inhabitants as much on interest as we can obtain, or may be needed, if in a year from now you will allow us, for the better security of the creditors, to receive the innkeepers or tapsters' impost here until the money, raised on interest, shall have been paid, with the interest, and not longer." Stuyvesant and the council, on the next day, agreed to the request, "except that besides the tapsters' excise granted" and to "begin in May, 1665," the "present and future revenues of the City" should, from that date, "be bonded for the payment of the money to be raised and that the fortifications" should "be planned and made with the knowledge and approval of the Director-General and Council."

On February 22d, the city court met and its propositions and the grant of Stuyvesant and the council were read. The president of the bench reported that Cornelis van Ruyven had offered a loan of a thousand florins and that Stuyvesant had promised at least as much on interest. The court then resolved unanimously "to summon not only the old Burgomasters and Schepens, but also the wealthiest inhabitants" to appear on the twenty-fourth; meanwhile the members of the city bench promised their individual loans on interest. On the twenty-fourth, "some of the burghers and inhabitants . . . being sent for to Court," the petition and grant were read to them. They were asked how much they would lend to the city on interest at ten per cent, "to commence when each" had "paid his last promised pennies," and continue until the principal was liquidated at the end of a period of not more than five years, and at the current rate in wampum of eight white and four black beads to a stiver. More than a hundred loans were made, aggregating 27,500 florins, which included a loan from the deaconry of 2,000 florins, the largest single loan. On the twenty-sixth the burgomasters estimated the amount raised to be "about 30,000 fl. in wampum" of the current rate. But before they undertook to accept the money, they requested Stuyvesant and the council for "a sealed warrant, showing that the impost on wine and beer, to be sold by the tapsters here from May 1, 1665," should "be paid to and remain in the hands of the Burgomasters until the money raised and to be raised" had been paid back with interest to the persons who entered into the agreement. Stuyvesant and the council gave this warrant on March 6th, under the provincial seal, it being also understood that "the monthly salaries of the City Messenger and other such employes, the sustenance of the negroes, etc., and other necessary expences" were to be paid out of the said revenues.

On March 7th, some men appeared before the burgomasters and offered their services "to cut wood for the palisades." The burgomasters then drew up the following proposals for the contractors: "The palisades are to be of oakwood, 13 feet long and at the thin end 8 inches square with true edges, that is at least 8 inches across for 1,000 palisades, 2,400 feet as ribs, one third 7 inches square, two thirds 7 inches by 4, all to be delivered near the stump at a place convenient to haul them: they may be thicker, but not thinner and at least 1,000 pieces together round wood and not split." The bidders demanded sixty florins per hundred, but were offered only forty. The men persisted in their demand and, after some discussion, the burgomasters yielded. The job was given to four men, who "signed a contract" and, upon their request, were promised ten florins each as an advance for their support, as soon as the work was begun. On the same day Hendrick Lambertsen Mol contracted with the city to quarry thirty to forty scows full of rock, at eighteen florins in wampum for each scow, and to begin his work by the end of the following week. These plans constituted the largest public contracts proposed during the Dutch régime in New Amsterdam; even if carried out, which seems questionable, they were too belated to save the city from capture.

With the signing of these contracts the city court renewed its activities. On the same day (March 7th), they addressed Stuyvesant and the council with respect to the imminent dangers of the province and requested the convocation of another "General Provincial Assembly as early as possible . . . to enact by a unanimous vote" whatever measures were deemed to be expedient "for the prosperity, quiet and peace" of the country. The provincial authorities gave their approval on the eighteenth and on April 1st issued a writ, summoning the several towns to send delegates to New Amsterdam on the tenth of that month. On April 8th, the city bench chose Burgomaster Cornelis Steenwyck and Schepen Jacob Backer as delegates from the city; the other settlements sent twenty-two delegates. The assembly met on the day named and drew up addresses to Stuyvesant and the council on the eleventh and twelfth, which were answered evasively. On the fifteenth, they sent a third address in which they asked permission to petition the West India Company and the States General for protection and redress of divers grievances, as well as to send agents to support their contentions, and then adjourned for a week. At the same time, Stuyvesant and the council submitted certain points for the consideration of the assembly, and on the twenty-second, when the delegates reassembled, Stuyvesant addressed them in person and communicated to them despatches from Holland with respect to the extermination of the Esopus Indians, the reduction to Dutch allegiance of the revolted English villages, and other matters. The delegates deliberated on these things, but found themselves unable to suppress the English rebels, because, they declared, the rebels were "six to one" and, aided from Hartford, would easily defeat the few Dutch soldiers that could be sent against them.

In May, peace was concluded with the Esopus Indians, at Fort Amsterdam, and on June 4th, the event was signalised by a general day of thanksgiving. On May 31st, several letters from Virginia were received by the provincial authorities of New Netherland, which gave warning of an intended attack on Dutch vessels from Manhattan by a privateer, commanded by Robert Downman; on June 6th the provincial council ordered the magistrates of New Utrecht to keep a watch for him, and, if he were discovered off the coast, at once to send word over to New Amsterdam.

On March 12–22, 1664,[1] King Charles II granted to his brother James, the Duke of York, a part of Maine, all of Long Island, Martha's Vineyard, Nantucket, "and all the land from the west side of Connectecutte River to the East side of De la Ware Bay," giving to him, "his heires and Assignes and to all and every such Governor or Governors or other Officers or Ministers as by our said Brother his heirs or Assignes shall bee appointed to have power and Authority of Governement, and Commaund in or over the Inhabitants of the said Territories or Islands that they and every one of them shall and lawfully may from tyme to tyme and att all tymes hereafter for ever for their severall defence and safety encounter expulse repell and resist by force of Armes as well by Sea as by land and all wayes and meanes whatsoever all such Person and Persons as without the special Lycence of our said deare Brother his heires or Assignes shall attempt to inhabite within the several Precincts and

[1] Double dates are given in the months for the remainder of the year 1664 in order to avoid confusion and error. The English dated their records according to the Julian calendar, which had its origin in the time of Julius Cæsar, and is known as "old style," to distinguish it from the Gregorian calendar, known as "new style," which was a reform in the reckoning of time that was instituted in Roman Catholic countries or countries under their influence, in February, 1582. The Dutch had then adopted the Gregorian system, while among the English it was not promulgated before September, 1752. In the seventeenth century, therefore, a difference exists of ten days. Most of the Christian countries, except Russia and Greece, now follow the Gregorian system. The later date is the modern equivalent.

Lymitts of our said Territories and Islands." This grandiloquent grant disregarded the rights of the Dutch over New Netherland, with whom England was then nominally at peace, and showed disrespect for the charters of Massachusetts and Connecticut, as well as ignoring grants that had been made to certain individuals in Maine and on Long Island.

We have seen how the English towns on Long Island revolted early in this year under the leadership of John Scott, "the usurper," and how the Dutch planned to fortify themselves against an attack from New England. While these things were happening, the Duke of York as Lord High Admiral of England began to organise an expedition to put his patent in operation. A fleet of four warships was assembled under the command of Colonel Richard Nicolls, who was appointed to be deputy governor of the Duke of York's territories. With him were associated as royal commissioners Sir Robert Carr, Colonel George Cartwright, and Samuel Maverick, to secure the assistance of the New Englanders in the reduction of the Dutch of New Netherland.

Information about the English designs was known in Boston as early as May 18–28 and was communicated to Stuyvesant by Captain Thomas Willett on June 28th–July 8th.[1] A hurried conference of provincial and city officials was held in the fort, where the imminent situation was gone over in detail, with respect to measures for defending the Dutch domain. The captains of sloops were warned not to sail up and down the Hudson River, unless they went "at least two in company" and were "properly manned." On July 25th–August 4th, Stuyvesant wrote to the Directors at Amsterdam that, owing to constant rumours of an English invasion, his government was "very circumspect, anxious and watchful." He said: "We keep the military force under our command as close together as possible, heighten the walls of our fort, strengthen it with gabions and make all arrangements for defense. It is not our least anxiety, that we have so little powder and lead on hand, there being only 2,500 lbs in the magazine and besides that not over 500 lbs among the militia and inhabitants here and at Fort Orange [Albany], as we are informed. You can easily judge, that this supply will not last long, for it is not more than two pounds of powder for each man able to bear arms and then we have nothing left for our artillery, if we have to sustain an attack." He demanded of them an immediate supply of "war materials: powder, lead, grenades and small arms," and said that for want of

[1] The Directors at Amsterdam had written to Stuyvesant on June 24th (N. S.), apprising him of the ships sent from England. That letter, of course, reached New Amsterdam some time after the fact had become known there.

ammunition everything would be lost, "to the dishonor and shame of the nation" and its "faithful officers." Meanwhile, reinforcements of ammunition and men were drawn upon from other places in the province. The rumours of an invasion persisted. The city fathers, on August 13–23, decided "to wait the time, in order to hear what demonstration the frigates" would make and "to regulate themselves afterwards accordingly." But they also voted "to demand twenty-five negroes" from the provincial authorities, to work eight days "at the City's works" and to begin "the next coming week." On August 15–25, the city court resolved that one-third of the inhabitants of the city should "appear in person," or provide each a substitute, "furnished with a shovel, spade or wheelbarrow, to labour every third day at the City's works," or be fined six guilders for failure to comply with the order. They ordered, also, that "the guard" should "be kept and a whole company paraded," that these measures should be begun immediately, and that each man who mounted guard should receive a pound of powder and one and a half pounds of lead. They stopped the brewers from malting "hard grain during eight days" and otherwise regulated their production. They preferred a petition to Stuyvesant and the council in which they declared that it was certain "that four frigates" had "arrived from Old England at Boston or thereabouts in N. England, provided with a considerable number of soldiers," who were "even now on their way to come here." They asked for "eight pieces of good and heavy cannon provided with their carriages, balls, swabs, brushes, picks and spoons." With this addition, they said, the city would be provided with a quantity of twenty-two pieces" and they requested also "for each piece fifty pounds of powder," as well as "ball in proportion, also six hundred pounds of lead for bullets, to be used by the Burghers for their muskets." They wanted the city's contingent to "be strengthened at first by soldiers and the Company's servants, and that the day watch" should "be kept by soldiers at both gates, and in case of being besieged or attacked . . . all the soldiers with the Burghery" should "repair to this City's walls, it being considered" that, if the city were lost, the fort would be untenable. On the same day, Stuyvesant and the council gave their hearty assent to these proposals, at once contributed the use of the Company's negro slaves and "the assistance of the corporal's guard of soldiers," sent six heavy cannon for the defence of the city, and forwarded 1,000 pounds of powder and 600 pounds of lead.

On August 18–28, the English squadron cast anchor in Nyack Bay, below the Narrows, between New Utrecht and Coney Island. This created a virtual blockade of the port and enabled the English to commit deprédations on shipping and at Staten Island. Stuyvesant, who had gone to Fort Orange, was urged to return and reached New Amsterdam on August 15–25, and four days later despatched bearers to Colonel Nicolls to "desire and entreate" him concerning the "meaning of their approach and continuing in the Harbour . . . without giving any notice . . . or first acquainting us wth their designe." This was of course the language of an evasive diplomacy. Nicolls replied on the following day by a peremptory summons, requiring "a Surrender of all such Forts, Townes, or places of strength" as were "now possessed by the Dutch," and expected an immediate answer at the hands of the English deputies who had conveyed his message. It was now, on August 22d–September 1st, that Governor Winthrop of Connecticut wrote[1] to Stuyvesant and the council from Gravesend, L. I., that he had "lately come hither upon the cōmād of the Right Honble Colonell Richard Nicolls Cōmāder in Cheife of his ma^ties^ forces now arrived heere, & other his ma^ties^ Honble Commissioners," who had come from England under a commission from King Charles II, "to reduce to his ma^ties^ obedience all such foreigners as have w^th^out his Maties leave, & consent seated themselves amongst any of his Dominions in America to the preiudice of his ma^ties^ Subiects, & diminution of his Royall authority." He added: "I vnderstand also that they have in his Maties name demanded the towne scituatt upon the Manhadoes, wth all the forts thereto belonging, to be surrēdred vnder his Maties obedience: I thought fitt to give you this freindly advertisemēt, That I vnderstand his Maties cōm̄and cōcerning this businesse is vrgent: and y^t^ although he hath sent over very considerable forces exceedingly well fitted wth all necessaries for warre wth such Ingineers, & other expedients for the forcing the strongest fortifications, yet hath also given them order to require assistance of all his Maties Colonies, & subiects in New Eng^l^and, & hath directed his particular cōmāds in his Royall letters to our Colonies: My serious advice therefore to your selfe, & all your people, as my loving Neighbours, & friends is this, That you would speedily accept his Maties gratious tender wch I vnderstand hath beene declared, & resigne your selves vnder the obedience of his sacred Matie, y^t^ you may avoid the effusion of blood, & all the good people of

[1] The text of this interesting letter is given verbatim from the original text preserved among the Winthrop manuscripts in the Massachusetts Historical Society (see Chronology).

your nation, may enjoy all the happinesse tendred, & more then you can imagine, vnder the protection of so gracious a prince: otherwise you may be assured, y[t] both the Massachusetts Colony, & Coñecticut, & all the rest are obliged, & ready to attend his Maties Service: And if you should by Wilfull protraction occasion a general rising of the English Colonies, I should be sorry to see the ill consequẽces, wch you will bring vpon your people thereby, of wch I hope & perswade (in reall compasion) y[t] you will not runne so great a hazard, to occasion a needlesse warre wth all the evills and miseries y[t] may accõpany the same, when nothing but peace & liberties & protection is tendred: I have desired m[r] Samuell Willis, & my son, wth Capt: Thomas Clarke & Capt: John Pinchon to attend your Hon[r] wth these letters, & to have further conference wth your hon[r] about the premises, & desire they may have friendly reception, and free returne wth their cõpany & attendance, & you shall receive vpon any occasion the civilities from your loving Neighbour and Servãt." With this letter Winthrop enclosed another letter from Nicolls, of the same date, in which he gave assurance: "If the Manhados be delivered to his Matie I shall not hinder, but any people frõ the Netherlands may freely come & plant there, or there abouts, and Duch [*sic*] Vessells of their owne country may freely come thither, and any of them may as freely returne home in vessells of their owne country, & this & much more is conteined in the priveledges of his Maties English subiects, & thus much you may by what meanes you please assure the Governour" [*i. e.* Stuyvesant]. The burgomasters asked Stuyvesant for a copy of the communication of Nicolls, which he refused. Then a delegation of the burghers went to him and demanded either a copy or the original. On the following day, the burgomasters requested him to communicate the contents of Winthrop's letter, but this he also refused peremptorily and tore the letter to pieces in their presence. They also demanded to be informed of the answer he had made to the letter of the commanders of the English fleet.

On August 22d–September 1st, Stuyvesant wrote to the Directors at Amsterdam a letter in which he told of the arrival of the English fleet, said that Long Island was lost, New Amsterdam was summoned to surrender, popular murmurs and disaffection existed, and the loss of the country was certain. Besides the depleted ammunition there was a scarcity of grain. The bakers of the city estimated that their united stock amounted to only 975 schepels. On August 26th–September 5th,

Stuyvesant consented to treat with the invaders and on the same day Nicolls accepted the proposal for a treaty of surrender in order "to prevent the effusion of blood, and to improve the good of the Inhabitants." The articles of surrender[1] were arranged by the joint Dutch and English commissioners at Stuyvesant's "Bouwery" or farmhouse at eight o'clock on the morning of August 27th–September 6th; they promised the inhabitants who wished to remain "liberty of their Consciences in Divine Worship and Church Discipline." The Dutch were also to "Enjoy their owne Customes, concerning their Inheritances." This secured their property rights. Article 16 provided as follows: "All inferior civill Officers and Magistrates shall continue as now they are, (if they please) till the Customary time of New Eleccon, and then new ones to be Chosen, by themselves, provided that such new Chosen Magistrates shall take the Oath of Allegiance to his Majesty of England, before they enter upon their Office." On August 29th–September 8th, the fort and town were formally surrendered to Nicolls; on the same day the city was named New York. This name was extended to the entire province, and Fort Orange was named Albany in honour of another of the titles of the proprietor.

On September 6–16, the burgomasters and schepens decided to apprise the Directors of the West India Company at Amsterdam of what had occurred. It had all happened, they said, "through God's pleasure thus unexpectedly," on account of the Company's "neglect and forgetfulness" of its promises. On the same day we find the earliest recognition of the name New York in the records of the city court. Fort New Amsterdam was renamed Fort James, after the Duke of York; perhaps the earliest use of this designation is found in a warrant of September 8–18. On October 18–28, the oath of allegiance was proclaimed by Governor Nicolls, namely, to be "a true subject to the king of Great Britain"; to be obedient to the king, to the Duke of York, and to such governors and officers as were appointed by such authority. Objections arose to the taking of this oath and during the squabble that ensued Nicolls "finally departed with his secretary from the meeting," and the meeting was adjourned. Nicolls sought by explanation to allay the fears of the Dutch. Two days later a general meeting was again assembled and the matter was settled amicably.

The burgomasters and schepens, having taken the oath, continued in

[1] See Chronology for reproduction of contemporary Dutch broadside giving the articles.

office. Pieter Tonneman, the city schout, however, asked to be relieved from his post in order to return to Holland. He was succeeded by Allard Anthony on November 22d–December 2d, but continued to sit with the city court until November 29th–December 9th, when he communicated "in writing his retirement from the Bench."

On November 24th–December 4th, the city fathers approved a letter written by their president to the Duke of York, in which they promised obedience and said they deemed themselves fortunate that the Duke had provided them "with so gentle, wise and intelligent a gentleman" for governor as Colonel Richard Nicolls, and that they were confident that "under the wings of this valiant gentleman" the city would "bloom and grow like the Cedar on Lebanon." This letter "was sealed with the Great Seal of this City impressed on Red Wax."

The members of the city court before the surrender were Pieter Tonneman, schout; Paulus Leendertsen vander Grift and Cornelis Steenwyck, burgomasters; and Jacob Backer, Timotheus Gabry, Isaac Grevenraet, Nicolaes de Meyer, and Christoffel Hooghlant, schepens. By the sixteenth article of capitulation they were continued in office, save that Tonneman resigned, as we have seen, and Hooghlant did not sit after July. That article stipulated that they should also thereafter name and elect their successors. Under the Dutch régime they had been allowed only to nominate a double number, while final selection, election, and confirmation were reserved by the director-general and council. On February 2, 1665 (old style), they proceeded according to the new agreement and "elected and confirmed" a new city court bench. This done, they submitted their action to Governor Nicolls, to learn "if he had any objection to these persons." He had not, and the board proclaimed the new bench to the commonalty of the city at the City Hall; whereupon the new members took the oath of allegiance to English authority. The city bench now consisted of Allard Anthony, continued as schout; Cornelis Steenwyck, continued and advanced to presiding burgomaster; Oloff Stevensen van Cortlandt, second burgomaster; Timotheus Gabry, president of the schepens, and Joannes van Brugh, Joannes de Peyster, Jacob Kip, and Jacques Cousseau, new schepens. They continued in office until the form of government was changed in June, 1665.

During the first months of the English régime a number of interesting events took place, which deserve mention. Episcopal services were held for the first time in the church in the fort. The first formal treaty with the Iroquois Indians was effected at Albany on September 24th–25th (O. S.) This treaty provided for mutual trade, and the English were not to give aid to certain New England Indians who had treacherously murdered a Mohawk chief, but they were to bring about a mutual peace with the River Indians. In October an adjustment of the West India Company's books and accounts was ordered to be made by Nicholas Bayard, as assistant to Cornelis van Ruyven, the late receiver-general of the Company. In the same month regulations for the shipping customs and duties were ordered. The New York and Connecticut boundary was established by joint commissioners on December 1st, but in a manner that caused much controversy for years thereafter. Hostilities having broken out between England and the States General, Nicolls, on December 24th, put under arrest the estate of the West India Company remaining in the hands of Stuyvesant and Cornelis van Ruyven, only to make a complete seizure thereof early in the following year.

The administration of Nicolls, signalised by reasonableness and justice, happily served to reconcile the Dutch of New Netherland to the change in jurisdiction. In the following chapter, the operation of the English system is set forth.

PL I

t' Fort nieuw Amsterdam op de Manhatans

t' Fort nieuw Amsterdam op de Manhatans

Vaste lant
Godenis bay
Noortzee
conzatz bay
paulbe bay

De MANATVS, op de Noort Riuier.

Noort Rivier

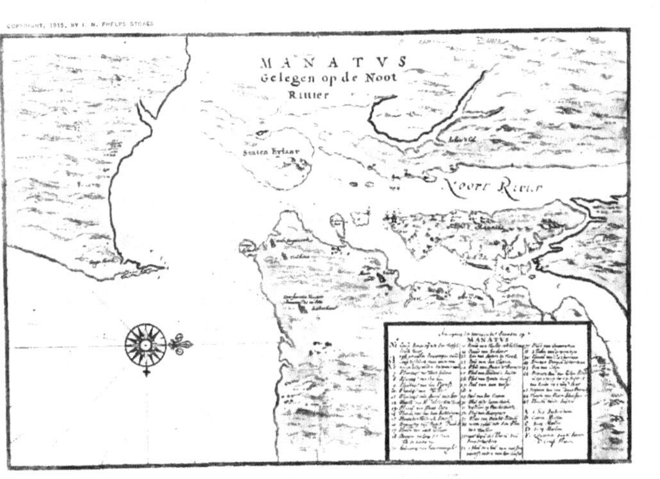

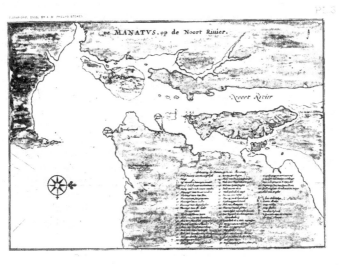

Novum Amst

Novum Ams

PL.4

PL 5

NIEU AMSTERDAM
Cum Privilegio Ordinum Hollandiæ et West-Frysiæ

Pl. 6

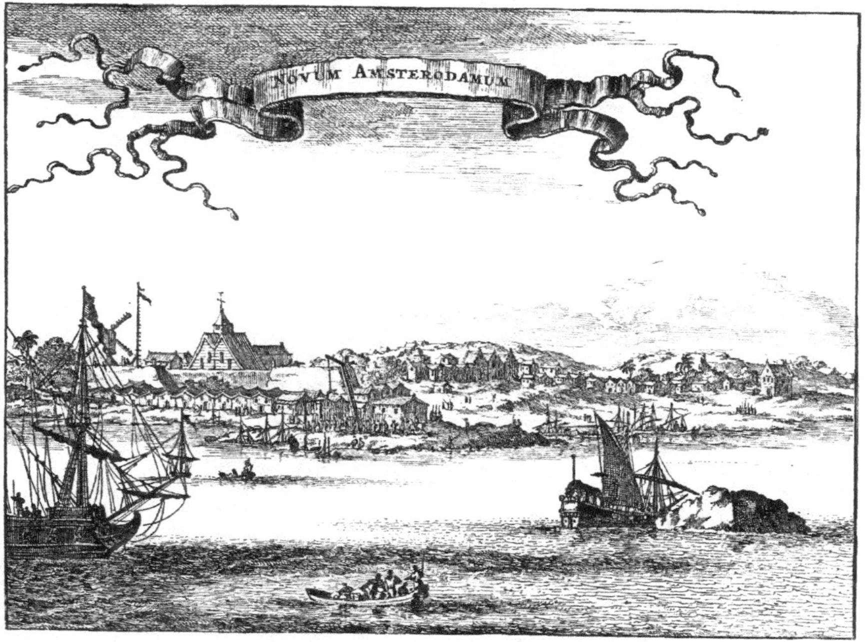

NOVUM AMSTERODAMUM

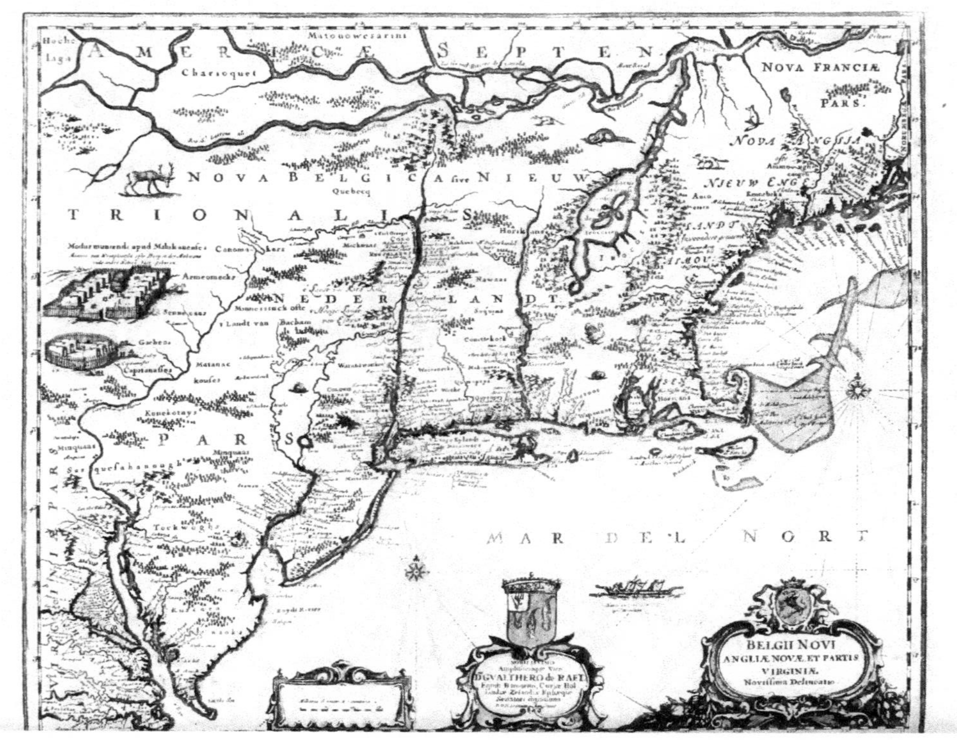
BELGII NOVI
ANGLIÆ NOVÆ ET PARTIS
VIRGINIÆ.
Novissima Delineatio
AMERICÆ SEPTENTRIONALIS PARS
NOVA FRANCIÆ PARS.
NOVA ANGLIA
NIEUW ENGELANDT
NOVA BELGICA sive NIEUW NEDERLANDT
MAR DEL NORT
Matouowesarini
Charsoquet
Quebecq
Hoche-laga
Armeomecks
Canomakers
Gachoos
Capitanasses
Matanac
Konekotays
Minquaas
Sasquesahanough
Tockwoghs
t'Landt van Bacham
Horikans
Nawaas
Sequins
Connittekock
Siwanoys
Monnessinck oste
Machkentiwomi
Mohawk

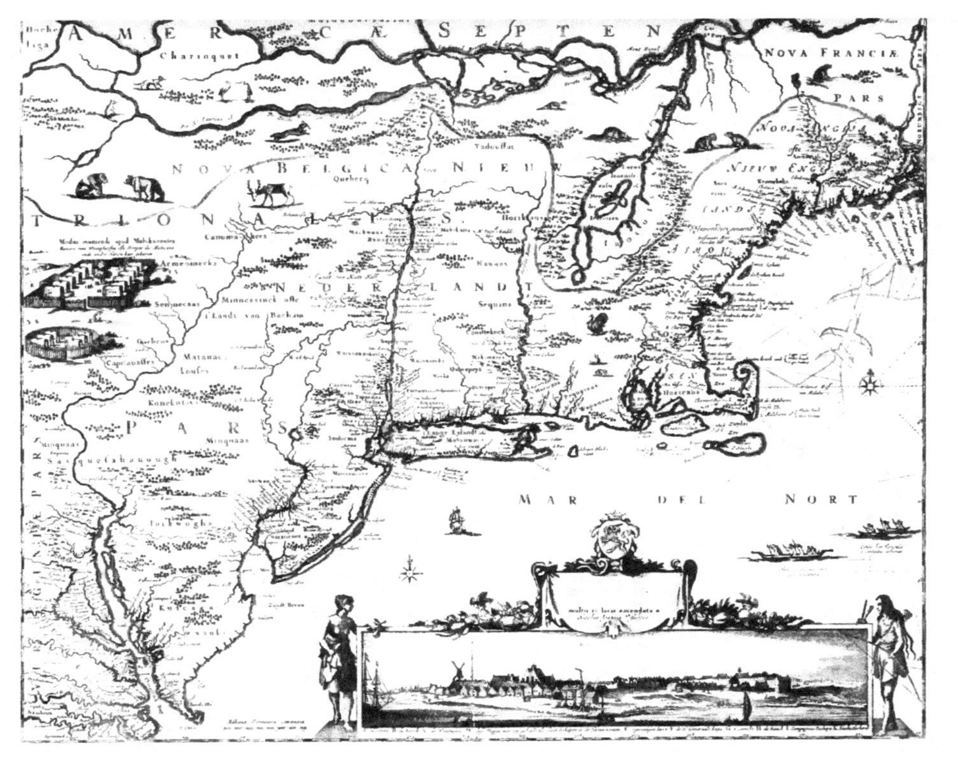

NOVA FRANCIÆ
PARS
NOVA BELGICA
NIEUW NEDERLANDT
Charioquet
Quebecq
Tadouffac
Minnessinck ofte 't Landt van Bacham
Sasquesahanough
Minquaas
Konekotay
Matanaes
MAR DEL NORT

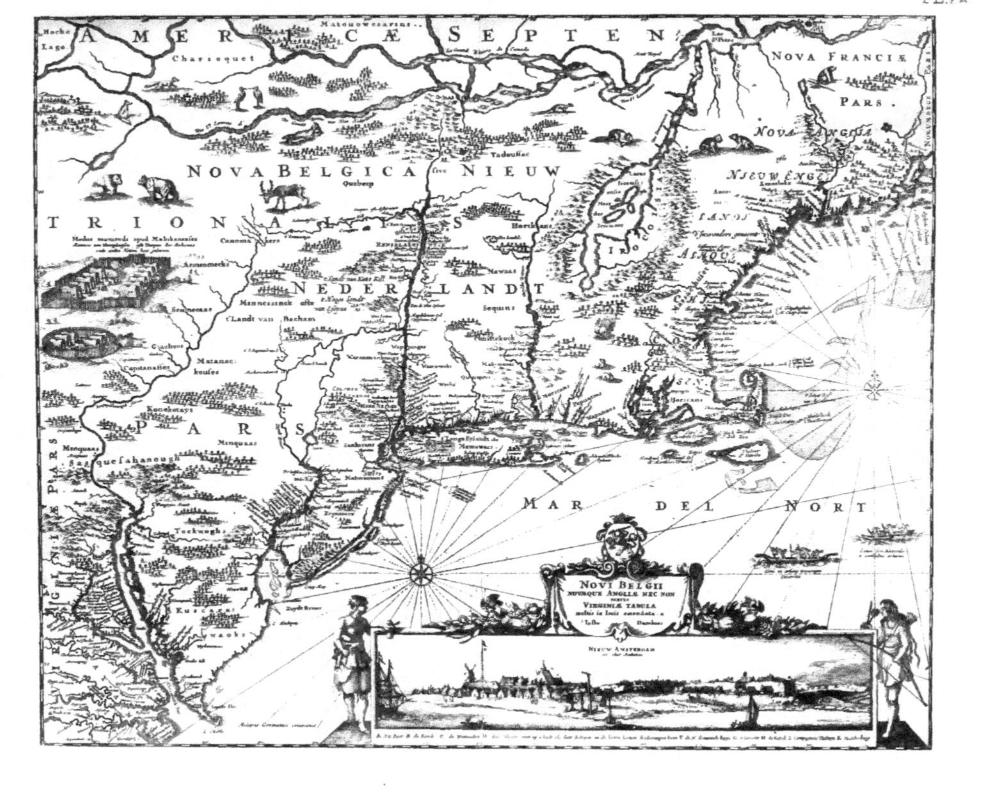
AMERICÆ SEPTENTRIONALIS PARS
NOVA FRANCIÆ PARS
NOVA BELGICA sive NIEUW NEDERLANDT
NOVA ANGLIA
NIEUW ENGLANDT
MAR DEL NORT
NOVI BELGII NOVÆQUE ANGLIÆ NEC NON PARTIS VIRGINIÆ TABULA multis in locis emendata
NIEUW AMSTERDAM
Charsoquet
Tadoussac
Quebecq
Canomakers
Armeomecks
Sennecaas
Mannessinck ofte t'Landt van Bachom
Matanackouses
Capitanasses
Konekotays
Minquaas
Sasquesahanough
Tockwoghs
Sequins
Horikans
Nawaas
Long Eylandt
Manatans
Zuyd Rivier

NIEUW AMSTERDAM
op t Eylant Manhatans

A. Het Fort B. de Kerck C. de Wintmolen D. dese Vlogge wert op gehaelt als daer Schepen in de Haven komen E. t'gevangen huys F. de N. Generaels huys G. t'Gerecht H. de Kaeck I. Compagnies Pachuys K. Stadts Herberch

Nieuw Amsterdam onlangs Nieuw jorck genaemt
en nu hernomen by de Nederlanders op den 24 Aug 1673

A. Fort Orangiensche oft N. Albanysche Jachten B. Vlagge soo daer de Vlag werdt opgehaelt als er comen Schepen in dese Haven C. Fort Amsterdam, genaemt Jeams-fort by de Engelsche D. gevangen huys E. Gereformeerde kerck
F. Gouverneurs Huys G. tmagazyn H. de Waeg I. Heeren gracht K. Stadthuys L. Lutherische kerck M. waterpoort N. Smides-valley O landtpoort P. Weg na t'versche Water Q. Wint-molen R. Ronduyten S. Stuyvesants Huys
T. Oost Rivier lopende tusschen t'Eylant Manhatans, en Jorckshire oft t'langs Eylandt.

Hugo Allardt Excud.

PL. 9

Pag. 1.
NOVA BELGICA sive NIEUW NEDERLANDT
Quebecq
Mackwaas
RENSELAERS WYCK
Minnessinck ofte
Landt van Bacham
Nawaas
Sequins
Horikans
Wappinges
Waranawankongs
Waoranecks
Wecke
Conittekook
Makimanes
Quiripeys
COLONIE VAN DE HEER NEDER
Tappaans
Sanhicans
Matovancons
Aquamachuques
Ermomex
Naraticons
Lange Eylandt
Matouwacs
MAR DEL NORT.
NIEUW AMSTERDAM

DESCRIPTION OF PLATES

FRONTISPIECE

AND

1–9

c. 1628–1664

THE PRINTED OR CONTEMPORARY MANUSCRIPT TITLES OF ALL MAPS, PLANS AND VIEWS ARE GIVEN IN CAPITALS AND SMALL CAPITALS. THE NAMES BY WHICH THE PRINTS ARE KNOWN TO COLLECTORS ARE GIVEN IN BRACKETS IN CAPITALS AND SMALL LETTERS. WHEN THE REPRODUCTION IS BEFORE LETTERS, OR WHEN IT IS GIVEN IN TRANSLATED FORM THE TITLE IS SUPPLIED IN PARENTHESES. THE DIMENSIONS, UNLESS OTHERWISE NOTED, ARE TAKEN BETWEEN THE INSIDE BORDER LINES.

FRONTISPIECE

NIEUW AMSTERDAM OFTE NUE NIEUW IORX OPT 'T EYLANT MAN
(New Amsterdam now New York on the Island of Man[hattan])
[The Prototype View]

Water-colour drawing on paper. 24¼ x 16⅝ Date depicted: 1650–3.
Date issued: Probably *c.* 1670.

Owner: Royal Archives, The Hague.

Provenance: Contained in a folio bearing the following title: *Verzameling van paskaarten dienende tot de vaart naar Oost-on West Indien meers alle uitvoerig met de pen getekent, benevens eenige afbeeldingen van voorname eijlanden steden en sterktens zo wel en de Spaansche Engelsche als Nederlands Indiën gelegen, alle zeer net naar 't leven met waterverven geschildert, in orde geschikt naar 't alphabeth.* (Collection of sea-charts relating to the navigation to the East- and West Indies, mostly drawn with the pen in detail; together with some pictures of important islands, cities, and fortresses, situated as well in the Spanish and English as in the Dutch Indies; all painted in water-colours very neatly from life and arranged in alphabetical order.)

This interesting view, which is here reproduced in the colours of the original, is, with the exception of the Castello Plan (Appendix, III), the finest and most important contemporary representation of New Amsterdam that has come down to us. It is bound up in a collection of 115 charts and views of the Dutch colonial possessions in various parts of the globe, apparently copies made in Holland in the second half of the seventeenth century from original sketches drawn *in situ.* The dates of the originals from which some of these copies were made have been approximately determined from internal evidence, and range from 1655 to 1696. No text accompanies the volume at The Hague which has, however, a manuscript table of contents. In May, 1869, this collection was sold at auction in Amsterdam by Frederik Muller, and was described in his Catalogue, dated May 18–22, 1869, as follows:

> [Item] 877 [For title, see above, under Provenance].
>
> One volume, very large folio, in atlas form, bound in calf, gilded, and accompanied by a very full index of 14 folio pages, in Dutch, written in manuscript about 1720.
>
> Such is the title in Dutch printed specially for this fine collection, which was drawn in Holland in the second half of the seventeenth century.
>
> The collection contains 4 maps of Europe; 11 maps and 29 views of Asia (of which 6 are printed); 7 maps and 11 views of Africa; 23 maps and 17 views of America. In addition there are 2 maps and 9 views of places situated in these countries, but unidentified. The maps and views represent in Asia: Atchin 2 pieces, Ceylon 4 pieces, Malabar 3 pieces, Goa, Dabul and Visiapour (Deccan) 4 pieces, Malacca 4 pieces, Samboppe (Makasser) 2 pieces, Eauweck (Cambodia), of the Dutch Indies 8 pieces, etc. In Africa: of the coast of Guinea, Cape Verde, etc. 9 pieces, of the Cape of Good Hope 3 pieces, of the Mosambique coast, etc. 3 pieces, etc. In America: a view of New Amsterdam almost identical with that on the N. Visscher Map of 1662; map of the River Powhattan (in New Netherland); 13 maps and 7 views of Mexico, Acapulco, Porto Rico, Hispaniola (10), Cuba, etc.; 9 maps and 9 views of Brazil, mostly of the theatre of war between the Dutch and the Portuguese, from 1636 to 1644, such as Fernambuco, Pariaba, Maragnan, Mauritiopolis, Olinda, Porto Calvo, the river Pousiock, etc.
>
> The dimensions of the maps and views vary between 410 and 470 millim. in height, and 500 and 870 millim. in length. Several of the maps are the originals which were used in the Atlas of C. Jz. Vooght (Nieuwe Groote Zee-fakkel), Amsterdam, 1696. This is also true of some of the views, as for instance that of Acapulco, which was used in the work of Montanus on America, Amsterdam, 1670. As for the beautiful drawing of New Amsterdam, it is quite possible that it is the original reproduced at a smaller scale by Visscher. This drawing of New Amsterdam is 620 millim. long and 425 millim. high, whereas the engraved view is only 310 by 65 mm. This view shows the town very much less extended than in the view made in 1679 and reproduced in the fine work, "Voyage to New-York in 1679 by Jsp. Dankers and P. Sluyter," translated and edited by H. C. Murphy, Brooklyn, 1867, and is also less extended than that found on the map by C. Allard [The Restitutio View, Pl. 8-b].
>
> This collection was brought together in the early years of the eighteenth century, and the index is apparently in the hand-writing of Mr. C. Beudeker, a distinguished Bibliophile of Amsterdam during this period.—*Catalogue de Livres Anciens, rares et curieux, parmi lesquels une collection remarquable sur L'Amerique.* Vente 18–22 Mai 1869 par le Libraire—Frederik Muller à Amsterdam.

The volume contains but part of a much larger collection, probably consisting originally of several hundred drawings, some of which have disappeared, but more than two hundred of which, besides several duplicates, have been traced and examined in connection with this work. The drawings are all on heavy paper with a water-mark consisting of a crowned shield and fleur-de-lis and the Jesuit monogram "I H S." Paper of the same manufacture, which was made in Angoulême, was used in Amsterdam for official registers, beginning with the year 1652. We find it also used by the cartographer De Graef for a number of manuscript maps made by him for the East India Company, about the year 1700. The water-marks vary slightly between these two dates. There are a number of other views of America and Asia in the volume at The Hague, all executed in much the same style, probably in the same atelier, the technique being bright colours and "gouache," usually applied to an outline carefully drawn in pen and ink. One of the last views in the book is unfinished, the outline sketch being complete but the colours only partly applied.

The New Amsterdam view here reproduced is, with a few slight variations, identical with that found on the Visscher Map (Pls. 7-b and 8-a), of which it may be a copy; although it is more likely that both were made from a common original as yet undiscovered or no longer in existence. The perspective of the Prototype is noticeably more correct than that of the Visscher View. This is apparent when we compare both views with the Map of Dutch Grants (Appendix, IV), especially in connection with the block of buildings on the Strand containing the three storehouses and the Old Church which, in the Visscher View, are so drawn that the church and the buildings to the right of it appear to stand considerably forward of the storehouses and the buildings to the left of them. The title "Nieuw Amsterdam ofte nue Nieuw Iorx opt 'T Eylant Man[hattans]" indicates, of course, that this particular drawing or copy was made after 1664, when New Amsterdam became New York. For a description of the various scattered groups of charts, maps, and views, once forming the great collection or family to which this water-colour and its companions doubtless originally belonged, see Cartography (Appendix, I), and The Manatus Maps (Appendix, II).

The Prototype Map (Pl. 7-a), in its first state probably published in 1650 or 1651, does not contain this view, which we may infer had not yet been made. When, however, a little later, but almost certainly as early as 1652-3, N. J. Visscher republished (Pl. 7-b) the Prototype Map, he added this view, correcting at the same time several errors in the original map; but Fort Kasimier, built in the summer of 1651, was not added on this first state of the Visscher Map (see Pl. 7-A and Vol. II, Addenda), which strongly suggests that the map and view were made, and probably issued at the end of 1651 or early in 1652; although it is possible that they were engraved later, and that the absence of Fort Kasimier is due either to carelessness or to the fact that information concerning its erection had not yet attracted attention in Holland. The map could not have been engraved prior to 1650, since the inset view of New Amsterdam shows conditions which did not exist until after that year, and probably as late as 1651 or 1652, and which will be referred to in detail hereafter.

The author of the Prototype View is unknown. It cannot be, as has sometimes been claimed, the drawing by Augustine Herrman, referred to under Pl. 6, because this Herrman drawing was not sent to Holland until 1660.

The view is taken from a point a little west of a line connecting the north end of Governors Island with Schreyers Hook, and shows the west shore extending in the distance to a point probably somewhat beyond Rector Street, the east shore being shown to within a short distance of Coenties Slip. The fore-shore, although doubtless somewhat exaggerated, is not so much so as in the other early views, taken from the same direction. Compare Pls. 4, a and b, and 6.

The appearance of the shore-front indicates a date prior to the erection of bulkheads along the river bank. As early as November 2, 1654, an order had been given for sheet-piling at the City Hall:

> Whereas the "Waal" in front of the City Hall is more or less washed away by the high water and heavy rain, so that finally the City Hall might be in danger; Resolved . . that the same . . . be properly protected with street [sheet] piles.—*Rec. N. Am.*, I: 261.

Again, on September, 25, 1656:

> Whereas the sheeting in front of the City Hall, and before the Waterport on the East River, and other places thereabout is finished and is further continued by others, and it is deemed expedient, not only for the welfare of this City in general, but of the neighbours resident about the beach in particular, that the sheeting be altogether erected and completed, the Burgomasters and Schepens do, therefore, order, and hereby, through the Court Messenger, give notice to,

all those who have any houses or lots on the East River, between the City port and City Hall properly to line with sheet planks their lots, according to the executed plan and survey, between this and the xvii. December next, under the penalty of fl. 25. to be paid by each one, who shall fail to perform the same, which shall then be done at the expense of those remaining in default.—*Ibid.*, II: 170.

In 1654, too, certain reconstruction work on the Graft, in the present Broad Street, was done, for we have a record, under date of August 24, of "Auken Jansen and Christiaen Barentsen, carpenters, being summoned to Court about the sheet-piling which they had constructed at the Graft and is again fallen down."—*Ibid.*, I: 231. Although the graft or ditch is not clearly defined in the view, there can be but slight doubt that its mouth is marked by the little indentation in the shore-line in front of the City Tavern, and from the point of view from which the sketch was drawn, its course would naturally have been concealed by its southerly or westerly bank. We know, however, that it must have passed between the houses of Hans Dreeper and Schellinger (nos. 45 and 46 in the view). It will be noticed that the graft is not shown in any of the views taken from this general direction.—Compare Pls. 4, a and b, and 6.

Moreover, there is no indication of the half moon of stone before the City Tavern, or Hall, the construction of which was recommended on June 13, 1654, along with other fortifications projected at this time because of rumors of an impending invasion by the English.—*N. Y. Col. Docs.*, XIV: 272–3. This fortification, however, was probably not built until much later, as it is not shown on the Castello Plan of 1661 (Appendix, III), although we know that it had been constructed prior to September 1, 1661, when it was described as having "3 smal bras guns, tho it be large enough to mount 8 guns on it."—*Description of the Towne of Mannadens*, 1661 (in Jameson's *Nar. N. Neth.*, 421).

Furthermore, it seems unlikely that an artist drawing a picture of New Amsterdam after 1653 would have stopped short of the "Wall" which was erected in that year, and which was so important a landmark in the city.

That the view was drawn after July 25, 1650, seems clearly proven by the fact that Vander Grift's storehouse (36) is shown completed, whereas, it was not until this date that he was granted permission to use the adjoining wall of the Company's Pack Huys in the construction of the building.

From the foregoing facts, as well as from those which follow, it is safe to assume that the original from which this important view was copied, was made some time between the autumn of 1650 and the summer of 1653; and there is, as we shall see, further good reason to believe that it belongs to the later half of this period.

In the centre foreground of the view is seen the little wooden wharf (31) erected at Schreyers Hook by Stuyvesant in 1648–9, shortly after his arrival (*The Representation of N. Neth.*, in Jameson's *Nar. N. Neth.*, 330) close to which are the crane (29) and the "gallows" (28), or rather the structure which has generally been accepted as such. No record, however, has been found of the erection or even of the existence of a gallows or gibbet at so early a date, although there probably was a gibbet, or something serving the purpose, as early as 1641, when a negro named Manuel Gerrit, the Giant, was sentenced to be hanged, although the rope breaking under his enormous weight, the sentence was never actually carried out.—See Chronology. It seems not unlikely that the structure here shown, which has been regarded as the gallows probably because it was so named on the Visscher and other engraved views, may have been used at this early period, before the erection, in 1654, of the weigh-house, for the purpose of weighing merchandise, etc. It is also possible that it may have served for drying or curing meat, or perhaps for its display previous to sale, although this seems on the whole a less likely assumption. If used to weigh merchandise, etc., it is probably the "beam" referred to in the early records.—See *Rec. N. Am.*, VII: 239–240, etc. Without doubt, the vicinity of the landing-place in these early times was the common meeting-place for barter and gossip. Prior to 1656, no regular market day had been established, and there was no definite site where country produce could be offered for sale. This lack of a regular market had resulted in considerable loss to the country people, and much inconvenience to the townspeople, to remedy which Stuyvesant, on September 12, 1656, passed the following ordinance:

> Whereas now and again divers wares such as meat, pork, butter, cheese, turnips, carrots and cabbage and other country produce, are brought to this City for sale by the outside people; with which being come to the Strand here, they are obliged frequently to remain a long time with their wares to their great damage, because the Commonalty, or at least the greater part thereof, who reside at a distance from the waterside, do not know, that such articles are brought for sale, . . . Therefore being desirous to remedy this evil, the Director General and Council, hereby ordain, that from now henceforward the Saturdays shall be Marketdays here within this City, on the beach, near or in the neighbourhood of Master Hans Kierstede's house, . . . —*Rec. N. Am.*, II: 169.

Kierstede's house (33), was on Pearl Street, west of the three storehouses.

Back of the wharf and of the crane and "gallows," or "beam," is a small building (30) which has been thought to represent the weigh-house which we know Stuyvesant caused to be "made and constructed" (*Laws and Ord., N. Neth.*, 174, 177), and which had been completed in this immediate vicinity by the spring of 1654. It is, however, altogether unlikely that this weigh-house had been erected at the period represented by the view, and much more likely that the little cabin was the old house of Jan Pietersen, who received, in 1647, a ground-brief for a lot situated at about this spot.—See Map of Dutch Grants (Appendix, IV). On March 18, 1653, Thomas Hall and Herman Smeeman, attorneys for Jan Pietersen, sold the house and part of the lot to Thomas Baxter, an Englishman (*Liber Deeds*, HH: 20), who turned pirate and was arrested by the English authorities. On February 14, 1658, Stuyvesant petitioned for Pietersen's lot, stating that he had "fenced, dammed and raised up, at great cost and labour, out of the water and swamp, certain abandoned lots" which had been granted in the year 1647 by Director General Kieft to "one Jan Pietersen, and conveyed by him, or his Attorney to one Thomas Baxter, a bankrupt and fugitive" from the Province. Stuyvesant said he had filled up these lots and erected upon them an "expensive and handsome building." He now petitioned the councellors and burgomasters for a ground-brief for these lots, which was granted.—*Rec. N. Am.*, II: 329–330. On the same date, Stuyvesant asked that the owner of the lot adjoining on the south be requested to enclose, fence, and improve his lot. This last-mentioned lot was granted, in 1647, to Joghim Kierstede, who was drowned on the "Princess Amelia." Stuyvesant stated that he did not know whether the same had "reverted to the Company" or continued "the property of Mr Hans Kierstede as heir of his brother Joghim Kierstede." It was thereupon ordered by the city authorities, that the heirs of Joghim Kierstede "sheet, raise and fence in" the lot, or surrender it.—*Ibid.*, II: 330–1. There seems to be no record of the transaction, but the lot was later in Stuyvesant's possession. The "gallows" and crane appear to stand upon the Kierstede lot.

There is no record, at the period of our view, of a house occupying the site of the small detached building seen north-west of the cabin near the crane and "gallows," but this may have been the abandoned shack of one of the early settlers.

The most conspicuous feature of the view is the Fort (2) within which are the church (6), the governor's house (7), the barracks (3), in the south-west corner, the building numbered "5," which was probably either a storehouse or the officers' quarters (*cf.* Pl. 23), and the "gevangen huys," or jail (4), between the barracks and the church. From the picture it is impossible to determine the condition of the Fort, although there is, perhaps naturally, no sign of the dilapidation described in a letter addressed by Stuyvesant to the Board of Nine Men, on November 15, 1651, wherein he speaks of his "vexation and disgust," when, on his return from Fort Casimir, he found the "new works, erected without the community's help, rooted up, trampled down and destroyed by the community's hogs, cows and horses." In the early part of 1653, the Fort was still in a down-trodden condition, but by July 28th, of that year, it had been almost entirely repaired.—See Chronology. It seems again to have been in need of attention in the following year for, upon rumor of an intended attack by the English, it was further repaired and strengthened. On July 11, 1654, an ordinance was passed, setting forth that whereas the works of the Fort had been "repaired and restored 2 or 3 times at considerable expense and labor and every time trod under foot and thrown to the ground by the Hogs," now, to protect the new works, the citizens were commanded to pen in their goats, sheep and hogs upon penalty of having them impounded if any were found twenty-four hours after the promulgation of the ordinance, "on the walls or constructed works of the Fort, either on the outer or interior works."—*Laws and Ord., N. Neth.*, 170.

The church within the Fort was erected in 1642, and stood until 1693, when it was torn down. In 1693–6 a new church was erected, which was finally destroyed by fire during the negro riots in 1741. According to this and other views of the period (see Pls. 5 and 6), the first chapel had, in the beginning, a double-peaked roof, which was later, probably in 1672, changed to a single roof. The governor's house and the soldiers' barracks had been built prior to 1643, when Father Isaac Jogues visited New Amsterdam. Writing in 1646, and referring to conditions on Manhattan Island, Father Jogues said: "Within the fort there was a pretty large stone church, the house of the Governor, whom they call Director General, quite neatly built of brick, the storehouses and barracks."—Jameson's *Nar. N. Neth.*, 259. Between the years 1643 and 1656 there is no record of the erection of the "gevangen huys," or jail, the small building to the left of the church, so named on the Visscher View (Pl. 8-a); but evidently, some time between 1643 and *c.* 1652–3, when the Visscher View was drawn, the jail had been erected, or one of the buildings within the Fort converted for use as a "gevangen huys."

There is no record extant of the erection of the wind-mill (1) north-west of the Fort. We know, from the Manatus Maps (Appendix, II), that there were two wind-mills west of the Fort in 1639, one a saw-mill and the other a grist-mill. Another saw-mill existed at this time on Nutten (Governors) Island. These may be the three mills referred to in *The Representation of New Netherland,* where, in stating the causes of the decay of the colony, the Nine Men declared that the West India Company, in the beginning, instead of seeking population, had run to great expense for unnecessary things, such as "building the ship *New Netherland* at an excessive outlay," and "erecting three expensive mills."—Jameson's *Nar. N. Neth.*, 321. In a deposition, dated April, 1639 (quoted in Chronology), it was declared that Governor Kieft, upon his arrival, on March 28, 1638, found, among other things "one grist and saw mill in operation, another out of repair and a third burned." Although ambiguous, this statement may indicate the existence at this time of two mills in operation—a saw-mill and a grist-mill—a second saw-mill out of repair, and a third burned, all of which mills seem to have been built prior to March, 1633, the date of Wouter Van Twiller's arrival. At any rate, no mention is made of their erection in the deposition of Gillis Pietersen van der Gouw, master-carpenter, dated March 22, 1639, which describes in detail the various buildings erected during Van Twiller's administration, including repairs to old buildings and the providing of "axes, arms and other requisites" for the "saw and grist mills."—*N. Y. Col. Docs.*, XIV: 16.

The wind-mill at the Fort was evidently an old mill in 1649, for in *The Representation* it was described as neglected "and, in consequence of having had a leaky roof most of the time,. . .considerably rotten," so that it could not go with more than two arms, and had been so "for nearly five years."—Jameson's *Nar. N. Neth.*, 326. In 1662, it was almost in ruins. In this year, Jan de Wit and Denys Hartogvelt, carpenters, entered into an agreement to build a wind-mill outside the City's Landport, near the Company's farm, on condition that they should receive at a reasonable price the stones and iron belonging to the Company's Old Windmill "whiche erelong would be in ruins." An agreement was accordingly made between the West India Company and De Wit and Hartogvelt, whereby the latter were to have the wind-mill stones, ironwork, etc., with liberty to grind in the wind-mill to be constructed by them "without contributing for it any share to the Company for the use of the wind." They were required to build the mill as soon as possible on the lot to be granted to them, and to grind for the Company "when there is no wind, 25 skepels of grain weekly, free of toll, if the Company require so much."—O'Callaghan's MS. Notes on Mills, in N. Y. Hist. Society.

There is no record of the demolition of the saw-mill near the Fort, and no definite reference to it other than that found upon the Manatus Maps. It may have been destroyed by fire, or by lightning, as was the Garrison Mill on the Commons, in 1689. Were it not for the fact that it is depicted in 1639 on the Manatus Maps, we might infer that it was the mill which was found burned upon Kieft's arrival in 1638.

At this period, the ground to the south and south-west of the Fort was covered by small houses which, later on, were mentioned by Stuyvesant as one of the reasons for surrendering the city in 1664, since they afforded easy access to the Fort. Colve remembered this, and when, in 1673, he recovered the city, one of his first acts was to cause the demolition of all the buildings around the Fort and near the fortifications along Wall Street.

The house at the extreme left of the view (8) probably belonged to Charles Morgan. The lot upon which it stood was conveyed to Morgan, on April 30, 1652, by Francis Doughty, the dissenting preacher, who had received his ground-brief in 1647. The conveyance makes no mention of a house, and we have no record of one prior to 1657, when Morgan deeded his "house and lot West of Fort Amsterdam on the North river" to Jan Dircksen. It is very likely, however, that Morgan built immediately after acquiring the lot in the spring of 1652, which, if true, would indicate a date for the view not earlier than the summer of this year. This house was one of those ordered demolished by Colve, in 1673, because it stood too near the Fort.

Next to Morgan's lot, on the south, at the period of our view, was a lot belonging to Paulus Heymanssen (9).—*Liber*, GG: 166. Doubtless a house was erected here several years prior to 1658, in which year the wife of Paulus Heymanssen mortgaged the property because her husband was "ill in bed."—*Book of Mortgages*, p. 94, in City Hall.[1] The third house from the corner (10) probably belonged to Sergeant Huybertsen (i. e. James Hubbard).—*Liber*, GG: 221. It later came into the possession of Andries Meyer. Jan Evertsen Bout owned the house (11) next to Huybertsen's (*Ibid.*, 170), and Lammert Van Valckenborch that next to Bout's (12).—*Ibid.*, 192. All three of these houses were demolished in 1673. In the ground-brief to Van Valckenborch, this lot was described as extending "next the road or on E. side 9 rods." This road was a passage-way to the Fort. That a street or lane existed at this point is further shown by the fact that there are in the view three houses, side by side, at right angles to the shore, which could only have been reached by a road. In 1656, Isaac Graveraet acquired the Van Valckenborch property. Evidently there was a house on this lot at the date of the ground-brief (1647), which gave the measurement on the south side as "in front of the house." It was referred to as "an old tenement," in 1670, when Graveraet conveyed the property to Pieter Jansen Slott.—*Liber Deeds*, B: 170.

Between the house of Van Valckenborch and the later Whitehall is seen a row of dwellings which must be the rear of those which we know occupied the lots on the south side of Pearl Street.—Map of Dutch Grants (Appendix, IV). Beginning at the small passage-way which led to the Fort, we have the house of Jurien Andriessen (13), which we know to have been in existence prior to 1653. The Company's bakery occupied this plot as late as 1647, for it is mentioned in a ground-brief granted in that year to Rem Jansen, for a lot adjoining to the east (14); but in 1649 Stuyvesant gave a ground-brief to Andriessen. Rem Jansen had built some time prior to 1656, when he conveyed to Laurens Jansen his "house and lot on Pearl Street between the house and lot of C. de Ruyter [16] on east side, and house of Thos. Lambertsen on west side."—*Liber Deeds*, A: 63. Claes Jansen Van Naerden, in 1644, received a grant east of Rem Jansen, of a double lot for two houses (15, 16).—*Liber*, GG: 97. There was evidently a house on the easterly half of this lot (16) at the date of the ground-brief, for the measurement on the north is given as "in front of the house." We have no record of the date of erection of the second house (15) on the west end of this lot, but it seems to have been built before the period of our view, for the lot is shown occupied. On October 29, 1652, when Van Naerden (Ruyter) deeded this lot (15) to Paulus Schrick, there was apparently no house here, and no house on Rem Jansen's lot (14), the conveyance being for a "lot in Pearl Street west of the said Claes Jansen Van Naerden's *house* [16], and east of Rem Jansen's *lot* [14]." By 1656, as above stated, and presumably much earlier, a house had been built on Rem Jansen's lot (14). In 1658, Schrick conveyed his lot (15) to Nickless Verlett, no house being mentioned. The apparent discrepancy between the land records, which fail to reveal the existence of a house upon this lot at this period, and the view here reproduced, which shows the lot occupied, can, perhaps, best be explained by supposing that the land records, which usually distinguish between vacant lots and those occupied by houses, in this instance failed to do so.

Cornelis Teunissen, a shoemaker, was, in 1647, given a ground-brief for the lot next to Claes Jansen van Naerden (or Claes Jansen de Ruyter).—*Liber*, GG: 215. There was an old house upon this lot (17) for, in 1659, when the property came into the possession of Jacques Cousseau, he recited that he had pulled the building down.—*Liber Deeds*, A: 171. Jan Jansen Schepmoes received, in 1643, a ground-brief for the next lot (18).—*Liber*,

[1] Since the plate descriptions were written most of the documents referred to as being preserved in the City Hall have been transferred to the Hall of Records or to the various departments housed in the Municipal Building.

GG: 59. Schepmoes died some time prior to 1659, in which year Willem Tomassen Cock who had married his widow, deeded to Francois Allard a house which from the description in the conveyance (*Liber Deeds*, A: 166) must have stood in the rear of the lot granted to Schepmoes, and just north of the lot of Director General Stuyvesant. It will be noticed that this house does not appear on the view. On the Castello Plan (Appendix, III) there appears to be a double house occupying about this site, which evidently faced a lane or passage-way to the west. In the deed above cited (Cock to Allard) the conveyance included "free passage-way west of house." Next to the Schepmoes lot on the east, was one (19) granted, in 1645, to Teunis Jansen Zeylmaker (sail-maker).—*Patents*, II: 45 (Albany). This lot was by mistake regranted to Jeuryaen Blanck, in 1647 (*Liber*, GG: 213), but the error was corrected, and Gillis Pietersen, who bought the lot from Jansen, was confirmed in his title. There is no mention in the records of a house upon this lot until 1667, although in all probability one had been erected prior to the date of the view. In a suit brought by Gillis Pietersen against Jurian Blanck, in 1667, Pietersen declared that he had bought a lot on Pearl Street from Teunis Jansen, sail-maker, whose ground-brief was dated July 4, 1645. He, the plaintiff, had "peaceably possessed for about 20 years" this lot which Blanck now demanded. The jury found in favour of Pietersen. It is extremely unlikely that an early settler would be allowed to possess a lot for twenty years without building upon it, and there is every reason to believe that Pietersen's reference to his twenty years' possession indicates that he had been living here since 1647.—*Rec. N. Am.*, VI: 73. Next to this lot was one owned by Egbert Van Borsum (20).—*Patents*, IV: 20 (Albany). No house is mentioned, but the grant was made in 1645 and a house without doubt was built. In 1643 Maretie Jansen received a ground-brief for the double lot to the east (21, 22) (*Ibid.*, IV: 32, Albany), but in 1653, through her husband, Govert Loockermans, who acted as attorney, deeded the "house and lot" to Pieter Cornellissen Van der Veen. In connection with this house and lot it is interesting to note that, in 1657, Van der Veen petitioned that a "Square" might remain in front of his house "at the corner of Pearl Street," as he had "incurred great expense" on the house, and was "about to make greater improvements as an ornament thereunto." Stuyvesant replied that the square was already disposed of and therefore the request could not be granted.—*Rec. N. Am.*, VII: 147, 149. This agrees with the appearance on the view of a vacant lot at the corner of Pearl Street.

The cluster of houses behind the crane cannot be positively identified. The three which appear to be on the north side of Pearl Street, at Whitehall, may be those of Peter Ebell (23), formerly Gillis Pietersen's (*Cal. Hist. MSS., Dutch*, 38), Cors Pietersen (24) (*Liber*, GG: 164), and Jochim Pietersen Kuyter (25).—*Ibid.*, 210. The building beyond (26) is probably not Geraerdy's Tavern, as stated by Innes, but the stable of the Fort. Note that, like the cabin near the crane and "gallows," or beam, it has no chimney, which probably indicates that it was not a residence.

The first building in the foreground, on the extreme right of the view (52), is the City Tavern, which was converted, in 1653, into the City Hall or "Stadt Huys," west of which is vacant ground belonging at this time to the city. On this vacant land, in 1670, Lovelace built an inn, joining it to the Stadt Huys by a bridge.—See Restitutio View, Pl. 8-b. Adriaen Blommaert owned the next lot (50) having received a ground-brief on September 20, 1651. The first conveyance of the property was in 1659, by which time a house had been erected. It was probably built by Blommaert at once, but the record is not in existence.

Directly back of Blommaert's house, on an elevation, is seen an old-fashioned hay-stack (51) which has by some writers been identified as the tower of the early horse-mill, erected in 1626, over which mill a loft was to be built for a church. There is, however, no reason to believe that the horse-mill occupied this site, or that it was in existence as late as 1651. See Manatus Maps (Appendix, II) and Chronology. This hay-stack appears to stand in the neighbourhood of the present Broadway and Wall Streets near which point a similar hay-stack is found on the Castello Plan (Appendix, III). Next to Blommaert's house is a vacant lot, belonging at this period to Govert Loockermans. We have no record of a house upon this lot until September 15, 1659.—*Liber Deeds*, A: 174. Cornelis van Tienhoven owned the lot next to Loockermans, but on October 12, 1654, he sold it to Jacob Hendricksen Verravanger, who resold the premises on the same day to Jacob Steendam, the poet of New Netherland, who built upon it between February 1, 1655, and September 23, 1656.—*Ibid.*, A: I, 6. The next lot on the Strand was owned by Mattheus de Vos, but there seems to have been no house upon it at this time. Next to De Vos was a house and lot owned by Sybout Claessen (49). We know Claessen had a house here, for, on November 9, 1654, he petitioned regarding the sheet-piling before his house on the Strand.—*Rec. N. Am.*, I: 264. The large building standing alone back of Claessen's house (48) is perhaps the brewery later known as Van Couwenhoven's on Stone Street. This brewery, at the period of our view, belonged to Govert Loockermans, who had received his ground-brief on September 15, 1646.—*Liber*, GG: 158, in office of Secretary of State, Albany. From the fact that on September 29th 1653, Loockermans brought suit to force Claes Pietersen Kos to make the roof of the brewhouse, as contracted,[1] it is possible that this brewhouse was not built until this year. It is, however, much more likely that the reference is to needed repairs or to a new roof, and that the damage feared refers to the contents of the brewhouse.

The two small houses at the corner of Broad Street and the Strand (46 and 47) probably belonged to Kuyter and Schellinger, the corner house at this time being Schellinger's. It was formerly the property of Cornelis Melyn. The names of Melyn and Kuyter are closely identified with the early history of New Amsterdam. Both were able men, of some prominence in Holland. In New Amsterdam they incurred the enmity of Governor Kieft by their opposition to his incompetent government. This ill-feeling continued under Stuyvesant, who imposed sentences of banishment and fines on both, for rebellious conduct and for other offences. Melyn and Kuyter took their grievances to Holland, in 1647, travelling on the same vessel with Kieft and Bogardus. The story of the destruction of the "Princess Amelia," the deaths of Kieft, Bogardus, and others, and the escape of Melyn and Kuyter are well known facts of history, and are recited in full in the Chronology. In 1644, during the Indian war which broke out after Kieft's wanton attack upon the Indians at Pavonia, both Kuyter and Melyn suffered the destruction of their farms and buildings at the hands of the Indians. Melyn, soon after, applied for and received a grant, inside the city, of a double lot extending five rods along the East River. The ground-brief recites that "through this aforesaid lot runs the Common Ditch, ten geometrical feet wide till into the East River."—*Liber*, GG: 92. Before 1647, Melyn had sold the western portion of this lot to Seger Tomassen, who was killed by the Indians. His lot was confiscated, according to Innes (*New Amsterdam and its People*, 107), and was later used for the purpose of widening the Graft. In this same

[1] "Govert Loockermans, pltf v/s Claes Pietersen Kos, deft. Deft. in default. As deft. had contracted to make the roof of a brewhouse, for the want of which great damage might ensue, . . ."—*Rec. N. Am.*, I: 121.

year (1647), Melyn sold to Jacob Loper a house and two lots (46), which were described as being situated between the Company's house and the lot sold by said Melyn to Seger Tomassen.—*Dutch Records, MSS.*, II: 158 (Albany). Jacob Loper died some time between 1647 and 1653, when his widow married Jacobus Schellinger (Innes, 351). The house was evidently directly on the Graft, for in June, 1656, Schellinger was exempted from constructing his portion of the sheet-piling along the East River, because his house "lies in the canal and on the road."—*Rec. N. Am.*, II: 113.

Kuyter also acquired a lot (47) from Melyn, but the conveyance is not of record. In 1658 the property was sold to Hendrick Van Der Vin, the deed reciting that the Orphan Masters had not been pleased to regulate the estate of Jochem Pietersen Kuyter and Leentje Mettens, his wife, both killed by the Indians.—*Liber Deeds*, A: 120.

The block west of Broad Street was one of the most interesting and important in the city at this time. It contained the storehouses of Vander Grift, the West India Company, and Augustine Herrman, all of which appear in our view, being the three tall buildings on the Strand. Another building of importance on the Strand was the Old Church, used as a storehouse after the Church in the Fort was erected, in 1642. It is, in all probability, the building appearing in the view with a side chimney, and situated just to the right of the storehouses. The westernmost of these three storehouses, which are so prominent a feature of the view, was that of Vander Grift (56), built in 1650–1 (*Patents*, Albany, II: 73), at which time Vander Grift petitioned for permission to use the party-wall of the West India Company storehouse (37), which was the middle one of the three and was erected in 1649 (*N. Y. Col. Docs.*, XIV: 105); the third (38), to the east, was that of Augustine Herrman who, on July 17, 1651, conveyed his property to the estate of Daniel Gabry, Amsterdam. This property, with the Pack Huys of the West India Company, was confiscated by the English on October 10, 1665.

The lot next to the Herrman storehouse was owned, in 1653, by Cornelis van Tienhoven, the Secretary of the West India Company, who had purchased it in this year from Jacob Haey.—*Liber*, HH: 32. The lot had originally been granted to Thomas Hall, in 1647.—*Liber*, GG: 219. Whether Hall or Haey built the small house (39) shown in the view is not known. There is a vacant lot next to Hall, which belonged, in 1650–5, to Jacob Hendricks Varravanger. In 1655 it, too, was acquired by Van Tienhoven, who built, probably in the same year, the house later referred to as Van Tienhoven's "Great House."—See Castello Plan (Appendix, III). Van Tienhoven, about whom it was declared in *The Representation of New Netherland* (Jameson's *Nar. N. Neth.*, 341), that the "whole country save the Director and his party," cried out "against him bitterly, as a villain, murderer and traitor" and that until he left there would be "no peace with the Indians," disappeared from New Amsterdam, in 1656, and was never heard of again. It may very naturally be assumed, therefore, that his house was erected prior to 1656. This house, of course, does not appear in our view.

Next to this vacant lot, was the Old Church (40) which, in 1656, was deeded to Jacob Wolphertsen van Couwenhoven, who, within a few months, conveyed it to Isaac de Foreest.—*Liber*, HH (2): 58; A: 71. Between the Old Church and the corner of the Graft (or Broad Street) there appears to be a solid row of houses of uniform size. Let us assume that the one next to the church (41) is that of Hendrick Jansen (De Boor). Jansen did not receive a ground-brief until 1656 (*Ibid.*, HH (2): 66), but he probably had a house prior to that date. His lot was a short one. Immediately back of it, on High (Bridge) Street, were a house and lot belonging to Hendrick, the smith, who received a transport of the lot in 1647 from Peter Lourensen.—*Liber*, GG: 202. Evidently there was some ill feeling between Hendrick Jansen (De Boor) and Hendrick, the smith, over a small wooden building which stood between the two houses, and which the city officials, on June 13, 1658, ordered Hendrick, the smith, to "break down within eight days."—*Rec. N. Am.*, VII: 188. Next to Hendrick De Boer's lot was one (42) owned by Samuel Edsall, the hatter, who also received a ground-brief in 1656. Nicolaes Backer, who received his ground-brief in 1656, owned the next lot (43).—*Liber*, HH (2): 52. On November 8, 1655, Nicolaes Jansen Backer petitioned the burgomasters and schepens for permission "to tap and to keep tavern and lodgings," pleading misfortunes, he having been driven away from his place by Indian troubles and his "means having burnt and lost."—*Rec. N. Am.*, I: 393. The lot to the east of Backer's (44) was granted to Frans Jans Van Hoogghten, on August 3, 1664, before the surrender (*Patents*, II: 171, Albany), but we have no record of its ownership at the date of the view. There was evidently a house upon it, if our drawing is correct. The corner house (45) is that of Hans Dreeper, who received his ground-brief on June 20, 1656.—*Liber*, HH (2): 54.

It will be noticed that the ground-briefs for several of the lots in this series are of date 1656. If houses were not erected before the patents to the land were obtained, the date of the view would, therefore, have to be placed at 1656 or later. The assumption of so late a date is, however, absolutely contradicted by the fact that a copy of the N. J. Visscher Map with the inset view was found in 1841 by Brodhead in the Royal Archives at The Hague, attached to the Proceedings of the South River, dated 1656, in which Proceedings reference is made to the map; and also by the appearance, in this year, of Vander Donck's *Beschryvinge*, which contains a copy of the same view. An earlier date is also indicated, negatively, as we have seen, by the absence of important improvements along the water-front, begun in 1654, and of the Wall, built in 1653, which improvements have already been referred to. It is conceivable, of course, that no houses had been erected upon these lots at the date of the drawing, and that the artist merely sketched them in to give to the view a more impressive appearance, but this is extremely unlikely, and it seems much more possible that they existed before the ground-briefs were granted.

The West India Company had from the beginning reserved the Island of Manhattan as its personal property, renting, leasing, or granting farms and lots according to its pleasure. Lots in the city upon which no improvements had been made were confiscated and regranted to those of the inhabitants who were willing to build. It was not until 1654 that the privilege of executing deeds and transports for city lots was placed in the hands of the Burgomasters and Schepens.—See Chronology, 1653, December 24, and 1654, May 18. On November 8, 1655, "divers petitions" were presented to the Burgomasters "by refugees and others" who wished to settle in New Amsterdam, for small lots within the city whereon they might erect houses. The matter being presented to the Director General, he answered that a "proper survey must be first made."—*Rec. N. Am.*, I: 393–4. On the 10th, Stuyvesant authorised the preparation of such a survey, which was to be made "without any regard to persons, gardens or places, so that settlers may be accommodated at a reasonable price," but, in case the survey ran through any private gardens, the owners were to be reimbursed for the property, which the surveyors were to value, but leaving to the Director General the approval thereof. It is quite possible that during the ensuing months a considerable number of lots changed ownership, and that those who occupied lots by virtue of some temporary arrangement with the Company, and had erected houses upon them, hastened to have their titles confirmed, and made permanent by deeds from the city. This would account for the existence of houses on lots for which ground-briefs had not yet been issued.

It is certain that back of the Strand, on High Street, there were, at this period, a number of houses. Hendrick Hendricksen Kip had a large house with a garden on the north side of High Street, almost directly back of the Old Church on the Strand, which probably conceals it from view.—*Liber*, GG: 57. Next to Kip was a house belonging to Anthony Jansen Van Fees (*Ibid.*, 94), and next to Van Fees a lot originally owned by Abraham Jacobsen Van Steenwick, who conveyed it to Hendrick Jans (Smith). Upon this lot in 1643, there was a house, probably a rude structure, belonging to one of the early settlers named William Heyl.—*Liber Deeds*, XXVI: 327. Next to this old house of Heyl's (although we do not know whether it existed at the date of our view) was a house which, in 1643, was in the possession of Teunis Cray (*Liber*, GG, 2: 214); and another dwelling, erected on the north end of the lot on the corner of the Graft, prior to 1656, was owned by Hendrick Willems, the baker.—*Liber Deeds*, A: 37. This row of houses does not appear on our view, unless we assume that all the land on Pearl Street between the Old Church and the Graft was vacant, and that the row of houses shown is this row on High Street, which is not at all likely.

West of the warehouses are four buildings. The corner one (32) is probably the old storehouse of the Company, facing towards the later Whitehall. Next to this is the house (33) of Hans Kierstede, surgeon (*Liber*, GG: 165), and between Kierstede's house and the warehouse of Vander Grift are the houses of Burger Jorissen (34), or perhaps Cornelis van Steenwick, who acquired the property in 1653 (*Liber*, HH: 38), and Pieter Cornelissen (Timmerman) (35), later owned by Joannes Nevius, who conveyed it, in 1658, to Cornelis van Steenwick.—*Liber Deeds*, A: 136.

It will be found very interesting to study this view in comparison with the Manatus Maps (Appendix, II) which depict conditions a little more than a decade earlier, and with the Castello Plan (Appendix, III), which shows every detail of the city as it existed exactly a decade later. *Cf.* also Map of Dutch Grants (Appendix, IV).

Reproduced and described here for the first time.

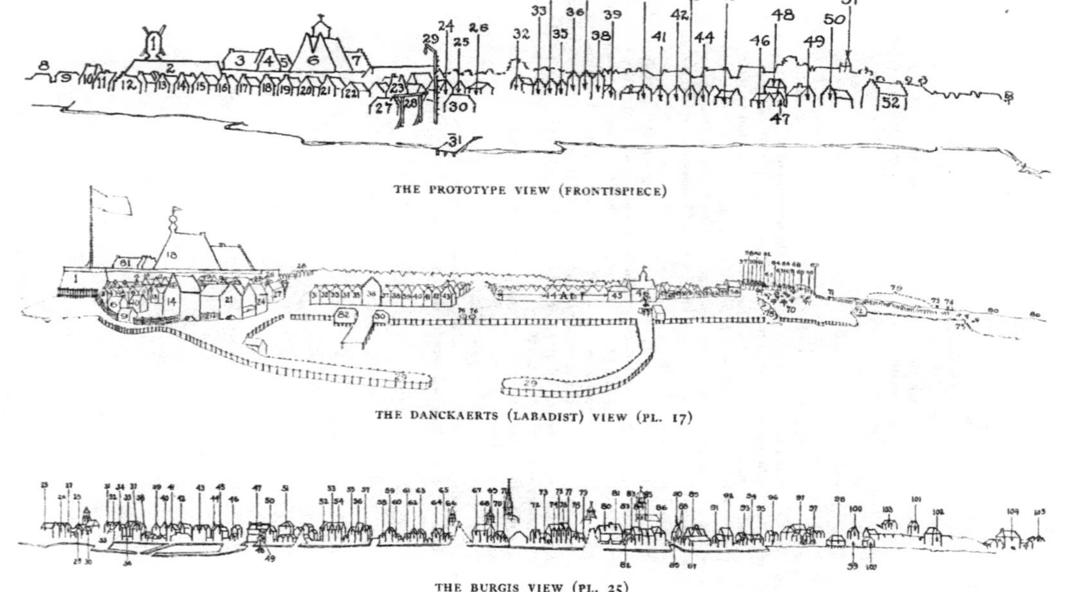

THE PROTOTYPE VIEW (FRONTISPIECE)

THE DANCKAERTS (LABADIST) VIEW (PL. 17)

THE BURGIS VIEW (PL. 25)

Plate 1–a

t' Fort nieuw Amsterdam op de Manhatans
[The Hartgers View]

Engraved on copper. 4¾ x 3¼ Date depicted: 1626–8?.
Date issued: 1651.

Provenance: From the *Beschrijvinghe Van Virginia, Nieuw Nederlandt* (etc.)
Published by Joost Hartgers, Amsterdam.
Author: Perhaps Kryn Frederycks (Cryn Fredericxsz).
Owner: I.N.P.S.
Other copies: N. Y. Public Library; N. Y. Hist. Society; Library of Congress, etc.

Earliest impression of the only known state. A later impression, from the same plate, and without any change, was used in Vander Donck's *Beschryvinge Van Nieuw Nederlant*, etc., 1st edition, 1655, p. 9. This picture, if authentic, is the earliest known view of Manhattan Island. Its authenticity, however, has been seriously questioned, and it is supposed by some to owe its origin to the fertile imagination of Joost Hartgers, and to have been concocted in the "tiny back parlor" of his shop on the Dam, purely as an embellishment for his little quarto volume. If, however, we accept the theory that the view has been reversed, the topographical features become so suggestive of reality that it seems much more likely that it actually had some basis in fact; and perhaps the most tenable theory is that it was intended mainly to show the Fort as originally projected, or, as is even more likely, to depict a proposed but never executed design, abandoned prior to the reconstruction of the Fort in stone with four bastions, commenced by Minuit in 1628, when the settlement, grouped about the Fort, was beginning to assume some little importance. It cannot have been drawn after the completion of the Fort, for it shows a fifth bastion to the south which was never built, although in *The Representation of New Netherland*, 1649 (in Jameson's *Nar. N. Neth.*, 331), it is stated that "From the first it has been declared that it [the Fort] should be repaired, laid in *five* angles, and put in royal condition." Moreover, we know from repeated references in the early records that the Fort, even at a much later period than 1628, was little more than a sodded earth-work.

There is a further reason for assigning a date not later than 1628 to this view. Michaëlius, in his letter of August 8, 1628 (in Versteeg's *Manhattan in 1628*, p. 69), says: "They are cutting wood and erecting another mill, for the purpose of exporting to the Fatherland whole cargoes of timber fit for building houses and ships"; and again, in his second letter, of August 11, 1628 (in Jameson's *Nar. N. Neth.*, 131), "They are making a windmill to saw lumber and we also have a gristmill." These two mills, one a saw-mill and the other a grist-mill, are without doubt those shown on the Manatus maps of 1639 (Appendix, II), *and are both there indicated as wind-mills.*

As it is clear from the Michaëlius letters that the grist-mill was the earlier of these two mills to be built, and that the saw-mill was not finished on August 11, 1628; and, as we know from *The Representation of New Netherland* (in Jameson's *Nar. N. Neth.*, 326), as well as from other sources, that the former stood near the north-west bastion of the Fort, where the single wind-mill in the Hartgers View is shown, it is evident that, if this view depicts any particular period, it must be before August 11, 1628. See Chronology, 1626 (Summer). See also monograph on the Fort, Chronology 1626-35, etc.

It is quite possible, and even probable, that the view from which this plate was made was drawn for Minuit by Kryn Frederycks, the engineer sent out in April, 1625, by the West India Company, "with particular instructions charging him with the construction of a fortification as well as houses in such suitable places as might be discovered by the Council" in New Netherland.[1]

The report of Isaac de Ragière (Rassieres), addressed to the Directors of the West India Company, and written in the fortress of Amsterdam on the Island of Manhattan, September 23, 1626 (item F of Muller's 1910 auction catalogue of MSS. belonging to the Van Rappard Collection:—see note), has even greater importance, although it is of general historical rather than topographical interest. It relates to the state of the colony as it existed on the arrival of de Rassieres, who states that very little progress had been made with the building of the Fort, that the government of the colony was in a bad state, and that great insubordination existed, which he had been forced to repress with a firm hand. The fines and punishments inflicted are stated, as is also the fact that a fort was being built at Orange (Albany) for the protection of the colonists trading with the Indians. He emphasises the fact that a better class of colonists should be sent out by the company if better results are to be looked for.

About thirty houses can be counted in the view, which corresponds with the number mentioned by Wassenaer as existing toward the end of the year 1626 (Jameson's *Nar. N. Neth.*, 83). Wassenaer states that the counting-house was kept in a stone building thatched with reed. This building probably stood on what afterwards was known as the Marckveldt, at the corner of the present Whitehall and Pearl Streets. It was referred to in 1638 as having been destroyed some time previously.—See Chronology, 1626. The counting-house may be the building with the stepped gable shown in the view, standing east of the south-eastern bastion of the Fort. This is the most substantial edifice in the view and occupies about the right location. Wassenaer, in the same passage, speaks of the other houses as being built "of the bark of trees," and adds: "The Director and *Koopman* live together; there are thirty ordinary houses on the east side of the river. . . . ." Writing on August 8, 1628, Michaëlius tells us: "A new fortress is in course of construction, not so much for protection against the savages. . . . as against enemies from abroad. They are meanwhile beginning to build new houses in place of the hovels and holes in which heretofore they huddled rather than dwelt."

[1] A contemporary copy of these original instructions, sold with other papers of New Amsterdam interest by Frederik Muller & Co. of Amsterdam, in 1910, is now in the possession of Mr. Henry E. Huntington. See Chronology, 1626, and Cartography, Chap. VI. Although it has not proved possible to secure access to these papers, which have been in storage since their purchase, the following brief summary of the "Instructions for the building of the Fort and Town in the New Netherlands," procured for the author at the time of the sale by Mr. Stiles, of the firm of Henry Stevens, Son & Stiles, gives an idea of their special interest and importance to our subject. We must, however, remember that no specific location is given for the Town and Fort, this being left to the discretion of those in command in New Netherland. The Fort was to be four-sided, of which one side was to face the water, but no definite position was assigned. The three sides facing landward were to be surrounded by a rampart and moat, the dimensions of which are given. A bridge over the moat was to give access to the Fort on one side, but which side it is difficult to determine as the references were lettered to correspond to an accompanying plan which was not attached to this copy of the specification.

All the male population were to be impressed into the work of building the Fort so that it should be completed as soon as possible. Indians were also to be employed and the sailors of the fleet, special rates of pay being given to the latter. Ten houses were to be built outside, under the wall, for the use of the architect and the foremen of the works. The dimensions and style of these houses are mentioned. A school, hospital, prison, and church were also to be built, and their dimensions are given. The Fort was to be named Amsterdam. A broad street was to lead down to one side of the Fort; and smaller streets, which were to be numbered, were to lead out of the broad street at regular intervals, the intervening ground to be used for growing supplies. The number of houses to be built on each street is stated and their general character and dimensions given. These instructions, as we know from other documents of the period, were never completely carried out.

It is interesting to note the existence of a small group of houses standing approximately on the block between Battery Place and Morris Street, on the west side of Broadway, a spot which tradition has long identified with the site of the first houses built on the Island.—See Chronology, 1613. It is also interesting to remember that at this period the horse-mill, in the loft of which the first church services were held, and in connection with which Wassenaer, writing in November, 1626, tells us that a tower was to be built to contain the bells brought from Porto Rico, was probably either still under construction or had just been completed.—Wassenaer's *Historisch Verhael* (in Jameson's *Nar. N. Neth.*, 83-4).[1] Nothing, however, has been found in the records to prove that the projected tower was ever added to the church. This tower has often been confused with the hayrick so clearly seen on the N. J. Visscher and other early views, where it appears just above and slightly to the left of the Stadt Huys. That this landmark was a hayrick and not a tower can be plainly seen by comparing its representation in the views referred to above with that of the hayricks clearly shown in several places on the Manatus Maps, Appendix, II. The character of these early Dutch hayricks is also very clearly depicted in etchings of the period by Rembrandt and others.

Notwithstanding the above reasons pointing to a date between 1626 and 1628, we must admit the strength of the arguments which exist for assigning a considerably later date to the original production of this view. For example, each feature of the little settlement as here depicted may be traced to some description contained in one or other of the writings upon which Hartgers drew for his text.—See Bibliography. It is undeniable, too, that the houses, as drawn, are much more substantial than we should suppose possible from the records of this period. It is also interesting to note the great similarity between the drawing of the canoes and Indians in this view and those on the map of "Nova Belgica et Anglia Nova" in Blaeu's *Atlas* of 1635 (Cartography, Pl. 32), which similarity, coupled with the better draughtsmanship displayed in their delineation on the map, must be considered as strengthening the argument that, in this respect, the Hartgers view was a copy and not the original, although it is of course possible that both were drawn from a common original. It is also difficult to account for the river seen in the view emptying into the Hudson opposite the mill, as no *river* exists in New Jersey at this point, although in the unreversed view its position would correspond pretty closely with that of Bushwick Creek, on Long Island. Two small *streams*, known respectively as Horsimus Creek and Hoboken Creek, did exist in this vicinity, in New Jersey, and can be seen on the Ratzer Plan (Pl. 41). They, however, were not nearly so important as the river shown in the view.

It is evident that the view has been reversed, for we know that the Fort was on the west shore of the island and not on the east as here shown. This may, conceivably, indicate that the picture was made by means of a camera obscura, as suggested by Mr. Innes (*New Amsterdam and Its People*, 2, Note 2), although it seems much more likely that it was carelessly engraved in Holland from the original sketch without reversing.

There are numerous process reproductions of this view, perhaps the best being that contained in Mr. William Loring Andrews's *New Amsterdam New Orange New York*. The earliest reproduction is probably that included as a frontispiece in the second volume of Yates and Moulton's *History of the State of New York* (1825). It is also reproduced by Asher, in his *Essay*.

[1] Michaëlius does not refer to a church *building*, but says, "From the beginning we established the *form* of a church. . . . Others had forgotten to bring their certificates with them, not thinking that a church would be formed and established here."—Jameson's *Nar. N. Neth.*, 124-5. See also Chronology, 1626 (Summer).

Plate 1-b

t' Fort nieuw Amsterdam op de Manhatans
[The Hartgers View]

Same as 1-a, but reversed to show the proper relation of the various topographical features.

Plate 2

[The Buchelius Chart]

Wash drawing on paper, outlined in green and yellow.	7¼ x 4½ (extreme limits of drawing)	Date depicted: 1630-4. Copied by Buchelius: *c.* 1640.

Provenance: Recently found by Dr. Johannes de Hullu, of the Dutch National Archives at The Hague, in a bound volume of manuscripts which had once belonged to Arend van Buchell (Arnoldus Buchelius), a Dutch antiquary who died in 1641, and who had been a director of the East India Company from 1621 to 1630, and was a brother-in-law of one of the first directors of the West India Company.

The handwriting on the chart is the same as that of the manuscript, and is evidently Buchelius's. The manuscript contains no reference to the chart and nothing which helps in determining its authorship or date, although, on folio 113vo, Buchelius gives a sketch of Minuit's arms, with the following brief description (translated): "Peter Minuit from Wesel, director in Nieuw Neerlant on the Island of Manhattan A° 1637 [evidently a reference to the year when the arms were copied by Buchelius]. On the helmet a bat." For a further discussion of this interesting document, see Cartography.

The inscription on the map may be translated as follows: "I have seen in a certain book by the hand of one who had had command in New Netherland or [New] Holland, the bay of the land, where our people have built [established] some colonies, thus:" Here follows what has been interpreted by Jameson and others to stand for the Dutch word "Siet," followed by "s̈" for south, meaning "look (or looks) south," a phrase which Jameson thinks is intended to inform the reader that the bay, the chief object referred to on the map, extends southward from the town; but which suggests, also, the abbreviated signature of Buchelius, "Buch s̈." If, however, "Siet" is accepted, the final sign, instead of an "s̈" seems rather to suggest a reference number (3 or 5?), perhaps to some subdivision of Buchelius's manuscript, and possibly to that part where Minuit's arms are found, although in this case it cannot be a page reference, as the arms are drawn on p. 113. From the words "one who had had command in New Netherland," it is altogether probable that the author of the drawing which Buchelius copied from memory was Pieter Minuit, who was governor from 1626 to 1632, during the period when Godyn, Coenratz, and Pauw, all of whose names appear upon the chart, were patroons of large tracts of land granted to them under the Charter of 1629. Godyn, on June 19, 1629, notified the Directors of the Amsterdam Chamber, of whom he was one, that he had undertaken "to occupy the Bay of the South River" and had so "advised the Director Pieter Minuet, and charged him to register the same there."—Notarial copy of extract from original papers, quoted in O'Callaghan's *Hist. of N. Neth.*, 479. It is not improbable that the rough drawing here reproduced is a copy of a draught prepared by Minuit to indicate the position of the grants to these three directors, Godyn, Pauw, and Coenratz. The original patent to Godyn and Blommaert is now in the office of the Secretary of State at Albany, where it was deposited by Brodhead, who found it in the West India House at Amsterdam in 1841. According to Brodhead (I: 200), it contains the only signatures of Minuit and his Council known to exist. This statement is, however, erroneous, as the original deed to Rensselaerswyck, bearing Minuit's signature, as well as those of Pieter Bylvelt, Jacobs Elbertsz Wissinck, Jan Janszen Brouwer, Symon Dircksz Vos, and Reyner Harmensen, is still in existence, in the author's collection. This very important document as well as the contract which preceded it, is reproduced in Wilson's *Memorial History*, I: 163–4. There are also several other documents signed by Minuit among the Van Rensselaer Bowier papers.

The similarity in the designation given to the principal features in the title of the Buchelius chart—the "bay of the land"— and that bestowed upon the Outer or Lower Bay on Minuit's Map of the Hudson River (C. Pl. 40)—"Landt Bay."—is also significant. A still further reason for believing the original drawing to have been prepared by Minuit is given by Mr. Innes, who discusses the chart at some length in the Preface to Jameson's *Narratives of New Netherland*. He believes such words as "bay" for "baai" and "cleine" for "Kleyn" to be German instead of Dutch forms, and thinks their use due to the fact that Minuit was by birth a German, and therefore naturally used German forms in writing. We are assured, however, by Mr. Dingman Versteeg of the Holland Society, and by other Dutch scholars, that the words upon the chart are all good old Dutch.

Because of the apparent reversal of some of the geographical features of the map, Mr. Innes believes, also, that the author of the Buchelius Chart was influenced in its preparation by the Hartgers View, a theory which seems to us rather far-fetched and unlikely.

It is a curious fact that Champlain's Great Map, completed in 1629 and published in the 1632 edition of his *Voyages*, and therefore corresponding exactly in date with the Buchelius Chart, is the only other known map to show a group of islands in the outer bay, the number corresponding exactly with those here indicated. It is also worthy of note that five well-defined *shoals* are found approximately in this location on the modern chart. For a further discussion of the Buchelius Chart, see Cartography, Chap. II.

Plate 3–a

DE MANATVS. OP DE NOORT RIUIER
[The Manatus Map—Castello Copy]

Manuscript on paper. $24\frac{7}{16}$ x $17\frac{1}{16}$ Date depicted: 1639.
Owner: Villa Castello, near Florence. Date issued: Probably *c.* 1670.

For full description of this and the following map, see Appendix, II.

Plate 3–b

MANATVS GELEGEN OP DE NOOT RIUIER
[The Manatus Map—Harrisse Copy]

Manuscript on paper. $26\frac{5}{8}$ x $18\frac{1}{4}$ Date depicted: 1639.
Date issued: Probably *c.* 1670.
Owner: Library of Congress, Harrisse bequest.

PLATE 4-a

NOVUM AMSTERODAMUM

Wash drawing in sepia and colour on paper. 19$\frac{1}{16}$ x 5⅞ Date depicted: 1650 ?.

Artist: Laurens Block.

Owner: N. Y. Hist. Society, the gift of Mr. C. E. Detmold, who procured it in Amsterdam in 1880 and presented it to the Society in 1881.

The drawing, which has a narrow brown washed border about ⅛ inch wide on three sides, and is on very thin old hand-made paper, without water-mark, is still in its original carved wood frame, as shown in the head-band of Chapter I. Although this frame is undoubtedly old, it dates probably from the eighteenth and not from the seventeenth century. The date of the view is fixed by the inscription in the lower left margin, which has always been interpreted to read: *In 't Schip Lydia door Lavrens Hermans Z^{n}. Block A^{o}. 1650.* (In the ship Lydia by Laurens Block, son of Herman, in the year 1650.) A careful examination under a glass *seems*, however, to indicate that the words "In 't Schip" really should be read "Faert Schip," or "Vaert Schip," or possibly "Vaart Schip," which, translated, would probably mean "passage ship" or "liner," presumably indicating that the large ship in the foreground was regularly engaged in carrying passengers or freight to and from New Amsterdam. If this reading is correct, it suggests interesting possibilities, although nothing has been found in the early records to justify the belief that there was at this time anything corresponding to a regular line of passage ships. Dr. Wieder does not accept this rendering, and states that the Dutch form would have been "Veerschip" or "Beurtschip," which terms were never applied to ships crossing the ocean.

Mr. R. H. Lawrence, in the *Catalogue of the Engravings issued by The Society of Iconophiles*, 64, speaks of a similar drawing, seen by Dr. Thomas Addis Emmet in Amsterdam in 1888, in the possession of Mr. Frederik Muller, the bookseller, who told Dr. Emmet that he had secured it from the cabin of an old teakwood vessel, which had formerly been in the Dutch navy and was one of the squadron which took New York from the English in 1673. This boat had been broken up only a few weeks before Dr. Emmet's visit. See article in *Magazine of American History*, January, 1890. In this article, Dr. Emmet states that, although he had not seen the view itself, but only a photograph, he had been told by Mr. Muller that it was painted on a teakwood panel 30 inches long, which was originally a part of the woodwork at the head of the companion-way, a statement which Dr. Emmet reiterates in a letter addressed to the author on November 24, 1912. There seems, however, to have been some misunderstanding, as Mr. Mensing, who was, in 1888, an associate of the firm of Frederik Muller & Company (Mr. Muller died in 1881), told the author, in 1911, that he distinctly remembered the drawing, which he had himself bought at The Hague in 1880. *He* had sold the view to Mr. Detmold, had never seen another of the same character, and was quite sure that no other had ever passed through the hands of his firm. He remembered the name of the dealer from whom he had purchased it and said that his reputation was such that he feared to leave the drawing with him overnight, and stipulated that it should be delivered on the same day, which, however, was not done, and he therefore went for it himself on the following day. It is possible that, in the meantime, or perhaps before the sale, a copy of this view was made. Indeed, it has occurred to the author that possibly the very similar view in his own collection (Pl. 4-b) may have originated in this way.

At first sight the view appears to depict a period considerably earlier than that of the Visscher View (Frontispiece and Pl. 8–a), but a careful examination shows that this impression is due chiefly to the fact that the portion of the town east of the Fort is very sketchily drawn. However, certain omissions, such, for instance, as that of the "gallows," which in the Visscher View appears near the crane, seem to indicate a somewhat earlier date. The little wooden wharf or pier, built by Stuyvesant, probably in 1648–9 (see Chronology), cannot be positively identified, but, no doubt, exists just south of the crane, where its presence seems to be indicated by a group of small boats. The three gabled buildings which are seen a short distance east of the Fort are the Company's Pack Huys and the two store-houses belonging, respectively, to Paulus Leendertsen vander Grift and Augustine Herrman, which stood on the Strand (Pearl Street), about 100 feet east of the Marckveldt (Whitehall Street). The Pack Huys was not finished before 1649, and the warehouse of vander Grift was probably not begun until after July 25, 1650, on which date he received permission to use the party wall of the Pack Huys. That of Herrman must have been built between 1645, when he received his ground-brief, and 1651, when he deeded his property to the Estate of Daniel Gabry, the deed mentioning the house. See Frontispiece.

The topographical features of the view are not very accurately depicted. For instance, there is far too much foreground between the water-front and the first row of houses along the Strand, and the Stadt Huys, which appears above the rock at the right of the view, is too far removed from the rest of the settlement.

The genuineness of this view has been disputed, and no record has been found of Laurens Block, or of the ship "Lydia." However, the general appearance of the drawing and of the frame is suggestive of authenticity. If a forgery, the view is undoubtedly copied from the Montanus View (Pl. 6). If genuine, it may *possibly* be the original sketch by Augustine Herrman, referred to by Stuyvesant in 1660 (see Chronology), although this was probably not made until some years later.

Engraved, in 1906, by Sidney L. Smith, for the Society of Iconophiles.

Plate 4–b

Novum Amsterodamum

Wash drawing in sepia, on paper. 17¾ x 7¾ Date depicted: 1642 ?.

Artist: Perhaps Laurens Block.

Owner: I.N.P.S.

This drawing was purchased in Amsterdam in 1909 from R. W. P. De Vries, who had procured it in exchange from Baron van Sypestein, a well-known amateur and collector of The Hague. The view, which resembles closely the Historical Society's drawing (Pl. 4–a), nevertheless differs from it in certain important particulars. For example, the City Tavern, which is a prominent feature of that drawing, does not appear in the present view. David Pietersz. de Vries, under date of "Anno 1642," writes in his Notes: "As I was daily with Commander Kieft, generally dining with him when I went to the fort, he told me that he had now had a fine inn built and of stone . . . I replied that it happened well for the travellers, but there was great want of a church, . . . " (Jameson's *Nar. N. Neth.*, 212). If we accept this statement of De Vries as accurate, considerable doubt is cast upon the genuineness of this drawing, which shows the church completed, but no sign of the City Tavern. On the other hand, the fact that De Vries, although "daily with Commander Kieft," apparently had no knowledge of the existence of a fine new stone inn, may indicate that the tavern was not actually completed, but only begun, at this period, a theory which is strengthened by the fact that the lease of the tavern to Philip Gerritsen, which ran for six years from January 1, 1642, was not executed until February 17, 1643.—*Cal. Hist. MSS., Dutch*, 21; Innes, 178. If the tavern was not completed until after the church was begun in 1642, the authenticity of the view, as representing the city at this date, becomes defensible, as the church, although begun in 1642 (*N. Y. Col. Docs.*, I: 299), and not roofed until 1643 (*Breeden-Raedt, etc.*, in N. Y. Hist. Society *Collections*, 1857, p. 261), may have been shown completed in accordance with the intended design, a form of license not infrequent in early views. This would fix the date as 1642. Why—on the same theory—the tavern, if begun, should not have been indicated, remains to be explained. If we accept this early date, we must suppose the row of buildings back from the Strand to be the Company's "five houses," on Winckel Street, and not the three store-houses on the Strand. It will be noticed that three wind-mills are shown west and north of the Fort, that the position of the crane, is different from that shown in the Historical Society's view, and that no flagstaff appears on the Fort. The first of these variations is very interesting and suggestive, and strengthens the claim of the drawing to be accepted as authentic and contemporary, as we know from the Manatus Maps (see Appendix, II) that in 1639 two wind-mills actually existed near the Fort, occupying approximately the sites indicated in this view. The more southerly of these two mills had disappeared before 1661, as it is found neither on "The Duke's Plan" (Pl. 10) nor on the Castello Plan (Appendix, III).

Baron van Sypestein unfortunately has no recollection of the source whence this drawing came into his possession, although he retains a distinct impression of the drawing itself, and, in a letter to the author, discusses it in considerable detail, and repudiates the suggestion of its being a forgery.

A careful comparison of the two drawings (Pl. 4, a and b) strongly suggests the same authorship, and there is so much independence and freedom in the treatment of each, and so many slight, but not impossible variations in the topography that it is difficult to believe that one could have been copied from the other. On the whole, however, although not convinced, I am reluctantly disposed to consider this drawing a clever modern forgery, based on the Historical Society's view and the Montanus print (Pl. 6). There exists, however, sufficient doubt to justify its reproduction here, for, if further study prove it to be genuine, it must be considered one of the most important documents which has come down to us from the Dutch period.

Reproduced and described here for the first time, except in the sales catalogue of R. W. P. De Vries, Amsterdam, 1909.

Plate 5

Nieu Amsterdam

Engraved on copper.	9⅝ x 7⅛, inside border.	Date depicted: 1643 ?.

Provenance: Unknown, but presumably from one of the numerous collections of views published in the later half of the XVII and early in the XVIII centuries.

Among the best known of these collections are those of Allard, Schenk, N. de Fer, Mortier, and Vander Aa.

Artist: Unknown.

Engraver: Unknown, although the Director of the Print Room in the Amsterdam Museum suggests that the two figures in the foreground closely resemble in execution the work of Peter van den Berge, whose work dates principally from the last third of the XVII century.

Owner: I.N.P.S.

This view apparently represents a period between 1643, when the City Tavern, which is shown, was probably finished, and was leased to Philip Gerritsen (De Vries's *Notes*, in Jameson's *Nar. N. Neth.*, 212; *Cal. Hist. MSS., Dutch*, 21), and 1654, when the sheet-piling of the Graft was repaired—this being the first reference to sheet-piling in this connection (*Rec. N. Am.*, I: 231)—the view distinctly showing the Graft in its original condition before any sheet-piling was placed. As there is no apparent sign of the little wooden wharf or pier on Schreyers Hoek, near which the weigh-house was built in 1653–4 (*Rec. N. Am.*, I: 56, 195, 246), and which is in all probability the same "little wooden wharf" that was built by Stuyvesant shortly after his arrival, probably in 1648-9 (*The Representation of N. Neth.*, in Jameson's *Nar. N. Neth.*, 330), and as the church is shown without a steeple or lantern, which was probably added in 1643 when the roof was completed (*Breeden-Raedt*, etc., in N. Y. Hist. Society *Collections*, 1857, p. 261), it is reasonably safe to assign to this important little view the date of 1643. With the possible exception of the Castello Plan of 1661 (Appendix, III), this is the only view in which the church appears without a steeple, which fact would seem to indicate that the steeple or belfry, found on the drawings (Pl. 4, a and b) and on the Visscher View (Pl. 8–a), was removed before 1661. It is possible that the small boat near the shore and just to the left of the Graft conceals the little pier, and also that the steeple or belfry was not added until 1647–8, when Stuyvesant took up the completion and general repair of the church, in which case the date would probably have to be placed between 1648 and 1650. We must admit that the presence of the gallows [1] near the crane, which former is not shown on the Historical Society's drawing of 1650 (Pl. 4–a) but is a prominent feature of the Visscher View, suggests the later date.

It must be borne in mind that the principal features of the town, from the Fort at the south-west to the Stadt Huys at the north-east, have been considerably condensed in this view, in order to bring them within the limited space available. This accounts for the Graft being found almost adjoining Schreyers Hoek, and for the Stadt Huys being shown much farther south than it actually stood. This also explains the relation between the Graft and the five stone buildings of the West India Company [2]—on the later Winckel Street—which appear just above it, although in reality they should be considerably to the west.

In the *Orbis Habitabilis*, etc., of Carolus Allard (see Bibliography), there is a view of Barbadoes, entitled "Engelse Quakers en Tabak Planters aende Barbados," the decorative accessories of which are almost identical with those of the present view. The Allard View,

[1] See Frontispiece.

[2] In the office of the Secretary of State at Albany is preserved a "Description of a survey of a piece of ground situated on the south side of Stoney street, known by the name of the ground of the five houses," etc. This description, which is dated December 2, 1680, and is signed by Phillip Welles, Governor Dongan's surveyor, is accompanied by a rough draft of the lots.—*Cal. Land Papers*, 21.

however, is larger, measuring 10⅝ x 8⅜, has numerous minor variations, and is very evidently a copy from our view, and not the original. It is signed by A. Meijer, as engraver.

With the exception of the Hartgers print, the view here reproduced is probably the earliest view of New York and is therefore of the highest interest and importance. The print belonged originally to the Holden Collection, and, so far as known, is unique. It is reproduced and described here for the first time.

Plate 6
Novum Amsterodamum
[The Montanus View]

Engraved on copper. 6⅜ x 5 Date depicted: *c.* 1650.
Date issued: 1671.

Provenance: From *De Nieuwe en Onbekende Weereld: of Beschrijving van America, . . . Door Arnoldus Montanus, t' Amsterdam, 1671,* p. 124.

Author: Perhaps Augustine Herrman.

Owner: I.N.P.S.

Other copies: N. Y. Public Library (Emmet Collection, 10414); N. Y. Hist. Society; etc.

Probably the earliest state. The same view, printed from the same plate in the same year, appears in Ogilby's *America* (etc.), published in London. Impressions from the same plate were also used in a German edition of Montanus, published in Amsterdam in 1673. An English edition, bearing the date 1670 and differing slightly in contents from the 1671 edition, is referred to in Sabin's *Dictionary*, XII: No. 50088. A copy with this date is in the Harvard University Library, and a frontispiece belonging to this edition is included in a copy of the 1671 edition owned by the N. Y. Public Library. This would seem to furnish ground for the belief that the English and not the Dutch edition was the first to be published; although, as the license to print was granted to Montanus on July 28, 1670, it is conceivable that a Dutch edition with the date 1670 (of which no copy has yet come to light) was printed first in that year, or that, although actually printed first, it was for some reason withheld and issued under a later date; or, finally, that the first English edition, although bearing the date 1670, was not published until 1671, a supposition which seems to be strongly supported by internal evidence, for discussion of which see Bibliography.

It is possible that this view is a copy of the drawing reproduced as Pl. 4-a, now the property of the New York Hist. Society (see also Pl. 4-b); or it may be the work of Augustine Herrman, one of the Nine Men, who made a sketch of the embryo city, which is referred to as follows in a letter dated October 6, 1660, addressed by Peter Stuyvesant to the West India Company:

> Honorable, Wise, Prudent and Very Worshipful Gentlemen.
>
> After closing our letter the Burgomasters have shown us the plan of this city, which we did not think would be ready before the sailing of this ship. In case you should be inclined to have it engraved and publish it, we thought it advisable, to send you also a small sketch of the city, drawn in perspective by Sieur *Augustin Heermans* three or four years ago or perhaps you will hang it up in some place or the other there. For the present we have no other wish, than that the place may gradually increase.—*N. Y. Col. Docs.*, XIV: 486.

A description, which is printed on the same page as the view, will be found in the Chronology.

For discussion of topography, see Pl. 4, a and b.

The same view, evidently from the same plate, is reproduced by Vander Aa in *La Galerie agréable du monde*, (etc.), [1729], Vol. 64. The plate, however, has been retouched, the large roof of the church and the front of the building in its rear, as well as nearly all the dark shaded buildings, having been cross-hatched. The clouds in the Vander Aa plate are much worn, which of course would not be the case if it were a new plate, and a French title has been added beneath the view.

Plate 7-a

Belgii Novi Angliæ Novæ et Partis Virginiæ Novissima Delineatio
[The Jansson or Janssonius[1] Prototype]

Engraved on copper.	19⅜ x 16½, inside border. 20¼ x 17⅜, plate measurements.	Date depicted: 1647-51. Date issued: Probably in 1660, or shortly thereafter.

Provenance: Probably published as a loose map. It is printed on heavy paper without text on the back. No copy of this state has been found in any atlas.

Publisher: Joannes Janssonius.

Owner: I.N.P.S.

Other copies: The only other copy known (an uncoloured impression) was also once in the author's collection, but is now in the N. Y. Hist. Society. An impression, which may be identical with one of these, was described in Muller's Catalogue, 1875, Part III, No. 2026.

This is in all probability the prototype of the Dutch series of maps of which the N. J. Visscher has usually been considered to be the first, although from the note in the title of the last-named map, "multis in locis emendata," some authorities have inferred that the Visscher Map was itself a later state of an earlier map. Asher, in his *Essay* (List of Maps and Charts, p. 9 *et seq.*), inclines to the opinion that the map of Joost Danckers, in its original state, was the first of this important series, although he suggests that it, as well as the N. J. Visscher Map, may have been a "counterfeit from an old plate." A copy of an earlier Danckers Map, without Philadelphia, has recently been found (Pl. 7-A), which would seem to strengthen this theory of Asher's, were it not for the fact that an early proof copy of the N. J. Visscher Map has lately come into the author's collection (found in Dortmund, by Frederik Muller & Co., in 1911), on which Fort Kasimier, founded by Stuyvesant on the Delaware River in 1651, is lacking. As Fort Kasimier is shown on the early Danckers Map, this proves almost beyond doubt that the N. J. Visscher is the earlier of the two. One of the arguments by which Asher arrives at the conclusion that the Danckers antedates the N. J. Visscher is what he describes as "the faulty course of the Delaware" on the Danckers Map, which he thinks indicates an earlier date than the "almost correct design of N. J. Visscher." As a matter of fact, the early issue of the Danckers, which was not available when Asher

[1] In 1644(?), after the death of his partner, Hendrick Hondius, Jan Jansson associated with himself his three sons-in-law, under the firm name of Janssonius.

made this assumption, shows approximately the same delineation of the Delaware as the Prototype and the N. J. Visscher Map. The later Danckers, upon which Asher bases this statement, shows changes in the drawing of this river, which is more correctly delineated than on either the early Danckers or the N. J. Visscher, this in spite of Asher's supposition to the contrary. For a further discussion of the priority of these two maps, see Pl. 7-A.

Frederik Muller, in his 1875 Catalogue of *Books on America*, Part III, No. 2026, describes this map of Joannes Janssonius as follows: "Highly interesting map of *New-Netherland*, quite differing from the reproduction of *de Laet's* map in *Jansson's* Atlas [published in 1639—No. 1887 of same catalogue. See also Phillips's *List of Atlases* No. 452], undoubtedly the original of those of later date by N. J. Visscher, H. Allardt, Danckers, Ottens, a.o. This map remained unknown to Mr. Asher, who however very sagaciously conjectured its existence (Asher's List, pp. 10, 11)."

Muller's 1910 Catalogue, *Geographie-Voyages*, offers a copy of this map (No. 802—the copy here reproduced), and states that the copy described in the 1875 Catalogue is the only other copy known. The date of this map is probably not later than 1651, as Fort Kasimier, built on the Delaware by Stuyvesant in that year, after he had destroyed Fort Nassau, is not shown. This map, in common with all the others of this series, contains the name Godyn's Bay, between Sandy Hook and Long Island. Asher, in his *Essay* (List of Maps and Charts, p. 11), erroneously states this location of Godyn's Bay at the mouth of the Hudson to have been a mistake, originating from a passage of Vander Donck's *Vertoogh*, published in 1650, p. 18 (erroneously cited as on page 9), which may be translated, "The bay was called New Port-May but at the present time is known as Godyn's Bay," the inference being that these names belonged to the neighbourhood of the South River, where Godyn owned a one-fifth share in Coenradus's patent. (Original draft of the first combination of colonies in New Netherland and shares each partner is to have in them, February 1, 1630. *Van Rensselaer Bowier Manuscripts*, 164.) The territory of this colony, which was abandoned before it was really established, may have extended as far north and east as Sandy Hook, but the association of Godyn's name with the Lower Bay and Sandy Hook is even earlier, being found in the 1625 edition of De Laet's *Nieuwe Wereldt* (etc.). Coenrad's Bay, although not mentioned by this name in this text, we are told by De Laet was formerly called by the Dutch sailors *Porte May*. The name Godyn's Punt, for Sandy Hook, appears on the Minuit "Pascaert van Nieuw Nederlandt," etc. (see Cartography, Pl. 40), and furthermore is mentioned as "godins puint" in 1637, in the log of the ship "Rensselaerswyck."—*Van Rensselaer Bowier Manuscripts*, 374. The reference in the *Vertoogh* does not, therefore, as Asher supposed, help to determine the date of the map.

Muller, in his Catalogue, *Geographie-Voyages*, 1910, No. 802, refers also to a reissue of this map without the dedication to De Raet, and with text on the back, which reissue is found in the *Maritime Atlas* of Janssonius, published in 1659 (also in 1657 ?), and remarks that the edition of this Atlas published in 1650 does not yet contain this map, from which, in connection with the building of Fort Kasimier in 1651, it would appear most probable that the map, in its original form, dates from 1650 or 1651. Dr. F. C. Wieder, Adjunct-Bibliothecaris of the University of Amsterdam, who has made a special study of this map, has been unable to find a copy of the edition without the dedication earlier than that in the 1657 edition of the Janssonius *Sea Atlas*, with Latin text (Vol. V of his General Atlas). It is not contained in the editions with Dutch and German text published the same year.

A careful comparison of the Prototype Map with the first issue of the N. J. Visscher Map, brings out the following facts: The Visscher contains all of the names shown on the Prototype with the exception of Ailfort, which seems to have been erroneously used for Milfort in the Prototype, Milfort in turn being used for Strotfort, which does not appear on the Prototype.

There are a few minor differences besides the above. "Zuyder Zee," found on the Visscher, is not contained on the Prototype. The same is true of "t' Kocks Rack," close to Manhattan Island, and of "Ounjure ofte Assareawe," south of the name Quebeck. Except as above stated, there are no names on the Prototype which do not occur on the Visscher.

An examination under the glass establishes the fact that the Prototype, the N. J. Visscher, and the Danckers Maps were all printed from separate plates.

For a discussion of the important and interesting series of which this is the Prototype, see Muller's Catalogue, *Geographie-Voyages*, 1910, p. 104 *et seq.;* Asher's *Essay* (List of Maps and Charts, p. 10 *et seq.);* and Andrews's *New Amsterdam New Orange New York*. See also Chronology, May, 1769, for interesting notes on the Visscher series, etc., by Du Simitière, and Cartography under Visscher Maps.

The authorship of this important map is unfortunately shrouded in mystery, but it is clear that the map itself represents a cartographical encyclopedia, combining materials from practically all of the known maps available at the time, as well as from others which have since been lost. It is very possible that the Prototype, in its present format, was reduced from a larger map, which idea is suggested by the fact that a great number of names are crowded together in a way which is often noticeable in reductions. Muller, in his 1875 Catalogue, Part III, No. 1964, refers to a large map by Blaeu on twenty-one sheets (over all, 303 by 171 centimetres), on which "by the enormous scale the different parts of the New World, f. i.: New-Netherland, Virginia, Florida, Nova Francia, etc. etc., are very distinctly delineated." This map is dedicated to Gasparo de Bracemonte et Guzman, Spanish Plenipotentiary to the Place of Munster, which dedication is dated 1648. Muller adds that he never saw another copy. [1]

We know from an entry in *N. Y. Col. Docs.*, I: 262, being certain observations on the Petition of the Commonalty of New Netherland to the States General, dated July 26, 1649, that the ship "Princess," in which Kieft, Bogardus, and others left New Amsterdam for Holland, perishing in her when she was lost September 27, 1647, had aboard "*very exact Maps;* fully a hundred different samples of Minerals and numerous Remonstrances and accounts of New Netherland." It is quite possible that these maps were remade with little delay and without material modification from the original notes, and that they were again sent to Holland and there formed the basis of the Prototype, or of the original from which it was copied, in which case this original would date from 1647.

Since writing the above, Dr. Wieder has suggested certain facts which, while not affecting the date of the original De Raet map, or that of the period delineated, seem to prove that the issue without the dedication, and included for the first time in the fifth volume of the 1657 edition of the *Sea Atlas*, antedates the issue with the dedication, here reproduced. These facts, briefly summarised, are as follows: (1) A careful comparison

[1] Dr. Wieder found in the British museum an imperfect copy of a map which he believes to be identical with the one referred to by Muller. On this map, however, the delineation of New-Netherland is not nearly so correct or detailed as on the Prototype. See Cartography, List of Maps.

of the two issues shows that traces exist on the latter (here reproduced) of a former inscription in the upper half of the cartouche bearing the dedication to De Raet, and that this inscription ("Canoo sive Navi cultae") corresponds to that found on the issue in the 1657 *Atlas* beneath a little picture of a canoe, which occupies the space later filled by the centre cartouche and the dedication. It seems evident, therefore, that the cartouche and dedication have been added on the copper-plate. (2) In the *Atlas Contractus* of Joannes Janssonius, Amsterdam, 1666, there is a map exactly similar to the one here reproduced, except that it has text on the back. This map also shows distinct traces of the deleted original title. In the same *Atlas*, there is a map of the Strait of Magellan, also dedicated to Gualterus de Raet, but his coat of arms here lacks the hand, and De Raet is styled "J. U. D." instead of "Knight Baronet." An earlier issue of this map of the Strait of Magellan, with the coat of arms—lacking the hand and without the dedication—is found in the Jansson *Atlas* of 1649, Vol. III, Frontispiece. From these facts, it appears that De Raet possessed a coat of arms as early as 1649, and that he afterwards received the title of "Knight Baronet," on which occasion the hand was added to his arms. The map of the Strait of Magellan dates from before his knighting; that of New Netherland in the *Atlas Contractus* of 1666 from afterwards.

J. B. Rietstap, in *Wapenboek van den Nederlandschen Adel*, Groningen, 1887, II: 85, states that Gualterus de Raet was born in Amsterdam on October 15, 1614, and died January 10, 1663. He was "Raadsheer in den Hove van Holland en West Friesland" (which is the same as "Curiae . . . Senatoris" on the map). On the 30th of May, 1660, he was knighted by the King of England. If this note is correct, the edition of the New Netherland map with the dedication to De Raet here reproduced must be dated after 1660. It will be remembered that Charles II, King of England, was in Holland at this time, just before his restoration in 1662.

It seems from the above facts altogether likely that our copy is the third, or perhaps an even later issue of this important map, and that its great rarity is due to the fact that it was published separately, shortly after De Raet was knighted, to commemorate that event. The map itself has not been altered from the 1657 issue, and in its original form certainly antedates any other map of the Visscher series, and may therefore properly be styled the Prototype of this important family. Although this interesting map has not been found in any atlas bearing a date earlier than 1657, it seems altogether likely, from the absence of Fort Kasimier and for other reasons, that it was originally issued, perhaps separately, and possibly in slightly different form, as early as 1651, perhaps even earlier, and that it is based on surveys made several years before this date.

The N. Y. Public Library has a copy of the Prototype identical with the one here reproduced except for a change in the name of the publisher, occurring in the cartouche under "Senatori dignissimo," which imprint has been changed to "D D D Petrum Schenk." The old lettering of Janssonius is still discernible. Beneath "Novissima Delineatio" is added "Prostant Amstelaedami apud Petrum Schenk, et Gerardum Valk C P." This is very evidently squeezed in. On the map itself, Fort Kasimier has not been added, nor has the erroneous placing of the three towns, Stamfort, Ailfort, and Milfort been corrected. This map, which is a later issue, is no doubt the one described under Asher's No. 11. The Library has assigned a date of 1690 to this issue, which Dr. Wieder believes to be approximately correct.

Reproduced and described here for the first time.

PLATE 7-b

NOVI BELGII NOVÆQUE ANGLIÆ NEC NON PARTIS VIRGINIÆ TABULA (etc.)

[The N. J. Visscher Map]

Engraved on copper, coloured by hand, and heightened with gold.	Map: 21$\frac{13}{16}$ x 18$\frac{3}{8}$ View: 12$\frac{5}{8}$ x 2$\frac{3}{8}$	Date depicted: Map: 1651–5. View: 1651–5 (probably late in '52 or early in '53).

Provenance: The state here reproduced was probably first issued by N. J. Visscher in an Atlas containing maps all of which bore his imprint. No copy, however, of this N. J. Visscher Atlas has been found. The N. J. Visscher Map is sometimes found bound up with the *Atlas Major* of Johan Blaeu, Amsterdam, 1662 to 1665, 10 vols.; also in the *Tooneel des Aerdriicx, Ofte Nievwe Atlas* (etc.) *Door Wilhelm: en Johannem Blaeu*, Amsterdam, 1649, to which, of course, it must have been added after publication; also in the Janssonius Atlas published in 1658, in 9 vols.; in a copy of his sea-atlas, with German text, published in 1657 (Königl. Bibliothek, Berlin); in the Latin edition of Jansson's *Atlantis Majoris*, etc., published in the same year (Phillips's *Geographical Atlases*, No. 465), and in the *Atlas Contractus orbis terrarum praecipuas ac novissimas Complecteus tabulas, Amstelaedami ex officino Nicolai Visscher*, without date. This Atlas has a printed index (1-91), in which the map is included as No. 90, "Novum Belgium & Nova Anglia" (copy in the University Library, Amsterdam).

Publisher: Nicolas Joannis Visscher.

Owner: Charles A. Munn, Esq.

Other copies (not illuminated): N. Y. Public Library; N. Y. Hist. Society; Library of Congress; I.N.P.S., etc. Although Asher, in his *Essay* (List of Maps and Charts, p. 12), speaks of this map as exceedingly rare, it is now very frequently met with. Probably 50 copies could be located without difficulty, at least half this number being in New York collections.

Second state(?). For description of a unique proof copy of an earlier state, doubtless the first, recently found by Frederik Muller & Co. at Dortmund, and now in the author's collection, see Pl. 7-A.

The date of the issue of the map here reproduced is between 1651, when Fort Kasimier on the South or Delaware River (which fort is shown on the map) was built, and January 24, 1656, the date of the report of the proceedings on the South River, to which the map was found attached in the Royal Archives at The Hague by Mr. Brodhead. As the data for the map must have been collected some months before the engraved copy could have been so used, it is safe to assign to it a date between 1651 and 1655. Dr. Wieder favors 1655 as the date of publication, first because in this year Fort Kasimier was captured and public interest in New Netherland was greatly stimulated in Amsterdam, which, in the following year, purchased this fort and its surroundings, and erected the colony of Nieuwer Amstel on Delaware Bay, which facts would account for the reconstruction and publication at this time by N. J. Visscher of the Prototype Map with a view of the city added; second, because in the first edition of Vander Donck, published in 1655, the early view of the city was used, whereas in the second edition, published in

1656, the N. J. Visscher View was substituted. In this connection, it is worthy of note that Vander Donck died in 1655.[1]

In some copies of this map (author's collection, etc.) the boundaries of New Netherland are outlined in colour, although not engraved.

Dr. Rosenbach, of Philadelphia, owned, in 1912, an impression of the N. J. Visscher, Map, once in the collection of Mr. Henry Stevens, of London, bearing the following endorsement in the hand of William Penn:

> "The Map by which the privy Council 1685 Settled the the [*sic*] Bounds between the Lord Baltimore & J & Maryland & Pennsylvania & Territorys or Amnexed [*sic*] Countys. W. P."

A reduced and somewhat cut-down copy of the N. J. Visscher Map without the dedication, with some geographical modifications, and with the title "A Map of New England and New York," was published in the 1676 edition of Speed's *Theatre of the Empire of Great Britain.* The British Museum possesses a copy of this map, evidently a "separate," printed on heavy paper and without text on the back. The Catalogue erroneously assigns a date *c.* 1660 to this map, which, however, must have been made as late as 1664, as it has New York instead of New Amsterdam. The only other known copy is in the author's collection and is in fine contemporary colouring.

A very accurate and beautiful copy of the N. J. Visscher Map was engraved in London in 1833. This map bears at the foot the following imprint: "A correct copy and imitation of the original Dutch map in the possession of S. Converse, publisher, N. Y. engraved by Thos. Starling Wilmington Square London, 1833." Size 21 x 17⅞. In this copy the date 1659 has been added under the cartouche.

For a fuller description of the view, which appears for the first time on the N. J. Visscher Map, see Frontispiece and Pl. 8–a. A later issue of this map was published, with many corrections and additions, by Nicolaas Visscher, about 1682 (Asher's *Essay*, List of Maps and Charts, No. 14). The Royal Library at The Hague possesses a copy (press-mark 395 C 3 No. 99), with the following title and imprint: "Novi Belgii . . . Nicolaum Visscher/Nunc apud Petr. Schenk Iun:" The view has the same title as that here reproduced.

For a further description of the origin of the Visscher series, see Cartography and Asher's *Essay* (List of Maps and Charts, 12).

Plate 7–A

Novi Belgii novæque Angliæ nec non partis Virginiæ tabula (etc.)
[Early issue of the Danckers Map]

Engraved on copper. 22 x 18 9/16 Date depicted: 1651–5.
Provenance: Probably issued separately.
Publisher: Joost Danckers (Amsterdam).
Owner: I.N.P.S.

Probably the first state. No other copy of this state is known, although the author once saw in the hands of a dealer and recorded an impression without Philadelphia, which probably was similar to the one here reproduced. The impression described in Muller's Catalogue, *Geographie-Voyages*, 1910, No. 805, is the identical copy here

[1] The recent discovery of an early proof impression of the N. J. V. Map, without Fort Kasimier, seems to discredit this theory, unless we accept the omission as due to carelessness. (See Frontispiece and Pl. 7–A).

reproduced, having come into the author's collection through Mr. Rosenbach of Philadelphia and Mr. Stevens of London. A comparison of this map with our N. J. Visscher (later state) brings out the following points:

The following names appear on the Visscher and not on the Danckers:

Russels I., in Chesapeake Bay	Sorico, island off Maine
Cinquack, " " "	Steurhoeck, in Renselaerswyck
Sennecas, s. e. of upper stockade	Carenay, south side Maquaas (Mohawk) River
Sauwanoos, on Zuydt (Delaware) River	Ruyters Eyl. in Versche (Connecticut) River
Patawomeck Flu, running into Chesapeake Bay	Gouwe, on Long Island
Rio Nassouw, in Roode Eylant	Naraticons, mouth of Zuydt River
Bevechier, off Cape Cod	

Mahikans, east of Renselaerswyck

Of these the following are not included in Asher's list as appearing on *his* N. J. Visscher Map:

Sauwanoos	Carenay
Steurhoeck	Mahikans

Naraticons

This may possibly indicate that the impression owned by the Royal Library at The Hague, which he refers to under No. 8 (Asher's *Essay*, List of Maps and Charts), but which cannot now be identified, was used in making up the list, and that it lacked these names. We know that they are not lacking on the only other copy which was known to Asher, the one attached to the report of the proceedings on the South River, referred to on p. 12 of his List of Maps and Charts, which, although lost for some years, has recently again come to light, and proves to be exactly similar to the copy reproduced as Pl. 7-b.

It therefore seems altogether probable that the early Danckers antedates the N. J. Visscher known to American collectors, although, of course, it is possible that the omissions represent carelessness in copying, and do not indicate an earlier date.

Muller's Catalogue, referred to above, describing a copy (No. 805) of the first edition of the Danckers Map (the impression here reproduced), draws attention to the fact that New Amsterdam (on the map) is spelled "Neuw" instead of "Niew" (Nieuw), from which mistake and from the technique of the vignette, the editor draws the conclusion that this map is copied from the N. J. Visscher, an argument which, it must be admitted, is strengthened by the fact that "Pequatoos" is erroneously spelled "Pepuatoos" on the Danckers.

In Asher's List, the following names do not occur under the N. J. Visscher Map, although they appear on all copies known to us:

Limbo (this is evidently an error, for, on p. 11, Asher refers to Limbo as being on the Visscher but not on the Danckers)
Sewapois
t Fort Kasimier
Minques Kill
Sauwanoos
Neve Sincks
C. Tragabigsanda

From all of the above facts, the logical conclusion seems to be that the earliest map of the series, except the Prototype (Pl. 7-a), is one of the two copies of the N. J. Visscher referred to by Asher (the only two which he knew), which apparently was an earlier issue than that known to modern collectors.[1]—Asher's *Essay* (List of Maps and Charts, p. 12). The early issue of the Danckers seems to be the second, and our edition of the N. J. Visscher (Pl. 7-b) the third.

The later issue of the Danckers Map, containing Philadelphia, and probably issued shortly after 1682, is unquestionably from the same plate as the early issue, but many new indications in relation to Pennsylvania have been added. This portion of the old plate has been entirely reengraved, the course of the Delaware considerably altered, and the State of Pennsylvania filled with representations of cows and other animals.—Asher's *Essay* (List of Maps and Charts, No. 19).

EARLY ISSUE OF THE N. J. VISSCHER MAP

Since writing the above a diligent search in Europe has brought to light a proof copy of the N. J. Visscher Map, on which Fort Kasimier does not yet appear, this being the only difference between the proof and the N. J. Visscher Map known to modern collectors. This proof copy, which was found by F. Muller & Co. at Dortmund, is evidently one of the earliest impressions taken from the plate, which had not yet been cleaned, and distinctly shows the light guide lines used by the engraver in placing the titles. The fact that Fort Kasimier is not here shown strengthens the proof that the N. J. Visscher Map was originally engraved before or very shortly after the founding of Fort Kasimier in 1651, and the fact that Fort Kasimier appears on the early Danckers is conclusive proof that this last map was later than the *original* N. J. Visscher. A further study and comparison of the Visscher Map with the first issue of the Danckers, and a comparison of both with the Prototype, seems clearly to indicate:

First, that the N. J. Visscher is the closer copy of the Prototype. Compare, for instance, the drawing of the fort of Quebec, the indications of the trees throughout, the spelling of names, such as R. Charlesr (alike on the Visscher and the Prototype, but corrected on the Danckers), etc., etc.

Second, that in many respects the N. J. Visscher and the Danckers, while closely resembling each other, differ materially from the Prototype, for instance, in the arrangement of the names in the peninsula formed by the "Chesapeack" and the Patawomeck. Note, for example, among many instances, the relation of the following names and the manner in which they are written, also the close resemblance between the Visscher and the Danckers, and the very evident difference between both of these and the Prototype:

Nacotchanck	Quomocac
Tauskus	Monanauck
Onnatuck	Cecomocomoco, etc.

Moreover, the change in the name and location of Strotfort and Milfort, alike on the Visscher and the Danckers, and differing from the incorrect arrangement on the Prototype, indicates that one has copied the other, as is further shown by the fact that the Visscher Map has introduced, between the two stockadoes, a group of Indians cooking over a fire, which group does not occur on the Prototype but does on the Danckers.

[1] Perhaps an issue prior to the addition of Fort Kasimier and similar to the author's proof copy described below, or possibly a still earlier edition, such as the one referred to above as lacking Sewapois, Fort Kasimier, etc.

Furthermore, a number of errors, some of which have been already referred to, such as "Quebecp" for Quebecq, "Pepuatoos" for Pequatoos, "Neuw" for Nieuw in Nieuw Amsterdam, the omission of "by" after landt in Nieuw Engelandt, etc., etc., occur on the Danckers but are not found on either the Prototype or the N. J. Visscher. All of these facts, together with the inferiority in drawing which is evident throughout the Danckers and especially in the figures supporting the view in the vignette, seem to afford conclusive evidence that the N. J. Visscher, in its earlier form at least, antedates the earlier Danckers, this notwithstanding the fact that the nomenclature of the Visscher is the richer, the Visscher Map containing at least fourteen names not found on the Danckers, as above indicated. A study of these fourteen names seems to show that their omission on the Danckers Map was due to carelessness.

The following do not refer to settlements, but to names of Indian tribes occupying the localities where the names occur:

Sauwanoos
Naraticons
Mahikans

In the following instances a settlement is shown on the Danckers Map, as on the Visscher, but the name of the settlement is omitted on the Danckers, probably through carelessness:

Carenay
Cinquack
Sennecas

The following are names of rivers; in the case of the Rio Nassouw the name occurs twice upon the Visscher Map and Prototype, while on the Danckers one has been omitted, probably intentionally, or deleted.

Patawomeck Flu.
Rio Nassouw

In the two following cases the engraver of the Danckers Map has either carelessly omitted the names or has deliberately left them out because of his failure to leave sufficient space for them:

Gouwe
Steurhoeck

It is hard to explain the omission on the Danckers Map of the names of the following three islands:

Russels I.
Ruyters Eyl.
Sorico

Bevechier, off Nieu Hollant, is the name of a cape. It is given on Minuit's "Map of New Netherland" (see Cartography, Pl. 40), as an alternate for Cape Cod: "Cape Col, Cap Iaems, Cape Schol, C. Bevesier."

Of all these fourteen names, not one can have any bearing upon the date of the maps, as indicating settlements made after the engraving of the Danckers plate, and inserted upon the Visscher Map.

Reproduced in Addenda, Vol. II, and described here for the first time.

Plate 8–a

Nieuw Amsterdam op t Eylant Manhattans

[The Visscher View]

Engraved on copper. $12\frac{5}{16} \times 2\frac{7}{16}$ Date depicted: 1651–5.
Provenance: Inset from the N. J. Visscher Map, Pl. 7–b.

This little view, which first appears in engraved form as an inset on the N. J. Visscher Map (Pl. 7–b), was used, also, in 1656, on the map of Adriaen vander Donck (Pl. 9), as well as, later, on the maps of Justus Danckers (Pl. 7–A), John Seller (Pl. 11–a), and several others. It is the third known engraved view of New Amsterdam. It is altogether likely that this view and the seventeenth-century water-colour in the Royal Archives at The Hague (reproduced as the Frontispiece of this volume), were made from the same original, which has since disappeared. For a discussion of the date, the topography, and the identity of the buildings, etc., see description of Frontispiece; see also Innes, p. 49 *et seq.*, and Map of Original Dutch Grants, Appendix, IV.

Plate 8–b

Nieuw-Amsterdam onlangs Nieuw jorck genaemt, en nu hernomen bÿ de Nederlanders op den 24 Aug 1673.

(New-Amsterdam lately called New York, and now retaken by the Netherlanders on the 24 Aug 1673)

[The Restitutio View]

Engraved on copper. $15\frac{1}{4} \times 2\frac{7}{8}$ Date depicted: 1673.
Provenance: Inset from the "Restitutio Map" (Pl. 16).

This is the fifth known engraved view of New Amsterdam, the earlier views being as follows:

1 t' Fort nieuw Amsterdam op de Manhatans
(The Hartgers View, Pl. 1)
2 Nieu Amsterdam (Unique Dutch View, Pl. 5)
3 Nieuw Amsterdam (Visscher View, Pl. 8–a)
4 Novum Amsterodamum (Montanus View, Pl. 6)

It is the eleventh in the series of early plans and views of Manhattan Island, i. e.,

1 The Hartgers View (Pl. 1)
2 The Manatus Map
 a. Castello copy (Appendix, II)
 b. Harrisse copy (Appendix, II)
3 The Unique Dutch View (Pl. 5)
4 The Novum Amsterodamum Drawing (Pl. 4–b)
5 The Novum Amsterodamum Drawing (Pl. 4–a)
6 The Visscher Prototype View
 a. The Inset on the N. J. Visscher Map (Pls. 7–b and 8–a)
 b. The copy in the Royal Archives at The Hague (Frontispiece)
7 The Montanus View (Pl. 6)
8 The Castello Plan (Appendix, III)
9 A Description of the Towne of Mannados ("The Duke's Plan," Pl. 10)

10 "The Island of Manhados" with inset plan of "The Towne of New York" (The Nicolls Map, Pl. 3)

11 The Restitutio View (Pls. 8-b and 16)

The Restitutio View was probably drawn, as the title indicates, shortly after the recapture of New York by the Dutch, on August 24, 1673. The presence of the soldiers on the quay and the firing of the cannon on the Fort seem to represent the moment of victory, although the fact that the Lutheran Church is shown within the wall would indicate that the view was drawn in 1674, or at least after October 17, 1673, when Governor Colve ordered the demolition of the old church (Cornelius Pluvier's house, converted for that purpose—*Liber* A, p. 11, temporarily deposited in N. Y. Hist. Society), together with other buildings "situate under the fortification and bulwarks of the city of New Orange" (*N. Y. Col. Docs.*, II: 634), and before November 10, 1674, when the city again fell into the hands of the English. We know from the records that a patent for lot No. 5, in the garden formerly belonging to the West India Company, and situated on the west side of Broadway just below the present Rector Street, was granted to the Lutheran Congregation by Governor Colve on May 22, 1674 (*Cal. Hist. MSS., Eng.*, 29); and it is altogether probable that they began at once the construction of their new church, although no reference to the building has been found until December 11, 1679, in a survey for George Cobbett.[1] In 1684 it is again referred to in an undated petition to Governor Dongan for a "patent of confirmation," for their church lot (*Ibid.*, 107; see also Chronology, 1684). This new church stood in approximately the location indicated in the view by the reference letter "L." It is possible, of course, that the old church was demolished in the autumn of 1673, and that, pending the erection of the new church, services were held temporarily in some private house, and that the letter "L" indicates the location of this building. For further details see notes on first Lutheran house of worship, Chronology, 1671.

The Restitutio View is henceforth found on the maps of Carolus Allard (second state), Ottens, Seutter, Seller (third and fourth states), etc., etc., replacing the Visscher View. It is also the prototype of the two Carolus Allard views from the *Orbis Habitabilis* (Pls. 13 and 14-b), of the view from the *Hecatompolis* of Peter Schenk (Pl. 15), of the Mortier View (Pl. 14-a), the "J^a Allard" View (Pl. 16-A), etc., etc.

The Church in the Fort appears here for the first time with a single roof, and a belfry on its southern gable. This change from the double-peaked roof was probably made in 1672, when the city voted an appropriation of five hundred guilders to "repair" the church roof (*Rec. N. Am.*, VI: 367-8). A similar portrayal of the church is seen in the Labadist View (Pl. 17).—*Cf.* also Castello Plan (Appendix, III).

This is the first view to show the Heere Graft in its completed state with the walls of the canal completely sheathed. It is also the first to show the tavern built by Lovelace, in 1670, just south of the City Hall, shown here without a cupola, which must be an error as we know from the Castello Plan that one existed before this time, having probably been added shortly after January 24, 1656, when the burgomasters petitioned Stuyvesant

[1] Survey for George Cobbett: "his house lott beg'g from the Broad St. at the house of Peter Stoutenberg; ranging thence NW'ly 50° by the said Peter's lot, 144 ft.; ranging thence NE'ly 44° by the Governor's Garden, 3 ft.; ranging by the Governor's Garden SE'ly 85° 116 ft. to the Dominie's Lott. Ranging thence by the Dominie's Lott, SW'ly, 45° 40 ft; ranging thence SE'ly 51° by the Dominie's lot *and the Church* 69 ft. Ranging thence by the street SW'ly 36°, 24 ft., 6 ins. to the said Peter Stoutenburge's.
Dec. 11, 1679. RO. RYDER, Surv.
—Land Papers, Secretary of State's Office, Albany, I: 161

for the bell which stood "idle in the Fort, either as a present or on valuation, to hang it, and make use of it, at the City Hall."—See Chronology. Three fortified roundouts are shown, corresponding with the statement in the *Description of the Towne of Mannadens, 1661* (in Jameson's *Nar. N. Neth.*, 421, and Chronology): "they then said they would build 2 halfe moons more between yt [the Stadt Huys] and the Northeast gate." These three roundouts can be discerned on the Danckaerts (Labadist) View, Pl. 17.

The view is seemingly inaccurate in many particulars, and was probably composed, in part at least, from a description of the city, or perhaps was "worked up" in Holland from a rough sketch made on the spot. Note, for instance, the exaggerated size of the roundouts or piers, which we know from the records are more faithfully portrayed on the Labadist View of 1679; the absence of the Burger's Path; and the built-up condition of the water-front near Wall Street, which, as we know from the same sources, was not so fully completed even as late as 1679. (For changes in the water-front after 1650, *cf.* description of Frontispiece.) The three tall buildings south of the canal or Graft are evidently intended to represent the three storehouses which are so prominent a feature of the Visscher and other early views, although the land records clearly indicate that these storehouses were separated from the ditch at this time by at least eight lots.—See Map of Original Dutch Grants (Appendix, IV). These errors are naturally repeated in the entire series of views of which this is the prototype.

An oil painting, evidently of seventeenth or very early eighteenth century origin, and closely resembling the Restitutio View, has recently been found in an old house on Staten Island, and now belongs to Mr. J. Clarence Davies. Unfortunately, the former owner had the picture restored in Paris, and the work was very badly done. The view contains some anachronisms for which it is difficult to account, even if we suppose that an attempt was made to bring it up to date some years after it was first painted. Nevertheless, it is an interesting document and merits careful study.

Plate 9

Nova Belgica sivc Nieuw Nederlandt
[With inset view of]
Nieuw Amsterdam op t Eylant Manhattans
[The Vander Donck Map and View]

Engraved on copper. Map: 7¼ x 12 Date depicted, map: 1651–5.
View: 7¼ x 1¼ " " view: 1651–5.
Date issued: 1656.

Provenance: From the *Beschryvinge Van Nieuw-Nederlant* (etc.), by Adriaen vander Donck, Amsterdam, 1656 (2d Edit.). Translated in the *Collections* of the New York Hist. Society, 2d Series, I: 129–242. The first edition (1655) does not contain the map but instead a restrike of "t' Fort nieuw Amsterdam op de Manhatans" (Pl. 1), from the same plate used by Joost Hartgers in his *Beschrijvinghe Van Virginia, Nieuw Nederlandt* (etc.), Amsterdam, 1651.

Publisher: Evert Nieuwenhof.

Owner: I.N.P.S.

Other copies: N. Y. Public Library; N. Y. Hist. Society, etc.

Earliest known state. A later issue of the map has lately been found in the Archives at Leyden. In the issue which we here reproduce it will be noticed that t' Fort Christina on the Zuydt Rivier (Delaware River) is twice shown and named, an error which is corrected on the later issue, where the more southerly of the two forts is correctly named t' Fort Casamirus (Kasimier). This is the only difference in nomenclature between the two maps. A number of accessories have, however, been added in the later issue: for instance, two stockadoes, one on either side of the Mohawk (Maquaas Kill, here and in the earlier state erroneously spelled Marquaa Kill), several groups of natives west of the Hudson River, a number of small animals between the Hudson and the Versche (Connecticut) Rivers, and a scale of miles, above which appear the words "Milliaria Germaniā Communia," the "c" in Germanica being apparently a later addition to the plate. There is no doubt that both impressions are taken from the same plate. Sabin's *Dictionary*, V: No. 20594, records the sale in London in 1860 of a copy of a second impression of the second edition of Vander Donck's *Beschryvinge*, with variations, although no mention is made of the map. It may be that the Leyden Map belongs to the later issue here described.

A note made at the time of the Hoe sale seems to indicate that Mr. Hoe's copy of the map, now owned by Mr. Henry E. Huntington, is similar to the Leyden copy, except that the title is differently divided, "Nova Belgica Sive" being printed in one line and "Nieuw" in a line by itself. Unfortunately, it has not proved possible to verify this note.

A comparison of the map here reproduced with the N. J. Visscher Map shows that it differs from the latter in the following particulars:

Fort Christina, as stated, appears in two places on the Vander Donck map. The name of Minques Kill, south of t' Fort Christina on the Visscher Map, is not found upon the Vander Donck, and this is also true of Kinderhoeck, south of Renselaerswyck, Herfort, t' Fort de Goede hoop, and Weeters Velt on the Versche Rivier (Connecticut River), although the last three are marked upon the map as settlements. The names of "De Gesellen" Island, off Long Island, and of Caep May do not appear upon the Vander Donck, while they are both shown and named upon the Visscher. With the exception of the above omissions, and of a few slight variations, such as Timmerk for Timmerkil on the Zuydt Rivier (Delaware River), and Marquaa Kill for Maquaas Kill (Mohawk River), north of Renselaerswyck, the two maps are alike.

Both ends of the view have been cut, eliminating the shipping and several houses north of the Stadt Huys. A number of insignificant variations occur in the drawing of the settlement and of the shore line. The large boats in the foreground are omitted and four small canoes introduced.

A close comparison leaves no reasonable doubt that this map and view are copied from the N. J. Visscher, and not the reverse, as has been sometimes claimed.

E. M. Ruttenber, in an article on *Indian Geographical Names in the Valley of the Hudson River*, etc., published in the *Pro. of the N. Y. State Hist. Ass'n, The Seventh Ann. Meeting*, 1906, discusses the location and probable meaning of many of the names found on this map, including those on Manhattan Island.

Reproductions:

Valentine's *Manual*, 1852, after title-page.

In part, only, in William Loring Andrews's *New Amsterdam New Orange New York*.

HISTORICAL SUMMARY

CHAPTER II

THE ENGLISH PERIOD

1664–1763

CHAPTER II

THE ENGLISH PERIOD

1664–1763

THE change from Dutch to English rule in New York was accomplished rapidly and with little friction. The Duke of York wished the Dutch inhabitants to remain within his jurisdiction, and, consequently, his representative, Colonel Richard Nicolls, acted with moderation and in a conciliatory spirit. The government was still that of a proprietary province, but instead of being in the control of a group of merchants, the Duke of York was the proprietor, with the right of establishing the government. He was under no obligation to grant a representative legislature to the people, but they were given the right to appeal to the King and to enjoy their property. The Dutch customs in the matter of inheritance and religion were recognised. The Duke of York appointed Colonel Nicolls as his first deputy-governor over the newly acquired territory. Nicolls, in turn, chose four men to be members of his council, and appointed Captain Matthias Nicolls secretary of the province and Captain Thomas Delavall collector of the customs duties. It was evidently intended that the English element should control. Two of the members of the governor's council were from England, and the other two were from the English towns on Long

Island. Both Delavall and Matthias Nicolls had accompanied Governor Nicolls from England.

English institutions were established as rapidly as possible, and English names were given to the divisions of the territory of the province. The land lying between the Hudson and Delaware Rivers was called Albania (New Jersey), and Long Island, Staten Island, and the present Westchester County were organised into a shire and named Yorkshire. This shire was divided into three ridings, and in each of these divisions a court of sessions was held three times a year by a board of justices appointed by the governor and his council for this purpose. In the same way, a high sheriff for the entire shire and an under-sheriff for each of the ridings were appointed. The highest court for the entire province was the court of assizes, which met once a year in New York and was composed of the governor, his council, the high sheriff, and the justices of the courts of sessions. The body of laws, usually called the Duke's Laws, was framed by the governor and his council sitting as a court of assizes and was proclaimed March 1, 1665, at Hempstead, before deputies from Westchester and the towns of Long Island, assembled in a general meeting called for this purpose. This code of laws was based very largely upon the laws of the New England colonies. It was designed principally for Yorkshire and was not enforced in New York, Esopus, Albany and Schenectady. The English form of municipal government under mayor, aldermen, and sheriff was substituted for the earlier form under schout, burgomasters, and schepens. This change was made in New York City by a proclamation of Governor Nicolls, issued June 12 (O. S.), 1665. He likewise appointed new officers to serve for one year. Thomas Willett became mayor; Thomas Delavall, Olof Stevensen van Cortlandt, Johannes van Brugh, Cornelis van Ruyven, and John Laurence, aldermen; and Allard Anthony, sheriff. Three of the governor's appointees were English; four were Dutch. Some opposition was made to this change on the ground that it was a violation of the articles of surrender; but Nicolls silenced these objections by declaring that the agreement of capitulation had been kept, and that instructions from the Duke of York required that the government of the city be made "conformable to the custom of England." The Dutch form of city government had been far from democratic, yet the English system was even less so; for in place of a board of magistrates which had the right to nominate its own successors, we find a magistracy appointed by the provincial governor.

On June 14th (O. S.), the governor's appointees took the oath of office, and on the following day the mayor and aldermen held their first meeting for the transaction of business. Joannes Nevius was continued in the office of secretary; Claas van Elslandt and Pieter Schaafbanck were also retained as town sergeants, and Hendrick Obe was chosen constable.[1] The English language was substituted for the Dutch and provision was made for jury trials. In deference to the majority some of the old customs were retained; and the procedure of the mayor's court, for instance, was long marked by peculiarities derived from the Dutch system.

The commission which Governor Nicolls had issued to the mayor and aldermen of New York declared that the city limits should include New Harlem and all the people living upon Manhattan Island, "as one Body Politique & Corporate." Consequently, the magistrates of New Harlem were discharged from their offices, and Resolveert Waldron was appointed constable in that division of the city. Waldron was authorised to choose three or four persons to form a court for the trial of cases involving sums to the amount of five pounds sterling. In 1666, Nicolls granted a patent to New Harlem, securing to the freeholders and inhabitants "the privileges of a Town, but immediately depending on" the city of New York "as being within the liberties thereof," on condition that the town should in future be known as Lancaster, and that the people should maintain a ferry. The people of Harlem were not pleased with this patent. They objected to the change in name, and as a matter of fact, the title Lancaster does not appear to have been used. They also objected because the patent failed to secure to them privileges which they had previously enjoyed, and put them under the control of the Duke of York in the matter of taxation. The patent was not recalled, as were some others, but the people were dissatisfied with it and simply waited an opportunity to secure another which should conform more nearly to their wishes.

In the meantime, Nicolls at New York was actively engaged in establishing his government and in trying to reconcile the citizens to the

[1] The events connected with the establishment of the English system are given in Brodhead, Vol. II. For a discussion of the government see Osgood, *American Colonies in the 17th Century*, Vol. II. Charles II's grant to the Duke of York and the latter's commission to Nicolls are printed, Brodhead, Vol. II, App., pp. 651-3. For the activities of Nicolls in 1664-5, see *N. Y. State Library Bulletin, History No. 2, General Entries*. The Duke's Laws are printed in *The Colonial Laws of N. Y.*, Vol. I, pp. 6-100. For information connected with the Hempstead meeting, see *N. Y. Col. Docs.*, Vol. XIV, pp. 564-6. For the changes in the government of New York City, see *Rec. N. Am.*, Vol. V, pp. 248-52. No attempt is made here to give authorities for detailed statements, since they may be found in the Chronology, arranged under the proper dates.

change. Regulations concerning import and export duties were carefully made, for much of the revenue of the province came from this source. The citizens were required to take an oath of allegiance to the king, Charles II, and to the Duke of York. Steps were taken to secure a report on the estate of the West India Company; and, in June, 1665, the whole estate was confiscated. Fort James had been in the governor's possession since the surrender of the town in 1664; but this confiscation gave to the Duke of York the store-houses, the store and weigh-house, and the farm that had belonged to the Company. In this way the "Company's Farm" became the "Duke's Farm." The Lutherans were given permission to secure a minister of their own faith; and when the salaries of the Dutch ministers at New York fell in arrears, Nicolls ordered the mayor and aldermen to secure a contribution of twelve hundred guilders for their support. Nicolls purchased the Esopus lands from the Indians and opened them to planters. He increased the revenue by decreeing that all patents of land must be renewed, and the quit-rents and fees from this source amounted to a considerable sum. This order was rigidly enforced, but in New York, where all land had been received from the Dutch West India Company, the payments for new patents were made as easy as possible. Nicolls exhibited prudence and discernment in the management of affairs; and, although there was some discontent evident, chiefly among the Long Island towns, and opposition to his changes in the municipal government at New York, still the governor's good judgment was appreciated and his influence grew stronger the longer he served.

In the winter of 1665–6, the people of Harlem undertook to build their first church. This was the Dutch church which stood on the north side of the Great Way (later known as the Church Lane) near the river, not far from the corner of the present First Avenue and 125th Street.—See Pl. 39.

Difficulties, however, threatened from without. The Dutch had never become reconciled to the loss of New Netherland, and their controversy with England developed into open war early in the spring of 1665. Governor Nicolls found it necessary to quarter one hundred soldiers in the burghers' houses, and required the city to allow five guilders weekly for each one. He was given a list of the inhabitants assessed for the purpose, which, next to the De Sille list of 1660, may be considered the earliest known street directory of New York. It contained 254 names.

The governor also urged upon the citizens of New York the necessity of strengthening the defences on Manhattan Island, and particularly the need of repairing the old works and of fortifying with palisades the west side of the town lying along the Hudson River. He even offered to furnish two thousand palisades and one thousand guilders for this purpose; but he accomplished little. "Som of the People answeringe, Said that the Towne was sufficiant anough; others that the[y] Could not worke before they had their Armes Restored to them againe & many other excuses, . . ." Later in the year the governor confiscated the property of Dutch subjects who had not taken the oath of allegiance to the King of England. This and the confiscation of the estate of the Dutch West India Company may be looked upon as war measures. New York itself escaped attack, and the war was brought to a close by the treaty signed at Breda in July, 1667. By this agreement each of the contestants kept the territory held when the treaty was made, whether it had been seized before or during the war. This gave New Netherland to England and certain possessions in the East were handed over to the Dutch.

News of the peace soon reached New York and was proclaimed by Governor Nicolls on January 1, 1668. He took advantage of the cessation of hostilities to reward certain of his English followers, giving Hog Island (Blackwells Island) to Captain John Manning and Barent's Islands (Great and Little Barn Islands, now Wards and Randalls Islands) to Thomas Delavall. For some time Nicolls had desired to be relieved of his government and to return to England. Finally, Colonel Francis Lovelace was sent out, and in August, 1668, Nicolls resigned the province into his successor's hands and returned home. As governor over a newly acquired province he had been very successful, and he left with the well-wishes of those who at first had hated him as their conqueror.

Colonel Lovelace brought with him a confirmation of the Duke's Laws and an order to make no change in the government which his predecessor had established. Consequently, his policy was largely a continuation of that of Nicolls.[1] In 1669 the Duke sent to Lovelace a seal for the corporation, a silver mace, and gowns for the mayor and aldermen. At this time, also, the governor re-introduced a practice which had obtained under the Dutch rule; that is, he allowed the mayor's court

[1] See *Minutes of the Executive Council of the Province* of New York, 1668-73, edited by V. H. Paltsits, Albany, 1910, for information regarding Lovelace's administration.

to nominate double the number of officers to be chosen, and from these he appointed the city's magistrates. The governor in 1670 decided to build an inn next to the City Hall and to join the two buildings with a bridge so that he might make "a doore to go from the upper-part of the house into the Courts Chambers." The next year a stone well was built in the yard of the City Hall at public expense. Overseers were appointed (April, 1670) to lay out and pave the streets of the city and their instructions directed them to lay out such streets "as level and even as possible," with a gutter through the middle of the street. The public roads, south as well as north of the Fresh Water, were under the care of these overseers, and at their request for a man who understood the work, Abram Jansen, master carpenter, was appointed to aid them. The roads were repaired by the country people, but the cartmen were compelled to help them in repairing those "over [beyond] the Fresh Water," which they used in hauling firewood from the public woods. The paved streets were cleaned by the householders on each street, who were obliged to gather the rubbish together every Saturday and load it upon the carts of the public cartmen. These cartmen had a monopoly of their business, in return for which they promised to fill up the breaches in the highways and cart the dirt from the paved streets gratis.

One of the conditions on which Governor Nicolls had granted a patent to the town of New Harlem was that it should maintain a ferry to the mainland. The ferry was established across the Harlem River at Harlem, but travellers began to use the road by Spuyten Duyvil instead, and in 1668 traders brought so many horses and cattle across there that the ferry-man and inhabitants of New Harlem sued for redress of grievances, and finally the ferry was moved to the wading-place of Spuyten Duyvil Creek, where King's Bridge was afterwards built. In 1669 a license was granted in New Jersey to Pieter Hetfelsen to run a ferry between Communipaw and New York.

The first exchange was inaugurated in 1670, the governor giving an order that merchants and "other artificers" should meet every Friday between eleven and twelve o'clock near the bridge over the Heere Graft. This was at the present Broad Street and Exchange Place, where the "curb market" of to-day transacts business out of doors near the Stock Exchange.

A general view of New York at this period is given in two descriptions of the place written in or about 1670. The first, by John Ogilby,

Esq., who was "Master of His Majesties Revels in the Kingdom of Ireland," says:

It is plac'd upon the neck of the Island Manhatans, looking towards the Sea; encompass'd with Hudson's River, which is six Miles broad; the Town is compact and oval, with very fair Streets and several good Houses; the rest are built much after the manner of Holland, to the number of about four hundred Houses, which in those parts are held considerable: Upon one side of the Town is James-Fort capable to lodge three hundred Souldiers and Officers; it hath four Bastions, forty Pieces of Cannon mounted; the Walls of Stone, lin'd with a thick Rampart of Earth; well accommodated with a Spring of fresh Water, always furnish'd with Arms and Ammunition, against Accidents.[1]

The second description, which is by Daniel Denton, states:

New York is built most of Brick and Stone, and covered with red and black Tile, and the land being high, it gives at a distance a pleasing Aspect to the spectators. The Inhabitants consist most of English and Dutch, and have a considerable Trade with the Indians, . . . here anyone may furnish himself with land, and live rent-free, yea, with such a quantity of Land, that he may weary himself with walking over his fields of Corn, and all sorts of Grain; and let his stock of Cattel amount to some hundreds, he needs not fear their want of pasture in the Summer, or Fodder in the Winter, the Woods affording sufficient supply. For the Summer-season, where you have grass as high as a man's knees, nay, as high as his waste, interlaced with Pea-vines, and other weeds that Cattel much delight in, as much as a man can press through; and these woods also every mile or half-mile are furnished with fresh ponds, brooks or rivers, where all sorts of Cattel, during the heat of the day, do quench their thirst and cool themselves; these brooks and rivers being invironed of each side with several sorts of trees and Grape-vines, the Vines, Arbor-like, interchanging places and crossing these rivers, does shade and shelter them from the scorching beams of Sols fiery influence.[2]

One interesting aspect of the life of the period which has been but little dwelt upon is reflected in the elaborate luxury and ceremony, recorded on certain occasions, especially in the governor's household. This is illustrated with surprising fullness of detail in a document found a few years ago among the Ashmolean Manuscripts in the Bodleian Library,[3] describing the funeral in 1671 of William Lovelace, the governor's young nephew. The "Partall or Entry" to the room, where the

[1] *America, Being an Accurate Description of the New World*, etc., Collected and translated . . by John Ogilby, London, 1670, pp. 169-70. Regarding the sources of this compilation, see the Bibliography under Montanus (Arnoldus).

[2] Denton, Daniel. *Brief Description of New York Formerly Called New Netherland* (Reprinted from original edition of 1670), 1902, pp. 40-1, 59.

[3] Published in the *American Historical Review*, Vol. IX, pp. 522-4.

body lay upon the "hearse," was "curiously adorned wth pictures Statues and other fancies in carved worke." Hung about the room, which was a "very spacious" one, were "Mourning and Escootcheons thereupon of his Paternall Coate to the number of 30." There were "Turkey worke chayres richly wrought," and a "Rich Cuphord of plate worth 200^{li}." "Round the hearse stood A black stand with Silver Candlestick wax Tap's and p'fumes burning night and day to the view of all people." Eight escutcheons covered the "Sheete and Pall"; and there was a canopy over the head embroidered with "deaths heads and bones." Over the centre of the hearse hung a "rich Garland" ornamented with "black and white Satten ribbands" and "an houre Glasse impending;" and at the foot there was a shield four feet square with "cotes of Armes quartered and gloriously gilt." Four attendants were on duty day and night. The funeral procession to the nearby chapel was led by "the Capt: of the dead," the "Minister," and the two "Preaching Ministers" (Dutch domines). "Two Maidens," who were "clothed in white silke" and "Cyprus Scarves," carried the garland. Six "Gentlemen Batchelers" carried the body, the pall being borne by six "virgins" dressed in white silk. The parents of the deceased, Thomas Lovelace and "his Lady," followed "in close Mourning"; then four halberdiers in velvet coats on which were embroidered the Lovelace crest, each coat being valued at "40^{li}." Governor Lovelace walked alone "in close Mourning." Then came Captain Dudley Lovelace, another uncle of the deceased, "in like mourning single"; the councillors; "the Mace with maior and aldermen in their black gownes"; "all the English and Dutch Women," in pairs; the chief English and Dutch men; "All Masters of Ships and Vessells," and about five hundred other English and Dutch men, most of whom were in black. After the funeral, all were provided with "wines Sweet meats and Biscuits and such Services" until ten o'clock that evening.

The first meeting of the Society of Friends (now called Quakers) held under a roof in New York City was in May, 1671, in an inn, though as early as August, 1657, the Quaker Records show the appearance of their preachers in the streets. These dates coincide with important years in the records of the Lutheran Church, for in 1657 the first pastor of that denomination arrived on Manhattan Island, and in 1671 their first church was established in the Cornelius Pluvier house "situate under the fortification and bulwarks of the City of New Orange."

In 1671, the inhabitants of Smith's Valley petitioned that the highway about the water-gate might be repaired, and Aldermen Lawrence and Van Brugh were appointed to inspect and report upon this and upon the "Corner Waal" which was to be built before the house of Long Mary. This was the beginning of Coenties Slip, where a wharf was soon afterwards constructed. In this year also the mayor's court at New York considered it necessary that a suitable road should be developed between the city and the village of New Harlem, and ordered that the magistrates of that village with the "overseers of the highways beyond the Fresh Water" lay out the one most suitable. This became a part of the Boston Post Road, which passed up the modern Broadway to Park Row, thence up the Bowery to Fourteenth Street, by Broadway to Madison Square, and from that point irregularly to the Harlem River at 130th Street and Third Avenue.[1] Governor Lovelace encouraged the building of this road; and it may be that he was influenced by a desire to establish a more adequate postal service between New York and Boston. At any rate, in December, 1672, he issued a proclamation for a post to go monthly from New York to Boston and back.

In the summer of 1672, Fort James was repaired. A month later the *kerckmeesters* (church-wardens) of the Reformed Church of the city petitioned the mayor's court for assistance in renewing the roof of the church in the fort, and the court decided to give 500 guilders for this purpose. Complaints were still made from time to time against certain persons who had neither paved the streets nor constructed the plank sheeting along the Strand. The Graft (or mote) in Broad Street was ordered to be "made up by ye Owners of ye houses or Lotts—uppon ye said mote" as far as the lane by Jacob Kip's;[2] the Slyck Steegh was ordered paved with stones from the house of Adrian Vincent to the house of Hendrick van Doesburgh, and from the house of David Jochems to the lot of Jacob van Couwenhoven, also Prince Street from the house of Jochem Beeckman to that of Mr. Bedloo.[3] A foot-path was also ordered paved on Pearl Street between Broad and Whitehall Streets; and the wharf or wall on the waterside and the half-moon before the City Hall, were ordered repaired. Peter Stuyvesant died at the age of eighty

[1] See Bridges' Map (Pl. 80). From 23d Street and Fifth Avenue it extended diagonally across Madison Square, crossing Fourth Avenue at 28th Street, and continuing northerly between Fourth and Third Avenues to 45th Street, and so on in a northeasterly direction across Third and Second Avenues, then northwesterly, recrossing these avenues, and continuing in an irregular course to Fifth Avenue at 97th Street, then again northeasterly to Third Avenue and 130th Street where it crossed the Harlem Bridge.

[2] Now Exchange Place.

[3] Beaver Street between Broad and William Streets.

years in February of this year, and was buried in a vault beneath the chapel at his bouwerie.

In July, 1672, news was received in New York that war had again broken out between the States General of the Netherlands and England. Lovelace bestirred himself to put New York into a position to defend itself. He called upon the towns of Long Island to assist and the citizens of New York to contribute money or work to repair Fort James. A third company of foot-soldiers and a new troop of horse were organised. Lovelace wrote to the officials at Albany of "the great preparac̄ons I am makeing here, as likewise . . . the chearfull & hearty concurrence both of the City and Countrey to assist mee by a voluntary Contribuc̄on to carry on the Worke." Nevertheless, all of these efforts were destined to be vain. Meanwhile, two Dutch admirals, Evertsen and Binckes, had been sent to attack the English possessions in the West Indies and on the mainland, and on August 7, 1673, appeared with the Dutch fleet in New York Bay. They came unexpectedly, while Governor Lovelace was away and Captain Manning was in command. The fort was not prepared to withstand such an attack, and on August 9th it was surrendered.[1] New York changed its name again and became New Orange; Fort James became Fort Willem Hendrick, both names being given in honour of the Prince of Orange. The two admirals appointed as governor Anthony Colve, a man who had been conspicuous in the attack on the fort, and re-established the Dutch municipal form of government under burgomasters and schepens. The old magistrates were released from their oath of allegiance to England and the new ones swore obedience to the States General and the Prince of Orange.

The necessity of putting the town in a proper state of defence was apparent, and new fortifications of earth and sod were begun. The houses and orchards lying close under the walls of the fort were ordered removed and the owners indemnified for their loss of property from the extraordinary impost levied on the peltries exported. Rules for a burgher-watch were made; the city gate was ordered closed at sundown, and people were forbidden to come upon the fortifications during the

[1] Manning, in defence of his conduct, declared that there were about seventy or eighty men in the fort and only four "ladles and spunges" for all the guns in the fort, without any platforms or any other necessaries fit for defence. "There was neither Bedd Spade Hanspike or other material to help to defend us." There were "4 bastions, 10 Gunns upon euery Bastion 4 curtains each curtain near 80 paces long and we had but between 70 and 80 men to help maintaine ye whole ground." Lovelace himself acknowledged that a more honorable defence should have been made. Manning was afterwards court-martialed, and declared incapable of holding office under the king's government.

night, or to leave the city except by the gates. In 1674 the Lutherans were given a lot "in the Company's garden," near the south-west corner of Broadway and what is now Rector Street, in exchange for the lot adjoining the wall and just inside the Land Gate where, in Cornelius Pluvier's house, their services had until now been held. See Castello Plan, Appendix III, and Map of Dutch Grants, Appendix IV.

All of these warlike preparations, however, were rendered unnecessary by the treaty of peace between Great Britain and the States General, signed at Westminster in the spring of 1674. By the terms of this treaty New Orange was restored to Great Britain, and on November 10, 1674, Sir Edmund Andros, whom the Duke of York had commissioned governor of New York, received the surrender of the town. The citizens were absolved from their oath of allegiance to the States General and their rights in property were confirmed.

The new governor brought with him as first councillor Anthony Brockholls, who had been appointed to succeed the governor in case he became incapacitated. William Dyre was appointed collector of customs, and the governor was authorised to form a council of not more than ten men. Andros was accompanied by a chaplain and one hundred soldiers, all in the pay of the Duke of York. The governor's house in the fort, which Lovelace had begun to rebuild, was not ready, and Andros chose to occupy Stuyvesant's former residence on the water front. The new governor had been instructed to follow a conciliatory policy. The grants and privileges made by the late Dutch government were confirmed November 9, 1675; and religious freedom and equality in justice were guaranteed to the English and Dutch alike. The Duke's Laws were again confirmed. Governor Andros re-established the government of New York City upon the English model by appointing a mayor, aldermen, and sheriff, and the citizens were required to take an oath of allegiance to the new government.

Various improvements were made in the city during this administration. A fair or market for the sale of cattle, grain, and other produce of the country was ordered held in November; and a night watch composed of the constables, soldiers, and citizens was established. A new dock, in front of the City Hall, was built, and paid for by taxing the citizens and all merchants trading to New York; the people living in the street called the Heeregraft (Broad Street) were ordered to fill in the graft to make it level with the street, and then to pave before their doors with stones. The maintenance of slaughter-houses and the killing of animals within the city limits were forbidden, and tan-pits were ordered removed from the city. Orders were issued that ruined houses or unimproved land should be appraised and sold to those who would build. A public slaughter-house for the use of the city was ordered built "over the Water without the Gate at the Smith's Fly near the half-moon," and several public wells were ordered constructed at specified places.

We are fortunate in having two descriptions of New York at this time, one written by Charles Wolley, the English chaplain who came back with Governor Andros when he returned from a visit home in 1678; the other, which is particularly interesting, by Jasper Danckaerts who, with Peter Sluyter, came to New York in 1679 looking for a place suitable for planting a colony of Labadists. Wolley was pleased with what he saw. He describes the city of New York as "a place of as sweet and agreeable air as ever I breathed in, and the Inhabitants, both English and Dutch, very civil and courteous as I may speak by experience, amongst whom I have often wished myself and Family."[1] Danckaerts and Sluyter were less favourable in their final judgment of the country, but they were, perhaps, too fanatical to be fair-minded judges. Danckaerts, who acted as scribe of the *Journal*, refers to their entrance to the town thus: "As soon as you are through the Hoofden [Narrows], you begin to see the city, which presents a pretty sight. The fort, which lies upon the point between two rivers, is somewhat higher; and as soon as they see a ship coming up, they raise a flag on a high flag-staff, according to the colors of the sovereign to whom they are subject, as accordingly they now flew the flag of the King of England. We came up to the city about three o'clock, where our ship was quickly overrun with people who came from the shore in all sorts of craft, each one enquiring and searching after his own, and his own profit. No custom-house officers came on board, as in England, and the ship was all the time free of such persons.[2] . . . Having then fortunately arrived by the blessing of the Lord before the city of New York, on Saturday, the 23d day of September, we stepped ashore about four o'clock in the afternoon . . . and went out to take a walk in the fields. . . . As we walked along we saw in different gardens trees full of apples of various kinds, and so laden with peaches and other fruit that one might doubt whether there

[1] Wolley, Charles, *A Two Years' Journal in New York*, London, 1701 (Reprinted, Cleveland, 1902), p. 65.
[2] *Journal of Jasper Danckaerts*, edited by James and Jameson, New York, 1913, p. 36.

were more leaves or fruit on them."[1] The travellers went to church and found there "truly a wild worldly world."—"The church being in the fort, we had an opportunity to look through the latter, as we had come too early for preaching. It is not large; it has four points or batteries; it has no moat outside, but is enclosed with a double row of palisades. It is built from the foundation with quarry stones. The parapet is of earth. It is well provided with cannon for the most part of iron, though there were some small brass pieces, all bearing the mark or arms of the Netherlanders. The garrison is small. There is a well of fine water dug in the fort by the English, contrary to the opinion of the Dutch, who supposed the fort was built upon rock, and had therefore never attempted any such thing. . . . In front of the fort, on the Long Island side, there is a small island called Noten Island (Governor's Island) around the point of which vessels must go in sailing out or in, whereby they are compelled to pass close by the point of the fort, where they can be flanked by several of the batteries. It has only one gate and that is on the land side, opening upon a broad plain or street, called the Broadway or Beaverway. Over this gate are the arms of the Duke of York. During the time of the Dutch there were two gates, namely, another on the water side; but the English have closed it, and made a battery there with a false gate. In front of the church is inscribed the name of Governor Kyft, who caused the same to be built in the year 1642. It has a shingled roof, and upon the gable toward the water there is a small wooden tower, with a bell in it, but no clock. There is a sun-dial on three sides. The front of the fort stretches east and west, and consequently the sides run north and south."[2]

The description of the custom-house is interesting: "All our goods which were between decks, were taken ashore and carried to the public store-house, where they had to be examined; but some time elapsed before it was done in consequence of the examiners being elsewhere. At length, however, one Abraham Lennoy [de la Noy], a good fellow apparently, befriended us. He examined one chest only, without touching our bedding or anything else. I showed him a list of the tin which we had in the upper part of our chest, and he examined it and also the tin, and turned up a little more what was in the chest, and with that left off, without looking at it closely. He demanded four English shillings for the tin, remarking at the same time, that he had observed some other

[1] *Jour. of Jasper Danckaerts*, pp. 43-4. [2] *Ibid*, pp. 45-6.

small articles, but would not examine them closely, though he had not seen either the box or the pieces of linen."[1]

Of Manhattan Island Danckaerts says: "It is almost entirely taken up, that is, the land is held by private owners, but not half of it is cultivated. . . . The west end on which the city lies, is entirely cleared for more than an hour's distance, though that is the poorest ground; the best being on the east and north side. There are many brooks of fresh water running through it, pleasant and proper for man and beast to drink, as well as agreeable to behold, affording cool and pleasant resting places, but especially suitable places for the construction of mills, . . . A little eastward of New Harlem there are two ridges of very high rocks, with a considerable space between them, . . . Between them runs the road to Spyt den Duyvel, . . . We went from the city following the Broadway, over the valley or the fresh water. Upon both sides of this way were many habitations of negroes, mulattoes and whites. These negroes were formerly the proper slaves of the [West India] company, but, in consequence of the frequent changes and conquests of the country, they have obtained their freedom and settled themselves down where they have thought proper, and thus on this road, where they have ground enough to live on with their families. We left the village called the Bowery, lying on the right hand, and went through the woods to New Harlem, a tolerably large village situated on the south side of the island, directly opposite the place where the northeast creek and the East River come together, situated about three hours' journey from New Amsterdam . . . As our guide, Gerrit, had some business here—we remained over night at the house of one Geresolveert Resolved Waldron, schout of the place . . . This house was constantly filled with people all the time drinking, for the most part that execrable rum." Leaving New Harlem, the travellers walked across the island, which took about three quarters of an hour, and came to the North River which they followed, walking a little within the woods, to Sappokanikke (Greenwich) and thence along the shore to the city.[2]

An idea of the military strength of New York may be gained from Danckaerts' account of a training and muster held there. "There was a training and muster to-day, which had not taken place before in two years because the small-pox had prevailed so much the last year. Some were on horseback, and six small companies were on foot. They were

[1] *Jour. of Jasper Danckaerts*, p. 48. [2] *Ibid.*, pp. 64-8.

exercised in military tactics, but I have never seen anything worse of the kind. They comprised all the force of New-York and the adjacent places."[1]

In addition to this description of Manhattan, the two Labadist travellers have left four sketches of the town. The first gives a view of the entrance to New York harbour; the second is a view of New York from Brooklyn Heights (Pl. 17), and shows the city frontage along the East River with the fort, the rows of closely built houses on Pearl Street, Broad Street, and the Strand, and the newly completed "Great Dock." The third (Pl. 18) is a view of the city from a point on the East River shore in the neighbourhood of Fulton Street; and the fourth (Pl. 19), a view looking south along the central ridge of the island and showing wind-mills and houses in fenced fields.

New York escaped one disaster which nearly ruined New England, the terrible Indian war of 1675–6, known as King Philip's War.

In 1680, the governor and council, in a meeting held at New York, ordered that in future no flour should be bolted or packed for exportation except at the city of New York. This measure proved of great benefit to the city, as it produced a monopoly which was credited, at a later day, with having very greatly increased its shipping and general prosperity. Officers were appointed to inspect the cleaning and packing of grain, because it was found that trade had suffered from the exportation of inferior flour. At this time an association of coopers was formed to raise the price of casks,—perhaps the first "trust" in American history.

Meanwhile, complaints were made to the Duke of York concerning the administration of Andros. That the revenues of the province had fallen off was a disappointment to the Duke. Consequently, John Lewin was sent over as a special agent to investigate the affairs of New York; and Andros, recalled to answer in London for his conduct, sailed in January, 1681, leaving Brockholls in command of the province. Trouble soon arose over the question of customs. The rates which the Duke's ordinance in 1674 had established for three years were renewed in 1677, but when this second period ended, in 1680, the Duke sent no new orders. The merchants refused to pay the duties and unloaded their ships regardless of the customs officers, who continued to demand the old duties. The officers of the province failed to coerce the merchants, and the government fell into confusion. The council of the province, the

[1] *Jour. of Jasper Danckaerts*, p. 239.

aldermen of the city, and the justices, at a special court of assize, urged that the only remedy for their grievances was the establishment of an assembly, and petitioned the Duke that in future the government of the province might consist of a governor, a council, and an assembly to be elected and chosen by the freeholders of the colony. Andros, although freed from blame, was not returned to New York, but his place was given to Thomas Dongan.

The request for a representative assembly was granted in the commission of the newly appointed governor; for it directed him to issue, as soon as possible after his arrival, writs for the election of delegates to a general assembly. Dongan followed his orders and soon after his arrival issued writs of election for all of the province of New York and its dependencies except that on the Delaware. The assembly met at New York City, October 17, 1683, and drew up a charter of liberties, provided for new customs duties, and claimed the taxing power for itself. These and other legislative bills were approved by the governor, and were put in operation provisionally until the Duke's consent could be obtained.

The Duke of York's instructions to Governor Dongan had ordered him to consider and report upon the advantage of granting to the city of New York "immunities and priviledges beyond w[t] other parts of my territoryes doe enjoy"; and on November 9, 1683, the mayor, aldermen, and commonalty of the city of New York petitioned the governor, reciting the privileges which they already enjoyed and asking their continuance, as well as the grant of several others, of which the most important were: (1) that the city might be divided into six wards; (2) that the freemen in each ward might annually elect their own officers;[1] (3) that there might be a mayor and a recorder, who with the six aldermen and six common councilmen should represent the whole body of the city and corporation and make laws for its government; (4) that the mayor,[2] recorder, coroner, town clerk, and sheriff might be appointed annually by the governor and council; (5) that the city magistrates might appoint a treasurer to collect the public revenues and pay all debts. Dongan acceded to most of these requests until the Duke, to whom he forwarded the petition, should make his wishes known; but he refused to enlarge the power of the magistrates, or to give them jurisdiction over the town of Harlem so as to curtail its independence.

[1] Aldermen, common councilmen, constable, overseers of the poor, scavengers, etc.
[2] The mayor was to be chosen from among the six aldermen.

Later in the month the magistrates of the city again petitioned the governor and council, this time for an extension of their revenues to include "ye benefitt of ye docke Wharfe & bridge markett & Markett house with ye fferry now between ye s^{d} Citty and Long Island," the granting of licenses to public houses, and the vacant lands on Manhattan to low-water mark. Dongan granted most of these requests. The ferries were granted, with the proviso that two boats for passengers and one for cattle should be kept on each side of the river. He also granted the dock and wharf to the city on condition that they be well kept and no duty paid upon the bridge.[1] He refused to grant them the privilege of issuing licenses, saying that this belonged to the governor; or the vacant lots on Manhattan, as they were already disposed of; but he said that the whole island had been ordered surveyed, and when this had been done, some lands in the woods, not yet disposed of, should be granted to the city.

A town house at Harlem, begun in 1680, was completed two years later. On December 8, 1683, the city magistrates agreed upon a division of the city into six wards,—the South, Dock, East, West, and North Wards, which included all the land south of the Fresh Water or Collect Pond; and the Outward, which took in the rest of the island including Harlem Village. The fuel used in the town at this time was brought from the woods on Manhattan Island and the neighbouring shores. In March, 1684, the Strand between the weigh-house and the corner of James Matthews, and the vacant ground before Mr. Van Brugh's and the Smith's Fly were appointed temporary places for storing and cording this wood. Pavements were newly laid in New Street, Smith's Street, and the Bever Graft during this year, and a paid night-watch was established in the five wards south of the Fresh Water. In 1685, Dongan ordained that a post office be established "for the better correspondence between the colonies" —a project started under the Dutch in 1652. It received further encouragement in 1692 by act of the legislature.

The death of Charles II, in February of 1685, brought his brother, the Duke of York, to the throne of England. This event made New York a royal instead of a proprietary province, and brought it directly under that committee of the King's Council to which oversight of trade and royal provinces was entrusted. The charter of liberties enacted by the legislative assembly in 1683 had not been finally approved by the

[1] Bridge Market and Market-house at the ferry.

Duke of York. He now took advantage of the change in government to decline to confirm the charter, and directed that the government of New York be "assimilated" to the constitution which should be agreed upon for New England.

The year 1686 was an important one in the history of New York, for the Dongan Charter was then received.[1] This instrument confirmed all rights and privileges that had been already granted to the city and all property grants to individuals. Public buildings, including the City Hall, two market houses, the bridge into the dock, the wharves, the new burial-place outside the city gate, and the ferry and all revenues therefrom were given to the mayor, aldermen, and councilmen. Fort James, the inn which Governor Lovelace had built, the governor's garden by the gate in the wall, and the land without the gate, called the King's Farm, with the swamp between it and the Fresh Water, were reserved to the crown. All of Manhattan Island was included in the city. The officers of the city were to be a mayor, recorder, town clerk, six aldermen, six assistants, a chamberlain, sheriff, coroner, clerk of the market, high constable, seven sub-constables, and one marshal. The mayor, recorder, town clerk, clerk of the market, and sheriff were to be appointed by the governor and council; the six aldermen, six assistants, and seven sub-constables were to be elected by the voters in the several wards; the mayor, recorder, and three or more of the aldermen and of the assistants composed the common council. The fourteenth day of October, the King's Birthday, was the date set for the newly appointed officers to take their oaths of office. The city was to have a new seal. Natural-born subjects of the king of England or those who had been naturalised might be made freemen of the city by the mayor, recorder, and aldermen. Only freemen could engage in commerce or ply a trade within the limits of the city. Provision was made for the erection of a court of common pleas to be held weekly, for the care of the prisons, and for the holding of a market three days each week.

For many years the Dongan Charter continued in force in the city of New York. In one respect it was less liberal than the Dutch and earlier English systems had been; for whereas previously the officers of the city had enjoyed the privilege of nominating some of those who should suc-

[1] The original charter is in the N. Y. Public Library. An imperfect impression of the provincial seal, granted in 1669 during Lovelace's administration and once attached to the document, is now preserved separately in a silver box. The text of the charter is given in the *Minutes of the Common Council* (Osgood ed.), Vol. I, pp. 290-305, where the date is stated as April 20, 1686.

ceed them, under the Dongan Charter the governor was left unhampered in his choice of a mayor, recorder, sheriff, town clerk, and clerk of the market. But, on the other hand, the choice of the aldermen, assistants, and sub-constables was given to the voters in the respective wards; this was an advance towards liberal government.

The new charter provided that the corporation of the city should have a "common seal." At a meeting of the common council on July 24, 1686, the mayor presented to the officials the new seal of the city. The corporation has never exercised the right, which the charter gave it, of *remaking* this seal, which, in its essential parts, is still the official seal of the city.[1]

The higher officials of the city received no salaries; the main expenses were for the city watch, for the salaries of the clerk, marshal, and public whipper, and for repairs to public property. Money for these expenses was obtained from licenses, freedoms, the dock and ferry, and from local taxes authorised by the assembly. At various times the city paid debts by selling part of its lands. Thus, on May 11, 1686, when the mayor reported to the common council that he had paid Governor Dongan three hundred pounds in return for signing the charter, the common council obtained the sum by selling fourteen lots on the water front between the dock and the City Hall for four hundred and seventy pounds, and sixteen acres on the North River shore near the present Gansevoort Street for fifteen pounds. Public improvements were made partly at the expense of the citizens, who were to be benefited by them. Thus, nine public stone wells were built in 1686, and the expense equally divided between the city and the inhabitants of the streets where the wells were situated.

In 1686 the city surveyors were ordered to survey the vacant land within the city near the dock, from the weigh-house to the City Hall, and to lay it out in lots of eighty feet deep by about twenty-four broad, leaving space for a new street, which was to be called Dock Street. The buildings on this street were to be made uniform.

[1] Numerous modifications, however, have been made from time to time. After the Revolution, the shape of the shield was changed, the legend was differently disposed, and the surmounting royal crown was superseded by an eagle rising from a demi-globe, a device taken from the arms of the State of New York adopted in 1778. James II granted a seal to the province of New York, August 14, 1687. In 1915, the seal was re-designed by Paul Manship in conformity with the recommendations of a committee of the Art Commission Associates, of which committee the author was a member; the revised seal and also a new city flag were formally adopted by resolution of the Board of Aldermen on April 27, and approved by the Mayor on May 1, 1915. For a brief history of the origin and development of city seal and a description of the new one, see *Seal and Flag of the City of New York*, ed. by John B. Pine, 1915. See also Chronology.

In 1687, Governor Dongan made a report to the Committee of Trade which well shows the conditions in New York at that time. The armed force of the entire province consisted of about 4000 foot and 300 horse besides one company of dragoons. The report reads:

At New York there is a fortification of four bastions built formerly against the Indians of dry stone @ earth with sods as a breastwork well @ pleasantly situated for the defence of the Harbor on a point made by Hudsons River on the one side and by the sound on the other, It has Thirty-nine Gunns, two Mortar pieces, thirty Barils of Powder five hundred ball some Bomb-shells @ Granados small arms for 300 men, one Flanker, the face of the North Bastion, and three points of Bastions @ a Courlin has been done @ are rebuilt by mee with lime @ mortar @ all the rest of the Fort pinnd @ rough-cast with lime since my coming here.

And the most of the Guns I found dismounted @ some of them yet continue to be soe which I hope to have mounted soe soon as the mills can sawe

I am forced to renew all the Batterys with three-inch Plank @ have spoke for new planks for that purpose

And the breast-work upon the wall is so moultered away that its likewise needful to make a reparation thereof. The Officers quarters had formerly a flat roof which I finding to be chargeable to maintain @ that it could not bee kept high, [dry?] have caused a new roof to bee upon it, as alsoe finding water to run through the arch of the Gate I have been forc't to put a Roof over it, I am forc't every day by reason of the roteness of the Timber @ Boards to bee making reparations in the Soldiers quarters or my own.

The ground that the Fort stands upon @ that belongs to it contains in quantity about two acres or thereabouts about which I have instead of Palisadoes put a fence of Palls which is more lasting. . .

The principal towns within the Governm[t] are New York Albany @ Kingston at Esopus . . . the buildings in York @ Albany are generally of stone @ brick. . . . New York @ Albany live wholly upon trade with the Indians England and the West Indies. The returns for England are generally Beaver Peltry Oile @ Tobacco when we can have it. To the West Indies we send Flower, Bread Pease pork @ sometimes horses; the return from thence for the most part is rumm which pays the King a considerable excise. . . . There are about nine of [or?] ten three mast vessels of about 80 or 100 tons burthen two or three ketches @ Barks of about 40 Tun: and about twenty sloops of about twenty or five @ twenty Tunn belonging to the Goverm[t]. . .

New York has first a Chaplain belonging to the Fort of the Church of England; Secondly, a Dutch Calvinist, thirdly a French Calvinist, fourthly a Dutch Lutheran—Here bee not many of the Church of England; few Roman Catholicks; abundance of Quaker preachers men @ Women especially; Singing Quakers, Ranting Quakers; Sabbatarians; Antisabbatarians; Some

Anabaptists some Independents; some Jews; in short of all sorts of opinions there are some, and the most part of none at all

The Great Church which serves both the English @ the Dutch [1] is within the Fort which is found to bee very inconvenient therefore I desire that there may bee an order for their building an other ground already being layd out for that purpose @ they wanting not money in Store wherewithall to build it

The most prevailing opinion is that of the Dutch Calvinists [2]

Early in 1687, the common council sought of Dongan and his council a confirmation of their new charter, which he had provisionally given to them, but final action on their petition was deferred; and it was not until forty years later that another charter, embracing this and other elements of local law, was granted by Governor Montgomerie.

Governor Dongan gave encouragement to the immigration of French Protestants and Irish into New York Province. In 1688, French Huguenots erected a church on what is now Marketfield Street.

Several of the English governors, in reporting the condition of the colony to the king, had pointed out the advantage which his interests would receive from uniting New York with other portions of his territory. In 1688 he acted upon this advice and annexed New York and East and West Jersey to New England, making Sir Edmund Andros, the former governor of New York, captain-general and governor-in-chief of the whole.[3] This union was destined to be of short duration, but the cause is to be found in England rather than in America.

In England, James's government had become extremely unpopular. The fact that he was a professed Catholic had caused the people to object to his accession, but they had been unable to force Charles II to agree to any bill excluding his brother from the throne. They were forced to receive James as their king, but they looked forward to the time when his death would re-establish the Protestant succession in Mary and Anne, his daughters. By a series of moves, politically unwise, James, in his effort to improve the condition of the Catholics, antagonised almost every class in his kingdom. His opponents realised that they had only to wait until he should die, when they could redress their grievances. At this juncture a son was born to James. The people foresaw a succession of

[1] Governor Andros brought over a chaplain with him in 1678 and inaugurated the custom of having the English service in the church in the fort at the close of the Dutch service.

[2] *Doc. Hist.*, Vol. I, pp. 96, 102, 116-17.

[3] Andros reached New York August 11th. As instructed by the king, he had the seal of the province, given to it only two years before, broken in the presence of the council. Thereafter the seal of New England served in its stead.

Catholic rulers, and invited William and Mary to become joint sovereigns of England. James was allowed to retire to France, whence with Louis XIV's aid, he made an unsuccessful attack on Ireland. In 1688(-9) William and Mary were established on the throne of England.

The revolution at home was accompanied by uprisings in the colonies. When the trouble broke out, Andros, the governor over New England, New York, and the Jerseys, had removed to the seat of government in Massachusetts, taking with him many of the city records; there he was forced to resign control and was imprisoned. Nicholson, the lieutenant-governor, was left in charge at New York.

Meanwhile, at New York, a widespread fear of the Papists, the danger of a French attack, and the uncertainty which resulted from William's failure to send directions for governing the province, caused the people to take matters into their own hands. The radicals, among whom was Jacob Leisler, a militia captain and merchant of some wealth, were active in stirring up the people against the existing government. Trouble broke out at the fort between the officers of the regular troops and those of the militia, which had been called in to help keep the peace in the city. The militia seized the fort and declared that they would keep it until a Protestant, appointed by the new government in England, should arrive. At last came news that William and Mary had been proclaimed in England, followed by William's proclamation continuing Protestants in the offices that they held. Nicholson, instead of taking control, decided to return home and report. This left affairs in the hands of the radicals, of whom Leisler was now the recognised leader. He wrested control of the city from the city magistrates; and Nicholas Bayard, a member of the royal council and leader of the conservatives, was forced to flee for safety to Albany. On June 26th, 1689, delegates from the counties met at the fort and appointed members of a committee of safety. On the 28th the committee appointed Leisler captain of the fort. In this capacity, he repaired the fortifications with sods and palisades, made a water port to the westward of the fort, and put New York in a "full posture of defence." On August 16th the committee commissioned Leisler commander-in-chief with virtually supreme control.

In the meantime William III had been too completely engrossed in European affairs to settle the government of his transatlantic colonies. Finally, on July 30th, he sent a letter to Francis Nicholson, lieutenant-governor and commander-in-chief in New York, and in case of his absence, to those in control, directing them to continue their authority until he should send further directions. In Nicholson's absence, this letter was delivered to Leisler; who thereupon, considering himself authorised by William to act as lieutenant-governor, appointed a council to take the place of the committee of safety. He also procured the election of Peter De Lanoy as mayor of the city of New York, who thus became the first mayor chosen by popular vote.

On November 14, 1689, William approved the appointment of Colonel Henry Sloughter to the governorship of New York; but there was a delay in fitting out his ships which postponed his arrival until a year later, and even then, it was not the governor who arrived first, but one of his subordinates, Major Richard Ingoldsby. Leisler's enemies seized this opportunity to make trouble for him by urging Ingoldsby to ask for the surrender of the fort. He demanded that Leisler admit his troops and stores; but as he could show no authority except his commission as a captain of a foot company, Leisler refused, and called out the militia to aid him in carrying out Their Majesties' directions to him. When Sloughter finally arrived, he found civil war already beginning between the Leislerians and Ingoldsby, who was supported by the anti-Leislerians. He immediately demanded the surrender of the fort, and after some delay, received it. Leisler, his son-in-law Milborne, and other leaders of his party were put into prison, and were soon brought to trial charged with treason. Leisler and Milborne were condemned, and executed May 16, 1691. That Leisler's conduct had been seditious may be granted, but it is hard to see how either he or Milborne had been guilty of treason. Sloughter reported to his home government that their execution was for the public peace. Instead of securing this, it resulted in the formation of bitter political factions that lasted many years.

Improvements in the city had not been stopped by the political disturbances. Leisler had repaired the defences and built at least one new battery. The lots lying between the City Hall and "the bridge"[1] were improved in 1691 by building a wharf, on which a "Ducking Stoole" was ordered erected before the "Towne house" in October of that year.

The purchasers of lots between the bridge and the dock were obliged to build the street according to the surveyor's directions and to construct "a good and Substantiall Stone Wall of three foot and one halfe Broad

[1] This was a pier, built in 1659 and extending into the East River from Pearl Street at about the present Moore Street. It divided the Great Dock into two basins.

Att the Bottome to batter one ffoote inwards on the Outside and to defend the Same from the rubbing of boates by driueing Spoiles or Stockadoes att Euery five foot distance of Seauen Inches Diameter and bound togeather by a plate att Topp. . ." The lots lying between the Burger's Path (Old Slip) and the block-house (probably the one standing on the shore near the water port) were ordered laid out into thirteen lots and sold with the condition that the front of each lot should be filled up entirely with one house, two full stories high, the front facing the street to be constructed of brick or stone. The lots belonging to the city from the Burger's Path to the foot of the hill by Mr. Beekman's[1] were also ordered laid out and sold, and a committee was appointed to lay out the "heere graft street" (Broad Street) to the waterside.[2] The plot of ground in Garden Street on which the new Dutch Church was to be erected was sold in 1691 for "one hundred and Eighty Currant p[s] of Eight Six Shillings p[r] p[s]." The deed was signed by the mayor to Samuel Bayard, who gave his bond to use the ground only for a church. The only butchers' shambles within the city in April, 1691, was at the green before the fort; butchers' meat could be sold at no other place. A few weeks later a second market for flesh was opened under "the trees by the slipp."[3] These markets were held on Tuesday, Wednesday, and Saturday of each week. No butchers' meat could be killed within the city gates. In 1692, the streets now known as Pine and Cedar Streets, and other streets above Wall, were laid out through the old Damen Farms. At this time also, a system of colonial post offices was organised under a patent, and Governor Andrew Hamilton of New Jersey was placed in charge.

Governor Sloughter's commission authorised him to call a legislative assembly, and shortly after his arrival in the province he issued writs for the election of deputies. The assembly met in the city of New York on April 9, 1691. It was empowered to pass laws conformable to the laws of England. The laws, if approved by the governor, were to be put into operation, and at the first opportunity, transmitted to England for the approval of the king. If he disallowed them, they became null and void. From this time on, the government of the province was in the hands of the royal governor, his council, and the assembly. The first assembly passed fourteen laws, which were promulgated at the City Hall.

[1] The modern Beekman Street.
[2] As this street had long been opened, the reference here must refer to the *improvement* of the old street.
[3] Old Slip, between Hanover Square and the East River.

Governor Sloughter's administration was brought to a close by his sudden death, on July 23, 1691. Ingoldsby acted as governor until the last of August, 1692, when the new appointee, Benjamin Fletcher, arrived. Fletcher's administration was marred by the enmity between the two political factions in the city and by the troubles along the frontier caused by the war between England and France.

In the city itself several events of interest occurred. Frederick Phillips was allowed to build a bridge at Spuyten Duyvil and to take toll of all passers, a method which the city took to get the bridge at a time when it could not undertake the expense itself. The governor in council ordered that "stockadoes" be prepared for building a platform upon the outermost point of rocks under the fort, whereon he intended to build a battery. Paving was laid down in a number of the city streets, and one alderman and one assistant in each ward were appointed to see that the work was properly done. For the first time in the history of the city a man was employed to supervise the cleaning of streets, when, in 1695, John Vanderspiegel was engaged at thirty pounds a year to do this work.

Up to this time no English church had been established in New York. Services in English had been held in the church in the fort, but they were not supported by a tax on the people. In 1693 the provincial assembly passed a "Settling Act" which provided for the maintenance of a minister in the city and county of New York, in Richmond, in Westchester, and in Queens Counties, the necessary money being secured by a tax on the freeholders. New York City was to raise the sum of one hundred pounds each year for this purpose. There was a proposal to build a church in one of the north bastions of the city wall;[1] but in March, 1696, Fletcher gave the managers of the Church of England permission to purchase a small piece of land lying outside the north gate of the city, between the king's garden and the burying-place, and to build a church there. Voluntary contributions to carry on the work were received, apparently from all classes. The church minutes of the time record the fact that Captain Kidd "lent a Runner & Tackle for the hoising up Stones as long as he stays here." In 1697 a charter of incorporation was granted, and Trinity Church was first opened for service on March 13, 1698. Governor Fletcher gave to the corporation of this church valuable lands that had formed a part of the "King's

[1] See Miller Plan, Pl. 23.

Farm" and built a pew in the church for his own use; the city magistrates also built a pew and thereafter were accustomed to attend service after taking their oaths of office, and to listen to a sermon by the rector. In the meantime Governor Fletcher had demolished the old chapel in the fort, which was so dilapidated that it was in danger of falling down, and the provincial assembly voted four hundred and fifty pounds to build a new edifice. The work went along slowly and had not been completed in the spring of 1696. The barracks in the fort were also rebuilt at this time.

We must not fail to mention the fact that Governor Fletcher was the means of establishing the first printing press in New York. In 1693, he persuaded William Bradford, of Philadelphia, to come to New York to fill the position of royal printer. Bradford spent the rest of a long life here. Other wise acts of Fletcher's administration were giving aid to the post-office and persuading the council to appoint a surgeon-general. An act of Parliament of great historic importance was passed in 1695, whereby the attainder of Leisler, Milbourne, and Gouverneur was reversed; the judgment of the court and of Governor Sloughter, who had caused the execution of Leisler and Milbourne in 1691, was completely overturned, and Leisler's seizure of the government was vindicated.

One misfortune which came upon the city at this time was the loss of the monopoly of bolting flour, which it had enjoyed for some years. A systematic attempt at lighting the streets of the city was made in December, 1697, when the common council ordered that, until the 25th of March in the dark of the moon, every seventh house should hang a "Lanthorn & Candle" out on a pole every night and that the expense should be borne equally by the seven houses.

By this time, however, Fletcher had aroused a strong opposition. To understand the cause of his downfall we must recall the conditions of trade in New York at this time. The Atlantic had never been free from pirates, but during the war with France (the so-called King William's War) their number had increased greatly. Many a ship sailed under the commission of a privateer, though in reality a pirate. Large fortunes were made, and many of the pirates hailed from New York, where they were well received by people of quality. The case of Captain Kidd illustrates this point. He was engaged by Bellomont, acting for a group of ministers high in English affairs, and including the King himself, to attack the pirates in their strongholds, and came to New York under a commission bearing the great seal of England. Unfortunately, he was unable to take any pirates, and in desperation, fearing to return empty-handed and dreading the temper of his crew, turned pirate himself, was captured, sent to England for trial, and executed; but we may well doubt if he would have been punished, if the matter had not been made a party issue in England. Governor Fletcher's enemies accused him of being too friendly with the pirates, and urged that he be recalled. The king finally decided to transfer him, and in 1697 commissioned the Earl of Bellomont to be governor.

Our knowledge of New York at this time is enlarged by a description and plans of the town and fortifications addressed to the Bishop of London in 1695 by the Reverend John Miller, who had been resident here for nearly three years as chaplain of the troops in the fort. Inasmuch as it was a time of war, he was most vitally interested in mentioning the fortifications that protected the province from the attack of the French. Of New York he says:

> The city of New Yorke more largely taken is the whole Island so called. . . . but more strictly considered & as a place of strength is only the part thereof within the fortifications & so is not in length or breadth above two furlongs & in circumference a mile. The form of it is triangular having for y[e] sides thereof the west & north lines & the East & South for its Arched basis the chief place of strength it boasts of is its fort situated on the southwest Angle which is reasonably strong & well provided with Ammunition having in it about 38 Guns mounted. on the Basis likewise in convenient places are three Batteries of Great Guns one of 15 call'd Whitehall Batterie, one of 5 by the Stadthouse [City Hall] & the third of 10 by the Burghers path [which extended from present Old Cotton Exchange to Old Slip]. on the North-east Angle is a strong block-house and halfe moon wherein are 6 or 7 guns this part buts upon the River & is all along fortified with a sufficient bank of Earth. On the North side are two large stone Points & therein about 8 Guns some mounted & some unmounted. on the North-west Angle is a Blockhouse & on the West side 2 Horne works which are furnished with some Guns 6 or 7 in number, this side buts upon Hudsons River, has a bank in some places 20 fadom high from the water by reason whereof & a stockade strengthned with a banke of Earth on the Inside (which last is also on the North side to the landward) it is not Easily Assailable. [1]

Miller continues with an account of the natural resources of the province, mentions some bad qualities of the inhabitants, and recommends an establishment of the English Church, and fuller measures for the de-

[1] Miller, J., *New York Considered and Improved, 1695* (Cleveland, 1903), pp. 35-7.

fence of the country against the French. His account is accompanied by a plan of the city of New York to which a key is appended which locates virtually all of the important places in the town. (See Pl. 23.)

Bellomont was a man of integrity and ability, but his administration was troubled by factional quarrels and opposition to his enforcement of the trade laws. His letters to the Lords of Trade are vigorous expressions of condemnation of official misconduct on the part of Fletcher and others; they reveal a masterly spirit, inspired by a love of honesty and efficiency in the administration of public affairs. An attack of the gout carried him off untimely in 1701. He was buried in the chapel in the fort; and when that was taken down and the ground levelled in 1790, the leaden coffin containing his bones was deposited in St. Paul's Churchyard.

The most important building operation undertaken by the city during this administration was the erection of a new city hall. First steps in the matter had been taken in 1696, when a committee of the common council was appointed to act with the surveyors of the city in making an estimate of the cost of a new city hall, and in determining the most convenient location for it and the best way of raising the necessary money. The next year the old City Hall was in such poor repair that men refused to serve on jury in it for fear it would fall, and a mason and two carpenters were employed to strengthen it with "Studds and Planke." In January, 1699, the committee appointed to report on the building declared that it considered the upper end of Broad Street the proper site for a new city hall, and that three thousand pounds would be enough to cover the expense of building it. The next spring the common council decided to follow the recommendation of this committee. The old City Hall was sold in the following August, the city reserving the right to retain the "Goale" within it for the space of one month ensuing.[1] At the same time the corporation petitioned John Nanfan, the lieutenant-governor, to exert his influence with the governor, so that they might have for the new building the stones of the fortifications and bastions from the East to the North Rivers along the line of Wall Street. These were in a ruinous condition and were useless because of the encroachment of houses. No contemporary view, plan, or description of this, the second City Hall, has been found, but we have an elevation and three plans, showing the

[1] John Rodman, a merchant of the city, bought it for £920, he being the highest bidder. The cage, pillory, and stocks, which had stood before the old hall, were ordered removed to the upper end of Broad Street and put up near the new one.

building as it was in 1745–7, drawn from memory in 1818 by David Grim. (Pl. 32-b.) Alterations and additions were made from time to time, the most extensive being in 1763, when a third story was added, and in 1789, when the entire building was remodelled for Congress.[1]

Governor Bellomont was succeeded by Edward Hyde, Lord Cornbury, a cousin of Queen Anne,[2], but a man of bad morals and a spendthrift, whom William III had appointed before his death. Cornbury reached his province in May, 1702. During this summer there raged in the city an epidemic so severe that some of the municipal officials could not be chosen in the manner that the charter directed, but were appointed by the common council. Many of the people fled into the country and Lord Cornbury himself retired to Jamaica, Long Island.

An unsuccessful attempt to establish a free school in New York had been made in 1695; in 1702 an act favourable to this project was passed by the provincial assembly. The common council petitioned that a part of the "King's Farm" be granted for the support of the school, and that the Bishop of London send over a teacher suitable for the position. Andrew Clarke was appointed in January, 1706.

In 1703 the population of the city and county of New York was 4,436. The common council in that year granted a burying-place to the Corporation of Trinity Church. In 1704, it declared it lawful to kill any swine running at large in the streets on the south side of the Fresh Water, and laid a fine on any one who should dig holes in the Commons south of that point. The French Church (l'Église du St. Esprit) was built in 1704 on the north side of Pine Street, east of Nassau. In 1705, pavings were ordered laid in the south end of Broad Street, in Queens, New, and Varlett's Streets, and about the dock and custom-house. "Nonconformist" ministers (Presbyterians) introduced their doctrines into New York early in 1707; they were imprisoned by Cornbury's order for spreading principles contrary to those of the Established Church. By their trial and acquittal religious toleration in the province was vindicated.

The most important event in this period of our review is the struggle between England and France, in Europe known as the War of the Spanish Succession (1702–13), in America as Queen Anne's War, a contro-

[1] In 1716 Stephen De Lancey gave to the city a four-dial clock, which was put up in the City Hall cupola. In 1718 the common council made provision for taking care of this clock. When the governor's council began to act as a separate house of the legislature, in 1736, they used the common council room, which was fitted up for them. Thus both houses of the legislature sat under one roof.

[2] Anne, second daughter of James II, became queen at the death of William III in 1702.

versy which had been bequeathed by William III to Anne when he resigned the crown to her. As in all of these wars against the French, the Iroquois Indians remained faithful to the English and served as a bulwark against attacks on the frontier. The city, however, was much disturbed by the danger of an attack by French privateers. The fort was repaired, and a line of "stockadoes" was run from the North to the East River; there and along the river-side a breastwork was erected. Three batteries were also built on the East River, of twenty-two, seven, and eight guns respectively. Three batteries were built on the North River of nine, five, and three guns, and one battery of eleven guns upon a point of rock under the fort. There were not enough guns for all of these places, but some were supplied by a Scotch man-of-war that lay at Amboy and some by merchants. The provincial assembly voted fifteen hundred pounds to fortify the Narrows, but Cornbury appropriated this to his own use. Later acts provided additional sums for the defence of the city and frontiers, but, made wise by experience, the assembly prevented the misuse of this money by appointing a treasurer of the province to receive and disburse all that might be collected for a special purpose. The treasurer was made responsible to the governor, council, and assembly. Thus the governor could no longer misuse the funds with impunity. During the summer of 1706 the citizens of New York were very much disturbed by reports that a French squadron under d'Iberville was coming to attack the city. One French privateer actually entered the harbour. All able-bodied citizens were called out to help throw up defences, but the city was not really attacked.

The appearance and customs of New York in 1704-5 are delightfully pictured by Madam Sarah Knight, who visited the city at this time, riding through the country from Boston.

> The Cittie of New York is a pleasant, well compacted place, situated on a Commodius River wch is a fine harbour for shipping. The Buildings Brick Generaly very stately and high, though not altogether like ours in Boston. The Bricks in some of the Houses are of divers Coullers and laid in Checkers, being glazed look very agreeable. The inside of them are neat to admiration, the wooden work, for only the walls are plasterd, and the Sumers and Gist are plained and kept very white scowr'd as so is all the partitions if made of Bords. The fire places have no jambs (as ours have) But the Backs run flush with the walls, and the Hearth is of Tyles and is as farr out into the Room at the Ends as before the fire, wch is Generally Five foot in the Low'r rooms, and the peice over where the mantle tree should be is made as ours with Joyners

work, and as I supose is fasten'd to iron rodds inside. The House where the Vendue was, had Chimney Corners like ours, and they and the hearths were laid wth the finest tile that I ever see, and the stair cases laid all with white tile which is ever clean, and so are the walls of the Kitchen w[ch] had a Brick floor. . .

They are Generaly of the Church of England and have a New England Gentleman for their minister, and a very fine church set out with all Customary requisites. There are also a Dutch and Divers Conventicles, as they call them, viz. Baptist, Quakers, &c. They are not strict in keeping the Sabbath as in Boston and other places where I had bin, But seem to deal with great exactness as farr as I see or Deall with. They are sociable to one another and Curteos and Civill to strangers and fare well in their houses. . .

They have Vendues very frequently and make their Earnings very well by them, for they treat with good Liquor Liberally, and the Customers Drink as Liberally and Generally pay for't as well, by paying for that which they Bidd up Briskly for, after the sack has gone plentifully about, tho' sometimes good penny worths are got there. Their Diversions in the Winter is Riding Sleys about three or four Miles out of Town, where they have Houses of entertainment at a place called the Bowery, and some go to friends Houses who handsomely treat them. . . [1]

The assembly had adjourned in the autumn of 1706 and was not convened again until August, 1708. The financial irregularities and extortions of Governor Cornbury led it to protest against the levying of money upon the freemen of the colony "without consent in general assembly." Fortunately in March, 1708, Queen Anne replaced Lord Cornbury by Lord Lovelace, who reached his province in the following December. With Lovelace came a company of Germans from the Palatinate, who had been aided by the English government in escaping the persecutions of Louis XIV. This administration, which began auspiciously, was cut short by the governor's death in May, 1709, and the government devolved upon Richard Ingoldsby, the lieutenant-governor, until his commission was revoked in 1709, and Lovelace's successor was appointed.

The new governor, Colonel Robert Hunter, reached New York in June, 1710. Settling the Palatines, many of whom accompanied him to America, was his first and one of his chief concerns. About 150 of these families settled in New York City. During his administration, which lasted until his return to England in 1719, several changes were made in the city. He refitted, for his own use and for the garrison, the old chapel in the fort, which Governor Fletcher had built

[1] *The Journal of Madam Knight* (New York, 1825), pp. 52-4.

on the site of the earlier Dutch church, and he won the enmity of William Vesey, rector of Trinity, by allowing the Reverend John Sharp, chaplain of the forces, to officiate there on Sundays for the benefit of the garrison and of those who found it impossible to secure accommodation in Trinity Church. Governor Hunter reported his action to the Bishop of London: "The ancient Chapell in the Fort (hinc illae lachrymae) for many years past a Bear Garden, I have at a great expence put in repair, so that it is now one of the most decent & most constantly frequented Houses of Prayer in all America." He also helped finish Trinity Church steeple by his liberal contributions and influence.

In 1711 the common council ordered the great bridge by the Custom-House finished and made convenient for shipping and landing merchandise, and the market-house at the south end of Broad Street near the dock repaired. In 1711 also, a market-place was established at the north end of Broad Street, between the City Hall and the cross street which extended from Broadway to the Dutch Church (Garden Street). The market-house at the Wall Street slip, which had been erected in 1709 or 1710, was appointed the place for hiring Indian and negro slaves, of whom there were many in the city. In 1712 they formed a plan to seize the town, but their conspiracy was frustrated by the prompt action of the governor, who captured them and brought them to summary justice. A census of New York was taken in 1712, and showed 5,840 people in the city and county, an increase of 1,404 over the number of inhabitants in 1703.

Early in October, 1714, came the news of Queen Anne's death, and the accession of George I, which was celebrated at a bonfire, with twenty gallons of wine to drink the king's health. The fort was now named Fort George. The Baptist denomination held their first sessions in New York in 1715 in a hired house on Wall Street. In 1718, the Presbyterians "purchased land in 'Stouttenburgh's garden' and the next year erected a church upon it and opened a cemetery beside the building." This church, standing on the north side of Wall Street between the present Nassau Street and Broadway, was the first Presbyterian Church in the city. While it was building, the common council allowed the congregation to worship in the City Hall, which stood near by.[1]

Governor Hunter, finding that his health would not permit of his remaining in America, arranged an exchange of offices with his friend,

[1] The Burgis View (Pl. 25) gives an excellent idea of the city at about that time.

William Burnet, by which he might return to England. Burnet reached his province in September, 1720, called the provincial assembly to meet at Fort George, where it voted a revenue for the government for the next five years, and prohibited the sale of Indian goods to the French. This dissatisfied the merchants of New York, who benefited greatly by this trade. Burnet was an excellent governor, but perhaps lacking in political sagacity, and his transference to Massachusetts in 1728 was brought about by enemies whom he had made through interfering in a quarrel between factions in the French Church, by unpopularity resulting from certain decrees which he had lately made in chancery, and by his stopping the French trade.

Several changes occurred in New York during this administration. In 1720 brickmakers and charcoal burners were forbidden to cut firewood upon the Commons. A census was taken in 1723, which showed the population of the city and county to be 7,248, of whom 5,886 were white persons. In 1723, also, the lots between high and low water on the North River, from the fort to Trinity Church, were ordered laid out and surveyed, and a committee was appointed to have this done. By 1729 these lots had been granted, and suggestions were made for laying out streets in the neighbourhood of the present Washington and Greenwich Streets.

On November 1, 1725, the first newspaper ever published in New York, *The New-York Gazette*, a weekly, was issued by William Bradford. No number of this paper is known earlier than the issue for Feb. 28–March 7, 1726, a copy of which is preserved in the Historical Society of Pennsylvania. The gaol in the City Hall had become a nuisance, and, as early as 1725, the common council considered the erection of a new one. In 1727 they petitioned the provincial assembly for leave to levy six hundred pounds upon the freeholders for this purpose. In 1725 slaughter-houses in the Outward were forbidden. The next year Wall Street market near the East River was declared the only place in the city where corn, grain, or meal could be sold. In 1727 the division line between New York and Harlem was run. The next year a powder-house was built on a little island in the Fresh Water. Two years later (1730) twenty-three cases of books containing 1,642 volumes were received from the venerable Society for the Propagation of the Gospel in Foreign Parts, and were placed in the City Hall, where they were to serve as a public library.

Governor Burnet was succeeded by John Montgomerie, who arrived in New York in the spring of 1728. In so far as New York was concerned, the most important event in this administration was the granting of a new charter to the city. The former city charter, granted by Governor Dongan in 1686, had been supplemented in 1708 by a charter from Governor Cornbury, which referred exclusively to the matter of ferry privileges. The Dongan Charter was sealed with the Duke of York's seal, and not with the great seal of England or the seal of the province; yet it was dated in the second year of King James. Governor Bellomont, in 1700, declared that it was therefore not a legal charter, and that "In strictness this is no city." In August, 1730, the corporation petitioned the governor and council for a charter to be issued under the seal of George II. The charter was sent to England for the king's signature, and on February 11, 1731, the document was delivered to the mayor and other city officers by the governor at Fort George.

The new charter confirmed all the rights and privileges granted in the preceding charters. It is important for the topography of the city, because it created a new ward, by dividing the Out Ward and naming the southern part Montgomerie Ward in honor of the governor. The territory north of Chambers Street was now called the Out Ward. The limits of the city's jurisdiction were laid down as the low-water line on the neighbouring shores. The officers of the corporation included a mayor, recorder, seven aldermen, seven assistants, a sheriff, coroner, common clerk, chamberlain, high constable, sixteen assessors, seven collectors, sixteen constables, and a marshall. The mayor was appointed by the governor, and in other details less authority was given to local opinion than at present.[1] The Bradford Map (Pl. 27) represents the city just at this time and shows the new division of the wards.

In 1731 an important step towards preventing paupers from settling in the city was taken by passing a law compelling shipmasters to report those whom they brought to the city, and lodging-house keepers to report those received into their houses. In the same year the common council agreed with Stephen De Lancey and John Moore, merchants, to procure for the city's use two fire-engines from London "with suctions, Leathern Pipes, and Caps and Other Materials thereunto belonging." One of these engines is still in existence, and is preserved by the Volunteer Firemen's

[1] This charter remained in use until after the formation of the United States. The original Montgomerie charter is preserved in the New York Public Library.

Association. The population of New York City and County had for some time been increasing steadily, and in 1731 was 8,622.

On May 31, 1731, Montgomerie's administration was brought to a close by the governor's sudden death. The executive function devolved upon Rip Van Dam, president of the governor's council, who exercised its powers until the arrival of the new governor. Van Dam was a wealthy trader of Dutch parentage, and even at this time could use English but imperfectly. Undoubtedly his elevation gratified the Dutch element in the city, and this feeling showed itself in the dedication to him of an engraving of the Dutch Church newly erected on Nassau Street (Pl. 28). During the year 1731 the laws and ordinances of the city were revised, and the common council had them printed and published by Bradford. Prominent among the newly developed laws were those relating to street paving and cleaning, carts and carmen, the prevention of fires, and the regulation of public markets.

The new governor, Colonel William Cosby, was appointed in January, 1732, but did not reach his government until the first of August. He was soon engaged in a lively controversy with Rip Van Dam over the division of the emoluments accruing to the governor's office during the thirteen months that the latter had performed its duties. Wishing to avoid the intervention of a jury, Cosby brought the case before the judges sitting as a court of exchequer, over which he himself presided. Cosby had already made himself unpopular by the ungracious manner in which he had received a gift voted to him by the provincial assembly, and his authority in creating such a court was at once questioned. Lewis Morris, who had served as chief justice of New York for nearly twenty years, declared against Cosby and was dismissed from office.

Cosby in this way aroused strong opposition; but on the other hand, he had the support of a faction called the court party, led by James De Lancey. The governor had an advantage in that he controlled the courts, the meeting of the legislature, and the press, which at this time consisted of Bradford's *New-York Gazette*. The opposition had no means of expressing its dissatisfaction. To overcome this disadvantage, there was established an opposition paper, called *The New York Weekly Journal*, edited by John Peter Zenger, in which Morris and others published articles expressing and defending their opinions. The first issue was published on November 5, 1733. From the beginning, the *Journal* defended the right of Englishmen to a free press and attacked Governor

Cosby's administration. Those who supported the governor were not spared. While the *Journal* was filled with these scathing attacks, the *Gazette* was equally bitter in terming them "false," "malicious," and "seditious."[1] Numbers 7, 47, 48, and 49 of the *Journal*, containing letters regarding the governor's adjournment of the assembly, which the writer thought unconstitutional, were found particularly objectionable; but what finally aroused the governor to take action, was a paragraph in the *Journal* for October 7, 1734, charging him with having interfered in the elections. He denied the charge and ordered the magistrates to bring the offenders to punishment. Zenger was arrested and certain numbers of his paper were ordered burned by the common hangman. At Zenger's trial, in New York, his counsel, James Alexander and William Smith, were disbarred, but Andrew Hamilton of Philadelphia defended him so ably that the jury pronounced him not guilty. The citizens showed their appreciation of Hamilton's services by giving him a dinner at the Black Horse Tavern, and the common council voted him the freedom of the city. The result of the Zenger trial was of great importance, for it freed the press from the control of the court party, and newspapers became the medium through which the people of the colonies secured a knowledge of their rights and liberties. Undoubtedly this helped the development of a spirit of independence and hastened the separation of the colonies from England.

In passing, it is interesting to notice that in 1733 Cortlandt Street was laid out, as the owners of the land through which it passed intended speedily to "lay out the Lands on both sides of the Said Street into Lotts for Buildings"; also, the first step towards draining the swamps near the Fresh Water was taken, when Anthony Rutgers, to whom the section had been granted, asked permission to lay a drain into the Hudson River. The land between high- and low-water marks in Kip's Bay and Turtle Bay was reserved by the city in 1733 "for the Harbouring of Vessells in the Winter time"; nevertheless, the following year, an individual grant of water lots was made to the captain of the king's ship-of-war, to enable him to build and own a pier at Turtle Bay "for his Majesty's Ships to Careen at."—See Addenda Plate. In 1733, the piece of land at the lower end of Broadway fronting the fort was leased to John Chambers, Peter Bayard, and Peter Jay at an annual rental of a pepper-corn for the

[1] The paper was directed by Alexander, Morris, and other leaders of the anti-court party. See *New York Weekly Journal* of Nov. 5, 1733, and following numbers.

purpose of enclosing it and making a bowling-green with "Walks therein, for the Beauty & Ornament of the Said Street." In 1735 a work-house was built on the Commons by the corporation. The building was finished in 1736, and put in the care of the church-wardens of the city, who were appointed overseers of the poor. In 1736 the street fronting the East River between Maiden Lane Slip (or Countess Key Slip) and Rodman's Slip was named Water Street.

Governor Cosby died in March, 1736. One of his last acts was to remove Rip Van Dam, his enemy, from the position of president of the council, so as to prevent his succeeding as acting governor. George Clarke, whom Cosby had appointed to Van Dam's place, secured the fort and by means of its garrison held the Van Dam partisans in check. Civil war was prevented by the arrival of an appointment for Clarke as lieutenant-governor of New York. Van Dam yielded to this decision, but the factional struggle continued throughout Clarke's administration.

In 1737 the population of New York County and City was 10,664, an increase of 2,042 over the number of inhabitants in 1731. The bulk of the people still lived below Wall Street, which now became the fashionable residence street. There were some fine houses in the city at this time, among them the De Lancey house, just above Trinity Church (on the site of the later City Hotel), and Abraham De Peyster's mansion on Pearl Street; there were, also, several fine country places, notably at Greenwich and Bloomingdale. Trinity Church was enlarged in 1735–7, and Robinson Street was opened. During these recent years the granting of water lots along the eastern shores of the city and the building of docks and bulkheads, made easy the later filling in and extension of the street system at the river fronts. At this time, the beginning of a quarantine was made. In June, 1738, ships were forbidden to enter the harbour farther than Bedlow's Island before being visited by a physician. This did not prevent many subsequent epidemics of small-pox and other contagious diseases. In 1738, the beginning of an organised fire department was made and men were regularly hired to work the fire engines.

In the spring of 1741 the town fell under the fear of a so-called negro plot. Several fires following each other in quick succession, in one of which the governor's house, the secretary's office, the chapel, and some other buildings in the fort were destroyed, [1] gave rise to the idea that

[1] The common council assigned its room for the keeping of the public books and records of the province during this exigency.

they were set by negroes who had formed a plot to seize the town, murder the whites, and set up a government of their own. It was easy enough to find witnesses, and on their evidence, much of which we now know must have been false, more than one hundred negroes were imprisoned, of whom twenty-nine were burned at the stake or hanged and eighty-eight transported. Three whites were executed.[1] To these troubles the danger of another war with the French was added; and the assembly of the province, meeting in the early summer of 1741, with this possibility in view, provided for building a new battery in New York City and for fortifying Oswego.

In 1743 Clarke's administration was brought to an end by the appointment of Commodore George Clinton as governor. He arrived at New York in September and soon found that his course was not to be easy. He made a serious mistake by appointing James De Lancey, who had been the leader of the court party, chief justice during good behaviour, thus putting him beyond his own direct control. He then quarrelled with his appointee, who immediately became the head of the opposition, and by means of his connection with the Archbishop of Canterbury, who had been his tutor, and Sir Peter Warren, his brother-in-law, who had won a great reputation by his share in the taking of Louisburg from the French in 1745, actually exercised more influence with the government in England than Clinton himself. It is not necessary here to go into all the points of difference between the governor and the opposition. The chief point, however, was the matter of granting revenues and appointing officials. Before this the provincial assembly had gained the privilege of granting a revenue for only a year at a time. Its next step was to grant the salary to the person and not to the office, thereby compelling the governor to appoint its nominees or find some other way of paying their salaries. The renewal of war between France and England further increased the difficulty. The Indians on the frontier were restless, and there was need of more fortifications, troops, and supplies. The assembly hampered the governor in the matter of voting funds, and accused him of appointing incompetent men to supervise the construction of fortifications at New York City. The war ended in 1748.

In spite of these difficulties, New York continued to grow. A census taken by Governor Clinton in 1746 showed that the population of the

[1] See *The Negro Conspiracy* by Daniel Horsmanden, Recorder of the City of New York, who had been one of the justices of the supreme court before whom these unfortunates were tried.

city and county was 11,717. The frequent recurrence of dangerous epidemics having directed public attention, in 1744, to the unsanitary condition of the streets, a committee appointed to investigate existing conditions reported on public nuisances to the common council. It declared that various slips (Burling's, Beekman's, and the Fly Slips) were intolerable nuisances and must be removed at the expense of the corporation. In May of the same year a law was passed forbidding the keeping of vats for skinners, leather dressers, and curriers south of the Fresh Water. Hatters were forbidden to pour their dye into the channels or gutters of streets, and starch makers, also, were specifically mentioned in a similar prohibition. More stringent regulations for the disposal of garbage were made at the same time. During 1744, and from then on, great activity was shown in making improvements in Montgomerie Ward. In September of that year a committee was appointed to lay out streets there. Francis Maerschalck, city surveyor, did much of his excellent work about this time.

Labor troubles were not unknown in New York even at this early date, and in a petition to the governor in 1747, about one hundred mechanics of various trades protested against the low wage-scale introduced by mechanics from neighbouring provinces. These workmen were doubtless the first to establish in New York a "union" for the purpose of increasing wages. In 1749, the owners of lots in the Swamp and Cripple Bush and in Montgomerie Ward declared that they had spent over two hundred pounds in making a street from Queen Street to their lots in the Swamp. This new thoroughfare became Ferry Street. Other streets in this section were laid out soon afterward. The development of the docks at Hunter's Key or "Rotten Row" was begun in 1750. Up to this time, making repairs to public wharves seems to have been done by committees of the common council, especially appointed for that purpose, but in 1755 the council made it a standing rule that the alderman and common councilman of the ward in which repairs were needed, should have liberty to do the work and charge the expense to the corporation.

In 1751, Trinity Church received a grant of land in the rear of its holding in the West Ward, extending two hundred feet beyond low-water mark in the North River, on condition that space be left for three streets, each to be forty feet wide, one at high-water mark, one at low water, and the third, two hundred feet beyond low water. In 1753 a new exchange was built at the lower end of Broad Street, with a second story surmounted by a cupola. In this period also several churches were built. On May 23, 1751, the Moravians informed Governor Clinton that they intended to built a church in New York City. It was soon afterwards erected on what is now Fulton Street. In 1752 Trinity Church built St. George's Chapel on the corner of Cliff and Beekman Streets, and Wednesday, the first day of July, was appointed for its formal opening.

By this time Governor Clinton had become tired of the continual struggle against De Lancey and the opposition, and in 1753 secured his own recall. His successor, Sir Danvers Osborn, arrived in the autumn of that year and took the oath of office on October 10th. We have a detailed account of this ceremony. Upon the parade before the fort (Bowling Green) the mayor and other officers of the corporation were assembled with the militia officers, clergymen, and leading citizens. The gate to the fort was thrown open and the two governors, Clinton and Osborn, appeared, preceded by a company of foot soldiers and followed by the governor's council. The procession, enlarged by those who had waited on the parade, marched up Broadway, whose sides were lined by a great concourse of people, until it reached Wall Street, and then marched down that street and halted at the City Hall. There the procession formed two lines between which the governors entered the building, where the new governor's commission was read. Cannon boomed, bells rang, flags waved in honour of the occasion, and in the evening illuminated windows and bonfires proclaimed the general joy. Governor Osborn, however, had been more impressed with the hatred which the populace had shown to Clinton, the retiring governor, than to the hearty welcome which he himself received. Evil forebodings, added to domestic affliction, overwhelmed a mind already unbalanced, and he hanged himself in the garden of Joseph Murray, where he was staying while his own house in the fort was being repaired. This unexpected event brought James De Lancey, the lieutenant-governor, to the governor's chair.

De Lancey had been a leader of the liberal or colonial party in the opposition to Governor Clinton. He now found himself called upon by the governor's instructions to work for what he had previously opposed; namely, a permanent revenue and appropriations, without the purpose for which they were to be used being specified. The appointment and arrival in New York in 1755 of the new governor, Sir Charles Hardy, relieved De Lancey from his difficulty, while permitting him to retain an influential position; as Hardy, frankly confessing that he knew nothing of law and was better fitted to command on the sea than on land, deferred to his judgment in many important matters.

In 1754, the country was again embroiled in the difficulties of war, the last of the series of struggles between France and England for dominion in America. The war began with the collision of French and Virginians in the upper Ohio valley. The English colonies made an attempt at united action in controlling Indian affairs and providing military forces to fight the French, by calling a convention of representatives of all the colonies to meet at Albany in the month of June, 1754. Virginia and South Carolina, however, failed to send delegates. Although the chief purpose of the meeting was to make an alliance with the Iroquois against the French, it is interesting to note that at this conference, the first formal proposal for a permanent union among the colonies was made by Benjamin Franklin, but met with scant approval both at home and in England. The first years of the war were disheartening to the English. Braddock's unlooked for defeat in western Pennsylvania in 1755 exposed the whole western frontier to the attacks of the French and Indians. The English attack on Crown Point in this same year was a failure, as was Shirley's attempt on Niagara; and in 1756, Montcalm actually took Oswego. The English were beaten back and so discredited that many of their savage allies deserted them for the French.

New York, from its central position, was vitally interested in these campaigns. The Earl of Loudoun, who had been made commander of all the English forces in North America, after the loss of Oswego, sent one thousand regulars to New York City for winter quarters. The old barracks in the fort were fitted up for them, and the officers were entertained among the unwilling citizens, who were forced to do this by the Earl's threatening to gather all his forces at New York and billet them upon the people. Fort George was repaired at this time.

A change in the misfortunes which had attended English operations in the early years of the war came when William Pitt assumed leadership in 1757. He prosecuted the war with a new vigour, which speedily brought its reward in the capture of Louisburg, Fort Duquesne, and finally Quebec and Montreal. In 1763 the Treaty of Paris ended the contest between France and England, and gave to England control of the lands in North America lying east of the Mississippi River.

Many changes in New York City itself had been made in these years of war. During this period the first college in the province was established. On October 25, 1751, the provincial assembly passed an act providing for the appointment of trustees to take charge of funds raised by lottery for founding a college. Trinity Church gave the land, consisting of that portion of the King's Farm lying on the west side of Broadway between Barclay and Murray Streets, extending to the Hudson River. A royal charter for the institution was granted October 31, 1754, and the first students were admitted to the institution, which was named King's College (now Columbia University). In the same year the Society Library was organised. In October, 1757, the common council decided to build barracks to accommodate eight hundred men, on some of the common lands of the corporation south of the Fresh Water, between the "New Goal House and the house of Catemuts." This project was hastened by the burning of the west barracks in the fort on December 15th. The next year, 1758, Aldermen Livingston and Lespinard, acting for the corporation, purchased Bedlow's Island of Archibald Kennedy for one thousand pounds, and the corporation built a pest-house upon it. In 1758, also, a third story was ordered to be added to the new Gaol, then "a building." The Gaol was finished so that the prisoners were removed to it from the City Hall in September, 1759. In 1760 Francis Maerschalck, city surveyor, surveyed the "Bloomingdall Road" leading from the northeast corner of Sir Peter Warren's land to "Bloomendall," and another road (Great George Street) in the West Ward of the city, beginning from the Spring Garden House and extending north to the ground of the late widow Rutger's. In 1761, provision was made for regulating and paving Vesey and Division Streets, part of Broadway, and Franckfort Street in Montgomerie Ward to Gold Street. Lamp-posts with oil lamps came into vogue in 1762, and continued in use until gas was introduced in 1825. In 1763 that part of the corporation's common lands called Inklanbergh (Incleberg), later Murray Hill, containing thirty-one lots of five acres each, was farmed at public outcry.

At the end of the English period, New-York was still a small provincial town of about twelve thousand inhabitants. The population was mixed—Dutch and English—and Dutch was the language still used by a large number of the inhabitants. The social and official centre of the town was Fort George, in which were the governor's residence and the offices of the provincial officials. The centre of the municipal government, however, was the City Hall, standing at the head of Broad Street. This was the headquarters of the mayor and common council. It was also the meeting-place of both branches of the provincial legislature, for which special rooms had been fitted up at the expense of the province. In 1763 there were seven wards in the city—East, Dock, South, West, North, Montgomerie, and the Outward. In the older wards considerable improvement had been made. Streets had been laid out and levelled, and considerable paving had been done. In the Outward, however, which lay north of the present Chambers Street, little had been accomplished. The bulk of the population still lived south of Wall Street, which remained one of the better residence streets. Places of amusement lay outside of the town, and there were various public gardens in different parts of the city. The chief interests of the town were centered in trade, and its most influential citizens were merchants.

By the next step in its development, New York ceased to be a provincial city, dependent upon England for the character of its government, and became one of the free cities of a new and independent nation.

A DESCRIPTION OF THE
TOWNE OF MANNADOS
OR NEW AMSTERDAM

THE MAINE LA

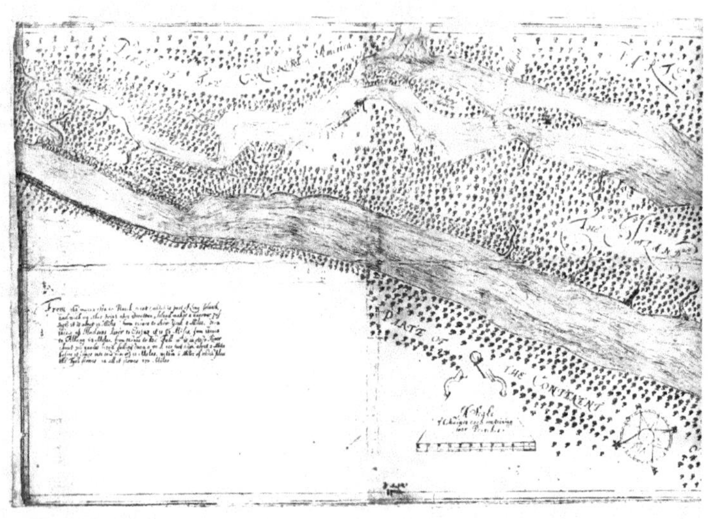

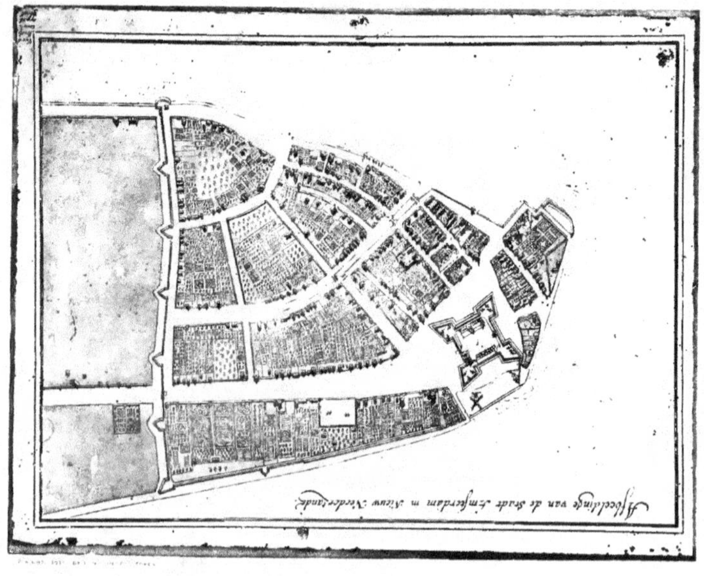

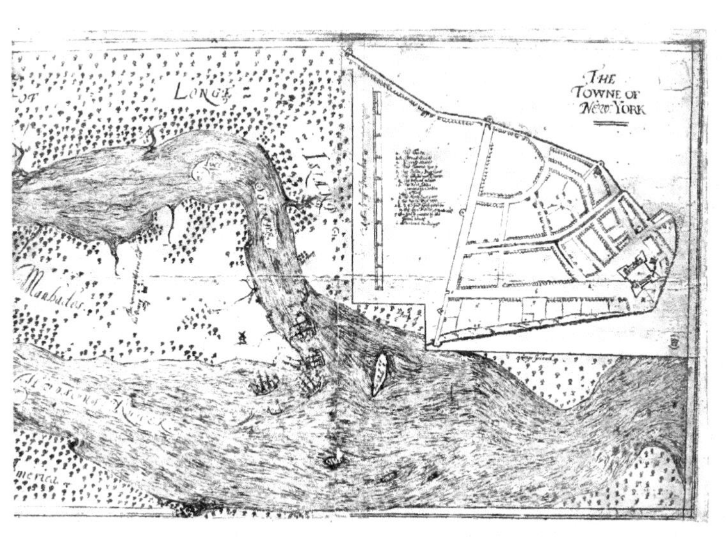
THE
TOWNE OF
NEW YORK
LONG
ISLAND
Manhatans
America

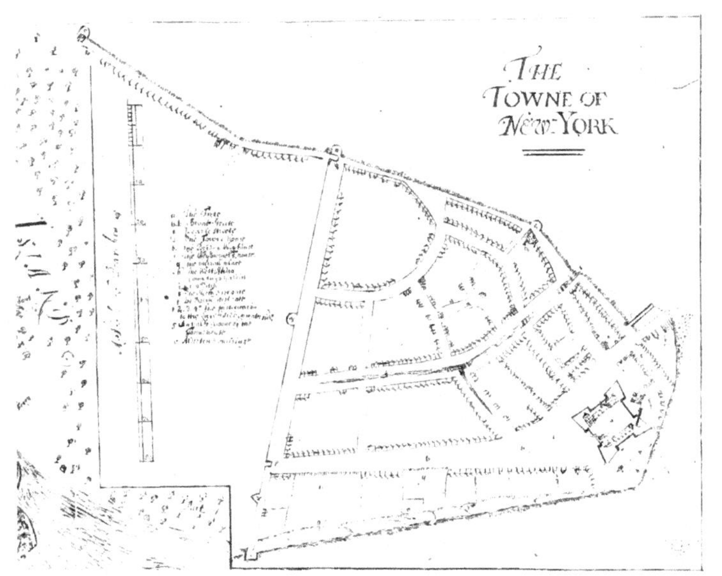
THE
TOWNE OF
NEW YORK

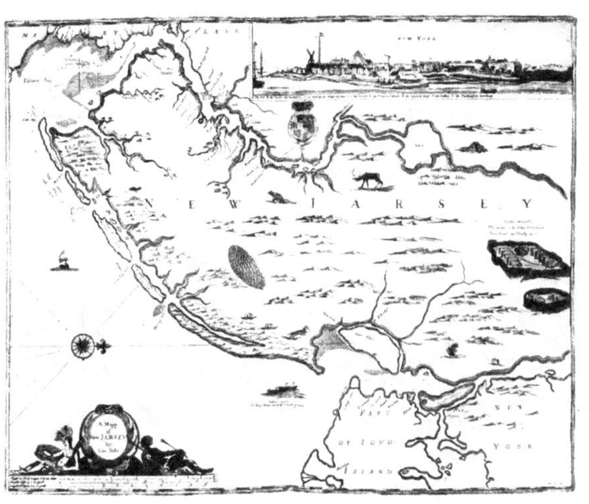
NEW YORK
N E W J A R S E Y
PART OF LONG ISLAND
NEW YORK

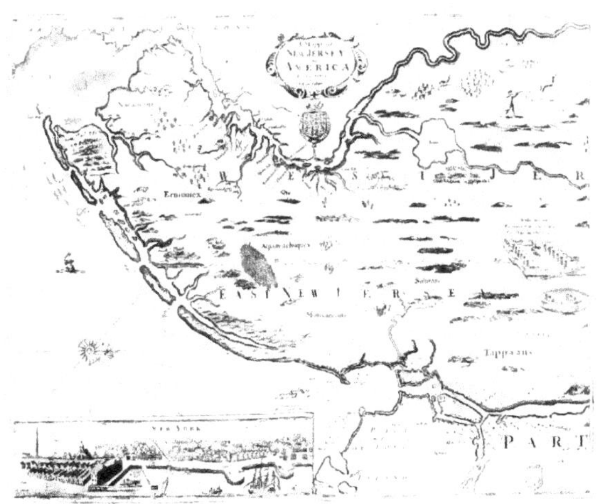
NEW JERSEY
AMERICA
EAST NEW JERSEY
NEW YORK
PART

AMSTELODAMUM NOVUM, Vrbs est in Noua Belgica inter Virginiam et Nouam Angliam, ab Hollandis extructa. Ita celebris es
habitantium multitudine, ac urbanitate, plenissimi portus amplitudine, Ædificiorum structura, Templorum Superbia, admira
bili Situ, Longitudineque et Latitudine sua, ut merito Belgæ eam Amstelodamy sui nomine insigniuerint. Caput est totius N
uæ Hollandiæ, Soli mira fertilitate sua maxime commendandi, Vitium Sylvestrium copia, Arborum ad Ædificia et Naues etiam r
[illegible] idoneorum abundantia, plantarum herbarumque multitudine, quarum quædam elegantissimos fructus ferunt, et quædam a
medicinam faciendam utiles iudicantur. Regionem hanc ab aliquot iam annis Hollandi sub auspiciis ordinum Confederatæ Belgicæ lu
[illegible] et patriæ suæ nomine appellarunt. Eadem ibi Politiæ forma quæ in ueteri Hollandia, cura prædictorum ordinum exercetur.
[illegible]

.E NOVVEL. AMSTERDAM, est une Ville bastie par les Hollandois en la Nouvelle Hollande en Lamerique, entre la Virginie et la Nouvel
Angleterre, elle est si celebre pour sa grandeur, son commerce, le grand nombre de ses habitans la longueur et la bonte de son Port,
belle Structure de ses Temples, et Superbes edifices, et pour son admirable Situation, que les Hollandois nont pas fait tort à leur
Amsterdam, de luy donner son Nom. Elle est la Capitale de la Nouvelle Hollande, que la fertilite de son Territoire rend recommanda
le. Elle abonde en Vignes, Arbres propres a faire Maisons et Vaisseaux, en plantes et herbes dont quelques unes portent de tres bons et tres-
eaux fruicts, et dautres sont propres pour la medecine. Le pais a este premierem.t decouuert par les Hollandois qui luy ont laissé
ur Nom. Elle est sous la puissance des Estats d'Hollande, qui y font garder la mesme police qu'en leur pais et ou les
tercontens se retirent souuent.

Jollain ex. — 71

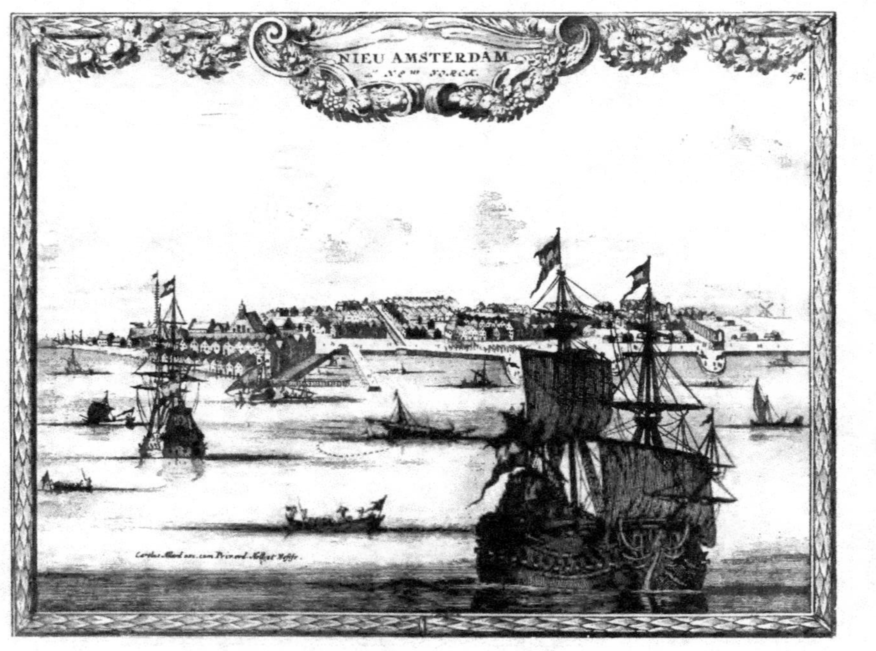
NIEU AMSTERDAM,
78.

Pl. 14

PL. 15

Nieu AMSTERDAM, een stedeken in Noord [illegible]
Nieu Hollant op het eilant Manhattan namaels N[illegible]
toen het geraeckte in t gebiet der Engelsen

AMSTELODAMUM recens, postea Anglis anno [illegible]
[illegible] norum Hollandiae novae, [illegible] Americae
Mexicanae [illegible] Septentrionalis appellatum.

[illegible] Amsteld. [illegible]

PL. 6

TOTIUS NEOBELGII NOVA ET ACCURATISSIMA TABULA.
AMERICÆ SEPTENTRIONALIS PARS
NOVA FRANCIÆ PARS
NOVA ANGLIA
NOVA BELGICA sive NIEUW NEDERLANDT
NIEUW ENGELANDT
NIEUW JORCK
NIEU JARSEY
MAR DEL NORT
oft NOORDT ZEE
VIRGINIÆ PARS
Charioquet
Quebecq
Canomakers
Armenmecks
Senecaas
Minnessinck offe 't Landt van Bacham
Gachens
Capitanasses
Maranac
koufes
Konekotays
Minquaas
Sasquesahanough
Tockwoghs
Horikans
Sequins
Mahikans
Wapenocks
Horicans
Nieuw Amsterdam

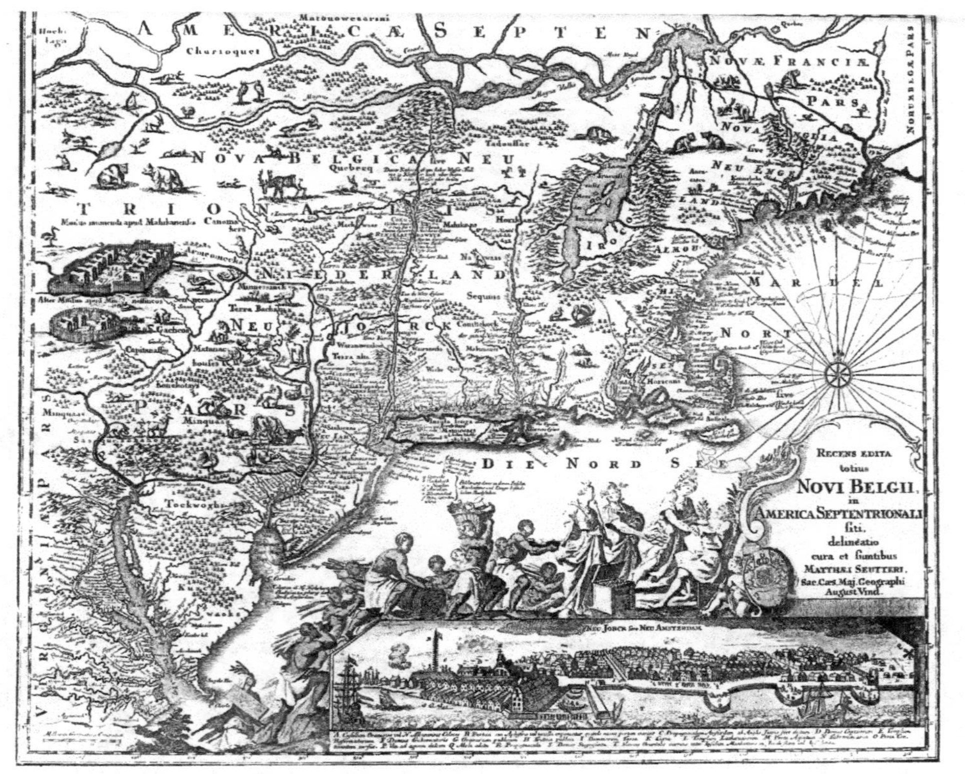
Recens edita
totius
Novi Belgii,
in
America Septentrionali
siti,
delineatio
cura et sumtibus
Matthæi Seutteri,
Sac. Cæs. Maj. Geographi
August. Vind.
Americæ Septentrionalis
Novæ Franciæ Pars
Nova Anglia
Neu Engeland
Nova Belgica sive Neu Niederland
Neu Jorck
Nova Suecia
Mar del Nort
Die Nord See
Virginia Pars
Norumbegæ Pars
Chartoquet
Matouweskarini
Quebecq
Tockwoghs
Minquas
Terra Bachan
Capitanasses
Sequins
Hochelaga
Neu Jorck sive Neu Amsterdam

PL. 16 A

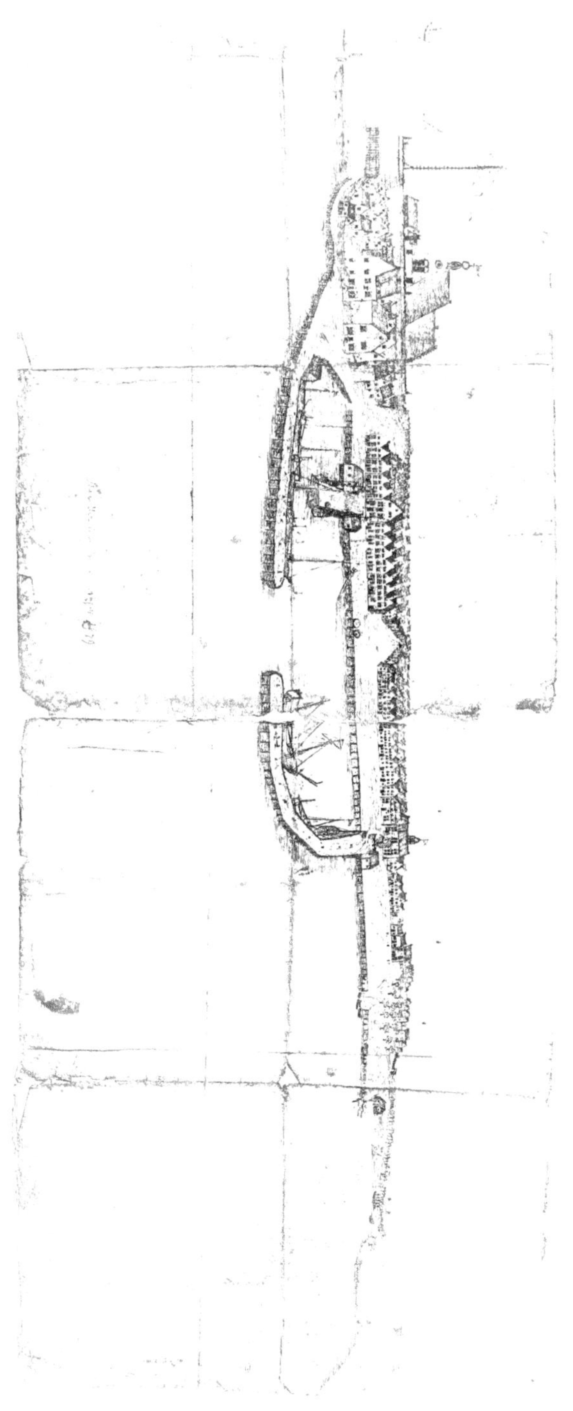

PL 18

Nyork van achteren of van de
noort kant,

PL. 20.

VIEW OF NEW YORK FROM THE NORTH. 1679

Pl. VIII.

[illegible]

Pl. 2

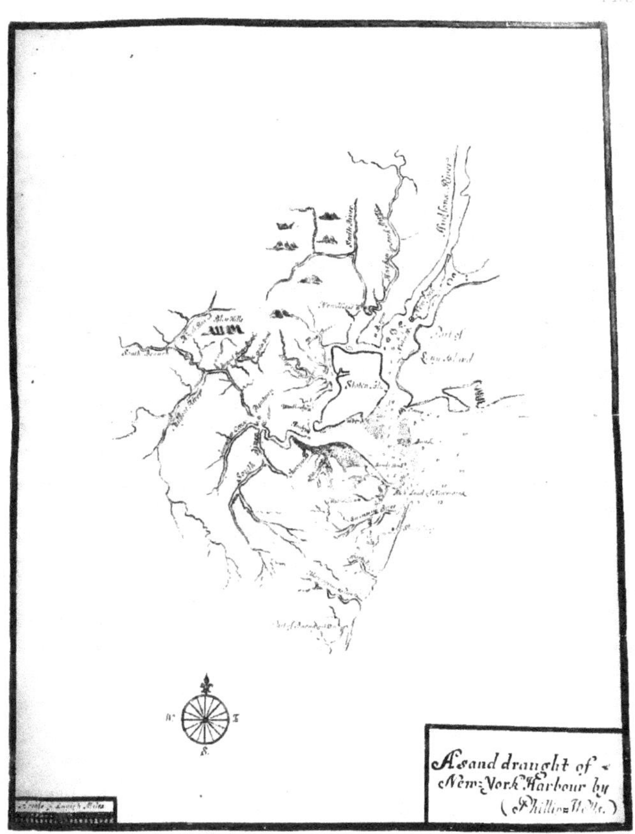
Hudsons River
Part of Long Island
Staten Is.
A sand draught of
New York Harbour by
(Phillip Wells.)

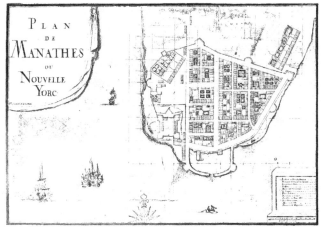

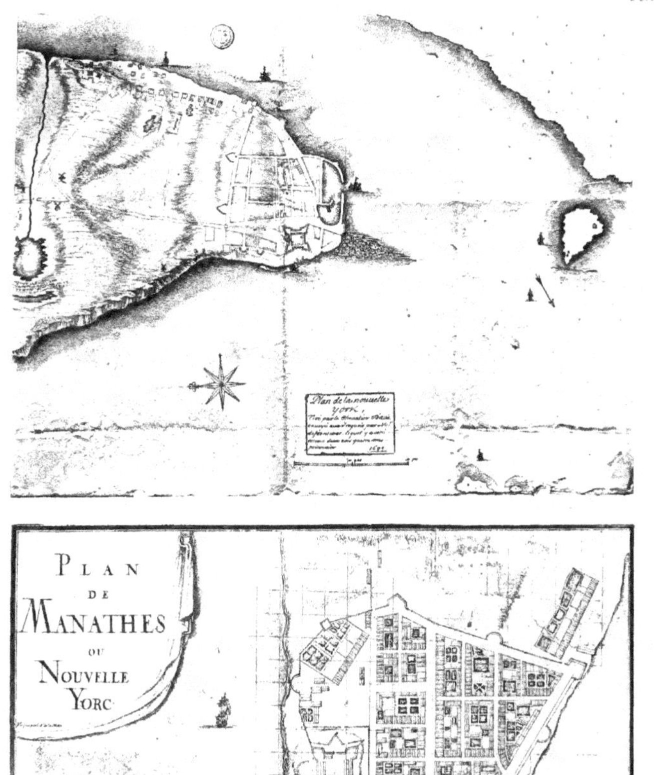
Plan de la nouvelle
york,
PLAN
DE
MANATHES
OU
NOUVELLE
YORC

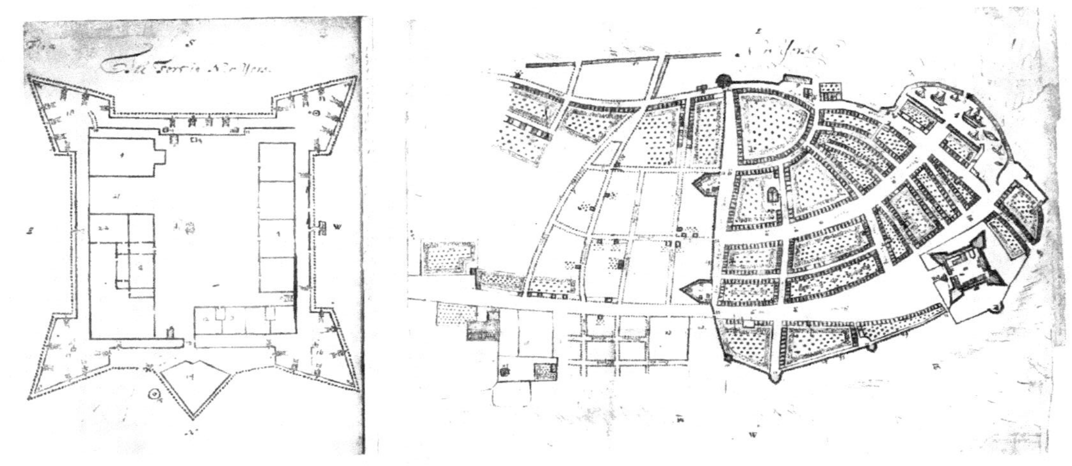

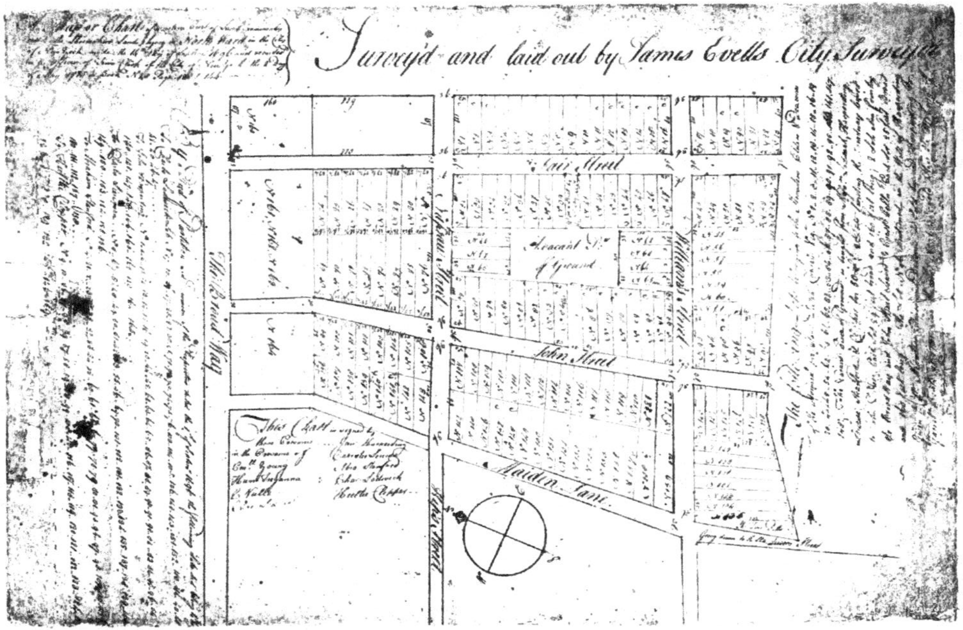

Surveyd and laid out by James Evetts City Surveyor

Fair Street

Nassau Street

Williams Street

John Street

Maiden Lane

Kip's Street

The Broad Way

Vacant Pc. of Ground

This Chart

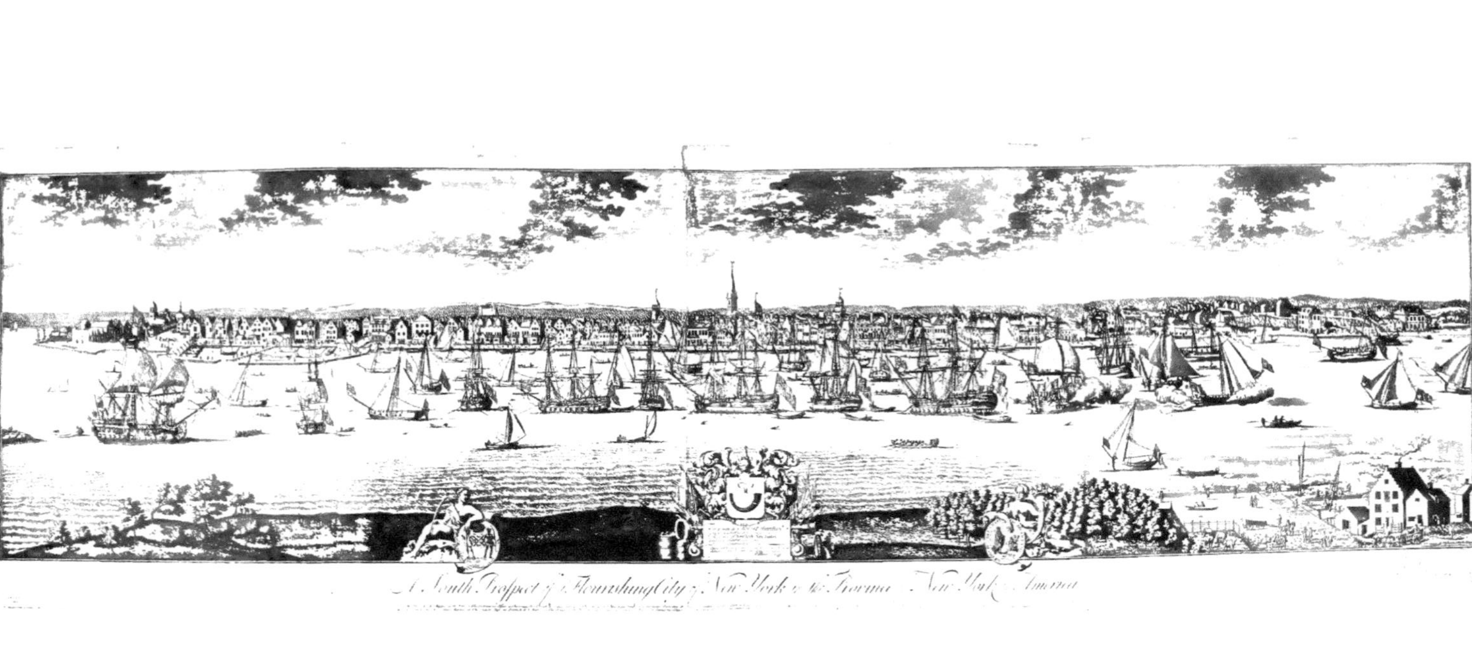

A South Prospect of ye Flourishing City of New York in the Province of New York in America

A PLAN
NEW YORK
James Lyne
HUDSON'S
RIVER
HARBOUR

Col. Robt. Lurting
MAYOR
JOHN MONTGOMERY ESQR.
Captain General and GOVENOR IN
CHIEF
PROVINCES
This Plan
CITY
NEW-YORK
RI

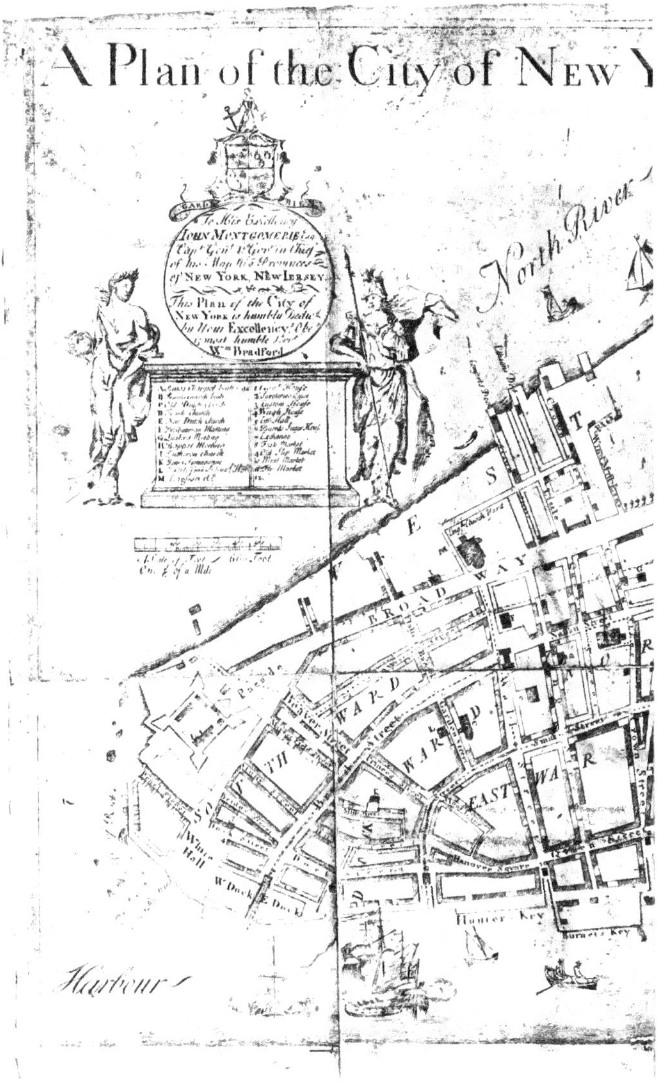

A Plan of the City of New Y

To His Excellency
JOHN MONTGOMERIE Esq
Capt Genl & Govr in Chief
of his Majesty's Provinces
of NEW YORK, NEW JERSEY

This Plan of the City of
NEW YORK is humbly Dedicated
to Your Excellency's Obedient
& most humble Servt
Wm Bradford

B
C
D
E New Dutch Church
F
G Quakers Meeting
H
I
K
L
M

1
2
3 Custom House
4
5 City Hall
6
7 Exchange
8 Fish Market
9 Old Slip Market
10 West Market
11
12

North River

Broad Way

Beaver Street

South Ward

East Ward

White Hall

Wt Dock

E Dock

Hanover Square

Hunter Key

Harbour

ORK from an actual Survey
Made by James Lyne
Col. Rob. Lurting
MAYOR
WARD
Kings Farm
COMMON
MONTGOMERIE'S
WARD

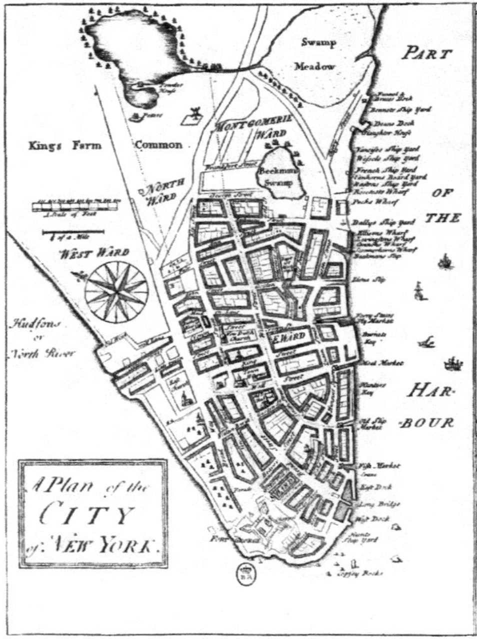

PL 27A

A Plan of the CITY of NEW YORK.

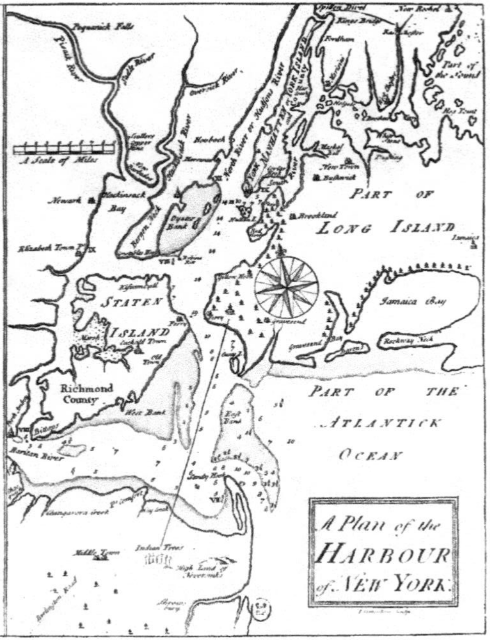

A Plan of the HARBOUR of NEW YORK.

Kings Farm

Common

Swamp

Meadow

MONTGOMERIE WARD

NORTH WARD

WEST WARD

Beckmans Swamp

Hudsons or North River

PART OF THE HARBOUR

A Scale of Miles

PART OF LONG ISLAND

STATEN ISLAND

Richmond County

PART OF THE ATLANTICK OCEAN

Jamaica Bay

This CHURCH
was founded
The Rev.
Mr Walter Du Bois
Mr Henry Boel
Ministers
To the Honourable
RIP VAN DAM. Esqr
PRESIDENT of His Majesty's Council for the PROVINCE of NEW YORK
This View of the New Dutch Church is most humbly
Dedicated by your Honours most Obedient Servt Wm Burgis

A
NEW MAP
of the
HARBOUR
of
NEWYORK
by a late Survey
Pequanock Falls
Elizabeth Town
Town pt.
STATEN
ISLAND
Woodbridge
THE CITY of PERTH AMBOY
RARITAN
PART
OF E
JERSEY
NEVER
SINK
HILL
Indian Trees
Shrewsbury
A Scale of Miles
HUDSON'S RIVER
PART
of the
SOUND
Flushing
PART OF
LONG ISLAND
Jamaica
JAMAICA
BAY
Rockaway Neck
BANK
NEWARK
BAY
Bergen Neck
Constables

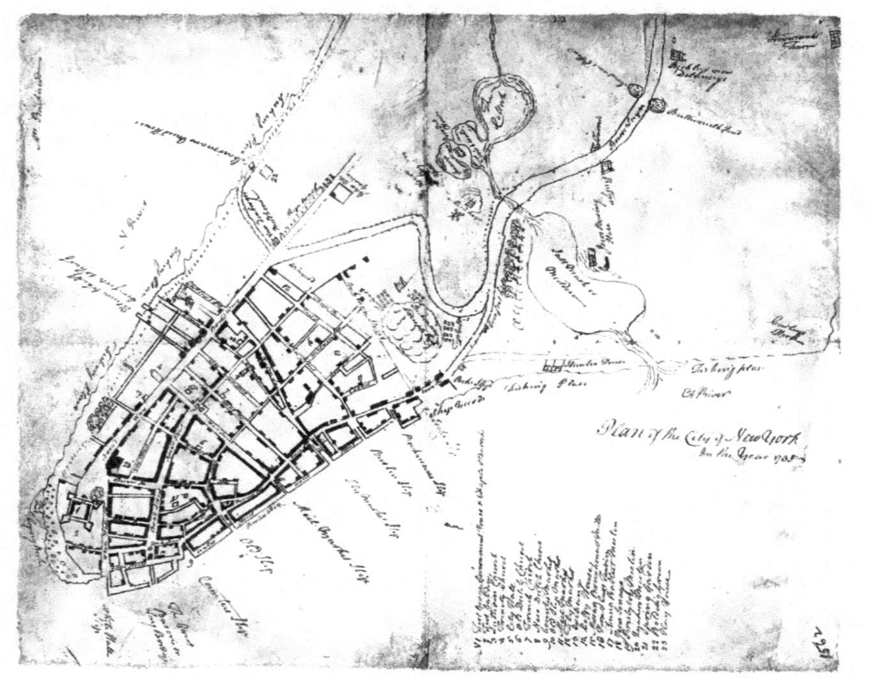
Plan of the City of New York

A View of FORT GEORGE *with th*

PL. 31.

CITY of NEW YORK from the S.W.

New York Historical Society
Fort George
Poor House
Lutheran Church
French Church
A PLAN OF THE CITY AND ENVIRONS OF NEW YORK

PL.

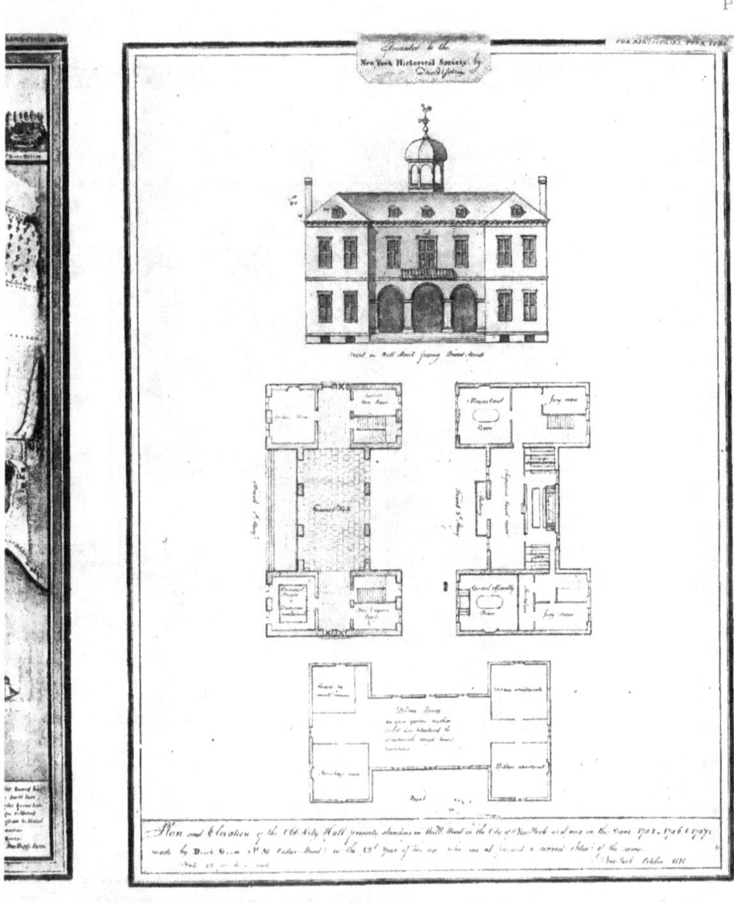
Presented to the
New York Historical Society by
Plan and Elevation of the Old City Hall

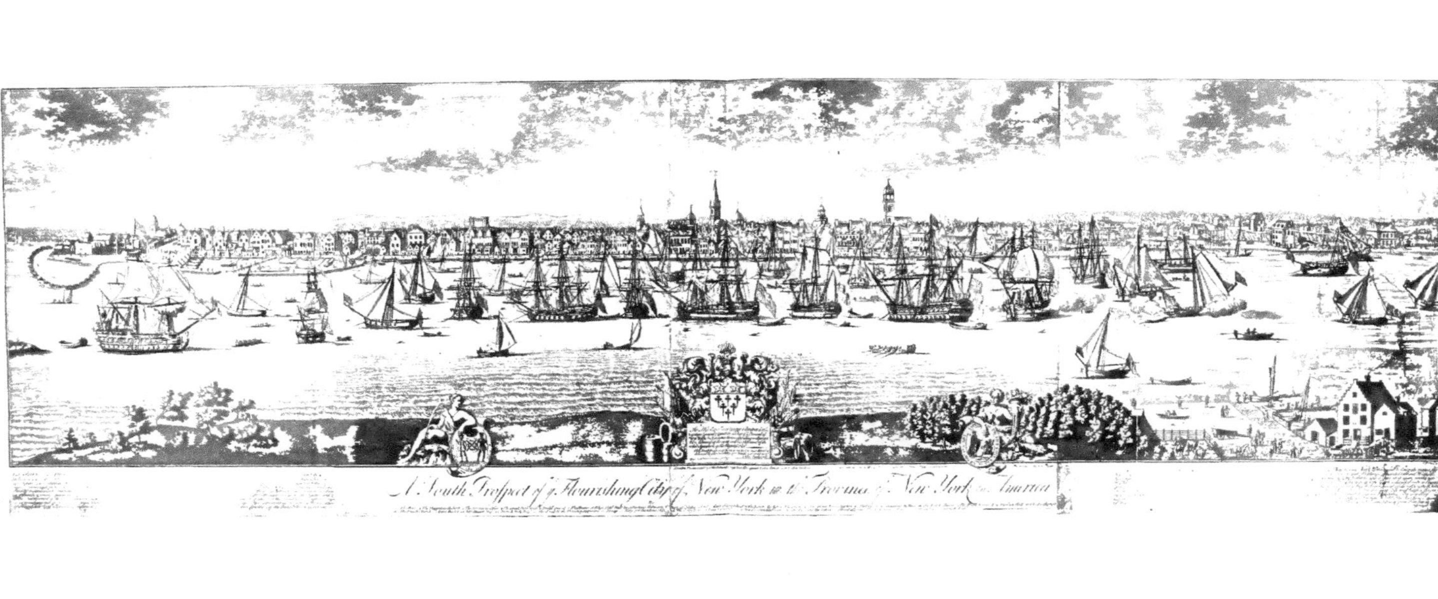
A South Prospect of y Flourishing City of New York in the Province of New York in America

A Plan of the City of New York from an
North River
Harbour
BROAD WAY
EAST WARD
Queen Street
William Street
Hunters Key
Common
Part of ye Kings Farm Lay'd Out in Lots

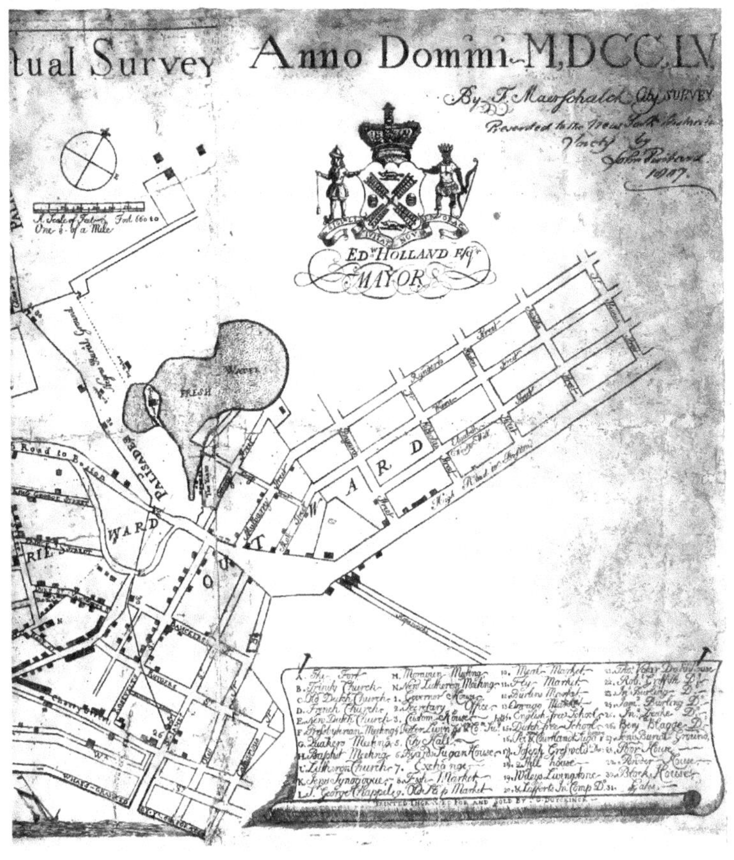
tual Survey Anno Domini MDCCLV
By F. Maerschalck City SURVEY
ED.W HOLLAND Esq.r
MAYOR
FRESH WATER
PALISADES
Road to Boston
WARD
OUT WARD
High Road to Boston
A. The Fort
B. Trinity Church
C. Old Dutch Church
D. French Church
E. New Dutch Church
F. Presbyterian Meeting
G. Quakers Meeting
H. Baptist Meeting
I. Lutheran Church
K. Jews Synagogue
L. St. George Chappel
M. Moravian Meeting
N. New Lutheran Meeting
1. Governor House
2. Secretary Office
3. Custom House
5. City Hall
6. Bayards Sugar House
7. Exchange
8. Fish Market
9. Old Slip Market
10. Meal Market
11. Fly Market
12. Burlins Market
13. Oswego Market
14. English free School
15. Dutch free School
18. Still house
19. Wileys Livingstone
28. Poor House
29. Powder House
30. Block House
31. Gallows
27. Jews Burial Ground

Pl. 35

PL. 36

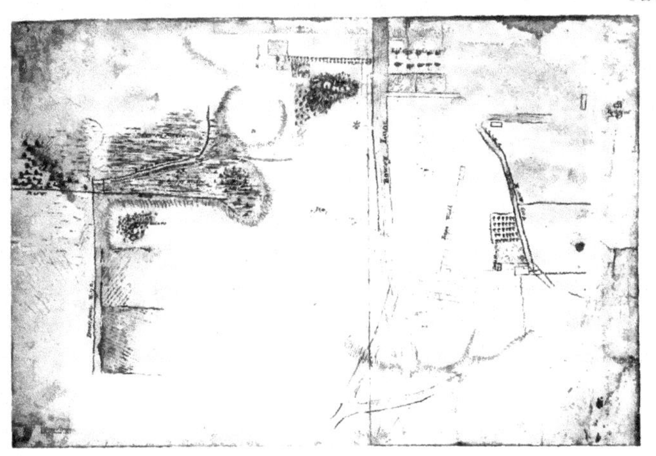

A South West View of the City of New York, in NORTH AMERICA. | Vue de Sud Ouest de la Ville de New York, dans L'AMERIQUE SEPTENTRIONALE

Drawn on the Spot by Capt. Thomas Howdell of the Royal Artillery. Engraved by P. Canot

PL. 38.

A South East View of the City of New York in NORTH AMERICA. Vue du Sud Est de la Ville de New York dans L'AMERIQUE SEPTENTRIONALE.

Drawn on the Spot by Capt. Thomas Howdell of the Royal Artillery. Engraved by P. Canot.

PL. 39

VIEW of HARLAEM from MORISANIA in the *PROVINCE* of NEW YORK *Septem.r 1765.*

DESCRIPTION OF PLATES

10–39

1664–1763

PLATE 10

A DESCRIPTION OF THE TOWNE OF MANNADOS OR NEW-AMSTERDAM

["The Duke's Plan"]

Wash drawing on heavy vellum, brilliantly coloured and heightened with gold.	27¼ x 21¾	Date depicted: September, 1661. Date issued: 1664.

Provenance: No. 35 in Vol. CXXI of the King's Collection of maps, plans, views, etc., contained in one hundred and twenty-four folio volumes, several of which are subdivided into two or more parts, and preserved in the British Museum. Vols. CXVIII, CXIX, CXX, CXXI, and CXXII contain documents relating to North America. Vol. CXXI (K. 121) refers to New York State only. This splendid collection was gathered by George III, and presented to the nation by George IV.

On the reverse side of the plan is written in a contemporary, or at least in an ancient hand, "A description of ye Towne of Mannados or New Amsterdam," also the words, "New Amsterdã" and the figure "3," an old number, and not the number of the volume in which it is now found.

Author: It is possible that this plan was drawn by Augustine Herrman, who did not remove to Maryland until 1661, or it may have been the work of Jacques Cortelyou or of William Hack, or perhaps of de la Montagne, whose Maps of New Guinea, accompanying the "[Jesse] de Forest Journal," it closely resembles, or more likely still, of some quite unknown draughtsman.

This beautiful and important plan, or rather bird's-eye view, which had lain unheeded for two centuries, was re-discovered in 1858 by George H. Moore, Librarian of the New York Hist. Society, who had a facsimile made (now in the Society's collections) which was reproduced by lithography at the same size as the original, in Valentine's *Manual* for 1859, p. 548. Mr. Moore gave to this view the name of "The Duke's Plan." This may be a copy of the original map surveyed by Jacques Cortelyou in the summer of 1660, or of his second map, surveyed in 1661, and drawn by Van de Water (see Chronology). The former was referred to by Governor Stuyvesant in a letter to the West India Company, dated

October 6, 1660.—*N. Y. Col. Docs.*, XIV: 486, and Chronology. In a letter acknowledging the receipt of this map, the directors comment upon the vacant lots between Smee (William) Street and Princes Gracht (Broad Street above Exchange Place), etc., "where the houses apparently are surrounded by excessively large lots and gardens; perhaps with the intention of cutting streets through them, when the population increases, although if standing closer together, a defense might be easier."—*Ibid.*, 489; see Chronology, June 7, 1660. See also *Nar. N. Neth.*, Preface, viii (quoted in Chronology, 1661), where Jameson draws attention to the close resemblance between the title on this map and that on the manuscript *Description* recently found among the papers of the Royal Society of London, Guard Book, No. 7, Part I.

It will be noticed that on the plan the gates of the Fort are correctly shown in the middle of its north and south sides, and not as stated in the *Description* "on the east and west." The church is erroneously shown in the north-west instead of in the south-east corner of the Fort. This is an error which it is hard to explain, as there is no reason to suppose that the church ever stood elsewhere than in the south-east part of the Fort. The date 1664 and the British flags on the ships, suggest that the map, although probably drawn by a Dutchman in 1661, or copied from a Dutch original, was redrawn or embellished by Governor Nicolls's instructions, and sent to his royal patron, the Duke of York, to show the condition of the city at the time of its capture.

The manuscript *Description* fits conditions not later than 1662, nor earlier than 1661, when Wiltwyck (Esopus), to which it refers, was formed into a stockaded village "a smal town of 60. Dutch families" (Jameson's *Nar. N. Neth.*, 422). The date of this text can, therefore, be fixed within narrow limits.

Why was this map inscribed "as it was in September 1661"? And why was the manuscript *Description* of Mannadens written "as it was in Sept: 1661"? Were both perhaps, the work of spies acting in the English interest?

In September, 1661, the English had designs for sending a force against New Netherland for its reduction, and proposals were made by the Dutch, upon receiving intelligence of the English scheme, to fortify the City of New Amsterdam and to strengthen Fort Amsterdam (dated September 22, 1661, *Cal. Hist. MSS., Dutch*, 229). Nothing came of this proposed invasion in this year, although some of the Long Island towns were annexed to New England in 1662. Was the manuscript *Description*, then, a spy's report of the state of New Netherland in September, 1661, when the English invasion was threatened, and has the *Description* a party relation to the so-called "Duke's Plan"? As we have already seen, the text and the map do not always agree, which would be singular if they had ever belonged together.

The most plausible solution of this interesting problem seems to be the following: From the Minutes of the Burgomasters it appears that Jacques Cortelyou, the surveyor-general, stated on January 26, 1662, that so far as his part of the work on "the map of the City" was concerned, it was done, and the results had "already been in the hands of van der Veen for 6 weeks; he [the second party, not Cortelyou] promises to have it ready this week." On March 3d, Jacob van de Water [not van der Veen] was "allowed . . . for making the map of this City" his pay. It seems evident that "van der Veen" is a slip in the records for "van de Water," and it would appear therefore that Jacob van de Water was the draughtsman. As he was paid 100 florins, wampum, for his work, while Cortelyou, who did the surveying and handed over to the draughtsman all his materials, was allowed, on March 10, but the same amount in heavy money, it seems clear that the drawing must have been an elaborate one, a fact which is further emphasised by Cortelyou's statement (Exec. Min. of Burgomasters, in *Min. of Orphanmasters Court*, II: 130.—See also Chronology 1662, March 10) that his work alone would have paid him in Holland as much as "100 ryksdaalders."

If we count back six weeks from January 26, 1662, we reach a date before the middle of December, 1661, as the time when Cortelyou had completed his part of the work and had handed it over to Jacob van de Water. This would make it quite possible that his survey had been completed a few months earlier, and actually showed the city "as it was in September 1661." If this theory be accepted, it seems altogether likely that the so-called "Duke's Plan" was founded upon Cortelyou's second survey, although it was probably not drawn until 1664, when the English took possession of the city and the English fleet was in the harbour. In this connection see remarks on Castello Plan (Appendix, III).

Prof. Archer B. Hulbert, of Marietta College, in his *Crown Collection of Photographs of American Maps*, V: 24, suggests that this plan may have been drawn by William Hack. According to Christopher A. Hack (*William Hack and his Descendants*—copy in Library of Congress), Hack settled in Taunton, Mass., about the year 1660. In 1664 he went to England to settle his affairs, leaving his wife and son here and intending to return the following summer, but he never came back. In June, 1667, his wife received from the court at Plymouth letters of administration (*Rec. Colony New Plymouth*, IV: 155).

A comparison of this plan with a collection of manuscript maps by William Hack, preserved in the Library of Congress and known as the "Buchaneer Atlas," develops many points of similarity. This similarity is especially striking in the title-page, which is signed by William Hack, but the handwriting throughout seems different. There is in the British Museum (Add. MS. 5415) an important map of North America north of Virginia by William Hack, which shows the French and English possessions. This map bears the date 1684, which apparently refutes the theory that Hack did not return to America. There is also, in the possession of the Pilgrim Society of Plymouth, Mass., a map in colour of New England, signed by William Hack, and dated 1663. Both of these bear a marked resemblance in technique to the present map. The latter is by some cartographers considered to be the original from which John Seller's important "Mapp of New England" was derived.

It is interesting to compare "The Duke's Plan" with the inset plan on the "Nicolls Survey" (Pl. 10-A). *Cf.* also Castello Plan (Appendix, III), and Map of Original Dutch Grants (Appendix, IV).

The Governours Garden, here shown on the west side of Broadway, and within the wall, extended about 70 feet north of the north side of the present Rector Street, by which it was intersected, and 150 feet south. It is worthy of note that the map shows no sign of the cemetery south of the Governours Garden, so prominent a feature on the Castello and Nicolls Plans. The mill north-west of the Fort is the well-known Fort mill, which appears here for the last time. The Governours House, seen at the east of the present Whitehall, was built prior to 1658 (see discussion of topography on Labadist View, Pl. 17). Just east of the Governours House can be seen Stuyvesant's little wharf, built in 1648–9 (see Chronology); and east of this, at the foot of the present Moore Street, the Custom House Bridge and the Weigh-house, which last was removed to this ocation in 1659.

The Stadt Huys, with the roundout in front of it, is a prominent feature on the shore, just east of the Graft. Note the Water Gate, designed by Captain Fredrick de Koningh in 1656.—See Chronology, February 1, 1656.

This is the first plan to show three bridges over the Graft at Beaver Street, only two appearing on the Castello Plan, the one below Beaver Street having, therefore, been built after the original of the Castello Plan was made, and prior to September, 1661, the date appearing upon the present drawing. These *three* bridges, as well as those near the mouth of the Graft, are also referred to in the *Description of the Towne of Mannadens, 1661* (quoted *in extenso* in Chronology):

> Within the towne, in the midway between the N. W. corner and N. E. gate, the ground hath a smal descent on each side much alike, and so continues through the town unto the arme of the water on the Easterside of the Towne: by the help of this descent they have made a gut almost through the towne, keyed it on both sides with timber and boards as far in as the 3. small bridges; and near the coming into the gut they have built two firme timber bridges with railes on each side. At low water the gut is dry, at high water boats come into it, passing under the 2. bridges, and go as far as the 3 small bridges.—Jameson's *Nar. N. Neth.*, 423.

Outside of the wall, to the east of the Land Gate, are a number of houses, part of the original Damen grant, referred to in the De Sille List (1660, July 10; see Chronology) as standing outside of the Heere Poort, on the road to Haerlem. The small square just north of these houses was probably the grant on the south-east corner of Maiden Lane and Broadway, belonging at this period to Abraham Verplanck, who had acquired it from the Damen heirs. Jan Pietersen Verbrugge's Garden is shown to the west of the Land Gate, just outside the wall. In 1662 this plot was petitioned for as a new burial ground. The beginning of the large square on the west of the Heere Straet (Broadway), and somewhat farther north, was probably intended to indicate the West India Company's land, later the Duke's Farm, etc., the southern boundary of which lay along Fulton Street. The irregularly shaped enclosed area stretching along the East River from the Water Gate to the ferry was the Smith's Fly, referred to in the De Sille List as the Voorstadt, or suburb. The street or passage dividing it was undoubtedly the present Maiden Lane. At the north-eastern extremity of Smith's Fly is seen "Alderton's" (Allerton's) Building, enclosed by a wall or palisade; the pier or roundout which appears at this point on the Nicolls Plan (Pl. 10A-a) had evidently not been built in September, 1661. The Passage Place on the shore a short distance further to the north was the Manhattan end of the ferry to "Breuckelen." The water-mill on the shore at the outlet of the Fresh Water, still further to the north, was Pietersen's mill, shown as "Old Mill" on the Nicolls Survey. It stood about at the intersection of the present Pearl and James Streets.

Reproduction: Valentine's *Manual*, 1859.

Plate 10 A–a

The Island of Manhados (with inset plan of) The Towne of New-York [The Nicolls Map or Survey]

Pen and ink drawing on paper. 54 x 18 Date depicted: 1664–8.
Owner: British Museum, Additional MS. No. 16371.

This interesting and accurate survey evidently depicts the Island and Town during the early years of the English occupation, as is plainly indicated by a note affixed to Stuyvesant's Bouwery: "The Governers that was last his Bowry." It was probably prepared for Governor Nicolls soon after his arrival. The Bouwery Church, probably built in 1660, is distinctly shown, being recognisable by its steeple (*Eccles. Rec.* I: 489, 490). East of the Church, near the shore, is a somewhat confused series of lines which may possibly be intended to represent the "Treffelyck Huys" (see Manatus Maps, Appendix, II), on the site of which "Petersfield" was later built.

The map is particularly interesting as showing the early road system at the southern end of the Island. There is, however, no sign of the wagon-road which was finally authorised by Lovelace on February 24, 1669, and ordered finished by "May next" (*Exec. Coun. Min.*, I: 230–1, edited by V. H. Paltsits). The settlement at "New Haerlem" is shown, as well as the various settlements and the ferry on Long Island. It is interesting, also, to note the "Old Mill" at the mouth of the outlet from the Fresh Water. This mill was probably erected in 1658, as, on April 2d of that year, Abraham Pietersen received permission from the Director and Council of New Netherland "to erect a water mill on the Fresh water, New Amsterdam."—*Cal. Hist. MSS., Dutch*, 193. On April 20, 1661, Pietersen sold this mill to Jan Cornelissen van Hoorn for 1700 guilders "good current wampum" (La Chair's *Register*). Van Hoorn, on September 7th of the same year, sold the mill to Cleyn Jan Cornelissen and Reyer Cornelissen Suysbergen, and on the following day Abraham Pietersen, "Molenaer," made a quit-claim deed to the last-mentioned parties, reciting: "Before us, the undersigned Schepens of the City of Amsterdam in New Netherland appeared Abraham Pietersen Molenaer, burger and inhabitant of this citty who declares by virtue of an appointment dated September 18, 1657, to cede and convey unto Cleyn Jan Cornelissen and Reyer Cornelissen Suysbergen his certain right to a water-mill and dependencies which he hath obtained on the 18th September, aforesaid [1657] from the Right Honorable Director-General and Council of New Netherlands . . . conveying the mill with all that is therein earth-fast and nail-fast . . . said mill standing on the shore of the East River at the Fresh Water east of the Potter's Bakery. Same as Jan Cornelissen van Hoorn who purchased said mill from Abraham Pietersen and sold it to Cleyn Jan Cornelissen and Reyer Cornelissen Suysbergen on September 7, 1661."—*Liber Deeds*, A: 241. O'Callaghan, in his notes on mills, preserved in the N. Y. Hist. Society, locates this mill "four rods from the Pottebacker's Hill," evidently from Albany records. See Chronology 1661, April 20, and 1664, August 27.

The partnership of Reyer Cornelissen [Suysbergen] and Jan Cornelissen Cleyn [Cleyn Jan Cornelissen] terminated the following year, the former having been accused by the latter of theft. On April 28, 1662, Cornelissen was found guilty and was condemned "to be taken to the place, where criminal justice is usually executed and there to be tied to a stake, severely scourged and banished out of this City's jurisdiction for the term of ten years; further in the costs and mises of justice."—*Rec. N. Am.*, IV: 69–70.

An interesting fact, although apparently erroneously connected by Mrs. Lamb and others with this mill, perhaps because of its comparative proximity to Stuyvesant's Bowery, where the Articles of Capitulation were signed on September 6, 1664, is that "the copies of the King's grant to His Royal Highness and the copy of His Royal Highness's commission to Colonel Richard Nicolls" were to be "delivered to the Honourable M. Stuyvesant, the present Governor, on Monday next by eight of the clock in the morning, at the Old Mill." It seems unlikely that Pietersen's mill [1] is here referred to, and much more likely that the reference is to the old mill at the Fort, which we know, from Albany records under date of November 2, 1662, quoted by O'Callaghan (MS. notes

[1] Mrs. Van Rensselaer (*Hist. of the City of N.Y. in the Seventeenth Century*, I: 526) accepts the theory that the capitulation took place at Pietersen's mill, because it was the nearest place to the ferry landing opposite which, on the Brooklyn shore, the English troops were assembled; the ships of the fleet being at anchor near Coney Island.

in N. Y. Hist. Society), would "ere long be in ruins." Note that the mill at the mouth of the Collect has disappeared in the "Plan de la nouuelle York" of 1693 (Pl. 22-a).

A close comparison of the inset plan of "The Towne of New York" with the plan of the "Towne of Mannados" ("The Duke's Plan," so-called), which is supposed to depict the town as it was in 1661, shows the former to represent a somewhat later period. For example, the Nicolls Plan gives the roundout at the eastern extremity of Wall Street, which does not appear on "The Duke's Plan." This roundout, as we know from the manuscript *Description of the Towne of Mannadens* (Jameson's *Nar. N. Neth.*, 421), was contemplated, although not built, in September, 1661. It must have been built shortly after this date, as it appears on the Castello Plan (Pl. 10A-b). This roundout appears also in the Allard series of views, beginning with the Restitutio View of 1673 (Pl. 8-b).

It is interesting also to note that the ground on the river front north of Coenties Slip seems to be filled in beyond the point shown on "The Duke's Plan," and an extra row of houses appears facing the Quay. As the West India Company's Garden is so named in the key, and as it, together with all of the possessions of the West India Company, was confiscated by Nicolls on June 22, 1665, it seems probable that the survey was made just prior to this date. The wind-mill, so prominently shown, was probably erected in the latter part of 1663. The first reference to it is under date of November 2, 1662, when Jan De Wit and Denys Hartogvelt, carpenters, proposed to build a wind-mill outside of the Land Gate of the City, near the Company's Bouwery, if they could obtain the burr-stones and ironwork of the Company's Old Mill (the wind-mill near the Fort).—*Cal. Hist., MSS., Dutch*, 241; see Chronology 1662, November 2, for contract.

On September 22, 1663, after due consideration, the Company agreed to allow them the use of the wind-mill stones and ironwork, the grantees to pay the Company nothing "for the use of the Wind," but to grind a certain quantity of grain for the Company each week, free of toll. They were also "bound to build the new mill as soon as possible on the lot to be granted to them."—*Liber Deeds*, B: 34. Hartogvelt was replaced on the day the contract was concluded with the Company, i. e., September 22, 1663, by Jan Teunissen, from Leerdam, and, on April 4, 1664, De Wit sold his interest to Claes Jansen (*Liber Deeds*, B: 34). The West India Company owned a half interest in the mill, machinery, horse, cart, etc. In the last-mentioned conveyance of De Wit to Jansen, the property is described as "A lot for a house and garden, as mentioned in the ground-brief aforesaid and also the Windmill standing thereon. . . . The said lot and mill are situate without the Land Gate of this City about the Fresh Water, answering to the line of the Great Highway. . . . " At this time (September 22, 1663) the "Great Highway" (Broadway) had not been extended beyond its junction with the Boston Post Road. The mill was standing in 1714 (*M. C. C.*, III: 57), but by 1723 had been demolished, as is shown by a later entry in the *Minutes*, under date of December 17, 1723 (III: 335), wherein reference is made to "Land lying near the Commons of this City, near the *late* Windmill of Jasper Nessepot." For comparison and further information, see Manatus Maps, Castello and Harrisse copies (Appendix, II), and Castello Plan (Appendix, III).

Reproductions:

Crown Collection of Photographs of American Maps, by Prof. Archer B. Hulbert.

Full size, in *Executive Council Minutes*, edited by V. H. Paltsits, Albany, 1910.

Valentine's *Manual*, 1863, Frontispiece.

Plate 10A-b

Afbeeldinge van de Stadt Amsterdam in Nieuw Neederlandt. [The Castello Plan—1660]. For full description, see Appendix, III.

Plate 11-a

A Mapp of New Jarsey

[The Seller Map]

Engraved on copper. Map: 21 x 17 Date depicted: *c.* 1664.
View: 11⅞ x 2⅝

Provenance: John Seller's *Atlas Maritimus*, published by "J. Darby, for the author," London, 1675, No. 44 (Phillips's *Geographical Atlases*, No. 487. See also Phillips's Nos. 505 and 529; also C. Pl. 52).

Engraver: Ja: Clerk.

Owner: Library of Congress, Div. of Maps and Charts.

Other copies: Boston Public Library (complete atlas); John Carter Brown Library (complete atlas); British Museum; Edward W. C. Arnold, Esq.; I.N.P.S., etc.

First state. As the name New York appears in the first state, the date must be as late as 1664, and as the arms of Carteret, whose patent to New Jersey was confirmed in 1664, do not appear, it is altogether likely that the map was made in that year. It is highly probable that it was prepared immediately after the reception of the news in England of the capture of New Amsterdam by Nicolls on September 8, 1664. This is the earliest English map to contain a view of New York (the Visscher View), and so far as known, is the earliest view of the city published in England. The English series of maps, of which this is the first, is one of the rarest and most interesting which we possess.

A second state of this map, also with the Visscher View, bears, almost in the centre of the plate, the arms of Sir George Carteret, with a dedication to him in an ornamental cartouche below the arms, and the Royal Arms (crown and shield) in the lower right-hand corner. There are also many changes in the geographical contours and in the nomenclature in the neighbourhood of New York; for instance, the forms of Staten Island, the Harbour, Manhattan Island, Long Island, etc., are completely altered. The Hudson River is now marked "Hudsons River"; "Manhattans Island" is written in two lines; New York City is marked "New York," in the water, and the city is indicated by a square, instead of a circular fort. Staten Island is so marked instead of "States Island," and bears the names of seven plantations, viz: three marked "Dutch Plantation," one "French Plant," one "Danne Plant," one "Dodelus Plant," and one "Lovelace his pla." In altering the shape of Long Island, East River, etc., all the names on the first state have been deleted, both on the mainland of New York Province and on Long Island, with the single exception of "Maresipe." The soundings in the harbour (shown in the first state) are also entirely deleted. Sandy Hook is now engraved on a pointed spit differing in form from that shown on any of the other issues, etc. The absence in this second issue of the names on Long Island and of the soundings in the harbour suggests, at first sight, that this is an earlier state of the plate, but Mr. Henry N. Stevens, of London, who compared for the author the various states in the British Museum, draws attention to the fact that in this state "numerous faint traces of the alteration on the copper plate clearly indicate a later issue. For instance, traces of the old coast-line and of the dotted sand-bank off Long Island are clearly to be seen; the old name 'Mispat' can be fairly made out in the middle of New York Harbour, and traces of the mountain ranges between the stockade forts and Staten Island are also discernible." The British Museum ascribes the date 1665 to the second state, which is probably approximately correct. It is quite possible, as Mr. Stevens in a letter to the author points out, that the Carteret Arms were added to the map soon after February 10, 1664 (5), when Berkeley and Carteret, to whom New Jersey had been leased by the Duke of York in June, 1664 (when it received its name), signed "The Concessions and agreements of the Lords Proprietors of New Jersey to and with all and every of the adventurers and all such as shall settle and plant there." The only copies in this state (second) known to the author are an impression in the British Museum and one (January, 1914) in the possession of Mr. Robert Fridenberg.

Reproduced and described here for the first time.

Plate 11-b

A Mapp of New Jersey in America

[The Seller-Fisher Map]

Engraved on copper.	Map: 21 x 17 in.	Date depicted: 1676.
	View: 11⅛ x 2⅞ in.	Date issued: 1676–7.

Publishers: John Seller and William Fisher.

Owner: Percy R. Pyne, 2d, Esq.

Other copies: Library of Congress, Div. of Maps and Charts; Boston Public Library; British Museum, etc.

Probably the third state of the map last described. The plate has been so strangely altered as to be almost unrecognisable, the most noticeable change being the substitution of the Allard for the Visscher View, and its removal from the upper right to the lower left corner. The north branch of the Delaware, named "The River Delawar or South River," is extended to the right-hand upper corner of the map. The title is removed from the lower left corner and is now found at the top, in the centre, just above the Royal Arms, which remain the same as in the earlier states. The Carteret Arms and the dedication of the second state are deleted.

The map itself is greatly altered. The old main lettering "New Jarsey" is gone, and in its place we find "West Jer" and "East New Jersey," with a broken line between, bearing the incomplete inscription—"This is the Partition Line Between East" . . . The shapes of Staten Island, New York Harbour, Manhattan Island, Hudson River, Long Island, etc., are again altered. Numerous soundings again appear in the Harbour, and also outside of Sandy Hook, in the sea. New York is written New York, in two lines, on the Island. The Island itself is written "Manhattans I," in one line. "Bowray" and two other places are marked on the Island. Numerous names of places now appear on both sides of the Hudson River and on Long Island. "Part" appears on the mainland of New York Province; Staten Island is now written "Staten I.," and no plantations are shown, as they were on the second state, the only place now named on the Island being "Dover." Sandy Hook is now called "Sandy Point."

This map cannot have been issued before 1676, for it shows the boundary line between West Jersey and East New Jersey, which was not run until that year. If issued separately, it is not likely that it was published later than 1676, because in 1677 the same map was reissued (fourth state?) with two side flaps and four columns of text added on a flap at the bottom, increasing the size to about 36¾ by 22¼ inches. These flaps were engraved on separate plates and the impressions pasted on the main map covering up the side borders of the original plate.[1] The text bears the title "The Description of the Province of West Jersey in America," and the imprint at the foot of column four: "London, Printed for John Seller at the Hermitage stairs in Wapping, and William Fisher at the Posterngate on Tower-Hill, 1677." The incomplete letterings of the third state on the main map are now completed on the wing on the right side, viz., "sey," "and West Iersey" and "of New York." Two copies only of this state are known, one (uncoloured), in the John Carter Brown Library, Providence, R. I., bound up with a collection of thirteen manuscript and thirty-five printed maps, forming a part of the important Blathwayt Collection, sold in London by Sotheby on April 25, 1910, the other (coloured) belonging originally to Mr. Henry Stevens, of Vermont and London, and lately offered for sale by Messrs. Dodd & Livingston.

A careful examination of this map (third state) discloses traces of the Carteret Arms above and below "ew" and "Jer" of East New Jersey. Traces are also discernible of the dotted line of the sand-bank near Staten Island, and in the lower left corner are distinctly seen traces of the lettering preceding the scale of miles under the cartouche of the first state, so that there can be no doubt that this is from the original plate.

A contemporary black-letter broadside, pasted on the inner cover of a copy of the John Seller Atlas (1675) in the Boston Public Library, in the name of King Charles, and under date 22d March, 167$\frac{0}{1}$, records the appointment of John Seller, "Hydrographer in Ordinary," and bestows upon him for thirty years the sole right to sell the *English Pilot* and the *Sea Atlas*, "two large Treatises of Navigation" which he "hath been for these several years last past Collecting and composing." This seems to prove that the *Sea Atlas* was originally published not later than 1671.

Reproduced and described here for the first time.

Plate 12

Nowel Amsterdam en l Ameriqve* 1672

[The Jollain View]

Engraved on copper. 19¾ x 12⅜ Dated 1672, although the title, the description, and the inset map all refer to the period of Dutch occupation.

Date issued: 1672?.

Provenance: No. 71, evidently from a book, or collection of views (see below).

Artist: Jollain.

Owner: I.N.P.S.

Other copies: Library of Congress, Div. of Maps and Charts (without number in lower right corner); British Museum; Holden Collection (imperfect copy), now

[1] Although Mr. Stevens is confident that the map here reproduced is a separate third state, and that the dated side flaps described below belong to a distinct later issue, it seems to the author quite possible that the so-called third state here reproduced is in reality only the centre portion (doubtless also issued separately, as seems to be proved by the fact that the border lines are continuous on all four sides) of the complete issue in the John Carter Brown Library, which theory is strengthened by the fact that, on the former, only the first three letters of the word "Jersey" appear.

(January, 1914) in the possession of Mr. Robert Fridenberg. These are the only copies known to the author.

Only known state, except as noted above. This, because of its early date, is by far the most interesting of the fictitious views of New York. A careful inspection of the original print reveals the existence of reference numbers, traces of about twenty of which can be made out with the aid of a glass. From the fact that these have been, for the most part, obliterated, it seems probable that the print was previously issued in some other combination, or collection, and was accompanied by a description corresponding to the reference numbers.

Notice Quebec and Le Chateau de Nassau, perched on little hills just outside of the city wall! Notice, also, in the upper right-hand corner, the ship surrounded by a wreath, probably intended to represent the "Half Moon."

In the Library of Congress (Phillips's *Geographical Atlases*, No. 477), there is an atlas bearing the title "*Trèsor des cartes géographiqves des principavx estats de lvnivers*" and the imprint "Paris, chez Jollain." A majority of the maps in this atlas are signed "Jollain excudit 1667." In Muller's Catalogue, *Geographie-Voyages* (1911), No. 4126, is described a "mappemonde" by Jud. Hondius, with the imprint of Jollain, Paris. Mr. H. N. Stevens, of London, and Mr. Soulsby, formerly head of the map-room of the British Museum, and now transferred to the South Kensington Branch, have made a careful search of all the collections of views of cities in the British Museum, but, although they discovered a similar view of Parma, bearing no reference number, but having an exactly similar imprint, and with Latin and French text below, they were unable to determine the provenance of this view. The Bibliothèque Nationale has no views or maps bearing the name of Jollain. Frederik Muller & Co. possessed in 1911, and recently sold to Mr. Arthur G. Doughty, Dominion Archivist, at Ottawa, a made-up atlas in old vellum, bearing the manuscript title, "Plans des principales Cites de l'Univers, Amsterdam, by Danker Dankerts," and containing fifty plates, mostly bird's-eye perspective plans. Among these, the following bear the name of Jollain, and have at the foot a description in Latin and French:

†[22] Besanson
[24] Boulogne
Seville
[31] London
[32] Stockholm
[49] Nowel Amsterdam en L Ameriqve* 1672.

Two only of these views are numbered,—Besanson, 26, and Nowel Amsterdam, 71.

The view of Seville has the address: "A Paris chez Iollain rue St. Jacques a la ville de Cologne." The view of Besanson is dated 1674. A view of Jerusalem, not noted by the author when he examined this collection in Amsterdam, but referred to by Dr. Wieder in a subsequent letter, has the address in Latin: "Paresiis apud Gerardum Jollain Via Jacobea Urbe Coloniae."

Besides the signed views, there are in this volume a number in the same style, but without descriptions, evidently copies from Jollain. One of these, "Olisippo Lisbona," is practically identical with the Nowel Amsterdam plate. Dr. Wieder recognised this

[†] This and the following numbers indicate the order of the views in this collection.

view (Olisippo Lisbona) as being an almost exact copy of one published in *Le Theatre de plusieurs Plans et Profils des plus renommeez Villes de l'Europe*, Amsterdam, Frederick de Wit, 1660–80. This latter view is, however, itself a copy from one originally published in the *Civitates orbis terrarum Coloniae*, Braun & Hogenberg, 1576–1618. Impressions of these two views are in the author's collection.

Of other fictitious views of New York, the best known form part of a series issued by F. X. Habermann in Augsbourg about 1776, for use in "Peep" shows. The subjects represented are as follows: 1 View of the Fort; 2 The Destruction of the King's Statue; 3 The Triumphal Entry of the British Troops at New York; 4 The Landing of the British Troops at New York; 5 The terrible Fire at New York, 1776. Size about 10 by 15 inches. A similar series was issued, somewhat earlier, by B. Fr. Leizelt, also in Augsbourg.

Reproduced here for the first time.

Plate 13

Nieu Amsterdam, at New Yorck
[The Carolus Allard View]

Engraved on copper. 10¾ x 8⅜ Date depicted: 1673.
Date issued: *c.* 1700.

Provenance: No. 78 of the *Orbis Habitabilis* (etc.) of Carolus Allard, for a description of which see Bibliography. Vander Aa, in his *Biographisch woordenboek* (etc.), states that Carolus Allard was born in 1649, became a medical doctor in 1673, established himself in Amsterdam in 1685, published two topographical works on The Netherlands in 1711 and 1716, and died in 1720; and Moes says that he applied in 1683 for a privilege for his publications. Although a pencil note on the fly-leaf of the copy of the *Orbis Habitabilis* in the N. Y. Public Library states that C. Allard lived in Amsterdam from 1683 to 1689, our conclusion, based upon other publications of Allard which can be dated, and from works edited by Dr. Smids, who wrote the descriptive notes contained in the *Orbis Habitabilis*, would indicate a date of publication for this work at least as late as 1700, and probably later.

Engraver: T. Doesburgh, who made most of the views without figures contained in the book. The views with figures were engraved by A. Meijer.

Owner: I.N.P.S.

Other copies: N. Y. Public Library (complete collection); N. Y. Hist. Society, etc.

Probably the earliest state. This view, except for the foreground, is practically identical with the Restitutio View (Pl. 8-b, which see for historical notes), and depicts the city in 1673. Notice, however, that there are several slight modifications; for instance, the weigh-house, correctly placed on the Restitutio View, is here shown to the south of the Custom House Bridge, on the site where, in 1677, Andros erected the Custom House Market. The Custom House pier seems here to have been lengthened.

This is a good example of copper-plate engraving and has always been considered one of the most pleasing of the early views of New York.

A variant of this print, almost surely a later state, is owned by Mr. Percy R. Pyne 2d. It bears the imprint "Covens et Mortier exc. cum Priv. ord Holl et Westfr." The words "In America" have been added under the cartouche, and the index number or cipher "1" substituted for the original number "78" in the upper right-hand corner. The dimensions are the same. The plate shows signs of much wear, especially in the sky.

Plate 14-a
N: Amsterdam, ou N: Iork. in Ameriq̃:
[The Mortier View]

Engraved on copper. 9⅝ x 7¼ Date depicted: 1673.
Date issued: *c.* 1700.

Publisher: P. Mortier.
Owner: Metropolitan Museum of Art, Huntington Collection.
Other copies: Only one other copy of this view is known to the author, that in the University Library in Amsterdam, which is referred to below.

This view probably belonged to a series similar to those of Allard and Schenk, and issued about 1700. No such complete collection has been found, although the Library of the Metropolitan Museum of Art contains several similar views of South American cities, bearing Mortier's imprint, and in the Library of the University of Amsterdam there is a set of nineteen similar views, without title, and in a modern binding. All of these views have the address "P. Mortier, cum Privil:". The following twelve are of America:

1 N: Amsterdam, ou N: Iork, in Ameriq̃: (exactly similar to our view)
2 Cartagena, in Ameriq̃:
3 Iuan de Porto Rico, in Ameriq̃:
4 Fernambuco, in Ameriq̃.
5 S.t Salvador, in Ameriq̃.
6 Kallas de Lima, in Ameriq̃.
7 Kurason, in Ameriq̃.
8 Mexico, in Ameriq̃:
9 Havana, in Ameriq̃.
10 S.t Augus de Floride, in Ameriq̃.
11 Quebec, in Ameriq̃.
12 Cuso, in Ameriq̃.

The following seven views are of European and Asiatic subjects:

7 Madrid en Spagne
8 Rome ou Roma
2 Mecha, in Asie
4 Galen, in Asie
8 Smirna, in Asie
10 Goa, in Asie
11 Constantinopole, in Asie

These last are similar in size and execution to the American views, but evidently belong to an incomplete series. They also are numbered in the lower right margin, instead of in the etiquette. This series may possibly be a part of Mortier's edition of 1702 (Phillips's *Geographical Atlases*, No. 537), although Phillips's description does not mention the New Amsterdam view (see description Pl. 14-b).

Without doubt, this view is based upon the Restitutio View (Pl. 8-b), from which it differs but slightly. The weigh-house, as in the views from the *Orbis Habitabilis*, is erroneously placed, on the south instead of the north side of the "Bridge," and one roundout or pier is missing, probably errors in copying. It is possible that the original view from which this plate was engraved antedates that reproduced on the Restitutio Map, in which case the date of the building of the third roundout, appearing on the Restitutio View between the two here shown, would be fixed between 1670, when Lovelace's tavern, which is also here shown, was built, and 1673, the date depicted by the Restitutio View.

Our reproduction is made from the photogravure in Mr. Andrews's *New Amsterdam New Orange New York*, as the original in the Huntington Collection cannot be found.

Plate 14-b

Nieu Amsterdam at New York

[The Carolus Allard View, with figures]

Engraved on copper. 10⅝ x 8⅜ with border. Date depicted: 1673.
Date issued: *c.* 1700.

Provenance: From the *Orbis Habitabilis* of Carolus Allard. The number 79 appears in the upper right-hand corner of the view, although scarcely discernible in our reproduction.

Engraver: A. Meijer, who signed most of the costume plates in this book.

Owner: I.N.P.S.

Other copies: N. Y. Public Library (complete collection); N. Y. Hist. Society, etc.

The same view was reproduced from the same plate, very much worn, in P. Vander Aa's *La Galerie agréable du monde*, Leyden [1729].—See Bibliography. Curiously enough, Vander Aa had already engraved the Allard View, in reduced size, for an earlier work, published in 1726, with the name *Les Forces de l'Europe, Asie, Afrique et Amérique ou description des princip. villes avec leurs forteresses* (etc.).—See *Bibliotheca* Petri Vander Aa (1729), p. 339, No. 1025 (copy in N. Y. Pub. Library). This earlier publication of Vander Aa was based upon a collection of views, etc., first issued in Paris, in 1694-7, by N. de Fer. This latter work contained only one plate relating to America, a map of Quebec.—Phillips's *Geographical Atlases*, No. 517a. Pieter Mortier bought the publication of de Fer and reissued it in 1702 (?) with several additional plates on America (*Ibid.*, No. 537), and, in 1726, Vander Aa, who had purchased the edition of Mortier, issued it in augmented form, always with the same title, and with the addition of sixteen plates on America, including the New Amsterdam view (Muller's *Catalogue of Books, Maps, Plates, on America*, Amsterdam, 1872, Part I, No. 2). Part 20 of this last issue of *Les Forces de l'Europe* (etc.) contains in the list of plates the following: No. 498, "Nouvel Yorck &

Habits", and No. 499, "Barbados & Habits." These and a view of Quebec are the only plates of North American interest in the book. Vander Aa's *Les Forces de l'Europe* (etc.) was published in Paris and also in Leyden. It is exceedingly rare; apparently no copy exists in an American collection, although a copy of the New Amsterdam plate is owned by Mr. R. T. H. Halsey, and one by Mr. Percy R. Pyne, II.

The reduced view of Nieu Amsterdam, contained in the 1726 publication of Vander Aa, is a close copy of the original Allard plate, but lacks the engraver's name and the privilege notice, as well as the engraved reference number. It bears the manuscript reference number 498. The plate measures 7⅞ inches by 6⅝ inches, including border.

The view here reproduced is almost identical with No. 78 of the same collection (Pl. 13), but the ships, occupying the foreground in the latter, are replaced in the present view by two figures of natives. It is a curious fact that this view is much rarer than the one with the ships, issued in the same book. For a description of Allard's *Orbis Habitabilis*, see Bibliography.

Reproduced in Mr. Andrews's *New Amsterdam New Orange New York*, opp. p. 53.

Plate 15

Nieu Amsterdam, een stedeken in Noord Amerikaes Nieu Hollant, op het eilant Mankattan: namaels Nieu jork genaemt, toen het geraekte in't gebiet der Engelschen

[The Schenk View]

Engraved on copper. $9\frac{13}{16}$ x $7\frac{7}{16}$ Date depicted: About 1673.
Date issued: 1702.

Provenance: *Petri Schenkii Hecatompolis* (etc.), 1702.

Owner: From the M. C. D. Borden Collection.

Other copies: N. Y. Public Library (complete collection); N. Y. Hist. Society; Library of Congress; I.N.P.S., etc.

Earliest known state. The same plate, except with the reference number 92 in the lower right margin, appears in the *Afbeeldinge van een-Hondert der Voornaamste en sterkste Steeden in Europa*, by J. Roman, Amsterdam, 1752. There has been some discussion as to which is the earlier impression, that bearing the reference number 92 or that without it. The N. Y. Public Library possesses both issues, each apparently in its original condition. That without the numerals 92 appears in the *Hecatompolis*, bearing the date 1702, which would be conclusive were it not for the possibility that either the title-page or the print itself has been transposed. That *neither* has been transposed, however, seems to be proved by the fact that a copy of the *Hecatompolis* in the author's collection, also apparently in its original binding and condition, and bearing the date 1702, has every plate without a reference number, and not one shows any sign of an erasure; whereas the copy of Roman's *Hondert voornaamste Steeden* (etc.), in the N. Y. Public Library, has every plate numbered. This, together with the fact that in almost every case the impression without the reference number is the stronger and finer of the two, is almost conclusive proof that the number was a subsequent addition, a conclusion which is shared by Mr. Henry N. Stevens, Dr. Wieder, and Mr. Nijhoff.

A comparison of plate 57—Amsterdam—in the *Hondert voornaamste Steeden* (etc.), with the corresponding view in the *Hecatompolis* shows the former to have been struck from an entirely new plate, differing in many minor points from the view in the *Hecatompolis*, of which, however, it is very evidently a copy. As all of these views were undoubtedly sold separately, and as naturally there would have been a greater demand for the Amsterdam view than for any of the others, the plate probably became worn before the issue, in collected form, of this later series, and it, therefore, became necessary to engrave a new plate.

The view of New Amsterdam is copied from the prototype view on the Restitutio Map (Pl. 8–b), which see for historical notes.

Reproduction: Valentine's *Manual*, 1851, opp. p. 136.

Plate 16–a

Totius Neobelgii Nova et Accuratissima Tabula
[The Restitutio-Allardt Map]

Engraved on copper. Map: 21 x 18⅛, including title at top; without title: 17½ View: 15¼ x 2$\frac{13}{16}$ Date depicted: 1673. Date issued: 1674?.

Provenance: No copy of the first, second, or third states of this map has been found included and indexed in a dated atlas, although a copy of the second state is bound up in an atlas without date, title-page, or index, owned by the N. Y. Public Library. The fourth state of the map is found in the *Atlas Minor, seu universi terrarum orbis geographicum compendium recentissimas* (etc.).—Phillips's *Geographical Atlases*, No. 523. A copy is also found in the second volume of an atlas in the author's collection with the title: *Atlas Minor: sive Totius Terrarum Orbis Geographica Delineatio; complectens Novissimas Tabulas* (etc.), Carolus Allard, Amsterdam, n.d. (a paster converts the name of "Carolus" Allard into "Abrahamum" Allard). A table of the seventeen Netherland Provinces, following the index in the second volume of this atlas, bears the date 1705.

Publisher: Carolus Allardt (Allard), who was presumably also the engraver, as he combined the professions of draughtsman, engraver, and publisher.

Owner: I.N.P.S.

Third state. Of the first state but three copies are known to the author, one in the collection of J. Clarence Davies, Esq. (Vol. II, Addenda), one owned by Robert Goelet, Esq., and one belonging to the collection of Edward W. C. Arnold, Esq. A copy described in Muller's Catalogue, *Geographie-Voyages*, 1910, No. 807, is probably one of these. Of the second state there are copies in the N. Y. Public Library and in the private collections of the late John S. Barnes, and R. T. H. Halsey, Esq. A third copy was, in January, 1914, in the possession of Mr. Robert Fridenberg. Of the third state, three copies only are known to the author, one plain and one coloured, in his own collection, and one belonging to Amos F. Eno, Esq.

The second state is exactly similar to the third state, here reproduced, except that it is signed by Hugo, instead of Carolus Allard. The loop of the "g" of Hugo can still be discerned, directly below the "u" of Carolus, the exact position in which it appears in the second state. In its original or first state this map closely resembles the N. J. Visscher Map, except that the name of Hugo Allardt appears in place of that of N. J. Visscher. Some slight variations, however, occur. For instance, Paucocomo, Kapaunich, and Ottachug, in Virginia, found on the Visscher, are lacking on the Allardt. The two maps are printed from different coppers.

In the first state of the Allardt Map the N. J. Visscher View is used. In this state the large running title extending across the whole top of the map is lacking. In common with the N. J. Visscher Map, which it closely follows in date of issue, the first state lacks also a number of features found on the later issues, for instance, Graef Hendric, south of Sewapois on the Delaware; the description of "Kahoos," near the high waters of the Hudson; the fleet of Evertsen, south of Long Island, and all of the small ships in New York Harbour and east of Block Island; the small figure of a running beaver south of the word "Armeomecks," near the large Indian village, as well as several other small animals; the reference letters on the Island of Manhattan, and the numbered references to which these refer, south of Long Island, etc., etc.

Both the second and the third states bear distinct traces of the erased references which appeared below the view in the first state. These can easily be made out between the word "Eylandt," just above the lower margin in the centre of the plate, and the signature of Carolus Allardt in the extreme right lower margin. The words "gevangen huys" are very clearly discernible just above No. 307 in the lower margin, and the words "Schepen . . . Haven komen" can be made out between degrees 305 and 306. Across the ankle of the figure of an Indian to the left of the inset view can also be traced the remains of the scale of miles found in the first state, etc., etc. Both the second and third states are before the publisher's imprint on the shield above the view, as well as before the addition of the third line in the title, "eindelijk aan de Engelse weder afgestaan" (finally again surrendered to the English), which seems pretty good proof that, in both states, the map was issued between the 24th of August, 1673, on which date New Amsterdam was recaptured by the Dutch, and the 10th of November, 1674, when it again fell into the hands of the English.

A later state of the map, probably the fourth, has the imprint on the shield, "Typis Caroli Allard Amstelodami cum privilegio," and the added line in the title above referred to, and was therefore issued some time after 1674. The same map, with the same title and etched view of New Amsterdam, and with the same elaborate vignette, probably by Romeyn de Hooghe, but with the address on the shield, "Apud Reinier & Josua Ottens Amstelodami," was issued much later, probably about 1740. An exactly similar edition, except with the inscription on the shield, "Typis Ioachim Ottens Amstelodami," is in the Library of the University of Amsterdam, Map Room, 28 A 19. Several further variations of this later issue exist. See Asher's *Essay* (List of Maps and Charts), Nos. 10, 13, 15, 16, 17, and 18.

For a description of the view, see Pl. 8-b. Notice has already been called to the presence off the south coast of Long Island of the fleet of Cornelis Evertsen, the Dutch Admiral who recaptured New Amsterdam in 1673, which event was undoubtedly the occasion for the republication of this map at this time with the addition of the Restitutio View.

The view on the Hugo Allard Map is the precursor of a numerous family of similar views, apparently issued over a considerable period of years. See, for example, Plates 11-b, 13, 14-a and -b, and 15.

PLATE 16–b

RECENS EDITA TOTIUS NOVI BELGII, IN AMERICA SEPTENTRIONALI (ETC.)
[The Seutter Map]

Engraved on copper. Map: 22 x 19¼ Date depicted: 1673.
View: 14 3/16 x 2 13/16 Date issued: *c.* 1740.

Author: Matthew Seutter.
Owner: I.N.P.S.
Other copies: N. Y. Public Library; N. Y. Hist. Society; Library of Congress, etc.

Earliest known state. This map is based upon the second edition of the Hugo Allardt Map (see Pl. 16–a), the Pennsylvania section, however, being copied from the second Danckers Map, reproduced in Andrews's *New Amsterdam New Orange New York*, xx. The impression here reproduced is before the copyright inscription below the title: "Cum Gratia et Privil. S. R. I. Vicariat. in part. Rheni; Sveviae et Juris Franconici." The same plate was later issued with the publisher's name altered to Tob. Conr. Lotter (Asher, No. 20). Copies also occur with the letters S. L. S. A. following the last words in the title "August. Vind." Several other slight variants of the original are known. The view, which bears the title, "Neu Jorck sive Neu Amsterdam," although the same as that on the Restitutio Map, has the references in Latin.

PLATE 16–A

NIEUW IORCK

Engraved on copper. 10⅜ x 7½ Date depicted: *c.* 1673.
Date issued: *c.* 1700.

Provenance: Unknown, but undoubtedly from a collection of views published at the end of the XVII or the beginning of the XVIII Century. The view is now found in Vol. I, Part I, of an extra-illustrated copy of the *History of the Navy of the United States of America*, by J. Fenimore Cooper. The specially printed title-page of this book bears the inscription at the foot: "Illustrated by John S. Barnes, New York, 1890." No other copy of this interesting view is known.

Owner: In the collection of the late John S. Barnes, now owned by James Barnes, Esq.

Publisher: J[a] Allard, who probably also engraved the view.

Artist: I. Harrewyn, probably Jacobus Harrewyn, a well-known Dutch artist, etcher, and engraver of the period.

This view is probably based upon the inset view on the Restitutio Map (1673–4), although there are more variations from the prototype than in any of the other copies, from which fact there is some reason to believe that this is an original view and not a copy. Among the variations note especially the very clear delineation of the houses on Marckveldt or Whitehall Street, and of those on the hill north of the Fort, which occupy almost exactly the position of the legendary first dwellings or huts spoken of by Beauchamp Plantagenet in *A History of the Province of New Albion* (etc.), the site of which has been associated by many writers with the present 39 and 41 Broadway, although without any real authority. Notice, also, the very clearly defined hills in the background, especially the one north-west of the stockadoes on Wall Street. Curiously enough, the weigh-house, which on the other views of this series, is erroneously placed, is here properly shown on the north side of the bridge. Note the distinctly marked cross on the flag, as well as the title, which denotes that the view is intended to depict the city after its re-capture by the English.

Reproduced and described here for the first time.

Plate 17

[The Labadist General View]

Pen and sepia ink drawing on paper. 31½ x 12½ Date depicted: 1679–80.

Provenance: Accompanying the MS. *Journal of a Voyage to New York*, 1679–80, by Jasper Danckaerts [1] and Peter Sluyter (the Labadist *Journal*), translated by Henry C. Murphy in Vol. I of *Memoirs* of L. I. Hist. Society (1867).

Artist: In all probability Jasper Danckaerts.

Owner: L. I. Hist. Society, which secured these views and the *Journal* which accompanied them, at the Murphy sale, in 1884, for $5.50 (No. 3054).

The view here reproduced is the most important and the largest of the three original drawings of New York accompanying the *Journal* (see Bibliography). Although we have no positive proof that these drawings were made by Danckaerts, the author of the *Journal*, there is every reason to believe that they were. On p. 129 of Murphy's translation, Danckaerts says: "Finding myself afterwards alone upon a small eminence, I made a sketch, as well as I could, of the land surrounding the great bay, that is, Coney Island, the entrance from the sea, *Rensselaer's* hook, and so further to the right, towards *Kil van Kol*." The sketch referred to is, almost without doubt, the one of the series accompanying the *Journal* which bears the following note (translated, p. 438): "Views of the land on the southerly and southwesterly sides of the great bay between the Neversincks and Long Island, 24 miles from New York. All as it appears from Jacques [Cortelyou's] house at Najak [Fort Hamilton] on Long Island." This view, which is not here reproduced, as it does not include Manhattan Island, shows a number of whales spouting in the outer bay. It is unquestionably by the same hand that drew the views of Manhattan Island. See also p. 163, where the author says: "I have wished several times that I could sketch in order to employ the art sometimes when it might be serviceable, especially upon this voyage. I, therefore, have practised it some, because it was convenient, and I thought I succeeded in it reasonably well, but I have done it, without any regularity or assiduity, and only to amuse myself occasionally."

On p. 361, Mr. Murphy in a note remarks: "Here occurs a break in the journal,

[1] In a note prefacing the *Journal of Jasper Danckaerts*, edited by Drs. James and Jameson, attention is called to the fact that "Danckaerts" is thus spelled by Danckaerts himself in his note prefixed to his copy of Eliot's Indian Old Testament; and that Mr. Murphy apparently adopted the spelling of "Jaspar Danckers" from outside references, as the *Journal*, except once in the case of Sluyter, gives only the assumed names, Schilders and Vorstman, by which alone Danckaerts and Sluyter were at first known in America. Domine Selyns of New York, in a letter to Willem à Brakel, gives their true names. This spelling is also used by the family "still or till lately extant in Zeeland."

embracing a period of five days, that is, from June 13th to June 19th, and filling twenty-four pages of the manuscript. . . . The missing part probably contained a general description of the city of New York." It is likely that the missing part also contained some reference to the drawings of New York. These drawings, made by a man whose only motive was to portray conditions as he saw them, are undoubtedly the most accurate and valuable pictorial records of the period which we possess, and are a mine of information to the careful student.

KEY TO 1679 VIEW

By the aid of the outline sketch accompanying the description of the Frontispiece and of the key printed below, the various topographical features may be readily recognised. The attribution of ownership to the buildings shown on this view was undertaken along the same lines and accomplished in the same manner as the determination of locations on the Map of the Dutch Grants. The Tax List of July 24, 1677 (*M. C. C.*, I: 50 *et seq.*), has been referred to, for the purpose of corroborating, and in some cases illuminating, the records of plain real estate history.

Modern street names have been used; and abbreviations are similar to those which precede the Key to the Map of the Dutch Grants.

LANDMARKS, ETC. (IN VARIOUS PARTS OF THE TOWN)

1 Fort James.

18 The King's Chapel in the Fort.

28 The houses on the west side of Broadway.

29 The Great Dock. First mentioned as "intended to bee buildt," January 15, 1675-6. (*M. C. C.*, I: 9.) Complete before October 8, 1679 (*Ibid.*, I: 73).

30 The Weigh House.

70 A group of trees. Site of the present Hanover Square.

71 The Water Gate.

72 The Slaughter House. February 16, 1676-7: "Itt is Ordered that for the Necessary and Publique Vse a Generall or Publique slaughter howse shall be Built for the Vse of the Cytie over the Water without the Gate att the Smiths fly Neare the halfe Moone" (*M. C. C.*, I: 46). Finished by October 8, 1678 (*Ibid.*, I: 68). Just beyond Wall Street on the south side of the present Pearl Street.

73 The Old Garrison Mill on the Common. Confirmed to William Aartsen and Jan Jansen Van Languedycke, October 3, 1667 (*Patents*, Albany, II: 116). It stood on a plot 248 feet square, in what is now City Hall Park, on Broadway opposite Murray and Warren Streets.

74 The Wind-mill of Captain Nicholas Demyre. The ground on which it stood was granted to him by Governor Edmund Andros, September 29, 1677 (*Patents*, Albany, IV: 126). Its exact location was on the present north-west corner of Duane Street and Park Row. The wind-mill plot was 8 English rods square.

75 "The sandy beach where a certain run of water empties itself into East river" (*Liber Deeds*, XXVI: 314, in N. Y. Co.). The outlet of the Fresh Water.

76, 76 Mill-stones.

77 The Half-moon or Battery in front of the City Hall.

78 The Burger's Path (William Street from Beaver Street to Pearl Street, then the Strand). The houses Nos. 57, 58, and 59 did not actually cross it, as the crude perspective of the view seems to indicate.

79 Houses along the Smith's Vly. The tax list of 1677 names twenty-seven owners here (*M. C. C.*, I: 50).

80 High hills on the Rutgers Farm, fortified during the American Revolution.

81 The Barracks in the Fort.

82 The New Market House; on January 29, 1676(7), "beinge now built by the Water Side neare the Bridge and weighhouse." (*M. C. C.*, I: 40.)

83 The Half-moon or Battery at the Water Gate (*M. C. C.*, I: 46). Shown also on Castello Plan.

84 Rondeel in front of Widow Loockermans. "Whereas the vessels lying in the harbor near the public Weigh-house of this city are considered to be seriously in the way should the enemy arrive, . . . therefore all skippers, barge and boat-men of this city, are hereby ordered and instructed to bring their vessels from said harbor inside the float, and to anchor before this city, and on the arrival of more than one ship at a time, to haul them behind the ship *Surinam* near the circular battery (*rondeel*) in front of the widow Loocquermans, on pain of having all vessels without discrimination burnt, which will then be found lying in the way. Done Fort Willem Hendrick, this 27th March, 1674."—*N. Y. Col. Docs.*, II: 702. The ship *Surinam* was the state ship on which Governor Colve returned home.—*Doc. Hist.*, III: 75.

THE BLOCK BETWEEN STATE, PEARL, AND WHITEHALL STREETS

No. 2 Thomas Lamberts, 1666–84 (*Patents*, Albany, IV: 10; *Liber Deeds*, XIII: 53, in N. Y. Co.).

4, 4a Pieter Jacobsen Marius, 1657 (*Liber Deeds*, A: 95, in N. Y. Co.). The tax list mentions two houses. Heirs still here in 1770 (*Liber Mortgages*, III: 24, in N. Y. Co.).

6 Jan Evertse Keteltas. He purchased on September 26, 1674, from heirs of Michael Tadens. (*Liber Deeds*, A: 50, in N. Y. Hist. Society).

8 Jacobus Van De Water. Confiscated lot of William Pattison; patented by Colve, 1673; confirmed by Andros, 1676 (*Patents*, Albany, IV: 106; quit-claim deed from Pattison's representatives, 1685; *Liber Deeds*, XIII: 82 in N. Y. Co.).

9 & 10 The great warehouse and the bake-house of Thomas Delavall, never heretofore noted, and pictured only on this view (Recited in conveyances cited on No. 14).

11 Thomas Fransen, 1661–85 (*Liber Deeds*, A: 244, in N. Y. Co.; *Ibid.*, XIII: 112).

12 & 12a Two houses built on the lot formerly of Jacques Cousseau. They were sold by Frederick Lubberse of Long Island to John Sconten, January 29, 1679 (*Liber Deeds*, XXVI: 321, in N. Y. Co.). It is recited in a mortgage, December 1, 1680 (*Liber Mortgages*, XII: 43 in N. Y. Co.), that Hendrick Arentsen then owned or occupied the more westerly house. The tax list places Henry Arients, Spaniard, there.

13 Thomas William Cock had two houses on his plot. The rear house (formerly of Stephen Genore, which had reverted to Cock, and in which Harmetie Janes lived in 1677) is the only one seen in the view. Cock's dwelling-house on Pearl Street is hidden by No. 14.

14 The house of Captain Thomas Delavall, Mayor of the City. This was the Great House of Director-General Stuyvesant, built by him prior to 1658 (see Chronology). On January 14, 1678, Judith Stuyvesant deeded the property to Delavall (*Liber Deeds*, Albany, V: 98), who subsequently sold to Jacob Milbourne and Samuel Swynock, on March 4, 1686. A week later, or on March 11, Milbourne and Swynock deeded the property to Thomas Dongan (*Liber Deeds*, XIII: 250–69). It was first called Whitehall during the occupancy of Gov. Dongan, subsequently the Earl of Limerick. The building was still in existence in 1715, when it was mentioned in a deed, but was destroyed, probably in a fire, by 1717, the date of the Burgis View (Pl. 25).

20 Gillis Pietersen, 1667 (*Patents*, Albany, II: 45). Assessed to Henry Jelleson on tax list.

21 & 21a Jacob Leisler, 1669–85 (*Liber Deeds*, B: 155, in N. Y. Co.; *Ibid.*, XXI: 34). In the tax list, No. 21-a is recited as vacant ground: "Mr Leisler Betweene Mr Darvall and his house Front to ye Bridge 24 foot 45 foot backward Ordered yt it shall not be built upon, as Mr Mayr Informed Mr Lewis" (*M. C. C.*, I: 52). Undoubtedly because of the agreement about the five-foot passage to be main-

tained between the houses, as recited in *Liber Deeds*, B: 155, in N. Y. Co.

24 Christopher Hooglandt, 1669–85 (*Liber Deeds*, B: 156, in N. Y. Co.; *Ibid.*, XXI: 34).

BLOCK ON NORTH SIDE OF PEARL STREET, BETWEEN WHITEHALL AND STATE STREETS

No. 3 Andries Claesen, 1672–1713 (*Liber Deeds*, B: 203, in N. Y. Co.; *Ibid.*, XXXI: 7). When the heirs of Claesen sell, they describe it as "All that certain house and lott of ground . . . near the stable of the Queen's Fort."—A unique reference.

5 Thomas Lawrence. Confirmed to him in 1668 (*Patents*, Albany, III: 13). He sold in 1707 (*Liber Deeds*, XXVIII: 514, in N. Y. Co.).

7 Juriaen Blanck. Confirmed in 1668 (*Patents*, Albany, II: 38). His widow still lived here in 1700 (*Liber Deeds*, XXIII: 216, in N. Y. Co.).

15, 16 Two houses of Warner Wessels. He died seized of this plot in 1701 (*Liber Deeds*, XXVI: 159, in N. Y. Co.). On tax list: Warner Wessels and William Allen.

17 Claes Bording. Confirmed in 1667 (*Patents*, Albany, II: 39). Heirs sell it, 1705 (*Liber Deeds*, XXVI: 73, in N. Y. Co.)

19, 19 Not accounted for. Probably redundancy on the part of the artist.

22 Andreas Bresteed, July, 1677 (*Liber Deeds*, XII: 77, in N. Y. Co.).

23 Michael Smith on the tax list of 1677. His administratrix sells in 1684 (*Liber Deeds*, XXXIII: 96 in N. Y. Co.).

25 Isaac Greveraet. Confirmed in 1667 (*Patents*, Albany, II: 105). Heirs sell in 1687 (*Liber Deeds*, XIII: 301, in N. Y. Co.).

26 Cornelis Van Borsum on tax list. Source of his title not traced. Jacques Cousseau here until 1670 (*Liber Mortgages* A: 90, in N. Y. Co.).

27 Cornelis Van Borsum, prior to April 30, 1672, when he petitioned for an enlargement of his lot on the back side of his house from the corner of his "Oold ffence a Long West Ward," etc. (*Rec. N. Am.*, VI: 368). Still recited here in 1685 (*Liber Deeds*, XIII: 154, in N. Y. Co.).

THE BLOCK BETWEEN WHITEHALL AND BROAD STREETS

A curious fact—proved by the real estate records—is that in this block, at the time of the view, there were actually four buildings to the left of the West India Company's Pack House (called at the period of the View the King's Warehouse and Custom House—No. 36), and eight buildings to the right of it, extending to the Heere Graft or Broad Street. The artist perhaps felt that the picture would balance better if the large structure were placed near the centre of the block. Premising that No. 35 was actually to the right of No. 36 and not to the left of it, the owners of the buildings were as follows:

No. 31 Heirs of Hans Kierstede, the original patentee, until 1710. (*Liber Deeds*, XXVI: 48, in N. Y. Co.) Peter Bayard, who is placed here in the tax list, was the husband of Blandina Kierstede (List of Dutch Church Members reproduced in Wilson's *Mem. Hist. of N. Y.*, I: 447).

32 Paulus Richard on July 3, 1667 (*Liber Deeds*, B: 134, in N. Y. Co.).

33 Domine Samuel Drisius on July 3, 1667 (*Liber Deeds*, B: 135, in N. Y. Co.).

34 Cornelis Steenwyck, by deed from Mary Varrevanger, widow of Jacob Hendricks Varrevanger, November 2, 1677 (*Liber Deeds*, Albany, VI: 44). Called Mary Jacobs in tax list.

35 Isaac Bedlow. Derived partly by deed from executors of Rachel van Tienhoven, December 3, 1669 (*Liber Deeds*, B: 163, in N. Y. Co.); partly by a patent from Governor Nicolls of Augustine Herrman's confiscated warehouse lot (*Patents*, Albany, III: 86).[1] The tax list shows

[1] About 10 feet of this lot was added to the Old Pack House when it became the King's Warehouse and Custom House, making it nearly 40 feet wide.

two houses here (one, a small house); probably by the time of the view one large house replaced them.

36 The Old Pack House of the West India Company, enlarged in English times. See footnote to No. 35.

37 Lucas van Tienhoven. Called "Van Tienhoven's Great House." Inherited from Cornelis van Tienhoven, who purchased here in 1655 (*Liber Deeds*, A: 21, in N. Y. Co.; *Ibid.*, XII: 144).

38 Allard Anthony. Formerly the Old Church, with the little lane added. Although the only deed of record into Allard Anthony is dated June 30, 1682 (*Liber Deeds*, XII: 93, in N. Y. Co.), he is known to have been here as early as 1660 (see Key to Castello Plan, Appendix, III).

39 John Hendricx de Bruyn, according to the tax list. The source of his title is not traced, but he is recited here in 1710 (*Liber Deeds*, XXXI: 53, in N. Y. Co.).

40 Samuel Edsall, on June 20, 1656 (*Liber* HH(2): 55). His heirs sell in 1710 (*Liber Deeds*, XXXI: 53, in N. Y. Co.).

41 Gulyn Verplanck. He purchased the house February 26, 1672(3) from Samuel Edsall (*Liber Deeds*, A: 7, in N. Y. Hist. Society).

42 Frans Jansen Van Hooghten. Confirmed here in February, 1667(8) (*Patents*, Albany, II: 171), and again in April, 1668 (*Ibid.*, III: 11). As late as 1699, Mary Francen is recited here (*Liber Deeds*, XXIII: 96 in N. Y. Co.). [Land next east]. The tax list calls this the property of Nicolas Jansen Backer, who had owned No. 41 until 1671 (*Liber Deeds*, B: 179, in N. Y. Co.). This is evidently an error.

43 James Mathews, who bought the house from Hans Dreeper, February 14, 1674 (*Liber Deeds*, A: 29, in N. Y. Hist. Society).

THE BLOCK BETWEEN BROAD STREET AND COENTIES ALLEY

It is a matter of record that there were, at the period of the view, but six houses between the Heere Graft and the King's House or Ordinary (No. 45). The view shows eleven houses. Beginning at the corner this range of buildings may be designated alternately from 44A to 44F.

No. 44A Olof Stevensen van Cortlandt, 1665–86 (*Liber Deeds*, B: 63, in N. Y. Co.; *Ibid.*, XIII: 269).

B Sybout Claessen. Confirmed to him August 6, 1667 (*Patents*, Albany, II: 88).

C Albert Bosch, 1672–1719 (*Liber Deeds*, B: 191, in N. Y. Co.; *Ibid.*, XXX: 434).

D Cornelis Jansen van Hoorne. Confirmed to him May 16, 1667 (*Patents*, Albany, II: 29). Recited here in 1682 (*Liber Deeds*, XII: 86, in N. Y. Co.).

E Sybrant Jansen. Confirmed to him March 29, 1667 (*Patents*, Albany, IV: 31). Still here in 1682 (*Liber Deeds*, XII: 86, in N. Y. Co.).

F Rem Jansen. Confirmed May 5, 1668 (*Patents*, Albany, III: 19). The tax list agrees with the above (*M. C. C.*, I: 51).

45 Tavern or Ordinary granted to Governor Lovelace before January 25, 1670 (*Rec. N. Am.*, VI: 215). Excepted as "messuage or tenement next the City Hall" by Governor Dongan in Charter of 1686. Evidently still government land in 1699, when it is called "The King's House now in the tenure of Joseph Davids" (*Liber* A of City Grants, p. 254, in Comptroller's Office).

46 The City Hall.

THE BLOCK BETWEEN COENTIES ALLEY AND WILLIAM STREET

No. 47 Lodowick Post. Confiscated land of William Pattison, granted to Post by Governor Colve. (Recited in *Liber Deeds*, XIII: 62, in N. Y. Co.) When Post sells in January, 1684, he recites that the next house is occupied by the widow of Clement Sybragh; evidently the "Clement the Cooper" spoken of in the tax list of 1677.

48 All of this property was included in the
49 ground-brief to Thomas Willett, whose
50 widow married Charles Bridges. Bridges
51 was confirmed here June 11, 1667 (*Patents*, Albany, II: 47).

48 Being vacant is not included in the tax list of 1677. It belonged to Thomas Willett, a son of Mrs. Bridges.

49 The house of Charles Van Brugh (Charles Bridges), occupied by Clement the Cooper.

50 The house of Charles Van Brugh, next to John Darvall's.

51 John Darvall on the tax list. The source of his title not traced.

52 Thomas Wandall. Purchased by him from Richard Smith, November 2, 1662 (*Liber Deeds*, A: 286, in N. Y. Co.).

53 Angeltie Burger. Sold as a vacant lot to the widow and heirs of the late Burger Joris, September 28, 1674 (*Liber Deeds*, A: 51, in N. Y. Hist. Society). Angeltie Burger sold to Johannes Burger, January 14, 1702 (*Ibid.*, XXVI: 106, in N. Y. Co.).

54 Gulyn Verplanck, 1674-83 (*Liber Deeds*, A: 52, in N. Y. Hist. Society; *Ibid.*, XIII: 1, in N. Y. Co.). The tax list gives John Shackerly. Evidently an error.

55 Evert Duyckingh, November 10, 1656 (*Liber Deeds*, A: 77, in N. Y. Co.). Confirmed here September 13, 1667 (*Patents*, Albany, II: 99). Sold by his heirs October 20, 1727 (*Liber Deeds*, XXXIII: 204, in N. Y. Co.).

56 Tryntie, widow of Abraham Martens Clock. Confirmed here October 10, 1667 (*Patents*, Albany, II: 117). Heirs of Clock until 1698, at least. (See recitals in *Liber Deeds*, XXX: 422, in N. Y. Co.).

THE BLOCK BETWEEN WILLIAM AND WALL STREETS

No. 57 Thomas Lewis. Bought from Burger Joris, July 2, 1668 (*Liber Deeds*, B: 144, in N. Y. Co.). Heirs of Lewis until 1713 (*Ibid.*, XXVI: 317, in N. Y. Co.; *Ibid.*, XXXIII: 47).

58 Johannes Van Brugh, who had married Caturina Roelofs, widow of Lucas Rodenburgh. She was confirmed there in 1667 (*Patents*, Albany, II: 72). The Van Brugh and Rodenburgh heirs sold to Peter Van Brugh in 1719 (*Liber Deeds*, XXX: 6, in N. Y. Co.).

59 Jacobus de Haert, June 1, 1673 (*Liber Deeds*, A: 22, in N. Y. Hist. Society). In November, 1701, heirs of De Haert partitioned it (*Ibid.*, XXIII: 340, in N. Y. Co.).

60
61
62
63 All property of Govert Loockermans's heirs. January 29, 1681, John Robinson purchased No. 60 (Recitals in *Liber Deeds*, XIII: 314, in N. Y. Co.). Govert Loockermans's old house, No. 61, was a part of his estate in 1687 (Recitals in *Ibid.*, XVIII: 27—on east side,—in N. Y. Co.). Nos. 62 and 63 were sold by the heirs of Loockermans to Cornelis Dirckse van Westveen (the son of Mrs. Loockermans by her second husband, Dirck Cornelissen), on April 18, 1674. (*Liber*, A: 31, in N. Y. Hist. Society.) Called in the deed "Their stone house and land." By reference to the Castello Plan, it will be seen that the large stone house stood back in the grounds and is not visible in this view. The house here seen seems to have been a lodge or some such small building. No. 63 is the garden belonging to No. 62. In later years, the Sloot (Sloat Lane) was cut through between Nos. 63 and 64.

64&65 Carsten Luersen, February 24, 1670(1), by deed from Rynert Reynoutsen Bell (*Liber Deeds*, B: 179, in N. Y. Co.). In the tax list two houses are noted on this land. In 1694 the water lot in front was granted to Castor Lieursen, Jr., at the request of his father, Castor Lieursen (*M. C. C.*, I: 362).

66 Andries Jochems, May 25, 1654. (Recited in *Liber Deeds*, B: 131, in N. Y. Co.). Andries Jochemsen mortgaged this house in 1667 (*Liber Deeds*, B: 131, in N. Y. Co.). His heirs were assessed here in July, 1677.

67 John Lawrence. He purchased a lot here with two houses on it, in August, 1659 (*Liber Deeds*, A: 172, in N. Y. Co.). One was on the Strand, the other in the rear. Only the former shows in this view. Still in his possession in 1677, according to tax list.

68 Balthazar De Haart. Jacob Jansen

Flodder's neglected lot, forfeited and re-granted to De Haart, June 28, 1667 (*Patents*, Albany, II: 56). Called De Hart's house on the tax list of 1677. Sold by De Hart to Daniel Veenvos in 1687 (*Liber Deeds*, XIII: 311, in N. Y. Co.).

69 Estate of Daniel Litscho. Three houses. Still owned by his descendants at the time of the view (*Liber Deeds*, XXI: 260, in N. Y. Co.; *Ibid.*, XXVI: 178; *Ibid.*, XXXIV: 397; *Ibid.*, LVI: 178). Assessed to Ann Litscho on tax list of 1677.

Reproduced in Murphy's translation of the Labadist *Journal*, published as Vol. I of the *Memoirs* of the Long Island Hist. Society.

Plate 18

YORK VAN TER SYDEN DAT IS VAN DE OOST KANT

Pen and sepia ink drawing on paper. 16½ x 12½ Date depicted: 1679–80.

Provenance: Accompanying the Labadist *Journal*.
Artist: Undoubtedly Jasper Danckaerts.
Owner: Long Island Hist. Society.

This view, bearing the inscription (translated) "York from the Side that is from the east side," appears to have been taken (as a modern pencil note, probably by Mr. Murphy, indicates) from a point on the East River near the foot of Fulton Street. The perspective is so faulty that it requires some patience to reconcile it with the general view (Pl. 17). However, from a careful comparison, the principal points of interest lying between the Stadt Huys (which, with its small cupola, can be distinguished at the land end of the Long Dock) and Wall Street, immediately north of which is seen the slaughter-house, built over the water on piles, can plainly be distinguished. Midway between the Stadt Huys and the slaughter-house can be seen the Burger's Path with two small boats moored at its water end, and between this point and Wall Street, Govert Loockermans' orchard (see Key to Pl. 17), so conspicuous a landmark in the general view. The large flag on the Fort and the smaller one on the tower of the church are seen directly above the east end of Wall Street. At first sight they appear to be much too far away from Stuyvesant's house (Whitehall), the large building at the extreme left of the town, but by a careful comparison of the drawing with the Castello Plan (Appendix, III), it will be seen that the respective positions of these various points are approximately correct.

Reproduced in Murphy's translation of the Labadist *Journal*.

Plate 19

N YORK VAN ACHTEREN OF VAN DE NOORT KANT

Pen and sepia ink drawing on paper. 12½ x 8⅛ Date depicted: 1679–80.

Provenance: Accompanying the Labadist *Journal*.
Artist: Undoubtedly Jasper Danckaerts.
Owner: Long Island Hist. Society.

This view, bearing the inscription (translated) "N york from behind or from the north side," is taken from a point near the Hudson River and north of the present City

Hall Park. It shows the great highway (present Broadway) and the two mills south of the Fresh Water, built respectively about 1664 and 1677.—See Chronology. This is a most interesting view and the only one which has come down to us showing the west shore and the backbone of the Island in the seventeenth century.

The tower on the church in the Fort is greatly exaggerated in this view. Indeed, the whole topography is much confused. This, however, will be readily understood by a reference to Mr. Brevoort's redraft (Pl. 20-a). Notice the whale spouting in the Hudson River. The small fenced parcel appearing west of Broadway and just north of the church is probably the new cemetery outside of the wall.—See Pl. 23-a, Ref. No. 23. For a description of the two mills, see Pl. 17, refs. 73 and 74. The wagon seen between these two mills is the first representation that we know of a horse-drawn vehicle on Manhattan.

Reproduced in Murphy's translation of the Labadist *Journal.*

Plate 20-a

View of New York from the North. 1679

[Brevoort Redraft]

Lithograph. $12\frac{1}{2}$ x $7\frac{9}{16}$ Date depicted: 1679-80.
Date issued: 1867.

Rectified redraft by J. Carson Brevoort of the view shown in Pl. 19.

From the lithograph by Hayward, reproduced in Murphy's translation of the Labadist *Journal.* The original drawing by Mr. Brevoort has been lost.

Plate 20-b

The Stadthuys of New York in 1679, etc.

[Brevoort Redraft]

Lithograph. $9\frac{1}{16}$ x $7\frac{1}{4}$ Date depicted: 1679-80.
Date issued: 1867.

Rectified redraft by J. Carson Brevoort of a portion of Pl. 17.

From the lithograph by Hayward in Mr. Murphy's translation of the Labadist *Journal.* The original drawing has been lost.

This view shows the Stadt Huys, and doubtless gives the best idea which we have of this important building during its most prosperous days. The opening into Coenties Alley is distinctly shown at the right of the Stadt Huys. The land end of the Long Dock is also depicted, as well as the battery, built probably in 1661, as it appears on "The Duke's Plan" of September, 1661 (Pl. 10), and not on the Castello Plan (Appendix, III) which was probably drawn earlier in the same year. It is also referred to in the manuscript *Description of the Towne of Mannadens.*—See Chronology, 1661.

Lovelace's tavern adjoins the Stadt Huys on the left. It is interesting to note that the St. Nicholas Society owns a copper wind-vane in the form of a cock, presented to them, in 1848, by Washington Irving, which wind-vane is said to have been removed from the Stadt Huys when it was demolished in 1700, and was afterwards used at Sunnyside, Sleepy Hollow, N. Y. Although this is, of course, possible, there is no official confirmation of this pedigree, and it seems more likely that the weather-vane really belonged to the later Federal Hall, on Wall Street, which we know from several contemporary pictures had a vane in the form of a cock. The cupola containing the bell, shown on the Stadt Huys, was probably erected in 1656. See Chronology, 1656, January 24 and March 29.

Plate 21

A sand draught of New-York Harbour by (Phillip=Wells.)

Pen and ink drawing on paper (described in the Brinley Catalogue as a water colour). 17 x 22 Date depicted: Probably 1686–9.

Author: Philip Wells (written Phillip Welles in *Cal. Land Papers*).

Owner: Edward E. Ayer, Esq., deposited in the Newberry Library, Chicago.

This survey of the Harbour was evidently made shortly after February 23, 1684, when Governor Dongan ordered the Surveyor-General (Philip Wells) to make a survey of Staten Island (*Cal. Hist. MSS., Eng.*, 154). Philip Wells's name first appears as surveyor in 1680 (*Cal. Land Papers*, 20) and is found attached to a number of surveys dating from this period, one of which (in the author's collection) shows a tract of land, patented to William Bickley, May 13, 1686, the site of the present Highbridgeville, and described as a "certain neck of land—lying upon the main, and adjoining upon Harlem river."—Riker, 395. (A certified copy of this patent, made for the Title Guarantee and Trust Co., from Liber 5 of Albany Patents, p. 413, gives the date as May 15, 1686.) Philip Wells had been Governor Dongan's surveyor, and was one of the commissioners appointed in 1684 to run the boundary line between the provinces of New York and Connecticut. A fine survey of Boston Harbour, also from the Brinley Collection, but unsigned, is now in the Boston Public Library.

J. Hammond Trumbull, in the Introduction to Winsor's *Memorial History of Boston*, II: 50–1, says that the draught of Boston Harbour and that of New York Harbour were undoubtedly drawn and lettered by the same hand and were probably executed at the same time, namely between 1686 and 1689. The two were found together in a parcel of the "Penn papers" sold in London by E. G. Allen in 1871. Trumbull refers to this survey of New York Harbour as a "Land Draught," and the same term is repeated in the Brinley Catalogue, V: No. 9317, although, as the survey shows particularly the shoals and sand bars at the entrance to the harbour, it seems more reasonable to suppose that it was intended to be a sand draught, and therefore is so designated on the survey. The drawing was purchased at the Brinley sale in 1893 by Dodd, Mead & Co., who sold it to Mr. Ayer.

There is in the British Museum (Additional MSS. 5414–19) a large map, 100 x 41½ inches, signed by "Phillip Wells," and dated 1686. This map shows the coast from the Bay of Honduras to Newfoundland.

Reproduced here for the first time.

Plate 22–a

Plan de la nouuelle york

MS. plan on paper. 33½ x 22$\frac{1}{16}$ Date depicted: 1692.

Author: The Chevalier d'Aux, who was sent to the Iroquois by Monsieur de Frontenac, and who also was the author of a fine, large plan of Boston and its environs, dated 1672, and preserved in the archives of the Dépôt de la Marine, Paris. The last-mentioned map is one of a set of French maps drawn by Franquelin, Pasquin, and others. See Pl. 22–b, which belongs to the same series.

Owner: Dépôt de la Marine, Paris.

The plan here reproduced is particularly interesting as giving a good idea of the fortifications existing at this period and of the road system outside of the walls of the city. It also shows very distinctly the positions of the three wind-mills. The wind-mill shown on the Hudson River, west of Broadway, was erected prior to 1686 by Peter Jansen Mesier, who acquired the lot upon which it was built from the heirs of Olof Stevensen Van Cortlandt. A lane about fifteen feet wide, belonging to Mesier and called in early records "Pieter Jansen's Lane," intervened between Mesier's property and the lot on the south. This lane was situated about 100 feet north of the present Liberty Street, and 110 feet south of Cortlandt Street, and was later referred to as "Old Windmill Lane," because it led from Broadway to the wind-mill, which stood about the middle of the present Cortlandt Street.—*Cf.* Lyne Survey (Pl. 27); see also Chronology, 1686, and O'Callaghan's manuscript notes on wind-mills, preserved in N. Y. Hist. Society.

The Collect is here erroneously shown on the west side of Broadway. Notice also that the Water Mill, or Old Mill, shown both on "The Duke's Plan" and on the Nicolls Survey, at the mouth of the outlet from the Collect, has disappeared.

Reproduced and described here for the first time.

Plate 22–b

Plan de Manathes ou Nouvelle Yorc
[The Franquelin Plan]

Manuscript on paper. 19$\frac{11}{16}$ x 13$\frac{13}{16}$ Date depicted: 1693.

Author: J. B. L. Franquelin.

Owner: Dépôt de la Marine, Paris, Pf. 135, Div. 1, Piece 1.

Verified by le Sieur de la Motte (probably the same Sieur, or Chevalier de la Motthe, who, on Sept. 15, 1688, as Major and second in command of Fort Niagara, signed a memorandum describing the condition in which said fort was on that date abandoned by order of the Governor-General.—*Doc. Hist. of N. Y.*, I: 168, citing Paris Documents, IV).

This plan is an inset in a large map by Franquelin of the coast of New England from Cape Anne to Point Nebresing. The full title of this beautifully drawn, although not altogether reliable, map is "Carte de la côte de la Nouvelle-Angleterre depuis le cap Anne jusqu'à la pointe de Nebresing, où est compris le chemin par terre et par mer de

Baston à Manathes, par I. B. L. Franquelin, hydrographe du roi, 1693." It measures $31\frac{15}{16}$ x $23\frac{9}{16}$.

The archives of the Dépôt de la Marine contain also a very interesting map entitled "Carte de la Ville, Baye, et Environs de Baston [Boston]," signed by Franquelin and also dated 1693. On this map, which is reproduced by Marcel (*Reproductions de cartes & de globes, etc.*, plate 22), appears a daintily drawn miniature view of Cambridge, showing the college. An inscription beneath the little view reads, "Cambridge, Bourgade de 80 Maisons, C'est une Université." This is probably the earliest known view of Cambridge and of Harvard College, and certainly the first reference to Harvard as a *University*. The Dépôt de la Marine contains several other interesting maps of the North East Coast, drawn by Franquelin in Quebec, and showing the Island of Manhattan, one of which, marked 4040^{B} 6bis, is dated 1681.

See Gabriel Marcel's *Reproductions de cartes & de globes*, etc., p. 27, and the accompanying portfolio (plate 6), for a reproduction of the "Plan de Manathes," from which reproduction our plate is made. See also the plan of the "Ville de Manathe ou Nouvelle-Yorc" in Bellin's *Le Petit Atlas maritime*, Paris, 1764, I: Pl. 33. This plan is evidently a direct copy from the Franquelin Plan.

It is quite probable that the plan here reproduced was made for military purposes, as the Paris Documents of this period contain many references to a contemplated but never executed attack upon New York by the French.

Plate 23-a
New Yorke
[The Miller Plan]

Manuscript on paper. $14\frac{1}{8}$ x $9\frac{7}{8}$ Date depicted: 1695.
Date issued: Probably 1696.

Provenance: From "New Yorke considered and improved Anno Dni 1695" British Museum, Additional MS. No. 15490).

Author: John Miller.

This interesting plan was drawn from memory by the Reverend John Miller, who, for three years, was chaplain to the King's forces in New York. He apparently reached New York in June, 1692, and left for England in July, 1695 (*Eccles. Rec.*, II: 1043; *N. Y. Col. Docs.*, IV: 182–3). The ship upon which he sailed, after some days at sea, was captured by a French privateer, and to save his valuable notes and drawings from falling into the hands of the enemy, Miller threw them overboard. He was taken to France and imprisoned, probably at St. Malo, where he wrote his account of New York, which he addressed to the Bishop of London. See letter prefixed to Miller's manuscript and printed in the edition published in Cleveland in 1903, and edited by Victor H. Paltsits, who also supplied the introduction. This is the most complete and accurate publication of the manuscript and plans. See also Bibliography.

In some manner, the manuscript and drawings later came into the possession of George Chalmers, the English antiquarian, and, in 1842, were sold at auction to John Rodd, who published the work in 1843 (see Bibliography). On April 5, 1845, the manuscripts were purchased from Rodd through Mr. Henry Stevens, by the British Museum.

The reference numbers on the plan refer to a list of references in the text, which are as follows:

1 The Chappel in the Fort of New Yorke
2 Leyslers halfe moone [built August, 1689, see Chronology]
3 Whitehall battery of 15 guns
4 The Old Dock
5 The Cage & Stocks
6 Stadthouse battery of 5 guns
7 The stadt-(or State-) house [Town-house]
8 The Custome house
8 8 The Bridge
9 Burghers or ye slip battery of 10 guns
10 The Fly blockhouse & half moon
11 The Slaughter houses
12 The New Docks
13 The French Church
14 The Jewes Synagogue
15 The Fort well & Pump
16 Ellets Alley
17 The works on the west side of the City
18 The Northwest Blockhouse
19 19 The Lutheran Church & Ministers house
20 20 The stone points on ye north side of the City
21 The Dutch Calvinist Church built 1692
22 The Dutch Calvinist Ministers house
23 The burying ground
24 A Windmill
25 The Kings Farm
26 Col^{l} Dungans Garden
27 27 Wells
28 The Plat of ground design'd for ye E. Min^{rs} house
29 29 The Stockado with a bank of earth on ye inside
30 The ground proper for ye building an E. Church
31.31 Showing ye Sea flowing about N. York
32.32 The City gates
33 A Postern gate

It is interesting to note, from reference number 30, that a location in one of the north bastions of the city wall was originally considered for the first Episcopal, or English, church. See Chronology under 1695(6), January 27, for first recorded proposal to build an English church (early unpublished manuscript minutes of Trinity Church). See also Chronology, 1690, May 19.

This is the first plan to show the layout of the streets above the wall, and for this reason is particularly interesting.

Reference number 24 shows the wind-mill, which stood about in the line of the present Cortlandt Street.—See Pl. 22-a.

For description of the city and fortifications, taken from Miller's manuscript, see Chronology, 1693. See also Chronology, 1688, November 15, for a very interesting account of the town and fortifications, made by order of Governor Andros by Francis Nicholson, Colonel N. Bayard, Wm. Beekman, S. Van Cortlandt, Matthew Plowman, and G. Minvielle.

Reproduction: Valentine's *Manual*, 1843-4, opp. p. 96.

Plate 23-b

The Fort in New Yorke

Manuscript on paper. $5\frac{15}{16}$ x $7\frac{13}{16}$ Date depicted: 1695.
Provenance: British Museum, Additional MS. No. 15490.
Author: John Miller.

The reference numbers in the Fort refer to a key of the Fort buildings, which is to be found in the text under the title "Fort William Henry. The Explanation of Fig. 2."

1 The Chappell
2 The Governours house
3 The Officers lodgings
4 The Soldjers lodgings
5 The necessary house
6 The Flag Staff & mount
7. 7. The Centry boxes
8. 8. Ladders to mount ye walls
9 The Well in ye Fort
10 The Magazine
11 The Sally port
12 The Secretary's Office
13 The Fortgate
14 A Hornworke before it
15 The Fort well & pump
16 Stone mount
17 The Iron mount
18 The town mount
19 19 2 Mortar pieces
20 A turn-stile
21 Ground for additionall buildings to ye G^rs house.
22 The Armory over ye Gov^rs Kitchin

This is the earliest known plan showing the Fort in detail. It is also the first plan to show the chapel in its new position, as reconstructed by Governor Fletcher, 1694-6. —See Chronology; *cf.* Pl. 46-A.

Reproduction: Valentine's *Manual*, 1843-4, opp. p. 96.

Plate 24-a

A Map or Chart of a certain Tract of Land commonly call'd the Shoemakers Land (etc.)

Pen and ink drawing on paper. $31\frac{1}{4}$ x 21 Date depicted: September 14, 1696.

Author: James Evetts, City Surveyor.
Owner: Preserved in the Archives of the Reformed Protestant Dutch Church, New York City.

This is probably a copy of the original survey, the present whereabouts of which is unknown. Another contemporary copy, differing somewhat from the one here reproduced, is recorded in *Liber Conveyances*, XXVIII: 145, in the N. Y. Register's Office, annexed to a deed of partition dated September 1, 1696, acknowledged January 20, 1700, and recorded May 2, 1715. The original draught from which this survey was made is apparently referred to in the *Minutes of the Common Council*, August 27, 1695, as being then in the possession of the Mayor. The map is reproduced here as being one of the earliest to show the division of a considerable acreage into city lots of a size and form which have since become typical.

The Shoemakers' Field consisted of about seventeen acres of land, bounded westerly by Broadway, southerly by Maiden Lane, and easterly by a fence which separated it from Van der Cliff's Orchard, approximately the centre line of the block between William and Gold Streets. Its northerly boundary was a line 117 feet north of and parallel with Fulton Street. The end of this fence intersected Broadway just at the obtuse angle in the St. Paul Building, south of Ann Street; then running easterly on the same line it struck Ann Street at the south-west corner of Nassau Street, and from that point easterly corresponded with the south line of Ann Street.

In its early days, the tract was a part of the plantation of the Dutch Colonial Secretary, Cornelis van Tienhoven. His grant from Director Wilhelm Kieft bears date June 14, 1644, and was confirmed to his creditors and heirs by Governor Nicolls, October 3, 1667.

On July 1, 1671 (*Liber* A, in N. Y. Hist. Society), Peter Stoutenburg and Jan Vinge, executors of the estate of Rachel van Tienhoven, the widow of Cornelis and Lucas van Tienhoven, and an heir of the deceased Secretary, conveyed to Jan Smedes, a carman, all that then remained of the Tienhoven grant. Jan Smedes, in turn, by two transactions, dated respectively April 30, 1673 (*Ibid.*), and March 20, 1675 (*Liber Deeds*, I: 126, in Secretary of State's Office, Albany), deeded to Conraet Ten Eyck, Caarsen Leersen, Jacob Abrams, and John Harpending, who were all tanners and shoemakers, a large part of the same land, "to be equally divided into four proportions or shares amongst them."

Cornelius Clopper, another shoemaker, threw his parcel, which adjoined, and which he had purchased from Oloff Stevensen Van Cortlandt, into the common field, and, in 1696, the proprietors, "finding the said land to be rentable for building of houses for an enlargement of the City, projected and laid out said lands into 164 lots."—See *Liber Deeds*, VI: 135, in Secretary of State's Office, Albany.

They caused a map to be made of it by James Evetts, C. S., and then partitioned the lots among themselves, by a deed dated September 14, 1696 (*Liber Deeds*, in N. Y. Co., XXVIII: 128). Cornelius Clopper being dead, his widow, Heyltie, took his share. Jacob Abrams, being also deceased, his son, Abraham Santvoort, as the family then was known, inherited his allotment.

John Harpendinck (his name is often so spelled) was the most prominent member of the Shoemakers' Guild. He was a wealthy man, and a great pillar of the Dutch Reformed Church. On his death, he left his lots in the Shoemakers' Field to that Communion. His will was dated February 7, 1723. Under this inheritance, the North Dutch Church and its graveyard later stood where the paint house of F. W. Devoe and C. T. Raynolds now is, covering lots 11 to 16 on the map here reproduced.

This Shoemakers' Field was a very cradle of churches. When, by Act of Parliament, in 1747 and again in 1749, the Moravian Church was recognised by the Church of England as a Protestant Episcopal Church, the Moravians were encouraged to come to America and to organise a congregation in New York City. In 1752, they built a church at 106-108 Fulton Street. They rebuilt on the same site in 1829, and the building was not demolished until 1845.

In 1758 the Reformed Dutch body recognised and encouraged a Calvinistic Church for Germans, this congregation establishing itself on Nassau Street between Maiden Lane and John Street; in 1765 they built a more substantial church edifice, which endured until 1822. The site is that of the present Nos. 64-66 Nassau Street.

Methodism in America was founded within this area. Early in 1767, Reverend Philip Embury, who had been preaching in a room in a building on City Hall Place (then called Barracks Street), hired the Rigging Loft in Horse and Cart Street (William Street).

In this building, now No. 120 William Street, the little congregation worshipped until 1770, when a plot was purchased on the south side of John Street (Nos. 44-46, between Nassau and William Streets, which it still occupies), "for a Methodist Preaching House forever." A second church was erected here in 1817 and the present structure in 1841 (see Pl. 43).

In 1769, the North Dutch Church was erected on the west side of William Street between Fulton and Ann Streets, and on the site of its old consistory, the meeting-place of the Fulton Street Prayer Meeting was built, at 113 Fulton Street, in 1869.

THE DE PEYSTER GARDEN

It was the original intention to reproduce, as Pl. 24-b, the very interesting map of the "De Peyster Garden" in 1718, from the original parchment, until recently in the possession of the De Peyster family, from which original the copy in Lamb's *History of the City of New York*, I: 505, was made. This, however, has not been possible, as the survey, apparently, is not among the papers bequeathed by the Honorable Frederic de Peyster to the N. Y. Hist. Society, and a search recently made among the family papers still in the possession of Mrs. Howard Townsend Martin (Miss Justine de Peyster) and elsewhere has failed to bring it to light. There is, however, among the De Peyster Papers in the Historical Society, a rough manuscript draught of a portion of the De Peyster Garden property, recently presented by the widow of Mr. Frederic de Peyster; and, in the Bancker Collection in the N. Y. Public Library, there is a plan of the lots on the north side of Wall Street, in 1774, which includes this property.

The land comprising what was later known as the De Peyster Garden was originally in the possession of Jan Jansen Damen, and was acquired, in part, from his heirs by Governor Dongan, through a dummy purchaser, Captain John Knight, on December 14, 1685 (*Liber Deeds*, XIII: 129-33, in N. Y. Register's Office). The remainder, which had been government propety (*i.e.*, the "Ditch" along the Wall), was granted by Dongan to Knight Feb. 10, 1685(6).—*Patents*, Albany, V:297. The Garden included the land lying north of Wall Street, 122 feet deep, and extending from Smith (William) to a point on Wall Street opposite New Street. On March 9, 1685(6) Knight transferred the property to Governor Dongan (*Liber Deeds*, XVIII: 64-71). On May 25, 1689, Dongan sold it to Abraham de Peyster and Nicholas Bayard (*Liber Deeds*, XXI: 25-7), who partitioned the land on October 4, 1695 (*Liber Deeds*, XXV: 61-2). On January 5, 1718, Abraham de Peyster and Samuel Bayard, son of Nicholas, sold a plot 88 feet wide to John Nicoles, Patrick Macknight, Gilbert Livingston, and Thomas Smith, Trustees of the Presbyterian Church, for £350 (*Liber Deeds*, XXVIII: 473-5); and on July 1, 1720, Smith and Livingston made a further deed of the same plot to the Reverend James Anderson and three other trustees. The statement in Lamb's *History*, I: 505, that this particular piece of property was sold to Gabriel Thompson, from whom it passed into the ownership of the Presbyterian Church, is thus shown to be erroneous.

In the *Minutes of the Common Council*, II: 99, under date of February 19, 1700, is the following entry: "Ordered that the sessions of the Mayor Courte & Common Council be held for the Citty att the house of Gabriel Tompson in the single Street [Cingel or Wall Street]. And that the Bell be hung there." Thompson is also referred to in the *Assembly Journal*, where his inn is called the "White Lion." It was probably in the immediate neighbourhood of the City Hall and may have occupied a building standing on the site of the later Presbyterian Church and leased to Thompson by De Peyster and

Bayard, but there is no record to prove this. There is a record, however, of the purchase, on November 23, 1701, by Thompson, of a lot on the north-west corner of Smets (William) Street and Wall (*Liber* XXX:184); this is shown on the map of the De Peyster Garden.

The City Hall was built (1699–1700) on a part of the De Peyster and Bayard property, but there seems to have been some contention as to the right of the city to appropriate this land; for on August 26, 1713, a petition of Colonel Abraham de Peyster and Mr. Samuel Bayard was read, "setting forth that part of the City Hall stands upon their land," and they desired "A Committee of this Court to treat with them Concerning the Premisses." A Committee was thereupon appointed to "Inspect the Title of the Petitioners and to make diligent search and Enquiry how the City Hall Came to be built upon the said Ground" (*M. C. C.*, III: 42). On September 29, 1713, the Recorder was ordered to appear for the Corporation at the next Supreme Court in an "Action of Ejectment brought ag[t] them by Coll Abraham Depeyster & M[r] samuell Bayard" (*Ibid.*, III: 46). There is no further mention of this case in the *Minutes*, and the probability is that it was settled in some manner. At any rate, the records seem to disprove the statement, in Lamb's *History*, I: 443, that the ground upon which the City Hall was built was donated by Colonel De Peyster, or at least that all of it was donated by him to the city.

It was only in 1689 that Dongan sold to De Peyster and Bayard his land north of Wall Street, including the strip 40 feet in width, to which he had no legal right, as it was clearly City property.[1] The transaction was a private one, and it is very possible that when the City came to build a new City Hall, ten years later, it did not recognise the validity of any claim of De Peyster and Bayard to this strip, and that when the city appropriated the property to which De Peyster's title was clear, he immediately took action.

Plate 25

*The title is almost entirely wanting in the only copy of this print known, but from a few words of descriptive matter which remain to the right and left of the inscription or legend below the view, and from fragments of the flourishes of some of the capitals in the title itself, it seems altogether likely that it is identical with that on the Bakewell reissue of 1746 (Pl. 33), i. e. "A South Prospect of y[e] Flourishing City of New York in the Province of New York in America," etc.

[The Burgis View]

Engraved on copper, and printed on four sheets of paper. 77 x 20½. Date depicted: 1716–18. Date issued: 1719–21.

Artist: Wm. Burgis.

Engraver: Probably I. Harris. The portion of the margin which in the Bakewell reissue (Pl. 33) bears this signature, is torn away in the N. Y. Hist. Society's unique copy of the original Burgis View, so that its engraver cannot be positively

[1] See Appendix, III.

[*] Since writing this description a perfect copy of the Burgis View has been found, and is now in the collection of Mr. Edward W. C. Arnold. While a reproduction of Mr. Arnold's impression has been substituted for the one originally prepared from the N. Y. Hist. Society's copy, it has seemed to the author advisable to retain here the original description written before this impression was found. A description of Mr. Arnold's perfect copy has, however, been added as a postscript.

identified. The print was photographed by Bierstadt shortly after it came into the possession of the Society, as a gift, through Berthold Fernow, about 1885, and before it was prepared for exhibition. The reproduction in Mr. Andrews's *New Amsterdam New Orange New York* was made at about this time and seems to show a portion of the margin, now lacking, which may have borne some part of the engraver's signature. It is therefore quite possible that if the Bierstadt negatives could be found the name of the engraver would appear, but, unfortunately, a careful search among the negatives which remain from the Bierstadt Collection has, up to the present, proved fruitless.

Owner: N. Y. Hist. Society. No other copy known.[1] For discussion of later states, see description of the Bakewell reissue of this plate (Pl. 33).

Mr. Andrews and other writers have described this important print as the earliest view of New York *engraved* in America. In his *New Amsterdam New Orange New York,* Mr. Andrews refers to it as follows: "The importance of this engraving in the pictorial annals of our city cannot well be over-estimated. It is beyond question an accurate representation of the place it claims to depict, and in the key at the foot of the print is embraced the name of every building of note of which the city at that time could boast."

There seems, however, to be every reason to believe that, while it was drawn by Burgis on the spot, the drawing was sent to England to be engraved. In the companion view of Boston the name of Wm. Burgis appears as "Delin." in the left lower corner below the description, while the imprint of "I. Harris, Sculp." appears below the border-line at the extreme right, exactly in the same place that it occupies in the Bakewell reissue of the Burgis New York view. On actually comparing the two views, New York and Boston, there can be no doubt that they are by the same hand. The style of the drawing and the character of the engraving determine this. We have ample evidence that the Boston view was sent to London to be engraved, as is proved by the several advertisements in the *New England Courant* of 1722 and 1723, and there is every reason to believe that the same course was followed in connection with the New York view.

The first advertisement of the Boston print appeared in the *Courant* for October 8, 1722, and reads as follows: "A View of the Great Town of Boston taken from a Standing on Noddles-Island, and designed to be cut on Copper will be carried on by Subscription as such expensive Works generally are. Those Gentlemen that would encourage such a Design may see the View at Mr. Price's Print and Map-seller over against the Town House, where Proposals are to be had and Subscriptions taken in." In the *Courant* of November 12, 1722, appears the first newspaper mention of Wm. Burgis that we have been able to find: "Whereas there has been an Advertisement lately publish'd of a Design to print a View of this Town of Boston, taken from Noddles Island, This is to certify, that the Undertaker, William Burgis, desires all Gentlemen to be speedy in their subscriptions, in order to send the Drawing to England this Fall, that he may conform to the Proposals to that end lately published. N. B. Sufficient Security is given to conform to the Conditions of said Proposals or to return the Advance Money." The Boston view was engraved by the summer of 1725, when in another advertisement in the *Courant* it was offered for sale by William Price.—See paper by Mr. John H. Edmonds, *Publ. Col. Soc. Mass.* (1910), XI: 245–62; also Winsor's *Mem. Hist. of Boston,* II: 531.

[1] See footnote, p. 239.

The first advertisement of the New York view antedated that of the Boston view by almost a year, appearing in *The Am. Weekly Mercury*, Philadelphia, under date of February 13–20, 1721/2. It reads as follows: "A Curious Prospect of the City of New-York, on 4 sheets of Royal Paper, to be sold by *Andrew Bradford*." Another advertisement appeared in the issues of the *New Eng. Courant* of August 20–27 and August 27–September 3, of the same year, as follows: "To be sold at the Picture Shop over against the Town-House in Boston, *an exact Prospect of the City of New York*, with all Sorts of Prints and Maps, lately come from London, in frames or without by Will. Price."

A careful search made in London by Mr. Henry N. Stevens fails to bring to light any evidence that our William Burgis, or anyone bearing the same name, resided or worked there during the period under consideration, although a "William Burgiss" engraved, at a much later period, a series of plates of English churches. This Burgiss was not born until 1735. I. Harris was a well-known English engraver who flourished between 1685 and 1739, being associated for many years with John Senex, who also issued maps and views of America. His name would naturally have been allowed to remain on restrikes, even if published years after the plate was engraved. It is, of course, conceivable, but not at all likely, that I. Harris's name was substituted for some other at the time of the reissue of the view in 1746, when Thos. Bakewell's name replaced that of Wm. Burgis in the dedication. We know that Harris died in 1739, and although it is also possible that he was succeeded by a son bearing the same name, this assumption seems scarcely worthy of serious consideration. A further argument in support of the theory that Burgis was the artist only and not the engraver of the 1717 view, is found in the fact that his Plan of Boston, although bearing his name in the dedication, was "Engraven by Tho[s] Johnson, Boston, N. E.," as is shown by the imprint. It was probably engraved in 1729, as it was first advertised in the *News-Letter* of July 3d of that year, as "lately published." It is true that Wm. Burgis did engrave a "View of the Light House" at Boston, which he signed "W Burgis del. & fecit," but the engraving of this print is very different from that of the New York and Boston views, and much cruder.—See Stauffer, Part I: 36–7, and Part II: No. 284.

The Burgis drawing was made from Brooklyn Heights, and evidently depicts the city on some special occasion, as is evidenced by the large amount of shipping present in the East River, by the firing of a general salute, etc. It may possibly represent the festal occasion of the celebration of the King's Birthday on June 4, 1717, just prior to Governor Hunter's departure for Albany.—See Chronology, 1717, June 10.

In a paper on "The Burgis Views of New York and Boston," read on February 17, 1914, before the Bostonian Society and printed in their *Proceedings*, for 1915, Mr. John H. Edmonds, of Boston, draws attention to the fact that the new province seal which, with the city seal and the coat of arms of Governor Hunter, bearing the date 1717, adorns the view, was not received in New York until July 1, 1718 (see Chronology, 1717, October 11, and 1718, July 1 and 7). He therefore concludes that 1717 is too early a date to assign to the publication of this print, the drawing for which, including the seals, could hardly have been completed before the later part of 1718.

The following interesting notes are taken from Mr. Edmonds's paper:

In an inventory of the effects of Thomas Selby, who died on September 19, 1727, are included "Two Prospect glasses, one brush for clothes, *one map of New York*, one pair of bellows £2 — 5 — 0"; and in an inventory of the personal effects of Gov. William Burnett, who died September 7, 1729, are included: a "*Prospect of New York* 10/ Ditto of Boston 10/." (The Boston view had originally been valued at 20 shillings, but was reduced to 10 shillings, evidently to conform with the New York view.)

Burgis was married on October 1, 1728, to Mehitable Selby, the widow of Thomas Selby, who was associated with him in the publication of the Boston View. Selby had been proprietor of the Crown Coffee House, at the Long Wharf, the present No. 148 State Street, near Chatham Row, Boston. Burgis evidently succeeded to the business for, on July 13, 1729, his petition to be "Tavernor at the Crown Coffee House" was approved and recommended to the Justices.

Reference to prints and copperplates, presumably of the Burgis drawings, is made in a suit brought on May 5, 1728, by Burgis against William Rendle (Randle), japanner, factor for John Greenwood, combmaker, "of London, but now of Boston," on bond of £100, dated April 8, 1723, the condition having been that Greenwood, after deducting what Burgis owed him, was to render a true account "of the neat [net] proceeds of *Certain Prints*, a Certain Note & *some Copper Plates*," which account he had failed to render.

Burgis, from the time of his marriage, was constantly in the courts. On September 17, 1730, an execution was issued in favor of John Smith, merchant, against Wm. Burgis, gentleman, and was placed in the hands of Deputy Sheriff W. Nicholls for collection. Nicholls returned this document on February 11, 1730/1, with the following endorsement, "I have found neither person or estate and return it in no part satisfied by reason it came to late to my hands." Burgis had probably left Massachusetts before this execution was granted. The last reference which Mr. Edmonds has found to him there is under date of July 20, 1736, in *Council Records* of Massachusetts: "A Petition of Mahetable Burgess of Boston, setting forth that her Husband William Burgess having gotten what he could of her estate into his hands about five years since left her, and has never returned into the Province again, nor taken the least care for her Support, and whether he be living or dead she knows not, and therefore praying for a Divorce or that the marriage may be declared void. Read & Dismissed." Unfortunately the original petition is no longer in the files.

A reduced copy of the Burgis View was published as an inset to the Popple Map, the first issue of which appeared in 1732 [see Pl. 29], and bears the signature of W. H. Toms, engraved above the reference letter "O" on the Brooklyn shore, near the Ferry. The view was also issued separately from the map, printed on a folio sheet with similar views of Quebec, Niagara, and the City of Mexico, but without signature.

A portion of the Burgis View was also engraved by Moll in 1741, together with views of nine other American cities, the views being introduced as marginal insets to a very rare map entitled "A new map of North America, wherein is exactly described all ye European settlements, with whatever else is remarkable in the West Indies, from the latest and best Discoveries: Adorn'd with views and plans of the most considerable Towns, Harbours &c." Apparently the same map, with the same views but bearing the imprint "Henry Overton at the White Horse without Newgate, London," was published in the same year. This map was dedicated to the Honble Edward Vernon Esq., and bears the title: "A New & Correct Map of the Trading Part of the West Indies including the Seat of War between Great Britain and Spain. Likewise the British Empire in America . . . Adorned with Prospects of ye most considerable Towns, Ports, Harbours, etc., therein contained from the latest and best Observations."

The earliest facsimile reproduction of the Burgis View is found in Mr. Andrews's *New Amsterdam New Orange New York* (1897), following p. 60.

Postscript:

Description of a complete and perfect impression of the Burgis View, belonging to Edward W. C. Arnold, Esq., and believed to be unique.

The view here reproduced is identical in every particular with that belonging to the New York Hist. Society. The title, references, and legend, however, which in the Hist. Society's copy are lacking, are here found complete, and are identical in all respects with those found on the Bakewell reissue (Pl. 33), except that the Burgis print lacks the imprint below the rectangle—"London Printed & sold by Tho. Bakewell Map & Print-seller, against Birchin Lane in Cornhill, where Merchants & others may be supplied with all sorts of Maps, Prints, & Pictures, at the lowest Prices. Published March 25th 1746"; and that it has in the left lower margin beneath the description the important additional line—"*W. Burgis Delit et Excud' Subscriptione Incolarum.*" As anticipated, "I. Harris, fec:" is found, as in the Bakewell reissue, in the right lower margin.

The print is in an immaculate state of preservation, almost as white, fresh, and crisp as when first printed, and all four of the sheets have wide margins and continuous plate marks. The history of this most important print is shrouded in mystery. It was offered to the author in June, 1913, by Mr. Harvey Minor, a well-known book-dealer of Cedar Rapids, Iowa, and was soon afterwards purchased by Mr. Robert Fridenberg, who sold it to Mr. Arnold. At the time of the sale it was reported that the print had been found in the possession of a family living in Iowa, who were supposed to have inherited it from an English ancestor. The author has, however, good reason to believe that the print was procured in England, and was brought over just prior to its sale, with several other important items of Americana, by Mr. L. Kashnor, of the Museum Book Store, London.

Reproduced and described here for the first time.

The Burgis View depicts the water-front along the East River from the turn in State Street west of Whitehall to a point a little north of Catherine Street. The shore line, which, in 1679, corresponded to the north side of Pearl Street, had at the time of this picture been extended a full block into the river, so that the street or wharf, on which the houses in the foreground of our view are aligned, is the present Water Street, which, in 1679, was the low-water line.

At the period of the view New York ranked as the third largest city in the colonies, being exceeded in size by both Boston and Philadelphia. Even as late as 1732, the estimated number of inhabitants of New York was only 8,624. It was not until 1790 that New York outstripped Boston and became the first city of the United States, with a population of 33,131.

Reference numbers 1 to 24 refer to buildings, etc., found in the Key printed below the view as follows (for additional information concerning these landmarks, see Chronology; see also outline Key Sketch, accompanying the description of the Frontispiece, p. 132).

"1. The Fort." Begun as Fort Amsterdam in 1626 or possibly earlier; rebuilt in 1628 and completed in 1635; many times repaired and strengthened; finally demolished in 1790. John Fontaine, who came to New York in 1716, refers thus to the Fort: "Oct. 27th. About nine I went and breakfasted at the Coffee-House, and at eleven I waited upon Governor Hunter, who received me very kindly, and invited me to dine with him. After dinner I walked with him about the fort, wherein he lives.

It is a small square situated upon a height above the town, and commanding it. The one side of it fronts the harbour, and hath a small curtain and two bastions; the land side hath but two half-bastions to it, so that it is a square composed of two whole and two half-bastions. There is a ravelin towards the land that lies on one side of the gate. It is but a weak place, and badly contrived. . . ."—See Chronology, 1716, Oct. 22.

"2. The Chappel in the Fort." Built in 1642; demolished in 1693; rebuilt, under Fletcher, in 1693–6. This is the first view to show the new church as rebuilt at this period. It was destroyed by fire in 1741. Compare this view with its delineation on the Carwitham View (Pl. 31).

"3. The Secretaries Office." Erected prior to 1658, as it is mentioned in January of that year in a proceeding of the city court. The building stood inside the Fort to the west of the gate, in which position it is shown, although not named, on the Castello Plan (Appendix, III). It was destroyed in the fire of 1741 and rebuilt outside the Fort.

"4. The Great Dock with a bridge over it." The "Bridge" (later the Custom House Bridge), also called the "pier," was constructed in 1659 at the foot of the present Moore Street, and was lengthened in 1660–1. In the latter year a basin or harbour was formed to the west of the Bridge by the construction of a pier running east from the extremity of the filled-in land in front of Stuyvesant's house at Whitehall. In 1676 the Great Dock was completed by the extension of the last-mentioned pier and the construction of a new pier running out from the Half-Moon Battery in front of the City Hall.

"5. The Ruines of White Hall built by Governour Duncan [Dongan]." Erected prior to 1658 by Stuyvesant. The ruins were still standing in 1769. See Du Simitière's MSS., Library Co. of Phila., Ridgeway Branch. For a history of Whitehall, see Pls. 17 and 35, and Chronology, 1658.

"6. Part of Nutten Island."—Governors Island.

"7. Part of Long Island."

"8. The Lower Market." Coenties Market or Fish Market, established at Coenties Slip in 1691. Demolished probably in 1780, in May, 1781, its site is designated as "the place where Coenties Market stood."

"9. The Crane." The successor to the original crane or hoist, a conspicuous object in all the early views of New York, and which stood somewhat farther to the south.

"10. The Great Flesh Market." Known later as Old Slip Market. Established April 18, 1691; built about 1701; enlarged in 1736; partially rebuilt in 1754, and demolished probably during the Revolution.

"11. The City Armes supported by Peace."

"12. The Dutch Church." The South Dutch Church on Garden Street (Exchange Place). Built in 1692; tower added in 1696; tower rebuilt from the ground in 1766–76; partly destroyed during Revolution; rebuilt in 1807; finally destroyed in the Great Fire of 1835.

"13. The English Church." Trinity Church, erected 1696–8; steeple finished in 1711; enlarged in 1724, and again in 1735–7; destroyed in the Great Fire of 1776. For subsequent history see Chronology.

"14. The City Hall." Begun in 1699 on site of present Sub-Treasury; third story added in 1763; remodelled in 1788–9 for the national Congress and called Federal Hall; torn down in 1812.

"15. The Exchange." Established in 1670 by Gov. Lovelace. In 1716, described by John Fontaine as "a small place that is planked and hath pillars of wood all round, which support the roof and leave it open on all sides." Thus shown in our view. In 1752, a new Exchange was erected on the same site.

"16. The French Church [Église du St. Esprit, Pine Street]." Erected in 1704 on the north side of Pine Street, east of Nassau. Rebuilt in 1796. In 1834 the property was sold.

"17. Upper Market." Called Fly Market from its location in the Smith's Vly (Valley) or Smith's Fly, now Pearl Street and Maiden Lane. Established in 1699, although the building was not erected until nearly seven years later; torn down in 1796; rebuilt in 1797; finally demolished in 1822.

"18. The Station Ship."

"19. From A to A, Warf."

"20. The Armes of the Province Supported by Plenty."

"21. Warfs for Building Ships."

"22. The Ferry House on Long Island side." This ferry was established some time prior to 1643, in which year Cornelis Dircksen (Hoochlandt) sold his house and garden with some sixteen or seventeen morgens of land on Long Island to William Tomassen, together with his right of ferriage.—*N. Y. Col. Docs.*, XIV: 42. That a tavern existed here as early as 1650 is shown by a statement in Van Tienhoven's reply to the *Remonstrance*, under date of November 29, 1650, that the taverns at the ferry and at Flushing were the only ones in the neighbouring towns.—*N. Y. Col. Docs.*, I: 425. Prior to 1654 the ferry was operated without particular oversight by the government of New York. In consequence, various abuses had arisen. People wishing to cross the ferry were sometimes obliged "to wait whole days and nights," and sometimes "to give up their journey not without gross extortion of double and higher fare, disputes and other unmannerly practices." To remedy these abuses, the Director-General and Council ordained, July 1, 1654, that thenceforth no one but the authorised lessee of the ferry should carry passengers or cattle. Fees were regulated, and the ferryman was ordered to have a sufficient number of boats with men to operate them. He was to be on duty in the summer from five in the morning until eight o'clock at night, and in the winter from seven until five, although he was not bound "except he please, to convey anyone over in a tempest, or when the Windmill hath lowered its sail in consequence of storm or otherwise." The ferryman was compelled, also, to maintain a "covered Shed or Lodge" on both sides of the river to shelter passengers. —*Laws and Ord. of N. Neth.*, 162–5. In the following year (1655) the first ferry-house was built on the Brooklyn side. The ferry was at this time operated by Egbert van Borsum, to whom the property had been conveyed in 1653 as "a house and lot by Wolpherts valley now called The Ferry."[1]—*Liber*, H H: 49. In 1661, Van Borsum was succeeded as ferryman by Albert James van Heemst, and he, some time before October 23, 1663, by Pieter Lucasen. The ferry was farmed out at "Publick Out Cry," and was operated later by different ferrymen. In February, 1699, various regulations for the ferry were prescribed by the Common Council, among them being the maintenance of two large boats for carrying cattle and two small ones for passengers, and a pound for cattle to be transported to New York. The Common Council also resolved, at this time, to erect "A good sufficient house of Stone and brick two Stories High," the old ferry-house being "Soe far gone to decay" as to be past repairing. In this new ferry-house, the lessee of the ferry was ordered to keep a "publick house of Entertainment" where

[1] This conveyance refers to the Ferry Terminus on the New York side.

men and horses might have "good Accomodation att Reasonable Rates."—*M. C. C.*, II: 64, 70–2. This house had been completed by December 27, 1700, when the ferry "with the New Brick house Barne and Pen thereunto belonging" was farmed out to Dirck Benson. At the time of our view, James Harding was the ferryman.

"23. Pen for Oxen and Cattel designed for the Markett." One of the conditions of the lease of the ferry to Dirck Benson, in 1700, was that he should keep a pen or pound for cattle, etc.

"24. Collonel Morris's Fancy turning to Windward with a sloop of Common Mould." This is probably the first view showing an American yacht—the noted "Fancy" belonging to Col. Lewis Morris.

WHITEHALL STREET

Jacob Leisler, who, with his son-in-law, Milbourne, was hanged for treason in 1691, had owned the two houses, Nos. 25 and 26. Mary Gouverneur, the widow of Milbourne, sold the premises in 1747 to Myndert Schuyler and Adam Dobbs.—[1] *Liber Deeds*, B: 155; XXXIV: 323; XXXIX: 308.

At No. 27 lived the heirs of the merchant, Daniel Veenvos (*Ibid.*, XXI: 34), and at No. 28 the widow of Christopher Hooghlandt.—*Ibid.*, B: 156; XXI: 34.

The north-west corner of Pearl and Whitehall Streets (29) was the property of William Teller at the period of the view.—*Ibid.*, XXVI: 380; CXIV: 305. Next westerly was the house where Domine William van Nieuwenhuysen had dwelt until his death (30).—*Ibid.*, XXVI: 380. The two houses on the north-east corner of the same streets (31 and 32) were at this time, respectively, in the possession of Stephen and Paul Richard.—*Ibid.*, XXVI: 481; LIV: 530.

FROM WHITEHALL STREET TO BROAD STREET

33. This broad plaza, which was known at the time of our view as Whitehall, later called Whitehall Street, was in 1731–2, diminished in width by the laying out of the block bounded by the present Whitehall, Pearl, Moore, and Water Streets.—*Liber*, B: 99, 104 (in Comptroller's Office).

As to the houses facing the Great Dock on Water Street as far as Broad Street, where the Exchange (15) stands, No. 34 belonged to one John Ellison, a "joyner," (*Liber Deeds*, XXIII: 142), and the building in the rear (35) was the warehouse of Col. Abraham de Peyster.—*Ibid.*, XXI: 164; CLI: 342. The vacant ground to the east (36) was the property of Isaac de Peyster.—*Liber*, A: 78 (in Compt. Office); *Liber Deeds*, XXXVIII: 82; XXXIX: 537. No. 37, the large house with a high stepped dormer belonged to Thomas Roberts.—*Liber*, A: 78 (in Compt. Office); *Liber Deeds*, XVIII: 121; XXXVIII: 82. Johannah Jamieson, the granddaughter of John Hendrix de Bruyn, lived at No. 38, the property having been devised to her by her grandfather in 1709.—*Ibid.*, XXXVII: 130; *Liber*, A: 23 (in Compt. Office). The next two houses (39 and 40) belonged, respectively, to Thomas Roberts and William Boyle, and fronted on Queen Street.—*Ibid.*, A: 18 (in Compt. Office); *Liber Deeds*, XXVI: 460; XXX: 74; XXXI: 206; XXXIV: 406. Nos. 41 and 42 were the property of Captain Cornelius de Peyster. The house with the stepped gables was his dwelling-house, erected in 1699, as he says, "to be ye ornament of ye sayde Citty."—*Liber*, A: 252 (in Compt. Office); *Liber Deeds*, XXX: 74; XXXIV: 406.

[1] Unless otherwise specified, all *Libers* here referred to are in the Office of the Register of New York County. *Liber* B of *Deeds*, however, has disappeared from the Register's Office; a duplicate may be found in the Library of the City Clerk. See Bibliography, Manuscript Sources. *Libers* A and B in the Comptroller's Office are *Libers of City Grants*.

FROM BROAD STREET TO COENTIES SLIP

No. 43 was the property of Philip Van Cortlandt and remained in this family until 1762.—*Ibid.*, XXXVI: 64, 131.

No. 44 belonged to Philip French, who had married Annetje, the daughter of Frederick Phillips (will of Frederick Phillips, dated October 26, 1700). The large house, No. 45, was devised by the will of Frederick Phillips to his son Adolphus, to whom he left "five houses and a warehouse in New York City."—*Liber*, A: 80, 87 (in Compt. Office); *Liber Deeds*, XIII: 278; XXIII: 111; XXXIV: 253.

Jacobus Van Cortlandt was the owner of No. 46, and held a patent, dated 1703, for all the land between Adolph Phillips and Coenties Slip.—*Liber*, A: 12, 84, 192 (in Compt. Office); *Liber Deeds*, XVIII: 46; *Land Papers* (Albany), III: 141.

FROM COENTIES SLIP TO THE BURGER'S PATH (FOOT OF WILLIAM STREET)

The house standing on the east side of Coenties Lane or Alley and on the north side of Pearl Street (47) belonged to Tobias Ten Eyck. It was a double dwelling under one roof, and remained in this family until 1784, when it was sold to Cornelius Ray, one of the most eminent New York citizens of his day.—*Liber Deeds*, XIII: 288; XLIII: 373. The north-east corner of Coenties Slip (48) was Conraet Ten Eyck's property. The Ten Eyck heirs did not remove from this site until 1801.—*Liber*, A: 229 (in Compt. Office); *Liber Deeds*, LIX: 542. No. 49 belonged to Johannes Outman (*Liber*, A: 41, 225, in Compt. Office; *Liber Deeds*, XXI: 40; XXXIX: 45); No. 50 to Helena Griggs (*Liber*, A: 247, in Compt. Office; *M. C. C.*, II: 111, 353, 354), and No. 51 to Jacobus Van Cortlandt. This last property included the large house which fronts on Queen (Pearl) Street, the small extension or gateway to the left of it, and the three small stores or buildings on the wharf. It remained in the possession of the Van Cortlandt heirs until 1775.—*Liber*, A: 47, 218 (in Compt. Office); *Land Papers* (Albany), III: 141.

Robert Livingston, the owner of No. 52, was at this period "of Albany." This wide lot, fronting on Pearl Street, on which appears the palatial residence with the high roof and two stacks of chimneys, had been granted to William Cox, in 1687, by the City. His widow married the notorious pirate, Captain Kidd, whose relations with Robert Livingston were very close. In 1693, Kidd and his wife, and in 1696 his wife's brother, Samuel Bradley, conveyed their holdings to Livingston, who, in 1725, died seized of the property shown in the view.—*Liber*, A: 40, 221 (in Compt. Office); *Liber Deeds*, XXI: 155, 158.

Nos. 53, 53a, and 54 are three similar houses. The first belonged to Cornelius Van Horne, the second to Abraham Lakerman, and the third to Lawrence Wessells.—*Liber*, A: 209, 239 (in Compt. Office); *Liber Deeds* XXXII: 159, 160, 162; CCIII: 123. Garrett Duyckinck owned No. 55.—*Liber*, A: 51, 380 (in Compt. Office); *Liber Mortgages:* II: 74. When the picture was made, Marten and Albertus Clock, heirs of Tryntie Clock, were the owners of Nos. 56 and 57. — *Liber*, A: 45 (in Compt. Office); *Liber Deeds*, XXXII: 189.

FROM BURGER'S PATH TO WALL STREET

Leonard De Klyn built on lot 58 in the year 1709; the building was subsequently demolished by order of the Common Council in order to widen Old Slip for public use.—

Ibid., XXXIII: 195; *M. C. C.*, II: 374, 375. When the slip had been so widened, Jacob Bolen's house (59) became the corner house.—*Ibid.*, XXIII: 323; *M. C. C.*, VII: 255, 263.

Barent Rynders owned No. 60 and Paul Richard No. 61, which latter remained in the Richard family until 1796.—*Ibid.*, XXVI: 286; XXXVI: 432; LVI: 324.

Nos. 62, 63. These two buildings, which had belonged to James Graham, Attorney-General of the Province, were sold by his executors in 1711 to the heirs of Peter Short, in whose possession they were at the period of the view.—*Liber*, A: 160 (in Compt. Office); *Liber Deeds*, XXVI: 506.

Andries Coeyman and Gertrude, his wife, were the owners of No. 64, which the latter had inherited from her father, Samuel Staats, "Chyurgeon."—*Liber*, A: 199 (in Compt Office); *Liber Deeds*, XXXIII: 511, 515; XXXV: 324. Nos. 65 and 66 belonged, respectively, to John Wandelaer (*Ibid.*, XXVIII: 104) and Albertus Bosch (*Ibid.*, XXXIII: 307, 308), No. 67 to Henry Courten or Coerten (*Ibid.*, XXXIV: 128; XXVIII: 497), and No. 68 to Andrew Fresneau.—*Ibid.*, XXVIII: 228.

Henry Carmer, Jr., was the owner of No. 69, which remained in the Carmer estate until 1772 (*Ibid.*, XXVI: 244; XLIV: 406). No. 70 was the property of Robert Sinclair's widow, Mary.—*Liber*, A: 156 (in Compt. Office); *Liber Deeds*, XXXVII: 378; *Liber Wills*, VII: 169.

Captain John Theobald owned and occupied the corner (71), referred to in many deeds and water-grants as "Captain Theobald's Corner."—*Liber*, A: 170 (in Compt. Office); *Liber Deeds*, XXXVII: 393.

FROM WALL STREET TO PINE STREET

The house with the two gables, one on Wall and the other on Water Street (72), is the dwelling of Thomas Clark. It did not stand directly on the corner of Wall and Burnet (Water) Streets, but 27 feet back. This location was always called, in water-grants and conveyances, "Clark's Corner."—*Liber*, A: 149 (in Compt. Office); *Liber Deeds*, XXX: 265; XXXII: 462, 464. The smaller house (73), which comes out to the wharf, belonged to Thomas Child, whose deed allowed him to "use the south east gable end of Thos. Clark's dwelling house for a partition wall, one half of which side wall doth stand on the premises sold [to Child]."—*Ibid.*, XXV: 48; XXXI: 428.

At No. 74 lived heirs of Richard Lawrence, perhaps his daughter Charity, the wife of Samuel Payton, to whom he bequeathed the property in 1712.—*Ibid.*, XXX: 265; XXI: 488. No. 75 is the "dwelling-house" of Rutgert Waldron (*Ibid.*, XXVI: 183; XXXIII: 348), and Nos. 76 and 77 the properties, respectively, of Peter Bresteade (*Ibid.*, XXVIII: 39; XXXIII: 348), and Isaac D'Riemer.—*Ibid.*, XXVIII: 18, 52. No. 78 was granted to George Heathcote, the founder of the family of that name, through whose extensive patent King (Pine) Street was cut. He was the uncle of the famous Col. Caleb Heathcote, who inherited this property from him. This same plot came afterwards into the possession of the Schuyler and Livingston families.—*Liber*, A: 187 (in Compt. Office); *Liber Deeds*, XXXIII: 355.

Joseph Baker, before his death, in 1711, had built three houses on his property (79) "which three tenements," as he observes in his will, "make the corner of King Street." These houses, which were bequeathed to Baker's son, William, obscure the corner of King (Pine) Street in the view.—*Ibid.*, XXIII: 233; XXX: 97; XXXI: 51.

FROM PINE STREET TO MAIDEN LANE

Nos. 80 and 81. These two fine houses fronted on Queen (Pearl) Street at the corner of King (Pine) Street. The view shows their rear elevations, balconies, and gardens. No. 80 was the residence of Garrett Van Horne (*Ibid.*, XXVI: 500; XXXI: 521) and No. 81 that of Colonel Abraham de Peyster, and was famous as one of the finest colonial houses of that day. The house was not, however, as will be noted, so extensive as tradition paints it. The large gardens originally belonging to it and adjoining to the east, had, by the period of our view, been covered by the buildings Nos. 82, 83, and 84, which remained the property of Colonel de Peyster.—*Ibid.*, XXI: 266; XLII: 281; XLVIII: 21; XXXI: 173.

The large double house (85) was undoubtedly that built, *c.* 1706, by Johannes Kip and Theunis De Key, in common. At the period of the view, Jannetie Tothill, widow of Jeremiah Tothill, owned the westerly part and De Key's heirs that to the east.—*Liber*, A: 128 (in Compt. Office); *Liber Deeds*, XXXI: 143, 173, 177, 191, 409.

The corner (86) was probably owned at this time by Rip Van Dam. Originally granted to William Merrit by the city (1692), it came to be well known, before 1721, as "Rip Van Dam's Corner."—*Liber*, A: 97 (in Compt. Office); *Land Papers* (Albany), VIII: 103–195; IX: 39.

FROM MAIDEN LANE TO FLETCHER STREET

The low building (87) on the corner of Countess Wharf (Water Street) and Countess Slip (Maiden Lane) belonged to Robert Lurting, Esq., a vestryman of Trinity Church, Treasurer of the City, and later Mayor.—*Liber Deeds*, XXVI: 302; XXX: 105.

The three small buildings on Maiden Lane, north of the corner (88), belonged to Abraham de Peyster (*Ibid.*, XXVI: 296; XL: 395; XLVIII: 524), while the two taller houses, numbered 89, and fronting one on Countess Slip and the other on Fletcher Street, were owned by Sampson Benson, who had bought them in 1711 from the eminent merchant Thomas Pearsall.—*Ibid.*, XXVIII: 4; XXXVII: 152.

No. 90 is the wind-mill of Pieter Jansen Mesier, near the corner of Cortlandt and Greenwich Streets.—See Pl. 22-a, and Chronology.

FROM FLETCHER STREET TO RODMAN'S SLIP (FOOT OF JOHN STREET)

Abraham de Peyster was the owner of No. 91.—*Ibid.*, XXVI: 296, 302; XLVI: 120. The large building, No. 92, and the smaller ones adjoining, belonged to the Schuyler family, whose ancestor, Captain Brandt Schuyler, had received the water-grant in 1692.—*Liber*, A: 124 (in Compt. Office); *Liber Deeds*, XXXI: 331, 332; XLV: 284; XLVII: 346.

Nos. 93 and 94 were, respectively, the property of Dr. John Rodman and William Huddleston.—*Ibid.*, XXXI: 110.

No. 95, at the period of the view, belonged to Matthew Benson, who had purchased it from Dr. Rodman and another of his partners, Thomas Stevenson. Because of Rodman's extensive holdings at the corner, the slip later became known as Rodman's Slip (now Burling Slip).—*Ibid.*, XXVIII: 190; XXXIV: 189.

FROM RODMAN'S SLIP TO BEECKMAN'S SLIP (FOOT OF FULTON STREET)

The ship-yard in the angle (96) belonged to Egbert van Borsum, whose heirs, in 1737, received the water-grant into the East River.—*Liber*, B: 296 (in Compt. Office).

The large house on the corner of Pearl Street (97), together with the smaller buildings fronting to the wharf (Water Street) as far as the corner of the slip, all belonged to the Van Cortlandt family. Stephanus Van Cortlandt had a wide water lot here in 1692, and the property remained in the possession of his heirs for the better part of a century.—*Liber*, A: 106 (in Compt. Office); *Liber Deeds*, XXXI: 199; XXXV: 438; XXXVII: 163; XLIII: 409; XXVIII: 295; XXXII: 105; *M. C. C.*, III: 206.

The small buildings between the ship-yard and the Van Cortlandt estate belonged to Joseph Latham. As he was a shipwright, he may also have been the proprietor of this yard. In 1719, he had a controversy with the widow Van Cortlandt about the fence shown in the view.—*M. C. C.*, III: 206.

FROM FULTON STREET TO BEEKMAN STREET

No. 98 was the slaughter-house of Johannes Beeckman, which had been built subsequent to the order removing the slaughter-houses from Queen Street, near the gate, June 23, 1696 (*M. C. C.*, I: 408) and prior to 1699 (*Liber*, A: 374, in Compt. Office).—See also *Liber*, B: 83 (in Compt. Office). It was ordered removed in 1721 (*M. C. C.*, III: 249-51). The river shore at this point was about midway between Water and Pearl Streets.

The land of John Cannon, called Cannon's Wharf in later days (see Pl. 27), is numbered 99.—*Liber*, B: 64 (in Compt. Office). The two houses at No. 100 belonged to Gilbert Livingston: one at the corner of Pearl and Beckman; the other at Water and Beckman Streets.—*Ibid.*, B: 50 (in Compt. Office).

Beyond Livingston's corner, the view seems to be somewhat inaccurate. There is no doubt that the house on the bluff (101), stood just west of what is now the northwest corner of Roosevelt and Cherry Streets, and that the large house on the shore (102) also stood at the corner of Roosevelt Street, on the river side, at about Water Street. At the time when the view was drawn, these two houses belonged to John Deane.—*Ibid.*, B: 76 (in Compt. Office); *Liber Deeds*, XXXII: 354; XXXIII: 431. In 1721, the City Slaughter House was established "a little to the westward of the new house of John Deane" (102).—*M. C. C.*, III: 249-51. A reference to Lyne's Survey (Pl. 27) will show the dock of John Deane, the slaughter-house, and the house on the north side of Cherry Street. In 1742, the Deane houses came into the possession of Joseph Latham, from the Deane heirs. A picture of the old Deane house is given in Valentine's *Manual* for 1855, p. 593.

The coach and horses (103) stand just at the intersection of Pearl and Cherry Streets (at that time, Queen and Sackett Streets) and the long fence running to the west was the Leisler boundary, near the present line of Frankfort Street, and parallel to it.

Although there remains no vestige of it in the 1717 view, the land between the Deane houses and the ship being built on the shore to the south, had been, a few years earlier, a famous pleasure-ground, called Sackett's Orchard or the Cherry Garden. The large ship on the ways, north of No. 101, lies just west of the old ferry point of Egbert van Borsum.

The artist has evidently not allowed sufficient distance between Livingston's corner at Beekman Street and John Deane's houses at Roosevelt Street, probably because of the limitations of the copperplate. Cherry Street is distinctly seen curving down to the river shore near the present James Street (*cf.* Pl. 27).

The big house on the shore (104) at the corner of Catharine Street, stands on ground once belonging to Captain Thomas Delavall. At the time of the view it was in the possession of Abraham Wendell, whose son, John Wendell, when he sold the tract of seven acres to Anthony Rutgers in 1743, recites that his father had "caused a house to be built and erected," which there is every reason to believe was the house here shown. —*Liber Deeds*, B: 193, 194; XXXI: 82; CLV: 250.

In 1732, Harmanus Rutgers purchased the land shown at the extreme right of the print. The two small houses under the brow of the hill (105) may be plainly seen on the Ratzer Map (Pl. 41).—*Ibid.*, XXXIII: 28.

Plate 26

A Plan of the City of New York

Wash drawing in pen and ink, and colour, on paper. 27 x 23¾ Date depicted: Probably 1730. Date Issued: ?

Author: Unknown, possibly William Bradford, from a survey by James Lyne.

Owner: I.N.P.S.

This very interesting drawing was purchased, about 1880, from a junk-dealer in Nassau Street by Dr. Thomas Addis Emmet. In a letter to the author, dated May 15, 1910, Dr. Emmet states that the plan when found was badly torn and that he had had it repaired by George Trent. It is difficult to find a plausible explanation of the origin of this mysterious document, which may possibly be the original drawing, from which the so-called Bradford Plan (Pl. 27) was engraved, perhaps even by the hand of William Bradford himself, in which case it would be one of the most important monuments in the cartography of New York. It will be noticed that the dedication bears the signature of William Bradford and an original seal. A comparison of this signature with an authentic copy of Bradford's discloses a close similarity, not sufficiently striking, however, to be conclusive.

The absence of a number of indications which are found on the engraved plan (Pl. 27) would seem to prove that the manuscript plan was made at an earlier date, were it not for the fact that a careful examination of the former shows that the most important of these additions are in manuscript and exist only on the impression of the plan owned by Mr. Andrews. These additions are described in detail in the description of Plate 27.

On the other hand, the manuscript plan, while lacking other indications found on all the known impressions of the engraved plan, contains a number of features not found on the latter, which fact seems to indicate that the manuscript was not a mere copy of the engraving. The most prominent of these are the parking of the space around the Fort, the addition of the paths and trees in Trinity churchyard, and the appearance of a new building on the north side of Fair Street, west of Cliff Street. The Dutch school belonging to the Old Dutch Church on Garden Street, and the English school belonging to Trinity Church (references L and M) are shown on this map, and apparently are not later additions. As these two schools were not built until 1748–9 (see Chronology), it is clear that the map cannot have been made before that date, unless, contrary to appearances, these were added later. Why it should not show certain other changes which we know had taken place in the city between 1730 and 1748, we are unable to explain. For instance, in 1735, the Almshouse was built on the Common, and in the same year the new Half Moon Battery was erected south-east of the Fort (see Pl. 32-a). The completion of the platform for this fortification was celebrated by the roasting of an ox, whole, upon the Battery, and by "Firing and Drinking of the loyal Healths, by a great many People, as is usual on such Occasions."—*The N. Y. Weekly Jour.*, July 21, 1735. Another important building, erected during this period, was the Broadway, or Oswego Market, at Broadway and Crown Street (see Chronology, 1738, April 13).

It is also curious that the Bowling Green, laid out in 1733-4, should not be shown. The plan seems to show Trinity Church after the additions made in 1735-7, at least so far as the south aisle is concerned. Why the new north aisle, which the records show was built at the same time, is not shown, it is difficult to understand.

The discovery of these heretofore unnoticed manuscript additions to Mr. Andrews's copy of the Bradford Plan removes the principal argument in favour of the priority of the manuscript over the engraved plan. Furthermore, a careful scrutiny of the former has revealed a partly erased inscription, probably a signature, in the left-hand lower corner, as well as the words "Made by J. Kall [or Kull, or possibly Katt or Kutt] Lon-[don]" on the scale to the left of the scroll in the right-hand lower corner. The former it has not proved possible to decipher definitely, although Mr. Paltsits thinks he sees in the deleted inscription the words "For the Commission, 1808."[1] This inscription and that on the scale, which is in gold, in minute block letters, had previously, for some inexplicable reason, escaped observation. An examination under the glass of the end of the scale, at the right of the scroll, reveals here also the existence, in the lower border, of some written characters. It proved impossible to decipher these until recourse was had to photography, when, after seventeen unsuccessful plates had been made, the eighteenth clearly revealed the figures 176– followed by either a "3" or a "5." These figures are in a running hand and do not seem to have any connection with the original block-letter inscription. They probably, therefore, represent a later addition, and may have no significance.

From all of the above facts, perhaps the most plausible assumption would be that this mysterious manuscript plan was copied in London from the engraved map at some time after 1748-9, in which years the two schools which it shows (references L and M) were built, and that these two buildings were therefore included. Why these should have been added, and the other variations from the engraved plan which have already been referred to, should have been made, while several important changes which had occurred in the city between 1730 and 1748-9 were ignored, we have found it impossible to explain, except by supposing that the author of the manuscript was for some reason particularly interested in these schools.

A number of slight differences occur in the spelling on the manuscript and engraved plans, which seems to indicate a lack of knowledge of the correct names on the part of the author of the former. Thus we find on the engraved plan the name "Vanases Ship Y^{d}," which is erroneously written on the manuscript plan, "Van Cises Ship Y^{d}." "Wessels Ship Y^{d}," on the engraved plan, is called "Weeds Ship Y^{d}" on the manuscript plan. "Vanderclifes Street," correctly spelled on the engraved plan, is "Vanderclises" on the manuscript. This is easily explained if we suppose that the "f" in Vanderclifes has been interpreted in the manuscript plan as an old-fashioned "s." Vanderclifes Street later became Gold Street. "Frankford" Street on the engraved

[1] This would suggest that the plan was prepared, perhaps with others for the use of the Commission of 1807-11.

plan, is written "Frankfort" on the manuscript. "Frankfort" is found on the Ratzen Plan and continues with this spelling down to the present day. "Beekmans Street," on the engraved plan, is changed to the more modern "Beekman Street" on the manuscript plan. "Meal Market," in the key of the engraved plan, is written "Meat Market" on the manuscript plan, an error which would not have been made by one with any knowledge of the city. Curiously, this same error is repeated on some of the facsimile copies of the engraved Bradford Plan. Note, also, that "Govenor," in the manuscript, is thus spelled, in both the key and the inscription. "Montgomery" is written on the manuscript plan, in place of "Montgomerie" on the engraved plan, although, as we find both spellings used as early as 1734, there is no special significance in this difference, except that, generally speaking, "Montgomery" is the more modern spelling. Note, too, that "Hanover Sqvare" and "Qveen Street" on the engraved map become the more modern "Hanover Square" and "Queen Street" on the manuscript.

It is, however, still conceivable that the manuscript plan was a contemporary copy of the original Lyne survey, and that it was afterwards partly brought up to date; or that it was made in London, after 1748–9, perhaps in 1763 or 1765, and possibly from the original survey. That it served as the intermediary between the original Lyne survey and the engraved Bradford Plan, although conceivably possible, is, on the whole, unlikely.

If we accept the theory that the plan was made by or for William Bradford or by someone else, and from the original survey, and that at some time subsequent to 1748–9 the two school buildings were added, without an attempt, in other respects, to bring the plan up to date, we must suppose the name on the scale to be that of the scale-maker, and the figures to be a later addition, and therefore to have no special significance. It must, however, be admitted that the character of the block lettering and the design of the frame or border strengthen the argument that the manuscript was made at a date even later than 1763 or 1765, their style being suggestive of the last part of the eighteenth century or the early nineteenth.

A very similar contemporary manuscript plan, preserved in the office of the Commissioner of Public Works, bears the date 1735 and the title "A Plan of the City of New York from an Actual Survey" (see Addenda). This plan is with little doubt a contemporary copy of the Bradford Map. To the lower edge of the map has been pasted a broad strip of paper, upon which is inscribed: "This Ancient Map Is respectfully Presented to The Honourable the Mayor and Common Council Of the City of New York By John Stanford A M 1828." The directories show that at this time John Stanford was a minister, and resided at 13 Lispenard Street.

The existence on the manuscript plan here reproduced and on the manuscript plan preserved in the office of the Commissioner of Public Works, as well as on the engraved Bradford Map, of the two schoolhouses built in 1748–9, and the omission of all reference to other improvements made between 1730 and 1749, has not been explained except by supposing either that Mr. Andrews's impression of the engraved map was copied from the manuscript plan here reproduced or from that in the Commissioner's office, or that these plans were copied from each other or from the identical copy here reproduced of Mr. Andrews's engraved map with the manuscript additions, and even this explanation is not complete or really satisfactory.

Reproduced and described here for the first time.

Plate 27

A Plan of the City of New York from an actual Survey Made by James Lyne
[The Bradford Map or The Lyne Survey]

Engraved on copper. 20¼ x 18 Date depicted: Probably 1730.
Author: Unknown; from a survey by James Lyne. Date issued: Probably 1731.
Engraver: Unknown; but possibly Thomas Johnson (Johnston; see Stauffer, I: 144), who engraved, about 1729, the Burgis Plan of Boston, which bears an ornamental dedication somewhat similar in character and execution to that on the Bradford Map, but much less crudely drawn. Another possible engraver is Charles Le Roux, the well-known silversmith and engraver, who, in 1715, 1716, 1719, 1734, and 1737 engraved bills of credit for the Province; those made in 1734 having been ordered delivered to William Bradford for printing (*MS. Coun. Min.*, II: 343, 346, in N. Y. State Library; *Assemb. Jour.*, Gaine Ed., I: 434 *et seq.; Laws of the Colony of N. Y.*, Chaps. 625 and 666), and who, on July 22, 1735, was ordered to make "a seal of the Office of Mayoralty of the City of New York."—*M. C. C.*, IV: 266. He was the eldest son of Bartholomew and Gertruyd Le Roux, a son-in-law of Gerard Beekman (Abstract of Wills in *Collections* of N. Y. Hist. Society, 1893, pp. 275–6), and a brother-in-law of Rip Van Dam.—*Ibid.*, 1894, p. 195. His father, too, was a well-known silversmith. For further information regarding the two Le Roux, see introductory Note on Early New York Silversmiths, by R. T. H. Halsey, in a *Catalogue of an Exhibition of Silver, Used in New York, New Jersey, and the South*, which exhibition was held at the Metropolitan Museum of Art in 1911. It is also possible that the plan was engraved by a certain "German Graver" who, as we know from a letter from Colonel Stephen Thomas to John Winthrop, dated New York September 15, 1713, was arrested in New York for counterfeiting paper-money and was sentenced to death. He was, however, pardoned, owing to the intercession of "most of the gentlewomen of this city," who addressed the governor "earnestly with prayers and tears."—*Boston News-Letter*, Sept. 21, 1713. Another possible assumption is that it was engraved by Francis Dewing, who arrived in Boston from England in 1715 and advertised his varied accomplishments in the Boston papers of the day. In 1722 he engraved and printed a large map or plan of "The Town of Boston in New England", which much resembles the Bradford Map in general character and technique. A proof copy of this rare plan is in the author's collection.[1]

[1] Although this print was long considered to be the earliest map or plan engraved upon copper in this country, it has been relegated to second place by the recent discovery of a map of the Raritan River, engraved nearly forty years earlier. This so-called "Map of the Raritan River", the first map or plan, indeed the first engraving on copper (of which we have any record), made in America, was engraved by R. Simson in 1683 from a plat or drawing by John Reid. It is fully described in a paper read by Charles Harper Walsh before the Columbia Historical Society of Washington, on March 21, 1911, and published by the Society in pamphlet form in 1912. But two copies of the map are known; one in the map division of the Library of Congress, the other in the collections of the New Jersey Historical Society. The latter bears two endorsements, the more important of which reads:

> "Mapp of some of the first Early Lands Patented to some of the Early Proprietors among the 24 Proprietors who sent over Stock & servants for the Setlement of the lands and building the Port Town of Amboy in the Province of East New Jersey In America.
> most Upon Raritan River, Milston & South Rivers &c anno 1683, 4, 5, 6."

Owner: William Loring Andrews, Esq.

Other copies: There are but two other copies of this important plan known, one in the possession of the N. Y. Hist. Society, presented to it by John Pintard in 1807, and one in the office of the Commissioner of Public Works (Bureau of Design and Survey; formerly the office of the Engineer of Street Openings). The latter is almost without doubt the impression formerly belonging to G. B. Smith, Street Commissioner, which was published in lithographic facsimile in 1834 by G. Hayward, which reproduction is also found in Valentine's *Manual* for 1842–3 where, however, the address is omitted.

Only known state. One of the earliest examples of the art of engraving on copper executed in New York, and almost without doubt the first *plan* of the city printed here. The earliest *map* engraved in New York was probably that published in 1724, also by William Bradford, in *Papers Relating to an Act of the Assembly of the Province of New York*, by Cadwallader Colden,—"A Map of the Countrey of the Five Nations," etc. (Vol. II, Addenda). Bradford published, also, in 1735, "A Map of the Harbour of New York" (Pl. 29). The Brinley catalogue, describing Mr. Brinley's copy of "A Map of the Countrey of the Five Nations," now in the N. Y. Public Library, which owns also an impression of the second state (Vol. II, Addenda), calls this edition superlatively rare. The only other copies in the first state known in America are a copy described in the 1912 catalogue of Mr. Charles E. Goodspeed of Boston, and an imperfect copy in the N. Y. Hist. Society. A reduced copy of the first state of the map is included in Colden's *History of the Five Nations*, London, 1747.—See Bibliography.

"A Map of the Countrey of the Five Nations" was first advertised in *The N. Y. Gazette* of February 20–27, 1726(7), and "A Map of the Harbour of New York" in the *Gazette* of March 24–31, 1735. An exhaustive search has been made, and every known copy of the *Gazette* for this period read, as well as all contemporary Philadelphia and Boston papers, and even the principal London papers, but no reference has been found to the Lyne Survey or Bradford Map. It is strange, indeed, that Bradford should not have advertised the publication or sale of this, his most important map or plan, in his own paper, although, as a number of issues are lacking between 1730 and 1733 (see Check-list of early New York Newspapers, Vol. II), it is of course possible that one of these may contain some notice of it.

The plan was probably surveyed and drawn in 1730, and issued some time between February 11, 1730(1) and July 1st, of the same year. It was on the former of the last two dates that the Montgomerie Charter, defining the boundaries of the wards and creating "Montgomerie's Ward," was given over to the city, although the charter had been in preparation since March 23d of the preceding year. On July 1st occurred the

John Reid, who compiled and drew the map, was a book-maker in Edinburgh, as is proved by his imprint on the title-page of *Scot's Model*, and was selected by the twenty-four original "Proprietaries" to take charge of a party of emigrants sent over in 1683. For his work in platting this map he received, in 1686, a grant of land, named "Hortensia," in Monmouth County where, having acted as Deputy-Surveyor and as a member of the General Assembly, and in 1703 as Surveyor-General of the Province, he died in 1723. Of R. Simson, the engraver, nothing is known beyond the fact that his name is attached to this map as engraver. That the map was engraved in the colonies, is proved by an agreement made between the then governors of East Jersey and West Jersey, which agreement was signed and sealed on Sept. 5, 1688. In referring to the neighbourhood of the Raritan River this agreement speaks of a "printed draught of the proprietors lands, surveyed in East Jersey and drawn by John Reid, *and since printed here*."

death, at Fort George, of Gov. Montgomerie, to whom, as "Capt Genl & Govr in Chief of his Majestis Provinces of New York, New Iersey &c," the plan is dedicated. It is almost certain, therefore, that it was drawn and engraved prior to this date, else the form of dedication would have been different. Colonel Robert Lurting, Mayor, whose name appears in the upper right-hand corner under the arms of the city, died on July 3, 1735.—*M. C. C.*, IV: 262.

Another indication that this plan could not, as has frequently been asserted, have been engraved, or even surveyed, as early as 1728, which date is found upon most of the early reproductions, is the fact that Bayard's Sugar House, on the north side of Wall Street east of Federal Hall, is shown (Reference No. 6), and this building was not erected until a short time prior to August 17, 1730, on which date *The New-York Gazette*, in an advertisement, referred to it in such a way as to indicate that it had just been erected.—See Chronology. Proof that the date of issue was not later than 1733 is found in the fact that Cortlandt Street, laid out and named in the spring of that year (*M. C. C.*, IV: 181), is not shown, as it almost surely would have been had the plan even been engraved after this date. Curiously enough, Cortlandt Street is shown on all the early facsimile reproductions of the plan except the first, issued by Longworth in 1817. Note, also, that the Bowling Green, laid out and named in 1733–4, is not found upon the plan. The first reference to the Bowling Green is contained in the *Minutes* of March 12, 1733 (*M. C. C.*, IV: 174, 179), where the Common Council resolved to lease the land for this use, and in those of October 1, 1734, where it was resolved "that the Bowling Green at the lower End of the Broadway in the West Ward of this City as it is now in fence be Leased unto Frederick Philipse Esqr Mr John Chambers and Mr John Roosevelt . . . at the yearly rent of one pepper Corne."—*Ibid.*, IV: 220–1. See Chronology.

The actual date depicted can with very little doubt be fixed at 1730, which is the date found upon the manuscript drawing reproduced as Plate 26. On August 13th of that year, a warrant was issued authorising Cadwallader Colden, Surveyor-General, to "survey, for the corporation of New York, 400 feet beyond low water mark, on Hudson's river, from Bestavers Killitie to the limits of the fort, from thence (leaving out, for the use of the fort, all the west side of the street that leads down to Whitehall) eastward along the East river, to the north side of Corlaer's hook."—*Land Papers*, X: 129, in Office of Sec'y of State, Albany. On September 15, 1730, the Common Council ordered the Treasurer to pay John Cruger the sum of forty pounds, "it being for the like sum by him disburst and paid to Cadwalladar Colden Esqr his Majesties Surveyor General of this Province as a Reward for his fees and service for the Return of his Survey and Certificate thereof, for the New Charter and Grant to this Corporation."—*M. C. C.*, IV: 24. This Warrant and Return are printed in full in Valentine's *Manual* for 1856, pp. 598–9.

The appearance at about this time of Bradford's Map, "from an actual Survey Made by Iames Lyne," is significant, and suggests the possibility that Lyne may have been one of the surveyors engaged upon the survey of Cadwallader Colden who, as Surveyor-General, probably did not personally take part in the field work. The fact that Bradford was at this time the provincial printer suggests also a possible official connection between his plan and the Montgomerie charter, although it is hardly likely that the Bradford Map reproduces, even in part, Colden's survey, which, as we know from the Return, was not begun before August 13th, and was completed not later than September 2d, a period of less than three weeks. We know, also, that its principal, if not its only object was to extend the boundaries of the city into the rivers and to determine the amount of land thus added, so that it probably contained no indication of the lay-out of the street system or other details of the city. Although it has not proved possible to connect the Bradford Map directly with the Montgomerie Charter or to assign to it an official standing, it is clear that it was at least a direct result of the interest aroused at this time in the boundaries of the city and in its redivision into seven wards, an interest which the enterprising Bradford did not fail to appreciate and take advantage of.

We have very little information concerning James Lyne. The first mention of his name that we find is in an advertisement in *The New-York Gazette* of August 31–September 7, 1730: "On the 15th of September[1] next at the Custom-House, in the City (where a convenient Room is fitted up) James Lyne designs to Teach in the Evenings (during the Winter) Arithmetick in all its parts, Geometry, Trigonometry, Navigation, Surveying, Guaging [*sic*], Algebra, and sundry other parts of Mathematical Learning." In Leeds's *The American Almanack For the Year of Christian Account, 1731*, printed and sold by William Bradford in New York and Andrew Bradford in Philadelphia, occurs the following paragraph: "Having occasion to go into Mr. Bradford's Printing-House at the time they were printing Mr. Birkets Almanack for the year 1731, and looking over the same, I found a Question proposed, in order to be answered, I sate down in said House, and in less than a quarter of an hour I found the Time since Noon (when Thomas met James) to be one seventh of an hour past Five. Ja. Lyne." Possibly the visit here referred to had something to do with the printing by Bradford of the Lyne Survey. In 1737, Lyne was elected a constable of the West Ward, although he never served, as he was appointed Adjutant of Militia in October of the same year.—*M. C. C.*, IV: 386, 390, 392.

Du Simitière, writing in June, 1769, and referring to the Montgomerie Charter's division of the city into seven wards, says:

> The boundaries of every ward are described in the charter, but they can not easily be understood without the help of the plan publish'd at that time by Wm Bradford & knowing also where Some places that Went by particular names, Obsolete now, Stood at that time. I shall mention a few, for instance, in describing the Boundaries of the West Ward. a lot of ground belonging to Charles Sleigh & the House & ground late of Thomas Elde are mentioned, Now these are Situated at the east end of the Street that goes from the Parade to the North River. one must be the Spot where Captn Kennedy's house Stands now & the other the House near the fort in possession of Th^s Coker at the time of Dongan's Charter & reserved to the King. the next mentioned is Domine Du Bois's house. it is the House where Domine Ritzema now lives it was at that time a Corner house there being no building from thence to the presbyterian meeting house, that house is Situated on the East Side of the Broad Way near the Corner of King's Street. Spring Garden house was a place of entertainm[ent] Situated on the east Side of the Broad Way at the entrance of the commons & exactly opposite to where St Paul's church now Stands, two new Brick houses are now erected on that Spot belonging to Some of the De Peisters. part of the old building remains yet but it had not been improved as a tavern for many years Bestayer's Killitie or Rivulet is a Small run of Water that takes its Sources in Mr Lespinard's land & after running thro its meadows, discharge itself into the North River.
>
> the South Ward include Nutten Island (now Call'd Governors Island, being appropriated as a Domaine to the governor for the time being) Bedloe's Island, Bucking Island and the Oyster Island. Bedloe's Island belong[s] to the Corporation, one Joseph Andrews a Pirate & murderer was hang'd in Chains on that Island the 23 of last month May.

[1] It is an interesting coincidence, that this is the very day on which the Common Council ordered the Treasurer to pay John Cruger forty pounds for a like sum paid out by him to Cadwallader Colden for the survey, as above noted.

> in the Dock Ward, mention is made of a place calld Marten Clock's corner and of a Small Street between the house, late of the Said marten Clock and the Slip
>
> in the East Ward I'll only observe that what is call'd in the charter Rodman's Slip is in the plan nam'd Lyons Slip & now Burling Slip
>
> the outward is the most extensive it comprehends all the rest of New York Island from the boundaries of the west, north South, Dock, East, and Montgomerie Ward all the Way to Kings bridge & include Great Barn Island little Barn Island & Manning Island as also part of the low water mark Shore on Nassau Island. it has two division, the Bouwerie Division & the Harlem Division for each of which two assessors & collectors & two constables are chosen. —Du Simitière's MSS., in the Loganian Branch of the Philadelphia Public Library (now the Ridgeway Branch of the Library Co. of Philadelphia).

These papers include also a manuscript copy of the Bradford Map, evidently made by Du Simitière himself. The ornamental cartouche (quite different from the one on the engraved map) containing the title, states the date depicted to have been "about 1731." This plan omits some details, but otherwise is evidently intended to be an exact copy.

Note on this plan what appears to be a short cut on the Road to Boston, between the wind-mill and the Fresh Water Pond. This short cut does not exist on the manuscript plan, dated 1735 (Pl. 30), nor does it appear that it was completed even as late as 1740; for we have a record in the *Minutes* under date of July 29, 1740, that a "Number of Gent. have Undertaken to finish the Street Already begun thro the Hill by the Windmill at their own Expence provided this Corporation Will give them Leave So to Do." Permission was accordingly given.—*M. C. C.*, IV: 496. There is no reference in the *Minutes*, or elsewhere, to the beginning of this street, or short cut, other than that contained in a Broadside dated September 8, 1734, where it is picturesquely referred to as follows (see Chronology):

> You are disappointed of your Hopes, says *Steep the Tanner*, but I am defeated of my Possession; for there is so many new Gimcracks made, that the old POND in the Neighbourhood, which used generously to give us its Water, to steep our Hides and wash our Shirts, is gone to take a New Habitation in the Dominions of his Elder Brother . . . And, say they, here we are summoned to make a Ditch thro' Fresh-water-Hill, as if there was such another Pond on the Top of it, as there is at the Botom; and when done, will cost more to keep it in Repair, than it did to dig it. And what the Use of it is I can't see (said one of them) unless it be to save the Governour's Coach, or some other great Men who are fond of it, the going about a Hundred Foot further, in a better and more convenient Road already made?

The fact that this street, or short cut, was made at private expense, shows that it was not a part of the High Road to Boston, which was in existence as a country road prior to 1735. On February 26, 1734(5), the *Minutes of the Common Council*, IV: 245–6, contain the following entry:

> Ordered that Alderman Fell, Alderman Burger, Mr Fred and Mr Byvanck or any three of them (Calling to their Assistance the surveyors of this Corporation) be a Committee to lay out the High Roads from Spring Garden Gate to freshwater and from the Gate at the End of Queen Street to the freshwater to meet the Other Road at freshwater, as the same was laid out by Act of Assembly by William Anderson, Clement Elswert, and Pieter Van Oblienis the 21th. day of June 1707 that they Cause a Draught to be made thereof; that the Said Roads may be Exactly Ascertained and publickly known, which are to be of the breadth of four Rodds at the least."—*M. C. C.*, IV: 245–6.

On March 22, 1736(7), a committee was appointed "to Ascertain and Cause to be Staked out, the Publick Highway from the Corner of Mr Freds House in Queen Street to Fresh Water."

The "better and more convenient Road already made" is without doubt the road which ran south from the wind-mill, curving northward to Fresh Water, although the road over the hill and past the wind-mill must also have existed at this time, probably as a rude and unregulated trail.

The allusion in the satire to the governor and his friends is undoubtedly to Governor Cosby, who lived at this time in the Rutgers House on the Bouwery, while the reference to the lowering of the water in the "old Pond" is a thrust at Rutgers, who in December, 1730, petitioned for the fee simple of the swamp and Fresh Water Pond adjacent to the Duke's Farm, consisting of seventy acres of ground, which petition was granted on December 31, 1733.—*Patents*, XI: 127. This patent provided for the draining of the swamp within a year, and reserved the remaining waters of the pond for the use of the inhabitants of the city. The drain laid by Rutgers, which extended to the Hudson River, is very clearly shown on the Ratzen Map (Pl. 42). Evidently, under the terms of his grant, Rutgers thought he had a right to drain the Collect Pond also. The objections of the tanners to this, shown in the Broadside above quoted, were carried to the Common Council on September 18th of the same year, when "A Great Number of Tanners and Other Inhabitants" represented that they were "greatly prejudiced by A Drain laid into the fresh Water Pond by the Order of Anthony Rutgers ESq[r]", which had "greatly drawn away the Water from the same Pond." Rutgers was, accordingly, ordered, before October 1st, to fill up the drain thirty feet from the Fresh Water "so as Effectually to prevent the same from Draining the said Pond."

The "ditch" mentioned in the broadside evidently does not refer to the drain laid by Rutgers, but to the short cut through Windmill Hill.

The impression of the Bradford Map owned by Mr. Andrews, and here reproduced, is in almost perfect condition, and may be described as "uncut," as the rough edges of the sheet upon which it is printed remain intact. A careful comparison of this copy with the copy in the N. Y. Hist. Society and with that in the office of the Commissioner of Public Works, clearly discloses the fact that Mr. Andrews's impression, probably shortly after 1748–9, was brought up to date by the addition in manuscript, in the table of references and on the plate, of "L. Dutch free School House," and "M. English d°," both of which were erected in these years; as well as by the addition to Trinity Church of the side aisles built in 1735–7, of the double outline of the block on the east side of Broadway facing Trinity Churchyard, the dotted line marking the boundaries of the New Dutch Church property on Nassau Street, between Queen (Pearl) and Crown (Liberty) Streets, and certain shaded portions representing buildings in the outline of the double block between Beekman Slip and Peck Slip or Wharf on the East River, including the closing of the east end of Beekman Street, etc.

The Bradford Map is the most important engraved plan that we have of the old City, which it depicts at a very interesting period of its development. Mr. Andrews, in a Postscript to his *James Lyne's Survey*, published in 1900, describes eight facsimiles of the original plan, but omits the earliest known reproduction, an inset plan about eight inches long, appearing in the left lower corner of the finely engraved and rare plan of the City issued by Longworth in 1817. He, however, mentions this inset in *The Bradford Map* (1893), although the date of publication is there given as 1825. There is a copy of this plan complete with the index of streets in the N. Y. Public Library; a proof copy, without the index, is in the author's collection.

Bradford's original tombstone, removed from Trinity Churchyard in 1863, when it was replaced by a modern copy, is preserved in the collections of the N. Y. Hist. Society, and bears a silver plate stating the stone to have been the gift of the rector, church-wardens and vestrymen of Trinity Church. The tombstone gives the date of Bradford's birth as 1660, the date of his arrival in America as 1682, and the date of his death as May 23, 1752. This inscription contains an error in that Bradford was born in 1663, according to Leeds's *Almanack* for 1739 (copy in N. Y. Hist. Society), wherein Bradford records, under date of May 20th, "The Printer born the 20th 1663." He was therefore 89 years old at the time of his death, and not 92, as stated on his tombstone.

Reproduction: Valentine's *Manual*, 1851, opp. p. 190.

PLATE 27–A
A PLAN OF THE CITY OF NEW YORK
[AND]
A PLAN OF THE HARBOUR OF NEW YORK

Engraved on copper. 17½ x 12 Date depicted: *c.* 1730.
Engraver: I. Carwitham. Date issued: *c.* 1735.
Owner: Bibliothèque Nationale, Paris, Print Department. Included in a collection mounted in four volumes, two of which contain loose maps, plans, and views of the United States, and two, similar documents relating to other parts of America.
No other copy known.

This interesting plan and map were evidently engraved by the same hand as "A View of Fort George with the City of New York from the S W" (Pl. 31), known from the name of its engraver as the "Carwitham View." They were apparently drawn at about the same period as Bradford's Plan of the City and Map of the Harbour, which they closely resemble, although some additions as well as omissions show that even if copied from these plans an attempt was made to bring them up to date. Note, for instance, in the Plan of the City, the "Potters" house, south-west of the Little Collect Pond. No such name appears on any other plan of the period, although Grim marks at about this same place on his plan, drawn from memory, two potters' houses—"Corselius' Pottery" and "Remmey & Crolius' Pottery"—and the Bradford Map has an unnamed building in this neighbourhood. We know that, later on, the city owned a pottery here, for we find in the *Minutes of the Common Council*, VI: 227–8, under date of October 30, 1760, the following reference: "Order'd that Alderman Filkin Alderman Bogart and Alderman Mesier, Messrs Roosevelt and Randell or the Major part of them be a Committee to Treat with Mr Henry Van Vlack Concerning the Rent of the Pott Bakers House Belonging To this Corporation near the Negroes Burying Place." This is probably the "Potters" house shown on our plan. On the Duyckinck Map of 1755 (Pl. 34), two "Pot Baker" houses are marked in this vicinity.

It is interesting to note that while there are a few additions on the Carwitham Plan of the Harbour, there are also some omissions. "Cuckold Town" on Staten Island, "Oversick River" in New Jersey, and "Bittops" (Billops) at the south point of Staten Island, are the most important additions. The most conspicuous omissions are "New Utrecht" (indicated but not named), "Jacques Bay," "Flatt Landt," and "Flatt Bush," all on Long Island. Note, also, on the City Plan, the crane and the ferry stairs at the Fly, as well as the practically continuous rows of houses surrounding the various blocks. The plan, however, is evidently not altogether accurate in this last particular, as we know from later plans that there were at this period a far greater number of vacant lots than are here indicated. A number of errors in spelling, while perhaps due to carelessness in copying, indicate also a lack of familiarity with the nomenclature of the places represented, which leads to the conclusion that the work was not done from original surveys. Note, for instance, on the Plan of the City, the very incorrect spelling of many place-names, and the corresponding names on the Bradford Map:

CARWITHAM	BRADFORD
"Scormerhorns" Wharf	"Schermerhorns"
"Levingstons" Wharf	"Livingston's"
"Rosetests" Wharf	"Roseveldts"
"Wastons" Ship Yard	"Waltons"
"Vancises" Ship Yard	"Vanases"
"East" Church	"Eng^{h}" Church (Trinity)

and on the Plan of the Harbour:

"Scullers" Copper Mine (in N. J.)	"Schuiler's"
"Kisvamcall" (n. end Staten Island)	"Killvancull"
"Spillen" Devil	"Spiten" Devil
Robins "Ritt"	Robins "Reeff" (?)
"Nullen" Island	"Nutten" Island

The Roman numerals, so characteristic a feature of the Bradford Map of the Harbour, are also used in the Carwitham Harbour Plan. It is interesting, too, to note the similarity of the Carwitham to the Popple Plan, drawn in 1727 and first issued in 1732 (see Pl. 29).

Perhaps the most interesting feature of the Plan of the City is the delineation in tiny bird's-eye perspective of a number of the most important buildings, such as the First Presbyterian Church, on Wall Street, the Dutch Church on Garden Street, and the Jews' Synagogue on Mill Street.

Reproduced and described here for the first time.

PLATE 28

NEW DUTCH CHURCH

(Known as the Middle Dutch Church after the construction of the North Dutch Church in 1767-9)

[The Rip Van Dam Church]

Engraved on copper. 9¾ x 13¾ (including title) Date depicted: Probably 1731, in which year, or shortly thereafter, the church building was completed. As the dedication refers to Rip van Dam as "President of His Majesty's Council for the Province of New York," and as he ceased to hold this office on August 1st, 1732, the print must have been issued before that date.

Author: Wm. Burgis.

Engraver: Unknown. Possibly Burgis himself, or Thos. Johnston, or Charles LeRoux.

Owner: William Loring Andrews, Esq.

Other copies: No other copy is known, although the Rev. Thomas De Witt, in his *Discourse Delivered in the North Reformed Dutch Church on the Last Sabbath in August, 1856*, gives a reproduction from an original copy of this view, then in the possession of the Rev. Mr. Strong of Newtown, L. I. It is, of course, possible, although not likely, that this is the same as Mr. Andrews's copy, which, he tells us in *The Bradford Map* (p. 21), he found about 1863 preserved in an old scrap-book, which contained, in addition, the Bradford Map and the Burgis "A View of Castle William by Boston in New England." The words "& is in Length 100 F in Breadth 75 Foot" have been added in pen and ink on Mr. Andrews's copy of the print of the church. They do not appear in De Witt's reproduction.

The street seen in the print to the right of the church is Nassau Street, and that on the left Crown or Liberty Street. The New Dutch Church was erected in 1727-31, and was, as the inscription on the print states, 75 feet broad and 100 feet long, exclusive of the tower, which stood on the north side of the building. The main entrances were on Nassau Street. Later, in 1764, when English preaching was introduced, it was found necessary to enlarge the church to accommodate the increased congregation, and galleries were accordingly added on three sides of the building. At the same time the pulpit was removed to the north side of the church, and the entrances were changed to the north and south sides. The interior of the building was almost totally destroyed during the Revolution by the British, who used it as a prison and also as a riding-school. It was repaired after the War and continued in use as a church down to August 11, 1844, when the last service was held within its walls (De Witt's *Discourse*, 53). In this year the United States Government leased and altered the building for a post-office. For a view of the building during this period of its existence, (see Pl. 130). In 1875 the post-office removed to its present building at the south end of City Hall Park, and thereafter the old church was remodeled and used as shops. In 1882 it was torn down to make place for the Mutual Life Insurance Company's building. For references and further historical data, see Chronology, 1726.

The church which is seen in the background of the view is the Église du St. Esprit, built in 1704 on the north side of King (Pine) Street, east of Nassau.—See Chronology. With the exception of the carriage shown in the Burgis View of 1717, the one here depicted is perhaps the earliest representation which we have of a New York carriage. It is presumably intended to represent that of Rip Van Dam, whose house was situated on Maiden Lane, east of Nassau Street.

Van Dam was one of the wealthiest citizens of his day. He owned the property now covered by 64-66 Nassau Street, where a theatre was erected in 1751, and which was later sold to the German Reformed Church, as well as all the land in that block south to Maiden Lane, and around the corner on the north side of Maiden Lane to the depth of about 150 feet. He also owned the land on the south side of Maiden Lane, 150 feet more or less on the Lane, extending to Nassau Street, where it had a depth of about 100 feet, besides other property. On the corner of Maiden Lane and Nassau Street, now No. 28 Maiden Lane, Van Dam built a house. This was evidently erected after September 11, 1732, when he bought from the city the gore fronting on Maiden Lane (15 by 103 feet) to straighten out his corner.—*Liber Grants*, B: 122 (in Comptroller's office). Van Dam probably lived here at one period, but at the time of his death, in 1749, according to a deed recorded in *Liber Deeds*, XXXVI: 28–33, he was occupying a house fronting on Maiden Lane, now 42, 44 and 44½ Maiden Lane. In the deed the property is described as "All that certain dwelling house, messuage, or tenement wherein the said Rip Van Dam lived at the time of his death." His executors caused a map to be made of his estate, by Maerschalck, and the property was advertised for sale in *The N. Y. Gazette* of December 4, 1749, the vendue being held December 18th.

The dial of the clock, removed from the tower at the time of the demolition of the Middle Dutch Church, is now preserved in the N. Y. Hist. Society.

Reproduction: Mr. Andrews's *New Amsterdam New Orange New York.*

This view was engraved on copper, in 1900, by Sidney L. Smith (from Mr. Andrews's copy) for the Society of Iconophiles.

Plate 29

A New Map of the Harbour of New-York by a late Survey

Engraved on copper. $9\frac{13}{16}$ x $12\frac{1}{16}$ Date depicted: *c.* 1734.
Date issued: 1735.

Published by William Bradford.

Owner: Henry E. Huntington, Esq., who purchased it, together with the entire library of the late E. D. Church, in April, 1911.

This map, which is believed to be unique, is bound up with a fine copy of the Charter of the City of New York, printed by John Peter Zenger, in 1735. In *The New-York Gazette* of March 24–31, 1735, Wm. Bradford advertised this map of the Harbour as follows: "There is now Published a new Map of the Harbour of New-York, from a late Survey, containing the Soundings and setting of the Tydes, and the bearings of the most remarkable Places, with the Proper Places for Anchoring [shown on the map by Roman numerals]. To be Sold by the Printer hereof."—See *Church Catalogue*, 920 A.

The name Greenwich appears here for the first time on a printed map.

A very similar draught of the Harbour had been issued in 1733 by William Henry Popple, as an inset to his large map of the British Empire in America. For a full description of this map, see *Lowery Catalogue*, No. 338. Winsor (*Nar. and Crit. Hist.*, V: 474) states that Popple's large manuscript draught is preserved in the British Museum, MS. 23615 (fol. 72), and that it is dated 1727. He also states that the first issue of Popple's engraved map appeared in 1732. No copy of this issue is known to the author.

Another map, similar in extent, appeared in the *English Pilot* for 1737, with the imprint of Page & Mount, on Tower Hill, London. Copies of this map exist with the date 1731 below the title, from which it seems evident that it was issued separately at that date. In the succeeding edition of the *Pilot*, issued in 1749, the same chart bears the name of Tiddeman. It was reissued with this imprint and without alteration down to 1767, the plate growing fainter and fainter till, in 1773, it was retouched, the water shaded, and the imprint altered to I. Mount, etc. Compare also, "A Plan of the Harbour of New York" by Carwitham (Pl. 27–A).

Reproduced here for the first time.

Plate 30

Plan of the City of New York In the Year 1735

Pen and ink drawing on paper. 18½ x 15¼ Date depicted: 1732–5.
Owner: I.N.P.S.; purchased at the Holden sale.

This very interesting manuscript plan contains references to buildings and topographical features not shown on any other known plan of the city. For example, No. 23, "Play House." This is the first plan upon which reference is made to a theatre; although we know that one was in existence as early as December, 1732, for the *Boston Gazette* of January 1, 1732(3), contains the following correspondence: "New York, Dec. 11 [1732], On the 6th Instant the New Theatre in the Buildings of the Honorable Rip Van Dam Esq; was opened, with the Comedy called The Recruiting Officer, the part of Worthy acted by the ingenious Mr. Thomas Heady, Barber and Perugue-maker to his Honour." Although a careful search through the title records fails to disclose any property on Broadway owned by Rip Van Dam at this period, it seems nevertheless probable that the advertisement quoted above refers to the "Play House" here shown, as, in *The New-York Weekly Journal* of February 2, 1740(1), we find another advertisement specifically referring to the "New Theatre" on Broadway: "On Thursday, Feb. the 12th at the new Theatre in the Broad Way will be presented a Comedy call'd the Beaux Stratagem," (etc.). Why the above notice is the solitary reference which we find to a theatre on Broadway in any of the New York papers of the period it is not easy to explain, except on the theory that in these early times theatres were not considered altogether reputable, and were not popular with the respectable, newspaper-reading community. At this period, too, the theatre was a transient institution, and plays and concerts were often given in the long-rooms of taverns, the place varying with almost every season. Thus, in 1736, the same play, "The Recruiting Officer," was given in a "new theatre" in Dock Street, possibly the long-room of a tavern. Van Denberg's Garden, to the west of Broadway, almost opposite the Vineyard, referred to on our map as "Van Denberger Meadhouse," was, in 1753, the site of what may have been a pavilion or out-door theatre, as is evidenced by the following advertisement in *The New-York Mercury* of August 13th of that year: "This is to inform the Publick, That there is just arrived in this City, and to be seen at a new House built for that Purpose, in Mr. Adam Van Denberg's Garden, This Evening being Monday, the 13th Instant, The Surprizing Performances of the celebrated Anthony Joseph Dugee. . . . "

From early records, we know that Van Dam at this time owned property on the east side of Nassau Street, between John Street and Maiden Lane, and also on both sides of Maiden Lane. He also owned the land on the corner of Maiden Lane and Pearl Street, which is the site referred to by T. Allston Brown in his *History of the New York Stage*, I: 7, as that occupied by the first theatre. Title records do not show when Van Dam acquired this latter property, but that he did own it as early as 1720 is proved by the following record from the *Calendar of Land Papers*, 134: "Caveat of the corporation of New York, against the granting of a patent to Thomas Clark and others, to gain upon the water between the house of Rip Van Dam, by the end of Maiden lane, and the corner, by Capt. Thomas Clarke, next the market house, at the lower end of Wall street." Another proof of the ownership by the Van Dam family of this property is found in Vol. IX of *Patents* (Albany), where, under date of March 7, 1722(3), Van Dam and others receive a patent for ground on the East River under water from Wall Street "to the southeasternmost corner of the lot of Rip Van Dam, Jr., which joins to the slip that leads from Maiden Lane."

In 1734, Judith Van Dam, widow of Rip Van Dam, Jr., applied for and obtained a water grant from the City (*Liber Grants*, B: 200, in Comptroller's Office), wherein it is described as "all that certain water-lot . . . being the corner lot on the westermost side of the slip commonly called Maiden Lane Slip or Countess Key Slip, opposite to a certain Messuage or tenement, fronting the street commonly called Queen Street Wharf [Pearl Street] belonging to said Judith Van Dam (the said street commonly called Queen Street Wharf lying between the tenement of said Judith Van Dam and the water-lot hereby to be granted)." There is nothing in this description, which refers to the building as a "messuage or tenement," to indicate that it was ever used as a play-house, or that it was suitable for such use. It stood on the present south-west corner of Maiden Lane and Pearl Street (197 Pearl Street and 104 Maiden Lane).

On the other hand, we know that, in 1750, a theatre was established in a "convenient room" in one of Van Dam's buildings on Nassau Street (see Chronology), and that on this same site a new theatre was built in 1753. *The New-York Gazette; or, the Weekly Post-Boy*, for September 17, 1753, states that "The Company of Comedians, who arrived here the past Summer, having obtained Permission from proper Authority, to act, have built a very fine, large and commodious new Theatre in the Place where the old One stood; and having got it in good Order, design to begin this Evening: As they propose to tarry here but a short Time, we hear they design to perform three Times a Week." The same paper contains, also, the advertisement of the play, "The Conscious Lovers," including "A New Occasional Prologue to be spoken by Mr. Rigby," and "An Epilogue (address'd to the Ladies) by Mrs. Hallam." The play was announced to begin, as did almost all plays of the period, at 6 o'clock.

The Nassau Street Theatre, which stood at the present 64–66 Nassau Street, was sold in 1758 to the German Reformed Church and, in 1765, was demolished.

Although from such records as are available at the present time, the date 1732 is the earliest to which can be definitely assigned the existence of a play-house in New York, we have reason to believe that plays as well as operas were given here at a much earlier date. As early as 1699, a petition was presented to Governor Hunter for a license to give theatrical performances (*Cal.Hist.MSS.,Eng.*,284). In the British Museum there is a very interesting little brochure entitled *The Fool's Opera; or, The Taste of the Age.* "Written by Mat Medley and performed by His Company in Oxford," etc.; printed in London for T. Payne, to which the Museum has assigned a date of 1730 with query. It was written by Mr. Anthony Aston, "commonly call'd Tony Aston," who describes himself as a "Gentleman, Lawyer, Poet, Actor, Soldier, Sailor, Exciseman, Publican; in England, Scotland, Ireland, New York, East and West Jersey, Maryland, Virginia (on both sides Cheesapeek), North and South Carolina, South Florida, Bahamas, Jamaica, Hispaniola, and often a Coaster by all the same."

Aston arrived at Charleston in January, 1703, where he says he "turn'd Player and Poet, and wrote one Play on the Subject of the Country." The following winter he was in New York. "There I lighted," he says, "of my old Acquaintance Jack Charlton, Fencing Master . . . after acting, writing, courting, fighting that Winter . . . my kind Captain Davis . . . gave me free passage for Virginia where the noble Governor Nicholson treated me handsomely till the fleet under Commodore Evans . . . convoy'd about 500 sail out of the Capes. The generous Captain Pulman . . . gave me my passage Home . . . We arriv'd in the Downs in August—up to London . . . " For a very interesting article on this subject, see O. G. Sonneck's *Pre-Revolutionary Opera in America*, in *The New Music Review*, VI: 438–44.

The first drama printed in English America is a farce entitled *Androboros*. It was written by Governor Hunter and "Printed at Monoropolis since 1st August, 1714," by William Bradford. The drama is a severe criticism of Trinity Church, including its rector, Dr. Vesey. Two copies only of this work are known, one in the collection of the Duke of Devonshire and another in a Scottish collection. Two manuscript transcripts of the play were made for Dr. Moore, about 1880, from the Duke of Devonshire's copy. One of these is now in the collection of Mr. Evert Jansen Wendell (see Bibliography).

Other places besides the "Play House," named on this plan and not on other maps, are the "Fishing Place," the name given to the east shore above Peck Slip and to the west shore above Morris Street; "Flat Rock," west of the Fort; "Buttermilk Pond" and "Sweetmilk Pond," on either side of the Bouwery Lane, etc., etc. These two ponds are shown nowhere else, except on the Holland survey (Pl. 36–b), where they are not named.

Cortlandt Street, laid out and named in 1733 (*M. C. C.*, IV: 181–2), appears for the first time on this plan. Notice the "Locust Trees" on the North River below the Lutheran Church, often mentioned in descriptions of the period, and shown also on the Carwitham View (Pl. 31); also the great tree on the north-east bastion of the Fort. For a description of Mesier's wind-mill, west of Broadway, between Cortlandt and Crown (Liberty) Streets, see Pls. 22–a and 23–a. Notice also the tan-yards, which are very clearly shown, surrounding Beekman's Swamp.

The house of Rutgers is shown on the "Bowre Layn," as is also the estate of De Lancey. The fact that De Lancey did not acquire this property from Bickley until September 15, 1744 (*Liber Deeds*, XXXII: 489), might seem to contradict the early date of 1735, which the map bears, but it is quite possible that De Lancey was a tenant of the property before he purchased it. We know that, in 1730, Colonel Gilbert occupied "the pretty House which Mr. Bickley built" on "the Bowery."—See Chronology, August 21, 1730. It is to be noted, also, that the exterior street, named Water Street on the plan, was not so named by the Common Council until 1736 (*M. C. C.*, IV: 331), but it is, of course, possible that this street was popularly called Water Street before it was officially so named.

The plan, curiously, omits any indication of the lane or alley shown on the Bradford Map immediately south of Trinity Church, and closed in 1739, when Robinson Street (now Rector) was opened a little to the south—*M. C. C.*, IV: 456. It also fails to show Frankfort Street. As on the Bradford Plan, there is no indication of the Almshouse, erected in 1735, or the Half Moon Battery, the platform for which was completed in the same year.

Although the map bears the date 1735, there are certain indications which seem to prove that it was drawn somewhat earlier. For instance, the Bowling Green, laid out and named in 1733–4, is not indicated; the shore line lying south and west of the

Fort seems to be more primitive even than on the Bradford Map, and there is no indication of the short cut through Fresh Water Hill, on the High Road to Boston, which was ordered constructed at about this date (see Pl. 26). That it could not, however, have been drawn prior to 1732 seems evident from the following facts: On August 26, 1731, a committee was appointed to "lay out the Land belonging to this Corporation lying on the West Side of the Dock, . . . leaving the Broadway and the Custom House Street each Sixty foot in breadth and Weigh House Street and Whitehall Street each forty foot in breadth . . . " We do not know exactly when these orders were carried out, but on March 24, 1731(2), the Common Council "Resolved that A Parcell of unimproved Ground belonging to this Corporation lying on the West Side of the great Dock and the Weigh House Street, Between the Said Dock and Street and the Street Called the Broadway, near the Custom House be laid out in seven Lotts and Exposed to Sale on Tuesday the twenty fifth day of April Next . . . ".—*M. C. C.*, IV: 130. Our map shows this property improved by buildings. A careful examination of the date on the plan brings out the fact that the last figure appears to have been altered, perhaps from a 2 or 4 to "5."

Note the very peculiar and apparently illiterate spelling throughout the plan, for instance: "Tavrin," "Meetin," "Jews Sinoge," "Bolding Green," etc. In the left-hand upper corner appears the name "Mrs. Buchnerd" (?), probably the original owner of the drawing.

The plan is drawn upon old hand-laid paper and has two water-marks, one a shield bearing the device of a horn and surmounted by a crown, beneath the shield the initials "G. R."; the other the name "I. Taylor."

Reproduced and described here for the first time.

Plate 31

A View of Fort George with the City of New York from the S W.
[The Carwitham View]

Engraved on copper. 17⅞ x 11¼ Date depicted: 1731–6.

Provenance: Unknown. Probably once included in a collection of views of cities, as is indicated by the reference number "V" in the upper right-hand corner.

Author: Unknown.

Engraver: I. Carwitham.

Owner: Library of Congress, Div. of Maps and Charts.

Other copies: No other copy known without an imprint.

While it is altogether likely that this state, without the imprint, is the earliest issue of the print, it is possible that it is a trial proof of a later state, taken after the erasure of the old imprint and before the engraving of a new one. Mr. H. N. Stevens, in his Catalogue of *Books Relating to America*, issued in February, 1901, describes an impression, now in the possession of Mr. R. T. H. Halsey (a similar state being also in the author's collection), with the Carington Bowles imprint and with a "V" in the upper right-hand corner. This is probably the second state of the print and must have been issued after 1764, at which date, as we learn from the London Directories, Carington Bowles succeeded to the business of Thomas Bowles. In the third issue, the "V" disappears from the upper right-hand corner and the numerals "35" appear in the lower left-hand margin. In this form the view occurs both with and without the reference numbers. Similar views of Boston and Philadelphia are known corresponding to this state and evidently belonging to the same series, bearing respectively the numbers "34" and "38." These three views are numbers 198, 199, and 200 of a collection of 271 perspective views in England, Scotland, France, Holland, Germany, Rome, Venice, Florence, America, etc., offered by Carington Bowles in a catalogue described more particularly under Pl. 37, and were designed to be used "in the Diagonal Mirror, an Optical Pillar Machine," or peep show. The price was "1 s plain, or 2 s, each beautifully coloured."

Carington Bowles, in his turn, was succeeded, in 1794, by Bowles & Carver, who carried on the business until 1832. During this period the print was apparently frequently reissued with the title changed to "A South West View of the City of New York in North America," with the number "35" in the lower left-hand margin, and without the reference numbers on the buildings. Mr. Stevens, in his Catalogue cited above, refers to copies of the Bowles & Carver issue printed on wove paper bearing the date in the water-mark 1825, and the author has in his own collection a copy with the water-mark 1809. The fourth issue sometimes appears with the English and sometimes with the American flag, but this change seems always to be in the colouring only and not in the engraving.

I. or J. Carwitham appears in Joseph Strutt's *Biographical Dictionary of Engravers* as having flourished as an engraver of book-plates, prints, and other work from about 1723 to 1741. We know, as mentioned above, that he engraved a view of Boston and one of Philadelphia uniform with the New York view. Both of these exist with the Carington Bowles and Bowles & Carver imprints. We have already referred to him as the engraver of A Plan of the City and A Plan of the Harbour of New York (Pl. 27-A). Some years ago, Mr. E. W. West, a veteran collector of early New York prints, spoke to the author of having seen, in the library of the British Museum, an octavo book, printed in 1739 for Carington Bowles and containing designs for floor decorations engraved by Carwitham, in which book was folded a copy of the Carwitham View of Boston. Mr. H. N. Stevens recently reported the existence of this book which, however, no longer contains the view. In the *Memorial History of Boston*, II: 530–2, Winsor discusses the date of the original Carwitham View of Boston, and reaches the conclusion, from internal evidence, that it was executed prior to 1743.

The date depicted by the New York view is between 1724, when Trinity Church was extended to the eastward (*Trin. Min.*, Apr. 11, 1722, and May 14, 1724), which enlargement distinctly shows in the view, and March, 1741, when the church in the Fort, which also appears, was destroyed by fire. These limiting dates are, moreover, narrowed down by the fact that the New Dutch Church (later Middle Dutch Church), finished in 1731, is shown completed. We know, from the Minutes of Trinity Church that, on July 2, 1735, it was ordered that "the North and South Sides of the Church [Trinity] be Enlarged and made Conformable to the New Building on the East End of the Church." By August 14, 1735, the foundations on either side had been completed and the vestry ordered that the side walls be raised six feet that autumn. The exterior work on the church was probably completed by the summer of 1736, for thereafter the Minutes refer only to work done on the interior of the church, which was not completed until 1738. It seems altogether likely that at this time (1736) the roof, as well as the sides, was made to conform with the new east extension, and as our view distinctly shows the roofs as they appeared after the building of this extension but before the original roof was raised, there can be little doubt that the date depicted is prior to 1736 (see Valentine's *Manual*, 1859, opp. p. 20, for a view of Trinity Church, original unknown, showing the church as it was in 1737; this view shows the roof without a break).

As it was a common custom at this period to show in views and plans important changes which had been decided upon, even if they had not actually been carried out at the time of publication, and as these changes in the roof, which were made in 1735, may have been determined upon earlier, it is possible that a still earlier date should be assigned to the Carwitham View, which may even have been drawn at the same time and by the same artist who made the plan, also engraved by Carwitham, referred to above, and reproduced as Pl. 27–A. This plan was probably drawn between 1731 and 1734.

The buildings shown in the view are as follows: 1 Trinity Church; 2 Lutheran Church; 3 New Dutch Church; the low building between Nos. 2 and 3 is probably the Presbyterian Church on Wall Street, very distinctly shown on the Carwitham Plan (Pl. 27–A), although it may possibly be intended for the Quaker Meeting on Liberty Place, or even for the new Poorhouse, which was built on the Commons in 1734 (see view of latter on Grim's Plan, Pl. 32–a); 4 The French Church du St. Esprit; 5 The City Hall; 6 The Old Dutch Church on Garden Street; 7 The Secretary's Office; 8 The Church in the Fort. It is interesting to compare this church, as here shown, with its delineation in the Burgis View, which is the earliest as well as the best picture which we have of the Church in the Fort, with its tower to the west as completed in 1696. The church in the Carwitham View seems to be quite different, although we have no positive record of any change in its plan having been made between 1717 (the date of the Burgis View) and 1730 (the earliest date to which we can assign the Carwitham View). We know, however, that on September 27, 1726, Governor Burnet spoke of repairs which, at that time, were urgently needed on the roofs of the chapel and the barracks which, he said, were "in a Condition entirely ruinous." On September 30, 1727, he referred to the fact that, although much had already been done to "beautify & repair the Buildings in the Fort," the soldiers' barracks were still in a "very ruinous Condition," and required immediate repairs. From this it seems quite probable that the changes in the chapel, shown in the Carwitham View, were made between these two dates. At all events they had been made before 1730, as the new arrangement is shown on the Bradford Plan of that year (Pl. 27). The wind-mill shown at the extreme left of the view is, of course, Mesier's. See Pls. 22–a and 23–a.

Notice the group of trees between the present Exchange Place and Morris Street, on the line of Church Street, generally referred to in the early records as the "Locust Trees," and shown on the 1735 Manuscript Map (Pl. 30). The large roof to the right of the Fort may be that of the De Lancey mansion, later Fraunces Tavern, corner of Broad and Pearl Streets, which was built in 1719 (*M. C. C.*, III: 199–200), or it may be one of the market houses so prominently pictured in the little Carwitham Plan (Pl. 27–A).

This is one of the most important, interesting, and sought-after prints of Old New York, and is rare in all states.

It is interesting to compare this view with the Bradford Map of the same period (Pl. 27), and also with Pls. 44 and 56, the only other known views of the city taken from the west in the eighteenth century.

Reproduction: Valentine's *Manual*, 1858, opp. p. xii.

A very good reduction, with slight variations, engraved on copper, 8⅜ x 5⅝ inches, appears in Russel's *History of America*, London, 1779.

PLATE 32-a

A PLAN OF THE CITY AND ENVIRONS OF NEW YORK
[Grim's General Plan]

Pen and ink drawing on paper. 22⅛ x 21⅞ Date depicted: 1742-3-4.
Date drawn: August, 1813.

Author: David Grim.
Owner: N. Y. Hist. Society.

This interesting plan was drawn from memory in the year 1813 by David Grim, then in his seventy-sixth year, and presented by him to the N. Y. Hist. Society. The original has been varnished and is in a very poor state of preservation. On the back of the plan is the following statement, written over the author's signature:

This plan of the city and environs of New York, I made for my amusement, with the intent that it be, on a future day, presented to the N. Y. Hist. Society. The number of houses in this city were, in the year 1744, as hereby particularized, viz.:

The west side of Broadway, to the river	129
The east side of Broadway, with the west side of Broad Street	232
The east side of Broad Street, with the west side of William Street	324
The east side of William Street, with the west side of Pearl Street	242
The east side of Pearl Street, to the East River	214
Total	1,141

I am perfectly clear there were not thirty houses, more or less, at that period, in the city of New York. Having a perfect recollection of the several spaces of vacant grounds and gardens that were at that time in the city, I could ascertain the number of houses with a tolerable certainty, by taking Retzer's [Ratzer's] Map as my guide, knowing the same to be correct, allowing twenty-five feet in the front, on the street, for each house, (some were more, others were less.) In order to prove my position, I carefully examined and counted the number of houses in several streets, and generally found them perfectly correct.

I will relate a few of the most remarkable occurrences that happened in this city, to the extent of my memory, which was that of the Negro-plot, in the year 1741, of which I have a perfect idea of seeing the negroes chained to a stake, and there burned to death.

The place of this execution was in the valley between Windmill hill and Pot-baker's hill, (now Augusta street,) about the centre of said street, and midway of (now) Pearl and Parley streets. The public executions were continued here for many years afterwards.

John Hustan, a white man, was one of the principal perpetrators of this horrid plot. He was tried, convicted, and hanged, in chains on a gibbet, at the south-east point of H. Rutgers' farm, bordering on the East river, not ten yards from the present south-east corner of Cherry and Catharine streets.

Caesar, a black man, a principal of the negroes in this plot, was also hanged in chains, on a gibbet, at the south-east corner of the old Powder-house, in Magazine street, (now Pearl street.) There were many of those negroes burned and hanged, and a great many of them were transported to other countries.

I remember the building and erecting the Palisades and Block-houses, in the year 1745, for the security and protection of the inhabitants of this city, who were at that time much alarmed, and afraid that the French and Indians were coming to invade this city, on which the General Assembly of this province voted a sum of money (£8,000,) to build a line of Palisades and Block-houses, from the East river to the North river. Those Palisades commenced at the house of Mr. Desbrosses, No. 57, in Cherry street, (which was then the last house on the East river, to Kip's bay.) From that place, it went in a direct line to Windmill lane, (late Catey Mutz;) from thence, in the rear of the Poor-house, and to Dominie's hook, at the North river.

Those Palisades were made of cedar logs, about fourteen feet long and nine or ten inches in diameter, were placed in a trench, dug in the ground for that purpose, three feet deep, with loop-holes in the same, for musketry, and a breast-work four feet high and four feet in width. In this line of Palisades were three Block-houses, about thirty feet square and ten feet high, with six port holes, for cannon. Those Block-houses were made with logs, of eighteen inches diameter. They were placed thus: the one was in (now) Pearl street, nearly in front of Bancker street; the second in the rear of the Poor-house, and the other between Church and Chapel streets. There were four large gates, or outlets to the city, the one at the head of Pearl street, Chatham street, Broadway and Greenwich street.

In the year 1746, (or nearly that time,) I remember having seen a concourse of Indians, of the Mohawk and Oneida tribes, come from Albany in their canoes, with their squaws and pappooses, (their wives and children,) a few hundreds, in order to hold a talk with the British Governor, George Clinton, Esq. They were encamped at the North river, in front of (now) St. John's Church. Those Indians, in a solemn train, marched from their encampment down the Broadway to Fort George, in which the Governor lived; in their parade they exhibited and displayed a number of human scalps, suspended on poles, by way of streamers, which scalps they had taken from the French and Indians, their enemies; after which the Governor, with the principal officers of the colony, and a large number of the citizens went in a procession, from the Fort to the Indian encampment, and presented to them the customary presents on those occasions. This was the last time the Indians came to New York to hold a conference; after which the Governor met them at Albany.

The winter in the year 1755 was so mild that the navigation on the North river was not impeded the whole of that winter. I remember having seen Sir Peter Hacket's and Dunbar's regiments, on their return from Braddock's defeat, in Virginia, embark on board of a large number of North river vessels, and sail to Albany in the middle of the winter.

Having spare paper here, and in order to fill that part I thought it might not be altogether improper to give an account here of the several slips in this city, and what gave rise to their several names. Those slips were formerly openings between two wharves, in the river, for horses and carts to enter, and there unload the wood boats; those boats would go into the slips at high water, and ground there, for the cartmen to enter from Pearl street, in order to unload them. I have often seen, at high tides, the water, by way of those slips, in Pearl street.

Whitehall slip took its name from Col. Moore's large white house. This house was adjoining to this slip, and was usually called the White Hall.

The next was called Coen & Antey's slip, (Conrad and Jane,) called so after Conrad Ten Eyck, and Jane, his wife; they lived at the corner of (then) Little Dock street and that slip.

The next was called the Old slip, being the first in this city.

The other was called Burling Slip, after the name of a Mr. Burling, a respectable family living at the corner of Smith's Flie, (now) Pearl street, and Golden Hill.

The next was called Beekman's slip, so named after a respectable family living at the south-west corner of Pearl Street and said slip.

The next and last on the East river, was called Peck slip, after the name of Mr. Peck, who was proprietor of the land on the side of said slip.

There was only one slip on the North River, at the foot of Oswego, now Liberty Street.

The statement quoted above is printed in the *Manual of the Common Council*, 1855, pp. 584-6, together with a reproduction of the Plan of the City Hall (Pl. 32-b). A reproduction of the Plan of the City is contained in the *Manual* for 1854, opp. p. 246.

Although drawn from memory, and at a period so remote from that represented, a comparison of this plan with the Bradford Map (Pls. 26 and 27) and with the 1735 Manuscript Plan (Pl. 30), shows it to be remarkably accurate; and it is important because it gives information which no other plan of the period contains. The small drawings of the churches above the map are in some cases the only record of the appearance of these edifices which we have. The course of the outlet of the Collect Pond into the East River is more clearly defined here than in any other map or plan that we possess.

Many of the reference numbers on the original are so faint as to be scarcely legible. They have, therefore, been strengthened in the photogravure plate.

PLATE 32-b

PLAN AND ELEVATION OF THE OLD CITY HALL (ETC.)

[Grim's City Hall]

Pen and ink drawing on paper. 15½ x 20⅞ (outside line) Date depicted: 1745-6-7. Date drawn: October, 1818.

Author: David Grim.

Owner: N. Y. Hist. Society.

This is the only record which we have of the external appearance and plan of the City Hall prior to its alteration in 1763 when a third story was added. The building, of course, appears in many of the general views, but at so small a scale as to make it impossible to judge of its architecture. The drawing was made by David Grim, from memory, in October, 1818, in the eighty-second year of his age. The original design of the City Hall was made by James Evetts, probably in 1698.—*M. C. C.*, II: 68.

So far as known, no representation of the City Hall exists between 1763 and 1788-9, when the building was altered by L'Enfant and became the Federal Hall (see Chronology), except a manuscript drawing by Du Simitière, made probably in 1769, and preserved, with other Du Simitière MSS., in the Ridgeway Branch of the Library Company of Philadelphia. For a reproduction of this drawing, see Vol. II, Addenda.

The Grim Plan and Elevation are reproduced in the *Manual of the Common Council*, 1855, opp. p. 584.

The N. Y. Hist. Society possesses a collection of Grim's reminiscences in the form of notes accompanying his General Plan and Plan of the City Hall (filed in a box under "N.Y., 1700-1760"). In addition to these manuscripts, Mrs. Sophia C. Minton, the granddaughter of David Grim, presented to the Society on June 7, 1864, a number of manuscript notes relating to the Tontine Coffee House, the Old City Hall, St. Paul's Chapel, the Brick Church, the Federal Table, and Federal Hall, and also a map of the Collect, a Plan of New York dated 1789, and a manuscript description of New York for the period covered by his recollections.

PLATE 33

A SOUTH PROSPECT OF Y^E^ FLOURISHING CITY OF NEW YORK IN THE PROVINCE OF NEW YORK IN AMERICA

[The Bakewell View, or the Bakewell reissue of the Burgis View, or the second state of the Burgis View]

Engraved on copper. 77⅜ x 20¾ Date depicted: 1717-46. Date issued: March 25, 1746.

Owner: N. Y. Hist. Society.

Only other known copies: New York Society Library; British Museum; Herbert L. Pratt, Esq. (title restored in photogravure); I.N.P.S.

Second known state. The Arms are changed and the dedication reads: "To His Excellency George Clinton Esqr Captain General," etc., instead of "To His Excellency Robert Hunter Esqr Captain General," etc. The date in the Province Seal is altered from 1717 to 1747, although the seal itself is still that granted by George I in 1718. "W. Burgis Delin^t^" etc., is erased, but "I. Harris fec." is left below the lower right-hand corner of the view above the legend.

The Whitehall Battery at the southern point of the Island, erected in 1734–41 (see Chronology), has been added, and also the Lutheran Church on the west side of Broadway below Trinity, built in 1727–9 (see Chronology), and the New Dutch Church on Nassau Street between Cedar and Liberty Streets, finished in 1731. Although the Church in the Fort and the Secretary's Office were burned in 1741, they still appear in the 1746 view. A comparison of the tower of the Lutheran Church, as here shown, with its representation in the Carwitham View (Pl. 31), in David Grim's reproduction (Pl. 32), and in the Banyer painting (Pl. 35), shows that this church has been drawn without an accurate knowledge of its architecture. The same may be said of the New Dutch Church, the most northerly of the group of churches shown in the view. Indeed, this church is quite erroneously drawn, as may be seen by comparing it with the Rip Van Dam View (Pl. 28) or with its delineation about ten years later in the Banyer painting. It will be noticed that the tower is shown on the south end instead of on the north as it should be.

It seems quite evident that Bakewell, wishing to bring the Burgis plate up to date, and not having authentic information at hand, made these changes largely from his own imagination. A minute comparison of the French Church as here shown with its representation in the Burgis View reveals the fact that it has been redrawn together with the small buildings immediately in front of it. In the original, traces of the change may clearly be seen with a glass. In redrawing this church the artist slightly altered the point of view, placing himself a little farther to the north, at the same time leaving out the reference number 16. It is hard to assign a reason for these changes. Although this reissue bears the date of publication "1746," attention has already been drawn to the fact that the seal of George I has not been altered. The reversed date in its lower border has, however, been changed from 1717 to 1747 (not 1746).

From the fact that the first part of the publisher's imprint, "London Printed and sold by Tho. Bakewell, Map and Print Seller against Birchin Lane in Cornhill" centres under the escutcheon and inscription of dedication, it seems likely that the remainder, "where Merchants and others may be supplied with all sorts of Maps, Prints & Pictures at the lowest prices," was a later addition, which fact would make this perhaps the third issue from the plate.

The first appearance of Thos. Bakewell in the London directories is in Osborn's fourth edition, of 1749, in which his address is given simply "Cornhill," without any designation of his trade. Mr. Soulsby, of the South Kensington Branch of the British Museum, has, however, a slip reference to an undated map of Berkshire, about 1730, with the imprint of "Tho. Bakewell next ye Horn Tavern in Fleet St. London," the same imprint which appears on the Bakewell reissue of the Burgis View. "Against Birchin Lane in Cornhill" appears too, in "A new and accurate Map of Scotland," by Bakewell, also dated 1746, and preserved in the British Museum. There are doubtless many other maps and views bearing Bakewell's name in the British Museum, but as the publishers are not separately indexed in the Catalogue, it is quite impossible, in a collection of many thousands of prints, to find them except by chance.

It may be interesting here to review the results of an examination of the London directories (first published in 1738), made for the author by Mr. Henry N. Stevens to establish the sequence of an important group of closely related publishers whose imprints appear on American views of the eighteenth century. In 1749, Bakewell's name first appears in Osborn's Directory, with address simply Cornhill and without any trade designation. In the same year, John Bowles first appears, with the same address. In

1752, Bakewell drops out but John Bowles continues. In 1753, the firm becomes John Bowles & Son, and this form continues down to 1763. In this last year, the firm of Bakewell & Parker, printsellers, Cornhill, first appears. In the directories from 1765 to 1774, the firm known as John Bowles & Son becomes again John Bowles, and for the same years the firm of Bakewell & Parker is superseded by Henry Parker, 82 Cornhill. Carington Bowles first appears in the directory for 1765.

The copy of the Bakewell View in Mr. Pratt's collection, which is in soft contemporary colouring, lacked practically the entire title, but this has been very skilfully restored in photogravure. The view itself was rather badly water-stained and a number of small pieces were gone, principally, however, from the sky and water, the city itself being intact. The print has been cleaned, rebacked, and very successfully restored by Mr. Hammond Smith of the Metropolitan Museum of Art, who also restored the copy owned by the Society Library. The author's copy was found mounted on a board, the resin from which had penetrated the paper, rendering it so brittle and dark that its successful restoration seemed almost hopeless. This, however, was finally accomplished with great skill, by Riviere & Son, of London. The print is still in its original hand-moulded frame. There is also in the author's collection a first section of the print, in contemporary colouring, but with the upper and lower margins trimmed.

A copper-plate reproduction of the Bakewell reissue, 20½ x 6⅛ inches, was published in *The London Magazine* for August, 1761. Three states of this view are known.

At the right and left of the title of the Bakewell View is engraved an interesting legend of the discovery of the colony and of its early history.

Valentine's *Manual* for 1849 contains a lithographic fac-simile of the print presented to the N. Y. Society Library, in 1848, by Mrs. Maria Peebles, of Lansingburgh, N. Y.

Plate 34

A Plan of the City of New York from an actual Survey Anno Domini M, DCC, LV

[The Maerschalck or Duyckinck Plan]

Engraved on copper. 33¼ x 17⅝ Date depicted: 1754.
Date issued: 1755.

Author: F. Maerschalck, City Surveyor.

Publisher: G. Duyckinck.

Owner: N. Y. Hist. Society, presented in 1807 by John Pintard.

Other copies: Library of Congress, Div. of Maps and Charts. This copy, which is the finest known, has an ornamental scroll border, of contemporary design but printed on separate strips. Trinity Church also possesses a copy, without border, and in rather poor condition, but complete. The only other recorded copy was destroyed in the State Library fire.

Only known state of the map as a whole, except as noted above. A microscopic comparison of this plan with the Bradford Map proves beyond the shadow of a doubt that the two were printed in part from the same plate. Du Simitière, writing in 1768, notes this fact (Du Simitière MSS. in Ridgeway Branch of the Library Company of Philadelphia). The plate, however, has been extended and very much altered, the joint being very easily distinguishable. The "P" of "Parade," north of the Fort on the Bradford original, is here still distinctly discernible. Reference No. 10, the market at the foot of Wall Street, and reference No. 11, the market at the foot of Crown Street, show distinctly a lengthening toward the East River. This is also true of the slips in front of them. The water contours of the Bradford Map show plainly in the neighbourhood of the little Bowling Green and Garden under "an" of the title of this plan. Note, among many other changes in the plate, that the lane just south of Trinity Church on the Bradford Map is not here shown. This lane was closed in 1739, and a new street, Robinson (Rector), was opened in its stead a little to the south. Robinson Street is shown on the present plan (see Chronology, 1739). Rotten Row (Hunters Key) appears here for the first time on a map. This also is the first printed map to show the fortifications built in 1745, during the war with France. They are thus described by Smith in his *History of the Province of New York* (1757), p. 188: "During the late War a Line of Palisadoes was run from *Hudson's* to the East River, at the other End of the City, with Block-houses at small Distances. The greater Part of these still remain as a Monument of our Folly, which cost the Province about 8000*l*."—See also Chronology, 1747, May 19.

This map was advertised by Duyckinck in *The New-York Gazette; or, the Weekly-Post-Boy*, under date of March 3, 1755, as "shewing the several Wards, Streets, Lanes and Allies, Churches, Meeting Houses, Markets, Sugar and Distilling-Houses, Water Lots, with the additional New Lots &c &c. to this present Year. Done from an actual Survey." Du Simitière, in his notes on maps (book No. 1412 Y, Ridgeway Branch of the Library Company of Philadelphia), states that copies of the Maerschalck Map had become (even in his day) very rare (see Bibliography).

A simplified copy of this map, on a reduced scale, was issued in 1763 as plate No. 1 of a collection of thirty engraved plans of American forts, published according to Act of Parliament, by Mary Ann Rocque, Topographer to His Royal Highness the Duke of Gloucester, in the Strand. The title of this copy, engraved at the top, is "A Plan of the City of New York, reduced from an actual survey by T. Maerschalckm 1763." (The "m" engraved here as part of the name evidently stands for maker.) The map was engraved by P. Andrews and bears at the bottom the imprint of M. A. Rocque, near Old Round Court in the Strand. In a copy of this book belonging to Mr. Grenville Kane, the "3" in the date has been re-engraved as a "5." A copy, in 1913 in the possession of Mr. Joseph F. Sabin, has the date untouched and bears no publisher's imprint or address. [1]

This little book contains also a "Plan of the Narrows about 10 miles from N. Y," showing the batteries, also the location on "Hated Island" (Staten Island) of a "Signal House proposed to receive y Signals from Sandy Hook and return them to New-York," and the location of "Alarm Beacons which Serves at present." The map of the city seems to have been issued separately, also, as a copy in the author's collection has evidently never been folded. There are two copies of the little Rocque album in the N. Y. Public Library.

Among the old surveys in the office of Mr. Francis W. Ford, City Surveyor (successor to Amerman & Ford), is an original survey by Maerschalck, dated 1751, and showing

[1] After this description had gone to press there appeared in a sale at Anderson's, on April 9, 1915, a copy of this map, identical in every respect with the first copy here described, except that it had the date 1755 in the title.

the city from Partition (Fulton) Street to Reade Street, and from Broadway to the North River. On this map is indicated the old line of fortifications and gates along Chambers Street, and also the "Boulding Green," between Warren and Chambers Streets near the North River. In the same collection, are a survey, also by Maerschalck, of the line between New York and Harlem Common, dated 1750, and a survey of the Bowling Green and Government House, showing many adjacent buildings (Vol. II, Addenda).

Among the miscellaneous manuscripts referring to New York City in the State Library at Albany, unfortunately lost in the fire of 1911 (Osgood's *Report to Public Archives Commission*, 108), was a map of New York City, 1749, in a folio volume, containing maps of pieces of land, mostly surveyed by Francis Maerschalck, City Surveyor. These maps were dated at different times between 1749 and 1754, one being a copy of a map made September 14, 1696.

Reproduction: Valentine's *Manual*, 1849, opp. p. 130.

Reference: Phillips's *Maps of America*, p. 521.

Plate 35

[A South-east Prospect of the City of New York]

Oil painting on canvas. 60 x 37½ Date depicted: 1756–7?.*

Owner: N. Y. Hist. Society.

Presented to the New York Hist. Society, on December 6, 1904, by Miss Cornelia Le Roy White, in the name of Goldsborough Banyer, a descendant of the original owner of the same name, who was Deputy Secretary of the Provincial Assembly at about the time depicted in the view. The water-front corresponds closely to the Duyckinck Map (Pl. 34), surveyed by Maerschalck and dated 1755. The vessels in the harbour are probably the French prizes which were brought to New York in May, 1757, and which are spoken of in *The New-York Gazette; or, the Weekly Post-Boy*, of May 30, 1757, as follows:

> Thursday and Friday last returned here from their Cruizes, the following Privateers, viz. the Brig Hawk, Capt. Alexander; the Sloop Charming-Sally, Capt. Harris, and Brig Johnson, Capt. Grig, each of 12 Carriage Guns; and bro't in with them five French Prizes, *to wit*. Three Ships, a Snow, and a Brig, which they took out of a Fleet of 27 Sail, between the 7th and 12th Inst. off the West Caucases . . . The Ships are of 14 Carriage Guns each, are Letters of Marque, stood a hot Engagement of some Hours, and our Vessels were obliged to board them before they struck;—they are at least 300 Tons, the Snow is about 250, and the Brig about 200 Tons, deep loaded with Sugar, Coffee, Cotton &c. And, we hear, one of the Ships has between 80 and 100,000 wt. of Indigo on board. The Whole, at the lowest Computation, is valued at about 70 Thousand Pounds Currency.

Were it not for the French flag on one of the vessels, we might suppose the fleet to be that referred to in *The New-York Mercury* of August 2, 1756: "We now have in this Harbour, fitted out, and fitting for Privateers, one Snow, two Brigs, one Schooner, and five Sloops; and we are told there are several large Vessels to be immediately put on the Stocks, and finished with all Expedition, in order to cruize against his Majesty's Enemies [the French]."

In the latter part of August, 1756, an English fleet visited New York on its way to Canada, and *The New-York Mercury* of August 23d contains a list of eleven of these

[*] While in press an entry has been found in the original MS. of Smith's *Memoirs*, which proves pretty conclusively that the fleet here shown was that of a hundred sail which, on November 19, 1761, left the Hook for Martinique on a secret expedition under the command of General Monckton.

English ships which "came up here from Sandy Hook where they arrived the Saturday night before." It is also possible that *this* is the fleet shown in the view, in which case the ship with a French flag was probably a prize. All of the others fly the English flag.

The steeples seen in the view, beginning at the south, are those of the Old Dutch Church in Garden Street, the Lutheran Church on Broadway south of Trinity, Trinity Church, the City Hall, the French Church, and the New Dutch Church. The Presbyterian Church, on Wall Street, although rebuilt with a cupola and bell in 1748 (see *Min. Presb. Ch.*, September 4, 1747; Smith's *Hist. Province N. Y.*, 1757, p. 192; and the old stone set up in the First Presb. Church on Fifth Avenue and 11th Street), is not here shown; possibly it is concealed by the cupola of the City Hall. The ruins of Whitehall are clearly seen, north of the Battery. These, according to Du Simitière's MS. notes, were still standing when he wrote, probably in 1769.—See Pl. 25.

The painting was engraved, in 1905, by F. S. King, for the Society of Iconophiles, with the title: "A South East Prospect of the City of New York in 1756–7, with the French Prizes at Anchor."—See *Catalogue of the Engravings issued by the Soc. of Iconophiles*, 62. A very good gelatine print by Bierstadt was issued in a small edition, about 1905.

Plate 36–a

[Manuscript Plan of the North-east Section of New York]

Pen and ink sketch on paper. 19 x 12¾ Date depicted: *c.* 1755–7.
Author: Unknown.
Owner: Library of Congress, Div. of Maps and Charts. This map probably once belonged to Montresor, whose name is stamped upon it.

A comparison of this drawing with the Holland MS. Plan or Survey, of 1757 (Pl. 36–b), shows that they represent about the same territory and belong to about the same period. The Rutgers house, built in 1754–5 on the East River, is shown on both, as are also the Bayard and De Lancey estates. A manuscript map or plan of the De Lancey Bouwery, as it was at the time of the Revolution, was, in 1877, in the possession of Edward F. de Lancey, Esq. This map was reproduced in Mrs. Lamb's *History of the City of New York*, I: opp. p. 617. The De Lancey property was confiscated after the Revolution. The original deed or indenture granting a portion of it to Nicholas Fish, made February 3, 1786, acknowledged October 2, 1794, by Isaac Stoutenburgh and Philip Van Cortlandt, Commissioners of Forfeiture; signed by the Mayor, Richard Varick, and recorded on April 9, 1796, is owned by the author. [1]

In the present drawing, the detail is more meagre than in the Holland Survey, and a number of errors exist. Note, for instance, the incorrect direction given to Love Lane (Henry Street), which is only faintly shown on the Holland Survey, but which may be plainly seen on the Ratzen Map (Pl. 42). The estate north of Love Lane and extending to the Rope Walk (Division Street), is marked "Dutch Ministers'." By correcting the position of Love Lane and the Rope Walk according to the more accurate outlines of the Ratzen Map, the Dutch Ministers' is found to correspond with the small house north of the Jews' Burying Ground, that is with the Rutgers house. At this period the house was

[1] This deed was for lots 180 to 211, inclusive, or the block bounded w. by Bowery Lane, n. by Rivington St., e. by 1st St. (Chrystie), and s. by Delancey St., in which block the mansion was located, as shown on the map.

rented, and may have been in the possession of one of the Dutch ministers, as Rutgers had no doubt by this time moved into his new house, built in 1754-5, at the north end of his estate (see Pl. 109). Or it may be that the name "Dutch Ministers'" had clung to the house long after its use as a parsonage had ceased, for at one period the property was evidently in the possession of Megapolensis and Drisius. This is shown by the following entry in Vol. III: 166, of *Patents* at Albany:

> A Confirmation Graunted to ye widdow & Relict of D^o^ Johannes Megapolensis & D^o^ Samuel Drisius for a peice of Ground upon this Island.
>
> FRANCIS LOVELACE Esqr &c WHEREAS there was a Patent or Ground-breife bearing date ye 23th [*sic*] day of January 1653 heretofore Graunted by ye late Governo^r^ Petrus Stuyvesant unto Lawrence Cornelisse^e^ & Isaack defforest for a Certaine Peice of Ground upon this Island lyeing & being neare ye ffresh water by ye Bowery N° 6 then in ye tenure or occupation of Cornelius Jacobs Stille beginning from ye fence & Conteyning in Length on ye North syde Eighty & in breadth behynde Thirty Rod being in all about Eleaven Acres or five Margen & a halfe & one hundred forty foure Rod leaving a Space for two Waggon Pathes as in ye said Groundbreife is Exprest Now ye said peice of Ground haveing beene since Sould & Transported in two Equall moyetyes or halfes unto D^o^ Johannes Megapolensis & D^o^ Samuell Drisius ffor a Confirmation unto [blank] ye widdow & Relict of ye said D^o^ Johannes Megapolensis & unto D^o^ Samuel Drisius in their Possession & Enjoym^t^ of each of them ye one Moyety or halfe of ye prmisses KNOW YEE &c.

The patent is dated August 25, 1670.

This description, which fits to scale the parallelogram on the Ratzen Map which lies north of Love Lane and east of the Highway, "beginning from ye fence and containing in length on ye north side 80 rods," gives us the exact length—1,000 feet—on Division Street, which was the fence line. Its breadth is exactly 30 rods or 375 feet. These are Dutch rods, following the original ground-brief.

The "Space for two Waggon Pathes" must refer to the later Division Street and to the lane which was very nearly on the line of Henry Street, unless possibly it refers to the highway, a portion of which was reserved in many grants.

Notwithstanding Stille's grant, this little domain had been carved out of his bouwery for the use and benefit of the Dutch ministers. Before 1728, Stille's heirs must have re-purchased it, for they sold the entire tract in this year to Harmanus Rutgers, citing it as being then in the possession of Stille (*Liber Deeds*, XXXIII: 19, 21). We know nothing of the house. It may have been built by the Dutch ministers, by Stille's descendant, Hendrick Cornelissen Van Schaick, or by Harmanus Rutgers.

This, the following map (Pl. 36-b), and the map reproduced as Pl. 30 are the earliest maps known to show in any detail this section of the city. This map is reproduced here for the first time. It has been described (with some inaccuracies) by Innes, in an unpublished letter addressed to Mr. P. Lee Phillips and filed with the sketch in the Library of Congress.

Reference: Phillips's *Maps of America*, 520.

PLATE 36-b

A PLAN OF THE NORTH EAST ENVIRONS OF THE CITY OF NEW YORK (ETC.)
[The Holland Survey]

Pen and ink sketch on paper. 21 x 12 Date depicted: 1757, Sept. 17.
Author: Samuel Holland.

Owner: State Library, Albany, N. Y., until destroyed in the fire of 1911 (Catalogue of Maps and Surveys, etc., Albany, 1859, p. 335).

This drawing, which covers approximately the same ground as the preceding (Pl. 36-a), is far more accurately drawn and shows much more detail. It was evidently made for military purposes and intended primarily to show the heights suitable for fortifications. The palisades and blockhouses built in 1745 under Governor Clinton, as a protection against the expected French and Indian invasion, are here shown. Note the Somerindyke house, east of the Bowery (High Road); so called from the fact that it was occupied at this period by Teunis Somerindyke, although the property belonged to James de Lancey. (No record exists in the New York County records of a deed to Somerindyke from De Lancey.) It was in this house that, in 1757, the year of the survey, the Assembly met, because of the prevalence of small-pox in the city.—*Assemb. Jour.* (Gaine Ed.), II: 525, 539. This property must not be confused with the Somerindyke Farm, which lay between 57th and 70th Streets, Sixth Avenue and the Hudson River, and which was sold by the Commissioners of Forfeiture (on attainder of James de Lancey) on July 27, 1785.

The slaughter-house, marked on the plan east of the Fresh Water, is that of Nicholas Bayard. It was built in 1750 and was for many years the public slaughter-house of the city (see Chronology). At this period Broadway was not laid out so far north. In 1760, Maerschalck laid out the extension of Broadway (known as Great George Street) from the Spring Garden (now the site of the St. Paul Building, Broadway and Ann Street) north "to the Ground of the Late Widdow Rutgers," whose house is marked upon the present plan. Note the Rutgers "Brew House," north of the Rutgers house on the East River, shown also on the Howdell-Canot South West View (Pl. 37). Another interesting feature is the fort shown on the North River beyond the palisades and inscribed "Ruins of the Battery." This fort or battery is shown on Grim's Map (1742-3-4) as a "Block House," and was erected, probably at about this time, on land belonging to Trinity Church (see Chronology, 1745, April 17).

A very good lithographic reproduction of the Holland Survey is contained in Valentine's *Manual* for 1859, opp. p. 108. The Fresh Water, which is scarcely discernible in our reproduction, is very clearly shown on the printed map.

The N. Y. State Library possessed also, until it was destroyed by the fire of 1911, a manuscript map by Holland of a "part of the province of New-York on Hudson's river, the west end of Nassau Island and part of New-Jersey." This map was prepared by direction of the Earl of Loudoun, and bore the same date as the plan here reproduced, i. e., September 17, 1757.

Reproduced photographically and described here for the first time.

Plate 37

A South West View of the City of New York, in North America
[The Howdell-Canot South West View]

Engraved on copper. 19¾ x 12½ Date depicted: *c.* 1763.
Date issued: 1768 ?.

Provenance: This is one of a pair of views, probably originally issued separately, but also found included as plates b. 3 and b. 4 in the *Scenographia Americana*, for full description of which see below.

Artist: Capt. Thomas Howdell, R. A.
Engraver: P. Canot.
Owner: William B. Osgood Field, Esq.
Other copies: N. Y. Public Library; N. Y. Hist. Society; etc., etc.

The view here reproduced is probably in the second or third state, and the original drawings from which it and its companion (Pl. 38) were engraved were apparently made about the year 1763. An earlier state, probably the first, bears the sole imprint: "Publish'd according to Act of Parliament by Thos. Jefferys at Charing Cross," and seems to have been issued separately, as there is no plate number (b. 3), as in our view. A blank space after the word "Parliament" appears to indicate an intended date, although the author has been unable to find a dated impression.

In a copy of "*Six Remarkable Views in the Provinces of New-York, New-Jersey, and Pennsylvania in North America*" etc., dated 1761, owned by Edward W. C. Arnold, Esq., and referred to more particularly hereafter, two undated New York views, which are laid in, have the Jefferys imprint alone, all of the other views having the date 1761, also with the Jefferys imprint alone. Although Jefferys appears for the first time in the London directories in 1764, several earlier publications bearing his name and with the same address are known. For example, "A Map of the South Part of Nova Scotia and its Fishing Banks Engraved by T. Jefferys [with an inset View of Halifax]" was "Publish'd according to Act of Parliament Jan. 25. 1750 price 1s Printed for T Jefferys at the Corner of St. Martins Lane Charing Cross." There is in the British Museum (K 119-67) "A Large and Particular Plan of Shegnekto Bay Publish'd according to the Act August 16th 1755 by Thos. Jefferys Geographer to his Royal Highness the Prince of Wales near Charing Cross." A Map of Virginia (2d edition) was advertised, in February, 1755, by "J. [T.] Jefferys, at the corner of St. Martin's-lane Charing Cross." Again, in April of the same year, "A Map of the British & French Dominions in N. A.," by John Mitchell, was offered for sale by "T. Jefferys, in the Strand"; and, in 1759, a "View of the action at the siege of Quebec" was advertised as "engraved, printed and sold by Thomas Jefferys at Charing Cross." These newspaper references are from the Upcott Collection of Clippings in the N. Y. Hist. Society.

As Governor Pownall, the author of the set of six plates referred to above, was in America from August, 1757, to June, 1760, and as his drawings were presumably engraved shortly after his return to England, it seems clear that all of the impressions bearing Jeffery's name alone are earlier than those with the joint imprint, especially as we know from the London directories that several of the firms appearing in the joint imprint were not in business until after 1761. From an analysis of the dates of the first appearance of these firm names, it seems safe to assume that the state here reproduced could not have been issued earlier than 1765, and, as will appear later, it was probably issued with the *Scenographia Americana*, published in 1768.

Scarcely any definite information has been found of Howdell in America. Duncan (Francis), *History of the Royal Regiment of Artillery*, London, 1872, gives much information of the doings of this regiment during the war with Canada, but no details are given of the junior officers, and no information regarding the time when the various companies came over or where they were assigned for service. We know, however, from the official records, that in 1763 Howdell commanded the Seventh Company, Third Battalion, in this Regiment, but the location of that company during the period under consideration is not given. From the English Army Lists, we know further that Howdell was commissioned as follows:

Lieut. Fire Worker	1 Sept. 1747	at 3 s 8 d	per day
2d Lieut.	29 Oct. 1755	" 4	Do
1st Lieut.	4 Feb. 1757		
Captain Lieut.	2 Apr. 1757	" 6	Do
(Full) Captain	18 Apr. 1763		

His name appears in the lists down to 1770 as Captain, and in 1771 among "Captains of Invalids"; after that it drops out altogether even from the half-pay list, which omission probably indicates that he had died.

If, as seems likely, a Captain Lieutenant would have been officially styled "Lieutenant" until he was commissioned full Captain, which latter title was not bestowed upon Howdell until April 18, 1763, it might be assumed that the views were not drawn before that date. On the other hand, it is quite possible that they were drawn at an earlier date, when he was still Captain Lieutenant, and engraved after his promotion, and therefore bore his new title.

Unfortunately, there is no internal evidence either in this view or in its mate which enables us to fix precisely the date depicted, although, as King's College is shown completed in the S. E. View; and, as we know from the college records that in 1760 "the College buildings were so far completed that the officers and students began to lodge and mess therein," the view must have been drawn as late as 1759 or 1760. In the former year the jail, which is here shown finished, was first used. If, as appears probable, Howdell was in America during the war with France and went home when the establishments were reduced at the Peace, the treaty for which was signed in Paris on February 10, 1763, two months before he received his Captain's commission, the New York views were probably engraved and issued shortly after this date. The first state of the S. W. View was certainly issued before May, 1766, at which time the reduced copy, referred to below, appeared.

The view is taken from the southern slope of Mt. Pitt, near the intersection of the present Henry and Montgomery Streets. The Rutgers house, seen in the foreground on the left, is the upper of the two Rutgers mansions and was built in 1754–5 (*cf.* Pl. 109). The meadow south of the Rutgers house is a prominent feature in many of the views and plans of the period. The reference number "1," which in the original appears midway between the mainland and Bedloes Island, has unfortunately disappeared in the reproduction.

It is interesting to compare this view with that by St. Mémin (Pl. 62), which was taken from nearly the same point (*cf.* also Ratzen Plan, Pl. 42).

A reduced copy of the view, $7\frac{1}{16}$ x $3\frac{11}{16}$, was published in the *Universal Museum and Complete Magazine* (etc.) for May, 1766, where it accompanied an article entitled "A Description of the Town of New York with a South West View of that City neatly engraved." Several other early reduced copies of the view are known, differing slightly in details and all published as illustrations to books or magazines.

SCENOGRAPHIA AMERICANA

The full title of the important and very rare series of prints, known as the *Scenographia Americana*, taken from the only complete copy found, which is owned by the Boston Public Library,[1] is as follows: *Scenographia Americana/or/A Collection of Views/in/North*

[1] See foot-note [2], on following page.

America and the West Indies / Neatly engraved by / Messrs. Sandby, Grignion, Rooker, Canot, Elliot, and others; / From drawings taken on the Spot, by several Officers of the British Navy and Army / Recueil / de Vues de / L'Amérique Septentrionale et des Indes Occidentales. / Gravées d'après les Desseins pris sur les Lieux par differens Officiers des Troupes et de la Marine Angloises / London: / Printed for John Bowles, at N° 13, in Cornhill; Robert Sayer, at N° 53, in Fleet-Street; Thomas Jefferys at the corner of St. Martin's Lane in / the Strand; Carington Bowles, at N° 69, in St. Paul's Church-yard; and Henry Parker at N° 82, in Cornhill MDCCLXVIII. [Just below this date is an erasure, perhaps originally an earlier engraved date, which explanation is also suggested by the fact that the present date is somewhat crowded up.]

A leaf bearing the printed table of contents is bound immediately after the title-page. The verso is blank; the recto reads as follows:

CONTENTS of the PRINTS in this Work: With the Separate Prices of each Sett. Six Elegant Views of the most remarkable Places in the River and Gulph of St. Lawrence, from the Originals drawn by Capt. *Hervey Smith*, Aid de Camp to the late General Wolfe. Price 1*l.* 1s.

1. The City of Quebec, the Capital of Canada. [a. 1.] [1]

2. The Falls of Montmorenci, and the Attack made by General Wolfe, July 31, 1759. [Plate missing, probably 2A, or a.2 on later state.] [2]

3. Cape Rouge, called by the French Carouge, Bay and River. [3A.]

4. The Bay of Gaspe. [No index number or cipher, probably 4A or a. 4 on later state.]

5. Miramichi, in the Gulph of St. Lawrence. [a5.]

6. The Pierced Island, a remarkable Rock in the Gulph of St. Lawrence. [6A.]

Two Views, Price 7s.

1. An East View of Montreal in Canada, drawn on the Spot by *Thomas Paton.* [b. 1.]

2. A View of Louisbourg, taken near the Light-house, when that City was besieged in 1758. [b. 2.]

Two Views drawn by Captain *Howdell* of the Royall Artillery. Pr. 7s.

1. A South East View of the City of New-York. [b. 4.]
2. A South West View of the City of New-York. [b. 3.] } [Transposed in binding.]

Two Views, Price 7s. 6d.

1. A View of the City of Boston, the Capital of New England, from an Original Drawing, taken by his Excellency Governor *Pownall.* Pr. 3s. 6d. [No cipher, probably b. 5 on later state.]

2. A View of Charles-Town in South-Carolina, from the Harbour. Price 3s. 6d. [No cipher, probably b. 6 on later state.]

Six remarkable Views in the Provinces of New York, New Jersey and Pennsylvania: Engraved after the Paintings made by Mr. *Paul Sandby*, from the Drawings taken on the Spot by his Excellency Governor *Pownall.* Pr. 1*l.* 1s.

[1] No index numbers or ciphers are found in the table of contents. These have been supplied, in square brackets, from the plates themselves.

[2] Although the copy of the *Scenographia Americana* in the Boston Public Library lacks two views, plate a. 2, the Falls of Montmorenci, and C. 4, the Great Cohoes Fall, impressions of these two plates, probably belonging originally to this set, are found in the Green Fund Collection, Nos. 289 and 492, so that the Library possesses the complete series.

1. A View in Hudson's River of the Entrance of what is called the Topan Sea. [C. 1.]

2. The astonishing Fall of Water on the Passaick (or Second River) in the Province of New Jersey. [C. 2.]

3. A View in Hudson's River of Pakepsey and the Cats-kill Mountains. [C. 3.]

4. The Great Cohoes Fall of Water on the Mohawk River. [Plate missing, probably C. 4 on later state.]

5. A View of Bethlem, the Great Moravian Settlement in the Province of Pennsylvania. [C. 5.]

6. A Design of the Beginning and Completion of an American Settlement or Farm. [C. 6.]

SIX VIEWS of the City, Harbour, and Country of the Havanna; from the Originals drawn by Engineer *Durnford*, Aid de Camp to the Earl of Albemarle. Price 1*l.* 1s.

1. The Harbour and City, taken from the Hill near the Road between the Regla and Guanavacao. [d. 1.]

2. The Entrance of the Harbour, from within the Wrecks. [d. 2.]

3. The Franciscan Church and Convent. [d. 3.]

4. The City, from the Road near Col. Howe's Battery. [d. 4.]

5. The Harbour and City, from Jesu del Monte. [d. 5.]

6. The Market Place. [d. 6.]

FOUR VIEWS, drawn on the Spot, by Lieut. *Archibald Campbell*, Engineer. Price 14s.

1. A View of Roseau in the Island of Dominique, with the Attack made by Lord Rollo and Sir James Douglas in 1760. [e. 1.]

2. A South West View of Fort Royal, with the Attack made by the British Fleet. [e. 2.]

3. A North View of Fort Royal, with the English Camp. [e. 3.]

4. An East View of Fort Royal. [e. 4.]

Sabin, in his *Dictionary of Books Relating to America* (77467), briefly describes this work, but refers to it by its French title only, which, as he quotes it, differs slightly from that given above. He correctly states the number of the plates as twenty-eight. Leclerc's *Bibliotheca Americana*, published in Paris by Maisonneuve et Cie, in 1878, No. 532, describes a copy of the *Scenographia Americana* as follows: "Recueil de vues de l'Amérique septentrionale et des Indes Occidentales. Gravées sur les desseins pris sur les lieux par différens officiers des troupes et de la marine angloises (par Sandry [*sic*], Grignion, Rooker, Canot et Elliot). London, printed for John Bowles, 1768, in-fol., max. cart. 1 fnc. [folio not paged in addition to title], 28 pl." In a footnote, the editor comments upon this set as follows (translated): "This magnificent album contains 28 large plates, engraved in a superior manner (it lacks the view of Charlestown)."

The complete titles of the twenty-eight plates in the *Scenographia Americana*, taken from the Boston Public Library's copy, are as follows:

a. 1. [1] A View of the City of Quebec, the Capital of Canada. Taken partly from Pointe des Peres, and partly on Board the Vanguard Man of War, by Captain Hervey Smyth. [Title also in French.] To the Right Honourable William Pitt, One of his Majesties most Honourable Privy Council & Principal Secretary of State. These Six

[1] The index letters and numbers, when given, are found in the lower right margin, directly below the rectangle. None of the early Jefferys states have ciphers.

Views of the most remarkable Places in the Gulf and River of St. Laurence are most humbly Inscribed, by his most Obedient humble Servant Hervey Smyth. Aid du Camp to the late Gen! Wolfe. P. Benazech Sculp. a. 1. 1. Gen! Wolfes landing. 2. St Charles's River. London Printed for John Bowles at N° 13 in Cornhill, Robert Sayer at N° 53 in Fleet Street, Thos Jefferys the corner of St Martins Lane in the Strand, Carington Bowles at N° 69 in St Pauls Church Yard, and Henry Parker at N° 82 in Cornhill. 19¾ x 12 7/16.

The British Museum possesses a copy of this state, to which the date 1764 has been assigned. It has also a copy with the sole imprint of T. Jefferys, near Charing Cross, published November 5, 1760 (K 119-39c).

Just outside the left margin of the engraving, 4⅛ inches from the bottom, appears the figure 1, in Arabic.

[a. 2]. [1] A View of the Fall of Montmorenci and the Attack made by General Wolfe, on the French Intrenchments near Beauport, with the Grenadiers of the Army, July 31. 1759. [Title also in French.] Drawn on the Spot by Capt Hervey Smyth. Engraved by Wm Elliot. / 1. Quebec. 2. Point Levy. 3. Orleans I. 4. Grenadiers. 5. Townshen'ds & Murray's Brigades. 6. Two arm'd Catts. 7. Centurion. 8. Beauport. 9. French Camp. / London, Publish'd according to Act of Parliament Nov. 5. 1760. by T. Jefferys the Corner of St Martins Lane. 20¾ x 13¼.

3A. A View of Cape Rouge or Carouge, Nine Miles above the City of Quebec on the North Shore of the River St Laurence. From this place 1500 chosen Troops at the break of Day fell down the River on the Ebb of Tide to the place of Landing 13 Sept., 1759. [Title also in French.] Drawn on the Spot by Capt Hervey Smyth. Engraved by Peter Mazell. 20 1/16 x 12¾.

Imprint same as a. 1. The British Museum (K 119-46) also possesses a copy with the Jefferys imprint only, published November 5, 1760.

[4A]. A View of Gaspe Bay, in the Gulf of St Laurence. This French Settlement used to supply Quebec with Fish, till it was destroyed by General Wolfe after the surrender of Louisburg in 1758. During the stay of the British Fleet in 1759, General Wolfe resided at the House on the Beach (1). (2) 1500 Quintals of Fish. [Title also in French.] Drawn on the Spot by Capt Hervey Smyth, Engraved by Peter Mazell. London, Publish'd according to Act of Parliament Nov. 5, 1760, by T. Jefferys the Corner of St Martins Lane. Printed for I.. Bowles, R.. Sayer, T.. Jefferys, C,,. Bowles, & H,, Parker. 20¼ x 12⅝. [It is interesting to note that, although published by T. Jefferys alone, it was printed for several other print-sellers as well.]

Probably second state. The British Museum (K 119-47) possesses a copy of the first state, with the Jefferys imprint alone, published November 5, 1760.

a5. A View of Miramichi, a French Settlement in the Gulf of St Laurence, destroyed by Brigadier Murray detached by General Wolfe for that purpose, from the Bay of Gaspe. [Title also in French.] Drawn on the Spot by Capt Hervey Smyth, Etch'd by Paul Sandby, Retouched by P. Benazech. 20¼ x 12 13/16.

Imprint same as a. 1. The British Museum (K 119-55) possesses a copy with the Jefferys imprint only, published November 5, 1760.

6A. A View of the Pierced Island, a remarkable Rock in the Gulf of St. Laurence.

[1] a. 2, 4A, b. 5, and b. 6, have been found only in impressions without ciphers. As, however, in each case the print occurs as one of a series, the other plates of which are consecutively numbered, the plain inference seems to be that these plates were also issued later with ciphers.

Two Leagues to the Southward of Gaspée Bay. [Title also in French.] Drawn on the Spot by Capt. Heny Smyth. Engraved by P. Canot. 20¼ x 12⅞.

The British Museum (K 119-48) possesses a copy with the Jefferys imprint only, published in 1760.

b. 1. An East View of Montreal, in Canada. [Title also in French.] Drawn on the Spot by Thomas Patten Engraved by P. Canot. 1. General Hospital. 2. The Recollects. 3. S. Sulpicius. 4. The Nunnery. 5. The Jesuits Church. 6. The Fort. 20 x 12½.

Imprint same as a. 1. The British Museum (119-42a) possesses a copy with Jefferys imprint only, published November 11, 1762.

b. 2. A View of Louisburg in North America, taken near the Light House when that City was besieged in 1758. [Title also in French.] Drawn on the Spot by Capt. Ince of the 35t. Regt. Engraved by P. Canot. 1. The City. 2. Gabarus Bay. 3. English Camp. 4. French Fleet. 5. Island Battery. 6. The Light House. 19¾ x 12½.

Imprint same as a. 1. The British Museum (K 119-95c) possesses a copy with the Jefferys imprint only, published November 11, 1762.

b. 3. A South West View of the City of New York, in North America. [Title also in French.] Drawn on the Spot by Capt. Thomas Howdell, of the Royal Artillery. Engraved by P. Canot, 1. The Harbour. 2. Nutting Island. 3. Staten Island. 4. Long Island. 5. Rutgers House. 6. South River. 7. Brewhouse. 19¾ x 12⅝.

Imprint same as a. 1. (B. M. K 121—38d. Jefferys imprint only. Publish'd . . . by Thos. Jefferys.)

b. 4. A South East View of the City of New York, in North America. [Title also in French.] Drawn on the Spot by Capt. Thomas Howdell, of the Royal Artillery. Engraved by P. Canot. 1. New Colledge. 2. Old English Church. 3. City Hall. 4. French Church. 5. North River. 6. Staten Island. 7. The Prison. 19¾ x 12½.

Imprint same as a. 1., except that there is no period at the end. (B. M. K 121—38c. Jefferys imprint only. Publish'd . . . by Tho. Jefferys.)

[b. 5]. A View of the City of Boston the Capital of New England, in North America. [Title also in French.] Drawn on the Spot by his Excellency, Governor Pownal; painted by Mr. Pugh, & Engraved by P. C. Canot. London; Printed for John Bowles, at No. 13 in Cornhill, Robt. Sayer, at No. 53 in Fleet Street; Thos. Jefferys, the Corner of St Martins Lane in the Strand; Carington Bowles, at No. 69 in St. Pauls Church Yard; & Heny Parker, at No. 82 in Cornhill. 20⅛ x 12¾.

[b. 6]. A View of Charles town the Capital of South Carolina in North America. [Title also in French.] Engraved by C. . Canot from an Original Painting of T. . Mellish, in the Collection of Mr. John Bowles. London. Printed for John Bowles at No. 13. in Cornhill, Robt. Sayer at No. 53. in Fleet Street, Thos. Jefferys at the Corner of St. Martins Lane in the Strand, & Carington Bowles at No. 69 in St. Pauls Church Yard. 20¼ x 13.

c. 1. A View in Hudson's River of the Entrance of what is called the Topan Sea. [Title also in French.] Sketch'd on the Spot by his Excellency Governor Pownal. Painted by Paul Sandby, Engraved by Peter Benazech. London. Printed for Jno. Bowles at No. 13. in Cornhill, Robert Sayer at No. 53 in Fleet Street, Thos. Jefferys the Corner of St. Martins Lane in the Strand, Carington Bowles at No. 69 in St. Pauls Church Yard, and Henry Parker at No. 82 in Cornhill. 19⅞ x 13.

The British Museum (K 121-116a) possesses a copy with the Jefferys imprint only, published May 20, 1761.

c. 2. A View of the Falls on the Passaick, or second River, in the Province of New

Jersey, The height of the Fall between Eighty and Ninety feet; the River about Eighty Yards broad. [Title also in French.] Sketch'd on the Spot by his Excellency Governor Pownal. Painted and Engraved by Paul Sandby. London, Printed for John Bowles at No. 13. in Cornhill, Robert Sayer at N° 53. in Fleet Street, Thos Jefferys the Corner of St Martins Lane in the Strand, Carington Bowles at N° 69. in St Pauls Church Yard, and Henry Parker at N° 82 in Cornhill. 20⅛ x 12¾.

The British Museum possesses a copy with the Jefferys imprint only, and without reference number, published May 20, 1761.

c. 3. A View in Hudson's River of Pakepsey & the Catts-Kill Mountains, From Sopos Island in Hudson's River. [Title also in French.] Sketch'd on the Spot by his Excellency Governor Pownal. Painted & Engraved by Paul Sandby. London. Printed for John Bowles at N° 13. in Cornhill. Robert Sayer at N° 53 in Fleet Street. Thos Jefferys the Corner of St Martins Lane in the Strand, Carington Bowles at N° 69. in St Pauls Church Yard. and Henry Parker at N° 82 in Cornhill. 20¼ x 12¾.

The British Museum (K 121–116b) possesses a copy with the Jefferys imprint only, published May 20, 1761.

c. 4. A View of the Great Cohoes Falls, on the Mohawk River; The Fall about Seventy feet; the River near a Quarter of a Mile broad. [Title also in French.] Sketch'd on the Spot by his Excellency Governor Pownal. Painted by Paul Sandby, & Engraved by Wm Elliot. / London, Printed for John Bowles at N° 13. in Cornhill, Robert Sayer at N° 53. in Fleet Street, Thos Jefferys the corner of St Martin's Lane and Henry Parker at N° 82 in Cornhill. 19⅞ x 12 9/16.

The British Museum (K 121–117) possesses a copy with the Jefferys imprint only, published May, 1761.

c. 5. A View of Bethlem, the Great Moravian Settlement in the Province of Pennsylvania. [Title also in French.] Sketch'd on the Spot by his Excellency Governor Pownal, Painted and Engraved by Paul Sandby. [Imprint same as c. 2 except as follows: N° 82. in Cornhill.] 20¼ x 12⅞.

The British Museum (K 122–23) possesses a copy with the Jefferys imprint only, published May 20, 1761.

c. 6. A Design to represent the beginning and completion of an American Settlement or Farm. [Title also in French.] Painted by Paul Sandby, from a Design made by his Excellency Governor Pownal. Engraved by James Peake. [Imprint same as c. 2 except as follows: London N° 82. in Cornhill.] 20⅛ x 12⅝.

d. 1. A View of the Harbour & City of the Havana, taken from the Hill near the Road, Between La Regla & Guanavacoa. [Title also in French and in Spanish.] To the Right Honourable George Earle of Albemarle, Commander in Chief of His Majesty's Forces on the late Expedition to Cuba; These Six Views of the City, Harbour, & Country of the Havana, are most humbly Inscribed, By his Lordships most Obedient & Devoted Humble Servt Elias Durnford, Engineer. 1. The Cavanos. 2. The Morro. 3. Entrance of the Harbour. 4. The Punta. 5. Redoubts. 6. Guadaloupe. 7. The Dock. 8. Gonzales Hill. 9. New Powder Magazine. 10. Isle de Puntas. 11. La Regla. 12. Landing place. a. The Mountain Aloe. 25 f.t high. b. The Plantain. 10. f.t high. c. The Plantain Fruit. [l.r.] W. Elliott sculpt [Imprint same as a. 1., but directly beneath rectangle.] 19⅞ x 12⅝.

The British Museum (K 123–28a) possesses a copy with the Jefferys imprint only, published August, 1764.

d. 2. A View of the Entrance of the Harbour of the Havana, taken from within the Wrecks. [Title also in French and in Spanish.] Drawn by Elias Durnford, Engineer. Engraved by Peter Canot. 1. The Signal House in the Morro. 2. Apostles Battery. 3. Shepherds Battery. 4. The Cavannos. 5. Ships sunk in the Entrance of the Harbour. 6. Man of War towing out between the Wrecks. 7. F[t] Punta. 8. N[th] Bastion. 20½ x 12⅝.

Imprint same as a. 1. The British Museum (K 123–28b) possesses a copy with the Jefferys imprint only, published August, 1764.

d. 3. A View of the Franciscan Church & Convent in the City of Havana, taken from the Alcalde's House in Granby Square. [Title also in French and in Spanish.] Drawn by Elias Durnford, Engineer. Engraved by Edward Rooker. 1. La Regla. 2. New Powder Magazine. 20 x 12¾.

Imprint same as a. 1. The British Museum (K 123–28e) possesses a copy with the Jefferys imprint only, published August 1, 1764.

d. 4. A View of the City of the Havana, taken from the Road near Colonel Howe's Battery. [Title also in French and in Spanish.] Drawn by Elias Durnford Engineer, Etch'd by Paul Sandby, & Engraved by Edw[d] Rooker. 19⅞ x 12¾.

Imprint same as a. 1, but no period at end. The British Museum (K 123–28d) possesses a copy with the Jefferys imprint only, published February 17, 1765.

d. 5. A View of the Harbour and City of the Havana, taken from Jesu Del Monte. [Title also in French and in Spanish.] Drawn by Elias Durnford, Engineer. Engraved by T. Morris. 20⅜ x 12¾.

Imprint same as a. 1. The British Museum (K 123–28c) possesses a copy with the Jefferys imprint only, published February, 1765.

d. 6. A view of the Market-Place in the City of the Havana. [Title also in French and in Spanish.] Drawn by Elias Durnford Engineer. Engraved by C. Canot and T. Morris. Imprint same as a. 1. 20¼ x 12⅞.

The British Museum (K 123–28f) possesses a copy with the Jefferys imprint only, published March 14, 1765.

e. 1. A View of Roseau in the Island of Dominique, with the Attack Made by Lord Rollo & S[r] James Douglass, in 1760. [Title also in French.] Drawn on the Spot by L[t] Arch. Campbell. Engraved by James Peake. 1. The Landing Place of the 1st Division. 2. The Ridge upon which the French had 3 Intrenchments a. b. c. & a Battery. 3. The Grenadiers under the Command of Col. Melvil supported by the rest of the Army. 4. Three Ships of the Line which covered the Landing. 5. A Detachment of the 1st Division to protect the Landing. 6. The 2[d] Division in Flat bottom Boats going to Land. 7. Transports. 19⅞ x 12¼.

Imprint same as a. 1. The British Museum (K 123–96–2) possesses a copy without imprint. This has not been cut off, as the plate mark is intact.

e. 2. A South West View of Fort Royal in the Island of Guadaloupe. [Title also in French.] Drawn on the Spot by Lieu[t] Arch. Campbell Engineer. Engraved by P. Benazech. 20 x 12⅝.

Imprint same as a. 1. The British Museum (K 123–92a) possesses a copy with the Jefferys imprint alone, published November 10, 1762.

e. 3. A North View of Fort Royal in the Island of Guadaloupe, When in possession of his Majestys Forces in 1759. [Title also in French.] Drawn on the Spot by Lieu[t] Arch. Campbell Engineer. Engraved by Grignion. 19¾ x 11⅜.

Imprint same as a. 1. The British Museum (K 123-92c) possesses a copy with the Jefferys imprint only, published August 10, 1764.

e. 4. An East View of Fort Royal in the Island of Guadaloupe. [Title also in French.] Drawn on the Spot by Lieu^t^ Arch. Campbell Engineer. Engraved by Peter Mazell. 19½ x 11⅛.

Imprint same as a. 1. The British Museum (K 123-92b) possesses a copy with the Jefferys imprint only, published November 10, 1762.

Sabin (76334) refers also, under Sandby (Paul), to *Twenty-seven Views in North America and the West Indies, with Descriptions in English and French. . . .* London, 1768. Oblong folio. This reference, which has caused much confusion, is probably incorrect, as no collection of *twenty-seven* views by Sandby is known. It probably originated from a catalogue description of an imperfect set of the *Scenographia Americana,* which we now know to have been identical with "Sandby's *Recueil,*" and not a separate publication as has often been stated. This error also occurs in *The First Proofs of the Universal Catalogue of Art,* etc., London, 1870, where we find, under Sandby (Paul), "Twenty-seven Views (by P. S. Grignon, and others) in North America and the West Indies with descriptions in English and French. Obl. fol. London, 1768. Another edition. Obl. 4to. London 1781." This latter edition was probably that composed of twelve quarto plates: "Twelve remarkable Views in North America and the West Indies," offered in Carington Bowles's Catalogue for 1790, and referred to more particularly hereafter. Sabin's description follows very closely the title given in the *Universal Catalogue,* and is perhaps taken from it.

The Catalogue of New-York State Library: 1856. Maps, Manuscripts, Engravings, Coins, &c., Albany, 1857, p. 136, describes and quotes the title of a copy of the *Scenographia Americana; or a Collection of Views in North America and the West Indies, Engraved by Messrs. Sandby, Grignion, Rooker, Elliot, Canot, etc., from drawings taken on the spot by officers of the British army and navy. London, 1768. 74 engravings.* 1 vol. fol. It will be noticed that this title differs only slightly from that of the copy with twenty-eight views in the Boston Public Library, already quoted. No other copy similar to the former is recorded, although most of the plates which it contains are known from impressions issued either separately or in smaller collections, [1] such as the collection of twenty-eight views described above and the *Six Remarkable Views in the Provinces of New-York, New-Jersey, and Pennsylvania in North America; sketched on the spot by his Excellency Governor Pownall, painted by Paul Sandby, and engraved by Sandby, Elliot, Benazech,* etc., Oblong folio, London, 1761. (Collection of Edward W. C. Arnold, Esq.) The State Library at Albany also contained (*Catalogue of the New-York State Library: 1856*) a set of these six views, to which were added twelve others, among them six views

[1] Probably the engraved title-page of the collection of twenty-eight views (*The Scenographia Americana*) served as a general title-page, although it is possible that a special title-page was printed for this collection. From the fact that the title-page is given in slightly different form in the 1850 and 1856 catalogues of the State Library, it might fairly be assumed that both were carelessly transcribed, and that the title-page was really identical with that of the twenty-eight views. It seems altogether probable that this was a special and unique collection made up of the twenty-eight views and of all the available smaller sets and separates. From the fact that the views of Belle Isle and Sauzon (hereafter referred to) were bound up in the N. Y. State Library copy, they were probably supposed to relate to Belle Isle, Newfoundland, whereas it is clear that they relate to Belle Isle on the south coast of Brittany, France, which was taken by the British under Admiral Keppel and General Hodgson in June, 1761. This is an additional proof that the *Scenographia Americana* containing 74 views, and belonging to the N. Y. State Library, was a made-up collection, as the original publishers certainly would not have issued *French* views as *North American.*

of the Island of Jamaica, not included in the series of seventy-four views owned by the same library. Unfortunately both of these collections were destroyed in the fire of 1911. Furthermore, in a book by William Sandby entitled: *Thomas and Paul Sandby, Royal Academicians, Some Account of their Lives and Works, London, 1892* (Copy in Library of Congress), occurs the following on page 30: "In 1761 were published in folio Eight Views on North America and the West Indies painted and engraved by Paul Sandby, from Drawings made on the spot by Gov. Pownell and others," etc. This may have been the same series as the six views referred to above, with the two New York views added later, as in Mr. Arnold's set, where they are found bound up with the others, but are not included in the printed index and were therefore evidently additions.

The N. Y. Historical Society has a collection of "*Six / Perspective Views/on/Belle Isle,/From Drawings made on the Spot,/At Command of Admiral Keppel,/By Richard Short, Purser of his Majesty's Ship the Prince of Orange. / Engraved by Messrs. Canot, Benoist, and Mason./*"(etc.)

London: Publish'd according to Act of Parliament, May 1, 1763. / Price One Guinea the Set to Subscribers: each Subscriber paying Half a Guinea receives Three Prints, the other Half Guinea on Delivery of the last three. / N. B. The other Three are in hand. [The titles of these views are quoted in full below.]

The seventy-four views, or, to be more accurate, seventy-three views and one map, belonging to the State Library's augmented copy of the *Scenographia Americana*, are listed in the Library's catalogues for 1850 and 1856 (published in 1857) as follows:

[1] Map of North America.
[2–8] Belleisle, town and fortress: seven views.
[9] Sauzon, town of.
[10] Landing of the New-England Expedition against Cape Breton.
[11–16] Halifax, Nova-Scotia, 1764: six views.
[17–38] Quebec: 22 Views of the city, public buildings and vicinity, 1759; *with* Views of the Battle between Wolfe & Montcalm; Falls of Montmorenci.
[39] Montreal.
[40] Louisbourg.
[41–42] New-York city: two views.
[43] Boston, Massachusetts.
[44] Charlestown, S. C.
[45] Hudson's river, Topan sea.
[46] Passaick falls.
[47] Pakepsey and the Catt'skill mts.
[48] Great Cohoes falls.
[49] Bethlem, Pa.: Moravian settlement.
[50] Beginning and Completion of an American settlement.
[51] Pisaiack falls, N. J.: north view.
[52] Niagara falls.
[53–55] Cataracts on the Casconchiagon, or Little Seneca's river on Lake Ontario: three views.
[56] Pensacola, West-Florida.
[57–66] Havana, Cuba: ten views.
[67] Roseau, Island of Dominica.
[68–70] Fort Royal, Island of Guadaloupe: three views.

[71-73] Antigua island: three views.
[74] Carthagena.

In addition to the twenty-eight views belonging to the completed Boston Public Library set, the titles of which have already been quoted in full, all other views which the compiler has been able to identify as belonging to this special collection are noted and described below in their proper sequence. Those not found are so marked.

[1] *Map of North America* [not found]. Perhaps, however, Pownall's Map: *A map of the Middle British Colonies in North America, first published by Mr. Lewis Evans of Philadelphia in 1755, and since corrected and improved, as also extended . . . from actual surveys now lying at the Board of Trade, by T. Pownall, M. P., Printed and published for J. Almon, London, March 25, 1776.* (Copy in N. Y. Public Library.)

[2-8] *Belle Isle* (seven views, one not found).

[l. l.] Serres Pinx. [l. r.] Canot sculp. / To the Honble Augustus Keppel, Rear Admiral of the Blue Squadron, of His Majestys Fleet, this Plate being an exact Representation of the First Attack, made by the British Fleet under his Command, 8 April 1761, / at Port Andro, on Belleisle [France, see note p. 16]. . . . Is most humbly Inscribed by his most devoted Servant, R. Short. / Drawn on ye Spot, Design'd & Published as the Act directs, by R Short May 1, 1763. (Copy in N. Y. Hist. Society.)

Serres pinx.—Canot sculp. / To the Honble Augustus Keppel, Rear Admiral, of the Blue Squadron, of His Majesty's Fleet, this Plate being an exact Representation of the second Attack, made at Fort d'Arsic on Belleisle, 22^d^ Apr^l^ 1761 . . . is humbly inscribed by his devoted Servant. R Short. / Drawn on the Spot & publish'd as the Act directs by R. Short May 1, 1763. (Copy in N. Y. Hist. Society.)

Serres Pinx.—Canot sculp. / To the Honble Augustus Keppel, Rear Admiral of the Blue Squadron of His Majesty's Fleet, This Plate representing St Foy nearly Locmaria Point, on Belleisle, the Place intended for a Feint 22 April 1761 . . . Is most humbly Inscribed by his most devoted Servant—R Short. / Drawn on ye Spot. Design'd & Publish'd as ye Act directs by R Short Sept 12. 1763. (Copy in N. Y. Hist. Society.)

Serres pinx.—Canot sculp. / To the Honble Augustus Keppel Rear Admiral of the Blue Squadron, of His Majesty's Fleet—This Plate representing the Watering-Place, Bomb-Battery, Redoubts near the Windmills— / The Breach in the Walls of the Citadel at Palais, The Land to Point - Trelafar on Belleisle / And Part of the Road for Ships, as appeared from Raminet Battery:— Is humbly Inscribed by his most devoted Servant, R Short. / Drawn on ye Spot Design'd & Published as ye Act directs by R. Short Oct. 8. 1763. (Copy in N. Y. Hist. Society.)

Serres pinx—Mason sculp. / To the Honble Augustus Keppel Rear Admiral of the Blue Squadron of His Majesty's Fleet, This Plate being an exact Representation of the Back Part or Land View, / of the Citadel and Town of Palais on Bellisle; . . . Is most humbly Inscribed by his most devoted Servant, R Short. / Drawn on the Spot, Designd, & Publish'd as the Act directs, by R Short May 1, 1763. (Copy in N. Y. Hist. Society.)

Serres Pinx^t^—Benoist Sculp^t^ / To the Honble Augustus Keppel, Rear Admiral of the Blue Squadron of His Majesty's Fleet This Plate being an Exact Representation, of the Citadel & Town of Palais on Belleisle, . . . Is most humbly Inscribed by his most devoted Servant, R. Short. / Drawn on ye Spot Designed & Published as ye Act directs by R Short Septr 12 1763. (Copy in N. Y. Hist. Society.)

[9] *Sauzon*, town of [in France; see p. 288, foot-note; no copy found].

[10] *Landing of the New-England Expedition against Cape Breton* (not found).

[11–16] *Halifax, Nova Scotia: 6 views* (three not found).

Serres Pinxit. R. Short delin^r^—Ja^s^ Mason sculpsit. / To the Right Honourable George Dunk, Earl of Halifax, His Majesty's Principal Secretary of State &c. &c. &c./ This Plate representing Part of the Town & Harbour of Halifax in Nova Scotia, looking down Prince Street to the / Opposite Shore shews the Eastern Battery, George & Cornwallis Islands, Thrum-Cap &c. to the Sea off Chebucto Head; [Title also in Fr.] Is most humbly Inscribed by his Lordship's most devoted Servant—R. Short. / 1 Pontack's 2 Governor's Summer House & Gardens. 3 Work House. Published Ap. 25th 1777 by Iohn Boydell Engraver in Cheapside London — 1 La Cabaret de Pontague. 2 La Maison de Campagne & Jardin du Gouverneur. 3 L'Hospital pour les Pauvres. (Copy in N. Y. Publ. Libr., Emmet Coll.)

Serres Pinxit. R Short delin^t^—Ja^s^ Mason sculpsit / To the Right Honourable George Dunk, Earl of Halifax, His Majesty's Principal Secretary of State &c. &c. &c./ This Plate representing Part of the Town & Harbour of Halifax in Nova Scotia. / Looking down George Street to the opposite Shore called Dartmouth,/ Is most humbly Inscribed, by his Lordship's most devoted Servant, R. Short. [Title also in French.] 1. King's Yard. 2. Barracks 3. Printing House. 4. Pontack's———Published Ap. 25th 1777 by John Bowdell Engraver in Cheapside London.——1. Le Magazin du Roy. 2. Les Barraques. 3. L'Imprimerie. 4. Cabaret appellé Pontaque. (Copy in N. Y. Publ. Libr., Emmet Coll.)

Serres pinx. R. Short delin^t^ / Ja^s^ Mason sculp. / To the Right Honourable George Dunk, Earl of Halifax, His Majesty's. Principal Secretary of State &c. &c. &c. / This Plate representing the Town and Harbour of Halifax in Nova-Scotia, / As appears from George Island looking up to the King's-Yard and Bason. / [Title also in French.] Is most humbly Inscribed, by his Lordship's most devoted Servant, R.. Short.

L. l. Published Ap. 25th 1777 by John Boydell Engraver in Cheapside London. (Copy in N. Y. Publ. Libr., Emmet Coll.)

[17–38] *Quebec:* 22 Views of the city, public buildings and vicinity. Besides the six views enumerated in the Boston Pub. Lib. copy of the *Scenographia Americana*, the following fourteen others are known:

A View of Quebec from the bason (see Bowles's Catalogue, p. 59—referred to more specifically hereafter—which states that this view was engraved by Canot from a painting by F. Swaine).

Cap. Her^y^ Smyth Delin Frances Swain Pinxit.—P. C. Canot. Sculp^t^ / A View of the Landing Place above the Town of Quebec, describing the Assault of the Enemys Post, / on the Banks of the River St Lawrence, with a Distant View of the Action between the British & French / Armys, on the Hauteurs D'Abraham. Sep^br^ 13th 1759. / Inscribed to the Right. Honble Field Marshall Lord Viscount Ligonier, Commander in Chief / of His Majesty's Forces / By his Lordships most Obed^t^ Servant,/ Her^y^ Smyth Aid de Camp to Gen: Wolfe. / London Printed for Robt Sayer Map & Printseller, at the Golden Buck in Fleet Street, T. Bowles in St Pauls Church Yard & John Bowles & Son at the Black House in Cornhil, E. Bakewell, & H. Parker opposite Birchin Lane in Cornhil. [From a painting by F. Swaine—See Bowles Catalogue, referred to below, p. 59.] To the left and right of the title are seventeen references. (Copy in

N. Y. Publ. Libr., Emmet Coll., and British Museum, Print Room, with assigned date 1766.)

A view of the taking of Quebec, in 1759, showing the manner of debarking the English forces and the scrambling of the infantry up the precipice [etc.]—Bowles Catalogue, 46.

The following twelve views, while included in this set, evidently form a separate series:

A General View of Quebec, from Point Levy/[Title also in French]. To the Hon[ble] S[r] Charles Saunders Vice Admiral [etc. . . .] These Twelve Views of the Principal Buildings in Quebec, are most Humbly Inscribed by his most Obedient Humble Servant, Richard Short/. Sept[r] 1st 1761 Publish'd according to Act of Parliament by R Short, & Sold by T. Jefferys the Corner of S[t] Martins Lane, Charing Cross. In right corner just under the engraving: Engraved by P. Canot.

A View of the Intendants Palace [Title also in French]. Drawn on the Spot by Rich[d] Short. Engraved by William Elliott. / Publish'd according to Act of Parliament, Sept[r] 1. 1761, by Rich[d] Short and Sold by Tho[s] Jefferys the Corner of S[t] Martins Lane. (Copy in N. Y. Publ. Libr., Print Room, and British Museum, K 119–39a.)

A View of the Bishop's House with the ruins as they appear in going down / the Hill, from the Upper to the Lower Town / [Title also in French]. Drawn on the Spot by Rich[d] Short. Engraved by J. Fougeron. / London Publish'd according to Act of Parliament Sep[r] 1. 1761, by Rich[d] Short, & Sold by Tho[s] Jefferys the Corner of S[t] Martins Lane. (Copy in N. Y. Publ. Libr., Print Room, and British Museum, K 119–39a.)

A View of the Treasury, and Jesuits College [Title also in French]. Drawn on the Spot by Rich[d] Short, Engraved by C. Grignion. / London, Publish'd according to Act of Parliament, Sep[r] 1. 1761. by Rich[d] Short, and Sold by Tho[s] Jefferys the corner of S[t] Martins Lane. (Copy in N. Y. Publ. Libr., Print Room, and British Museum, K 119–39a.)

A View of the Jesuits College and Church [Title also in French]. Drawn on the Spot by Rich[d] Short. Engraved by C. Grignion. / London Publish'd according to Act of Parliament, Sep. 1. 1761 by Rich[d] Short, & Sold by Tho[s] Jefferys the Corner of S[t] Martins Lane Charing Cross. (Copy in N. Y. Publ. Libr., Print Room, and British Museum, K 119–39a.)

A View of the Cathedral, Jesuits College, and Recollect Friars Church, / taken from the Gate of the Governors House. [Title also in French.] Drawn on the Spot by R. Short Engraved by P. Canot. / Published according to Act of Parliament by R Short and Sold by T. Jefferys the corner of S[t] Martins Lane Charing Cross. Sep[r] 1.1761. (Copy in N. Y. Publ. Libr., Print Room, and British Museum, K 119–39a.)

A View of the Orphan's or Urseline Nunnery, / taken from the Ramparts. / [Title also in French.] Drawn on the Spot by R. Short. Engraved by James Mason. / Sept[r] 1st 1761. Published according to Act of Parliament by R. Short and Sold by T. Jefferys the Corner of S[t] Martins Lane Charing Cross. (Copy in N. Y. Publ. Libr., Emmet Coll., and British Museum, K 119–39a.)

A View of the North West part of the City of Quebec, taken from S[t] Charles's River [Title also in French]. Drawn on the Spot by Rich[d] Short. Engraved by P. Benazech / London Publish'd according to Act of Parliament, Sep[r] 1, 1761, by Rich[d] Short, & Sold by Tho[s] Jefferys the corner of S[t] Martins Lane. (Copy in N. Y. Publ. Libr., Emmet Coll., and British Museum, K 119–39a.)

A View of the Inside of the Recollect Friars Church. [Title also in French] / Drawn on the Spot by Rich[d] Short, Engraved by C. Grignon / London, Publish'd according to Act of Parliament, Sep. 1, 1761, by Richd Short, & Sold by Thos Jefferys the Corner of St Martins Lane, Charing Cross. (Copy in British Museum, K 119–39a.)

A View of the Inside of the Jesuits Church. / [Title also in French.] Drawn on the Spot by Richard Short, Engraved by Anthony Walker. / Publish'd according to Act of Parliament by Richd Short, and Sold by Thos Jefferys the corner of St Martin's Lane./ (Copy in British Museum, K 119–39a.)

A View of the Bishops House with the Ruins as they appear/in going up the Hill from the Tower, to the Upper Town. / [Title also in French.] Drawn on the Spot by Richard Short. Engraved by A. Benoist. Imprint same as that of "A General View of Quebec," the first view of this series, above. (Copy in British Museum, K 119–39a.)

A View of the Church of Notre Dame de la Victoire; Built in / Commemoration of the raising the Siege in 1695, and destroyed in 1759 / [Title also in French]. Drawn on the Spot by Richd Short. Engraved by A. Bennoist. Imprint same as "A View of the Inside of the Recollect Friars Church," above. (Copy in British Museum, K 119–39a.)

[39]	*Montreal* [Titles quoted in full above.]	(In *Scenographia*	*Americana*,	Boston P. L.)
[40]	*Louisbourg*	"	"	"
[41–42]	*New York City:* two views	"	"	"
[43]	*Boston, Mass.*	"	"	"
[44]	*Charlestown, S. C.*	"	"	"
[45]	*Hudson's river, Topan sea*	"	"	"
[46]	*Passaick Falls*	"	"	"
[47]	*Pakepsey and the Catt'skill mts.*	"	"	"
[48]	*Great Cohoes falls.*	"	"	"
[49]	*Bethlem, Pa.*	"	"	"
[50]	*Beginning and Completion of an American Settlement*	"	"	"

[51] A North View of the Pisaiack Falls, in the Province of New Jersey in North America, / The Height of the Fall 67 Feet. Drawn on the Spot by Thos Davies Capt Lieu^{t} of the Royal Reg^{t} of Artillery. (Above title the imprint: "Sold by R^{t} Wilkinson N° 125 Fenchurch Street.") (Copy in N. Y. Publ. Libr., Print Room.)

[52] *Niagara Falls*

(l. r.) J. Fougeron sculp. / To his Excellency Lieu^{t} Genl Sir Jeffrey Amherst, Knight of the Most Honourable Order of the Bath, &c. &c. &c. / These Six Views are most humbly Inscribed, by His Excellency's most devoted Servt Thos Davies. / An East View of the Great Cataract of Niagara. / Sold by R^{t} Wilkinson N° 125 Fenchurch Street. (to left of pub. line): Perpend^{r} Heigth (*sic*) of the Fall 162 Feet, Breadth about a Mill & Quarter (To r. of pub. line): Drawn on the Spot by Thos Davies Capt. Lieut^{t} in the Royal Reg^{t} of Artillery. (Copy in N. Y. Hist. Society.)

[53–55] *Cataracts on the Casconchiagon or Little Seneca's river on Lake Ontario: three views* (one not found.)

A South East View of the Lower Cataract on the Casconchiagon or Little Seneca's River on Lake Ontario. Perpendicular Height 75 Feet. Drawn on the Spot by Thos Davies Capt Lieut^{t} of the Royal Regiment of Artillery. (l. r.): Morris Sculpsit. Sold by R^{t} Wilkinson N° 125 Fenchurch Street (In N. Y. Public Library).

A South East View of the Great Cataract on the Casconchiagon or Little Seneca's River, on Lake Ontario, Perpendicular Height of the Fall 105 Feet Drawn on the Spot by Thos Davies Capt Lieutt of the Royal Regiment of Artillery. (l. r.): Mazell Sculpsit. (Directly under rectangle): Sold by Rt Wilkinson No 125 Fenchurch Street. (In N. Y. Public Library.)

[56] A North View of Pensacola, on the Island of Santa Rosa, Drawn by Dom. Serres. 1. The Fort. 2. The Church. 3. The Governors House. 4. The Commandants House. 5. A Well. 6. A Bungo. (Copy in British Museum, K 122-97.)

[57-66] *Havana, Cuba.* 10 views [two not found].

Besides the six enumerated above in the Boston Public Library copy of the *Scenographia Americana*, the following two views have been found:

A Prospect of the Moro Castle taken within the Entrance of the Harbour. Published according to Law & Sold by R. Willock Bookseller, in Cornhill, & J. Boydell Engraver in Cheapside. Drawn upon the Spot by an Officer. P. C. Canot sculp. N. B. The original drawing is preserved with this in the King's Collections. (Copy in British Museum, K 123-28i.)

A Prospect of the Moro Castle and City of Havana from Sea. Imprints, &c, exactly same as foregoing. (Copy in British Museum, K 123-28b.) The original drawing also is preserved in the British Museum.

[67] *Roseau, Island of Dominica* (In *Scen. Am.* in Boston Public Library; Title quoted in full above).

[68-70] *Fort Royal, Island of Guadaloupe:* 3 views (In. *Scen. Am.* in Boston Public Library; Title quoted in full above).

[71-73] *Antigua island:* three views [not found].

[74] *Carthagena* [not found].

As has already been noted, one of the views of Quebec is added from a sales catalogue issued by Carington Bowles in 1790. This interesting catalogue, which belongs to Mr. R. T. H. Halsey, contains (p. 75) a description of "Twenty-eight Sea and Land Views in North-America, and the West-Indies, drawn on the spot by several officers of the British Army and Navy, and neatly engraved by Sandby, Grignion, Rooker, Canot, and others: each print is about 20 inches wide and 14 inches deep the whole half bound. Price 4 l. 4 s. or, each set separate at the prices affixed"; and (p. 59) "The Siege and Reduction of the Havannah, or Britannia's triumph in the year 1762, being a series of 12 capital sea-pieces, representing the operations of His Majesty's fleet and army, employed in the attack and conquest of the Havannah." These latter prints, which are 25½ x 18 inches, evidently do not belong to the *Scenographia Americana*.

The catalogue describes also (p. 136) a collection of "Twelve remarkable Views in North America and the West Indies, viz. 1. A View of the city of Quebec, the capital of Canada. 2. A view of the water falls of Montmorenci, and the attack made by general Wolfe, on the French intrenchments near Beauport, with the Grenadiers of the army. 3. A View of Cape Rouge, or Carouge, 9 miles above the city of Quebec, on the north shore of the river St. Lawrence. 4. A view of Gaspee Bay, in the Gulf of St. Lawrence. 5. A view of the Pierced Island, a remarkable rock in the Gulf of St. Lawrence, 2 leagues southward of Gaspee Bay. 6. An east view of Montreal in Canada. 7. A view of Louisburgh, taken from the Light-House, when that city was besieged. 8. A south west view of the city of New York. 9. A view of Charles Town, the capital of South Carolina.

10. A view of the great Cohoes Falls, on the Mohawk River; the fall, about 70 feet, the river a quarter of a mile broad. 11. A view of Bethlehem, the great Moravian settlement in the province of Pennsylvania. 12. A view of the entrance of the Harbour of the Havannah, taken from the wrecks."

These views are described (p. 129) as printed on half sheets of demy paper, twelve prints in a book, each eleven inches wide and seven inches deep, price 3 s. plain or 8 s. each set coloured. No. 8 of this series, "A south west view of the city of New York," is an exact reduction from the Howdell-Canot View, except that a group of three men and a dog has been added in the meadow south of the Rutgers house. Two copies of this print, one coloured and one plain, are in the author's collection. A note in the catalogue, p. 144, explains: "The preceding sets of demy prints are adapted to be viewed in the diagonal mirror, and are kept properly coloured for that purpose; or to frame and glaze for furniture: also designed to instruct, amuse and draw after." There was a complete set of these quarto views in the collection of the late William F. Havemeyer.

Plate 38

A South East View of the City of New York in North America
[The Howdell-Canot South East View]

Engraved on copper. 19¾ x 12½ Date depicted: About 1763.
Date issued: 1768 ?.

Provenance: Pl. "b. 4" from the *Scenographia Americana*, for a description of which see Plate 37.

Author: Capt Thomas Howdell.

Engraver: P. Canot.

Owner: Wm. B. Osgood Field, Esq.

Other copies: N. Y. Public Library (Emmet Coll., 10718); N. Y. Hist. Society; Library of Congress, Div. of Maps and Charts (1st State), etc.

Probably the second or third state. The same remarks as to states, etc., apply to this plate as to the preceding.

A study of this view in connection with the Montresor Plan (Pl. 40), or with the Ratzen Plan (Pl. 42), enables us to identify the various prominent buildings as follows, beginning from the east: St. George's Church (Beekman Street), Jail, New (later Middle) Dutch Church (this is erroneously designated in the reference as the French Church), French Church, South Dutch Church (Garden Street), City Hall, Presbyterian Church on Wall Street, erroneously shown with a *spire*, which was not added until the church was rebuilt in 1835, the church at the time of this view having a tower and cupola, built in 1748 (see description Pls. 105 and 111, Pls. 117 and 123-b, St. Mémin's Panorama, Pl. 80-b, and remarks, Pl. 44). The next buildings are King's College, with cupola, and Trinity Church.

The view is taken from a point about midway between Ranelagh and Mr. Lispenard's (see Ratzen Plan, Pl. 42). An interesting view of this neighbourhood, drawn in 1785 by Dr. Alexander Anderson, is reproduced in Wilson's *Memorial History*, III: 17. The original drawing belonged, in 1910, to Miss Mary King, of New York.

Behind the more distant of the two fences seen in the foreground appear the palisades built in 1745 and shown on the Maerschalck Map (Pl. 34). The westernmost blockhouse and gate which protected this line of fortifications can be seen at the right of the view. The large building between the block-house and Trinity Church is probably Vauxhall. See Montresor Plan (Pl. 40).

Reproduced in Mr. Andrews's *New Amsterdam New Orange New York*, opp. p. 67.

Plate 39

View of Harlaem from Morisania in the Province of New York Septem^{r} 1765

Water-colour sketch on paper. $11\frac{5}{16}$ x $6\frac{11}{16}$ Date depicted: 1765.

Owner: British Museum, King's Collection. The War Office possesses, among its collections of American maps and views, several sketches similar to this one, and evidently forming part of the same set. Among these are two very interesting views of Albany.

The church shown in this view is the second Dutch Church at Harlem, known as the Reformed Church, the foundations for which were begun on the 29th of March, 1686.—Original *Harlem Records*, 470 (see Bibliography and Chronology). The specifications for this church, which are contained in the *Harlem Records*, quoted in Riker's *History of Harlem* (p. 453), read as follows:

> Specifications of the *Church* at *Harlem:* The size of the church, across in either way, is 36 Dutch feet; upon which William Hellaker undertakes to construct the roof, with an arch therein, and a small steeple upon it, and to cover all properly with shingles, and to make a scuttle thereto; upon condition that the people of the town shall be obligated to deliver the timber at the building place. For which the Constable and Magistrates promise to pay the aforesaid William Hellaker, the sum of Seven Hundred and Fifty Guilders, in Wheat, to be paid in the month of January following this year, 1686, the wheat to be delivered at the current price. Thus arranged and agreed to in the presence of the after-named witnesses, and which, with our usual hand, is subscribed. Done at New Haerlem, this 30th of March, 1686.

This church stood about two hundred feet south-west of the original site of the first Dutch Church and on the other side of Church Lane.—See Randel's Survey, Pl. 79; also Landmark Map, Vol. II, Appendix, and Randel's Map of the Farms (Pl. 86). Under date of January 15, 1687, the Harlem "Schult Boeck" or Ledger, page 74, records a credit to Jan Delamater of f. 9 for "*Aen een ketel tot de haen van de toorn*" (A copper weathercock on the steeple). This second Dutch Church was destroyed during the Revolutionary War, and was rebuilt in 1788. When the latter church was taken down, in 1825, and a new one built on the present site (the north-west corner of Third Avenue and 121st Street, part of the old Church Farm), the old vane bearing the date 1788 was removed to Judge Ingraham's barn on Second Avenue (Riker, 191).

Until the organisation of St. Mary's Episcopal Church at Manhattanville, in 1823, this was the only church building in Harlem or its vicinity.

In the immediate foreground of the view is seen the landing of the ferry to Bronkside or Morisania. The cove which appears at the left of the settlement lay at the foot of the present 123d Street.

There is no proper record of the organisation of the first Dutch Church at Harlem, which, however, we know dates from about 1660. Although Stuyvesant's letter to the Directors in Holland, dated October 6, 1660, states that at that time Harlem had no minister and no religious service, within about a month thereafter the services of Domine Michel Zyperus had been engaged. Jan la Montagne, Jr., who acted as deacon of this first Dutch Church organisation, served as such until November 30, 1662, and as the usual term of service was two years, we can be reasonably sure that the organisation dates from the close of the year 1660 (Riker, 198). Furthermore, as the magistracy was not instituted until this year, a church organisation could hardly have existed previously. Zyperus left Harlem, probably early in 1663, and Montagne for a time acted as *voorleser* and schoolmaster at an annual salary of fifty guilders, paid by the Company. Services were evidently held in a private house, as the first church building was not begun until 1665. Montagne's accounts, as treasurer, showing what the deacons expended for labor and material, are still in existence—*Harlem Records*. The first entry is under date of January 23, 1665, and the last, January, 1668, the total cost being f. 369.18.—Riker, 247–8; see also Chronology.

The first Dutch Church was situated on the north side of the Old Church Lane, south of the graveyard. It stood in the bed of the present 125th Street, just west of First Avenue, and within a few hundred feet of the river (see Randel Map of the Farms, Pl. 86, where it is shown as a little rectangular building; Bridges Map, Pl. 80-b; also Landmark Map, Vol. II, Appendix). It was used jointly as church and schoolhouse, and contained a second story or loft, which was sometimes rented at public auction.—Riker, 263. The old Ingraham home, which stood on the church lot, and not on the Turnure lot as stated by Riker, p. 532, occupied the exact site of the first church.

The view was lithographed by Hayward for Valentine's *Manual*, 1863, and appears opp. p. 610.

HISTORICAL SUMMARY

CHAPTER III

THE REVOLUTIONARY PERIOD

1763–1783

CHAPTER III

THE REVOLUTIONARY PERIOD

1763–1783

THE treaty of 1763 closed one chapter in the development of the English colonies in America and ushered in a period in which new conditions and forces co-operated to determine the destiny of the country. Up to this time the colonies had been threatened continually with the encroachment of the French and their savage allies; and, quite naturally, they had looked to the home country for help and encouragement in the struggle against these relentless enemies. The treaty of 1763 removed this danger, and from that time forward, there was apparently to be no barrier to their westward progress. The removal of their fear of the French made the colonists realise more fully the opportunities which their position gave them. They were naturally a hardy, self-reliant people, from whom the hardships and dangers of frontier life had largely eliminated the timid, the weak, and the unfit. Their increase in wealth and population had been rapid, and already some of them were looking forward to the time when their influence, by reason of both numbers and wealth, should be greater than that of England itself. These changing conditions could not fail to weaken their feeling of dependence upon the mother country.

That the removal of the French from America would be followed by the union of the colonies, and ultimately by their winning independence from England, had long been foreseen by careful observers. More than thirty years before this, Montesquieu had foretold that England, because of her laws restricting trade and navigation, would be the first nation to be abandoned by her colonies. Vergennes, on hearing the terms of the treaty of 1763, remarked, "The consequences of the entire cession of Canada are obvious. I am persuaded England will ere long repent of having removed the only check that could keep her colonies in awe. They stand no longer in need of her protection; she will call on them to contribute toward supporting the burdens they have helped to bring on her; and they will answer by striking off all dependence."

Even at this time, and for many years before, evidences of friction between the colonies and England had not been wanting. There had already been controversies in practically every one of the colonies over providing supplies for the government, quartering troops upon the people, the questions of free speech, a free press, and the independence of the judiciary. Some of these questions had aroused violent feeling during the late war, as was noticed in connection with providing for the troops in the command of the Earl of Loudoun at New York City. In addition to these causes of friction, there was the notion, held so naturally by England and Englishmen, that the colonies were dependents, and the colonials inferiors. This feeling had been manifested during the war by many English soldiers in their contempt for the provincial troops and officers. Even such disasters as Braddock's defeat did not materially modify their opinion. On the other hand, the provincials were not the type of people to endure such contemptuous treatment without feeling keen resentment.

The great weakness of the colonies lay in their lack of unity. Up to this time intercolonial jealousies and enmity had kept them effectually apart, and the connection between the individual colonies and England was undoubtedly stronger than that among the colonies themselves. This condition of estrangement was increased by the physical conditions of the country, which made travelling slow and difficult, and inter-colonial communication of little effect in welding the separate colonies into one body, united by a feeling of common interest against a common foe. Some recognition of a common peril and the resulting need of union, had been shown in 1754 at the Albany convention in Franklin's plan for a union of all the colonies to control Indian and military affairs; but the fear of France was not strong enough to make the colonies forget their mutual jealousies and individual interests so far as really to bring them together. England herself was destined to provide the force that should drive her colonies into a union firm enough to enable them to throw off her control over them.

If the close of the French and Indian War in 1763 was accompanied by a change in the feeling of the colonies towards England, it was no less marked by a change in England's treatment of the colonies. Up to this time England's plan had been to regulate their trade in her own interest, a policy which resulted in the enactment of a series of navigation laws designed to control the imports of the colonies from abroad, their exports to other countries, their traffic with each other, their carrying trade, and their manufactures. The importation of goods from any part of Asia, Africa, or America, whether British or foreign, was confined to English or colonial ships. No commodities of foreign growth or manufacture could be brought into Great Britain or Ireland unless they came directly from the producing country. Foreign carriers were absolutely excluded from the colonies, whether carrying their own goods or not. The coasting trade was entirely closed to foreigners, and no one except a British citizen could act as a merchant in the colonies. Finally, certain enumerated commodities, such as sugar, tobacco, cotton-wool, and indigo, might not be carried, even in English ships, to any place other than Great Britain, Ireland, and the British plantations.

Fortunately for the prosperity of the colonies, England had never been in a position to enforce these restrictions on trade. During the reigns of the Stuarts, domestic affairs had largely monopolised the energies of the government. Both at that time and later, the fear of France in Europe and America had distracted England's attention from her colonial administration. In fact, colonial affairs had been treated with what has been termed "salutary neglect." This policy permitted the colonials virtually to disregard such regulations as worked injury to their trade (notably the Molasses Act of 1733, which had never been anything but a dead letter), and to engage in a very lucrative trade with the French, Spanish, and Dutch. This trade was, in the eyes of the law, simply smuggling, but the fact that it had been permitted for many years, served to justify the colonials in thinking that they had a right to enjoy its benefits. The end of the French wars in 1763 made it possible for England to reorganise her whole policy, so far as her treatment of her dependencies beyond seas was concerned.

There was some occasion for this. Since the time when Braddock began his march to the reduction of Fort Duquesne, England's yearly expenditure had increased threefold. The land tax was constantly rising, and the means for paying it were not growing proportionately. An army in the colonies to protect them from the Indians was necessary; it could likewise be used to overawe the colonists into submission to the control of the government, as well as to provide employment for officers and younger sons. These considerations largely determined England's plan of colonial reorganisation in 1763. Under the leadership of Townshend, a plan was developed proposing: (1) to enforce the acts of navigation and trade rigorously, (2) to raise a revenue in the colonies by both direct and indirect taxation, (3) to use this revenue for the support of a standing military force in America and for paying colonial officials independently of colonial assemblies. In execution of this policy, ships were despatched to America to prevent smuggling, and by a clever device, all the commanders of British ships of war serving in American waters were authorised to act as custom-house officers with the usual share in the contraband and confiscated cargoes. Admiralty courts, which were invariably regarded with disfavour and suspicion by the colonists, were established to try cases connected with the service; and writs of assistance, authorising officers to search houses suspected of containing smuggled goods, were issued. To make colonial officials less fearful of local opinion and more dependent upon the home government, they were required to answer for the maladministration of their offices, not to local courts, but to English tribunals; and the policy of paying their salaries from England, instead of by grants from the colonial assemblies, was adopted.

Unfortunately for the harmony between England and the colonies, the occasion chosen by England for putting into operation this new policy for a stricter control over her colonial possessions was the very time when they were least willing to endure such restrictions. Until 1763 they had been threatened constantly by a cruel and savage enemy, and had looked to England for protection and aid. The danger from the French and Indians disappeared with the Peace of Paris, and with it passed the old feeling of dependence. Consequently, England's plan of exercising more complete control over the colonies was inaugurated at the very time when the colonies themselves were placed in a position to assert greater independence. Under these circumstances, only a policy profoundly wise and carried out in a spirit of conciliation could prevent a clash between England and her colonies.

Neither the crown nor the ministers were able to direct affairs satisfactorily. The young king, George III, who since 1760 had occupied the English throne, although of upright character in private life, proved to be a bad ruler. Narrow-minded, ignorant, arbitrary, with an unbounded confidence in his own judgment, and an exaggerated idea of his prerogative—which, indeed, he intended to make still greater—determined to control his ministers and force them to follow his dictation, he was particularly unable to direct the colonial policy of the government to a successful issue. He believed thoroughly in the new plan to exercise a stricter control over the colonies. It was the king's intention, also, to govern in fact as well as in name. He was entirely unwilling to occupy the position of a figurehead in public affairs, as his immediate predecessors had been content to do. Relying on the Tories, he hoped to build up a party of the king's friends by whom he could control Parliament and consequently the entire government. In this he was successful for a time. In 1762 Pitt lost his position. The Earl of Bute, and later Lord North, became prime minister. Both of these men represented the personal policy of the king, and each was kept in power because he was supported by the party of the king's friends. This party, in turn, was held together by the granting of pensions, places, and even by gold. The royal patronage was freely used to bind men to the loyal support of the king's policy. It was this organisation which the king used to enforce England's new colonial policy. Fortunately for America, the Liberals in England, as well as on this side of the water, were filled with apprehension at the increase of the royal power, and the effort of the colonies to prevent the enforcement of the new colonial policy was closely connected with the attempt of the Liberals in England to limit the royal prerogative at home. The policy which George III and his ministers had adopted relative to the colonies could scarcely have been carried out, even under the most favourable circumstances, without trouble. That it could be executed under the direction of the king with the conditions existing in 1763, without causing a clash between the English government and its colonies overseas, was virtually impossible.

On two points especially the interests of England and the colonies were opposed to each other. These were: (1) the enforcement of the navigation laws, which would ruin a lucrative trade, illegal to be sure, but one which the colonies had enjoyed without let or hindrance for a century or more; (2) the measures of the government designed to secure a permanent revenue from the colonies, such as the Stamp Act of 1765 and the Townshend Acts of 1767. The colonies objected to these on the ground that they inaugurated a new kind of taxation; they levied taxes within the country, and consequently were internal taxes, whereas the revenues derived from the Navigation Acts were external taxes. From opposing the new laws, because they levied a new kind of tax, the colonists quickly passed to the contention that they could not be legally taxed at all, except by their representatives, and, that since they could not be represented in Parliament, that body had no right to levy taxes upon them. Only their own assemblies had the right to do this.

In New York City, where trade with the Indians and overseas was the very mainspring of prosperity, where the merchants were among the wealthiest and most influential citizens, of whom the most respected did not hesitate to break the navigation laws, and, in fact, not infrequently built their houses with secret chambers for the concealment of smuggled goods, the attempt of the English government to enforce a new colonial policy, which must necessarily injure trade, could not fail to awaken a strong feeling of dissatisfaction, which soon produced a powerful party opposed to the crown.

This party was not new. It had existed in greater or less strength for many years. In fact, it is hard to trace this opposition to its source. In the Leislerian period, the party opposed to the court had been strong and violent, and the feeling aroused then long continued. Zenger's trial stirred up the old hostility again. Later, the question of the tenure by which the colonial judges held their positions, whether during good behaviour or the king's pleasure, served to keep the feeling alive. This question was settled for the time in 1744, and the judiciary was relieved of its dependence on the king's government by the withdrawal of the commission of James De Lancey, the chief-justice, by which he had held office during the pleasure of the king, and the issuing of a new commission by which he retained office during good behaviour. The opposition was further kept alive by quartering troops on the citizens without pay during the French and Indian war, and by the impressment of seamen for the British navy from the market and wood boats, as well as from the merchantmen lying in the harbour of New York.

The organ through which the party of the opposition made its will known was chiefly the provincial assembly, which it very largely controlled. The struggle resolved itself into a contest between the king's government, as represented by the governor, and the assembly, each trying to gain control for itself. During this struggle the assembly made successive advances in power. It secured the right to a provincial treasurer, who should be responsible to it, as well as to the governor and council, for the conduct of his office. It secured the right of being represented before the home government by an agent of its own selection and under its own control. It gradually assumed control of Indian affairs and of the commissioner who had them in charge. It claimed and exercised the right of deciding what fortifications were needed in the colony, and of controlling the time and manner of their construction. It claimed exclusively the right to originate all bills for the raising of revenue in the colony. It refused to provide a permanent revenue for the king's use, but provided for a single year only. It disposed of the revenue by specific appropriations to each individual, instead of by a general appropriation, controlling by this device the conduct of every officer in the province.

The policy of governing the colonies more strictly, adopted at the close of the war in 1763, could not fail to awaken among the colonists the fear of an opposition which had already shown itself active and aggressive. In fact, the new policy had been foreshadowed before 1763. Two years before, on the death of James De Lancey, who for many years had been chief-justice of New York, the crown made an effort to regain control of the provincial judiciary by appointing Benjamin Pratt, a Boston lawyer, to the position "during the King's pleasure." When the assembly refused to grant him a salary, the government directed that it be paid from the royal quit-rents. In this way, what was thought a necessary right by Englishmen, namely, that the judges be safeguarded against being turned out of office by the crown, was denied to Englishmen in the provinces. In 1764, the lawyers and judges in New York were further aroused over a change in the manner of making appeals from the common law courts of the province. Hitherto appeals had been made by writs of error to the governor and council, and thence to the king. In this year, the system was changed so that an appeal to the king in council could be made on the merits of the case, and not simply on the law and action of the courts. The members of the legal profession in New York united in violent opposition to the change. It may be that their opposition, as Lieutenant-Governor Colden asserted, was partly due to the fact that the change tended to lessen their power in the province; but undoubtedly their conduct was also influenced by the conviction that this was merely another device of the crown to increase its prerogative by taking the provincial common law courts completely under its control. The fears of the people were aroused, and they became even more thoroughly opposed to the policy of a strict control over the colony, to which the king's government had evidently committed itself.

But the British government soon discovered that even a strict enforcement of the Navigation Acts could not provide enough revenue to maintain the establishment of His Majesty's government in America. To provide for this deficiency, Lord Grenville's ministry in 1765 passed the Stamp Act, laying a tax on all legal documents executed within the colonies. Unfortunately for the success of this measure, its weight fell most heavily on the men best fitted to organise resistance, namely, on the lawyers and men of property. These were prompt to use their influence with the public against a measure which they found obnoxious; and in this case, the public, whose interests coincided with their own, was ready to be led. The organisation of societies called the Sons of Liberty, and of committees of correspondence was the result. It is often said that the passage of the Stamp Act in 1765 was violently opposed. This is not true. It attracted little attention in either the House of Commons or the House of Lords, and even colonial agents (of whom Franklin was one) who had been sent to England to oppose its passage, felt that there was nothing to do but to submit.

The opposition started in America as soon as news of the passage of the act was received; newspapers and broadsides stirred public opinion. Lieutenant-Governor Colden, writing from New York to Secretary Conway, under date of September 23, 1765, said: "Soon after it became known that Stamp Duties were by Act of Parliament to be paid in the Colonies, virulent papers were published in the Weekly Newspapers, fill'd with every falshood that malice could invent to serve their purpose of exciting the People to disobedience of the Laws and to sedition. At first they only denied the authority of Parliament to lay internal Taxes in the Colonies, but at last they have denied the Legislative Authority of the Parliament in the Colonies, and these Papers continue to be published."

In New York, the incident of Zacharias Hood, the stamp officer of

Maryland, who, driven from that province by the Sons of Liberty, sought safety in New York, first in the King's Arms Tavern and then in the fort, where Colden took him under his protection, although later the Sons of Liberty forced him to resign his office, shows the spirit of the opposition. The regular newspapers of the city and occasional publications such as the *Constitutional Courant* served to keep the spirit of the people inflamed, and ballads, written for the occasion, were sung about the streets of the city. The designs of the opposition were undoubtedly aided by the fact that there was no governor in the province and that Lieutenant-Governor Colden, a man far advanced in years, lacked the decisiveness which had marked the actions of certain other provincial governors. Colden and his council believed it imprudent to investigate, for fear of rousing the mob, and thought that any danger was preferable to the risk of inciting open rebellion. News of the riots in Boston, and the threats of citizens frightened James McEvers, who had been appointed stamp officer in New York, into resigning his office. Colden wrote to General Gage, then acting as commander-in-chief of His Majesty's forces in North America, asking for a small force to protect the government; and on September 3d he asked Captain Kennedy of the British ship "Coventry," then lying in the harbour, for help in protecting the stamps from the destruction which had been planned for them on their arrival. In this same month, Sir Henry Moore, Baronet, was appointed governor of New York and arrived in the province on November 12th.

In the meantime the committees of correspondence had kept the colonies in touch with each other. A proposal for a general congress found favour, and one was called to meet in New York early in October, 1765. On the seventh, delegates from all the colonies except New Hampshire, Virginia, North Carolina, and Georgia met in the City Hall, and drew up an address to King George, a memorial to the House of Lords, and a petition to the House of Commons. In these they declared that His Majesty's subjects in the colonies owed the same allegiance and were entitled to the same "inherent rights and liberties" as "his natural born subjects" in Great Britain, and acknowledged due subordination to Parliament; but objected to being taxed except by their own assemblies, and also to the establishment of admiralty courts. Its work accomplished, the assembly adjourned on October 25th.

The stamps for New York were shipped secretly on the ship "Edward," which arrived in New York harbour October 22, 1765. Here a difficulty arose. The stamps had been shipped as merchandise. To land them with the rest of the cargo would insure their destruction by the mob on the wharf. To keep the ship out of dock until the cargo could be overhauled and the stamps landed separately by barges was impracticable, because the master of the ship would thereby render himself liable to suit by every one who had merchandise on board; and furthermore, no one would lend his barge for such a purpose. The stamps were finally landed through the assistance of the crews of the men-of-war lying before the city, and were placed in the governor's house in the fort.

The arrival of the stamps caused the Sons of Liberty to take measures to prevent the Stamp Act from being put into operation on November 1st. On the twenty-third of October, manuscript placards were pasted upon the door of every public office, and at the corners of the streets, forbidding anyone to distribute or use the stamped paper. On one of the placards was written: "Pro Patria The first Man that either distributes or makes use of Stampt Paper let him take Care of His House, Person, & Effects. Vox Populi We dare." On October 31st, the lieutenant-governor took the oath to carry the law into effect; and Major James, who had entered the city with two companies of artillery, prepared to defend the fort. In the evening of this same day, the merchants of the city met at the City Arms Tavern [1] and agreed not to import goods from England after January 1st unless the Stamp Act was repealed. The resolutions were signed by "Upwards of Two hundred principal Merchants"; the retailers also agreed not to buy any goods shipped from Great Britain after the first of January. An inter-colonial committee of correspondence was appointed to secure the co-operation of the merchants of other colonies, its five members being Isaac Sears, John Lamb, Gershom Mott, William Wiley, and Thomas Robinson. On the same day, the tradesmen, mechanics, and other workingmen met at "the Fields" (City Hall Park), marched down Broadway to the fort, and through other streets of the town, but they did no damage.

The next day, November 1st, was the day on which the Stamp Act was to go into effect. The government, acting through Major James, had taken precautions to prevent disorder by bringing troops from neighbouring posts to the fort and by placing the cannon so as to command the town. A guard was put around the jail and around Major James's residence. The people, on the other hand, were active. Handbills had

[1] Which occupied the site of 115 Broadway.

been distributed during the day threatening anyone who should distribute or use the stamped paper. A letter threatening Colden was put up in the Coffee House, remained there all day, and at night was delivered at the fort gate. In the evening a great crowd gathered in the Fields "and after it became dark they came up to the Fort Gate with a great number of Torches, and a Scaffold on which two Images were placed, one to represent the Governor in his grey hairs, & the other the Devil by his side. This scaffold with the immages was brought up within 8 or 10 feet of the Gate with the grossest ribaldry from the Mob." As they went from the gate, they broke open the governor's coach-house, took his coach, put the effigy on top, and went back towards the Fields. All of the crowd then went to the Bowling Green, where they tore away the palisades, marched to the middle of the Green, and with the palisades and planks of the fort fence and a chaise and two sleighs from the Governor's coach-house, burned "the coach, gallows, man, Devil, and all to ashes." A detachment of the mob then went to the house of Major James, destroyed every article in it, and defaced the house itself.[1]

This demonstration was followed by threats of violence from the mob and remonstrances from the magistrates and principal men of the town, urging Colden to suspend the execution of the act. Under the advice of his council, he promised that no stamped paper should be distributed, but that it should be delivered to the new governor, Sir Henry Moore, whose arrival was expected daily. Some were contented with this arrangement, but the leaders were still dissatisfied and proposed that the paper be put on board the "Coventry" in the care of Captain Kennedy. It was supposed that they planned to force Kennedy to deliver the paper to them by threatening to destroy his houses in the city; for he and his wife owned a considerable number. At any rate, Kennedy declined this suggestion. The mob continued its threats and declared that they would assault the fort for the purpose of getting the paper into their possession. The more sober-minded citizens objected to this plan, for they knew that it must result in the destruction of life and property. The common council of the city settled the difficulty by petitioning Colden to deliver the paper to them to be deposited in the City Hall under the care of the city watch. He accepted this offer, and informed the mayor and aldermen that if they would attend at the gate of the fort, the paper should

[1] This house was known by the name of Vauxhall, and stood on the square bounded by Warren, Chambers, and Greenwich Streets, and West Broadway.

be delivered to them; soon afterwards, accordingly, accompanied by a prodigious concourse of people of all ranks, they appeared at the gate of the fort, when the governor ordered the paper to be given up to them; upon its receipt they gave three cheers, carried it to the City Hall, and dispersed, after which tranquillity was restored to the city. Shortly afterwards, November 12, 1765, the new governor, Sir Henry Moore, arrived, and endeavoured to placate the people by dismantling the fort and removing the artillery stores which Major James had placed there.

The events attending the arrival of the stamped paper and the attempt to put the Stamp Act into operation in New York were disastrous to the prestige of the king's government. The people had successfully opposed the operation of the law, and the government was unable, or afraid, to use force. Governor Moore, writing to the Earl of Dartmouth, January 16, 1766, described the situation: "By the Minute of Council here inclosed your Lord[p] will see our true situation, and that the disorders have become so general that the magistracy are afraid of exerting the powers they have [been] vested with, and dread nothing so much as being called upon in these troublous times for their assistance . . . though every individual suffers greatly by the total stop put to all kinds of business, such is the general combination, that the execution of the Stamp Act still continues suspended, in spite of all efforts I can make to enforce it."

During this agitation, the leadership of the people was in the hands of the Sons of Liberty. Among these, new and more radical men came forward, and partly took the places of the earlier and more conservative leaders, among whom were such men as William Smith and William Livingston. Isaac Sears, Alexander MacDougall, John Lamb, and Marinus Willett became prominent at this time. The struggle for leadership between these two groups was bitter, and ended only with the definite defeat of the radical element in the election of the committee of fifty-one, May 19, 1774.[1]

The other colonies received the stamped paper in much the same way as did New York. It was soon apparent to the British ministry that the cost of collecting the tax would offset the revenue derived from it. Moreover, the methods by which the colonies were expressing their op-

[1] A large number of citizens, who believed in opposing the enforcement of the Navigation Acts and the later Stamp and Townshend Acts, were unwilling to go so far as to make open war upon England or to adopt the Declaration of Independence. Some of them joined the British and remained in New York until 1783. Others remained neutral and took no active part in the Revolutionary War.

position to it appealed to the interests of British merchants; and a general dissatisfaction in England, as well as in America, convinced the party in Parliament opposed to the government that this was a good opportunity to discredit and defeat Grenville. The result of the agitation was the repeal of the Stamp Act, on March 18, 1766;[1] but although the Stamp Act was repealed, a declaratory act was passed expressly asserting Parliament's right to tax America. In spite of this, the colonies received the news of the repeal with great joy and paid little attention to the declaratory act.[2]

Unfortunately, the government was unable to turn to proper advantage the renewed loyalty which followed in America the repeal of the Stamp Act, and the joy of the colonists was destined to be of short duration. From the first, some of the colonists favoured united opposition to the declaratory act, and events soon occurred to revive discontent and distrust. The question of billeting troops was one of the questions that reopened the agitation. The billeting act had been renewed by the government in England. This was opposed in the colonies as being both unconstitutional and unjust: unconstitutional in that by it a command was laid by one legislative body upon another; and unjust, because the whole burden of providing for the troops would fall upon the colony where they chanced to be stationed. New York especially felt the injustice of this measure, for it was the headquarters of the British forces in America. The New York assembly passed a bill making part provision for the troops, but carefully avoided any admission of the legality of the act. The governor, Sir Henry Moore, approved the bill, and reported the matter to the ministry in England; to which Shelburne, then secretary of state, replied that the king expected obedience to the act in its full extent and meaning. The provincial assembly persistently refused this. The result of this conduct appears in the Townshend Acts of 1767.

The repeal of the Stamp Act did not indicate that the policy of which it was a part had been abandoned permanently. In 1767, the Townshend ministry determined to secure a revenue from America in much the same way, but with this difference, that, while the Stamp Act had been an internal tax, the new measure should provide for an external tax on imports. In May, the ministry secured the passage of three laws:

[1] Broadside printed by Hugh Gaine at New York May 20, 1766 (reproduced in Chronology).

[2] As a reward for William Pitt's activity against the Stamp Act at this time, the citizens of New York erected a statue in his honour in Wall Street. A wave of loyalty swept over the city, and George III was similarly honoured by a statue placed in Bowling Green.

one suspended the New York assembly until it should comply with the mutiny act; another established a board of commissioners of customs with large powers to administer the trade laws; a third laid a duty on all paint, paper, glass, and tea, imported into the colonies. It was intended that the revenue obtained from this measure should be used in paying colonial governors and judges.

The new tax proved to be as obnoxious to the colonies as the Stamp Act had been; it was received in America with protests, resolutions, and memorials. The most feasible method by which the colonies could make England feel the force of their opposition was to form non-importation agreements among themselves. In 1769, an inter-colonial non-importation agreement was adopted. As a matter of fact, the Townshend Acts were a failure. They brought the colonies to the verge of rebellion, and the revenue derived from them was far less than the increase in the amount expended on the military force required in the colonies. Consequently, in March, 1770, Lord North, the new prime minister, secured their repeal, except in the matter of the tax on tea. This item was retained to assert Parliament's right to levy the tax, but the government declared that it would not try to secure a revenue from the colonies, and allowed the hated billeting act to expire by limitation.

The death of Governor Moore in September, 1769, again placed Lieutenant-Governor Colden at the head of the New York government, a position which he held until the new governor, the Earl of Dunmore, arrived, in October of the next year. When the assembly met, in November, 1769, Colden demanded that it make further provision for the troops. The assembly refused to grant this until a plan to issue paper currency to the amount of one hundred and twenty thousand pounds was incorporated with it. Colden signed the bills, which, however, were afterwards rejected by the government of England, and he was reprimanded for his action. The passage of these bills was marked by the appearance of inflammatory placards and handbills. One of these, addressed to "the betrayed inhabitants of the City and Colony of New York," called for a meeting in "the Fields" to protest against the bill providing for the troops. John Lamb spoke at this meeting, and was chosen to head a committee appointed to present an address to the assembly condemning its action. The assembly refused to receive the document and voted the handbills seditious. The leaders of the popular party were especially aroused over the action of the assembly on these bills, because they saw in the arrangement a clever scheme by which Colden and the friends of the government had undermined the opposition of the assembly to the bill for billeting the troops, by joining to it the measure for emitting bills of credit, a measure very much desired, since it would improve the balance of trade with England, and would furnish a medium of exchange, of which the colony was in great need. The assembly had long been looked upon as the people's chief defence against the crown's encroachment upon their liberties. Consequently, the popular leaders were thoroughly aroused over its apparent defection.

After supplies for the troops had been secured, the officers were less careful than they had been to restrain their soldiers from violence, and an attack was made on the liberty pole, January 13, 1770, by members of the Sixteenth Regiment, who tried to blow it up with gunpowder. Some citizens who had gathered while this was being done were driven at the point of the bayonet into a tavern nearby on Broadway, kept by La Montagne, and used as a rendezvous for the Sons of Liberty. Finally, an officer came and ordered the soldiers to their barracks. Repeated attempts to destroy the pole ended in success on January 17th, and its shattered fragments were piled up before La Montagne's door. The next day a meeting of more than three thousand citizens adopted resolutions, one of which declared that all soldiers found armed in the streets after roll-call should be treated as "enemies to the peace of the city," and a committee of the Sons of Liberty was appointed to enforce these resolutions. On January 18th, the soldiers retaliated by posting placards about the city ridiculing the citizens' action. Three soldiers were caught in the act of posting these bills, and were marched towards the mayor's office. On the way some twenty soldiers met them and tried to rescue their comrades. A fight followed in which the soldiers were forced to retreat towards Golden Hill,[1] where they were met by reinforcements, and a scrimmage ensued, in which one man was killed and several wounded. The conflict was ended by officers, who appeared and ordered the soldiers to their barracks. The next day there were skirmishes in the morning and afternoon. On the twentieth the mayor forbade the soldiers to leave their barracks unless accompanied by a non-commissioned officer; the officers and some of the most influential citizens supported the measure and order was secured. The Sons of Liberty asked the corporation for permission to erect a new liberty pole on the site of the

[1] The section bounded by John, William, Fulton, and Cliff Streets.

one destroyed, and when their request was refused, purchased a plot of ground on the western edge of the Commons (opposite the present 252 Broadway), and erected a new pole there, on February 6, 1770.

By 1770, the colonies had fallen away from their agreement not to import English goods. Georgia, Carolina, Maryland, and Virginia had increased their importations. Pennsylvania and New England were importing nearly half as much as usual; and only New York was really keeping to the contract. Here merchants were suffering from the failure of the other colonies to stand by their agreement, and were anxious to resume the importation of all commodities except tea. A canvass of the wards, taken in the summer of 1770, showed that eleven hundred and eighty voters out of fourteen hundred and eighty wished to confine the agreement of non-importation to tea only, about three hundred declined to express an opinion, and a few were opposed to all importation. In July, the merchants sent out orders for everything except this commodity. Exception was made in the case of tea, because the Townshend Acts had been repealed in all points except this; but even this general capitulation failed to satisfy public opinion. The tax on tea continued to be obnoxious to the people, especially to the merchants, who objected, not so much on account of the principle involved, or even because it would raise the price of tea, as because it established the East India Company's monopoly of the business, and deprived the merchants of a lucrative trade.

The effect of the tax on tea in the American colonies is too well known to require discussion here. At New York, the persons to whom the tea was consigned were induced to decline to receive it, and the tea was sent back to London. All the colonies resisted,[1] but only Boston was singled out for punishment. Her port was closed to commerce from June 1st, 1774, and soldiers were sent to maintain order. The effect of these measures was to draw all the colonies together, for each felt that the interests of Massachusetts were equally its own.

Boston appealed to the other colonies to join her in resistance and in another non-importation agreement. On May 16th, the "more considerable Merchants & Citizens" of New York, fearing that the more radical citizens, who had been the leaders in the opposition to the enforcement of the Stamp Act and the Townshend Acts, might adopt extreme and dangerous measures, gave up their earlier indifference, and

[1] See Chronology for reproduction of broadside printed in New York, April 19, 1774.

attended the first meeting of the people called in New York after the Boston Port Bill was published there. They secured the dissolution of the former committee, and the appointment of a committee of correspondence of fifty-one members, among whom the moderates had the controlling voice. Three days later, a meeting was held at the Coffee House to confirm the earlier action. Isaac Low was made chairman of the committee and John Alsop deputy-chairman. The committee was approved by the body of the mechanics of the town who also were organised, under the chairmanship of Jonathan Blake. Low, MacDougall, Duane, and Jay were appointed to answer the communication from Boston. The answer must have been disappointing to its recipients; for, while it condoled with them over their misfortunes, it refused to enter into another non-importation agreement, and declared that New York would abide by the decision of a general congress, to be held to discuss what should be done in the matter. The New York committee sent letters to Philadelphia and to the supervisors in the different towns in the province, telling them what had been done, and calling on them to appoint committees of correspondence. On July 4, 1774, the committee met at the Exchange, nominated Philip Livingston, John Alsop, Isaac Low, James Duane, and John Jay as representatives to the general congress, and called a meeting of the inhabitants for the seventh of July at the City Hall, to concur in the choice of this committee or to choose another.

Up to this time the committee had been dominated by the more conservative citizens. Their action displeased certain of its members because it was too moderate. This radical faction issued handbills calling for a meeting of the people in "the Fields" on Wednesday, July 6th. This meeting, of which Alexander MacDougall was chairman, adopted a set of resolutions far more radical than the action of the committee of fifty-one. Non-importation was advocated, and a subscription was set on foot to help the sufferers in Boston. But the next day the committee of fifty-one disavowed the action of the meeting in "the Fields." This resulted in the withdrawal of eleven members from the committee of fifty-one. The remaining members of the committee adopted resolutions of sympathy with Boston, but declined to enter into another non-importation agreement unless that measure should be adopted by the general congress which was soon to meet; they declared that an agreement only partially observed, as the last had been, was more injurious than beneficial. Both parties, however, united to elect the five delegates who had previously been nominated to the congress soon to be held at Philadelphia. For some time thereafter the New York committee remained under the control of the conservatives.

The general congress of the colonies met at Philadelphia early in September, 1774, and there adopted the "Association," an agreement which pledged the colonies to the non-importation of British goods. The New York committee of fifty-one appointed a day on which the freeholders should choose a committee of observation to enforce this agreement. When the new committee, which was composed of sixty members, was organised, the committee of fifty-one dissolved. The chief business of the committee of sixty was to see that the agreement, or Association, was enforced.

News of the battles of Lexington and Concord reached New York on Sunday morning, April 23, 1775.[1] The radical leaders of the citizens went to the City Hall, seized the arms there, and distributed them among the most active of their number, who formed themselves into a voluntary corps and assumed the government of the city. They took possession of the keys of the custom-house and of all public stores; and two of their number, Isaac Sears and John Lamb, headed a band which seized the cargo of a sloop about to sail with supplies for the troops at Boston. The confused and unsystematised manner in which things were done showed the necessity for a more stable city government. The committee of sixty called a meeting of the citizens at the Merchants' Coffee House, where it was agreed that the government should be placed in the hands of a new committee until other provision should be made by a general congress of the colonies. On the first of May, this action resulted in the election of a committee of one hundred, of which Isaac Low became chairman, and to which was given increased authority to deal with the situation. In the meantime, the lieutenant-governor and his council decided to follow a waiting policy, believing that as soon as the grievances of the people were redressed, the disturbance would subside. Up to this time New York had held no revolutionary congress for the province, but in May, 1775, delegates were chosen from the different counties, who met in New York City early in June. This meeting authorised the enlistment of troops and planned the fortification of positions on either side of the Hudson and at Kingsbridge. Even New

[1] See Chronology for broadsides printed in New York announcing these battles.

York City was forced to yield to the provincial congress which, although not determined on independence or even war, desired an assurance of the continuation of local self-government, which it felt was being threatened.

At this time, however, the efforts of England were being directed against Boston, and in June the few British soldiers stationed at New York and quartered in the barracks on Chambers Street were ordered to that city. As they were marching down to the transport, they were stopped at the corner of Broad and Beaver Streets by Marinus Willett, who told them that the committee had not consented to the removal of the spare arms, which they had loaded on carts and were taking away with them. During the altercation friends came to Willett's assistance; the arms were taken from the soldiers, and were put in the yard of Abraham Van Dyck, at the corner of Broadway and John Street, and afterwards were used by the troops raised in New York. Washington passed through New York on June 25th on his way to take command of the army in Boston, and on the same day Governor Tryon, who had succeeded Dunmore in 1771, returning from a visit in England, arrived at the city. Each was warmly greeted by the faction that supported the particular cause which he represented.

Later in the summer the cannon were removed from the Battery and taken to the Highlands, and during this movement a skirmish occurred in which some houses near Whitehall were injured. On October 19, 1775, Governor Tryon, believing that it was no longer safe for him to remain in the city, went on board the Halifax packet lying in the harbour. The winter of 1775-6 was one of grave anxiety and distress. Many left the town and business was at a standstill.

New York's political situation was peculiar. The committee in control was undoubtedly true to the patriot cause; but there was also a large party of Loyalists, who planned to give the city over to the English, and their presence made it necessary for the committee to act with caution. Later, when the patriots feared that British troops would be sent to take possession of the city, it was necessary to call on forces outside of New York itself to build fortifications and to secure the town from capture. In February, 1776, General Charles Lee was sent to New York by Washington to supervise the construction of defences there, and with him came a regiment of Connecticut men commanded by Colonel Waterbury, and four companies of Jersey troops under Lord Stirling. Lee's approach threw the committee in charge of affairs at New York into consternation. They feared that, when it became known that patriot troops from a distance were fortifying the town, the British ships lying in the harbour would bombard the place. They, therefore, sent to Lee, begging that he would remain outside the city. He, however, disregarded their request and began erecting new defences. These circumstances aroused great fear among the citizens, and many of them, anticipating an immediate collision, left the city. The general distress was further increased by the weather, which was intensely cold.

Lee's plan for fortifying New York provided for blocking the passage of Hellgate by a fort at the foot of the present East 88th Street, and by another on the shore opposite. Batteries were planned for both sides of the river at the entrance to the harbour. A battery was located at the intersection of Catherine and Cherry Streets, and a stronger work was placed on Rutger's Hill, just above it. Another battery was placed at Coenties Slip, a short distance below Wall Street. The side of Fort George facing Bowling Green was demolished, so that, if captured, it might not serve as a citadel to the enemy; and a battery was built under the southern walls of the fort. Batteries were planned, also, for various points along the Hudson River shore, and barricades were erected in the streets leading up from the water. A breastwork was thrown up around King's College, which had been converted into a general hospital. A chain of fortifications to protect the town from an attack from the north was erected on Jones's, Bayard's, and Lispenard's Hills. It was clearly recognised that New York's peculiar position made it practically impossible to hold it against an enemy that controlled the harbour, but it was thought that it would serve as an excellent battleground.

Early in March, Lee was ordered south, and the construction of the defences in New York was entrusted to Lord Stirling. Washington wrote to the latter on March 14th urging him to hasten the completion of the works in every possible way, for it had become evident that the British were about to evacuate Boston, and he thought their next point of attack was likely to be New York.

The British evacuated Boston on March 17th and Washington hastened to New York, where he arrived on April 13th, accompanied by all but five regiments of the army which he had had in New England.[1] His headquarters in New York were at the Richmond Hill House, on

[1] See Chronology, April 17, 1776, for the "Secret Intelligence" sent to England from New York, regarding the strength of Washington's army in men and guns; and a schedule of the batteries and guns at New York, which the same person reported about this time.

the block now bounded by King, Varick, Charlton, and MacDougall Streets. General Sir William Howe, with his fleet of about one hundred and thirty sail and an army of between nine and ten thousand men, arrived from Halifax at Sandy Hook late in June, and there awaited the reinforcements which his brother, Admiral (Viscount) Richard Howe, was bringing from England. Admiral Howe reached Sandy Hook on or about July 12th; and during the first week in August, General Clinton and Lord Cornwallis arrived, bringing with them the army from South Carolina. These reinforcements increased the British force before New York to about twenty-five thousand men.[1]

In the meantime Washington was prosecuting measures of defence with all possible vigour. The works already begun were strengthened, a fort was built at the north end of the island on the Hudson shore and named Fort Washington,[2] and strong works were constructed at Kingsbridge under the direction of General Mifflin. Within the city, Washington had to contend with disaffected citizens, some of whom he put in jail, and later removed to a distance, and with all the disadvantages that must accompany the command of a poorly disciplined, poorly paid, and poorly equipped fighting force. On August 8th, he had on Long Island, on Governors Island, at Paulus Hook, and at New York, 10,514 men fit for duty, and with these he had to defend extended lines against a superior force. His entire force was about eighteen thousand.

During this period of excitement the Continental Congress, on July 4th, proclaimed the Declaration of Independence, which had been adopted two days before. The New York provincial congress ratified this action and adopted the Declaration on July 9th, and by Washington's order it was read at the head of each brigade of the army in or near New York. This threw New York definitely on the side of the patriot cause, and for the time being Loyalists were forced to leave the town or remain in retirement. Public enthusiasm rose to such a pitch that the populace pulled down the gilded equestrian statue of George III, which had been erected on the Bowling Green after the repeal of the Stamp Act. On July 18th the Declaration was publicly proclaimed from the City Hall in Wall Street.

Early in August, the last of the British reinforcements had arrived,

[1] See Chronology, 1776, for extracts from unpublished Journals of the operations of the British army in America under General Sir William Howe. See also Pls. 45-b, 46, and 50 for the location of fortifications erected at this time.

[2] After it was captured by the British it was called Knyphausen; the northernmost work of this fortification was called Fort Tryon.

and, on August 22d, Howe made a landing on the Long Island shore, at Gravesend Bay. On the twenty-seventh, the battle of Long Island occurred, and as the British were greatly superior to their opponents in numbers, equipment, and training, they were everywhere victorious. By two o'clock in the afternoon they had taken the outer line of defence, and the Americans were driven within the fortified camp on Brooklyn Heights, where they were in grave danger of being captured. Heavy rains on August 28th kept both sides inactive. The rain continued on the twenty-ninth, but during the night Washington, favoured by a dense fog, succeeded in removing his entire force across the river to the Manhattan side.

The result of the battle of Long Island made it impossible for Washington to hold New York, and the question of what should be done with the city had to be settled without delay. Should it be burned or left for the British to occupy as winter quarters? Washington consulted Congress, and that body promptly replied that no damage should be done to the city, as it would undoubtedly be recovered, even if the enemy should gain possession of it for a time. To prevent the church bells and brass knockers from being appropriated by the enemy, and to secure their use if needed for cannon, the provincial convention authorised Washington to have them removed from New York to Newark. The bells were restored to the city after the war. At Richmond Hill, on the seventh of September, Washington held a council of general officers, which voted for a defence of the city. On the tenth, Congress voted to leave the decision to Washington. He called a second council of war on the twelfth to reconsider the earlier action. At this conference a large majority of those present, including Washington himself, voted to evacuate the city.

Preparations were accordingly made to withdraw from the entire island at once. There were two general routes leading from the southern end of the island to the north; one, the Boston Post Road, diverged from Broadway just below the Commons and followed Park Row, the Bowery, and an irregular course north of the present 23d Street, between Third and Fifth Avenues, to the Harlem River at 130th Street; the other, lying farther west, was an extension of Broadway as far as the present Union Square, whence it followed the Bloomingdale Road as far as Kingsbridge. Over these roads the retreat was conducted. On Sunday morning, September 13th, three British ships passed up the Hudson River as far as Bloomingdale, cutting off the transportation of stores by water. On Sunday the fifteenth, there were evidences that the British were about to execute an important movement, and soon the men-of-war in the East River began firing upon the defences at Kip's Bay, near the present 34th Street, preparatory to the approach of the landing party. The fire was so severe that the Americans were unable to stay in their works, but fled in a disorderly manner at the enemy's approach, without firing a shot, and leaving behind the greater part of their stores and cannon. Washington rode with all possible speed toward the landing place, but was unable to rally the troops. The British landed at eleven o'clock at the house of Mr. Foxcroft, the postmaster-general, at Kip's Bay, and started a force westward to cut off the retreat of the Americans' rear-guard. The British general and staff stopped at the Robert Murray house at Inclenberg, or Murray Hill, for the noonday meal, and tarried so long that Putnam's division, guided by Aaron Burr, was able to escape northward along the present Eighth Avenue to the Bloomingdale Road near the present 60th Street. Lieutenant-Colonel Kemble, a British officer, recorded in his journal after the landing:

> On a survey of their Works the Day after, find the whole Coast from Kipp's Bay to New York on the East River, and from New York to Little Bloomingdale on the North River, fortified with a Line of Entrenchment, except where the Marshes obstructed it, with a Chain of Redoubts and Works from Jones's House, across the Island to Lispenard's and Mortimers House by Bayard's Mount, on which they have a Fort called Bunkers Hill, the only work of any consequence or strength on the Island, and tolerably well finished. It is made of Sod. All the rest of their Works (which are innumerable) appear Calculated more to Amuse than for use.

Washington encamped his army on the Heights along the Hudson above Bloomingdale and Manhattanville, making the Morris house, at the present 161st Street, his own headquarters; while the British General, Lord Howe, took up his headquarters at the Apthorpe mansion at Bloomingdale, which Washington had just vacated.[1] A position near the Blue Bell Tavern, which was at the present 181st Street and Kingsbridge Road, was strongly fortified by the Americans and named Fort Washington. British troops occupied an eminence commanding McGown's Pass. On the sixteenth occurred the battle of Harlem Heights, and here the Americans gained confidence in themselves, for they were able to hold their

[1] After the battle of Long Island, Washington had moved his headquarters from the Richmond Hill House to the Apthorpe Mansion at Bloomingdale.

own. Knowlton's Rangers met the attack. Colonel Knowlton himself and twelve men were killed and forty wounded, while the British, who were forced to retreat, suffered more heavily. The high ground along the river, where now stand Grant's Tomb, Columbia University, Teachers' College, and Barnard College, and southward to 103d Street, was the scene of the action. Howe became convinced that these heights were impregnable and prepared to turn Washington's rear by way of Westchester.

Meanwhile, the British had taken possession of New York City. Governor Tryon was present, surrounded by officers of rank and a great concourse of people, and the Tories expressed their joy in loyal addresses to Lord Howe. All property that belonged to Royalists was marked and the rest confiscated. The soldiers of General Howe's army plundered the City Hall and looted the library of King's College, which had been removed there when the Americans converted the college into a hospital. From this time on, until the evacuation in 1783, New York was the refuge of Tories from all parts of the country. The defeated Americans left, or, if they dared to remain, were subjected to the insolence and violence that had been heaped upon the Tories during the months preceding the surrender.

On September 21st, a fire broke out near Whitehall Slip, ranged up Broadway and Broad Street to the City Hall, and destroyed virtually all of the buildings between Broadway and the Hudson River as far north as St. Paul's Church. Fortunately, its progress northward was ultimately checked by the open space about the college grounds at Barclay Street. The origin of this disastrous conflagration has been attributed both to English and to American incendiaries, but probably it was purely accidental.

On the following day, Nathan Hale, a member of Knowlton's Rangers, was executed as "A spy from the enemy," as the British orderly-book states, "by his own full confession," having been "apprehended" the night before. According to the latest authority, Professor Henry Johnston,[1] Hale was captured within the British lines on Manhattan Island, and the place of his execution was "in front of the Artillery Park," near the Dove Tavern, which stood on the west side of the present Third Avenue at 66th Street. The headquarters of General Howe were then at Lieutenant-Colonel James Beekman's House on the East River near Turtle

[1] *Nathan Hale 1776* (1914), pp. 157-63.

Bay at the present 51st Street. His troops threw up intrenchments "from Jacob Walton's country-seat at Horn's Hook at Hell Gate across the whole Island to Humphrey Jones House on the North River." The advanced post of the British was at the Black Horse Tavern.

Early in October, Howe began his northward movement. As it was impossible to blockade either the Hudson River or Long Island Sound, it became necessary for Washington to abandon his fortifications on Harlem Heights and to retreat. A garrison was put in Fort Washington, and Washington retired to White Plains, while Howe's Army moved up to Kingsbridge. On November 16, Fort Washington was attacked and taken, yielding 2,637 American prisoners to Howe and securing him in the possession of the entire Island.

New York remained in British hands until the close of the war, and the civil government, under a mayor and common council, gave way to a military establishment. At the head of the government was the commandant of the city, who controlled all departments of the administration. The office of mayor was continued, and David Mathews, who had held the office at the time the town was captured, was retained in the position, although he seems to have exercised but little authority. Leading citizens of New York and refugees from other provinces formed themselves into twenty independent companies as early as November, 1777, adding to the strength of the British; and they served as a relief to the king's troops, which were thereby employed elsewhere. Mayor Mathews was in command of one of these companies. Many houses that had belonged to rebels or rebel sympathizers were seized by the military government and offered for rent. "Mr. Nicholl's House opposite the three-mile stone" and "the house of Messrs Peter & Nicholas Stuyvesant in Bowery Lane" were among those appropriated, but "Mr Murray's House on the Heights of Inklenberg" was exempted. No taxes were levied on the citizens, the expenses of administration being defrayed from the moneys received as dues at the wharf, in payment for tavern licenses, and the like. The cost of living was much increased. Landlords, encouraged by the increased demand for houses, raised their rents, on an average to four times the amount the same houses had rented for before the rebellion; and "the markets were raised eight hundred per cent for the necessaries of life."

The fire in September, 1776, caused a great deal of distress among the poor, and this was further increased by the severe weather of the following winter. On December 27th, General Robertson, then commandant at New York, appointed nineteen citizens to serve as a vestry, with power to collect money and use it for the relief of the poor. They asked that they be permitted to levy a tax to secure money. This request was refused, but the mayor and the overseer of the poor were added to the committee, and the out-door poor, the almshouse, the city pumps, and the cleaning of streets were placed under its care. In addition, it was empowered to collect the rents of the houses formerly owned by rebels, but now occupied by tenants of the Government. Later, the money received for tavern licenses, as well as the fines levied on all those who broke the police regulations, were handed over to the vestry. It had a secretary and treasurer, whose accounts were subject to inspection by the commandant, and to that of his superior, the commander-in-chief. The reports of the treasurer of the vestry show what it paid for the support of the poor, the salaries of city officers, the repair of buildings, ferries, pumps, lamps, and fire engines, the care and paving of streets, cleaning the arms of the militia, and for other expenses. In fact the vestry seems to have performed many of the functions exercised by the common council during the civil régime. Strict orders were issued by both Major-General Robinson and Major-General Pattison for keeping the streets clean, and against washing clothing in the Fresh Water Pond or otherwise polluting its waters.

In imitation of the queen and peeresses of England, who equipped ships of war at their own expense, a privateer named the "Royal Charlotte" was fitted out by the ladies of New York and commissioned by Governor Tryon early in February, 1779. During the six months prior to this, beginning September, 1778, when the first privateers were commissioned, 142 vessels, valued at £200,000, had been taken under letters of marque, and brought into this port.

While government under British military control was thus developing in New York City, the representatives of the state, in convention at Kingston on April 20, 1777, adopted a constitution. It was the first that gave the choice of governor to the people. George Clinton was elected governor in June and inaugurated July 30th; John Jay was elected chief justice, and Robert R. Livingston, chancellor. The first legislature met in September, until which time the committee of safety exercised authority.

Life went on in New York during the British occupation much as it had before. All who sympathised with the patriot cause had, of course, left the city, and their property had been confiscated. As these people were, for the most part, Dissenters, their churches were appropriated by the military government and put to various uses. The Presbyterian, Dutch Reformed, and Huguenot churches were used for prisons, stables, hospitals, storehouses, or riding schools. Among these was the North Dutch Church, which was begun in 1767 and completed two years later by the English-speaking members of the Dutch congregation. It stood on the west side of William Street, occupying with its grounds the entire block front from Fulton to Ann street. Services in the English churches were continued, and the charity school flourished. Refugees and others who could not obtain seats in the English churches were given accommodations for Sunday service in the large court-room of the City Hall. The students of King's College resumed their studies in a house on Wall Street, as the college building had been converted into a hospital. Merchants continued their activities and we find them still advertising their commodities as newly arrived from abroad. Although the *New York Journal* and the *Packet* were obliged to seek other localities when the city was captured, there were excellent newspapers which supplied information to the Royalists in New York. The *Mercury*, first published by Hugh Gaine in 1752, remained during the war (a few issues being published under other control), and was then discontinued. *Rivington's New-York Gazetteer*, which suspended publication for two years at the beginning of the war, resumed in October, 1777, first as *Rivington's New-York Loyal Gazette* and then as *The Royal Gazetee;* but at the close of the war, having taken the fourth title of *Rivington's New-York Gazette, and Universal Advertiser*, it was forced to suspend a month after peace was declared. There were two other less noteworthy publications in New York during the Revolution. (See Check-list of Early New York Newspapers, Vol. II, Appendix.)

A spirit of gayety seems to have pervaded the city, and we hear of many social functions and sporting events, by which the British officers tried to relieve the tedium of garrison duty in a provincial town. There was a "bathing machine" at the North River near Vauxhall. A "stage wagon" made regular trips between New York and Kingsbridge. At the little theatre in John Street, comedies were presented in which officers of the army and navy performed, among whom were Major André and Captain De Lancey. The orchestra from the theatre played in

Trinity Churchyard, where the walks which passed the ruins were railed off, benches being placed there and lamps fixed in the trees for an evening promenade. Cricket was played between English and American teams on the parade ground near the Jews' cemetery; and bull-baiting was occasionally offered as a special diversion. In September, 1781, Prince William Henry, the third son of the English sovereign, paid New York a visit. He was received with cordial honours, and was provided with apartments in Wall Street. He was the first person of royal lineage to visit America. The queen's birthday was regularly celebrated in the winter time, instead of in summer when it really occurred, the change of date serving, as Baroness Riedesel, a participant, explained, "to give more custom to the tradespeople, as every one upon those days appears at court in gala-dress."

In spite of relief measures, there was much suffering among the poor. Many had lost their homes in the fire, and others had been thrown out of employment by the war. The Americans taken at the capture of Fort Washington and in the skirmishes around New York were confined in various buildings in the city, used for prisons, under conditions that are too horrible to relate. Dishonest commissaries appropriated the money designed to purchase the provisions for the prisoners, and consigned their charges to slow starvation. Prison ships, loaded with diseased and dying men were anchored in Wallabout Bay, where about twelve thousand perished miserably.

New York was at first comparatively free from danger of attack. During the winter of 1780, however, the weather was so severe that the Hudson River froze over entirely, and General Pattison, then in command, feared that Washington might make an attempt upon the town by crossing on the ice. Forty companies of the citizens were enrolled and uniformed at their own expense, and the old volunteer companies were augmented. The fortifications were strengthened, the citizens joining in the work with hearty good will; and a code of signals was adopted to rouse the town in case of attack. There was at this time some danger of an attack by the French fleet, which was hovering off the coast, as well as by Washington, who, with his troops, was watching the city from the north. Their departure to attack Cornwallis at Yorktown again left the town free from immediate danger. After Cornwallis had surrendered, in October, 1781, Washington returned to the neighbourhood of New York, but did little besides sending out parties to make forays. In 1782, Sir

Guy Carleton was put in command of New York. He treated the Americans with less severity than his predecessors, and adopted the plan of conciliating them. He also reformed the administration of justice and ended many of the frauds from which New Yorkers had long suffered.

With the surrender of Lord Cornwallis, the speedy advent of peace was foreseen. The king, however, remained firm in his policy of attempted control of the colonies; although, on February 28, 1782, Parliament decided against continuing the war. Then followed the disruption of the British ministry, the resignation of the prime minister, Lord North, and the slowly developing negotiations of a treaty of peace between the contending nations. Proclamations of peace were published in the American newspapers early in August, but it was not until November 30th that provisional articles "for treating of peace" were agreed upon in Paris and signed by the commissioners representing Great Britain and the United States. The king's proclamation of peace delivered from St. James's Palace on February 14, 1783, reached New York on April 5th, and was read at noon on April 8th by the town major at the City Hall. Congress issued a proclamation on April 11th, declaring the cessation of arms by land and sea; this was read at Newburgh on April 19th, dispatched to all the outposts of the American army, and communicated to Sir Guy Carleton on April 21st. The definitive treaty was signed at Paris on September 3, 1783, expressing finally the desire of both nations "to forget all past misunderstandings and differences," and "to establish such a satisfactory and beneficial intercourse between the two countries, upon the ground of reciprocal advantages and mutual convenience, as may promote and secure to both perpetual peace and harmony." The American commissioners who negotiated and signed this treaty were John Adams, Benjamin Franklin, and John Jay. The official copy arrived in New York November 19th, to be conveyed to the president of the congress. English newspapers containing it arrived on November 23d, and their presentation was the one to be given to the public here on November 26th, in *Rivington's New-York Gazette and Universal Advertiser.*

Washington met Sir Guy Carleton and Admiral Digby on May 6th at Tappan to arrange preliminaries for the evacuation of New York City. In June, the Continental Congress appointed a commission to co-operate with those chosen by Carleton in superintending the embarkation of Loyalists for Nova Scotia. Twelve thousand or more embarked from

New York. Carleton evacuated the city on November 25th, 1783, after calling in the British troops from McGown's Pass (now in Central Park at about 107th Street) and from Kingsbridge. The ceremonies of this day were conducted in accordance with the preliminary plans arranged by Washington, and those of a committee appointed to receive him. (See the broadside of November 24, reproduced in the Chronology from the original in the collection of Mr. Stokes, which is the only copy known.) Early in the morning a detachment of troops under General Knox, accompanied by General Washington and Governor Clinton, marched from Harlem to the Bowery Lane near the Fresh Water Pond. They remained there until about one o'clock. When the British troops retired from the posts in the Bowery, the American troops, consisting of infantry and artillery (including a battalion of Massachusetts soldiers), preceded by a corps of dragoons, marched into and took possession of the city. The American standard was hoisted on the flag-staff on the fort, and a salute of thirteen guns fired, while the British were embarking on their transports. After the troops had taken possession of the city, General Washington and Governor Clinton made their public entry, with their suites, on horseback. Following them, in procession, were the lieutenant-governor and members of the council (for the temporary government of the Southern District); General Knox and the officers of the army; the speaker of the assembly, and citizens on horseback and on foot. They were escorted by a body of Westchester light-horse, as a compliment to the governor and civil authority. The procession marched down Queen Street and through Broadway to Cape's Tavern. Governor Clinton gave a public dinner at Fraunces Tavern, with which the celebration of the day was closed. Perfect order and quiet prevailed from the beginning to the end, and no untoward incident (except the difficulty of hoisting the flag on the fort on account of the flagstaff having been "slushed" by the British) occurred to mar the interest of an occasion which had been so long wished for and was so joyfully welcomed.

A few days later (December 4th), Washington bade farewell to the principal officers of the army, then in town, who had assembled for this sad occasion at Fraunces Tavern. A contemporaneous newspaper account of the event quotes the illustrious commander, who, having filled a glass of wine, thus addressed his brave fellow-soldiers: "With a heart full of love and gratitude, I now take leave of you; I most devotedly wish, that your latter days may be as prosperous and happy as your former ones have been gracious and honorable." After bidding each an affectionate adieu, Washington passed through a line of light infantrymen on his way to Whitehall, and there embarked in his barge for Powles Hook (Jersey City), accompanied by General Steuben. He went first to Philadelphia, then to Annapolis to resign his commission "into the hands of the Continental Congress from whom it was derived."

The physical progress of New York City during the years 1763-83[1] had been much retarded by the war. During the first years of this period the population had increased rapidly. In 1771 the number of inhabitants of the city and county was given as 21,863. New streets were being opened, pavements were being laid, and the city was moving northward at a rapid pace. The needs of the growing population required more churches and a number were erected: St. Paul's Chapel, in 1764–5; the Brick Presbyterian Church, in 1766–7, on ground now bounded by Park Row, Beekman and Nassau Streets; a Lutheran church, later known as the Swamp Church, at the corner of William and Frankfort Streets, in 1767, and the Scotch Presbyterian Church, in 1768, on the south side of Little Queen Street (the present Cedar Street). In the same year the first Methodist Church, which stood on the south side of John Street between Nassau and William Streets, was dedicated. Milestones were purchased by the city in 1769. A monument having been erected, near the site of the present Eighth Avenue and 15th Street, to the memory of General Wolfe, who was killed in the assault upon the Heights of Quebec on September 13, 1759, the long road leading to it from the Boston Post Road was recorded as a permanent public road in 1768. This road was shown as early as 1766 on the Montresor Map (Pl. 40); but the monument, then in evidence, an obelisk, did not appear on the War Map of 1782 (Pl.50), and, although it was a prominent landmark for about twenty years, no other record of its construction, appearance, or location now remains. Nor do we know when or for what reason it was removed. A careful study of these circumstances has been made by Mr. Edward Hagaman Hall, who reaches the conclusion that it was erected between 1760 and 1767 by General Oliver De Lancey, on whose land it stood, and that he had it removed when the British evacuated the city[2]

[1] The Ratzer Map (Pl. 41), published from a survey made in 1766-7, gives an accurate representation of the city at the commencement of the war, and the War Office Map (Pl. 50) gives an interesting survey of the entire island just before the close of the war.

[2] *Nineteenth Ann. Rep., 1914, Am. Scenic and Hist. Pres. Soc.*, pp. 121-6.

In 1768, after years of controversy, water-lots began to be extensively granted at Hunters Key. The Chamber of Commerce was formed that year for the promotion of industry and trade. One of its first acts (1769) was to engage David Rittenhouse and Captain John Montresor to ascertain the exact latitude of the city at Fort George; the southwest or flag bastion was found to be in 40° 42′ 8″ N. L. That year, also, the Marine Society was formed for the promotion of maritime knowledge and the relief of the widows and orphans of sea-captains. A stage-coach was first operated between New York and Boston in 1772, its terminus at this end of the route being "Mr. Fowler's Tavern at Freshwater." The need of a hospital in the city had been felt as early as 1771, when a charter was granted for the New York Hospital. A plot of ground was secured at Ranelagh and a building erected, but, unfortunately, fire destroyed it early in 1775. It was rebuilt, but before it could be opened the war came on, and the building was used as a barracks in turn by both Americans and British. It was not opened as a hospital until 1791. King's College, which had been erected in 1756–60 on the plot bounded by Murray, Chapel, Barclay, and Lumber Streets, was used as a general hospital during the military activities in the neighbourhood in the summer and autumn of 1776.

The question of the adequate security of public records was raised by Governor Tryon in 1772, when he found the secretary's office unsuited to the purpose and submitted a plan for a new building. The following year, the Governor's house in the fort, which had recently been extensively repaired at his solicitation, was destroyed by fire, including all the contents, except "a little Furniture out of the Parlour," the papers belonging to the surrogate's office, and the great seal of the province, which was raked out of the ruins. The public and private papers in the Governor's possession, family jewels, tableware, furniture, and cash were burned. He and his family, except a housemaid who perished, barely escaped with their lives, his daughter being compelled to jump from a second-story window into a snow-bank. The assembly voted an allowance of £5,000 to cover his private losses. In December, 1775, when the threats of Sears and other Sons of Liberty became alarming, Tryon ordered that the public records of the province be placed on board the "Dutchess of Gordon." There were "two Boxes containing Records of Patents, Records of Commissions, ettc and Minutes of Council." Shortly after this, for better security, they were put on board the "Asia," then on the "Eagle" and taken to England in 1778. These records were returned to the secretary's office in November, 1781, except those relating to Indian sessions, which had been lost. The city records, having been placed for safety in private houses in Westchester County, the provincial convention ordered, on October 15, 1776, that they be removed under guard. Augustus Van Cortlandt being the city clerk, had them placed, it is believed, in the family vault near the mansion which still stands in what is now Van Cortlandt Park.

In 1783 the City Hall at the head of Broad Street still served the needs of the city, but the prisoners, who formerly had been confined in its upper stories, had been removed in 1759 to the Commons (the present City Hall Park), where they were accommodated in the Gaol (erected in 1757–8) and later in the Bridewell prison (erected in 1775). A workhouse stood next to the Gaol. The city had grown northward, so that the Commons, perhaps more popularly known as "the Fields," were conveniently near, and served as the meeting-place of the citizens when some public crisis or other event brought them together. It was here that the new liberty pole was erected after the old one had been destroyed by British soldiers.

New York suffered severely during the war. Before its capture by the British in 1776, extensive fortifications had been erected on the East River, at the Battery, and on the Hudson River shore. When the town was abandoned, all patriots, or Whigs, left, and their property was confiscated. For years, home manufactures had flourished. David Hunt began to make fire-engines in New York in 1767; and, in 1768, a "nailery" and a paper-mill had been established. Such industries, however, must have been completely disorganised, at least temporarily, by the capture of the city. But all of these injuries were trivial when compared with the devastation caused by the conflagrations which swept over the town on September 21–3, 1776, and on August 3, 1778. The first of these fires, which has already been referred to, started in the southern part of the city and spread northward, devastating all the buildings on the east side of Whitehall Slip and the west side of Broad Street to Beaver Street. The buildings on both sides of Beaver Street were burned, as well as those on both sides of Broadway as far as Rector Street, among them Trinity Church, the charity school near it, the rector's house, and the Lutheran Church. St. Paul's Chapel and King's College were saved. It was estimated that one-fourth of the town was lost in this disastrous fire. The second great fire, although not so extensive as the first, burned over sixty dwellings, besides many stores, near the wharf and in Little Dock and Dock Streets. The following day, an ordnance ship, lying in the East River near Wall Street, was struck by lightning, and the 260 pounds of gunpowder on board blew up the ship and damaged near-by buildings.

Even the evacuation by the British in 1783 brought a measure of disaster to the city. New York had long been the home of a large party well disposed to the English government and, since the autumn of 1776, the city had been a haven of refuge to Tories from neighbouring sections, many of whom were men of ability and refinement. Now, however, with the evacuation of the city, thousands of these people went into voluntary exile, and the benefit of their presence was lost forever to the province. At the close of the Revolution, New York's population was little if any greater than it had been in 1771. However, the triumphant patriots came flocking back and began to repair the damages of war, and to reestablish their homes. By December 5, 1783, the harbour having been finally cleared of the British flag, New York was on the threshold of a new era of growth and prosperity, greater than any she had yet enjoyed.

PLATES

40–51

1763–1783

PLATE 40

PL.40.

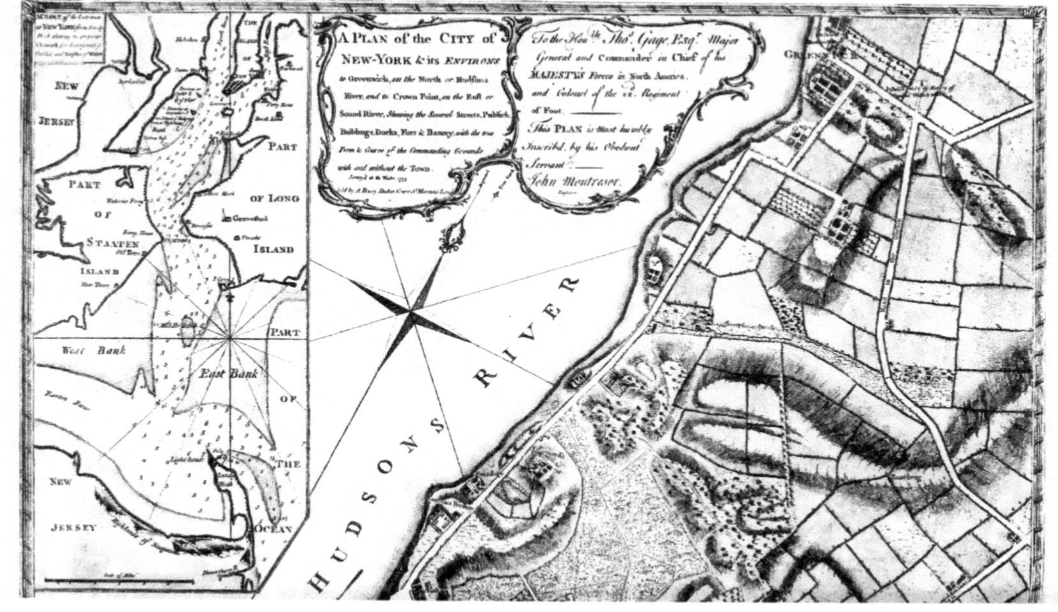
A PLAN of the CITY of
NEW-YORK & its ENVIRONS
to Greenwich, on the North or Hudsons
River, and to Crown Point, on the East or
Sound River, Shewing the Several Streets, Publick
Buildings, Docks, Fort & Battery, with the true
Form & Course of the Commanding Grounds
with and without the Town.
To the Hon.ble Tho.s Gage, Esq.r Major
General and Commander in Chief of his
MAJESTY'S Forces in North America,
and Colonel of the xx. Regiment
of Foot.
This PLAN is Most humbly
Inscribed, by his Obedient
Servant
John Montresor.
HUDSONS RIVER
NEW
JERSEY
PART
OF
STAATEN
ISLAND
PART
OF LONG
ISLAND
West Bank
East Bank
PART
OF
THE
OCEAN
NEW
JERSEY

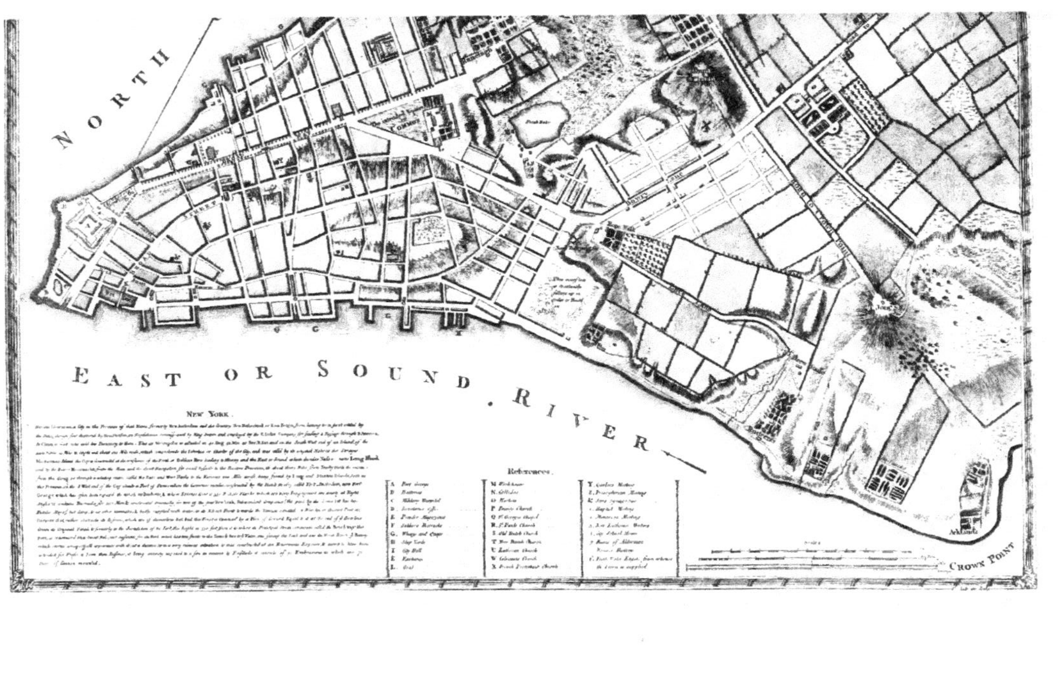
NORTH
EAST OR SOUND RIVER
NEW YORK.
References.
A Fort George
E Powder Magazine
F Soldiers Barracks
H Ship Yards
I City Hall
P Trinity Church
Q St. Georges Chapel
R St. Pauls Church
S Old Dutch Church
T New Dutch Church
V Lutheran Church
X French Protestant Church
Y Quakers Meeting
Z Presbyterian Meeting
CROWN POINT

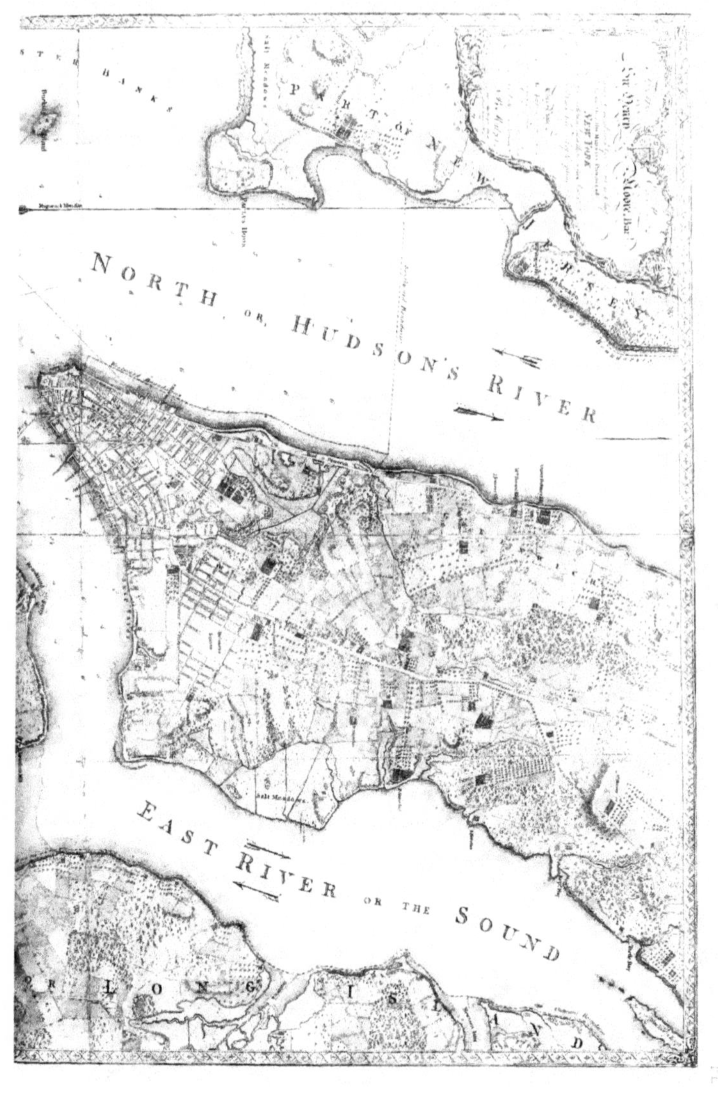

NORTH OR HUDSON'S RIVER
EAST RIVER OR THE SOUND
LONG ISLAND
PART OF NEW JERSEY
BANKS
Salt Meadows
NEW YORK

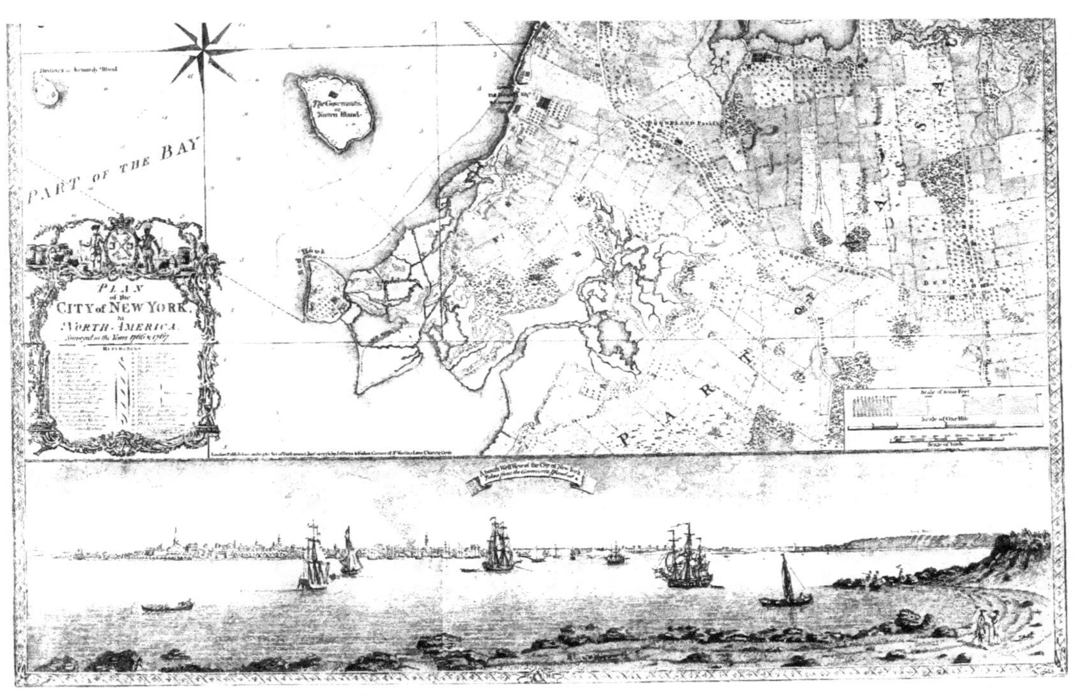
PART OF THE BAY
PLAN
of the
CITY of NEW YORK,
in
NORTH AMERICA.
Surveyed in the Years 1766 & 1767
REFERENCES
PART OF

PL. 42

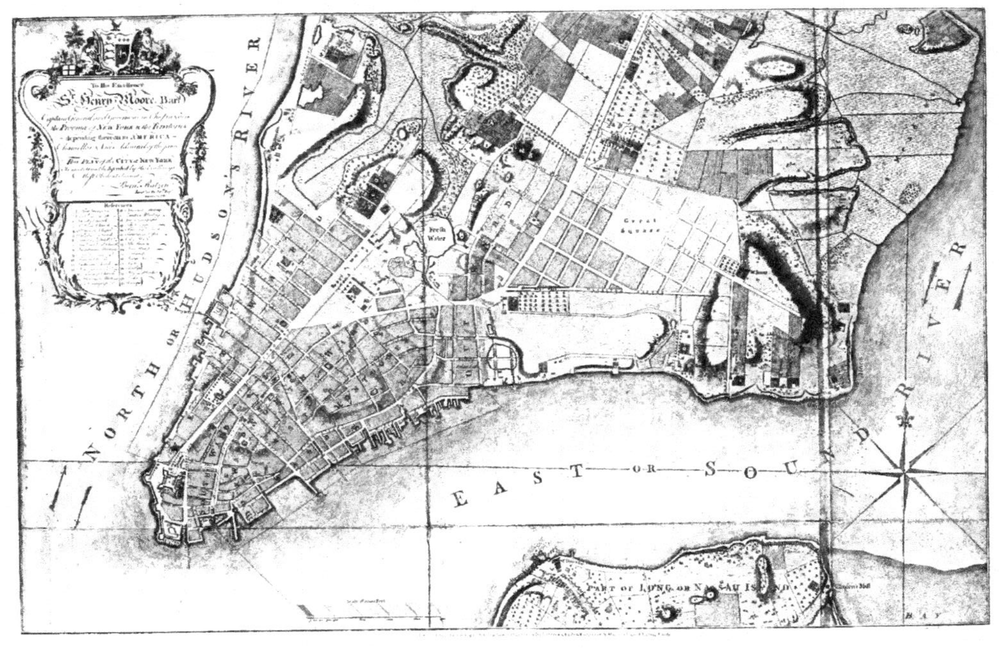
To His Excellency
Sr. Henry Moore, Bart.
This PLAN of the CITY of NEW YORK
References
NORTH OR HUDSON'S RIVER
EAST OR SOUND RIVER
Fresh Water
Great Square
PART OF LONG OR NASSAU ISLAND
BAY

PL.43

A Correct View of the OLD METHODIST CHURCH in John Street N. York

The first [illegible] in America, Erected A.D. 1768

PLATE 44

PL.44

PL.45.

NEW YORK with the ENTRANCE of the NORTH and EAST RIVERS.

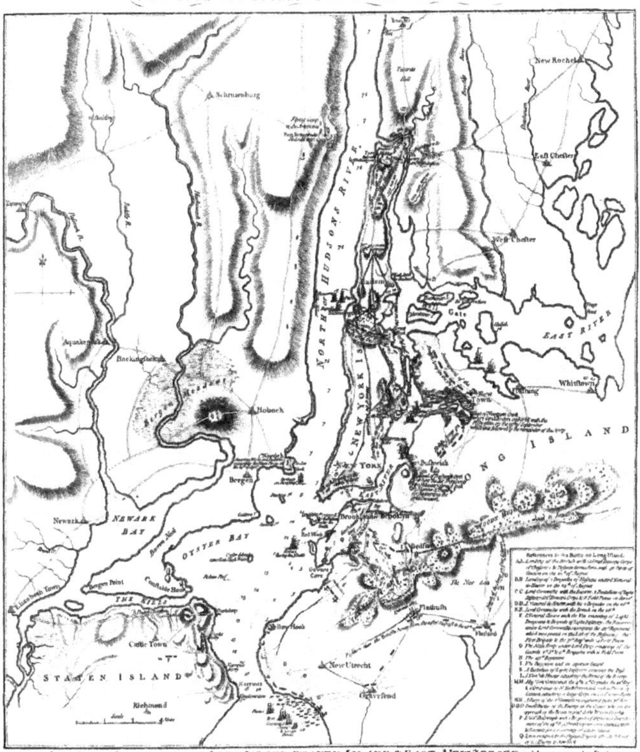

A PLAN of NEW YORK ISLAND with part of LONG ISLAND, STATEN ISLAND & EAST NEW JERSEY, with a particular Description of the ENGAGEMENT on the Woody Heights of Long Island, between FLATBUSH and BROOKLYN, on the 27th of August 1776 between HIS MAJESTY'S FORCES Commanded by General HOWE and the AMERICANS under Major General PUTNAM. Shewing also the Landing of the BRITISH ARMY on New-York Island, and the Taking of the CITY of NEW YORK &c. on the 15th of September following, with the Subsequent Disposition of Both the Armies.

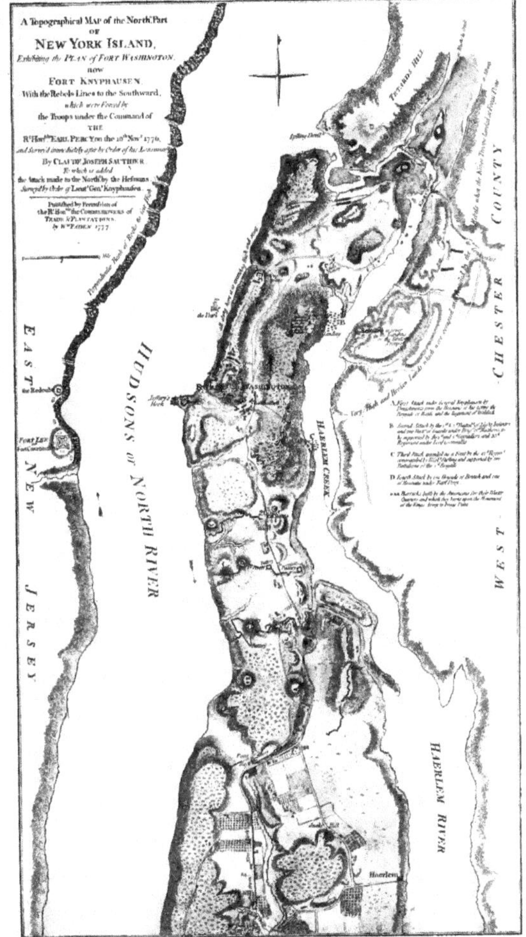
A Topographical MAP of the North^n Part
OF
NEW YORK ISLAND,
Exhibiting the PLAN of FORT WASHINGTON,
now
FORT KNYPHAUSEN.
With the Rebels Lines to the Southward,
which were Forced by
the Troops under the Command of
THE
By CLAUDE JOSEPH SAUTHIER.
the Attack made to the North by the Hessians
Surveyed by Order of Lieut^t Genl Knyphausen.
HUDSONS OR NORTH RIVER
EAST NEW JERSEY
WEST CHESTER COUNTY
HAERLEM CREEK
HAERLEM RIVER
TETARDS HILL
Fort Lee
Haerlem

PL. 46A

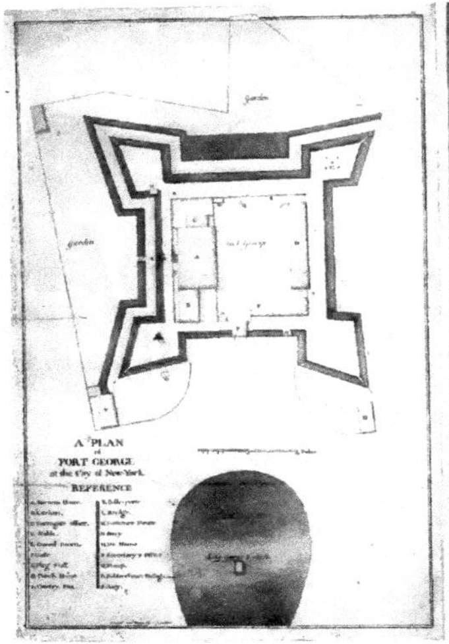

A PLAN
of
FORT GEORGE
at the City of New-York.
REFERENCE

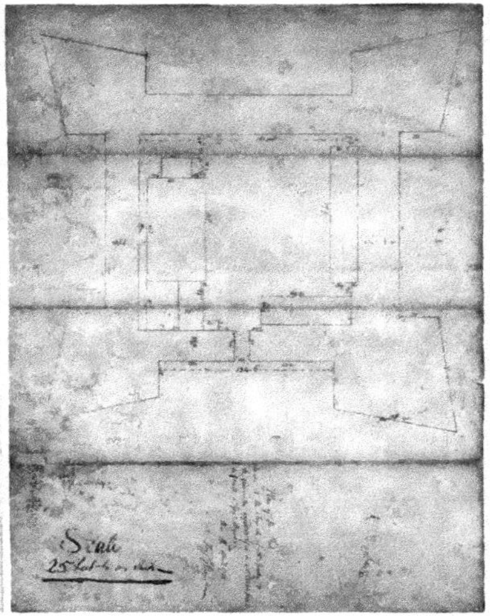

Scale
25 [illegible]

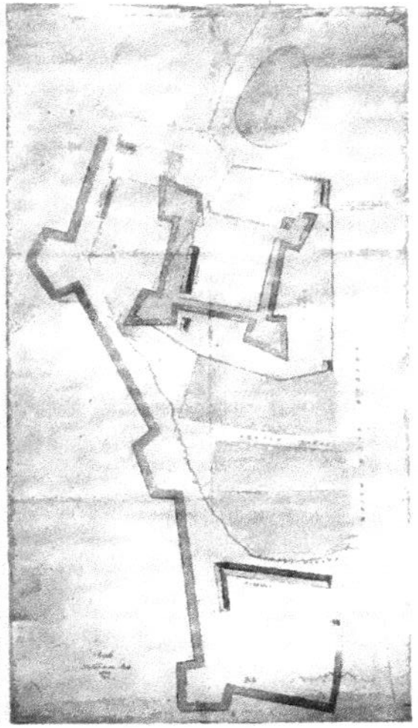

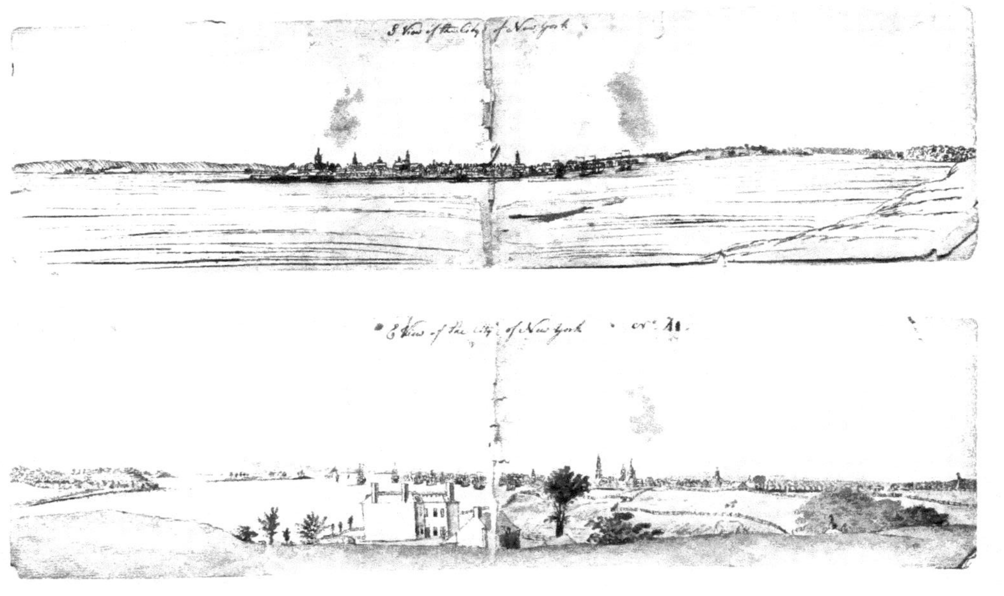
A View of the City of New York
A View of the City of New York

PL.48

PL. 49.

An original sketch of the ruins of [illegible] during the Revolution.

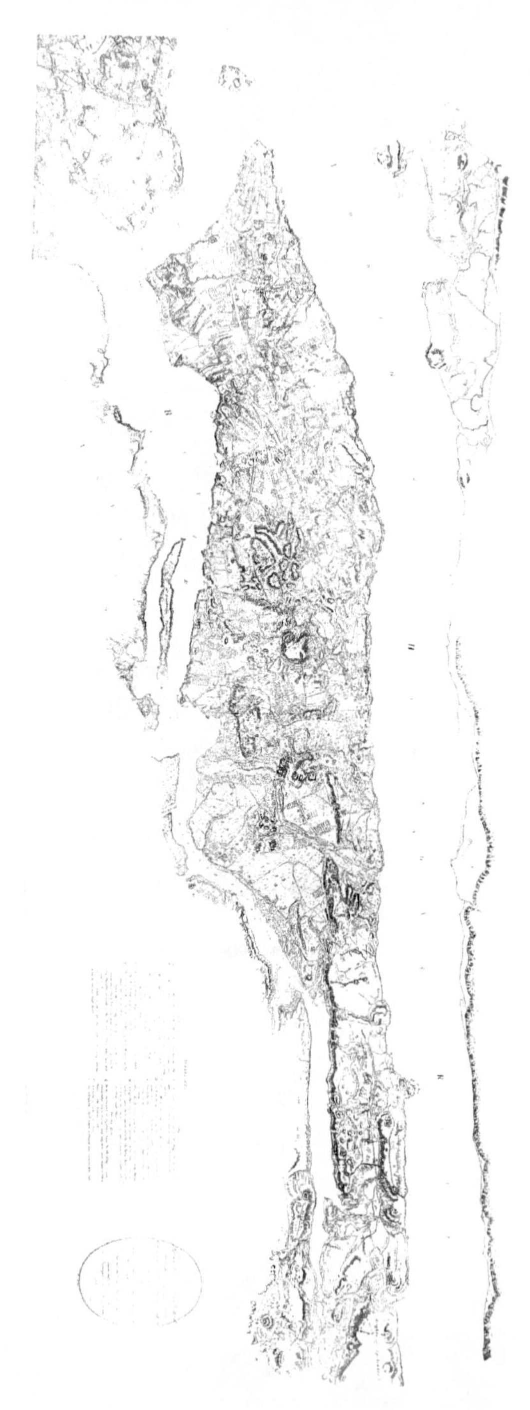

PL. 51.

DESCRIPTION OF PLATES

40–51

1763–1783

DESCRIPTION OF PLATES
40–51
1763–1783

PLATE 40
A PLAN OF THE CITY OF NEW-YORK & ITS ENVIRONS TO GREENWICH, ON THE NORTH OR HUDSONS RIVER, (ETC.)
[The Montresor Plan]

Engraved on copper. 20⅝ x 25⅜ Date depicted: 1766.
Date issued: 1775.

Author: John Montresor.
Engraver: P. Andrews (who engraved also the Maerschalck Map).
Owner: I.N.P.S.
Other copies: N. Y. Public Library; N. Y. Hist. Society; Library of Congress, Div. of Maps and Charts, etc.

Second known state. This plan was first issued under the date of 1766. The earlier issue, which is very scarce (N. Y. Hist. Society; I.N.P.S. Collection, etc.), is identical with that of 1775, except for the date, and for the publisher's imprint which is lacking. The survey, according to Montresor's notes, was made between December 16, 1765, and February 8, 1766, and was dedicated to the Commander-in-Chief, General Gage, by whom it was ordered made. Without doubt it was prepared for military purposes, for at the time New York was in the midst of the Stamp Act Riots.

It may be of interest to quote a few extracts from the *Journals* of Captain Montresor at this period, preserved among the family records of Colonel Henry Edward Montresor, of Stonely Grange, Huntingdonshire, England, and printed in the *Collections* of the N. Y. Hist. Society for 1881, pp. 341–5.

1765, Dec. 7th

Requested by the Commr in Chief to let him have the perusal of the General Draught of this Province and also to procure him one of this place and Enciente with its environs. . .

8th The Sons of Liberty as they term themselves, openly defying powers, office and all authority sole rulers.

16th . . . Placards seditious and infamous as ever. The Commander in Chief requested of me to Sketch him a Plan of this Place on a large Scale with its environs and adjacent country together with its harbour, but particularly to shew the ground to the North and North East of the Town &c.

17th Advertisements stuck up everywhere Libellous and rebellious. This night about 8 o'clock the Effigies of Lord Colville Mr Grenville and General Murray were paraded several times through the streets amidst a large concourse of people who halted first where the Governor was in company and gave 3 Huzzas, they were carried to the Common and there burnt. Their numerous attendants the Mob were furnished all with Candles which they forced from the Houses as they went along, threatening to set them on fire if Refused. I continued on the General's Draught and daily taking the Bearings & distances & Sketching in the country about this place.

On January 7, 1766, Montresor notes: "Waited on the Comm[r] in Chief & shewed him my Brouillon that he might see the Progress I had made on the Survey. . . . I received General Gage's thanks for the above. . . . Continued on my Survey *Sub Rosa* as observations might endanger ones house and effects if not ones life. . . . " This enforced secrecy probably accounts for numerous inaccuracies and omissions on the plan, among the most flagrant of which are the omission of the smaller Collect Pond, most of the street names, and a number of piers lying along the water-front of the East River.

Du Simitière, writing in about the year 1768, refers to the Montresor Map as "extremely uncorrect [*sic*] and full of gross errors."

Montresor finished the survey on February 8, 1766, and on the 14th "Began reducing the large Plan to ½ the scale." We know from his *Journals* that he spent the summer of 1766 on this and other surveys in New York, and on October 30th embarked for England, returning to New York in August, 1767. While abroad, he notes, under date of May 2, 1767: "Got 2 of my plans of New York and Environs with the Hook and Channel from the Engravers being just finished. Engraved by La Roque, in the Strand, upon the Examination of it found Thirty one Erratas."—*Ibid.*, 392.

A fine trial proof copy of the Montresor Map, in the author's possession (forming part of a small collection of maps originally belonging to Montresor), is before the title and cartouche, half of the description, the references, and a number of buildings had been engraved. It is possible that this is one of the imperfect prints referred to above.

In the Library of Congress, Faden Collection, No. 54, is a manuscript map, in water-colours, which, at first sight, might be taken for Montresor's original, but a careful examination reveals the fact that it was drawn at a later period, probably about 1776. For instance, the small pond in the Battery, south of the Barracks, or the "Military Hospital," which pond was ordered filled in on May 26, 1773, has disappeared; the Bowling Green, which was laid out as an oval in 1771, is so shown; the Oswego Market, taken down before April, 1772, has disappeared, etc., etc.—See Chronology.

For a discussion of the priority of Montresor's Plan to those by Ratzer, see Pl. 42.

A French edition of this map, entitled "Plan de New-York et des Environs Levé par Montresor Ingénieur en 1775," was issued at Paris by le Rouge, rue des Grands Augustins, in 1777.

The author's collection contains a large manuscript map or survey of the inner harbour, entitled "Plan of Governors, Kennedeys [Bedloes], and Browns [Ellis] Islands and Red Hook together with part of the Bay and Soundings shewing the position they bear to each other and to New York, Sept. 1766. By order of his Excellency Major General Gage, Commander in Chief of his Majesty's Forces in North America. [Signed] John Montressor [*sic*], Engineer." The preparation of this plan is minutely described in Montresor's *Journals* from September 1 to September 17, 1766.—See *Collections*, N. Y. Hist. Society (1881), p. 386.

Reproduction: Valentine's *Manual*, 1855, opp. p. 482.

PLATE 41

[MAP] PLAN OF THE CITY OF NEW YORK, IN NORTH-AMERICA
[VIEW] A SOUTH WEST VIEW OF THE CITY OF NEW YORK, TAKEN FROM THE GOVERNOURS ISLAND AT*

[The Ratzer Map]

Line and stipple engraved on copper.	Map: 35 x 47⅜ over all, including border. View: 34 x 7½	Date depicted: 1766–7. Date issued: January 12, 1776.

Publishers: Jefferys & Faden, London.
Author: B. Ratzer.
Engraver: Thos. Kitchin, whose name appears at the foot of the dedication and is barely legible in our reproduction.
Owner: I.N.P.S.
Other copies: N. Y. Public Library; N. Y. Hist. Society; Library of Congress, Div. of Maps and Charts (coloured copy), etc.

An amplification of the so-called Ratzen Plan (Pl. 42). Probably the second state, as we know from advertisements in contemporary newspapers (see Pl. 42) that the map was issued as early as 1770. It is a strange fact that no copy of the early issue has come to light.

This is one of the most beautiful, important, and accurate early plans of New York. It is printed on two sheets of equal size, the joint passing through the Wallabout Bay. On the under lap of the upper sheet the publisher's imprint appears in two places, once as Jefferys & Faden, and once as Faden & Jefferys. The view is unusual, very attractive, and beautifully executed. The cloud of smoke in the sky just south of St. George's Chapel has often been taken to indicate the fire of 1776, from which it has been argued that the view was a subsequent addition to the original map. A careful examination, however, reveals the fact that the smoke emanates from a small fire on the shore-front, just to the south of which a ship is careened undergoing repairs, and the fire is evidently from a tar-kettle used in this connection. That this cannot be the great fire of 1776 is further proved by the fact that the map and view were advertised for sale as early as 1770.

A lithographic facsimile of this map, but without the view, was issued by Perris, New York, in 1853. The execution is so good that it is often mistaken for a copperplate.

Ratzer is the author of a Survey of New Jersey, made in 1769, and included in the *North American Atlas*, printed by Faden in 1777. Sauthier in his map of the Province of New York, also included in the Faden *Atlas* of 1777, bases the New Jersey section of the map upon Ratzer's surveys.

Du Simitière, in his notes on maps (Book No. 1412 Y, Ridgeway Branch, Library Co. of Philadelphia), speaking of the Ratzer Map, says that Ratzer proposed to issue this plan by subscription. He adds that the plan of the town by Lieutenant Ratzer arrived at New York from London in July, 1769, and says (translated): "It is the largest and the most correct which has ever been made and is engraved by Kitchin. There is also a large view of N. York, printed, I think, in London."

Reproduction: Valentine's *Manual*, 1854, opp. p. 320.

Plate 42

Plan of the City of New York
[The Ratzen Plan]

Engraved on copper. 33 x 23 Date depicted: 1766–7.
Author: Bern[d] Ratzen (Ratzer). Date issued: January 12, 1776.
Engraver: T. Kitchin.
Publishers: Jefferys & Faden.
Owner: I.N.P.S., from the Holden Collection.
Other copies: N. Y. Public Library; N. Y. Hist. Society, etc.

Probably the second state. The N. Y. Public Library, the N. Y. Hist. Society, and the Library of Congress (Div. of Maps and Charts) have each a copy of what may be the first state of this plan. This state has "T. Kitchin sculp[t]" beneath the rectangle, at the right, but lacks the line containing the publisher's imprint and date. In the copies in the N. Y. Public Library and the Library of Congress, Ratzer's name is correctly spelled, although this is, apparently, a manuscript correction, as both show signs of erasure.

In the Army Lists, Bernard Ratzer's name appears as a Lieutenant in the 60th Regiment; his name also appears in the *Calendar of Land Papers* where, under date of January 19, 1767, General Gage certifies that Bernard Ratzer served as assistant engineer during the war with France. The 60th Regiment, to which Ratzer belonged, was formerly the 62d, but, in 1756, the title was changed to "The 60th, or the Royal American Regiment of Foot." It is interesting to note that J. W. F. des Barres also served in this regiment as a lieutenant, until 1776, when he was made a captain. Ratzer became a captain in 1773.—See Wallace's *A Regimental Chronicle and List of Officers of the 60th or the King's Royal Corps* (etc.), London (1879), p. 2 *et seq.* No mention can be found in the records of the name "Ratze*n*," which is no doubt an engraver's error.

The first advertisement offering this plan for sale (evidently the first issue) is probably that contained in *The New-York Gazette; and the Weekly Mercury*, of August 21, 1769, and is as follows:

> Just published, and to be sold by H. Gaine,
> (Price, 16 s. coloured, and 8 s. plain)
> A Plan of the City of New-York, Dedicated to His Excellency Sir Henry Moore, Bart. The above Plan is done on a Sheet of Imperial Paper, the Streets laid down very exact, with the Names of each, the Wards, Wharfs and all the publick Buildings in and about the City properly distinguished, and the whole carried considerably farther than Corlear's Hook.

The first advertisement of the Ratzer Map (which is undoubtedly based on the Ratzen Plan) is contained in the same newspaper, under the later date of October 15, 1770, and reads as follows:

> To be sold by the Printer hereof,
> A Plan of the City of New-York, and its Invirons, surveyed and laid down in the Years 1766, and 1767, with a South Prospect of the same, taken from the Governor's Island. In this Plan is taken in Powlis-Hook, Red-Hook, the Long Island Shore, and the Islands in our Bay, &c. &c.

In the same paper, under date of January 4, 1773, and in subsequent issues, is found the following advertisement:

> Ratzer's large and small Plans of the City of New York, to be sold very cheap by the Printer hereof [Hugh Gaine].

Added to the fact that the first newspaper advertisement undoubtedly refers to the Ratzen Plan, its priority to the Ratzer Map is apparent on a careful examination of the plans themselves. For instance, the Methodist Meeting, which was completed in 1768, is not shown on the Ratzen, but is found on the Ratzer Map. Beekman Street, incorrectly written "Deekman's" Street on the Ratzen, has been corrected on the Ratzer; and this is also true of Cliff Street, which on the Ratzen Plan is written "Clist" Street. "Wyne Coop" Street, on the Ratzen Plan, has been changed on the Ratzer Map to the more modern appellation of Bridge Street. Many unnamed streets in the neighbourhood of Delancey Square, called Great Square on the Ratzen Plan, are designated by name upon the Ratzer Map. We know from Major Holland's Plan of the City in 1776 that as late as that year Delancey Square retained its name.

This last-mentioned plan, which was engraved for Sayer & Bennett and issued by them in August, 1776, as an inset to a large map entitled "The Provinces of New York and New Jersey with part of Pensilvania" (etc.), was reproduced in Valentine's *Manual* for 1863. The Map and Plan were also included in Jefferys' *American Atlas* of 1778. The "Ropewalk," shown on the Ratzen Plan, extending along the line of Division Street, has disappeared on the Ratzer Map, and Judith Street, on the former, has, on the latter, been merged in Anne Street. According to Post (*Old Streets*, etc., p. 25), "Judith" was never accepted by the city authorities as the name of this street and was in use only for a brief time. Many other points might be cited, indicating the priority of the Ratzen Plan over the Ratzer Map.

In the author's collection, there is a coloured copy of the Ratzen Plan, which once formed part of a small collection of maps belonging originally to Montresor. On this copy of the Ratzen Plan are laid down, in manuscript, a number of fortifications, probably those erected during the Stamp Act Riots, and referred to by Montresor in his *Journals*. They are found on the Battery and scattered all through the city. On this plan is also shown, in manuscript, the extension of the East River front at Hunter's Key, which extension was "allowed" in 1767 (*M. C. C.*, VII: 80–1).

The priority of the Montresor to the Ratzen Plan is clearly proved by a comparison of the two. Note, for instance, that on the Montresor Plan "Delancey's Great Square" has not yet been laid out, nor Division Street opened. It was not until October 31, 1765 (*Liber Deeds*, XLVIII: 364–7), that Rutgers and De Lancey agreed on the division line between their properties. The street was in part laid out during the succeeding year, for it shows on the Ratzen Plan of 1766–7, and is laid out in its entirety on the Ratzer Map. Note, also, that streets have not been cut through the "overflow" in the Montresor Plan. The New Presbyterian Meeting, in the Vineyard, begun in the autumn of 1766 and completed by January 1, 1768, is not shown on the Montresor, although it is found on both the Ratzen and Ratzer Plans. This is also true of the Theatre on John Street, finished in December, 1767; the new Dutch Church on William Street, between Ann and Fair (Fulton), the corner-stone of which was laid on July 2, 1767, and which was dedicated on May 25, 1769; the German Lutheran Church on the corner of King George (William) and Frankfort Streets, established in 1767, etc., etc.

The Ratzen and Ratzer Plans are the most accurate and reliable which we have of New York at this period, and are even to-day much used in searching titles.

Reproduction: Valentine's *Manual*, 1854, Frontispiece.

PLATE 43

A CORRECT VIEW OF THE OLD METHODIST CHURCH IN JOHN STREET N. YORK

Coloured aquatint. 13⅞ x 10¼ Date depicted: 1768.
Date issued: 1824.

Provenance: Frontispiece to *A Short Historical Account of the Early Society of Methodists, Established in the City of New York in the year 1763*. Published, N. Y., 1824. Sold by Myers & Smith, 59 Fulton St. Apparently also issued separately, printed on heavy paper (Collection of the late Wm. F. Havemeyer).

Artists: I. [J.] B. & P. C. Smith.

Owner: I.N.P.S.

Other copies: N. Y. Public Library; N. Y. Hist. Society, etc.

Only known state. This is the first Methodist Church erected in America, although services were held from 1766 to 1768 in a rigging-loft at 120 William Street. See Chronology, 1767. The dimensions of the church were 42 feet wide and 60 feet long. The house shown in the view to the right and partly in front of the church was the parsonage, which contained a library, and was built many years before the church. "According to the colonial law, none but the established service could be performed in what was commonly called a church; and places for public worship belonging to dissenters therefore were to have some appendage about them which should cause them to be classed among ordinary dwellings. Whence it became necessary to affix a fire-place and chimney to the methodist *church*, merely for the purpose of eluding so preposterous a regulation. The walls were constructed of ballast-stone, and the face was covered with a light blue plaister." The church was called Wesley's Chapel.—*A Short Hist. Account of the Early Soc. of Meth.*, 6-7.

A fine lithograph of this church, 17½ x 12¾ inches, was published, probably shortly after 1844, by Endicott & Co., from a drawing by Joseph B. Smith and with the title and inscription: "The First Methodist Church and Parsonage in America. / John Street New York / Church Edifice dedicated by Philip Embury 30th October 1768." There is also a scarce, tinted lithograph by the same artist and lithographers, 27¼ x 18¾ inches, copyrighted in 1844, and showing the old rigging-loft, the first church, erected in 1768, the second church as rebuilt in 1817, and the present building, constructed in 1841. On this print, besides the views of the churches, there are three tablets containing the names of the boards of trustees. The lithograph is inscribed to the trustees and members of the First Methodist Episcopal Church in John Street, New York, by Joseph B. Smith.

An interesting oil painting of the south side of John Street, from William to Nassau Street, about 60 x 30 inches, is owned by the family of the late Rev. F. G. Howell, of Brooklyn, and depicts conditions as they existed prior to 1817. This painting was engraved on steel by Lewis Delnoce and published in 1868 by Jos. B. Smith & Co. The engraving, which measures 17½ x 10¼ inches, reveals only about two-thirds of the original painting. Mr. Howell's family possesses also an original note-book mostly in the autograph of Mr. Smith and containing the names and many of the signatures of the original 259 subscribers to the large lithograph, which was issued at five dollars per copy, as well as the names of 202 subscribers to the lithograph of the church alone, issued at two dollars per copy. Mr. Howell once owned a water-colour sketch of the south side of John Street (Vol. II, Addenda), probably the original from which the painting was made. This drawing, which is now in the N. Y. Historical Society, is doubtless the sketch referred to in a leaflet advertising the Delnoce steel engraving of 1868 as having been "made by him [J. B. S.] upon the spot when a mere youth." A copy of this leaflet and also the original copyright of the plate, dated July 27, 1868, are still in the possession of Mr. Howell's family.

The author possesses a lithograph, 9 x 11¼, published by H. R. Robinson, September, 1846, showing "The Rigging House," 120 William Street, with an historical notice printed below the view. The Borden Collection and the Neill Collection each contained an impression of this view, these being the only other copies known.

Du Simitière, in his description of public buildings in New York in 1769 (Du Simitière MSS. in Ridgeway Branch, Library Company, Philadelphia), refers to the early Methodist Church as follows: "a Tabernacle for one Webb a half pay officer & Barrack master in N. Y. in Golden Hill."

In early days that portion of the city bounded by the present William, John, Fulton, and Cliff Streets was known as Golden Hill, the highest point, which is still in existence, being directly behind the buildings at Nos. 19–23 Cliff Street, at the head of Ryders Alley; John Street, east of William, was during this period called Golden Hill Street. In the immediate neighbourhood of the old rigging-loft occurred the "Battle of Golden Hill," wherein was spilled the first blood shed in the American Revolution. For an interesting contemporary account of this affray, see *The New-York Gazette; or, the Weekly Post-Boy* of February 5, 1770; see also Chronology.

No. 120 was not demolished until the summer of 1900 (Records in Title Guarantee & Trust Co.), although the building was remodelled and two stories added some time between 1846 (the date of the lithograph in the author's collection, above referred to) and 1861, the date of a view reproduced in Valentine's *Manual* for 1862, in which view a high building occupies the site of No. 120. The site is now covered by a twelve-story loft building, occupied by Lehn & Fink, wholesale druggists. The house adjoining it to the north (No. 122), also shown in the lithograph of "The Rigging House," is still standing, and is one of the oldest buildings in the city. According to a letter from Thomas B. Gilford, dated July 8, 1887 (quoted in Bartram's *Retrographs*), this house was purchased, in 1773, by his grandfather, Samuel Gilford, who resided there until the beginning of the Revolution, returning after the war and occupying the house until his death, in 1821. In this letter, Mr. Gilford says that the house, when purchased in 1773, was very old. "It was built of bricks imported from Holland, and laid in a cement that is as imperishable as the bricks themselves." Bartram, writing in 1888, describes this house and that at No. 126, which was built by Gilford shortly after the Revolution, as follows:

> In the basement of each house are two of the famous old Dutch ovens, forming the base of immense stone chimneys, which were the house anchors and pride of the Knickerbockers. The kitchens, in the basements, were after the English models, and the immense mantels, upon each floor, were elaborately inlaid with tiles of porcelain, about six inches square, in various colors and designs; each tile containing a representation or illustration of some historic, religious, or secular event, and all combined to produce a singularly-beautiful and striking effect. . . . It has been asserted by several of the oldest citizens (though the writer has no documentary evidence to sustain the assertion), that one of the buildings, at various periods prior to the Revolution, was used as a hotel and coffee-house, numbering among its patrons such patriots as Washington, Lafayette, . . .

The author has been unable to find any record of an inn or tavern on this site prior to the Revolution, although it is quite possible that the old building at No. 122 William

Street was so used before its purchase by Gilford in 1773. The house was occupied by the Gilford family as late as 1829. It was probably thereafter leased for business purposes, for we find it given as the address of Benjamin Lawrence, stationer, from 1848 to 1854. From 1870 to 1891 the house was occupied as a restaurant by Louis Heckman or his heirs.

Although, as stated, no reference has been found to an early inn or tavern on this site, we know that on the opposite side of the street, somewhat nearer to Fair (Fulton) than to John Street, stood in pre-Revolutionary days a famous inn known as the Horse and Cart Tavern. The Horse and Cart is referred to in *The New-York Gazette* as early as 1732, and is also named upon the Manuscript Map of 1735 (Pl. 30). In 1754 it was run by Edward Willett, who in this year removed to the Province Arms in Broadway.

Reproduction: Valentine's *Manual*, 1857, opp. p. 400.

Plate 44

(A View of New York from the North West)

[The large Atlantic Neptune View, or The Wooded Heights View]

Aquatint, in sepia. 16⅛ x 8¼ Date depicted: Probably shortly before 1773.

Date issued: Probably 1777.

Provenance: From the *Atlantic Neptune* (Impression supérieure), Vol. II, Pl. 112.

Owner: Edward W. C. Arnold, Esq., who bought it at the sale of the M. C. D. Borden Collection (February, 1913).

Other copies: British Museum; Bibliothèque Nationale; R. T. H. Halsey, Esq., with title as above (from the Bourinot copy belonging originally to the King of Sardinia, and sold at auction in New York in 1906); I.N.P.S. The Sydney Collection, sold by auction in England, in June, 1915, contained a fine impression of this view with the manuscript title as above. These are the only copies of this view known to the author. Collections of the *Atlantic Neptune* are found in the N. Y. Public Library (two copies), in the N. Y. Hist. Society, in the Library of Congress (eight copies), in the Boston Public Library, in the John Carter Brown Library, in the Library Society, Charleston, S. C., in the Library of Yale University (two copies), in the British Museum, in the Bibliothèque Nationale, and in the I.N.P.S. Collection. All of these copies have been examined by the author. There are also two sets in the Admiralty Archives, London.

Proof before letters. The view must have been drawn between 1763, when Des Barres first visited New York after his appointment as engineer in charge of the preparation of the *Atlantic Neptune*, and 1773, when the Governor's House (Mansion House) in the Fort, which appears in the view, was destroyed by fire, this house never having been rebuilt inside the Fort. Although it has not proved possible to assign a definite date between these limits, the general appearance of the view in comparison with the various maps of the period seems to indicate that it was drawn shortly before 1773.

This view is generally considered one of the most attractive and interesting representations of New York in the eighteenth century. Although the height of the bluff on which Trinity Church stands has evidently been exaggerated (Broadway in front of the church is actually only about thirty-five feet above high water), the contour of the land is, nevertheless, probably more accurately depicted than on the Carwitham or any other early view of the city. This is natural, as we know that special pains to secure accuracy were taken in the preparation of the plates of the *Atlantic Neptune*, which were intended primarily for military purposes.

The view shows very clearly the Fort and the buildings which it contained at this period. By a comparison with the Ratzen Plan (Pl. 42), it is easy to recognise the principal buildings throughout the entire city. The little settlement at the extreme left clusters around Paulus Hook Ferry, which is the slip just south of King's Wharf, the central of the three wharves seen in the view. The houses rising steeply one above the other in line with the most southerly of these three wharves are on Crown (Liberty), Little Queen (Cedar), and Stone (Thames) Streets. The church at the summit of the bluff is of course Trinity, just south of which, across Rector Street, may be discerned the building of the Free English School. The small steeple south of Trinity is that of the Lutheran Church, on Broadway below Rector Street. Next to this is seen the Middle Dutch Church. The positive identification of the next tower and steeple presents some difficulties. They are probably intended to represent the Wall Street Presbyterian Church, which we know from Smith's *History of the Province of New York* (1757), p. 192, had a "Steeple" 145 feet high. Kalm, too, writing in 1748–9, says the church had a "steeple and a bell in it." From views of the period, notably from the large view forming part of the Ratzer Map (Pl. 41), and from the manuscript view made after the fire of 1776 (Pl. 48), we know that the *steeple* of this church at this time was surmounted by a cupola, and not by a spire. Indeed, the only churches having pointed spires were Trinity Church, the old Lutheran Church on Broadway below Rector Street, and the South Dutch Church in Garden Street. The only other church having at this period a tall steeple or tower was St. George's Church on Beekman Street, and, from a glance at the Ratzen Plan, it will be seen that from the point from which the view is taken it is not possible to bring this steeple into range with that of the Presbyterian Church, and, besides, the point of view is so low that the steeple of St. George's could not have appeared above the cupola of the Presbyterian Church. Furthermore, the steeple of St. George's differed materially from the representation in the view (see Pls. 45–a and 80–a). The most likely explanation seems to be that the tower and cupola of the Wall Street Church, which we know were tall and attenuated, have been erroneously depicted in this view, which perhaps was elaborated from a hasty sketch (see remarks under Pl. 38).

Next appear the tower and cupola of the French Church du St. Esprit in King (Pine) Street. Some little distance to the south the cupola and flag of the City Hall are clearly discernible, and south of this again we recognise the spire of the South Dutch Church in Garden Street. The large building in the Fort is the Mansion House referred to above; the low building in front of it, the stables. These buildings are very distinctly shown on the plan of the Fort drawn by Sauthier (Pl. 46–a). The two houses between the stern of the ship and the north-west bastion of the Fort are apparently the same two which appear prominently in this location on the Bradford and Ratzer Maps and in the Carwitham View. The northerly and larger of the two was occupied at this period by Christopher Blondel, store-keeper of the Fort, who received a lease of the lot on November 16, 1752, for ninety-nine years at 2s. 6d. per year. This house occupies the same site on which "Gen. Hunter was pleased to permit Thomas Elde the Armourer of the Fort to erect a small tenement" about forty years earlier, as Christopher Blondel recites in his petition. He adds: "the house is become ruinous and a sort of pest house for the sick of the city."—*Land Papers* (Albany), XV: 25. See also Chronology, 1752, November 15. It is possible that our view shows this house enlarged, or, more probably, a new building altogether. In 1792, the house, which had come into the possession of Thomas Joseph Smith, was purchased for £750 by the City of New York, as it interfered with improvements then being made at the Battery.—*M. C. C.* (*MS.*), X: 280, 284, 294.

The small house just to the south seems to have stood on government property; it was apparently enlarged and converted into stores before 1788, when it appears so designated on the survey of the Fort in the office of the State Engineer at Albany (see Pl. 46 A-c). Both of these buildings are clearly seen on the smaller view from the *Atlantic Neptune* (Pl. 45-a). A roof, probably that of the Secretary's Office, appears between and just above these two houses. The high roof slightly to the left and behind the more northerly of the two is probably that of the Kennedy House, No. 1 Broadway, built about 1760 by Archibald Kennedy on the site of two smaller houses facing Marketfield Street. The house just north, at No. 3 Broadway, which belonged to Kennedy's father, was occupied in 1745 as the Custom House. The Custom House was moved to Whitehall in 1769 (*The New-York Gazette; and the Weekly Mercury*, May 8, 1769), but in 1776 seems to have been temporarily at least brought back to this locality, as it is shown on the Holland Plan of that year (reproduced in Valentine's *Manual*, 1863, opp. p. 532) just west of No. 1 Broadway. However, as this plan also shows the Governor's House in the Fort, which house we know was destroyed by fire in 1773, its reliability appears somewhat questionable. For a further discussion concerning the location of the Custom House during this period, see Chronology, 1756, August 26.

The line of posts between the Fort and the shore evidently marks the remains of the outer defences, so prominent a feature in the Carwitham View. These posts or pickets were still standing in 1784, when the Assembly requested the Governor to give orders that the poor be allowed to use them for fire-wood (*Assemb. Jour.*, February 13, 1784). The screens themselves had been demolished by Montresor on November 1, 1765, during the early days of the Stamp Act Riots, as they interfered with the raking fire of the flanking guns.—Montresor's *Journals* in *Collections* N. Y. Hist. Society (1881), p. 336.

The battery forming the outer breastwork south of the south-west bastion of the Fort can be discerned at the extreme right of the view. *Cf.* Maerschalck Plan (Pl. 34), and Plan of the Fort, etc. (Pl. 46 A-c). *Cf.* also a manuscript "Plan of the Ground in the South Ward of the City of New York, which has lately been taken in as part of the Battery; surveyed Sep. 8, 1775, by Gerard Bancker," now owned by the N. Y. Hist. Society, which acquired it at the sale of the Holden Collection (No. 1750). This is item No. 2533 in the catalogue of the Bancker papers sold originally by Henkles in Philadelphia in 1899.

The little pavilion with the pyramidal roof, which is seen on the shore in range with the Lutheran Church, can be recognised on the Ratzen Plan. It was built at the south-west angle of a walled garden seen in the view and owned at this time by the heirs of Sir Peter Warren and Oliver De Lancey.—Recitals in *Liber C of Grants*, in Comptroller's Office, pp. 302-8. (In the Warren papers in the N. Y. Hist. Society Library is a sketch of Sir Peter Warren's lots from Broadway to the farthest extent of the water grant, 77 ft. on Broadway, 81 ft. in the rear.) The garden was in the rear of numbers 59, 61, 63, and 65 Broadway. At this period the river shore was at Greenwich Street, so that the summer-house stood where the Adams Express Company building west of Trinity Place now is, The little building at the foot of the bluff below Trinity is also found on the Ratzen Plan just to the south of a narrow lane, all that remains of the little street shown on the Maerschalck Plan just below Trinity Church. It stood in the rear of the school-house plot on land belonging to the church.

THE ATLANTIC NEPTUNE

No two copies of the *Atlantic Neptune* have been found containing exactly the same collection of plates, and no complete list exists of the plates which were issued from time to time in connection with this most important publication, which Rich, in his *Bibliotheca Americana Nova*, I: 249, refers to as the "most splendid collection of charts, plans and views ever published." The *Atlantic Neptune* exists bound in two forms—in folio, the full size of the plates, and in narrow folio, with the plates folded vertically. A notice of its publication appears in *L'Esprit des journaux*, Paris, 1784, III: 459-74. This notice contains also a description of the work as published in its final form and a full collation. This description, freely translated, reads as follows:

> There has recently been placed on sale at The Hague by P. F. Gosse, court book-seller and printer, a superb Atlas, which we take this first opportunity to describe in detail. This work, which is indispensable for the navy, is the result of nineteen years' labour and has cost the English government more than a hundred thousand pounds sterling, in addition to the considerable expenses which the author himself has discharged for its execution. The work is of the highest degree of beauty and superior to everything of the kind that has heretofore been published.
>
> It is entitled:
>
> Plans of the coast and of the harbours of North America, entitled: the Atlantic Neptune, executed, engraved and published by the order of the government for the use of the royal navy of Great Britain, by Joseph F. W. Desbarres, Esq., under the direction of the very honorable lords commissioners of the admiralty.
>
> Sunt ingeniorum monumenta, quae saeculis probantur.
>
> This work, of the highest possible utility for navigation and commerce, is offered to the public at a price considerably below its value, and the enormous expenses of its execution, in acknowledgment of the protection and assistance which the author has received from parliament.
>
> The first part contains the original plans by the author, of the coast and the harbours of Nova Scotia with soundings, maritime remarks, etc. on LXXXIV leaves of royal paper.
>
> The second part consists of charts composed of different plans, observations and remarks of officers of the navy and army employed by the government as follows:
>
> The coast and the harbours of the gulf and river St. Lawrence and of the islands of Cape Breton, St. John, etc. on XXXVI leaves of royal paper.
>
> The coast and the harbours of Connecticut, Rhode-Island, the bay of Massachusetts, New-Hampshire, etc. on XLVIII leaves of royal paper.
>
> The charts of the harbours and the coast between New York and the entrance of the Missisipi river on XXVI leaves of royal paper.
>
> The price of this atlas bound in one volume in calf is 160 f. and as the work is sold for the account of the author it will be delivered only on receipt of cash.
>
> Address Pierre-Frédéric Gosse, court book-seller and printer to S. A. S. who alone is authorised by the author to dispose of this work in foreign parts.
>
> The same Atlas (impression supérieure)
>
> Large size on imperial paper with the addition of several pictures superbly printed in colours representing views of the coasts, the river banks (*rivages*) and interior portions of the country, views of towns, remarkable places, etc. the whole accompanied by numerous interesting plans and views of military operations occurring during the war in North America,
>
> In two Volumes
>
> The price of this work complete in CCLVIII sheets on imperial paper is 252 f. money of Holland, payable in cash.

Mr. Henry N. Stevens has recently prepared a very full description of various states of the *Atlantic Neptune* plates, from copies in public collections in London, as well as from several incomplete sets in his own possession, one of which, General Gage's personal copy, is in six original parts, or so-called "Deliveries," uncut and flat, in the original coarse pink paper wrappers. The charts and views of this set are not even pasted up. The first four "Deliveries" have each a printed slip pasted on the outside wrapper "Contents of the First Delivery" (Second, Third, and Fourth ditto). The Contents of the Fifth and Sixth Deliveries do not seem to have been printed, but the wrappers of these two parts bear manuscript inscriptions in a contemporary hand "Fifth Delivery 1 April 1781," and "Sixth Delivery 1 May 1781." These six deliveries contain 84 sheets, including a general letter page in Part I, Vol. I, 1780. Each part bears the addressed inscription "Hon. General Gage Portland Place" with the Book Ticket of W. Babbs.

In a very rare folio pamphlet in the N. Y. Public Library, entitled *A Statement submitted by Lieutenant Colonel des Barres for consideration*, etc., etc. (1795), which is a sort of brief in a suit brought against the Government for the reimbursement of moneys personally expended by the plaintiff, on the first and last pages occur references to the preparation of 257 plates of charts and views, engraving and printing the same, etc. It will be noticed that this agrees within one with the number enumerated in *L'Esprit des journaux*. As this suit was apparently brought in 1795, and as no plate in the *Atlantic Neptune* bears a date later than 1784, the above collation would appear to be complete were it not for the fact that a number of charts and views are known which it does not contain. The author's own collection includes all but two of those enumerated and upwards of thirty additional plates, exclusive of varying "states." We know from this pamphlet (p. 5) and from other sources, that the work extended from 1763 to 1784, that the printing began in 1774, and that editions were printed in 1777, 1780, and 1781, as well as in 1784. It is therefore probable that for the final (1784) edition the author selected what he believed to be the most interesting and attractive charts and views and suppressed a number which had appeared in earlier editions.

It is evident that special copies of the *Atlantic Neptune* were from time to time made up containing only selections from the complete set of charts and views. These were doubtless intended for the use of masters of vessels who required only the particular maps and views of the parts of the coast which they purposed visiting. It may be of interest to quote some statements made by Des Barres in his little book above referred to:

> Earl Howe, in the View of benefitting Navigation and Commerce and of acquiring for the use of His Majesty's Service in the Operations of War necessary Information, had in Contemplation to establish a Depôt and institute an Office in the Admiralty, for the Purpose of forming an arranged Collection of all useful Surveys, Charts, Plans, and Descriptions of Countries, Coasts, Harbours, Fortresses, Commercial Places, &c., that could be procured.
>
> * * * * *
>
> The said Surveys, Charts, Plans, &c: were to be minutely examined in order to ascertain their respective Degrees of Accuracy. The defective or dubious Parts therein were to be pointed out, for the Purpose of putting Navigators on their Guard, and that the same be, by subsequent Observations, rectified; and, in the Object of averting as far as practicable the Disaster to which Navigation might be exposed from the delusive Use of erroneous Draughts, it was proposed that the thus examined Charts, &c: should be distinguishable by some Official Stamp Mark.
>
> At the fitting out of any Fleet, Squadron, or particular Ship of War, wheresoever destined, the Commanding Officers were to be supplied from the said Depôt, with such Surveys, Charts and Plans, of the Coasts, Harbours, and Places, to which they were to be sent, and with such Extracts of Observations, Journals, &c: as should be thought requisite for their Information

and the Service they might be ordered upon—All which, on the Return of said Fleet, Squadron, or Ship from their Expedition or Voyage, were to be rendered into the said Depôt, together with all Discoveries made in respect to Longitudes, Latitudes, Banks, Rocks, Shoals, Soundings, Currents, Tides, Variations, &c: and whatever Alterations or Additions might be perceived in the Fortifications or Strength of Places, their Policy or Government &c: And for the easier and more effectual Performance whereof, and that the same might at all future Times be readily recurred to, Books prepared for that peculiar Use were likewise proposed to be furnished to said Commanders.

* * * * *

Having proposed the undertaking to senior Officers, who declined it on account of the difficulties, he [Rear Admiral Spry] mentioned Des Barres to the Admiralty as an officer qualified to undertake it.

In the meantime [1763], Des Barres had repaired to Head Quarters in New York, by order of the Commander in Chief Lord Amherst, who he understood, had an idea to employ him in excursions to different parts of the Colonies, with a view to report military observations of the grounds; but his Lordship returned to England, and was succeeded by General Gage.

Admiral Spry was succeeded also, in the Command of the squadron by Lord Colvill, who, having received instructions from the Admiralty to employ Des Barres in the survey projected by Admiral Spry, wrote to General Gage for leave for him to undertake it.

Des Barres no sooner arrived at Halifax accordingly, than he was set to commence, with the strongest assurances, of being rewarded in a manner adequate to his diligence and ability.

* * * * *

Having exerted himself in this arduous Service until the End of 1773, he returned to England and laid his Performance before the King. His Majesty was pleased to order the same to be engraved.

Nautical Charts of several other Parts of the American Coasts being much wanted for the Operations of War, he was, in pursuance of the Royal Commands, farther engaged in the Construction and Completion thereof until the Year 1784.

Under the dates of 1774–1783, Des Barres notes:

The Officers destined to conduct the Fleet in the reduction of the Colonies, being also desirous of correct Charts of the North American Coasts from Florida to the Gulph of St. Lawrence, Des Barres became involved in the intricate task of selecting, correcting and adapting, the surveys of others to Nautical Purposes, and of publishing the whole under the title of the Atlantic Neptune, which cost ten years more of incessant labor.

* * * * *

Messrs Holland and Debrahm, engaged in 1764, and were employed under the directions of the Board of Trade and Plantations to carry on Surveys of land in America (which they commenced in the following year).

* * * * *

In order to enable the Public to enjoy the Benefits of his Performance, at the mere Cost of the Materials and printing, Desbarres received from the Bounty of Parliament, the sum of £8188 18s 3d on Account of the Expence for engraving 257 Plates, (contained in the Atlantic Neptune, begun and completed in the Period from 1774 to 1784, and charged, in conformity to the Allowance settled therefor by Government, at 35 Guineas for each Plate) amounting to £9444 15s 0d.

On the last page of this folio is a statement, under the headings "Salary" "Contingencies" and "No. of Assistants employed," showing that Des Barres, for "Carrying on surveys of the Coasts and Harbours of Nova Scotia, from 1764 to 1773—preparing the same, and constructing sundry nautical charts, for Publication, from 1774 to 1784," received a total salary of £6883. In a contemporary hand is added in manuscript, perhaps by Des Barres himself, "incessant Employment."

It is interesting to note that in the years 1776 to 1779 he had from 20 to 23 assistants each year, while in all other years his assistants numbered only a very few, never more than 7. The statement shows also that Holland, for "Carrying on Land Surveys in the

Northern District, from 1765 to 1774—preparing the same for Publication in 1775 and 1776," received a total salary of £4749, with "Contingencies" amounting to £12963 16s., and that Debrahm, for "Carrying on Land Surveys in the Southern District, from 1765 to 1774—preparing the same for Publication in 1775 and 1776," received a total salary of £4749, and £9861 1s. "Contingencies."

A partial catalogue issued by W. Babbs, bookseller and stationer (No. 31) Oxford Street, 1781, is contained in the Library of Harvard University. This pamphlet has fifteen numbered pages and gives the price of most of the plates, some few being supplied in manuscript. The following note appears on the 8th and also on the last page: "For the conveniency of Navigators, and the public, any Chart or View comprehended in this Work may be had singly of W. Babbs, Bookseller (No. 31) Oxford St."

The view here reproduced was engraved, in 1906, by Sidney L. Smith for the Society of Iconophiles, with the title: "View of New York in 1775."

Plate 45-a

New York, with the Entrance of the North and East Rivers
[The small Atlantic Neptune View]

Aquatint in colours. 18⅝ x 4$\frac{5}{16}$ Date depicted: *c.* 1776.
Date issued: October 4, 1777.

Provenance: *Atlantic Neptune*, Vol. II, Pl. 113.

Owner: From the M. C. D. Borden Collection.

Other copies: N. Y. Public Library, Map Room (two copies), and Emmet Collection: 10577 (earlier state); N. Y. Hist. Society; Library of Congress, Div. of Maps and Charts; I.N.P.S. (earlier state), etc.

Probably the second state. Another state (probably earlier) exists, lacking most of the shipping, and with the hills on the Staten Island shore much lower. Manhattan Island and the City, however, are identical. This is the third of five views printed on the same page. The others are:

"A View of the Highland of Neversunk, N. W. b. W. four Miles distant with the Light House, on Sandy Hook, N. W." (etc.).

"The South Shore of Long Island, ten leagues Eastward of Sandy Hook, four Miles distant."

"The Light House on Sandy Hook, S. E. one Mile."

"The Narrows, (between Red and Yellow Hook, on Long Island & the East Bluff of Staten Island,) bearing S. b. W."

In addition to these views and the view shown on Pl. 44, the *Atlantic Neptune* contains the following plates of particular interest to our subject:

A chart of the coast of New York, New Jersey, Pennsylvania, Maryland, Virginia, North Carolina, etc., three sheets.

A chart of the Harbour of New York, one sheet.

A view of the naval engagement between the Phoenix and the Rose on Aug. 16, 1776, one sheet. This view, which is extremely rare, exists in two states, one showing the Palisades and one without. The N. Y. Public Library and the Bibliothèque Nationale possess each a copy of the former, and the N. Y. Hist. Society, the British Museum, and the author, each an impression of the latter state. The title of the view is: "The Phoenix and the Rose / Engaged by the

Enemy's fire Ships and Galleys on the 16 Aug^st 1776 / Engraved from the Original Picture by D. Serres from a Sketch of Sir James Wallace's / Pub. April 2 1778." The location of the encounter is shown on the Chart of the Harbour.

A chart of the west passage near the East River in the straits of Long Island, two sheets.

A chart of Hellgate with an inset view, and a chart of the neighbourhood of New York entitled: "A Sketch of the Operations of His Majesty's Fleet and Army under the command of Vice Admiral the R^t H^ble Lord Viscount Howe and Genl Sr Wm Howe K. B. in 1776" (with references A to Q and a separate paragraph of interesting particulars regarding the position of the opposing forces, etc.), one sheet. This map, which was issued Jan. 17, 1777, closely resembles the Howe War Plan (Pl. 45-b). For the most complete published list of plates belonging to the *Atlantic Neptune*, see *L'Esprit des journaux*, referred to under Pl. 44.

There is also, in the possession of Mr. Robert Fridenberg, a folio view without title but with the word "Hellgate" inscribed below the rectangle, in pencil. This view is printed on paper exactly similar to that used in the *Atlantic Neptune* and having the same water-mark. The character of both the drawing and the engraving is very similar to that of some of the views in the *Atlantic Neptune*. This interesting view, which shows several ships passing through the straits on both sides of a small island, is known only by this one impression. It seems likely that it was intended to be included in the series, but that for some reason it was not used. The print was originally in the collection of Mr. Edward Dexter of London. It was sold with the collection of his son, Mr. Elias Dexter of New York, to Mr. John Anderson, Jr., from whom Mr. Fridenberg bought it, about 1905. A copy of the *Atlantic Neptune*, purchased by Mr. Henry N. Stevens, in 1915, contained two plates hitherto unknown, one with three views and the other with three plans of Forts Clinton and Montgomery. These plates are now in the author's collection.

Plate 45-b

A Plan of New York Island, with part of Long Island, Staten Island & East New Jersey, with a particular Description of the Engagement on the Woody Heights of Long Island, between Flatbush and Brooklyn, on the 27th of August 1776 (etc.)

[The Howe War Plan]

Engraved on copper. 16 11/16 x 18 3/4 Date depicted: 1776.
Date issued: October 19, 1776.

Provenance: Sometimes found bound up with Faden's *North American Atlas* (1777). Also issued separately.

Engraved and published by William Faden, London.

Owner: I.N.P.S.

Other copies: N. Y. Public Library (fourth state, two copies, one with and one without text, and fifth state); N. Y. Hist. Society (first state, two copies, one with and one without text); Library of Congress, Div. of Maps and Charts, etc.

The John Carter Brown Library possesses a nearly complete set of the various states of this interesting and important series of maps, and the author's collection contains the first, fourth, and fifth states, all with the descriptive text.

Fourth state. Five distinct states of this plan are known, and each state, except the fifth, exists both with and without the descriptive text at the foot. No copy of the fifth state without the text has been recorded. In the fifth state, which is very rare, the text has been reprinted, the set-up being different. In every state except the fourth the text relates to the attack on Long Island. In the fourth state (with text), which is the rarest, the text is an account of the taking of New York on September 15, 1776.

Mr. Henry N. Stevens has carefully compared and collated the five known states, all of which have the imprint: Wm. Faden, October 19, 1776. The following notes for identifying the different states have been condensed from his fuller descriptions:

In the first state, the fourth line of the title has only four words, *viz.* "Disposition of both Armies." The sea coast, harbour, and rivers are shown in single outline only, without any shading. The most northerly place marked on Hudson River is "Tetard's Hill." The Heights on Long Island are twice lettered simply "The Heights." When without text, the paper measures, uncut, 19½ x 24 inches, and has two water-marks:—the initials "R G" in the left half; and a device of a shield with fleur-de-lis at the top and initials "G R" below, in the right half. When with text, the paper is much thicker—and measures, uncut, 22½ x 30½; and the water-marks are "W F" in the left half, and a coroneted shield with the fleur-de-lis inside and "G R" below, in the right half.

The second state has exactly the same title as the first state, but the sea-coasts, harbour, and rivers now have the outline shaded with several lines. The most northerly place now marked on Hudson River is "Younker." The Heights of Long Island are marked as in the first state.

The third state has the title altered in the third and fourth lines, the fourth line now having thirty words—beginning and ending thus: "British Army . . . Both the Armies." Fort Washington does not yet appear. The Heights of Long Island are now lettered—on the left, "The Heights of Guana," on the right, "The Woody Heights of Guana." Three lines of lettering have been added on the Jersey shore opposite the head of New York Island, viz:

Flying Camp
of the Americans
Redoubt with Cannon

In the fourth state, the title is the same as in the third state, but the text below is quite different, being an account of the taking of New York on September 15, 1776. Fort Washington is now marked, being lettered in the river near the head of New York Island. On the Jersey shore, opposite the head of N. Y. Island, Fort Independence is added, making four lines of lettering instead of three as in the third state, thus:

Flying Camp
of the Americans
Fort Independence
Redoubt with Cannon

From a rather confused, and apparently conflicting, description of an impression of the fourth state which Mr. Stevens has seen, he thinks it likely that this state also was issued with the printed text of the attack on Long Island, August 27, 1776.

In the fifth state, the title is the same as in the third and the fourth. In the text below, however, in the description of the attack on Long Island, August 27, 1776, although the same matter is given as in the foregoing editions, the type has been reset throughout. In this state, the last line of the imprint reads: "Mr Wallis Bookseller in Ludgate Street." In the former impressions the last line reads: "of Mess Wallis and Stonehouse Booksellers, Ludgate Street." In this state, "Younker" at the top of the map, is deleted, and the word "Fort" inserted. Fort Washington is now shown about three inches below the head of New York Island, adjacent to a point in the river now marked "Jefferys Hook." The Fort is now lettered "Fort Washington," on the island itself, and not on the river, as in the fourth state. Fort Lee or "Ft Constitution" is now marked on the Jersey side a little south of a point opposite Jefferys Hook. The old four-line lettering "Fort Independence," etc., etc., as described above in the fourth state, is now deleted. Very numerous alterations appear in this edition, both on the land and in the shape and course of the Hudson River. There is reason to suppose that this state also may have been issued with the descriptive text of the taking of New York on September 15th, but no copy with this text has been seen either by Mr. Stevens or by the author.

Reference: Phillips's *Maps of America*, 526.

PLATE 46

A TOPOGRAPHICAL MAP OF THE NORTHN PART OF NEW YORK ISLAND, (ETC.)

Engraved on copper. 10 3/16 x 18 3/8 Date depicted: 1776.
Date issued: 1777.

Provenance: Although usually appearing as a separate map, this plate is sometimes found bound in *The North American Atlas*, published by Wm. Faden, London, 1777. No copy of the Atlas, however, has been found in which this map appears in the printed index.

Author: Claude Joseph Sauthier.

Owner: I.N.P.S.

Other copies: N. Y. Public Library; N. Y. Hist. Society; Library of Congress, etc.

Mr. Phillips, in his *Maps of America*, describes two issues of this map, each apparently containing slight variations in the title from the copy here reproduced. However, in a letter to the author, dated May 19, 1913, from the Library of Congress, Div. of Maps and Charts, the statement is made that the titles and imprints are all exactly the same, although, in "cataloguing the maps for the 'List,' unnecessary capitals were evidently eliminated . . . there are [however] some differences in the maps themselves." In the same letter, attention is drawn to the fact that the separate map, mentioned on p. 526 of the "List," and the copy in Vol. 3 of *American Maps* agree with the copy here reproduced; while on the copy in Vol. 5 of *American Maps*, as well as on the one in Faden's *North American Atlas, 1777*, slight differences appear, such as the addition of the line of march of the "Hessian Column" and that of the "British Column commanded by Earl Percy."

The most beautiful, and probably the most accurate map of the upper end of Manhattan Island at the time of the Revolution. Sauthier's original drawing is in the Library of Congress, Div. of Maps and Charts. Three manuscript plans of the attack on Fort Washington—one of them surveyed by Sauthier on the day of the battle—are also owned by the Library of Congress, and are preserved in the Faden Collection (MSS. 59, 60, and 61).

The N. Y. Hist. Society possesses a very interesting original water-colour map covering this same territory, and bearing the title "Attacks of Fort Washington by his Majesty's Forces under the Command of Genl Sir Willm K:B. 16 Novr 1776." There is also reproduced in the *Collections* of the N. Y. Hist. Society for 1882, Plate VI, an interesting bird's-eye view of Harlem and the north end of the Island, the original of which forms part of Van Krafft's Journal, which, in 1882, was in the possession of Mr. Wm. Callender, of Washington, D. C. A recent attempt to locate the Journal, or Wm. Callender, or his heirs, was unsuccessful.

During the year 1776, Sauthier prepared also a map of the Province of New York. An advertisement of this map in *The New-York Gazette; and the Weekly Mercury*, of December 9, 1776, describes it as "exhibiting all the Grants of Lands made in that Province with The Proprietors Names inserted on each Grant: Compiled from actual Surveys by Claude Joseph Sauthier," etc. This map is also found in the Faden *Atlas* of 1777.

It is interesting to compare the map here reproduced with "A Military Topographical Plan of Harlem Heights and Plain," drawn by Wm. J. Proctor, and constructed under the direction of General J. G. Swift by Captain James Renwick. This plan is found reproduced as Pl. 82-A.

Reproduction: Valentine's *Manual*, 1859, opp. p. 120.

Plate 46 A-a

A Plan of Fort George at the City of New-York

Wash drawing on paper. 17 x 27½ Date depicted: *c.* 1773.
Author: Claude Joseph Sauthier.
Owner: Library of Congress, Div. of Maps and Charts (Faden Collection, No. 95).

This plan is the most complete and detailed representation of the Fort that we possess. It must have been drawn prior to December 29, 1773, when the buildings in the Fort were destroyed by fire, and after August 16, 1770, as it shows the statue of George III, erected on that day in the Bowling Green. This statue was demolished on July 10, 1776, although the pedestal remained until 1818 (see Pls. 51 and 52).

The stone base of this statue and the tail of the King's horse are now in the possession of the New York Hist. Society. The mutilated head, according to Montresor's *Journals* (N. Y. Hist. Society *Collections*, 1881, p. 123), was forwarded to Lord Townshend "to convince them at home of the Infamous Disposition of the Ungrateful people of this distressed Country."—See Chronology, 1770, August 16.

The kitchen building here shown was built prior to January 24, 1756.—*Assemb. Jour.* (Gaine Ed.), II: 477.

Reproduced and described here for the first time.

Plate 46 A-b

Plan of the Fort Made at the Request of Mr. Speaker & the Committee appointed to fix on a Suitable plan to build a Govt. House

Pen and ink drawing on paper. 14⅝ x 19¼ (size of sheet) Date depicted: April 12, 1774.
Author: Gerard Bancker.
Owner: I.N.P.S.

This very interesting survey was made by Gerard Bancker, City Surveyor, as is stated on the plan, "at the Request of Mr Speaker [John Cruger] & the Committee appointed to fix on a suitable plan to build a Gov[t] House." The erection of a new house for the Governor became necessary because of the destruction by fire, on December 29, 1773, of the Governor's, or Mansion House in the Fort, shortly after it had undergone extensive repairs, for which, as well as for repairs on the Fort and Battery, the Colony had, on February 18, 1773, allowed £1,764, 14s., 2d.—*Assemb. Jour.* (Buel. Edit.), 69. After the fire Governor Tryon made his residence in Broad Street.—*Ibid.*, 43, February 8, 1774.

Action was first taken towards rebuilding the Governor's House on February 26, 1774, when Colonel P. Livingston "moved for leave to bring in a bill to raise £6000 by lottery or lotteries, towards building a province house for the residence of the Governor or Commander in Chief, for the time being, and a secretary's office, for the security of the public records of this colony."—*Ibid.*, 71. On March 11th, the House appointed a committee to "fix on a suitable place for building a government house, and to prepare a plan and an estimate of the expense."—*Ibid.*, 91–2. The plan here reproduced, as stated above, was evidently made in conformity with this action of the Assembly, which, on March 15th, passed an Act to raise £12,000 by lottery for the erection of a province house and secretary's office. The bill passed by the Assembly was read in the Legislative Council on the same day and committed, but no further action was taken.—*Legis. Coun. Jour.*, 1931, 1933. About a year later, or on March 7, 1775, Mr. De Lancey, in behalf of the committee appointed for the purpose, submitted plans for the Government House and an estimate of its cost. The committee recommended that the building be erected in Fort George "either in the front towards the broad way, or in the rear near the back curtain, provided the front curtain be pulled down."—*Assemb. Jour.* (Buel Ed.), 59–60. The Government House, as projected at this time, was, however, never built.

After the Revolutionary War and during the period when the seat of government was in New York, a Government House was begun (1790) south of the Bowling Green; but before its completion Philadelphia had become the capital city, and it was therefore never occupied by the President, although it served as the residence of the Governors of the State of New York from 1791 to 1797. For its subsequent history, see Chronology.

This sketch was part of a collection of surveys and other papers belonging formerly to Gerard Bancker and sold at auction in Philadelphia in 1899. It was probably the first rough draught for an almost exactly similar but more finished plan, belonging to the N. Y. Hist. Society and filed with the Swift Report on fortifications erected and projected in 1814. In the latter there are some slight changes in figures, a little more detail, and the buildings are coloured red. There are also preserved with the Swift Report two copies of this original survey, one made by Isaac I. Ludlam, October 4, 1817, and the other copied on September 29, 1817—by whom is not stated. This latter copy has a pencil note in the centre of the south-west bastion reading "S. 19 W 340 feet from Kennedys corner." A similar note in the centre of the Fort reads: "Lat. 40′ 42″ N. as taken by Gov. Burnet 1721." There is also an early copy of the original survey in the office of the successors of Mr. Francis W. Ford, City Surveyor.

The N. Y. Hist. Society owns an important collection of Bancker surveys, belonging originally to the Bancker Collection, sold in Philadelphia May 4, 1899, and acquired by Mr. E. B. Holden, at the dispersal of whose collections they were bought by Mr. Samuel Verplanck Hoffman, who presented them to the Society.—See Holden

Catalogue, items 1750 *et seq.* The author's collection contains a beautiful "Plan of the Ground between Coenties Slip and White-Hall Slip, made by Gerard Bancker City Surveyor November 10th 1772." This plan, which is mounted on silk and bound with silk ribbon, is endorsed, "This Survey adopted by the Common Council Augt V. Cortlandt Clk."

About 1300 other surveys and plans by Bancker, mostly of sites on Manhattan Island and acquired at the Bancker sale, are now in the N. Y. Public Library, filed in nine boxes, indexed alphabetically by street names, etc. A few of the most interesting of these are as follows:

"A Plan of the Ground contiguous to the Poor House, Surveyed the 22d June 1774 by G Bancker CS." (This is important as showing the exact location of the Liberty Pole.)

An interesting survey of the land on Broad and Mill Streets, showing the Jews' Synagogue., dated 1793; and another Survey of the property of the Synagogue, dated Jan. 21, 1808, showing that even at that date Mill Street passage was most irregular.

"A Survey of the Calk or Fresh Water Pond on the Ice by Order and in the presence of a Committee of the Corporation this 25 February 1771" by F. M. [Francis Maerschalck] & G. B. [Gerard Bancker] C. S. Also, a copy of the same by E B. [Evert Bancker] Feby. 17, 1790.

"A plan of the Tan yards," which were in the vicinity of the Fresh Water, "Surveyed and Divided march 23, 1773, by Frances & Andrew Marchalk, Copyed (from one annexed to a deed to Jacobus Quick, by A. Hardenbrook George Shaw Abram Maseir Hugh Gaine) by Everett Bancker Jun Sept 9, 1785."

"A Plan of Mount Pitt in the Out Ward of the City of New York in the County & Province of New York in North America. The Seat of The Honble Thos Jones Esqr, Judge of the Superior Court of Said Province Surveyed August 10, 1782. By E. Bancker, Jun." (This is a quaint and interesting sketch with trees, the mansion, outbuildings, etc.)

"Plan of Dye Street" "Surveyed by Francis Marcallack [*sic*] City Surveyor New York May 12 1748. Copyed from one of Richard Varick, Esqr E. Bancker." (What is apparently the original of this survey is in the Historical Society, the date being exactly one week earlier, i.e. May 5th. This latter is an important map, for it fixes the exact south line of the King's Farm.)

Sketch showing the Sugar House on the south side of Liberty Street adjoining the new Dutch Church. Not dated.

A Study of the School House lot at Greenwich "Surveyed at the Request of the Honble O. D. L. the 8th Octo. 1774. G. B., C. S." (This is part of the Warren property and shows Lady Warren's school-house. "O. D. L." was the Hon. Oliver de Lancey, Lady Warren's brother.) *Cf.* a plan of this property in the Warren papers in the N. Y. Hist. Society.

"Plan of a parcel of Ground together with the Buildings erected thereon lying between Maiden Lane and John Street in the North Ward of the City of New York surveyed at the Request of Mr Anthony Rutgers, this 27th May 1772 by G B C S." This is the present 43–59 Maiden Lane.

A Survey of the Land of Jacob Walton on Hanover Square, January 16, 1772.

A Sketch or Survey of the "Bounds of Mr Barcly & L Lispnard on the Kips & Corporation." No date. (This shows the exact location of the Powder House at the Fresh Water Pond.)

"A plan of a piece of Ground belonging to James De Lancey Esqr near fresh water surveyd feb. 20 1781." (This survey shows the "old House" on the "Kings High Way" or Bowery.)

A Sketch of Chatham Square, undated, showing the "Plow and Harrow." Attached is a memorandum that Mr. Bancker re-surveyed this property for the Commissioners of Forfeiture, Aug. 19, 1784, and made a map of it for which he rendered a bill to the Commissioners of 1 pound 12 s.

A Sketch showing the White Conduit house. No date. (For a picture of the White Conduit House, see *Manual*, 1857, opp. p. 420.)

A Sketch showing the Air Furnace. No date.

"Draught of Andrew Elliots Seat in Bowry Lane," Nov. 1, 1783. (The Survey is bounded on the west by the brook called "Bestavors" Rivulet, i. e. the Minetta Brook. This was "Minto,"

Paymaster-General Elliot's home, afterward that of Robert Richard Randall, and now belonging to the Sailor's Snug Harbor.)

A Complete Survey of Nicholas Bayard's Land, July 1, 1769, covering 175 acres, 1 rood 4 perches.

Draught of the Mansion of Captain de Lancey. Surveyed September 18, 1784. (This shows the precise location of General de Lancey's house.)

A Description of Mortier's Lease (Richmond Hill), for 99 years of part of Old John's land, 26 acres, 3 roods, 36 perches. (A survey of the same property, undated, is in the collection of Francis W. Ford.)

A Sketch of Alderman Nicholas Bayard's lots contiguous to his barn and garden, April 15, 1795. (Shows the barn at the north-east corner of William Street and an un-named street, the present Crosby and Broome Streets, and the fence lines on both sides of Crosby and Grand Streets.)

Survey showing the English School House and the Old Lutheran Church, Broadway and Rector Street, dated N. Y. Apr. 27, 1749. Surveyed and protracted at a scale of 16 feet to an inch, by Brandt Schuyler.

A plan of lots on the north side of Wall Street from Nassau to William Street, showing the location of the City Hall; drawn in 1774.

Plan of the Bear Market, between Division and Vesey Streets, near the North River; undated.

"Copy of a Map (in the Town Clerk's Office) of the White Hall Lots, as they were sold by the Corporation in the year 1732," showing the neighbourhood of "Custom House Street," "Weigh House Street," "Broad Way Street" (Broad Street), and the Great Dock. On the back of this sketch is "A Survey of the White Hall Lots," made August 28th, 1772, in which White Hall Street appears as "Water Street."

"Plan of a parcel of Land situate and lying in the West Ward of the City of N Y purchased from Mr Anthony Rutgers by the Governors of the Hospital to be erected in said City." Dated May 20, 1772. The ground here shown extended from Broadway west to Church Street, and from Anthony Street on the south to the block above (440 feet on Broadway and 327 to 340 feet west to Church Street). Thomas Street now passes through the centre of this property.

The draft of a survey of New York, showing the seven wards. Undated; but depicts the city between 1791 and 1803, as in 1791 the wards were given numerical designations, and in 1803 their number was increased to nine. The "Arch-bridge" on Broadway at Canal Street is here shown by name for the first time on any map or plan known.

"A plan of a Parcel of Ground lying in Montgomerie Ward in the City of New York lately purchased by the People called Quakers for erecting an House of Public Worship, surveyed 12 Octo. 1774." It shows the ground plan of the Quaker Meeting-house on Queen Street, measuring 48 ft. 7 in. by 68 ft. 8 in.

Sketches of the State Prison grounds, dated 1796 and 1797.

"Plan of Mrs. Ann White's estate known by the name of the Vineyard," drawn by James Willson, January 1795, and copied by "E. B." in 1797.

A sketch of lots on the west side of Broadway, between Robinson and Murray Streets, showing the location of "Machanick Hall." Dated 1798.

Sketch of grounds occupied by a "Circus or Theatree," lying below Rector Street between Washington and Greenwich Streets. (See Pl. 56.)

A plan of lots on Great George Street, endorsed "Mr Dugans Ground near the Stone Bridge G. G. Street." The bridge is not shown on the plan; the "Air Furnace" is indicated, and a "White House" is mentioned at the corner of Great George Street and another street (probably Canal).

The Bancker Collection also contains certain miscellaneous manuscripts, including: "A List of the Farms on New York Island West Side of Bowry & Blooming Dale road," and on the "West Side of Bowry lane," undated; a description of the "Harlem Line," surveyed by Bancker and Maerschalk, and dated April 11, 1773; and two lists of proprietors and tenants on Water and Pearl Streets, dated September 3, 1794 and June 14, 1803.

This plan of the Fort is reproduced and described here for the first time.

Plate 46 A-c

[A Plan of the Fort, Bowling Green, etc.]

Wash drawing on paper. 40 x 74 Date depicted: 1788.
Owner: State of New York, Office of State Engineer, Albany.

As stated in a note on the drawing, the red line (surrounding all but the north-west bastion of the Fort) distinguishes the property of the state as defined by an Act passed March 16, 1790 (*Laws of New York*, Chap. 25). The Government House was erected on this property by the state in 1790–1. This same Act defined the boundaries of the land in the Battery to be reserved for the city's uses (see Chronology). This survey was evidently prepared in anticipation of the agreement between the state and the city, as described in this Act.

Notice the contour line showing the original shore of the North River. Notice also the exterior fortifications, which are more accurately shown here than on any other plan. No description has been found of the erection of these fortifications, which do not appear on the Maerschalck Map of 1755 (Pl. 34), but are clearly shown on the Montresor and Ratzen Plans of 1766–7. (Pls. 40 and 42.) We know, however, that an Act was passed on February 19, 1755, to raise £45,000 for putting the Colony "into a proper Posture of Defence; for furthering his Majesty's Designs against his Enemies in North America, and other the Purposes therein mentioned" (see Chronology, February 4, 7, 19, 1755; July 2, September 27, 1756), and it is quite evident that the fortifications here shown were erected in conformity with the provisions of this Act.

It is interesting to compare this plan with a manuscript plan drawn in 1827 by Colonel John Van Dyk, a captain of artillery in the American Army during the Revolutionary War, and showing, from memory, the Fort and Battery as they were just prior to the Revolution. This last plan is reproduced in Mr. Andrews's *The Iconography of the Battery and Castle Garden.*

The plan here reproduced and the 1817 copy of the Bancker sketch referred to under Pl. 46 A-b are the only documents known to the author which definitely establish, by actual figures, the location of the state property and of the Fort in relation to the surrounding street system. The figures on the plan here reproduced connect the south-east corner of the dwelling of Capt. Archibald Kennedy, which stood on the north-west corner of Broadway and Marketfield Street, with the north-west angle of the state reservation, and are given as "South 37° 40′ E. 86 feet."

Reproduced and described here for the first time.

Plate 47–a

S View of the City of New York

Pen and ink drawing on paper. 16 x 4½ Date depicted: September 15–21, 1776.

Owner: Library of Congress, Div. of Maps and Charts.

This view is taken from a point on Long Island in the vicinity of Red Hook, and was probably drawn between September 15 and September 21, 1776.—See Pl. 47–b.

A part of the English fleet is seen in the foreground, anchored off the north end of Governor's Island, which the English captured on September 2d.—"Journal of the Operations of the American Army under General Sir William Howe from the Evacuation of Boston to the end of the Campaign of 1776" (British Museum, Egerton MSS., 2135 f 7).—See also Chronology.

Reproduced here for the first time.

Reference: Phillips's *Maps of America*, 525.

Plate 47–b

E View of the City of New York

Pen and ink drawing on paper. 16 x 4½ Date depicted: September 15–21, 1776.

Owner: Library of Congress, Div. of Maps and Charts.

This view is drawn on the reverse side of the same sheet as the preceding (Pl. 47–a), and is numbered in pencil 569. The building in the foreground is the Rutgers house. *Cf.* Pl. 37.

It will be noticed that a fleet is shown lying off the city, probably the English frigates "Rose," "Roebuck," "Phoenix," "Orpheus," and "Carysfort," etc., which, under Admiral Lord Howe, convoyed transport ships from the Bay into the East River between the 3d and the 14th of September, on which latter date the fleet anchored under the Long Island shore. On the 15th they sailed up the river to Kips Bay within close range of the American guns. The English transports then crossed the river and the troops disembarking forced the Americans to retreat. The City of New York on the afternoon of this day fell into the hands of the British. The view must have been drawn after the 15th, as it shows this fleet lying off shore before the city, and prior to September 21st, as it shows the steeple of Trinity Church, which was destroyed in the fire of that date.

See Chronology, especially extracts from "Journal of the Operations of the American Army under General Sir William Howe," referred to under 47–a.

Reproduced here for the first time.

Reference: Phillips's *Maps of America*, 525.

Plate 48

A view of the City of New York from Long Island

Wash drawing on paper. 17 x 11 Date depicted: 1778 ?.

Owner: Library of Congress, Div. of Maps and Charts.

This view was evidently drawn during the English occupation, as the harbour is full of ships of war, and Trinity Church appears without its steeple, which was destroyed in the fire of September 21, 1776.—See Chronology. On May 18, 1784, the remains of the tower were ordered pulled down (*Trinity Minutes, MS.*), and on June 15 a large part of the church walls, which had become a menace, was demolished.—*Independent Jour., or the Gen'l Adv.*, 1784, June 16. The final demolition of the building did not, however, take place until 1788.—*The Daily Adv.*, 1788, June 18.

The North Dutch Church, built in 1767–9, is distinctly visible in the view, being the second church from the north, with a tower but without a steeple. Just south of this church a careful examination reveals the roof and pediment of St. Paul's Chapel, built in 1764–6. The church farthest to the north, with a tower and steeple, is St. George's Chapel. South of St. Paul's, the Middle Dutch Church, the French Church, Federal Hall, the Wall Street Presbyterian Church, and Trinity are all clearly discernible.

This drawing has the name of Montresor stamped on its back, and although the workmanship seems rather too crude, it may be his. If Montresor was the author, it must have been drawn between the fire of September 21, 1776, and July 20, 1777, when he left with the fleet for the South; or between July 1, 1778, when he returned with the fleet to New York from the Delaware, and October 19 of the same year, when the fleet with Montresor on board sailed for England.—See Chronology for extracts from Montresor's *Journal*.

The Library of Congress, Div. of Maps and Charts, has two other somewhat similar manuscript drawings of about this period: one of "Bunker's hill on N. York island," 20 x 7 inches, with the name of Montresor on the reverse, showing very clearly the water-front and the formation of the Island from a point a short distance below Bunker's Hill to the Belvedere House; the other "A View from Paulushook of Horsimus on the Jersey shore & part of York Island," 17 x 10 inches, also marked with Montresor's name.

The view here reproduced was engraved, in 1912, by Sidney L. Smith for the Society of Iconophiles.

Reference: Phillips's *Maps of America*, 527.

Plate 49

An original sketch of the ruins of Trinity Church N. York—Taken by an English Officer during the Revolution

Water-colour sketch on paper. 10⅝ x 6⅞ Date depicted: *c.* 1780.
Author: Perhaps Lord Rawdon.
Owner: N. Y. Public Library (Emmet Collection, 10961).

This sketch must have been taken between September 21, 1776, when the great fire occurred in which Trinity Church was destroyed, and 1784, when the ruins of the tower were torn down (*Trinity Minutes, MS.*, May 18, 1784; see also description, Pl. 48). In all probability, as it was drawn by an English officer, it was made before the evacuation in 1783.

The cupola shown on the right is evidently that of the City Hall on Wall Street.

The original inscription on the back of this sketch, written in a contemporary hand, has faded almost beyond recognition. It has been rewritten on the back as well as added under the view by Dr. Emmet.

The Emmet Collection contains three other interesting wash drawings (Nos. 2583, 2584, and 7815), purchased at the sale of the effects of the Marquis of Hastings, a grandson of Lord Rawdon, who is supposed to have been their author. The technique and colouring are very similar to those of the view here reproduced, which is doubtless by the same hand. Lord Rawdon was, at this time, an officer on the staff of Lord Cornwallis. One of these sketches represents the landing of the British forces in the Jerseys and shows the Palisades with the soldiers making the ascent from boats; of the other two, one was drawn just previous to the landing of the English Army at Gravesend on Long Island, and the other just after the Battle of Long Island, as is stated in faded manuscript on each. The first depicts a night scene with indistinct shore-line; the second shows five of the British ships-of-war, Governor's Island, and a part of the Long Island shore.

Mr. Percy R. Pyne, II, owns a charming early lithograph of the ruined church, very similar in composition to the drawing here reproduced, but taken from the north-west instead of from the south-west. It shows one corner of the tower still standing, probably the portion which was ordered demolished on May 18, 1784.—See Pl. 48. This lithograph was originally in the collections of the late William F. Havemeyer and is the only impression known. It measures 12 x 10⅜ inches, including border and title and has the following inscription: "Ruins of Trinity Church./As seen after the memorable Conflagration of Septr 21st 1776, by which Four hundred and ninety three buildings comprising about a sixth part of the City of New York was laid in ashes.—From a sketch taken on the Spot by the late Thomas Barrow, Esq^{e} one of the Vestry of said Church. [l. l.] On Stone by J. Evers. [l. r.] Litho. & Published by J. Childs, N. Y."

The lithograph was probably made from an original water-colour drawing presented to the Corporation of Trinity Church by James Barrow in 1841. This drawing now hangs in the Corporation Room at 187 Fulton Street. The view is reproduced in Valentine's *Manual*, 1861, p. 694.

Plate 50

[British Headquarters MS. Map of New York and Environs]

Original drawing on paper. 120 x 48 Date depicted: 1782?.
Owner: The War Office, London.

The original of this fine map of Manhattan Island, made during the English occupation, is in so bad a state of repair that the authorities at the War Office recommended that the reproduction be made from the facsimile lithograph published in 1900 by Mr. B. F. Stevens of London. This facsimile is in twenty-four sheets, and in making the reproduction it was thought best to obliterate the joints and to rearrange somewhat the position of the descriptive matter. The reference numbers have been enlarged so as to be more distinctly discernible.

This map is particularly interesting as showing all of the fortifications on the Island and upon the adjoining mainland, as well as the road systems and settlements. It is a veritable topographical encyclopedia of the Island during the Revolutionary Period.

The archives of the War Office contain two other similar maps, one of them evidently a comparatively late copy, and the other possibly an earlier original than the one from which the map reproduced by Mr. Stevens was copied.

It is interesting to compare the map here shown with the Commissioners Map (Pl. 79) and the Map of the Farms (Pl. 86). *Cf.* also Landmark Map, Vol. II, Appendix.

In this same year (1782), John Hills completed the survey of a map of the lower part of Manhattan Island, which was drawn up in 1785. The original of this interesting map was presented to the Corporation of the City by John Lozier, and was deposited for safe-keeping in the N. Y. Hist. Society. It is in such bad condition and is so water-stained that it was found impossible to reproduce it. Fortunately, however, it is preserved by its reproductions in Valentine's *Manual* for 1848 (opp. p. 291) and 1857 (Frontispiece). A finely engraved reduction of this map, 12¾ x 11⅞, was issued by Stiles, Sherman, & Smith (Emmet Collection, 10990).

Some interesting notes, hitherto unpublished, regarding the "State of the Fortifications at New York" in 1771 and 1777, copied from the British Admiralty Records, will be found in the Chronology.

Plate 51

[Trumbull's Washington]

Oil painting on canvas. 72 x 108 Date depicted: November 25, 1783.
Date painted: 1790.

Artist: John Trumbull.

Owner: New York City. The portrait hangs at the west end of the Governors' Room in the City Hall. It was originally in Federal Hall, where it was seen, in 1793, by John Drayton, and described in his *Letters*, published in 1794.

Trumbull, in his *Autobiography*, p. 164, says that in July, 1790, he returned to New York, where he was requested "to paint for the corporation a full length portrait of the President." He "represented him in full uniform, standing by a white horse, leaning his arm upon the saddle; in the background, a view of Broadway in ruins, as it then was [1783], the old fort at the termination; British ships and boats leaving the shore, with the last of the officers and troops of the evacuating army, and Staten Island in the distance." According to the *Minutes of the Common Council* (*MS.*), X: 13, Trumbull received from the City for this painting the sum of £186 13s. 4d.

The signature and date, which are not discernible in the reproduction, are in the left lower corner.

The original sketch (20 x 30 inches), by Trumbull, from which the portrait was made, was owned in 1892, by Edmund Law Rogers of Baltimore, Md. This sketch is referred to in the will of Martha Washington (owned by J. Pierpont Morgan): "Item I give and bequeath to my granddaughter, Elizabeth Parke Law the dressing-table and glass that stands in the chamber called the yellow room, and General Washington's picture painted by Trumbull."—*Hist. of the Centennial Celebration of the Inauguration of George Washington* (etc.), 545.

Washington's *Diary* contains several references to this sketch; for example,

> Tuesday, July 8th, 1790, sat from 9 o'clock till after ten for Mr. Jno. Trumbull, who was drawing a portrait of me at full length which he intended to present to Mrs. Washington.
>
> Monday 12th Exercised on horseback between five and six in the morning. Sat for Mr. Trumbull from nine till half after ten.

Engraved in mezzotint, 1899, by S. Arlent Edwards and copyrighted by Jos. F. Sabin.

HISTORICAL SUMMARY

CHAPTER IV

PERIOD OF ADJUSTMENT AND RECONSTRUCTION

NEW YORK AS THE STATE AND FEDERAL CAPITAL

1783–1811

CHAPTER IV

PERIOD OF ADJUSTMENT AND RECONSTRUCTION
NEW YORK AS THE STATE AND FEDERAL CAPITAL
1783–1811

NOT all of the inhabitants of New York City remained to welcome General Washington. Twelve thousand Tories, as we have seen, left with the British, choosing rather to go into a voluntary exile than remain to face the punishment which they had good reason to expect at the hands of the victorious patriots. Of these, some removed to Canada, where they became the nucleus of another English colony, and some returned to England. At the same time, those inhabitants who had been forced to leave the city when it surrendered to the British, came back; and the pastors of the non-conformist churches with their congregations, who had sought refuge in other places, returned to gather together the property which they had been obliged to leave at the time of their flight. In March, 1784, Cornelius Bradford, proprietor of the Merchants' Coffee House, opened a registry of returning citizens, "where any gentleman now resident in the City"—so his advertisement stated—"may insert their names and place of residence." Its purpose was to enable anyone who desired to locate missing relatives and friends to consult a convenient list, alphabetically arranged for this purpose.

There were many questions to be settled. Claims against the British for property which they had used during the war, and for the slaves that they had carried away with them at its close, were met by counter-claims against the patriots for debts still owing to the Tories. Questions over land titles had been complicated to a high degree by the sudden changes during the years of war. The estates left by the fleeing Tories were not inconsiderable, for many of the large land-owning families had supported the British cause. These were taken in charge by commissioners of forfeiture appointed for the purpose. A law passed by the legislature of New York on May 19, 1784, provided for the speedy sale of confiscated and forfeited estates, and under it many sales were effected. The large city estate of James De Lancey, lying in the district bounded by the Bowery, Rivington Street, Division Street, and the East River, was sold, and De Lancey himself was attainted. Family quarrels, which sometimes became so important that they acquired considerable political significance, as in the case of the Livingstons and the De Lanceys, had existed for many years; but the bitterness with which they raged was largely increased by disputes over the ownership of property resulting from the general confiscation at the end of the war.

The returning patriots found the city in a distressing condition. Houses had been injured; churches used as riding halls, hospitals, barracks, and prisons; public buildings, as military headquarters or as storehouses for ordnance and other supplies. Fences had been torn down, and trees cut for firewood. Intrenchments and breastworks had been made along both river shores; forts crowned nearly every considerable eminence on Manhattan Island, and barricades had been made at the intersections of important streets. In addition to these natural consequences of war, the city had suffered peculiarly from the terrible conflagrations in 1776 and 1778, which had laid waste large sections. We do not know the number of New York's inhabitants at the time of the return of the patriots, but three years later their estimated number was 23,614, and the number of houses in the city was 3,340.

The changes which occurred in New York at the close of the war were political as well as social and economic. All property in the city which had formerly belonged to the English government, as represented in the person of the royal governor, now became the property of the state of New York. This included Fort George and all other fortifications in the city. Before the Revolution the city had been governed by a charter granted by the king. Under this charter the mayor, sheriff, and coroner had been appointed annually by the royal governor of the province; and the aldermen, assistants, assessors, collectors, and constables, elected each year by the freemen in their respective wards. During the British occupation, the city had been governed by military law, administered by a military governor, who was directly responsible to the commander of the British forces. At the end of the war the city found itself governed under the old charter, in which, however, certain important changes had been made. The executive officers, such as the mayor and the sheriff, were still appointed, but by the governor and the council of appointment of the state of New York, instead of by the royal governor. Aldermen, assistants, and constables were elected by the freemen of the city, as formerly had been the custom. This did not indicate, however, that there was manhood suffrage in the election of these officers, for the right to be a freeman was restricted to men who could satisfy certain fixed property qualifications. This system concentrated the patronage of the city in the hands of the governor and the council of appointment of the state, instead of giving it to local authorities, as is done at present. In some respects the city had greater liberties then than now. The aldermen formed a real local legislature and the city treasurer was accustomed to issue paper money on the credit of the municipality. The city seal was altered in 1784, so as to show the political change which had taken place, the royal crown being removed and an eagle rising from a semi-globe substituted in its stead. The first mayor after the Revolution was James Duane, who was appointed in 1784, during the administration of Governor George Clinton.

The government of the United States, of the state, and of the city, was centred in New York in 1785. Congress, at Trenton, in December, 1784, having resolved to meet in New York on "the 11th of Jan'y next" (an honour for which several cities had competed), the common council offered for the use of Congress such parts of the City Hall and other public buildings as might be necessary, and Congress accepted all the apartments in the City Hall except the court and jury rooms. The president of Congress (Richard Henry Lee) and other members "made their entrance into this city, under a discharge of cannon," on January 8th; they were greeted by Governor Clinton and others at Whitehall, and conducted to the governor's house in Queen Street, which had been assigned to him by the commissioners of forfeiture. On the appointed day the sessions began, though a quorum was not present for several days. One of the first transactions of Congress in New York was to take a two years' lease of Fraunces Tavern. The regular sessions were held in the City Hall, in spite of the noise of passing carriages which compelled the common council to order that chains be drawn across the streets during business hours.

The legislature was to meet in New York on January 6, 1784, according to a proclamation of the governor issued on December 9, 1783, but a quorum could not be gathered until January 21st. With the exception of five sessions, their meetings were continued here until November, 1796, after which they were held in Albany. The exceptional years were 1788, when the sessions were held at Poughkeepsie and Albany; 1789, at Albany; 1794, at Albany; and 1795, at Poughkeepsie. The place of meeting in New York was the Exchange on Broad Street.

An important change in the status of religious organisations followed the close of the Revolution. Previously only the two churches which in turn had been the state church, had been incorporated. These were the Dutch Reformed Church and the Church of England. The non-conformist churches had suffered severely because of their inability to hold property, and in one case, that of the Presbyterian Church, had deeded their property to the authorities of the Church of Scotland, rather than subject it to the uncertainties involved in granting it to individual members or to trustees of the church. On April 6, 1784, the legislature of the state passed an act allowing all religious bodies to be incorporated. This placed all churches upon an equal footing. The laws which made the exercise of the Roman Catholic forms of worship illegal in Great Britain were equally binding upon New York until the close of the Revolution, and up to this time there were no Roman Catholic churches in the city. For a time the Catholics worshipped in a chapel fitted up in the French embassy, and in a building owned by Trinity Church in Vauxhall Garden, near the North River, between Warren and Chambers Streets; but on October 5, 1785, the corner-stone of St. Peter's Church, the first Roman Catholic church in New York City, was laid on a site purchased from Trinity Church, at the south-east corner of Church and Barclay Streets. The first bishop of the Protestant Episcopal Church in America was Samuel Seabury of Connecticut, who was consecrated by three Scottish bishops at Aberdeen on November 14, 1784. On June 22d, of the following year, the first convention of this church in the state of New York was held in New York City. As soon as certain difficulties concerning the consecration of American bishops by bishops of the Church of England were settled, Dr. White of Pennsylvania and Dr. Provoost, rector of Trinity Church, New York, were consecrated in Lambeth Chapel, London, on February 4th, and arrived in this city on Easter Day, 1787. The Rt. Rev. Samuel Provoost, D.D., thus became the first bishop of New York, just ninety years after Trinity Parish was chartered by Governor Fletcher; and the Protestant Episcopal Church in New York was duly organised as a self-perpetuating branch of the Church in the United States.

At first the citizens of New York were appalled by the extent of the destruction that had come upon their city, but gradually they began to take heart and commenced extensive repairs. In spite of the devastation of the city, and the want and distress of the inhabitants, there was gratitude to Providence (expressed by Governor Clinton in his message to the legislature on January 21, 1784) that the war was over, and that "our ports so long withheld from us" were now "open to all the world." A month later, there sailed from this harbour the "Empress of China," the first American vessel to venture into Asiatic waters, carrying the American flag which had been adopted in 1777. The first important step taken by the city to repair the damages wrought by the war, was when it exercised the power granted to it by the legislature on May 4, 1784, of appointing five commissioners to lay out streets in the section that had been burned over in 1776. The alterations and development carried out at this time in the streets west of Broadway, were largely in accord with the recommendations of Anthony Van Dam, a public-spirited citizen of New York who was a port warden before the Revolution and was now sojourning in Bermuda.[1]

The various church organisations, also, immediately turned their attention to the restoration of their damaged church edifices. Of the Dutch Reformed churches, the North Church had been used as a prison and hospital, and the Middle Church, first as a prison, and later as a riding academy. The entire interior of the latter was destroyed, leaving only the bare walls and the roof. The church in Garden Street, although it had been used by the British temporarily as a military hospital, had escaped without serious injuries; this church was restored to its owners before the evacuation, and services were resumed. Soon after the close

[1] See Chronology, March 3, 1784.

of the war, the North Church was restored and again opened for use, and the Middle Church was re-dedicated in 1790. The Presbyterian and the Huguenot churches had suffered similarly. The Brick Church was repaired and reopened in 1784, and the Wall Street Church, which had been used as barracks and had suffered more severely, was later restored. Until these repairs could be made, Trinity Church gave the Presbyterians the use of their chapels, St. George's and St. Paul's. Trinity Church itself had been burned in 1776, so that only the charred walls remained. Part of these walls fell in 1784. During 1788, the rest were taken down, and on August 21st the corner-stone of a new building was laid; the edifice itself was dedicated on March 25, 1790. The subject of completing the tower of St. Paul's Chapel was considered in 1784-5, as was that of supplying it with a clock and bell, in 1790; but the steeple was not built until 1794, and the clock and bell were not procured from London until 1799. The monument to General Montgomery was placed by the city on the Broadway front of the Chapel in 1787.

The legislature, on May 1, 1784, incorporated the "Regents of the University of the State of New York" in place of the "Governors of the College of the Province of New York," which had been established by letters patent under the great seal of the province on October 31, 1754, one provision of the act of 1784 being "That the College within the City of New York, heretofore called King's College, be forever hereafter called and known by the name of Columbia College."

In 1784 the Bank of New York, the first banking institution in the city, was organised. Alexander MacDougall was its first president and Alexander Hamilton served on its first board of directors. It was chartered in 1791. In 1785, the Commons or Fields were enclosed and established as the Park. A curious bit of local history is found in a petition of this year, made to the common council by Isaac Sears, who succeeded in proving that he had a good title to the ground "bounded westerly in front by the Broad Way, southerly by the Green commonly called the fields, easterly by the Ground belonging to this Corporation & occupied by the Poor House, and northerly by other ground of the said Corporation." It was thereupon ordered that the mayor execute a city bond to cover the price of £80 which Sears asked for this property. Miss Booth, in her *History of the City of New York* (1860), p. 581, states that payment was never made, and that therefore, "the grounds to the northwest of the City Hall still belong to the heirs of the New York Liberty Boys."[1]

Bowling Green at this time presented a dilapidated appearance, and hogs roamed over it. Chancellor Livingston, in 1786, offered to plant shrubbery there and keep the place in repair, if the common council would plant trees around it, replace the scattered fragments of the iron fence, restore a missing lamp, and take down the pedestal which had remained ever since the ardent soldiers of Washington secretly pulled down the leaden statue of King George on July 10, 1776. The common council accepted Livingston's offer, with the understanding that he would have it "well laid down as a Green." Another place of picturesque interest at this time was "Canvas Town," so called because of the temporary construction of the houses, built after the great fire of 1776 between Broad Street and the East River. It figured in the news of the day, from 1785 to 1797, as the abode of dissolute characters and the scene of frequent disorder and even crime.

The first printed city directory made its appearance in 1786. Not more than ten or twelve copies are now known; indeed, it was spoken of as "a rarity" in 1846, by Watson, who in his *Annals* thus commented upon its contents: "The very names of that day are curious; so few then who were foreigners. Such was the novelty or uselessness of a directory then, when every man knew his neighbour, that no other was attempted till the year 1793." This is, of course, an error, as directories were issued in 1788,[2] 1789, 1790, 1791, and 1792.

The first hackney-coach was introduced in 1786 by James Hearn, whose stand was at the coffee-house of Cornelius Bradford at Old Slip. The coffee-house served the purpose of an exchange, the leading newspapers of the United States, London, and Paris being on file there, as well as a registry of vessels which entered or left the port. It was in 1786 that the "Society of Tammany or Columbian Order in the City of New York" was established. As early as January 25th of that year, a toast was offered at a dinner of the Marine Society, held at the Merchants' Coffee House, to "St. Tammany and the New Constellation." The society held its first anniversary on May 1, 1787. The chief purpose of

[1] The results of a careful examination of the records, very kindly undertaken for the author by the Comptroller's office, will be found in the Chronology, under 1789, June 10, on which day the common council ordered the city treasurer to "pay off the Bond from this Corporation to Isaac Sears, deceased [for his interest], assigned to Thomas Ten Eyck, as the state of the Revenue Fund shall permit."—*M. C. C. (MS.)*, IX : 224. A further search, to April, 1803, has not disclosed any warrant issued for the cancellation of this bond.

[2] The only known copy of the 1788 directory is in the N. Y. Hist. Society. It is possible that a directory was issued also in 1787, although no copy for this year is known.

its organisers was probably to offset the aristocratic and monarchical tendencies of the Society of the Cincinnati, by an organisation which should foster democratic and republican institutions. At first it served a social and philanthropic purpose only; but in later years, under the skilful manipulation of Aaron Burr, it became the powerful political factor which it still remains. This was not the first Tammany organisation in the United States, however. One having the name "Sons of King Tammany" was established in Philadelphia in May, 1772, which had various titles and branches in later years, and was the parent stem from which other similar societies sprang. The "Saint Tammany" idea was adopted also in Virginia and New Jersey before it appeared in New York.

In 1787, the first fire insurance company was organised—the Mutual Assurance Company—after unsuccessful attempts to establish one in previous years; in 1845, it became the Knickerbocker Fire Insurance Company. King's College, whose building had been used as a military hospital during the war, resumed its exercises in 1784, and received a revised charter in 1787 as Columbia College. All schools had suffered serious disorganisation by the Revolution. It was in this year, also, that a structure of considerable interest was built on Broadway, in connection with its extension northward, called Great George Street. This was the stone bridge over the drain at Canal Street, shown on Pl. 83–b. Instead of being a military work designed by the British during their occupation of the city, as Valentine and other writers have supposed,[1] this bridge was built in 1787 under the direction of Nicholas Bayard, alderman of the ward in which it was situated, as appears by payments made that year by the common council for stone and lime used in its construction.

In 1788 the so-called Doctors' Riot interrupted the quiet flow of life. The hospital, which had been commenced before the war, was turned into a barrack in 1776. It remained untenanted after the evacuation, except by a few doctors who used it for occasional lectures and for dissecting. Some boys, prowling about the grounds on Sunday, April 13th, were horrified at seeing a student at work dissecting a human body. They hurried to inform their fathers, who soon raised a mob and attacked the place. The doctors had to flee for their lives. Finally, the mayor quelled the riot by ordering the militia to fire into the crowd. Five persons were killed and many wounded.

The most important and interesting event in national politics during

[1] *Man. C. C.*, 1865, p. 604.

these years was the struggle over the formation and adoption of the Federal Constitution. The Articles of Confederation[1] under which the states were being governed were found to be entirely inadequate to the exigencies of the situation, and thoughtful men viewed with alarm the state of anarchy into which the country was rapidly drifting. As a result, a convention of the states met in Philadelphia and drew up a constitution, which Congress transmitted to the several states, asking that it be acted upon by conventions of delegates chosen by the people of each state. The New York Convention was organised at Poughkeepsie, June 17, 1788, and chose George Clinton, governor of the state, to be its president. Governor Clinton led the party opposed to the adoption of the Constitution. This party contained many individuals who had been leaders in the War for Independence. They were opposed to the Constitution because they did not wish the states to give so much power to the central government, as they believed it would subvert the rights of the people. The party in favour of adoption, in New York, was led by Alexander Hamilton; John Jay, also, was a staunch supporter of the measure. To bring their opinions before the people of the state and to convince them of the need for a strong central government, as well as of the excellence of the proposed constitution, the leaders of this party, in collaboration with James Madison, prepared a series of essays on the nature of the Constitution, entitled *The Federalist*, the first number of which appeared in *The Independent Journal* of New York on October 27, 1787. This publication exerted at the time great influence on the public mind, and still remains the ablest exposition of our national instrument of government.

When the debates were at their height, there was held in New York, on July 23, 1788, a remarkable civic parade under the direction of Major L'Enfant, "in honor of the Constitution of the United States." As a great popular demonstration it ranks with the foremost in the annals of the city, and was the forerunner of the torchlight processions and fireworks which are to-day prominent features of presidential and other political campaigns in all American cities. Although the convention's chief objection to the proposed instrument of government was that it contained no bill of rights to safeguard the liberties of the people, popular feeling in New York showed itself in this parade strongly in favour of

[1] The Articles of Confederation, adopted during the war, established a loose union of the states, and vested the government in a congress composed of delegates from the several states. The states retained a large amount of power under this system, and the central government was almost impotent.

the Federalists. All classes, including members of Congress and notable foreigners, took part. Among the marshals and assistants were Colonel William S. Livingston, Captain Stagg, Major Bleecker, John R. Livingston, Daniel Le Roy, Edward Livingston, and Staats Morris. Members of the mechanical trades and of learned societies, in distinctive costumes, carrying various symbols of their occupations, as well as banners and mottoes, and hauling emblematic floats, made up the procession. The principal feature was the federal ship "Hamilton," which had been "launched" on July 18th. This was a miniature frigate of thirty-two guns, measuring twenty-seven feet keel and ten beam, the gift of the ship carpenters. It was complete in every particular, and was manned by officers and men under the command of Commodore James Nicholson. Drawn through the streets by ten horses, it fired salutes of ten and thirteen guns at Bayard's Hill and at the fort, and was finally deposited at the Bowling Green, where it remained until the following year.

The convention having agreed that a bill of rights should be added later, the Constitution was at last adopted on July 26th. New York was thus the eleventh state to ratify the Constitution. When this news was received on the evening of the twenty-sixth, "the bells of the city were immediately set a ringing and from the Fort and the Federal ship 'Hamilton' were fired several salutes. The merchants at the Coffee House testified their joy by repeated huzzas; and a large body of citizens, headed by a number of the first characters, went to the houses of the Members of Congress, and gave three cheers, as a testimony of their approbation of the glorious event brought about by their united, unremitted, and toilsome exertions."[1]

Congress resolved, on September 13, 1788, "that the first Wednesday in January next be the day for appointing electors in the several states which, before the said day, shall have ratified the said Constitution; that the first Wednesday in February next be the day for the electors to assemble in their respective States and vote for a president; and that the first Wednesday in March next be the time, and the present seat of Congress the place, for commencing the proceedings under the said Constitution." Immediately the common council of New York undertook to make improvements in the City Hall and the Exchange, the former to be used by Congress and the latter by the courts and common council. The extensive alterations and repairs begun on October 6, 1788, at the

[1] New York letter in *The Pennsylvania Packet*, July 30, 1788.

City Hall were after designs by Major L'Enfant, and were paid for by taxation, loans, and lotteries. Enlarged, remodelled, and newly decorated, the building was thereafter popularly known as Federal Hall. The first Congress under the Constitution met there on March 4, 1789, before the improvements were completed.[1] On the previous evening, as the sun was setting, the guns of the Battery were fired to bid farewell to the old confederation; and at daybreak, at noon, and at six o'clock on the fourth of March, guns were fired and the bells of the city were rung to celebrate the commencement of the new era. A quorum not being present, owing to the exigencies of travel, and in spite of repeated appeals to absent members to hasten, business could not proceed until April 6th. On that day, these electors chose Washington president by a unanimous vote of sixty-nine; and John Adams vice-president, he receiving thirty-four votes, while his nearest competitor, John Jay, received but nine votes.

Accompanied by a committee of senators and representatives, Washington arrived at New York on April 23d, having been conveyed from Elizabethtown in a barge made for the occasion and manned by thirteen "pilots" in white uniforms. High government officials followed in other boats. Salutes were fired from ships at anchor and from the Battery. It was one of the most animated and festive spectacles ever seen in the harbour. On landing at Murray's Wharf at the foot of Wall Street, Washington was greeted by Governor Clinton and a great concourse of civil and military dignitaries, and was escorted to the Walter Franklin house, on the corner of Cherry Street and Franklin Square, which had been prepared for his reception.

The inauguration of Washington as President of the United States occurred on April 30, 1789, on the balcony of Federal Hall,[2] the oath of office being administered by the Hon. Robert R. Livingston, chancellor of the state of New York. "I do solemnly swear," Washington replied to Livingston, "that I will faithfully execute the office of President of the United States, and will, to the best of my ability, preserve,

[1] See the Chronology for a letter written by Alexander Hamilton to James Duane, and reproduced here for the first time, dated simply "Tuesday" but evidently written on March 3, 1789, urging the mayor to convene the common council on that day, "to pass an act for appropriating the City Hall to the use of Congress," to publish such act in the papers, etc. Such action was taken, and the following notice appeared in *The Daily Advertiser* of March 4th, and in the *New York Journal, and Weekly Register* of March 5th: "The Corporation of this city having appropriated the City Hall for the accommodation of the Congress of the United States, and the same having been elegantly improved and repaired for that purpose, the Common Council have resolved that the Recorder communicate the same to the Congress of the United States accordingly." Hamilton's finesse, attention to detail, and fine sense of the proprieties were never more timely and appropriate.

[2] See Chronology for full account of the ceremony; see also Frontispiece, Vol. II.

protect, and defend the Constitution of the United States." He bowed his head and kissed the Bible,[1] and, in deepest reverence, added, "So help me God." The chancellor thereupon exclaimed, "Long live George Washington, President of the United States!" The discharge of thirteen cannon, and the shouts of the immense crowds of people in Wall and Broad Streets, instantly echoed the proclamation. After the ceremony Washington returned to the senate chamber and delivered a short inaugural address. Then, with the vice-president and other principal officers of the government, he repaired on foot to St. Paul's Chapel, where prayers were read by Bishop Provoost, the chaplain of the senate. It was a day of general rejoicing, continued into the evening by illuminations and fireworks.

During his short residence in New York, Washington gave his counsel and help in shaping the policies and practices of the new republic. The debates in Congress regarding the location of the permanent seat of national government were continued here from previous sessions. Local rivalries provoked long and acrimonious discussion until the Residence Act was finally passed, on July 16, 1790, establishing the territory on the Potomac, afterwards named the District of Columbia, which was considered conveniently central for all sections of the country; and providing for the development by commissioners, under the personal direction of Washington (who later called L'Enfant to his assistance), of a model city and of government buildings, which were to be ready before the first Monday in December, 1800. Until that time, the sessions of Congress were to be held in Philadelphia, beginning with the next session; Congress met for the first time in Washington on November 17, 1800.

Addresses of welcome were presented to Washington soon after his arrival, by the Chamber of Commerce, the mayor and common council of the city, and the legislature. On May 7th, a few days after the inauguration, the Dancing Assembly gave "an Elegant Ball and Entertainment" in his honour, at Burns's Coffee House. The brief newspaper report of the event stated that

> His Excellency the Vice-President, most of the Members of both Houses of Congress, the Governor of New York, the Chancellor, and Chief Justice of the State, Hon. John Jay, and the Hon. Gen. Knox, the Commissioners of the

[1] This Bible, which was borrowed for the occasion from St. John's Masonic Lodge, is still preserved in the headquarters of the order in New York.

> Treasury, His Worship the Mayor of the city, the late President of Congress, the governor of the Western Territory, the Baron Steuben, the Count de Monstier, Ambassador of his Most Christian Majesty, and many other foreigners of distinction were present. A numerous and brilliant collection of ladies graced the rooms with their appearance. The whole number of persons was about three hundred. The company retired about two o'clock, after having spent a most agreeable evening. Joy, satisfaction and vivacity were expressive in every Countenance—and every pleasure seemed to be heightened by the presence of a Washington.

He attended the theatre in John Street in May, in company with the vice-president, the governor, members of Congress, and many of the principal citizens of New York, the President's box "being elegantly fitted up and distinguished by the arms of the United States." The play was "The School for Scandal," and was followed by a comic opera. Mrs. Washington arrived at New York on May 27th with Mrs. Robert Morris, who accompanied her from Philadelphia; she was met at Elizabethtown by the President, Mr. Morris, and others, and was rowed to the city on the "Federal barge." A salute was fired from the Battery, and when the boat arrived at Peck's Slip, the presidential party was conducted through the welcoming crowds by the City Troop of Light Horse. The President and Mrs. Washington held a levee in the Franklin Square mansion on May 29th. They attended the theatre on June 5th, when, as on the former occasion of the President's visit, several other prominent men and women "honored the Theatre by their presence." Washington went to the theatre again on November 24th, when an after-piece by William Dunlap, entitled "Darby's Return," was presented. Dunlap wrote later regarding the event that Washington "indulged in that which was with him extremely rare, a hearty laugh." Trumbull, the painter, arrived from Paris in November, and early in 1790 began to paint the portraits of as many signers of the Declaration of Independence as were then in New York for the second session of Congress. Washington sat frequently for his portrait to both Trumbull and Savage. The portraits of Washington and Clinton were painted by Trumbull in a room adjoining the senate chamber in the Federal Hall. Both portraits occupy places of honour in the present City Hall.

The sports and pastimes of the period, commencing with the inauguration year, are of more than passing interest. A yacht race, held off Sandy Hook on August 13, 1789, was the forerunner of our international cup-races of to-day. This race was between the pilot-boat "York" of New York, and the Virginia-built schooner "Union" of Curaçao. Fourteen leagues (forty-two nautical miles) were run in a light breeze in five hours, the "York" winning. In September, there was horse-racing in Greenwich Lane. Fox-hunting with "March's hounds" between the five-mile stone and Kingsbridge (King's Bridge, or Kings Bridge), around Fort Washington, or at "Kissing Bridge" near the six-mile stone, alternating with runs near Gravesend or Jamaica on Long Island, was a favourite pastime of the spring or autumn.

The organisation of the United States courts was effected while New York was the federal capital, the first term of the Supreme Court being held in the Exchange, at the foot of Broad Street, commencing February 1, 1790. This odd-looking but commodious structure, standing upon arches and surmounted by a cupola with a bell, was built by the city in 1752. It had been used for various purposes—for the sale of merchandise and of land at "public vendue"; for meetings of organisations (the Chamber of Commerce, Sons of Liberty, Marine Society, and others); for public lectures, concerts, and dinners; for private schools of dancing, fencing, military science, and mathematics; and, as occasion required, for meetings of the common council and of the legislature. The opening of the United States Circuit Court for this district occurred in the consistory room opposite the Dutch church in Garden Street, on the day after the Supreme Court was opened in the Exchange.

Washington found time for occasional diversions from his absorbing official duties. His favourite walk was "round the battery," and he took long drives in the family coach with Mrs. Washington and the two Custis children, "the fourteen miles round" being covered between breakfast and dinner-time. This tour led over the Bloomingdale Road to Harlem Heights, thence by a cross-road to Kingsbridge, returning along the Boston Post Road. On one of his rides, he called on Baron de Polnitz to see the operation of Winlaw's threshing-machine. At another time, having formed a party consisting of the vice-president and Mrs. Adams, their son and a Mrs. Smith, the secretaries of state, the treasury, and war, "and the ladies of the two latter," all the gentlemen of his own family, Mrs. Lear, and the two children, he visited "the old position of Fort Washington." These simple diversions were varied in June, 1790, by a fishing trip at Sandy Hook, that he might have the benefit of the sea air, which his health required. He had changed his place of residence in February, on his fifty-eighth birthday, to the house of Alexander Macomb, Nos. 39-41 Broadway, which had been lately improved and occupied by the Minister of France. Here President and Mrs. Washington gave receptions and dinners, with the graciousness of personal cordiality and the simple dignity that were best suited to a state function on the part of the chief magistrate of a republic. With the close of the second session of Congress, on August 12th, and the departure of the President on August 30, 1790, New York ceased to be the federal capital, the government being then transferred to Philadelphia, where the sessions of Congress began on December 6, 1790, and continued until 1800.

In 1790, the first federal census showed that the population of New York was 33,131. The city was "every day growing into symmetry, elegance and beauty."[1] Improvements at the Battery were the most conspicuous, and these progressed for several years. The shore from Greenwich Street toward Whitehall was filled in at this time and a bulkhead or wharf was built "from the corner of Kennedy's wharf into the northwest bastion of the Battery." Early in 1790, the legislature had authorised the demolition of Fort George, which, with the adjacent battery, was now useless for purposes of defence. At the same time, commissioners were appointed to erect a building on a part of this land "for the use of the government of this State, and to be applied to the temporary use and accommodation of the President of the United States of America, during such times as the Congress of the United States shall hold their sessions in the City of New York." The rest of the state lands at the Battery was given to the city to be used for public buildings and works of defence. On removing the earth where the church in the fort had stood, before it was burned in 1741, three vaults were uncovered, one of which contained the remains of Lady Hunter, who died in 1716, and the other held two leaden coffins, one bearing the arms of Lord Bellomont. The former was removed to Trinity Churchyard, and the latter two to St. Paul's. There was also found on the same historic ground a square stone bearing in Dutch an inscription, of which the English translation reads: "1642, Willem Kieft, being Director-General, the congregation caused this church to be built." The stone was removed to the belfry of the Garden Street Church, and was destroyed in the fire of 1835.

[1] *The Daily Advertiser*, Nov. 23, 1790.

The corner-stone of the Government House, on the site of the fort, was laid on May 21, 1790, while the federal government was still in New York. Naturally, disappointment and regret were widely felt and expressed when Congress decided against New York as the permanent national capital. Although not destined to become the residence of the president, the Government House, as was originally intended, was occupied by governors of the state, both Clinton and Jay, in turn, making it their home, the building containing not only their residential apartments but also the executive offices. The state capital having been transferred to Albany in 1797, Governor Jay removed from the Government House about May 1, 1798; and the state then leased the building to one Avery, for a family hotel. With a superb view of the harbour and opposite shores, and facing the Bowling Green, it was aptly named the "Elysian Boarding House." On May 1st of the following year, it was temporarily leased to the federal government and converted for use as the Custom House. The city sought to purchase the property in 1806; failing at first in this, it secured a lease in 1809 for a term of years, and finally, in 1812, acquired full title.

While these improvements at the Battery were in progress in 1791, Governors Island was being transformed from a neglected spot into an attractive and convenient resort for a summer day's outing. Groves, gardens, and walks were laid out on its seventy-five acres, thousands of trees were planted, and a house and pavilion erected. A prospectus published in the newspapers stated: "The City of New York (the Naples of America) exhibits from this place an elegant appearance, which will daily become more so, as the improvements are completed in the neighbourhood of the old battery, and new buildings erected in the room of the stables, barracks, and other petty edifices, which ought always to be in the background or less noticed parts of a large city."

The John Street Theatre, which stood on the north side of John Street between Broadway and Nassau Street, and which had first opened its doors to the public in 1767, reopened, after the Revolution, in 1785, with the Old American Company, which had left the city ten years before for a voluntary exile in Jamaica. In 1786, a strong protest against the theatre was made to the legislature by many citizens of New York, who considered it inimical to the interests of morality and frugality. Whatever effect this may have had on the character of the productions, the theatre continued, and on April 16, 1787, there was presented here the first professional performance given in New York of a play written by an American. This was "The Contrast," by Robert Tyler, a native of Massachusetts, who later became the chief justice of Vermont. The John Street Theatre finally closed in January, 1798, and a few days later in the same month the first performance was given in the new Park Theatre on Park Row, which enjoyed for nearly fifty years the reputation of being the principal home of the drama in New York. The Grove Theatre, the Italian Theatre, the Lyceum (renamed, successively, the Amateur Theatre and the Theatre of Arts), and the Olympic were playhouses which enjoyed temporary celebrity between 1804 and 1812.

A voluminous history might be written about the taverns of New York during this period as influential centres of political and social life. The "long room" was the meeting-place of societies of all kinds, and the scene of celebrations, public dinners, balls, concerts, and the drama. One of these hostelries was the old Province Arms Tavern, on the west side of Broadway, between Thames and Cedar Streets, originally the De Lancey mansion. It had a notable career, under various titles[1] and several successive proprietors from 1754 to 1794, after which the Tontine City Tavern, later known as the City Hotel, was erected on the same site. Before the Revolution it was a rendezvous of the Sons of Liberty, and deserves enduring fame as the place where the non-importation agreement of 1765 was signed. Soon after the British evacuated New York, Washington, Clinton, and other officers of the American army were banqueted here by the citizens returned from exile. It was at this time called the State Arms. Another noted tavern, the Merchants' Coffee House, at the south-east corner of Wall and Water Streets, enjoyed a distinguished career under various owners and lessees from 1772 to 1804, having been established some years prior to 1738 on the diagonally opposite corner. Fifty organisations, political, commercial, benevolent, and social, from time to time made this their headquarters for dinners and meetings. It was destroyed by fire in 1804, but rebuilt the following year and named the Phoenix Coffee House. The Tontine Coffee House, on the north-west corner of Wall and Water Streets, the original site of the Merchants', was begun in 1792, and was a prominent business exchange and tavern for more than a generation. There were other taverns conveniently located throughout the city. One, of much interest, was Martling's, at 87 Nassau Street, corner of George (Beekman)

[1] See Landmark Map and Chronology.

Street, opposite the Brick Meeting House. It was the Free Masons' Hall and a "wigwam" of the Tammany Society before the erection of their own hall in 1811, which was later converted into the "Sun" building.[1] Plays and acrobatic performances were given at Martling's in 1796 and 1797, one of which, having evidently a political significance, was entitled "Citizen Democrat, Mons. Aristocrat, and Miss Moderate, or the Speaking Fair." A hotel farther north, deserving special mention, was the Belvedere House,[2] built in 1792 and opened the following year near the corner of the present Cherry and Montgomery Streets, overlooking the East River. A number of gentlemen designed it for a clubhouse—perhaps the first built specially for such a purpose in New York—but they later changed their plans, enlarged their place, and made it a house of public entertainment for dinners and dances as well as a club. It became a centre of pro-British influence and was the home of the British ambassador during his transient visits in New York.

There were also numerous pleasure gardens, several of which were successively named "Vauxhall" or "Ranelagh," from the two well-known places of recreation in and near London bearing these names. In 1765 Ranelagh was established in the mansion of Anthony Rutgers, near the place where the New York Hospital was built in 1773, on the west side of Broadway opposite Pearl Street (where now Thomas Street is situated). There, for the first time in America, set pieces of fireworks were exhibited. The name Vauxhall was first applied by Samuel Fraunces, before the Revolution, to the estate of Major James at the foot of Warren Street. A Mrs. Amory opened another Vauxhall in Great George Street in 1793, and illuminated it "in the Chinese style with 500 glass lamps." Vauxhall was opened at No. 5 Pearl Street in 1797 (or earlier), and renamed Ranelagh in 1798; while in 1807 (or earlier) the same name (Ranelagh) was given to the house and garden which had been called Mount Pitt before and during the Revolution, when this place was owned by Judge Jones. After the Revolution, it was owned successively by Morgan Lewis and John R. Livingston.[3] Joseph De Lacroix, a French restaurateur, opened the Vauxhall Garden in May, 1797, at 112 Broadway, where ice cream was served and *al fresco* concerts given. He established still another garden of this name in 1798 at the Bayard mansion, near Bayard's Mount or Bunker Hill and

[1] This building, which stood at the south-east corner of Park Row and Frankfort Street, was torn down in September, 1915. [2] See Pl. 60-a. [3] See Pl. 62.

extending east to Mary Street (which was later named Centre Street). The remote location compelled him to set up lanterns in the evening along the Broadway approach. Here he gave not only concerts, but also plays, circus performances, and fireworks. A notable feature of this resort, in 1803, was a bronzed equestrian statue of General Washington, life size, with uplifted arm pointing his sword toward the Narrows, through which the British retired when they withdrew from the harbour. With his sons, De Lacroix again moved northward in 1805, and established the Vauxhall on the Sand Hill Road, between the Bowery and Broadway, below the present Astor Place. This was said "to rival in point of elegance and beauty any place of the same kind in the European world." In the shade of old trees, beside gravel walks, were private boxes and pavilions, with tables where visitors could take refreshments and listen to the music or watch the progress of a play or allegorical fête. De Lacroix had a temporary rival in Joseph Corre, proprietor of the Columbia Garden at the Battery, who in 1800 opened the Mount Vernon Garden Theatre at the north-west corner of Broadway and Leonard Street, where he gave dramatic and musical entertainments, balloon ascensions, and displays of fireworks.

The circus was not introduced into New York until after the Revolution, although there had been exhibitions of wild animals as early as 1763. Thomas Pool, an American equestrian, exhibited feats of horsemanship in 1786 on the hill near the Jews' Burial Ground; and again, in 1788, on the hill above the shipyards, where he had established a menagerie. In 1793, another horse-fancier, Jacob Ricketts, started a circus on the east side of lower Greenwich Street, in the rear of the Macomb houses, one of which Washington had occupied when President. The following year, he opened a "new equestrian amphitheatre" at the corner of Broadway and Oyster Pasty Lane, adjoining the Macomb houses on the north. In 1797 Ricketts built, on the west side of Greenwich Street, a third amphitheatre, circular in form and with a stage and scenery, which proved an attractive resort where both equestrian and dramatic performances were given. French players appeared there during the first season, in an "heroic pantomime." It became known as the French Theatre, and later as the Pantheon, and was destroyed by fire in 1799. These early ventures were followed in 1801 by De Lacroix's Vauxhall Circus, just mentioned; and by a circus in the Bowery, where bull-baiting and wild animal combats were the chief attractions. A circus was established at Corlear's Hook in 1808, and another the same year at the corner of Broadway and Anthony Street. It was at a circus in Anthony Street (evidently the one last mentioned) that, in 1809, the Federal Republicans held their convention.

There were also several museums, menageries, panoramas, and galleries of paintings. The most notable of these was the Tammany Museum, founded by John Pintard in June, 1790. Its original purpose was the purely antiquarian one of collecting everything of interest relating to the history of the United States. It first occupied a room in the City Hall, by the consent of the common council, and later one in the Exchange on Broad Street. Its enterprising keeper, Gardiner Baker, exhibited works of art and nature, including wax-works and a patent steam-jack, and also established a menagerie on a vacant lot on the corner of Pearl Street and the Battery. The Tammany Society, in 1795, relinquished the museum to Baker, who then began selling French and English prints and showing electrical apparatus. In 1797 he opened a panorama at 222 Greenwich Street, and on Washington's Birthday, 1798, exhibited Gilbert Stuart's portrait of Washington at the new City Hotel on Broadway. After Baker's death, his collections, already famous, passed into other hands until John Scudder acquired them and established the American Museum, first in Chatham Street and then in the converted Almshouse. This was considered "the most amusing and striking place of public resort in the City." The Museum was finally acquired by P. T. Barnum, who, in 1835, housed it in a white marble building at the south-east corner of Broadway and Ann Street.

The legislature passed an act on February 28, 1791, defining anew the boundaries of the wards of the city, and changing their names from Dock Ward, East Ward, etc., to First, Second, Third, and so on, up to the Seventh Ward. This year was one of those memorable for pestilence and fire. Yellow fever, which had appeared forty years before, occurred now for the first time with notable malignity and fatality. The Hospital, which had been erected in 1773, destroyed by fire in 1775, and only partially rebuilt, was now completed and opened for patients. There was a big fire in September of this year, in Mill Street. The block of buildings between the Jews Alley and Duke Street, bounded on the north by Mill Street, and some buildings adjoining the Custom House were destroyed. In December, a permanent fund was started for the relief of firemen injured in the performance of their duty. Another large fire occurred early in the following year, on Front Street between the Fly Market and De Peyster Street.

An agreement among stock brokers, on May 17, 1792, effected the organisation which developed later into the New York Stock Exchange. From 1792 to 1817, the dealings of the members were conducted in various places, the trading out of doors being usually done near a buttonwood tree which stood in front of the dividing line between 68 and 70 Wall Street. After the completion of the Tontine Coffee House in 1793, at the north-west corner of Wall and Water Streets, the brokers for a time met there.

Ordinances were passed by the common council in 1792, requiring that the streets lying in the tract of land called the Meadows be filled in. Others provided that pavements be laid down in parts of Greenwich Street, in Crown Street, Little Queen Street, and Thames Street from Broadway to Greenwich Street; in Barclay Street from Greenwich Street to the bulkhead at the river; in Great Dock Street, Little Dock Street, and Front Street from Coenties Slip to Whitehall Street; in Moore Street from Great Dock Street to the river, and in Broad Street to the south side of Water Street. Improvements were also made in the streets near Chatham Square.

In 1793, the common council ordered that all buildings be regularly numbered in accordance with a prescribed method. The new numbering first appears in the city directory for 1794. In 1793, the building of the Society Library, at the present No. 33 Nassau Street, was begun, and was completed two years later. It was very similar in architecture to the Government House. The library books were moved to this new building from a room on the upper floor of Federal Hall which had long served as their home. The City Tavern, which stood on the west side of Broadway between Little Queen (Cedar) and Thames Streets, was demolished in 1793 to make way for the new Tontine City Hotel, which was the first building in New York to have a slate roof. The first Episcopal body to leave Trinity Parish and establish a separate organisation was incorporated this year under the name of Christ Church, and laid the corner-stone of a building of its own on the north side of Ann Street between William and Nassau Streets. It was taken over by Trinity in 1802.

The city's drinking water was so poor in quality as to be for many years a menace to health, and the supply was so limited as to constitute a serious handicap in fighting fires. This condition naturally grew worse with the growth of the city. As early as 1749, Peter Kalm, the Swedish naturalist, had written that the well-water here was so bad that horses did not like to drink it. People were obliged to drink the water from the Tea Water Pump, which was carted in casks to their houses. The location of this famous spring was mentioned in 1782 as next to the Old Punch House which stood at No. 25 Chatham Street. The property was sold in 1784 by the executors of Gerardus Hardenbrook. Even the once pure water of this well had become contaminated, by 1785, through its proximity to the polluted waters of the Fresh Water Pond, which had come to be a general receptacle for refuse. Christopher Colles, because of the Revolution, had failed to give the city the promised supply of water, with his pump, reservoir, and wooden pipes, and after the war other inventors and public-spirited citizens advanced various schemes for the same purpose. Samuel Ogden in 1785, and Robert Livingston in 1786, were two of these. The following year the city advertised for proposals. In 1788, consideration was given to a plan for completing the water-works begun by Colles; and in 1789 the Rumsian Society of Philadelphia offered still another plan, but no definite relief was undertaken at that time. The Tea Water Pump, which was again sold with the adjoining property in 1793, still supplied the city with drinking water.

In 1794, Bellevue Hospital for contagious diseases was established on land purchased from Brockholst Livingston, on the East River "opposite the three mile stone"; and the common council appropriated ground at the junction of the Post and Bloomingdale Roads for the use of the Almshouse for a burying-ground. The names of several streets which had been given in honour of royalty, such as King, Queen, Crown, and Prince Streets, were changed in 1794 so as to be more in keeping with republican institutions, becoming respectively Pine, Cedar, Liberty, and Rose Streets. At the same time, several short streets were joined together to form one longer street; thus, Pearl Street, Great Dock Street, Hanover Square, and Queen Street became the present Pearl Street; while Broadway, beginning at Government House and ending at Vesey Street, and Great George Street from Vesey Street to the Sand Hill Cross Road (Astor Place) were united to form Broadway. That part of Broadway which lay between Trinity Church and St. Paul's was commonly called Jarvis's Parade. It was recommended in the spring of 1794 that, as trees were being set out in streets in various parts of the town, they be planted also along this section of Broadway. The places appointed for the election of charter officers at this time were city buildings and churches. In the First Ward, Trinity Church was named; in the Second, City Hall; in the Third, the North Dutch Church; in the Fourth, St. Paul's; in the Fifth, the Friends' Meeting House; in the Sixth, the Almshouse; and in the Seventh, the Methodist Church. In November and December of 1794, the sportsmen of New York had a new diversion in buffalo hunts with hounds, starting on one occasion from Lambert's Tavern at Greenwich, and once from the Sign of the Huntsman and Hounds, five miles from town on the Kingsbridge Road. The buffalo had been brought from Kentucky.

International complications were threatening on account of the conflict recently developed between England and France. Edmond Charles Genet, minister plenipotentiary of France to the United States, arrived in Charleston on April 9, 1793, bringing the French declaration of war against England. The seventeenth article of the treaty of commerce between France and the United States guaranteed the exclusive right of shelter for her ships-of-war and privateers, and for their prizes. Washington, nevertheless, issued immediately a proclamation of neutrality, and this awakened ill-feeling in the United States among the partisans of France. The French minister attempted to fit out cruisers from our ports. This the President opposed. Genet was charged with having said that he was resolved to appeal from the President "to the people, the real Sovereigns." Following the appearance in New York Harbour, on April 22d, of the French frigate "L'Ambuscade," with M. Genet on board, partisan feeling was deeply aroused in this city. A keen controversy was developed through letters to the press, commencing with one, signed jointly by John Jay and Rufus King, in *The Diary; or Loudon's Register* for August 12, 1793, charging Genet with unfriendly acts and words regarding the neutrality of the United States. It was evident that Genet's mission was to involve this country in a war with England. His recall was demanded by Washington. He found many enthusiastic sympathisers, nevertheless, among whom was Governor Clinton, with whose daughter he fell in love. Although recalled, he remained after the excitement subsided, married, and made New York his home for the rest of his life.

Early in 1794, volunteer work was begun under federal commissioners for the erection and repair of fortifications in the city and its vicinity. An appeal to the patriotic spirit of the citizens brought relays of men in large numbers to the task, many of whom were unused to such heavy manual labour. The principal scene of their exertions was Governors Island. Militiamen, cartmen, members of the St. Andrew's, Tammany, and other societies, English Republicans, ship carpenters, Columbia students, journeymen hatters, lawyers, peruke-makers and hair-dressers, schoolmasters, grocers, tallow-chandlers—in fact, all classes of citizens, organised by trades, societies, etc.—carried on this work on days assigned for their respective groups. The fortifications were reported completed two years later.

Meanwhile the federal government had been labouring under serious difficulties. One of these resulted from its failure to secure any agreement with England respecting trade. In 1794 John Jay concluded a treaty with Lord Grenville, the representative of the British government, which, among other provisions, permitted a limited trade between the United States and British possessions, but failed to settle the question of England's claim to the right of searching American ships, and seemed to give England benefits in trade without securing adequate compensation to the United States. The treaty greatly curtailed the carrying trade of the United States and was excessively unpopular in New York, where it was thought that prosperity would be seriously affected. Popular demonstrations were made against the treaty; and on July 18, 1795, when Alexander Hamilton addressed the crowd from a stoop at the head of Broad Street, speaking in favour of the treaty, some of the citizens threw stones at him, broke up the meeting, burned the treaty on the Battery, and adopted resolutions condemning it.

The corner-stone of St. Mark's Church was laid by the Right Reverend Samuel Provoost, bishop of New York, on April 25, 1795, and the building was completed and opened for worship on May 9, 1799, occupying the site of Governor Stuyvesant's old Bouwery Chapel. In 1795, New York was again visited by yellow fever, and 732 deaths resulted. The new Almshouse, in Chambers Street, completed this year, was used as a hospital during the epidemic, in addition to the New York and Bellevue Hospitals. By the first of November the fever had run its course, and Governor Jay, in gratitude for the city's deliverance, issued a proclamation appointing Thursday, November 26th, as a day of thanksgiving. His political opponents looked upon this as another evidence of his aristocratic or federal notions of government, and declared that he had exceeded his prerogatives as governor.

The first coloured congregation of New York was formed in 1796, by the negro members of the Methodist Church. The New York Missionary Society was also formed this year, by a number of the clergy and laity of the Presbyterian, Dutch Reformed, Associate Reformed, and Baptist Churches.

The Collect Pond, in 1796, was the scene of John Fitch's historic experiment with the first steamboat using the screw propeller, after the successful experiments with steam-propelled paddles on the Delaware River ten years before (see Pl. 58–a). New building laws were enacted in 1796 for the more effectual prevention of fires; that they were needed was proved, later in the year, by a fire that consumed forty buildings on Wall Street and along the east side of Front Street between Murray's Wharf and the Fly Market. Already at the beginning of the year, the common council had determined to provide some suitable plan to secure for the city an abundant supply of good water, and a committee, of which Robert Lenox was chairman, advertised for suggestions. Proposals were received from time to time, and a model of the suggested water-works was exhibited in the City Hall in March, 1797, but no definite arrangements were made. On the average, 110 hogsheads of water (of 130 gallons each) were drawn daily from the old Tea Water Pump, which amount was increased in summer to 216 hogsheads.

The "foundation stone" of the United States Branch Bank was laid on June 13, 1797, at No. 38 Wall Street, east of William Street. A few days later, the corner-stone of the New York Bank was laid at No. 32 Wall Street on the north-east corner of William Street (see Pl. 72–b). The State Prison, begun in 1796 near the Hudson River, in the block afterwards enclosed by Washington, West, Christopher, and Perry Streets, was so near completion by December 1, 1797, as to receive prisoners. This building, given up as a prison in 1828 when Sing Sing was opened, was standing as late as 1881, being then used as a brewery. Part of the old building still remains on Weehawken Street. In the spring of 1798, the street department of the city government was placed in charge of three commissioners instead of a committee of the common council as formerly; the following year, a single commissioner took the place of the three, and for many years this important office was thus constituted until finally it developed into the present department of public works. In July, 1798, the yellow fever again suddenly appeared, and in the two months ending October 20th there were 1,310 deaths from this cause. Earlier in the year, the legislature had provided for the appointment of three commissioners of health for the city. Many of the victims were buried in the new burial-ground established the year before "on the road leading from the Bowery Lane at the two-mile stone to Greenwich," where, thirty years later, Washington Square was laid out. Some of the materials of the old Almshouse, which was demolished in 1797, were used in constructing a superintendent's house there.

Broad, practical wisdom on the subject of supplying the city with pure water was presented in a report of a committee of the common council on December 17, 1798, stating that they inclined to the opinion "that the Bronx River will afford a copious supply." This was in accord with a project which had been submitted to the board by Doctor Joseph Brown. The committee recommended that William Weston, an engineer employed by some of the canal companies in this state, "be requested to examine that river with the situation of the grounds to be employed in the aqueduct." Weston's report was submitted to the common council on March 16, 1799, and printed by John Furman the same year. The Bronx River plan was one of great magnitude, complicated and costly. Over forty years actually elapsed before it was finally put into operation in the form of the Croton Aqueduct and Reservoirs. In the meantime, a commercial scheme to provide the city with water was launched as a private enterprise by a group of promoters who incorporated the Manhattan Company, under the leadership of Aaron Burr, and included Doctor Brown, John B. Church, John Watts, and other prominent citizens, with David Ludlow as president and J. B. Prevost as secretary. They obtained from the legislature a charter conferring unusually comprehensive powers. While their main purpose, no doubt, was to supply the city with water, and they undertook to do so by the method previously attempted by Christopher Colles, another object, of quite as much importance to the organisers, was to carry on a banking business. This was provided for by a clause in the charter stating that the surplus capital might be used in the purchase of stocks, "or in any other monied transactions or operations not inconsistent with the Constitution and laws of New York or of the United States." This was the first instance in New York of a practically unlimited act of incorporation, a monopoly in effect, given to a private stock company, and it is doubtful whether such broad powers would have been granted had the incorporators openly stated their intention to engage in a regular banking business. The capital stock of the Manhattan Company was $2,000,000. By 1800 a reservoir and steam pump had been erected at the corner of Reade and Centre Streets, where the reservoir was maintained until 1915 to guarantee the validity of the company's charter. About six miles of wooden pipes were laid through the principal streets, and more than four hundred houses supplied with water. The system was extended later, but the machinery, pipes, and supply of water proved inadequate and the quality of the water not very good. The frequent complaints of the citizens compelled the common council, in 1804, again to appoint a committee to consider the availability of the Bronx River and Rye Pond in Westchester County. Still the Manhattan Company's operations continued, and in 1828 they substituted iron pipes for logs, but were unable to meet the needs of the growing city.

Early in 1799, the legislature passed an act for the gradual abolition of slavery in New York State. It provided that any child born of a slave after the 4th of July of this year should be deemed free-born, but should be a servant until twenty-eight years of age if a male, or twenty-five if a female, as if such slave had been bound to service by the overseers of the poor.

Although Washington had begun his administration with the desire and purpose that it should remain non-partisan, it soon became apparent that the federal government was to be conducted along party lines. Washington sympathised with the principles of the Federalist party, which had secured the adoption of the Constitution, and which believed in a strong central government; and in making appointments to public office, he naturally chose men in sympathy with its principles. As his administration drew to a close, he became even more thoroughly a Federalist. His retirement from the presidency in 1797 did not result in his party's losing control of the government; for John Adams, also a Federalist, was elected to succeed him. Washington's death occurred on December 14, 1799. The citizens of New York of all parties wore mourning emblems; and on December 31st, one year before the end of the century in which he had been perhaps the most conspicuous figure, they held appropriate obsequies, with a civil and military funeral, in honour of the national hero, whose many high qualities of character and illustrious accomplishments were already universally acknowledged.

Adams's administration was marked by trouble with France, and by the passage of a group of measures known as the Alien and Sedition Laws, which were designed to curb the freedom of the press, and to provide for the punishment of anyone who should attack the government. These laws became unpopular and this helped to discredit the Federalists. The party was further weakened by the quarrels between two of its leaders, John Adams and Alexander Hamilton. Hamilton had controlled New York for several years, and it became clear that in the approaching election in November, 1800, this state would decide the contest. New York City controlled the state; it therefore became the pivot on which the whole election turned. Aaron Burr, one of the keenest politicians of the time, manipulated the Republicans in the city (the Democrats of that time) so cleverly that his party won by about five hundred votes. The national election was indecisive, and the choice went to the House of Representatives, where Hamilton's influence helped to make Jefferson (a Republican) president, and Burr vice-president.

In 1800 the second federal census was taken, and showed New York's population to be 60,515, an increase of 27,384 over that of 1790. An organisation of much local interest at this time was the thriving Philharmonic Society, which gave semi-annual concerts at the City Hotel. Although the present society of that name was founded as early as 1842—nearly seventy-five years ago—its purposes were thus anticipated by more than forty years. The last year of the century (1800) was one of notable progress in building operations throughout the island. The frigates "New York" and "President" were launched in April. The Coles or Harlem Bridge, a non-taxable toll bridge, was erected over Benson's Creek. "Claremont" was built by Doctor Post; and "The Grange" was planned by Hamilton and completed two years later. In October there were more than fifty three-story buildings and nearly as many of two stories being constructed in various parts of the city. The most important building undertaken during this period was the new City Hall, first projected by the common council in 1800, although not actually begun until three years later. This building, ever since its completion in 1815, has been the seat of municipal government. The land selected as its site was "the vacant space of ground between the goal and the bridewell," the common council requiring "that the wings in front range with Murray Street, on a parallel line with the fence in front of the Alms-house & the Cupola range in a Line with the Cupola of the Alms house." The site therefore included that originally occupied by the first Almshouse, which was built in 1735 and demolished in 1797, the same site on which, in 1798, the horse-market was established by direction of the common council.

In the spring of 1801, George Clinton was elected governor of New York by the Republicans. Thus, for the first time, this party controlled the nation, the state, and the city. In the city the party has maintained this control almost without interruption to the present time. The Federalists among the city office-holders were removed, and Republicans appointed in their places. Edward Livingston thus became mayor in the place of Richard Varick, who had filled the office for more than a decade. The common council took measures in 1801 to complete the old mile-stones on the Post Road from the City Hall to Kingsbridge, and to extend the series of mile-stones on the Middle Road from the three-mile stone to the new Coles Bridge across the Harlem River. In that year, also, the office of commissioner of police was established for the city of New York, and the United States government acquired the property at the Wallabout, in Kings County, for a Navy Yard. There were three important daily newspapers in the city at this time: the *New York Evening Post*, founded in 1801 and edited by William Coleman, supported Hamilton; the *American Citizen* (1801), edited by James Cheetham, supported Jefferson and Clinton; and the *Morning Chronicle* (1802), which was edited by Peter Irving, whose younger brother, Washington, sometimes contributed to its columns, was especially friendly to Aaron Burr. All three were violently partisan and indulged in personal abuse of rival candidates, in a manner which would not be tolerated to-day.

The idea of a bridge across the East River was first advanced in 1802, in a petition to the legislature from citizens of New York. It met with opposition and ridicule; the chief objection to its construction being that, whether built upon piers or floats, it was certain to encroach upon navigation. Moreover, the means of communication between New York and Brooklyn, with twelve ferry-boats in operation, having a working force of twenty-four men, were believed by ferry owners to be already adequate. The corner-stone of the hall of the General Society of Mechanics and Tradesmen was laid that year at the north-west corner of Broadway and Robinson Street (now Park Place); as also that of the first building erected in New York by the Masonic Order, St. John's Hall, on Frankfort Street in the rear of the present World Building. The proposal was first made at this time to use hearses at funerals in this city in place of bearers.

In 1802 the study of art received special encouragement by the organisation of the New York Academy of Fine Arts, which exhibited during the following summer, in the rotunda of the Pantheon on Greenwich Street (formerly Ricketts' Circus), a collection of reproductions of classic statuary from Paris. The Society of the Cincinnati, in 1802, decided to place a bronze equestrian statue of Washington in the Park, but the plan proved the first of several patriotic but futile efforts in the first half of the nineteenth century to erect a public statue or monument in New York to the honour of one whose living memorial was in the hearts of the people. Nevertheless, the following year, De Lacroix installed in his garden at Bayard's Hill the statue already referred to, "by an able artist," which was similar to the one proposed by the Society of the Cincinnati. A sufficient fund could not be raised to erect such a monument in the Park, although in 1826 the Italian sculptor Causici placed on exhibition there a full-size model of an equestrian statue, which remained four or five years (see Pl. 100); nor did one appear elsewhere in the city until 1856, when that designed by Brown and Ward was unveiled in Union Square.

Doctor David Hosack, professor of botany at Columbia College, received from the common council in 1802 a grant of about fourteen acres within the boundaries of Fifth and Sixth Avenues, 47th and 51st Streets (as the streets were afterwards laid down in the Commissioners' Map of 1811). This land was to be used for a public botanical garden. Hosack developed there a large collection of choice plants, trees, and shrubs, both native and exotic, and named it the Elgin Garden; he then sold the property to the state, which later conveyed it to Columbia College. It has since become one of the most valuable residence and business sections of the city, and one of the chief sources of revenue to the college.

The problem of disposing of the Collect Pond, which had been a public nuisance for many years, and which, in 1796, the Mangin brothers, engineers, had proposed to convert into "a safe harbour for shipping," was solved in 1802 by the common council's adopting the proposal of William Beekman, that it be filled in with "good and wholesome earth." An order to this effect was given in 1803, and at the same time it was ordered that a drain or tunnel be dug to the East and North Rivers. More than ten years elapsed before the pond had entirely disappeared. The laying out of Canal Street, one hundred feet wide, from Collect Street between Pump and Hester Streets, and extending north-west to the Hudson River, was done under commissioners appointed by the legislature in 1809, who reported their plans completed in 1810.[1] An open ditch or canal, eight feet wide, was accordingly built in 1811,[2] through the centre of the street, spanned at Broadway by the Stone Bridge. Plans were drawn in November of the same year to convert this canal into a covered sewer,[3] and the work on this was begun in 1816 and completed in 1819. The long-continued uncertainty and vacillation in connection with the plans for city development, and the frequent assessments for public improvements became, in 1810 and 1811, the cause of strong public protest, which did not altogether subside when the commissioners of streets and roads submitted their report and plan on March 22, 1811.[4]

The legislature passed an act in March, 1803, equalising the wards of the city and increasing their number from seven to nine. The most notable event of this year, in the physical development of the city, was the laying of the corner-stone of the present City Hall, on May 26th, by Mayor Livingston. While the award in the public competition held for the purpose of securing the best designs for the building, had been given on October 4, 1802, to Joseph Fr. Mangin and John McComb, Jr., jointly, the latter, on March 22, 1803, was appointed the sole supervising architect and master builder, and so remained, through many difficulties, until the edifice was completed in 1815. The vicinity of Hudson Square (later called St. John's Park), a wild and marshy spot, was laid out in streets, and lots there were offered for sale by Trinity Corporation with certain restrictions. The corner-stone of St. John's Chapel was laid on the east side of this square on September 8, 1803, and the edifice was completed four years later. Yellow fever raged this year from July to November, and caused a general suspension of business and about six hundred deaths.

The "Louisiana Purchase" was celebrated in New York on May 12, 1804, by a general holiday, the display of flags, firing of salutes, ringing

[1] See plan No. 195, in the Bureau of Design and Survey. [2] Plan No. 161, *Ibid.* [3] Plan No. 155, *Ibid.*

[4] Mrs. Lamb, referring to the levelling process that began at this period, says: "All that was romantic in scenery and prepossessing in cultivated grounds immediately above Canal Street was quickly doomed. The city was on the march, and every form of hill and dale and pleasant valley must be sacrificed."—*Hist. of the City of N. Y.*, II: 569.

of bells, and a civic parade. The gubernatorial election this year resulted in the choice of Morgan Lewis and the defeat of Aaron Burr, but is best remembered for the fatal duel which grew out of the struggle. Burr attributed his defeat to Hamilton's influence, challenged him to a duel, and shot him fatally, on the Weehawken shore, July 11, 1804. All of New York joined in honouring the memory of the fallen statesman. The merchants of the city closed their shops during the funeral; the Bar Association, the Cincinnati, and even the Republican Society of Tammany joined in the general mourning. Burr was forced to leave the city, and his home, Richmond Hill, was sold to satisfy his creditors.

On November 20, 1804, a group of New York gentlemen met in the picture-room of the City Hall in Wall Street, and organised the New York Historical Society. John Pintard was the leader of this movement, and Doctor Hosack his chief associate. A fire in December of this year consumed over forty buildings, including the Merchants' Coffee House. The region burned over was from the west side of Coffee House Slip, on Water Street, to Gouverneur's Lane, thence down to the East River, and east across Wall Street to the farther side of the slip.

The year 1805 was another one of fatalities due to yellow fever. The post-office was removed to Greenwich Village, as the banks and custom-house had been during previous epidemics; and so large was the emigration from the city that a tent colony was established between Greenwich and Broadway. New York's schools up to this time had been maintained either by private individuals or by religious and charitable organisations. On February 19, 1805, a meeting at the house of John Murray, Jr., in Pearl Street, resulted in the formation of a society for establishing a free school, for the education of poor children who were not provided for by any religious society. This society opened its first school in May, 1806, in a house in Madison Street, near Pearl Street. Five years later, the common council gave to the Free School Society the arsenal on the corner of Chatham Street and Tryon Row, on condition that the children of the Almshouse should be instructed without expense to the city. This building, which had been erected in 1798, was entirely rebuilt above the foundations by the society, and was the first one in New York constructed especially for use as a free public school. It was opened on December 11, 1809, with an address by De Witt Clinton, president of the society.

An interesting description of New York as it appeared at this time is given by John Lambert,[1] an English visitor to New York in November, 1807:

> New York is the first city of the United States for wealth, commerce, and population; as it also is the finest and most agreeable for its situation and buildings. It has neither the narrow and confined irregularity of Boston, nor the monotonous regularity of Philadelphia, but a happy medium between both. When the intended improvements are completed, it will be a very elegant and commodious town, and worthy of becoming the capital of the United States, . . . New York has rapidly improved within the last twenty years; and land which then sold in that city for fifty dollars is now worth 1500.
>
> The Broadway and Bowery Road are the two finest avenues in the city, . . . The first . . . is upwards of two miles in length, though the pavement does not extend above a mile and a quarter; the remainder of the road consists of straggling houses, which are the commencement of new streets already planned out. The Bowery Road commences from Chatham street, which branches off from the Broadway to the right, by the side of the Park. After proceeding about a mile and a half it joins the Broadway, and terminates the plan which is intended to be carried into effect for the enlargement of the city. Much of the immediate spaces between these large streets, and from thence to the Hudson and East rivers, is yet unbuilt upon, or consists only of unfinished streets and detached buildings.
>
> The houses in the Broadway are lofty and well built. They are constructed in the English style and differ but little from those of London at the west end of the town; except that they are universally built of *red* brick. In the vicinity of the Battery, and for some distance up the Broadway, they are nearly all private houses, and occupied by the principal merchants and gentry of New York; after which the Broadway is lined with large commodious shops of every description, well-stocked with European and Indian goods, and exhibiting as splendid and varied a show in their windows as can be met with in London. There are several extensive book stores, print-shops, music-shops, jewellers and silver-smiths, hatters, linen-drapers, milliners, pastry-cooks, coach-makers, hotels, and coffee-houses. The street is well paved, and the foot-paths are chiefly bricked.
>
> The City Hotel is the most extensive building of that description in New York; . . . The ground-floor . . . is, however, converted into shops, which have a very handsome appearance in the Broadway. Mechanic Hall is another large hotel at the corner of Robinson street, in the Broadway, . . . There are three churches in the Broadway: one of them called Grace Church, is a plain brick building, recently erected; the other two are St. Paul's and Trinity; both handsome structures, built with an inter-mixture of white and brown stone. The adjoining churchyards, which occupy a large space of

[1] John Lambert, *Travels through Canada and the United States of North America in the years 1806, 1807, 1808.* London, 1814, Vol. II, p. 55 *et seq.*

ground, railed in from the street, and crowded with tomb-stones, are far from being agreeable spectacles in such a populous city. At the commencement of the Broadway, near the battery, stands the old Government-house, now converted into offices for the customs. Before it is a small lawn railed in, and in the centre is a stone pedestal upon which formerly stood a leaden statue of George the Third. . . .

The City Hall where the courts of justice are held, is situated in Wall Street, leading from the coffee-house slip by the water side into the Broadway. It is an old heavy building, and very inadequate to the population and wealth of New York. A Court-house on a larger scale, and more worthy of the improved state of the city, is now building at the end of the Park, between the Broadway and Chatham street, in a style of magnificence unequalled in many of the large cities of Europe. The exterior consists wholly of fine marble, ornamented in a very neat and elegant style of architecture; and the whole is to be surmounted by a beautiful dome, which, when finished, will form a noble ornament to that part of the town, in which are also situated the Theatre, Mechanic Hall, and some of the best private houses in New York. The Park, though not remarkable for its size, is, however, of service, by displaying the surrounding buildings to greater advantage; and is also a relief to the confined appearance of the streets in general. It consists of about four acres planted with elms, planes, willows, and catalpas; and the surrounding foot-walk is encompassed by rows of poplars: the whole is enclosed by a wooden paling. Neither the Park nor the Battery is very much resorted to by the fashionable citizens of New York, as they have become too common. The genteel lounge is in the Broadway, from eleven to three o'clock, during which time it is as much crowded as the Bond street of London: and the carriages, though not so numerous, are driven to and fro with as much velocity. The foot paths are planted with poplars, and afford an agreeable shade from the sun in summer.

Among the pleasure-places in New York Lambert mentions the theatre on the south-east side of the Park, Vauxhall, and Ranelagh. He calls the theatre a large, commodious building. "The outside [is] in an unfinished state, but the interior is handsomely decorated, and fitted up in as good style as the London theatres, upon a scale suitable to the population of the city. It contains a large coffee-room, and good sized lobbies, and is reckoned to hold about 1200 persons." He rates Vauxhall and Ranelagh as but poor imitations of their prototypes near London, but calls them "pleasant places of recreation for the inhabitants." The Vauxhall garden of this period was situated on the Bowery Road about two miles from the City Hall. It is described as "a neat plantation, with gravel walks adorned with shrubs, trees, busts, and statues. In the centre is a large equestrian statue of General Washington. Light musical pieces, interludes, &c., are performed in a small theatre situate in one corner of the garden: the audience sit in what are called the pit and boxes, in the open air. The orchestra is built among the trees, and a large apparatus is constructed for the display of fire-works." Ranelagh, usually known by the name of Mount Pitt, was a suburban hotel surrounded by extensive grounds, situated near the intersection of Division and Grand Streets, and commanding extensive and beautiful views of the city and its environs. According to Lambert's account, New York contained at this time thirty-three places of worship, thirty-one benevolent organisations, numerous banks and insurance companies, a public library with ten thousand volumes, and three or four reading-rooms and circulating libraries.

Lambert was evidently impressed by the part of the city lying between Broadway and the East River, which, he writes:

> . . . is very irregularly built; being the oldest part of the town, and of course less capable of those improvements which distinguish the more recent buildings. Nevertheless, it is the chief seat of business, and contains several spacious streets crowded with shops, stores, and warehouses of every description. The water side is lined with shipping which lie along the wharfs, or in the small docks called slips, of which there are upwards of twelve towards the East river, besides numerous piers. The wharfs are large and commodious, and the warehouses, which are nearly all new buildings, are lofty and substantial. The merchants, ship-brokers, &c. have their offices in front on the ground floor of these warehouses. These ranges of buildings and wharfs extend from the Grand Battery, on both sides the town, up the Hudson and East rivers, and encompass the houses with shipping, whose forest of masts give a stranger a lively idea of the immense trade which this city carries on with every part of the globe.

When Lambert arrived in New York in November, 1807,

> the port was filled with shipping, and the wharfs were crowded with commodities of every description. Bales of cotton, wool, and merchandize; barrels of pot-ash, rice, flour, and salt provisions; hogsheads of sugar, chests of tea, puncheons of rum, and pipes of wine; boxes, cases, packs and packages of all sizes and denominations, were strewed upon the wharfs and landing-places, or upon the decks of the shipping. All was noise and bustle. The carters were driving in every direction; and the sailors and labourers upon the wharfs, and on board the vessels, were moving their ponderous burthens from place to place. The merchants and their clerks were busily engaged in their counting-houses, or upon the piers. The Tontine coffee-house was filled with underwriters, brokers, merchants, traders, and politicians; selling, purchasing, trafficking, or insuring; some reading, others eagerly inquiring the news. . . . the

> coffee-house slip, and the corners of Wall and Pearl streets, were jammed up with carts, drays, and wheel-barrows; horses and men were huddled promiscuously together, leaving little or no room for passengers to pass. . . . Everything was in motion; all was life, bustle, and activity. The people were scampering in all directions to trade with each other, and to ship off their purchases for the European, Asian, African, and West Indian markets. Every thought, word, look, and action of the multitude seemed to be absorbed by commerce. The welkin rang with its busy hum, and all were eager in the pursuit of its riches.

This prosperity was, however, seriously checked by the gigantic struggle in which Europe was at this time engaged. The bitter contest between Napoleon and England soon began to disorganise the commerce, not only of the combatants but of neutral nations as well. Napoleon had failed in his attempt to wrest the control of the sea from England and therefore could not launch his *grande armée* directly against his antagonist, because the Channel, controlled by English men-of-war, separated him from his goal. He, therefore, determined to bring England to terms by attacking her through her commerce. The French Empire and all its dependencies were forbidden to admit English goods into their ports or to trade with England in any way. England retaliated with her orders in council; Napoleon answered with his Berlin and Milan decrees. The result was that virtually all neutral shipping was declared lawful prize by either France or England. As the United States was, at this time, the most important neutral commercial state, it suffered severely from the European conflict. President Jefferson and our government were unwilling to engage in a war which the country was poorly prepared to endure, which would surely increase the national debt, and might result in the loss of national independence. They, therefore, resorted to pacific measures of defence and passed the Non-Importation Act of 1806, which provided that certain specified goods should not be imported from the ports of Great Britain after November 25th following. This act failed to wring the desired concessions from England, and was followed by the Embargo Act of 1807, which forbade the departure for any foreign port of any merchant vessel, except foreign vessels in ballast, and required vessels in the coasting trade to give heavy bonds to land their cargoes in the United States. The embargo was as unsuccessful in winning concessions from England and France as the Non-Importation Act had been, and the commerce of the United States continued to feel the bad effects of the European conflict until its close in 1814-15.

New York as the foremost trading centre in America felt the hardships of this situation severely. Lambert, who described the commercial activity of New York before the embargo went into effect, later contrasts with that picture conditions under the embargo.

> The coffee-house slip, the wharfs and quays along South-street presented no longer the bustle and activity that had prevailed before. The port indeed was full of shipping; but the ships were dismantled and laid up. Their decks were cleared, their hatches fastened down, and scarcely a sailor was to be found on board. Not a box, bale, cask, barrel, or package, was to be seen upon the wharfs. Many of the country-houses were shut up, or advertised to be let; and the few solitary merchants, clerks, porters, and labourers, that were to be seen, were walking about with their hands in their pockets. Instead of sixty or a hundred carts that used to stand in the street for hire, scarcely a dozen appeared, and they were unemployed; a few coasting sloops, and schooners, which were clearing out for some of the ports in the United States, were all that remained of that immense business which was carried on a few months before.

The coffee-house was almost empty; the streets near the water side were almost deserted; the grass had begun to grow upon the wharves. The scene was so gloomy and forlorn that had it been September instead of April, Lambert would have thought that a malignant fever was raging in the place; "so desolating were the effects of the embargo, which in the short space of five months had deprived the first commercial city in the States of all its life, bustle, and activity; caused above one hundred and twenty bankruptcies; and completely annihilated its foreign commerce."

During this period, New York was described in petitions and reports to Congress as "defenceless." Permanent fortifications, war-ships, and a naval arsenal were demanded. Many plans for works of defence were proposed in 1806 and succeeding years, and these plans were discussed at great length in newspapers and pamphlets. In April, 1806, there was an attempted blockade of the harbour by the British. The British ship "Leander" fired upon the American sloop "Richard" off Sandy Hook, killing the captain's brother. Public meetings of protest and of demands for defence were held. The harbour was surveyed under the direction of the Secretary of War, who decided to build fortifications at Governors, Bedloes, and Ellis Islands, and at the Battery and the foot of Duane Street. A citizens' committee of defence was appointed on October 16, 1807, and in November the common council authorised the conveyance to the United States of as much land within its jurisdiction as was needed for the proposed fortifications, the Duane Street site being changed for one at the foot of Hubert Street. All these defensive works were commenced in 1808, under the direction of Colonel Jonathan Williams, of West Point, and an arsenal was built by the state on the land bounded by Elm, Sugar Loaf, and White Streets. The fort on Governors Island, completed in December, 1810, was named "Castle Williams" in honour of its designer. The fort at the Battery served many useful purposes in later years, and is now the Aquarium. From 1807 to 1810, Robert Fulton invented and developed the submarine torpedo, and demonstrated its utility by experiments and published descriptions.

The city, with astonishing enterprise, began, in these years of foreign conflict, to make extensive internal improvements, and these have been continued with unabated vigour to the present time. Building operations first began to multiply in 1806 and 1807. Manhattanville, on the Hudson River at Harlem Cove, was surveyed and laid out in 1806. The number of new houses built in 1807 was greater than in any previous year. Many private residences were erected in the "suburbs." Besides Grace Church, mentioned by Lambert, the corner-stone of which was laid in 1806 at the south-west corner of Broadway and Rector Street, there were three other new churches planned or already begun in 1807 —a new Dutch church in Garden Street on the site of the old one, just burned, a Presbyterian church in Cedar Street, and a Roman Catholic cathedral adjoining the burial-ground owned by this congregation on the southern half of the block bounded by Houston, Prince, Mulberry, and Mott Streets. The new City Hall was now built to the base of the second-story windows. Mechanics of every class found ample employment on these buildings, and also in constructing wharves and paving the streets. In this year the common council placed the extensive "Dove Lots" on the market, reserving in the centre a square which they named after Alexander Hamilton, and which, when the present plan of the city was laid out, was bounded by Third and Fifth Avenues, 66th and 68th Streets. The future development of the city depended chiefly upon the laying out of the streets and avenues throughout the upper part of the island, and to accomplish this most important purpose, a commission was appointed by the legislature on April 3, 1807. The operations under this commission, and the plan which it devised, are dealt with in detail in Chapter V.

The first New York City guide-book made its appearance in 1807. This was Dr. Samuel Mitchell's *The Picture of New York . . . By a gentleman Residing in this City.* It became the subject of Washington Irving's satirical humour, for he soon began writing what Mrs. Lamb calls "an extravagant burlesque" of it—*A History of New-York . . . By Diedrich Knickerbocker*, which was published in 1809. While very evidently never intended as a history, this work of Irving's has, nevertheless, contributed more than any other book to an interpretation of the Dutch character as false as it is widespread.

An event of great interest in the history of New York and of the world was the successful trip of Robert Fulton in the steamboat "Clermont" from New York to Albany. This trip was made from a dock near the State Prison near the foot of the present Christopher Street, starting at one o'clock on the afternoon of Monday, August 17, 1807. Fulton's own account of the journey, published in the *American Citizen* on August 22d, states:

> I left New York on Monday at 1 o'clock and arrived at Clermont, the seat of Chancellor Livingston, at 1 o'clock on Tuesday, time 24 hours, distance 100 miles; on Wednesday I departed from the Chancellor's at 9 in the morning, and arrived at Albany at 5 in the afternoon, distance 40 miles, time 8 hours; the sum of this is 150 miles [*sic*] in 32 hours, equal nearly 5 miles an hour. On Thursday, at 9 o'clock in the morning, I left Albany, and arrived at the Chancellor's at 6 in the evening; I started from thence at 7, and arrived at New York on Friday at 4 in the afternoon; time 30 hours, space run through 150 miles, equal 5 miles an hour. Throughout the whole way my going and returning the wind was ahead; no advantage could be drawn from my sails—the whole has, therefore, been performed by the power of the steam-engine.[1]

The Tammany Society of New York performed an act of generous patriotism in 1808 by erecting a vault at the Wallabout in Brooklyn to contain the remains of the seamen, soldiers, and citizens who perished on British prison-ships during the Revolution. The corner-stone was laid on April 6th, and the funeral was held on May 25th. A Roman Catholic See was created in New York on April 8, 1808.

Albany was now the state capital.[2] A line of stages began on January 4, 1808, to make daily runs from New York along the east side of the Hudson. John Stevens now sought encouragement from the legislature for the construction of floating bridges across the North and East Rivers, but, as in the case of earlier attempts, the plan did not meet with public favour. The steamboat, however, with his potent help and that of Chan-

[1] Fulton's calculation, or the newspaper reproduction of it, is evidently in error, there being a discrepancy of ten miles, which would reduce the rate to about four and a half miles an hour. [2] See *ante*, page 370.

cellor Livingston, soon began to extend its service in every direction. The "Phoenix" was the first vessel propelled by steam to make regular trips on the ocean. Leaving New York on June 8, 1809, she arrived at Philadelphia on June 17th. Improvements in ferry-boats were also undertaken. In November, 1809, there was put into operation between New York and Brooklyn a passenger ferry-boat propelled by paddle-wheels operated by men turning the shaft with a crank; but this method was replaced the following year by the introduction of steam ferry-boats. The first was the "Rariton," which began regular trips from the Battery to Elizabethtown Point and Perth and South Amboy in May. In December, 1810, the common council entered into a contract with Fulton for the permanent employment of his steamboats at the Powles-Hook Ferry. These boats were to be so constructed that eight or ten loaded wagons could be driven into them with safety. They were put into commission in 1811.

Among the more prominent buildings that were being constructed at this time, besides the City Hall, may be noted the Cedar Street Church, which was opened with a sermon by Reverend Doctor Rogers on November 6, 1808; the First Congregational Presbyterian Church, on Elizabeth Street, which was dedicated on December 18, 1808; St. Patrick's Cathedral, already mentioned, the corner-stone of which was not laid until June 8, 1809; and Washington Hall, at the south-east corner of Broadway and Reade Street, designed by John McComb, the corner-stone of which was laid by the Washington Benevolent Society on July 4, 1809. In honour "of the late signal triumph of Federal policy," in the restoration of commercial intercourse with Great Britain, a day of celebration was held on April 24, 1809, with illuminations, the ringing of bells, and the firing of salutes. The year 1809 was also the two-hundredth anniversary of the discovery of the Hudson River by Henry Hudson, and this event was celebrated on September 4th by a meeting of the New York Historical Society in the City Hall, where the Reverend Doctor Miller delivered an address, and by a banquet in the City Hall.

At the end of the decade, the federal census showed that the city had a population of 96,373, an increase of more than thirty-three thousand since the preceding federal census of 1800, and of over eighteen thousand since the municipal census of 1805. Between six and seven hundred dwellings and stores were begun in the spring of 1810. Among these were the Latin School of the Jesuit Fathers, opposite the Elgin Garden, on the present Fifth Avenue at 50th Street; St. James's Episcopal Church at Hamilton Square, which was consecrated on May 17, 1810; and a Presbyterian church in Spring Street, the corner-stone of which was laid on July 9th of the same year. A trade review, published in *The Repertory* on September 25th, stated:

> Business along our streets and docks is now unusually brisk, and the warehouses and stores begin to be crowded with European and India goods. The importations this season are like to be larger than for many years past, and are arriving on time. No less than five ships arrived here yesterday from the single port of Liverpool.

The country dealers sold their produce at good prices, and were able to make prompt and satisfactory remittances on their purchase of imports. Thus the wealth of the city increased with the population. An element which began now to have an increasing importance in this prosperity was the introduction of coal, a factor in the future development of the whole country then undreamed of. Coal had long been imported in considerable quantities from Liverpool, but as a result of experiments beginning in 1798 in the use of Lehigh River coal for fuel, the American product came gradually into favour. Lackawanna coal from Wilkes-barre was first burned in New York at the City Hotel on Broadway, in November, 1810.

We have now reached the point where the old city, which had grown up at haphazard, with crooked streets, wooded hills, and fertile valleys traversed by streams and winding country roads, begins to be absorbed into a new city, in which antiquity and nature are no longer respected, with streets laid out in accordance with a carefully considered, symmetrical plan—that evolved by the commissioners of 1807—which was submitted and adopted in 1811. Unfortunately, this plan, although possessing the merits of simplicity and directness, lacked entirely the equally essential elements of variety and picturesqueness, which demand a large degree of respect for the natural conformation of the land. The new plan was entirely deficient in sentiment and charm, and with its gradual development, little by little, the individuality, the interest, and the beauty of one choice spot after another have been swept away; until now, except in Central Park and at the extreme north of the island, scarcely anything remains to remind us of the primitive beauty and the fascinating diversity of natural charms which we know Manhattan once possessed. The year

1811 marks the end of the little old city and the beginning of the great modern metropolis.

This transition, corresponding as it does almost exactly with the War of 1812–15, makes a fitting point to pause before passing to the consideration of the next stage in the development of the modern city.

PLATES

52–79

1783-1811

This Plate … RESPECT … CONGRESS … the United States.

PL. 53

New York Magazine

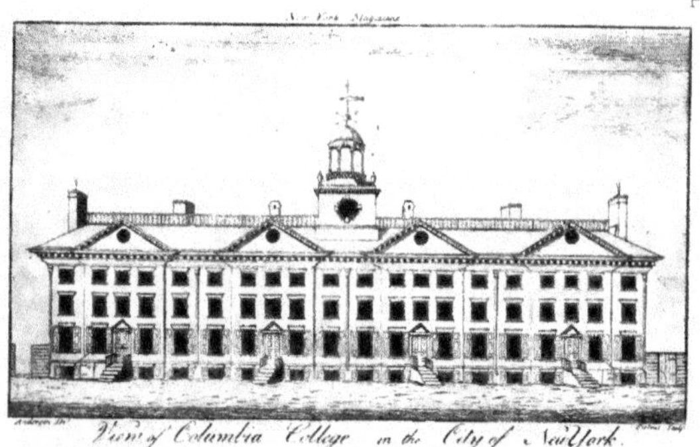

View of Columbia College in the City of New York.

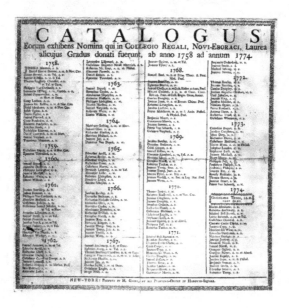

CATALOGUS

Eorum exhibens Nomina qui in COLLEGIO REGALI, NOVI-EBORACI, Laurea alicujus Gradus donati fuerunt, ab anno 1758 ad annum 1774.

[illegible]

NEW-YORK: PRINTED BY H. GAINE, AT HIS PRINTING-OFFICE IN HANOVER-SQUARE.

PL. 54

Engrav'd for the NEW YORK MAGAZINE, January 1790

An E. View of TRINITY CHURCH. N YORK

I. Anderson del. Scoles sculp

A View of St. Pauls Church New-York

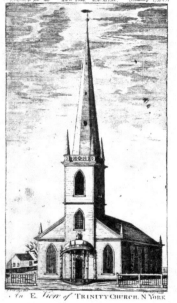

New York Mag. June 1790

A View of the present Seat of his Excel. the Vice-President of the United States

GOVERNMENT HOUSE.

PLATE 56

NEW

ORK.

PL. 57

C. Tiebout Delineavit & Sculpsit.

A Perspective View of the City Hall in New York taken from Wall Street

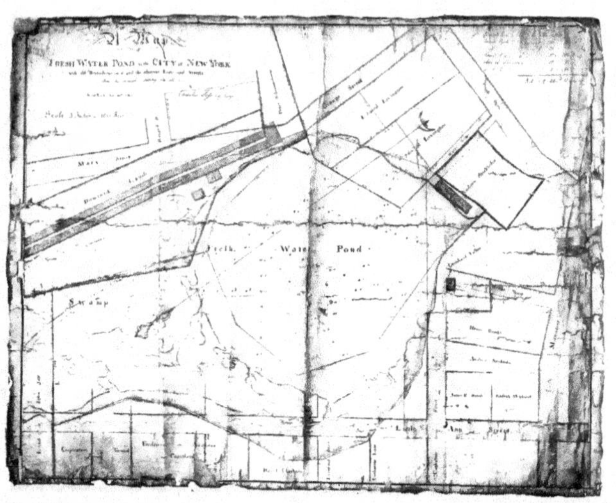
A Map
FRESH WATER POND in the CITY of NEW YORK
Fresh Water Pond
Swamp
Mary
Domenick
Little Ann Street

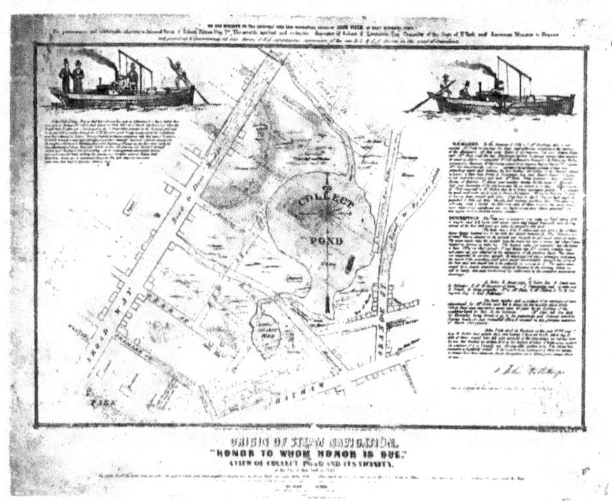
COLLECT
POND
BROAD WAY
PARK
CHATHAM
ORIGIN OF STEAM NAVIGATION.
"HONOR TO WHOM HONOR IS DUE."
A VIEW OF COLLECT POND AND ITS VICINITY,

PL 59

J Drayton Delin. S Hill Sc. Boston

A View of the BATTERY and HARBOUR of New York, and the AMBUSCADE FRIGATE:

VIEW of BELVEDERE HOUSE.

View of the City of New York
taken from Long Island

PLATE 62

...stance of New York
... Pitt
... Livingston Esq.

Custom House, New York.

PLATE 64

A New & Accurate PLAN of the CITY of NEW YORK in the

State of NEW YORK in NORTH AMERICA. Published in 1797

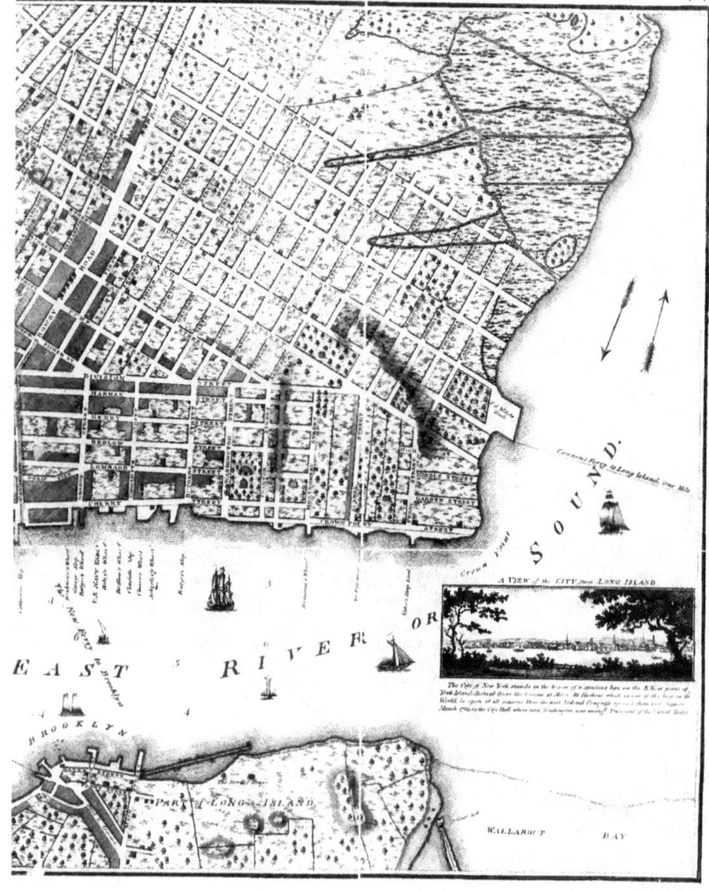

New York — FROM LONG ISLAND

PL. 67.

Pl. 6[illegible]

PLATE 70

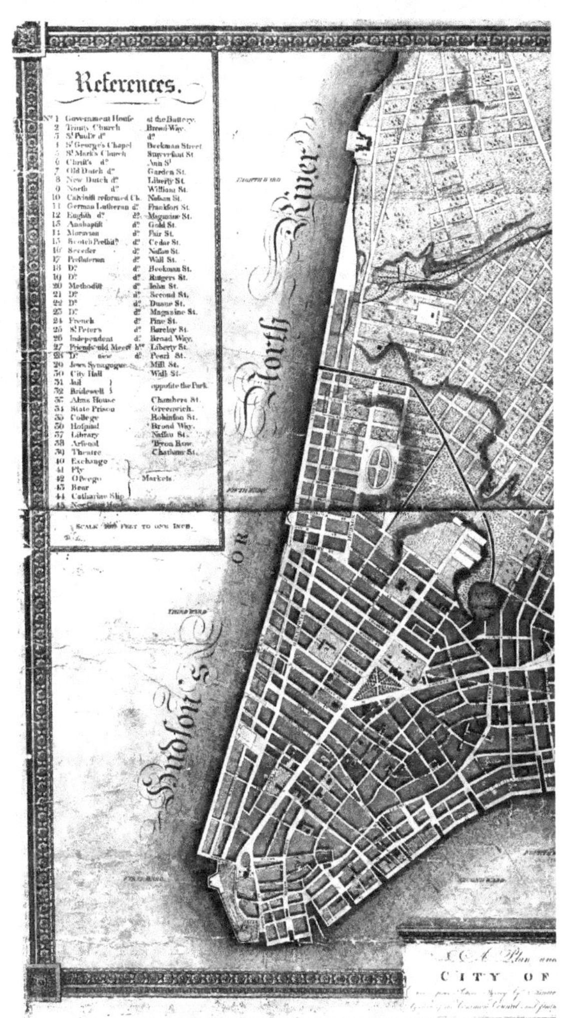
References.
Nº 1 Government House at the Battery.
2 Trinity Church Broad Way.
3 St Paul's dº dº
4 St George's Chapel Beekman Street
5 St Mark's Church Stuyvesant St
6 Christ's dº Ann St
7 Old Dutch dº Garden St.
8 New Dutch dº Liberty St.
9 North dº William St.
10 Calvinist reformed Ch. Nassau St.
11 German Lutheran dº Frankfort St.
12 English dº dº Magazine St.
13 Anabaptist dº Gold St.
14 Moravian dº Fair St.
15 Scotch Presbytn dº Cedar St.
16 Seceder dº Nassau St.
17 Presbyterian dº Wall St.
18 Dº dº Beekman St.
19 Dº dº Rutgers St.
20 Methodist dº John St.
21 Dº dº Second St.
22 Dº dº Duane St.
23 Dº dº Magazine St.
24 French dº Pine St.
25 St Peters dº Barclay St.
26 Independent dº Broad Way.
27 Friends old Meetg hse Liberty St.
28 Dº new dº Pearl St.
29 Jews Synagogue Mill St.
30 City Hall Wall St.
31 Jail
32 Bridewell opposite the Park.
33 Alms House Chambers St.
34 State Prison Greenwich.
35 College Robinson St.
36 Hospital Broad Way.
37 Library Nassau St.
38 Arsenal Tryon Row.
39 Theatre Chatham St.
40 Exchange
41 Fly
42 Oswego
43 Bear
44 Catharine Slip
Markets.
Scale feet to one inch.
North River
Hudson's or
City of

PL. 79

PLAN OF THE CITY OF NEW-YORK,

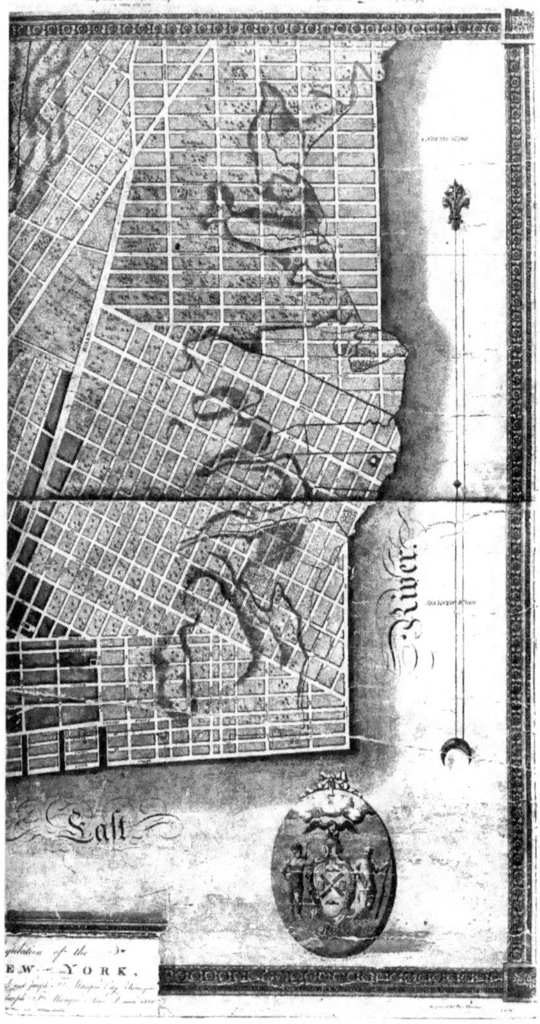

PL. 71.

STATE PRISON, on the Bank of the North River NEW YORK

St. Paul's Church & New Presbyterian Meeting New York

Two Banks & Insurance Office Wall Street New York

New York

PL. 74

NEW YORK, from LONG ISLAND

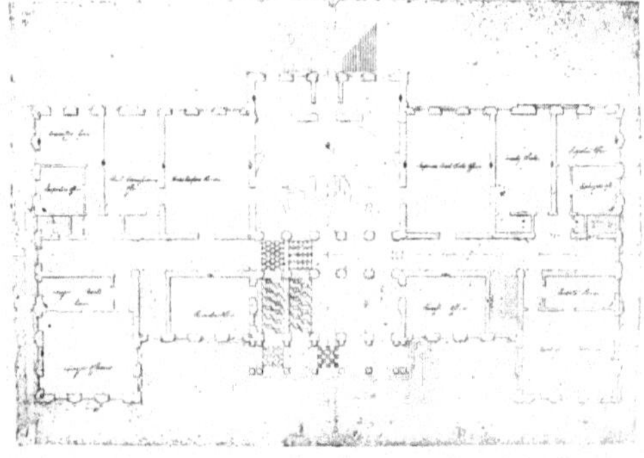

The City of
New York in the State of New York, North America

The City of
New York IN THE STATE OF NEW YORK North America

PL. 78

Imprim.ie Lithograph. de F. [illegible] à Dijon.

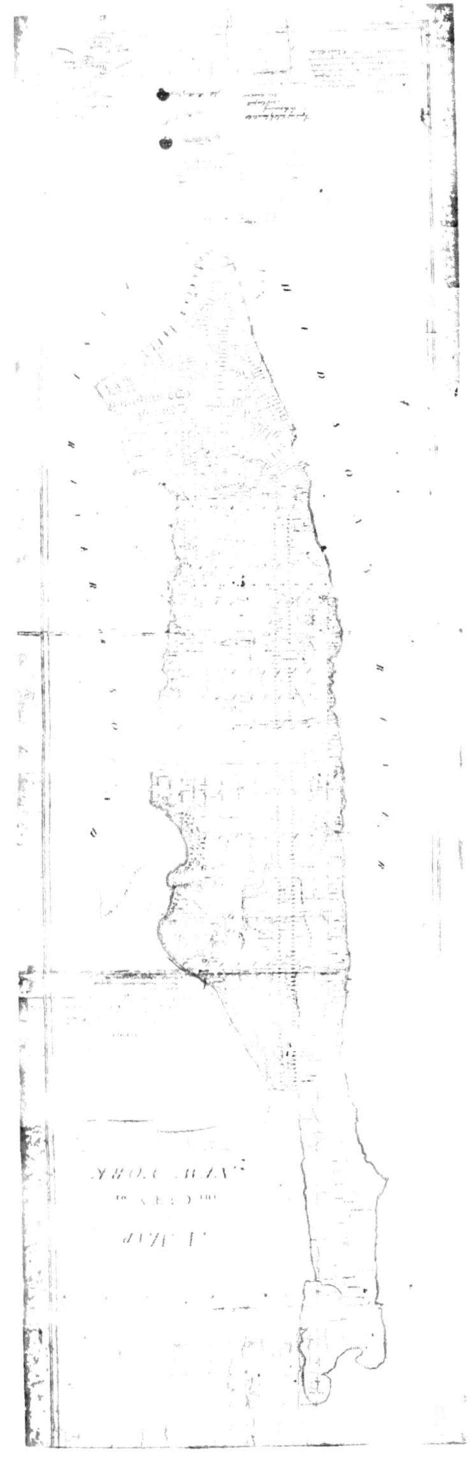
A MAP
of the CITY of
NEW YORK
HUDSON RIVER
EAST RIVER

DESCRIPTION OF PLATES

52–79

1783–1811

DESCRIPTION OF PLATES

52–79

1783–1811

PLATE 52

[The Bowling Green Washington]

Engraved on copper. 21¾ x 25⅛ Date depicted: November 25, 1783.
Artist: Charles Buxton, M. D.
Engraver: Cornelius Tiebout. Date issued: 1798.
Publisher: Charles Smith, N. Y.
Owner: I.N.P.S. (From the Holden Collection.)
Other copies: Library of Congress; Collection of the late Wm. F. Havemeyer, etc.

Second state. An earlier state exists, identical with this except that it was struck before the addition of the publisher's line beneath the title. A copy of this early state is in the collection of Charles W. McAlpin, Esq.; another copy, formerly in the Lossing Collection, was sold by Anderson, in 1912, to J. Clarence Davies, Esq.

The view in the background depicts the Fort, the Bowling Green with the pedestal of the statue of George III, and the Kennedy House, No. 1 Broadway. The British troops and ships are seen evacuating the city.

A copy of this engraving, with some variations, was printed on cotton in Glasgow by "C. G." in 1819 (author's collection, etc.).

Reference: Stauffer, 3196.

PLATE 53–a

VIEW OF COLUMBIA COLLEGE IN THE CITY OF NEW YORK

Engraved on copper. 6¾ x 3$\frac{13}{16}$ Date depicted: Probably 1790.
Provenance: *The New-York Magazine; or, Literary Repository*, May, 1790.
Author: (J.) Anderson.
Engraver: (Cornelius) Tiebout.
Owner: Charles A. Munn, Esq.
Other copies: N. Y. Public Library; N. Y. Hist. Society; Library of Congress, Div. of Maps and Charts, etc.

Only known state. Columbia College, or King's College, as it was originally called, was erected in 1756–8 on ground bounded by Lumber (Church), Murray, Chapel (College Pl.), and Barkly (Barclay) Streets.

In the text accompanying the cut in the magazine, the original college building is described as being only one-third of the intended structure—"an elegant stone edifice, three complete stories high, with four stair cases, twelve apartments in each, a chapel, hall, library, museum, anatomical theatre, and a school for experimental philosophy." It was "surrounded by a high fence, which also enclosed the court and garden, and was about one hundred and fifty yards from the Hudson River . . . The college edifice has received no additions since the peace [1783]. The funds produce, annually, about £1000. The library and museum were destroyed during the war. The philosophical apparatus cost about 300 guineas. The plan upon which it was originally founded, was contracted, and its situation unfavourable. The former objection is removed, but the latter must remain." The first commencement took place on June 21, 1758. For a further description, see Chronology, 1756. See also Moore's *Historical Sketch of Columbia College*, published in 1846; John B. Pine's brief history of *King's College: now Columbia University, 1754–1897*, published in the *Half Moon Papers;* and *History of Columbia University* by J. Howard Van Amringe, 1898, in *Universities and their Sons*, Vol. I.

Plate 53–b

[First Catalogue of King's College]

Printed from movable types by Hugh Gaine. Date issued: 1774?.
Owner: Columbia University.

No other copy known. This is a list of graduates from 1758 to 1774, and was probably printed in 1774. It is the earliest known broadside catalogue of the University.

Plate 54–a

An E. View of Trinity Church, N. York

Engraved on copper. 3⅞ x 7$\frac{3}{16}$ Date depicted: 1789.
Provenance: *The New-York Magazine; or, Literary Repository*, January, 1790.
Author: I. (J.) Anderson.
Engraver: Cornelius Tiebout.
Owner: Charles A. Munn, Esq.
Other copies: N. Y. Public Library; N. Y. Hist. Society; Library of Congress, etc.

Only known state. A description of Trinity Church, accompanying the above engraving in *The New-York Magazine*, explains that as the church "is not yet complete, a description in its present form would convey . . . but an imperfect idea of the whole edifice. The representation here given was drawn from a view in Broadway. The portico in front, and the balustrade and towers at the foot of the spire, were, however, taken from the builder's plan, and are supposed to be pretty correct." The description also states that the church "was built by Mr. J. Robinson, carpenter, and Messrs. Moore and Smith, masons." This same combination of names occurs in connection with the building of the Government House, and we know from *Trinity Minutes, MS.* (1778, June 11), that a resolution was passed to rebuild Trinity Church "upon the Plan proposed by Dr. Bard & delineated by Mr Robinson," showing Robinson to have been the architect.—See Pl. 55–b.

This is the second Trinity Church edifice, and was built in 1788–90 and demolished in 1839. The modest little building seen south of the church occupies, as nearly as can be judged, the position of the public school, sometimes called the Charity School and sometimes the English Free School. The original school building was erected in 1748–9, destroyed by fire in 1750, and rebuilt in the following year at an expense of £375.—See Chronology, 1748, May.

There hangs in the basement of the Trinity Corporation Offices at 187 Fulton Street a large, crudely drawn painting on wood similar to this engraving and evidently contemporary.

Engraved on copper, in 1900, by Sidney L. Smith, for the Society of Iconophiles.

Reference: Stauffer, 3232.

Plate 54-b

A View of St. Pauls Church, New-York

Engraved on copper. 3⅝ x 5⅛ Date depicted: 1795.
Provenance: *The New-York Magazine; or, Literary Repository*, October, 1795.
Author: I. (J.) Anderson.
Engraver: I. (J.) Scoles.
Owner: Charles A. Munn, Esq.
Other copies: N. Y. Public Library; N. Y. Hist. Society; Library of Congress, Div. of Maps and Charts; I.N.P.S., etc.

Only known state. The view shows the church shortly after the erection of the steeple, which was finished in 1794. The following description of the building accompanies the engraving in the magazine:

> The annexed view of *St. Paul's Church* is very judiciously taken from the Park, where the foliage of the young trees embellishes the accuracy of the design. This church was built about thirty-five years since, and is esteemed the most elegant in the city. The front is an Ionic portico, the pediment of which contains a statue of St. Paul in a niche in the centre; and the inside is finished in the Corinthian order, with columns supporting an arched ceiling. The great window in front is adorned with the monument erected by order of Congress to the memory of General Montgomery: the pulpit and altar are designed and executed with a remarkable degree of taste, and the only imperfection appears at the west end, by the deficiency of an organ, the preparations for which, entrances, etc. which it was intended to conceal, are at present a blemish.
>
> The steeple, which was finished last year, completes the external appearance of the building: it is something more than 200 feet high from the ground: above the tower rises a quadrangular section, or story, of the Ionic order, with the proper columns, pilasters and pediments; the two next sections are octangular, of the Composite and Corinthian orders, supported by columns at the angles: the whole is crowned with a spire. The church, tower, and first section of the steeple are of stone, the rest is of wood. As no expense has been spared, and the several parts have been directed by persons of taste and capacity, the structure is generally esteemed preferable to most of the kind in the United States.

The house in the foreground, which stood on the corner of Vesey Street and Broadway, and occupied a part of the site of the Astor House, belonged to Walter Rutherfurd, who describes its location as "far up the street with an open square in front and good air, as there are but few houses in the neighbourhood." Here Walter Rutherfurd lived until his death in 1804.—*Family Records and Events*, by Livingston Rutherfurd (1894), p. 109.

See Pls. 68-b and 100 for further description of residences on Broadway in this neighbourhood.

The "post and rail" fence seen in the foreground was built surrounding the "Fields" in 1785.—*M. C. C. (MS.)*, VIII: 279; see also Chronology. It was replaced in 1818 by an iron railing.—*Ibid*, XXXVI: 8, 108.

Engraved on copper, in 1901, by Sidney L. Smith, for the Society of Iconophiles.

Reference: Stauffer, 2848.

Plate 55-a

A View of the present Seat of his Excel. the Vice President of the United States

Engraved on copper. $6\frac{11}{16}$ x $3\frac{13}{16}$ Date depicted: 1790.

Provenance: *The New-York Magazine; or, Literary Repository*, June, 1790.

Drawn and engraved by Cornelius Tiebout.

Owner: Charles A. Munn, Esq.

Other copies: N. Y. Public Library; N. Y. Hist. Society; Library of Congress, etc.

Only known state. This beautiful country seat, known as Richmond Hill, occupied a site near the present Charlton and Varick Streets. An interesting history of the building, written by General Prosper M. Wetmore, is contained, as Appendix II, in Stone's *History of New York City*. See also Chronology, 1760.

It has often been stated that Richmond Hill House was built shortly after 1760, and so named by Major Abraham Mortier, an English officer who bought the property at the close of the Canadian campaign, and took great pride in improving and beautifying it. It seems probable, however, that the house was not built before 1767, as it is not mentioned in the description of the lease, dated May 1, 1767, contained in the Bancker Papers in the N. Y. Public Library (Box R-W, folder R). From this paper, which is endorsed, "Bounds of Farm—Richmond Hill Trinity Church Commenced May 1," the following extracts have been made:

> And whereas the said Rector & Inhabitants of the City of New York in Communion of the Church of England as by Law established by a certain Indenture of Lease under the said seal bearing date the first of May in the year of our Lord 1767, did demise unto the said Abraham Mortier in his Lifetime, his Executors administrators & assigns for the Term of Ninety nine years to be computed from the date thereof . . . being part of the Land commonly called and known by the name of Old Johns Land . . . containing 26 Acres Three Roods & 36 perches of Land—under the yearly Rent of Two pounds current money of New York aforesaid for each acre thereof . . .

For the second period of 33 years he was to pay three pounds per acre annually, and for the third period four pounds per acre.

Although the estate appears as "Mortier's" upon the Montresor Plan, drawn in 1766, this does not prove that the house had been built at this time or even that the lease had been signed, as it is quite possible that it would have been so included and described on the plan had the lease been pending at the time. There is, however, in the collection of Francis W. Ford, C. S., an original survey of these premises, dated June 10, 1767, showing a house, and a road one rod wide (now obsolete), leading to the Greenwich Road. See also map No. 30 in N. Y. Register's Office, surveyed March 1, 1798, by Charles

Loss, C. S. On this map, a large building called the "Mansion," and evidently intended to represent Richmond Hill House, is shown lying directly in the bed of the later Charlton Street, west of Varick Street. The lease to Mortier seems to have been cancelled at the time of the Revolution, probably because of his British sympathies, or perhaps, as has been stated, because of his untimely death. After the Revolution and during the period when New York was the seat of government, Richmond Hill was occupied for a short time by John Adams, Vice-President of the United States. For an interesting description of the estate, written by Mrs. Adams in a letter to Mrs. Shaw, under date of September 27, 1789, see Chronology.

Aaron Burr acquired the property in 1797 on a 69-year lease from Trinity Church, and, in 1803, sold it to John Jacob Astor. From this time on, the property was allowed to deteriorate and finally, in 1822, became a public garden. In 1831, a new wing was added in the rear of the house, which had been moved when Charlton Street was cut through in 1813, and the whole was converted into a theatre; but the situation of Richmond Hill was not well adapted for this purpose and after about ten years the theatre closed its doors. In 1849 the building was demolished.

In 1913, seven blocks of buildings on Varick Street were torn down for the purpose of widening Varick Street, and in a stable (probably the converted building added in the rear of Richmond Hill House in 1831) were found traces of the old stage of the Richmond Hill Theatre.—*The N. Y. Times*, December 11, 1913.

Engraved on copper, in 1901, by Sidney L. Smith, for the Society of Iconophiles.

Reproduction: Valentine's *Manual*, 1854, opp. p. 468.

Reference: Stauffer, 3202.

Plate 55-b

Government House

Engraved on copper. $5\frac{13}{16}$ x $3\frac{1}{2}$ Date depicted: Probably 1793.

Provenance: *The New-York Magazine; or, Literary Repository*, January, 1795.

Drawn and engraved by I. (J.) Scoles.

Owner: I.N.P.S.

Other copies: N. Y. Public Library; N. Y. Hist. Society; Library of Congress, etc.

Only known state. This view, which shows the west elevation of Government House, was taken from the north-west corner of Battery Park. It was probably drawn after September 5, 1791, when the special committee on the improvements at the Battery and Government House was ordered to erect a fence "to complete the Improvem[ts] in front of the Gov[t] House." This wooden fence, which was in line with the northern elevation, is shown on this view as completed in apparently the same form as in the Milbourne View of 1797 (Pl. 66). The drawing cannot well be later than 1793, for, on January 28th of that year, the committee was ordered to "cause an Iron Railing to be put on the circular Breast Work in the Street in front of the Government House."—*M. C. C.(MS.)*, X: 336. This breastwork and railing were evidently not constructed at the date of our view, but had been added prior to the making of the Milbourne drawing.

Our assumption that the date of the view may be fixed as 1793 is strengthened by the fact that Scoles, who signs the plate as "del." as well as "sc.", does not appear in the New York directories until the year ending May 1, 1794, nor do we find any record of his having been in New York prior to 1793.

The corner-stone of the Government House was laid on May 21, 1790, and the building was completed in the spring of the following year. It was erected by the State of New York as a residence for the President of the United States, but before it was finished the seat of government had been transferred to Philadelphia. For a summarised history of Government House, see Chronology, 1790.

Although we have no positive knowledge of the identity of the architect, it is probable that the design was prepared by James Robinson, who in 1792 appeared in *The New-York Directory and Register* as a house carpenter and master builder, with shop "near Trinity Church, Broadway." In an article accompanying the present view in *The New-York Magazine; or, Literary Repository*, is the following statement: " . . . the whole of the building appears to be executed in a stile which reflects much credit on the professional abilities of those who had the direction of it, Messrs. Robinson, Moore and Smith." In the same magazine for January, 1790, in an article accompanying an engraving of Trinity Church (Pl. 54-a), it is stated, as earlier quoted, that the "new Church was built by Mr. J. Robinson, carpenter, and Messrs. Moore and Smith, masons." We know, also, from the Minutes of the Vestry of Trinity Church (1788, June 11), that a resolution was passed to rebuild Trinity Church "upon the Plan proposed by Doctor Bard & delineated by Mr Robinson," showing Robinson to have been the architect of that building. Designs for the Government House were invited in public competition, and a selection had been made prior to April 26, 1790.—See Chronology.

Among the McComb drawings in the N. Y. Hist. Society, are two unsigned and undated sketches of the Government House, a north elevation and a plan, both of which, especially the plan (Vol. II, Addenda), are suggestive of the executed design. These were perhaps McComb's competition drawings and may have influenced the final design. *Cf.* also survey by John S. Hunn, Street Commissioner, and Amos Corning, City Surveyor (Vol. II, Addenda).

Engraved, in 1901, by Sidney L. Smith for the Society of Iconophiles.

Stauffer, No. 2832, describes an engraving of Government House, N. Y., with the title: "The Government House on lower Broadway," perhaps intended for this view. It, too, was drawn and engraved by Scoles.

Reproduction: Valentine's *Manual*, 1852, opp. p. 180.

Plate 56

New York

Line engraving on copper, coloured. — 21⅛ x 15¼ — Date depicted: Probably 1796 or 1797.

Artist and Engraver: Unknown, but possibly St. Mémin, whose style is suggested by the drawing of the city. Other New York artists of this period who are known to have drawn views of or in the city, and the character of whose work is such as to entitle them to consideration in connection with the authorship of this drawing, are Archibald and Alexander Robertson, John Wood, J. J. Holland, George Holland, Francis Guy, and Cornelius Tiebout (see also below —description of water-colour drawing belonging to Mr. Van Kleeck). It is, however, quite as likely that the view was drawn by some visiting artist, perhaps a foreigner, and that it was engraved abroad.

Owner: Amos F. Eno, Esq.
The only other copy of this print is in the collection of Percy R. Pyne, 2d, Esq.

The only known state of one of the most accurately drawn and interesting views of the city, which it depicts shortly after the period of Washington's residence. Neither the author nor the engraver of the print is known, nor has it proved possible definitely to determine either the exact date depicted or the place of publication. From the fact, however, that Government House is shown apparently completed, and the "mound" or embankment surrounding the Battery finished, it is evident that the drawing was made after 1791. A somewhat later date than this may be assigned from the following facts: During the period between 1791 and 1793 extensive improvements were made at the Battery. In the course of this work, several old buildings were demolished, one of them being the old barracks, or hospital, shown on the Montresor and Ratzen Plans (Pls. 40 and 42), south-east of the Fort. On July 9, 1792, these barracks were ordered demolished, and the materials used in the improvements being made at the Battery.—*M. C. C.* (*MS.*), X: 267. On July 30th, "such of the Materials of the Barracks as may be necessary" were ordered appropriated "for the erection of a Watch House at the City Hall."—*Ibid.*, X: 273. Although we find no definite record of the demolition of these barracks, it is likely that they were torn down at once, as they were an obstruction to the work of improving the Battery. Certainly they had been removed prior to July 29, 1793, when the Watch House at the City Hall was begun.—*Ibid.*, XI: 49. There is no trace of them in this view, nor are they shown on the St. Mémin View of 1796 (Pl. 61).

Another building, demolished during this period, was the house of Thomas Joseph Smith, which stood on the Battery west of the Government House. It was purchased by the city, on September 10, 1792, for £750.—*Ibid.*, X: 280, 284, 294. No vestige of this house, which may be seen on the large Atlantic Neptune View (Pl. 44), remains in the present view. The fence around the Battery, here shown, was evidently built after August 29, 1792, when the Committee on Improvements at the Battery submitted "a Plan of the Ground with a sketch of the manner in which the Committee contemplated to fence in the said Ground."—*Ibid.*, X: 284. Among the improvements made at the Battery during this period, although not specifically referred to in the *Minutes*, must be included the erection of the flag-staff, or "churn," referred to more particularly under Plate 59. It will be noticed that the flag on the "churn" has fifteen stripes instead of thirteen, a change which was not authorised by Congress until January 29, 1794, when it was enacted that from and after the first day of May, 1795, "the flag of the United States, be fifteen stripes, alternate red and white. That the Union be fifteen stars, white in a blue field."—*Acts Passed at the Third Congress of the U. S.* [Phila., 1794], Chap. I. It is, of course, possible that the change from thirteen to fifteen stripes was made by the engraver, after the passage of the new law, or the flag with fifteen stripes may have been in use before its formal ratification by Congress, a supposition which receives support from the fact that the flag in the Drayton View (Pl. 59) also has fifteen stripes (although only thirteen stars), and that this view appears in a book which was published in 1794.

The ship of war in the foreground has not been identified. Although the eagle and the shield in the figurehead suggest an American emblem, it seems hardly possible that she could have belonged to the United States, as there was at this period no American navy, the last ships belonging to the old navy—the "Deane," "Washington," and

"Alliance"—having been sold in 1785, and the first ships of the new navy—including the "Constitution," the "United States," the "President," and the "New York"—not having yet been completed.[1] One of the ships listed in the American navy in 1798 was a fourteen-gun revenue vessel called the "Eagle." This description does not, however, seem to correspond with our view.

The ship, if the drawing depicts an actual vessel, was therefore probably a foreigner, and may very likely have belonged to France, which was still on friendly terms with the United States at this period. It would be interesting to see in her the "America," one of the finest vessels of the period, a seventy-four gun line-of-battle ship, built at Portsmouth, N. H., in 1782, after having been six years on the stocks, and presented to Louis XVI by the United States government to replace the French ship "Magnifique," lost in Boston Harbour the same year. We have, however, no record of a visit of this ship to New York, although in James's *Naval Hist. of Great Britain,* I: 110, the author states that on July 30, 1793, when the "Boston" was awaiting the expected encounter with the "Ambuscade," twelve ships, reported to belong to the French squadron bound for New York, appeared in the south-west, two of which were seventy-four gun ships, stated to be "L'Eole" and the "America." A French fleet did arrive in New York on August 2, 1793 (*The N. Y. Jour. & Patriotic Register,* Aug. 3, 1793), and remained in the harbour until October 5th, but the "America" was apparently not in this fleet which, however, also included two seventy-four gun vessels, "L'Fole" (L'Eole) and "Le Jupiter."—*The Daily Adv.,* Oct. 7, 1793. We know, too, from a description written by Captain Paul Jones, that the "America" had, as a figurehead, a woman crowned with laurel, although it is, of course, possible that this may have been changed.

On April 22, 1793, the frigate "Ambuscade" (variously described as mounting 32, 38, and 40 guns) having on board M. Genet, the newly appointed French Ambassador to the United States, arrived from France via Charleston. She remained in the harbour but a few days, as we know from Dunlap's *American Daily Advertiser* of April 29th that she was sighted off Wilmington on April 26th, and on May 2d arrived in Philadelphia.—*Ibid.,* May 3, 1793. On June 10th, she returned to New York and anchored in the North River.—*The Daily Adv.,* June 11, 1793. Under the dates of June 15th and 25th, we have an interesting description accompanied by a view (Pl. 59) of the "Ambuscade Frigate" and the Battery, by John Drayton (*Letters Written during a Tour through the Northern and Eastern States of America,* Charleston, South Carolina, 1794). This description of the Battery corresponds closely with our view, and in his drawing the "Ambuscade" resembles the ship shown in the view. Drayton, in his description of the Battery (p. 8), says: ". . . the Battery . . . has no merlons, or embrasures; but the guns (which are thirteen in number) are placed upon carriages on a stone platform, *en barbette,* some few feet above the level of the water. Between the guns and the water is a public walk; made by a gentle decline from the platform: and going round the ground upon which the battery is placed. Some little distance behind the guns, two rows of elm trees are planted, which in a short time will afford an agreeable shade." There is apparently a contradiction in the fact that some of these newly set out elm trees, to the

[1] The "Constitution" was built at Boston in 1797. Her figurehead was at first Hercules; later changed to Andrew Jackson. The "Constitution" today lies in the harbour at Boston. The "United States" was built at Philadelphia in 1797, the figurehead being a woman's figure wearing a crest adorned with a constellation. This was changed later to a billet-head. The "New York" and the "President" were built in New York and launched, respectively, on April 21 and April 24, 1800 (see Chronology). The "New York" was a 38-gun frigate but her figurehead is not known; the "President" was a 44-gun vessel with the figurehead of John Adams.

north of the Battery, which are distinctly shown in the Drayton View, do not appear in the view here illustrated, an omission which would seem to indicate that the latter, if belonging to this period, was drawn before June 10th, the earliest date on which Drayton's view could have been made, as he did not arrive in New York until Sunday, June 9th, the day before the return of the "Ambuscade." The only way in which we can account for this apparent contradiction is by supposing that the trees were set out between April 22d and June 15th (which happens to be the usual planting season for deciduous trees), and that the present view was drawn before, and the Drayton View after they were thus set out; or that the view was made during the third visit of the "Ambuscade," when she remained in New York from August 2d until October 7th. In this case, we must suppose the absence of these trees to be due to the fact that they had been removed or destroyed before our view was made. In this connection it may be noted that on March 18, 1793, the Committee on Battery Improvements resolved to empower "proper Persons to prevent Injury to the Trees and Fences at the Battery."—*M. C. C.* (*MS.*), X: 347.

From other internal evidence, which will be considered later, it does not, however, seem at all likely that the view depicts so early a period; and it is, therefore, probably safe to dismiss, as possibilities, the "Ambuscade," "Jupiter," "L'Eole," and other war vessels which visited New York in this year. It is also very unlikely that the boat is one of the English fleet of five vessels, including the "Thetis" of 38 guns, which lay in the Harbour of New York, in December, 1795.—*The Argus, or Greenleaf's New Daily Adv.*, Dec. 10, 1795. The "Thetis" visited New York again in 1796, as did also the "Thisbe," "Spencer," "Hussar," "Hunter," and other English vessels; but it is not possible to connect any of these with the war ship shown in the view.

The author has consulted some of the best naval authorities, including the Hon. Franklin D. Roosevelt, Assistant Secretary of the Navy; Rear Admiral Caspar F. Goodrich; Rear Admiral Charles H. Davis, and Mr. Robert Wilden Neeser; no one of whom, however, has been able to identify this mysterious ship, although Admiral Davis is confident that she is "not a frigate, but a seventy-four, i. e. a line-of-battle ship," and, because of the figurehead, unmistakably American. He inclines to the opinion that, whereas the view was evidently intended principally to show the city, the ship was put in purely as an embellishment, in the delineation of which the artist drew freely upon his imagination.

The date 1796-7 is in keeping with information obtained from a study of the view in connection with the Taylor-Roberts Plan (Pl. 64), from property records of the period, and from the city directories, which study has also made it possible to determine with some accuracy the location and identity of the principal buildings, as follows:

The building at the extreme left, the south end only of which appears in the view, is without doubt the new Tontine City Hotel on the west side of Broadway between the present Cedar and Thames Streets, erected in 1793-5, while the low building next to it is the old Van Cortlandt Mansion (see Pl. 68-a). The drawing of Trinity Church corresponds closely with other views of the church made during this period.—See, for example, plates 54-a (1790) and 68-a (1799). The latter view shows the railing ordered erected around the roof in 1797.—*Trin. Min.*, Aug. 14, 1797. The present view was apparently drawn before this railing was added. The buildings immediately south of Trinity are probably Hunter's Hotel, at No. 69 Broadway, and the Livingston mansion at Nos. 65 and 67. Livingston acquired this property in 1791, at which time it had several houses upon it. In the directories for 1794, 1795, and 1796, we find Livingston at 67 Broadway, and a Mrs. Barham, who kept a tavern and boarding-house, at No. 65. She disappears from the directory in 1797, and in the following year Dr. Hosack is found at this address. It seems very likely that this fine residence, or at least the northern half of it, was built just prior to Dr. Hosack's occupancy.

To the right of the ship's mast may be seen the upper story and the dome of the City Hall on Wall Street. The Presbyterian Church is probably hidden by the mast.

The large block of houses just south of the City Hall was on the west side of Broadway, south of Exchange Place. The northerly of the group occupied the site of the present No. 45 Broadway, and the most southerly that of No. 35. The property between Nos. 39 and 45 was forfeited by Oliver De Lancey and sold by the Commissioners of Forfeiture to Isaac Roosevelt in 1784. On May 8, 1786, Alexander Macomb acquired this property, which at that time was vacant land.—*Liber Deeds*, XLVI: 6. On June 20, 1787, "Messrs. Macombe Lynch, Livingston, &c., proprietors of Lots in the Broadway bounded on the River," petitioned that measures be taken "for compelling Augustus Van Courtlandt to wharf out in front of his lots, to the end that Greenwich Street may be continued on & continued [*sic*] to the Battery." By October 10, 1787, Macomb's house or houses apparently had been completed, for a committee of the Common Council was on that date appointed "to direct the Breadth of the Area in front of the new Buildings of Messrs. Macomb and others in the Broadway."—*M. C. C.* (*MS.*), IX: 4. Macomb's house at 39-41 Broadway, afterwards called the Mansion House, and later still Bunker's Mansion House, was occupied, in 1790, as the official residence of President Washington. It is interesting to note that this house occupied the site of Paulus Leendertsen vander Grift's, afterwards Mayor Rombout's house (see Castello Plan, Appendix, III), and also the legendary site of the first houses on Manhattan Island, referred to in Beauchamp Plantagenet's now discredited book (see Bibliography). It was fifty-six feet wide, while the houses at Nos. 43 and 45 were each twenty-five feet wide, so that together they have the appearance in the view of four houses instead of three. Macomb later became financially embarrassed, and, on October 10, 1792, made a deed in trust to William Edgar and Daniel McCormack.—See *Liber Deeds*, XXIV: 437, in the Secretary of State's Office, at Albany. On April 22, 1793, the Macomb property was advertised for sale in *The Diary; or, Loudon's Register:*

> For Sale, Those three elegant four Story Houses in Broad-Way, formerly the Property of Alexander Macomb, now occupied by Mr. Macomb, Mrs. Graham and Mr. Ricketts. These Houses are so well known as to render a particular Description unnecessary. The Purchaser may have Possession of the House occupied by Mr. Macomb, the 1st of May next; the House occupied by Mrs. Graham, is let to the 1st of May, 1794, for 200 l. the House occupied by Mr. Ricketts is under Lease for four Years, from the 1st of May next, at the annual Rent of 150 l. and the Taxes. For Particulars and Terms of Payment, apply to William Edgar.

This advertisement is somewhat misleading, as Macomb had not sold all his property at this time. As a matter of fact, he did sell the large house to Isaac Clason, a "dummy" purchaser, who turned it over to William Edgar, on April 29, 1793, for £5,700.—*Liber Deeds*, DXXVI: 506, 508. The Edgar family retained this property until 1849. The house at No. 43 reverted to Macomb, who did not dispose of it until 1799, when the executors of Cornelius Clopper, who had evidently lent money on the property, took a deed for it.—*Ibid.*, LXVIII: 271. The house at No. 45 remained in Macomb's possession until it was sold under foreclosure in 1811 by Dominick J. Blake, Master in Chancery.—*Ibid.*, XCV: 182.

The vacant lots north of Macomb's buildings, and adjoining Oyster Pastie Street (present Exchange Alley), belonged to William F. Smith. They had not been built upon in 1795, when Smith recites that he has the privilege of inserting beams in the house of Alexander Macomb when he builds, using it as the party wall.—*Liber Mortgages*, VIII: 225. They were still vacant in 1800, when the Smith heirs sold the property to William Lawrence and Wynant Van Zandt (*Liber Deeds*, LIX: 142), but had probably been built upon by December 19, 1801, when Van Zandt and Lawrence partitioned the property and recited that they had made improvements on said lots.—*Ibid.*, CV: 301. On January 19, 1802, William Lawrence sold to Margaret Jones, widow of Thomas Jones, M. D., a certain "Messuage or tenement number 49 Broadway bounded south by the house and lot now used and occupied by Alexander Macomb." The Jones house was later known as No. 47 Broadway. All of these deeds recite Macomb's occupancy, in these years, of the house at No. 45 Broadway.

Referring to the directories of this period, we find that, in 1791, Mrs. Graham conducted a boarding-school for young ladies at No. 19 Broadway; in the same year Alexander Macomb's residence is given as No. 18 Broadway, and Mr. Jacob Ricketts is at No. 20. In 1792 and 1793 their residences are the same except that Mr. Ricketts's address is given, probably erroneously, as No. 19 instead of No. 20. In 1794 we find Mrs. Graham removed to Liberty Street, and Mr. Ricketts to 142 Greenwich Street, while Alexander Macomb is at No. 39 Broadway. It is quite evident that this last number is the same as No. 18 in the earlier directories. Furthermore, we know that the street numbering was changed in 1794 by a resolution of the Common Council passed December 30th, 1793, which defined in detail the method to be adopted.—See Chronology.

The changes made at this time in the numbering of the houses on Broadway may be further illustrated by a few examples: From 1787 to 1793 James Hallet, a coach-maker, appears in the directory at No. 43 Broadway, which we know from an advertisement in *The Daily Advertiser*, of November 16, 1798, was "adjoining the theatre in John-street." After the renumbering of the street, Hallet's address is No. 194 Broadway. S. Buskirk, a "tinman," was, in 1786, at No. 39 Broadway, which we know from later directories was on the corner of Partition (Fulton) Street. His renumbered address, in 1795, was 209 Broadway. James Anderson, a shoemaker, at No. 65 Broadway from 1786 to 1793, is given at No. 144 Broadway in 1794, etc.

In 1796, William Edgar occupied the old Macomb house at No. 39, and Edward Livingston the house at No. 43 Broadway. Although Macomb's name does not appear in the directory for 1796, it is very probable that he occupied No. 45 (or, as it was then called, No. 47), as he is found here in the following year.

Jacob Ricketts, the lessee of the property at No. 20 (45) Broadway, was a noted equestrian and had a circus on Greenwich Street back of his house in 1793. In 1794 he built a new circus on Broadway, corner of Oyster Pastie Street (Exchange Alley). The ground upon which this circus stood is described in detail in an advertisement of the property, which was offered for sale on February 7, 1795.—*The N. Y. Jour. & Patriotic Register*. In March, 1797, Ricketts opened a new circus on the west side of Greenwich Street, which was described in the newspapers of the day as far surpassing any other of the same description in the United States.—*The N. Y. Gaz. & Gen'l Adv.*, March 3, 1797; *The Diary*, March 20, 1797. This circus is shown on a Bancker Survey of the property of Remsen & McKenny, dated August 3, 1799.—Folder G of Bancker Surveys, in Manuscript Room, N. Y. Public Library. In this survey, Washington Street is shown laid out south of Rector.

The lots immediately south of Lynch's house, Nos. 33 and 31 Broadway, were acquired, on April 3, 1798, by Garrit Van Horne for $6,500, at which time they contained no houses.—*Liber Deeds*, LIX: 512. Van Horne must have built immediately, for in the directory for 1798 his address is given as No. 31 Broadway. On March 3, 1801, Van Horne sold to Thomas Streatfield Clarkson, for $12,000, the north-west half of the property which he had acquired in 1798, together with the dwelling-house.—*Ibid.*, CXIV: 454. As the view shows no buildings at these numbers, it must have been drawn prior to 1798.

On the opposite side of Broadway is seen a continuous row of houses corresponding with numbers 30 to 42 Broadway, or thereabouts. In 1796, No. 30, according to the directory of that year, was occupied by John Delafield; No. 32, by James West and William Hamersley, M. D.; No. 34, by John Charlton, M. D.; No. 36, by Peter J. Munro, an attorney; No. 40, by Mrs. Sarah Livingston; and No. 42, by Mrs. Mary Allen.

Passing to the Battery, and beginning at the south, we find a row of low buildings, evidently occupying the block on the east side of Whitehall between Front and South Streets. All of these buildings existed in 1797, and some of them several years earlier. They seem to have been occupied as small shops and as lodging-houses, with a constantly changing tenancy. Dr. Bayley, the health officer, referred to this neighbourhood in a report to Gov. Jay, dated December, 1796, as being occupied by old and decayed houses, where people of the poorer kind were crowded together.

The point of view is such that the houses standing between Nos. 1 to 5 State Street are concealed by the large three-story and attic house, the western gable of which with its two chimneys is so clearly seen in the view, and which was No. 6 State Street (present No. 7). We know, however, that No. 1 was later the residence of John B. Coles, who bought the property in 1797, and who evidently built within the next few years, as his name appears in the directory for 1800 at this address. No. 2 was not built upon at the date of the view. No. 3 was first occupied in 1800, when it is given as the address of H. Overing. The property is still held by the Overing estate. No. 4 was built, according to land records, by January 30, 1795, in which year it is given in the directory as the residence of D. Penfield. No. 5 was erected prior to March 20, 1797, when it was sold by James Watson to Elkanah Watson, of Albany, for £6,000 (*Liber Deeds*, LIV: 510), the deed reciting that at the time of the sale the house was occupied by Philip Livingston.

No. 6 State Street first appears in the directory for 1794 as occupied by James Watson. In the deed of James Watson to Moses Rogers, dated May 4, 1805 (*Liber Deeds*, LXXI: 397), this property is described as follows:

> Beginning at State Street at the Southwest Corner of the dwelling house of John Hunter and comprising half the wall which seperates [*sic*] the premises from the dwelling house of the said John Hunter and running thence along the centre of the same Northerly to the lot of [blank] Hunt then Westerly along the said lot of said Hunt to the Southwestern Corner thereof then Northerly along the Western line of said lot to Pearl Street thence Westerly along Pearl Street thirty one feet to Stephen Smith's lot then Southerly along the Eastern line of the said Stephen Smith's Lot to the Southeastern Cornern [*sic*] thereof as the fence now runs from thence Southerly to a point in the line of the front of the Coach house extended to the dwelling house which point shall be in the direction of said line ten feet Westwardly from the brick wall of the said dwelling house and from thence to State Street thirty feet Westwardly of the Southwest Corner of the

dwelling house to be measured on the exterior part of Coping Stone of the intermediated [*sic*] Wall (etc.)

From this description, it is evident that even as late as 1805 the western portion of the lot remained vacant. A careful examination of the present No. 7 State Street (which is still standing) shows clearly that the eastern wing of the building, 22 ft. 10½ in. wide, is the original No. 6 seen in our view, and that the westerly portion together with the colonnade and loggia were later additions. That they were built before 1824 is proved by their presence on a manuscript survey of the Battery of that date by Gerard Bancker, in the collections of the N. Y. Public Library. The measurements of the lot and the distance referred to in the deed between the south-west corner of the lot and the south-west corner of the original dwelling-house correspond. Furthermore, the interior arrangements clearly indicate that the western elevation of the original house had the same architectural treatment as that shown in the drawing. Reference to the map shows that the garden of this property came just at the point of the turn in State Street.

It seems likely that the three houses at Nos. 4, 5 and 6 State Street were built by Watson shortly after he had acquired the property. In an article in *The Commercial Advertiser*, of March 28, 1801, the writer draws attention to the various improvements in the city, and enumerates, among others in the period around 1791–2, the "elegant Houses in State street" erected by Mr. Watson.

The house at No. 8 State Street was sold, in 1793, under foreclosure, by the sheriff, Marinus Willett, to James Watson. In 1788 this property was occupied by three small dwelling-houses, as we know by a recital in a mortgage made by Dr. Price. Evidently, before the date of the foreclosure, these three buildings had been replaced by a single house, which stood towards the rear of the lot and does not appear in our view.

The large residence with well-defined string-courses, seen just at the left of No. 6 State Street, occupied the lots Nos. 9 and 11 State Street. According to title records, these lots belonged to Carey Ludlow, and were, by his will, dated 1814, bequeathed to his wife. A very good picture of the Ludlow house is found in Lamb's *History of the City of New York*, II: 445. No. 9 State Street appears first in the 1797 directory, where it is given as the address of J. Watson and Carey Ludlow, although, during the following three years, Joseph Corre, the tavern-keeper, seems to have occupied the building. The properties at Nos. 9 and 11 had a frontage of 55 feet, more or less, and adjoined, there being at the time no No. 10. The three-story single-chimney house, with the blank north wall, adjoining No. 9–11, was No. 12 State Street, and was deeded, on May 21, 1793, by Belinda Hunt, widow of Obadiah, to Joseph Corre. It was then described as having a messuage or dwelling-house upon it "wherein the said Obadiah Hunt formerly lived."—*Liber Deeds*, XLIX: 351. Curiously, the directories do not give this property as occupied prior to 1800.

North of No. 12 was Corre's Columbia Garden, which extended from No. 10 Pearl Street west to the Battery and through to State Street—Corre's house, as already noted, being at No. 12 State Street. The Garden was opened in 1798, when Corre advertised that he had completed "the above garden, adjoining his house facing the Battery."—*The Daily Advertiser*, May 5, 1798. In *The Picture of New-York*, published in 1807, there is an account of the pleasant walk about the Battery, where the citizens could enjoy the fresh breezes from the bay, the shade of the trees, and the delightful view. "And if more gratification is desired, musick, ice-creams and other delicacies, are provided in the evening, at Mr. Corrie's public garden, not far from the centre of this exquisite place of recreation." Corre's gardens were not partitioned off until after 1809. The low buildings north of No. 12 State Street are probably inside the Garden; possibly one of them is the building in which, according to the directory for 1796, David Jostler had a "menage of living animals." In May, 1797, this menage was run by Gardner Baker.—*The Daily Adv.*, May 9, 1797. On October 30, 1797, the "menage or place for the keeping of wild animals" at the corner of Pearl and State Streets was declared a nuisance, and the tenant ordered to surrender the property.—*M. C. C. (MS.)*, XII: 256.

The large three-story building north of No. 12 State Street is probably No. 14 Pearl Street. It belonged to Stephen Smith and at the time of the view was in the tenure of Joseph Jacobs, who conducted a "porter-house." Title records indicate that, in 1791, lots Nos. 10 and 12, west of this, were occupied by small houses.—*Liber Deeds*, XLVII: 41–2. These had probably been demolished prior to the date of the view. They were evidently not in existence in 1809 when, in a conveyance made by the heirs of Joseph Rose to John Clark, the property at No. 10 Pearl Street is described as bounded north by Pearl Street, east partly by land belonging to the grantors and partly by land belonging to Carey Ludlow, south by land belonging to Corre, and west by Corre's land; no mention being made of any houses.—*Ibid.*, LXXXII: 330–1.

The next large house, of which we see the westerly gable with two chimneys, is undoubtedly the residence of John Shaw, merchant, at No. 9 Pearl Street. Shaw acquired this property from John Stevens and William Alexander for $2,545, in 1795, at which time it had no house upon it. He evidently built at once, for his name appears in the directory for 1798 at this address. He had a store at No. 15 Pearl Street, and back of his lots at Nos. 11 and 13, a store-house, which was reached by a cartway between Nos. 13 and 15. On March 4, 1814, Shaw conveyed the property at No. 9 Pearl Street for $23,250, to Helen Elizabeth Gibbs, of Boston, who later became the wife of Luther Bradish and who lived here until her death. Annexed to this conveyance is a very interesting survey of the property, by Bridges & Poppleton, dated February, 1814, which shows the plan of the house and of the yard, with coach-house, outhouses, and store-house.—*Liber Deeds*, CVI: 266. In 1836 the house was occupied by Thomas Ludlow Ogden. The store-house, which is seen in the view back of the Shaw house, was apparently still standing in this last-mentioned year, when the three dwellings at Nos. 11, 13, and 15 Pearl Street "and the two Store houses in the rear of said dwellings" were sold by David B. Ogden, executor of the Shaw property, to Joseph D. Beers, for $38,700.

The large house to the left of the flag-staff and adjacent to the garden of the Government House was known as No. 1 and No. 3 Pearl Street. It belonged to Edward Livingston in 1796, as is shown by a mortgage recorded in *Liber Mortgages*, VII: 522–4, where it is referred to as "all that Messuages & Lot or Lots of Ground situate in the first Ward of the City of New York part of which is now in the Tenure of James Wells [Mills] and Elizabeth Cotterall," etc. In 1798 the directory gives No. 1 Pearl Street as the address of Samuel Mills, tavern-keeper, Richard Cottrel, cooper, and John Carlton, boatman; and No. 3 as the address of Philip Ferguson, porter, Andrew McPherson, chandler, and the "widow Flanagan." The house depicted in the view was probably built after the Revolution. It existed in 1789 when, as No. 2 Pearl Street, it is given as the address of Mrs. Wade, who conducted a school there. In 1792 and 1793 Thomas Cotteral, a mariner, occupied No. 2 Pearl, while in 1794 he is at No. 3 Pearl Street. As we know that the street numbering was changed in 1794, it is evident that No. 3 Pearl Street was formerly known as No. 2. The house stood on the east side of State

Street, just south of the present Bridge Street, which was opened in 1808, although in the view it is drawn much too near the Government House to allow for the intervening garden. It was built well back from Pearl Street, from which it was separated by an extensive private garden. This site was originally occupied by the house of the mid-wife, Tryntie Jonas (see Vander Gow's Report in Chronology, 1638), and in 1755 is shown on the Duyckinck Map as a sugar-refinery belonging to Joseph Griswold. It had been acquired in 1743 by Gulien Verplanck (*Liber Deeds*, XXXII: 452), from whom it descended to his granddaughter, Mary Livingston. In 1804 this property came into the possession of Archibald Gracie (*Liber Deeds*, CXX: 200), who erected upon it a fine residence, the outline of which is clearly drawn on the manuscript Bancker Survey, above referred to.

Although in the view no trace appears of a house at No. 5 Pearl Street, east of the Livingston property, it may be hidden by No. 1, or may be the little wooden cottage shown in the foreground of No. 9, we know that a house existed here in 1796 and later. In the mortgage given by Livingston, already referred to, the property at No. 1 Pearl Street is bounded east "by a house and Lot of Ground formerly in the Possession of Mrs Blaau." In the directory for 1794, Uriah Blaau is given at No. 5 Pearl Street; in 1798 C. G. Fontaine lived at this address, and in 1801, Daniel Dickson. In 1804 the property was sold to Robert McCullen, the deed referring to it as a "certain lot or parcel of ground," no house being mentioned.—*Liber Deeds*, LXIX: 67-9. As no house was cited in the conveyance to Gracie of the old Livingston property, it is possible that both of these houses had by this time been destroyed by fire.

There is in the view no indication of the apse-shaped extension south of the Government House which appears in McComb's plan of April 27, 1808 (Vol. II, Addenda), as well as on two surveys made by Amos Corning and owned by Mr. Ford, C. S.; and no record has been found of the subsequent erection of this wing. North of the Government House is seen the Kennedy mansion, on the north-west corner of Broadway and Battery Place. For a brief history of this house and property, see Pl. 98.

The large building near the shore front at the extreme left of the view resembles closely the fine old house still standing at No. 22 Lumber Street, corner of Edgar Street, and running through to Greenwich Street. Furthermore, the distance from Edgar Street to the Battery, measured on the modern map, is about 750 feet, agreeing very closely with the view, which shows between Edgar and Marketfield Streets, about 28 or 30 lots of a probable average width of 25 feet. However, property records apparently indicate that this house was not built until after 1809. A careful comparison of the original of this view with the Taylor-Roberts Plan of 1797 (Pl. 64) shows that the water-front corresponds very closely on both. The bulkhead in the view is apparently flush with the wall of the Battery, as on the plan, and the little projecting bulkhead midway between Market Street and Beaver Lane, which can easily be distinguished in the original view, is also prominently shown on the plan. The new wharves were completed in 1794 (see Chronology); and as the buildings along the water-front evidently occupied the new ground reclaimed at this time between Greenwich Street and the shore, it seems obvious that the view was drawn after this year. It is possible that the large building to the extreme left may be one of the store-houses of William Edgar who, in 1792, acquired from Alexander Macomb property extending 205 feet along the west side of Greenwich Street, covering numbers 56 to 70, and running through to the Hudson River. We do not know when these store-houses were erected, but it is very likely that they were built soon after Edgar came into possession of the property. At the period of the view they would, if built, naturally appear on the water-front. Later on, when the water lots were reclaimed and Washington Street was extended through to the Battery, they occupied a position on the east side of Washington Street. Their location is thus described in Edgar's will, wherein he bequeaths to his daughters his houses at 62, 64, and 66 Greenwich Street with the store-houses in the rear on Washington Street. The directories of 1796 and 1799 have been searched for mention of a house at one of these numbers, but none apparently existed at this time. In 1801, we find J. Marks, a merchant, at No. 62 Greenwich Street, where he continued to reside for a number of years.

A water-colour drawing, perhaps the original from which the engraving was made, is in the possession of Mr. Charles M. Van Kleeck, of New York. This drawing was inherited by Mr. Van Kleeck from his mother and it has always been a tradition in the family that it was painted by his great-grandmother, (Mrs.) Agnes Boyd Van Kleeck, a number of whose drawings and water-colours show a somewhat similar technique. The drawing is on hand-laid paper of the period, with a fleur-de-lis and Whatman water-mark. It measures 22¾ x 16¼ inches.

Although it is possible that this drawing was copied from the engraving, a very careful comparison of the two seems to indicate that this was not the case, but rather that such variations as exist were the result of additions or modifications on the part of the engraver, especially of technical details in connection with the ship, with which he might naturally have been more familiar than the artist. The most noticeable of these variations are the following: The water-colour shows the pinnacles at the main corners of Trinity Church, which we know existed at this time (see Pl. 54–a), and omits the mullions in the apse window; the dormers and panels above the windows of Government House are omitted; the flag on the "churn" has a different outline and the pole is lower; and the side elevation of No. 6 State Street is somewhat different. On the Battery there are but six small clumps of trees, the southerly small clump shown in the engraving being merged with the larger double clump. In the drawing of the ship the water-colour omits entirely the guns on the forecastle, and also the streaks. The shield in the figurehead has the stars and stripes, and there are a number of variations in the drawing of the jib-boom, shrouds, and cordage. The figure in the small boat alongside is omitted. The shipping in the East River extends to a point above the flag-staff. In the row-boat, off the Battery, both men are shown rowing. Generally speaking, the variations are of a character which suggest an original drawing made on the spot rather than a copy.

A view which may possibly be a later state of the engraving here reproduced is known only through its reproduction in Valentine's *Manual* for 1862 (frontispiece), where it bears the inscription: "New York, about 1790./ Presented to D. T. Valentine, by Edw. Crommelin, 195 Prince St New York." In this view there are many slight variations, some of which seem to indicate a slightly later period than the one depicted in the view here reproduced. The fact, however, that the ship in the foreground and the sloop rounding the Battery still appear, must be accepted as a strong point in the argument that the view presented to Mr. Valentine was a drawing made from our engraving, or possibly from the water-colour above referred to, and that the additional ships which it shows lying off the Battery were added by the artist merely as embellishments. This theory, however, leaves several variations in the town itself to be accounted for, such as the screen or breastwork in front of the flag-staff, which does not appear in the engraved view here reproduced, and which did not exist at the time of Drayton's visit in 1793, as he distinctly refers to the guns as being mounted "en barbette." This screen or breastwork may have been erected in 1798 when a number of fortifications were built at the Battery and on the islands in the harbour (see Chronology). On January 30, 1805, the wooden bastions at the Battery and at Rhinelander's Wharf were given by the State to the City of New York to be used as fuel for the poor.—*Laws of N. Y.*, 1805, Chap. III. A small additional house in front of the group of buildings at the southern end of the Battery also appears in the reproduction of Valentine's view, in which, too, a group of trees at the southern extremity of the Battery appears more mature, and a tree to the north of the Government House somewhat higher than in the engraved view here reproduced.

Valentine reproduces, also, our engraved view in the *Manual* for 1851, to which he assigns the date 1787. Evidently he considered that this was a different view from the one which had been presented to him, or at least that the latter was a later state. Our own conclusion is that both were copied from the same original, and that Valentine's view is only a dressed-up copy of the original, and the apparent variations in the town itself the result of carelessness in copying.

It is interesting to note that the copy of the view here reproduced was sold at auction in the winter of 1910–11 for $660, the highest price which up to that time had been publicly paid for any printed view of New York, whereas Mr. Eno paid only $15 for his copy, about fifteen years earlier.

Engraved, on copper, in 1906, by Sidney L. Smith, for the Society of Iconophiles, with title: "A South West Prospect of the City of New York (1806)."

Plate 57

A Perspective View of the City Hall in New York taken from Wall Street
[The Tiebout City Hall View]

Engraved on copper. 20½ x 14¼ Date depicted: Probably 1791–3.
Drawn and engraved by Cornelius Tiebout.
Owner: N. Y. Hist. Society.
Other copies: N. Y. Stock Exchange Lunch Club (defective), and a copy belonging to the Lossing Collection, and sold at Anderson's, in 1912, to George D. Smith (now in the collection of Percy R. Pyne, 2d, Esq.). These are the only copies known.

Only known state. This interesting view and the Lacour-Doolittle print (Vol. II, Frontispiece) together give us an almost complete picture of the exterior of the Federal Hall, as remodelled by L'Enfant in 1788–9 for the accommodation of Congress, at which time the extension seen in the rear of the hall was added. The drawing must have been made either between 1789, when the restorations were completed, and 1793, or between 1796 and 1799, as Tiebout was absent in London from 1793 to 1796, from which year until 1799 his name appears continuously in the New York directories. As *City* and not *Federal* Hall is used in the title, the view must have been made after December 6, 1790, when the seat of national government was removed to Philadelphia. It will be noticed that Trinity Church is shown completed, as it was early in 1790; also that the three-story building, shown at the north-east corner of Wall Street and Broadway in the Holland water-colour sketch of 1799 (Pl. 68-a), does not yet appear in this view.

The building seen at the left of Trinity Church, on the south-west corner of Wall and Broad Streets, was at this time in the possession of Nathaniel McKinley. On May 16, 1796, the city bought this property from McKinley's heirs for the purpose of widening Wall Street at this point.—*M. C. C.* (*MS.*), XI: 379. This proposed work, as we know from descriptions in later deeds, was never carried out. The building at the extreme right is the Verplanck mansion, replaced in 1823 by the U. S. Branch Bank.—See Chronology, 1822. In 1836, on the failure of the Branch Bank to obtain a renewal of its charter, the building was purchased by the Bank of the State of New York, and, in 1844, part of the property was sold by this institution to the Bank of Commerce. In 1853, the building again came into the possession of the U. S. Government and was converted for use as the Assay Office, for which purpose it continued to be used until 1912, since which time it has been unoccupied.[1]

The omission from the view of the steeple or cupola of the Presbyterian Church, which should appear above the City Hall, is worthy of note.

On the back of the Historical Society's copy of this view is the following inscription: "Presented to the New York Historical Society by John Pintard on the 15th May 1812, the day on which this building was prostrated, the materials having been sold at auction to Mr. Jinnings for four hundred and twenty-five Dollars."

The New-York Magazine for March, 1790, published a perspective view of the Federal edifice, which has been attributed by Stauffer and others to Tiebout, and our view was probably taken shortly after this date. It is interesting to compare the view here reproduced with the Du Simitière sketch (Vol. II, Addenda), made probably in 1769 after the third story was added to the building; see also Pl. 72-b for description of a very similar, but somewhat later water-colour view belonging to the N. Y. Hist. Society.

Engraved on copper, in 1902, by Sidney L. Smith for the Society of Iconophiles. See *Catalogue of the Engravings* issued by this Society (pp. 49-50) for a list of early engravings of the City Hall in Wall Street.

Reproductions:

A lithographic reproduction of this view, approximately the size of the original, was published, without date, in Buffalo, by Clay & Richmond, and is now very scarce.

Valentine's *Manual*, 1847, Frontispiece.

Reference: Stauffer, 3223.

Plate 58-a

A Map of Fresh Water Pond in the City of New York (etc.)

[A Manuscript survey by Charles Loss, City Surveyor, made on the ice]

Manuscript on paper. 38 x 30 Date depicted: 1801.

Owner: City of New York, Office of the Bureau of Design and Survey (formerly the Office of the Engineer of Street Openings), Department of Public Works (Manhattan).

[1] On April 20, 1915, the demolition of this interesting and charming little building was begun (under the supervision of the present writer) to make room for the Wall Street wing of the new Assay Office on Pine Street. The stones of the facade were carefully taken down, cleaned, marked for identification, and stored on a vacant lot at No. 519 E. 69th Street, the intention being to re-erect the facade at some future time, when an appropriate use can be found for it.

This is the earliest actual survey of the Collect Pond that the author has been able to find, although in the Bancker Collection in the N. Y. Public Library (Box B–F, folder E–F) there is a "Survey of the Calk or Fresh Water Pond on the ice by order and in the presence of a Committee of the Corporation this 25 Feb. 1771," by F. M. (Francis Maerschalck) and G. B. (Gerard Bancker), City Surveyors, copied by E. B. (Evert Bancker) February 7, 1790. This survey does not, however, depict the outlines of the pond, nor does it give the surrounding streets.

The *Manual of the Common Council* for 1856 contains a reproduction of an interesting sketch drawn from memory by David Grim, showing the pond and its immediate vicinity as it was in 1742.[1] The *Manual* for 1860 contains a view of "The Kolch or Kalch-Hook Pond, as it was in Olden Times," probably purely fanciful. There is also, in the *Manual* for 1861, an interesting "Ancient View of the present junction of Pearl & Chatham Sts" which has the appearance of having been copied from an older view. A pencil drawing on tracing-paper, in the author's collection, differing in some details from this view, may possibly be the contemporary original, or a tracing from it. Otherwise, no early contemporary view of the Collect has survived, or at least no such view is known to exist.[2] This seems very extraordinary, as the Collect was one of the most important and interesting topographical features of the old city, and was during a long period a popular resort for fishing and boating in summer, and for skating and coasting in winter.

In *New-York as it was, during the latter part of the last Century*, Mr. Wm. Alexander Duer (p. 13) gives an interesting description of the Collect Pond as he remembered it in 1783:

> Its southern and eastern banks were lined with furnaces, potteries, breweries, tanneries, rope-walks, and other manufactories; all drawing their supplies of water from the pond. Besides, it was rendered ornamental as well as useful. It was the grand resort in winter of our youth for skating; and no person who has not beheld it, can realize the scene it then exhibited in contrast to that part of the city under which it now lies buried. The ground between the Collect and Broadway rose gradually from its margin to the height of one hundred feet, and nothing can exceed in brilliancy and animation the prospect it presented on a fine winter day, when the icy surface was alive with skaters darting in every direction with the swiftness of the wind, or bearing down in a body in pursuit of the ball driven before them by their *hurlies;* while the hill side was covered with spectators, rising as in an amphitheatre, tier above tier, comprising as many of the fair sex, as were sufficient to adorn, and necessary to refine the assemblage.

On February 22, 1796, a proposal of Joseph Mangin and other engineers was submitted to the Common Council for "making a Dock or Basin in the low Grounds at the fresh Water Pond as a safe Harbor for shipping & to drain and carry off the Water from that Quarter into the Rivers."—*M. C. C. (MS.)*, XI: 346. Nothing ever came of the project, and the Collect was later (1803–11) filled up. For a more complete history of the Collect, or Fresh Water Pond, see Chronology.

Reproduced and described here for the first time.

[1] The original Grim sketch is in the N. Y. Hist. Society (box labelled, "N. Y. 1700–1760"). It was presented by Mrs. Sophia C. Minton, June 7, 1864.

[2] Mr. Arnold's collection contains a set of twenty-nine original water-colour drawings, about 6 x 8 in. (Nos. 7 and 16 missing), many of which are signed "Wm P. Chappell," and dated variously from 1806 to 1810. No. 23 of this interesting series has on the back the following contemporary inscription: "Collect Ground Arsenal & Stone Bridge Garden. Militia Drilling. View from the East side of Orrange & pump St. N. Y. 1812." The south end only of the Pond is shown in this view. See Vol. II, Addenda.

Plate 58-b

ORIGIN OF STEAM NAVIGATION
"Honor to Whom Honor Is Due."
A View of Collect Pond and its Vicinity, in the City of New York in 1793 . . . . (etc.)

The remainder of the title, which in the print here reproduced is in part obliterated, reads as follows:

> On which Pond, the first boat, propelled by paddle wheels and screw-propellers, constructed by John Fitch, six years before Robert Fulton made trial of his boat upon the River Seine, in France, and ten years prior to his putting into opperation (*sic*) his boat Clermont in New York; with a representation of the boat and its machinery, on the Collect pond.
>
> By John Hutchings
>
> N? 3, Wesley Place, Williamsburgh, L. Island, 1846

Lithograph. $23\frac{11}{16}$ x $15\frac{15}{16}$ Date depicted: 1793-6.
Date issued: 1846.

Drawn on stone by J. Penniman.
Lithographer: F. Michelin.
Publisher: John Hutchings.
Owner: I.N.P.S.
Other copies: N. Y. Public Library; N. Y. Hist. Society; etc.

This is the earliest form in which this print appears. A later state (copy in N. Y. Public Library) omits the third line in the upper margin. The oarsmen also have been omitted from the two boats in the upper corners of this print, traces of the oar on the right-hand boat remaining plainly visible. Beneath the boat, at the left, a number of testimonials have been added, the area of the map being correspondingly decreased. Below the Collect, in this later state, appears a representation of "John Fitch's First Boat Perseverance, as seen on the Delaware, Phi[a] 1787, speed 7 miles an hour," and another small boat "The Model Boat at Bardstown, 1797-8."

The print was redrawn and issued with modifications in at least two other forms, in one of which it was mounted on rollers as a wall map. All of these prints bear the date of issue 1846, and all were probably copied, in part, from a map or survey made in 1793, possibly from one by Gerard Bancker now preserved among the Bancker Papers in the N. Y. Public Library. See Pl. 46 A-b.

The publisher of this lithograph, John Hutchings, as the inscription relates, when a lad, in the summer of 1796 or 1797, assisted Mr. Fitch in experiments on the Collect Pond with his steamboat, which it is here claimed was the first boat propelled by paddle wheels and screw-propellers.

Fitch had been experimenting with steam boilers for propelling boats for over ten years. As early as July 27, 1786, he made a trial trip in Pennsylvania, in a steamboat of his own invention, and, on August 22d of the following year, with a new and larger boat, gave a demonstration which was witnessed by "all the members of the convention for framing the Federal Constitution, except General Washington." From 1790 to 1792, regular trips were made with Fitch's steamboat between Philadelphia and Trenton.—Bullock's *The "Miracle" of the First Steamboat*, in *Jour. Am. Hist.* (1907), I: 33-48.

The boat used in connection with Fitch's experiments on the Collect Pond is thus described by William Alexander Duer, an eye-witness, in his *Reminiscences* (pp. 46-9):

Passing on one occasion with a companion across the fields near the "Kolck," we were startled by a sound, which, for a moment, I mistook for the blowing of a shoal of porpoises which had found their way from the river. But on proceeding to the bank overlooking the pond in the rear of Broadway, we descried a boat, which I supposed at first to be on fire, but soon perceived that not to be the case, as her movements were regular, and produced by paddle-wheels at her sides, which, in my wisdom, I supposed to be driven by the smoke issuing in a thick volume from her pipe, after the manner of the Jack for roasting, in my father's kitchen.

My more intelligent companion, who had seen the boat before, informed me, however, that it was a "*steam boat*," and belonged to one Fitch, a Yankee, who had contrived that mode of rowing boats by the steam arising from a close kettle of boiling water, which he had on board, and to which the fire that caused the smoke was applied. My wonder and curiosity being thus excited, I advanced to the point at the foot of the hill, to which the boat appeared to be approaching, and reached the spot as she touched the shore. I there saw several persons land from her, among whom I recognized Chancellor Livingston, Colonel John Stevens, of Hoboken, and a Mr. Roosevelt, . . .

There remained on board a man, whom I understood to be Mr. Fitch, and a boy, whom my companion accosted as Jack Hutchins. Of the former he asked and obtained permission for us to go on board the boat, and were shown her machinery by the latter. She was a ship's long boat, or common yawl, about eighteen or twenty feet in length, and six in width. She had cross seats as usual, between which were placed a large iron pot, with a heavy plank cover, set upon a sort of grate or furnace, and a square vessel of copper was annexed to the pot. Forward of this apparatus, were placed, at some distance from each other, two casks, of different sizes, and between them, at about the center of the boat, an upright bar of iron, with another lighter one fixed horizontally upon it, so as to vibrate like a scale beam. At each end of this beam depended a perpendicular rod, which played up and down in the casks, through orifices in their heads, and a third rod, stouter than the others, was attached at one end to the horizontal beams, about half way between its centre and one of its extremities. This was fastened, at its other end, to a crank, in an iron shaft running across the boat, and passing through her sides so as to form the axis of her water wheels. There was another iron that passed longitudinally out of the boat's stern, and upon asking the use of it, the boy told us that Mr. Fitch found the wheels splashed so much, and the paddles in rising held so much water, that he meant to use the screw lying on the shore in their stead, and fix it under water at the stern, "so as to scull her."

Fitch, failing to arouse public interest in his experiment, abandoned his boat in the Collect and left New York. He died in Kentucky in 1798, or thereabouts. While he was not the first successfully to demonstrate the practicability of navigation by steam, his experiments marked a decided advance in the working out of the problem, although, as pointed out by Dickinson (*Robert Fulton Engineer and Artist. His Life and Works*, p. 132), "he was unable to build a boat large enough, or an engine quite light enough for the work; nor was transportation so important a question then as it quickly became." In a letter written in June, 1792, to one of his share-holders, Mr. Rittenhouse, Fitch remarks: "This, sir, *will* be the mode of crossing the Atlantic in time, whether I shall bring it to perfection or not."

Fitch's manuscript autobiography is in the Franklin Institute in Philadelphia.

PLATE 59

A VIEW OF THE BATTERY AND HARBOUR OF NEW YORK, AND THE AMBUSCADE FRIGATE

[The Drayton View]

Engraved on copper. 5¾ x 3⅞ Date depicted: June 10–20, 1793.

Provenance: Opposite p. 20 in *Letters Written during a Tour through the Northern and Eastern States of America;* by John Drayton, Charleston, South-Carolina, 1794.

Artist: J. Drayton.
Engraver: S. Hill, Boston.
Owner: William Loring Andrews, Esq.
Other copies: N. Y. Public Library; N. Y. Hist. Society; I.N.P.S., etc.

This is the only known state of the print.

From an analysis of Drayton's *Letters*, it is evident that he arrived in New York on Sunday, June 9, 1793, and left, or intended leaving, on June 26th. He reached Boston on July 2d via Newport and Providence. His two letters from New York are dated June 15th and June 25th. In the latter he describes the Tontine Coffee House, which, he says, was visited by a "vast throng" every evening when the Ambuscade Frigate was in New York. According to *The Daily Advertiser* of June 11, the "Ambuscade" had arrived on the preceding day, or June 10th, at about noon, and anchored in the North River. On this occasion the frigate remained in New York ten days, or until June 20th.—*Ibid.*, June 21, 1793. She was in command of Captain Bompard.

Prior to this visit, the "Ambuscade" had, on April 22d of the same year, conveyed the French Ambassador, Edmond Charles Genet, to New York, whence he left by land for Philadelphia, on April 23d.—*Ibid.*, April 23, 1793. On July 14, 1793, the frigate made a third visit to New York, and, on August 1st, fought an engagement with the British frigate "Boston" off Sandy Hook. An interesting account of this engagement may be found in *The Daily Advertiser* of August 2, 1793. This account was also printed, probably for quick circulation, on a handbill, the only known copy of which was recently purchased at the sale of the Jonathan Trumbull Collection by Mr. George D. Smith.

The frigate lay off New York from August 2d until October 7th, repairing the damage sustained in her encounter with the "Boston." It may be of interest to add that on October 12–13, 1798, the "Ambuscade" was captured by the British in an engagement off the Irish coast. She is described by James in his *Naval History of Great Britain*, I: 59, as a "36 gun frigate; on 1st or main deck 26 twelve-pounders; on quarter-deck 8 six-pounders and Brass carronades No. Prs. 2; on Forecastle 2 six-pounders, Brass Carronades No. Prs. 2; Total 40; Compliment 300."

For Drayton's description of the Battery, and for a discussion of the date as affected by the design of the flag, see Pl. 56.

This is the first print in which the flag-staff, likened by Washington Irving to the handle of a gigantic churn, appears. No record of its erection can be found in the *Minutes of the Common Council*, or elsewhere. In 1790, the old Fort was demolished, and a "committee for improving the Battery" was appointed, under which the old buildings were removed; an embankment of earth was constructed around the Battery to prevent the encroachment of the water, and other improvements were made. When the Fort was demolished, the flag-staff, which stood on the south-west bastion (see Sauthier's Plan of the Fort, Pl. 46 A-a), of course, disappeared, and it is altogether probable that immediately thereafter the "churn" was erected for the display of the official flag. A letter in the *New-York Commercial Advertiser* of June 30, 1831, seems to confirm this theory. The letter, which is written by an old Revolutionary army officer, contains an interesting account of the evacuation of New York by the British and of the entry of the American army.—See Chronology, November 25, 1783. In this letter the writer says: "I lived in the vicinity of the Battery and Fort, and I never knew a flag staff on the Battery, until the Corporation of New York had one put up at or after the taking down of Fort George." Under date of July 16, 1793, the *Minutes of the Common Council* contain the following entry: "Ordered that Mr Mayor Issue his Warrants on the Treasurer to pay, Joseph Griffiths for altering & improving the Flagg at the Battery £8 4 6"—*M. C. C.* (*MS.*), XI: 46. These alterations and improvements probably included changes in the flag-staff or "churn".

The earliest record of the use of the flag-staff as a refreshment-stand is contained in the *Minutes of the Common Council* under date of June 17, 1805, when the corporation permitted Mr. Keefe, keeper of the Battery, to erect a temporary shed around the flag-staff and an awning "above the stonework surrounding the same."—*Ibid.*, XV: 248. The emoluments arising from the sale of "soft drinks," etc., were evidently not inconsiderable, for, in 1808, the widow of Keefe offered to pay for the privilege of being continued keeper of the flag-staff, and it was agreed that she should pay $225 per annum, in quarterly installments.—*Ibid.*, XVIII: 299, 376-7. In 1809, Andrew J. McLoughlin had charge of the flag-staff, around which he had "at great expense" erected a pavilion. On July 31st of this year, the Superintendent of Repairs reported the flag-staff to be "in a decayed State and dangerous to the inhabitants." It was thereupon decided to repair it or to erect a new one.

At this time Castle Clinton was being erected by the United States Government, and the "churn," which stood directly in line with the causeway, was found to be an obstruction. Accordingly, on September 11th, a committee was appointed to select another site. On September 18th, the committee recommended that the flag-staff be erected "within the scite of the former Bastion neare the south point of the Battery."—*Ibid.*, XX: 305-6. It was to be "constructed in the same manner as the former flag Staff except that the columns" were "to be new & turned in such a manner as to admit of two steps so that if the Common Council should at a future period think it necessary to have it floored it may be done." The committee further reported "that in their opinion so much of the old materials as can be used to advantage be applied to the construction of the new flag Staff."—*Ibid.*, XX: 349-50. According to a paragraph in the *New-York Gazette & General Advertiser* of October 25, 1809, the new flag-staff was to be of the same dimensions, height, and circumference as the old one, but would "possess more conveniences for the Subscribers to the Spy-Glasses, as every accommodation that they could wish, will be erected. . . . "

The old flag-staff appears on the Longworth Map of 1808, but not on the Commissioners' Map of 1811, which shows the new one at the south-eastern extremity of the Battery, as well as Castle Clinton. The new flag-staff, like the old, was leased as a refreshment-stand and, as late as 1819, had a pavilion around it. See Wall's view of New York from Governor's Island (Pl. 89). This pavilion, octagonal in shape, was removed some time before August 16, 1824, as no trace of it remains in the Imbert view of the landing of General Lafayette (Pl. 94-b), or in the panoramic view in Colden's *Memorial* (1825) (Pl. 95-a); and the "churn" itself was finally removed in 1826. —*M. C. C.* (*MS*)., LVI: 248-9.

The collection of Mr. Edward W. C. Arnold contains a small vignette view of the "churn" and refreshment-stand, as well as an artist's proof copy of the same before letters. There exists also a very similar small engraved vignette, dated 1820, drawn by C. Burton and engraved by G. B. King (I.N.P.S. Collection, etc.). A similar view is reproduced in Mr. R. T. H. Halsey's *Pictures of Early New York on Dark Blue Staffordshire Pottery*, 106, which work contains also a very interesting description of the

Battery in the early nineteenth century. See also Mr. Andrews's *Iconography of the Battery.*

Engraved on copper, in 1903, by Sidney L. Smith, for the Society of Iconophiles.
Reference: Stauffer, 1387.

Plate 60-a
View of Belvedere House

Engraved on copper. $5\frac{15}{16}$ x $3\frac{1}{2}$ Date depicted: 1794.
Provenance: *The New-York Magazine; or, Literary Repository*, August, 1794.
Artist: J. Anderson.
Engraver: I. (J.) Scoles.
Owner: Charles A. Munn, Esq.
Other copies: N. Y. Public Library; N. Y. Hist. Society; Library of Congress; I.N.P.S., etc.

This view, according to the text accompanying the engraving, was taken from Long Island, over a mile distant. The house shown to the south of the Belvedere House is probably the Rutgers mansion. Belvedere House was first opened by John Avery in May, 1792.—*New-York Daily Advertiser*, May 20, 1793. Accompanying the above engraving is a description of the building of this period: "Belvedere House . . . is situated on the banks of the East river, about a quarter of a mile beyond the pavement of the eastern extremity of the city of New York [on grounds bounded by the present Montgomery, Clinton, Cherry and Monroe Streets]. It was built in the year 1792, by thirty-three gentlemen, of whom the Belvedere Club is composed. The beauty of the situation induced them to extend their plan beyond their first intentions, which were merely a couple of rooms for the use of their Club; and they erected the present building, as well to answer the purposes of a public hotel and tavern, as for their own accommodation."

The east wing of the building comprised a large room on the ground floor for public entertainment and a ball-room on the second floor; the west wing contained two dining-rooms, a bar-room, card-rooms, and bed-chambers. A bowling-green, shrubbery, and gravel walks ornamented the grounds. "The want of extensive grounds," says the writer in the article above quoted, "is, however, much compensated for by the commanding view which the situation gives of the city and adjacent country. The prospect is very varied and extensive; a great part of the city, the bay of New-York, Long-Island, the East river as far as Hell-Gate, the island of New-York to the northward of the city, and a little of the North river, with its bold and magnificent bank on the Jersey side, altogether compose a scenery which the vicinity of few great cities affords."

Mr. J. Clarence Davies owns an engraved view of the Belvedere House, $8\frac{3}{4}$ x $6\frac{1}{2}$ inches, undated, but probably belonging to about the same period as the view here reproduced.

Engraved on copper, in 1903, by Sidney L. Smith, for the Society of Iconophiles.
Reproduction: Valentine's *Manual*, 1864, opp. p. 748.
Reference: Stauffer, 2824.

PLATE 60-b

HAERLEM TOWN

Pen and ink drawing on paper. 15¾ x 12¾ Date depicted: August, 1798.
Author: Archibald Robertson.
Owner: N. Y. Public Library, No. 11262 in portfolio containing large views, maps, etc., transferred from the bound volumes of the Emmet Collection.

This view shows the Dutch church at Harlem which, according to some notes written by A. J. Robertson above the church, had a red spire and roof, the door being yellow, the cornice, pillars, and pediment white, and the walls gray.

This was the third church in Harlem, and was built in 1788 (Riker, 459), and taken down in 1825. The view is taken looking down Church Lane toward the Harlem River. The church stood between 124th and 125th Streets just west of First Avenue. See Bridges' Map (Pl. 80), Randel's Map (Pl. 86), and the Landmark Map (Vol. II, Appendix). For a brief history of the first and second Harlem churches, see Plate 39.

Two other interesting drawings by Archibald Robertson, preserved in the Emmet Collection and numbered respectively 12047 and 12048, are "In Haerlem Lane" (north-east corner Eighth Avenue and 120th Street), showing the "Kimmel Tavern," and "at Haerlem, late the Ferry House."

PLATE 61

VIEW OF THE CITY OF NEW YORK TAKEN FROM LONG ISLAND

[St. Mémin's General View]

Engraved on copper. 18¾ x 12⅞ Date depicted: 1796.
Date issued: 1796.

Artist and engraver: Charles-Balthazar-Julien Févret de Saint-Mémin.
Owner: R. T. H. Halsey, Esq.
Other copies: N. Y. Hist. Society (two copies, one coloured and one uncoloured); Harris D. Colt, Esq.; J. Clarence Davies, Esq. (imperfect). These are the only copies known.

Only known state, except the modern re-strike described below. Mr. Halsey's copy is very beautifully coloured by a contemporary hand, undoubtedly St. Mémin's. The print has been cut to, but not into, the engraved surface, and carefully mounted in the prevalent French manner of the period, with mitred bands and borders drawn by hand with a ruling-pen, the bands being washed in with a delicate blue colour. The mounting was almost certainly done by St. Mémin himself and is a beautiful piece of work. The mitres, however, are only apparent, the mount being a single sheet, although in one corner a delicate shadow has been washed in to give the appearance of a real mitre. The etiquette bearing the title has been printed separately and applied, which fact can be detected only by the use of a glass.

The N. Y. Hist. Society's collections contain a coloured impression and a plain impression, both identical with the copy here reproduced so far as the engraving is concerned, except that the uncoloured copy has the title in a single line below the rectangle. The plate-mark is about five-eighths of an inch from the rectangle all around. Both of these impressions are on old hand-laid paper, and the uncoloured copy has a large water-mark consisting of a crown above a shield with a fleur-de-lis, and the royal initials "G R," beneath which is the word "Patent." Mr. Colt's copy is exactly similar to the one just described, but not so strong an impression.

The copperplate of this engraving is still in existence, having been found in Philadelphia about 1905. It is owned by Mr. Halsey, and modern impressions from it are in circulation, about twenty-five copies having been pulled before the plate came into the present owner's possession. The re-strike is printed on soft paper about half an inch larger all around than the rectangle, so that the joint passes through the title. The paper, which is of poor quality, has taken the ink very unevenly, so as to give a rather "fuzzy" look to the print.

A careful comparison of this re-strike, of the two impressions in the Historical Society, and of Mr. Colt's copy, with Mr. Halsey's print here reproduced, and with the copperplate, brings out the fact clearly that, except for the change in the title, nothing has been done to the plate from the time when the earliest known impression was pulled down to the present day.

The signature of the artist and the date are plainly discernible on the print, in the foreground just below the second fence-post from the right (St. Mémin del. et Sculᵗ. 1796).

It will be found very interesting to compare this view with the so-called St. Mémin Panorama (Pl. 80-a). The "drawing" from which this panorama was engraved, and which is referred to in its descriptive title as belonging to J. Carson Brevoort, may have been an enlargement made by St. Mémin himself with his "physionotrace" from the view here reproduced. It seems, however, more likely that this panorama was enlarged for Mr. Brevoort, or perhaps by him, directly from the original engraved view, which was long mistaken for a drawing. This panorama was probably made between 1850 and 1860.

For the names of the important buildings in this view, see Pl. 80-a.

Engraved, in 1912, by W. M. Aikman for the Society of Iconophiles.

Reference: Stauffer, I: 231-2; II: 2735.

Plate 62

View of the City and Harbour of New York, taken from Mount Pitt, the Seat of John R. Livingston, Esqre

[St. Mémin's View from Mount Pitt]

Engraved on copper. 18⅜ x 12¾ Date depicted: 1794.
Date issued: 1796.

Artist and engraver: Charles-Balthazar-Julien Févret de Saint-Mémin.

Owner: R. T. H. Halsey, Esq.

Other copies: N. Y. Public Library; N. Y. Hist. Society; Daughters of the American Revolution, in the Van Cortlandt Mansion (print originally owned by Mrs. J. A. Glover); Harris D. Colt, Esq.; Percy R. Pyne, 2d, Esq. (recently acquired from Mrs. David A. Hengst, of Pittsburgh). These are the only copies known.

Only known state, except a proof before letters, of which an impression is owned by the N. Y. Hist. Society, and one by Mr. Harris D. Colt. Mr. Halsey's copy has been cut close to the rectangle and mounted exactly similarly to the General View, described under Pl. 61. The uncoloured impression of this view owned by the N. Y. Hist. Society has the etiquette blank but printed from the same plate. The etiquette differs slightly in form and dimensions from that used on the mounted copies. The Historical Society's copy has a two-inch margin at the bottom and one inch at the top and sides, but the plate-mark shows only at the sides, about three-quarters of an inch from the rectangle.

A careful comparison of the last-described impression with Mr. Colt's copy, which is identical with Mr. Halsey's coloured impression here reproduced, clearly establishes the fact that all are in the same state, except that on Mr. Halsey's copy the title has been added in two lines, being neatly engraved on an applied etiquette.

This comparison also shows that the uncoloured impressions are not unfinished proofs, as has sometimes been stated, but contain every line of the needle found on the coloured impressions. The apparent difference in shading is entirely a matter of applied colour, and it is very evident from the comparison that the artist intended the plates for colouring, as they are more lightly cut than would otherwise have been the case, and there is practically no shading. This is particularly true of the Mount Pitt View, some slight shading having been done with the needle on the General View (Pl. 61).

These two engravings are perhaps the most beautiful views of New York that exist. Mr. Halsey's pair, undoubtedly coloured and mounted by St. Mémin himself, are of unrivalled delicacy, freshness, transparency, and beauty. They were acquired at the auction sale of the engravings belonging to the estate of Professor Charles E. West of Brooklyn, which sale took place in New York, at the American Art Galleries, on March 27, 1901, and were thus described in the catalogue, under item 725:

> A view of the city of Montreal and the river St. Lawrence from the mountain. Engraved by John Bluck after E. Walsh. View of the city of New York taken from Long Island. View of the city and harbor of New York taken from Mount Pitt. Three pieces, one lot.

The auctioneer's catalogue used at the sale records an order from a well-known collector of $10 for the lot (!) which, however, brought $305. Although not so described in the catalogue, the views were, at the time of the sale and for some years afterwards, believed by many to be drawings. They are said to have once belonged to the collection of Mr. J. Carson Brevoort.

St. Mémin's unfinished original pencil sketch for the view from Mount Pitt is owned by the N. Y. Hist. Society, who acquired it in March, 1909, from Mr. John Anderson, Jr., who had bought it in 1901 from a book-dealer on the Paris quays. The sketch is on paper exactly similar to that used for the prints and has a water-mark identical with that found on the uncoloured impression of the General View owned by the Society, except that it lacks the word "Patent."

The view here reproduced, as the title states, is taken from Mount Pitt, the seat of John R. Livingston, Esq., which he acquired on February 3, 1792, from Morgan Lewis (*Liber Deeds*, XLVII: 376), who had purchased it on August 2, 1785, from the Commissioners of Forfeiture (*Ibid.*, XLIII: 36), after the original owner, Thomas Jones, had been attainted.

The view was evidently drawn from a point just in front of the Livingston house, perhaps from the porch. Grand Street, which, although carried through the Livingston property just in front of the house, was at this time little more than a country lane, is seen in the immediate foreground, running almost parallel with the river. The road along which the two figures in the foreground are walking is a continuation of Clinton Street; the fence in the middle distance runs along Division Street, upon which thoroughfare a coach is proceeding in a northerly direction.

The house at the extreme right, which Valentine, in the description beneath the lithographic reproduction of this view in his *Manual* for 1850, says was still in existence at that date, stood at the junction of Arundel (Clinton), Eagle (Hester), and Division Streets, and was owned by John R. Livingston as late as 1815. The roof of the Rutgers house is seen at the left of the view just under the point of Long Island. The little hamlet in the centre of the view clustered around the U. S. Navy Yard and lay between Catherine and Rutgers Streets.—See Taylor-Roberts Plan (Pl. 64). Valentine, in the descriptive title of his reproduction above referred to, notes that the house with the rail around its roof, which can be distinguished in the middle of this little group, was also standing in 1850—on Water Street east of Pike Street (originally Charlotte St.), and belonged to the estate of Isaac Claussen (Clason).

All of the above points become clear after a comparison of our view with the Taylor-Roberts Plan, the manuscript map of De Lancey's Farm, reproduced in Lamb's *History of the City of New York*, I: opp. p. 617, and the two interesting manuscript surveys of the Mount Pitt property contained among the Bancker papers in the N. Y. Public Library. A comparison with the Howdell-Canot South West View (Pl. 37) will also be found interesting.

The following notes regarding St. Mémin's life, which throw some light on the production of the two views here reproduced, are taken from *Notice historique sur la vie et les traveaux* de M. Févret de Saint-Mémin, by Ph. Guiguard, Bibliothecaire de la Ville de Dijon, MDCCCLIII, which *Notice* was read at a meeting of the Academy of Dijon on March 16, 1853, a little more than a year after St. Mémin's death. The *Notice*, which covers twenty-two pages, was issued as a brochure and is now very rare. There is a copy in the N. Y. Public Library.

Charles-Balthazar-Julien Févret de Saint-Mémin was born March 12, 1770. In 1793, accompanied by his father, he started for St. Domingo by way of Holland, England, Halifax, Quebec, Montreal, Lake Champlain, the Hudson, and New York, at which place they abandoned their idea of going to St. Domingo, having learned from refugees of the disastrous condition of affairs on that island. In New York, aided by a devoted servant who had attended them from home, they tried to gain a livelihood by cultivating a small garden, but, their means proving insufficient, St. Mémin took up drawing and mechanics. One of his earliest friends (John R. Livingston) gives the following account of his début in New York: "Mm. de St. Mémin did not delay in associating themselves intimately with my family. They had come to stay with us in a charming house, situated outside New York, dominating the town, and from which one enjoyed a superb view which on one side included the entire harbour. Charmed by the beauty of the landscape, M. de Saint Mémin made a very exact drawing of it. [As] there existed no other [on the market], we suggested to him the idea of engraving and spreading it. I introduced him myself to the public library, where he learned from the Encyclopedia the first principles of engraving. He soon made himself a master of this art. He was endowed by nature with a strong will and a trained mind; had an extraordinary aptitude for all the sciences, remarkable skill, and perseverance equal to any proof." M. de St. Mémin completed the engraving of two views of New York, which he then coloured (p. 9).

Every object and detail in these views was shown with scrupulous care, and made quite an impression. At this time he produced some etchings of public buildings for a new town which was to be called Asylum. To this period also belong his first portraits, made by means of the "physionotrace," invented by Chretien in 1786. These drawings were reduced to the required size by means of the pantograph. St. Mémin's price for a life-size portrait in black crayon on red paper, framed, a small copperplate, and 12 proof impressions, was $33.

In 1798, his mother and sister came to New York and shortly thereafter settled in Burlington, Delaware, where they established a girls' school.

There are known by St. Mémin nearly 900 pieces, of which 818 are portraits. Although specialising in portraiture, he did not neglect on his voyages to depict the most remarkable places; among them Niagara Falls, which he drew in crayon by means of the camera obscura (p. 13). He engraved also a charming little plan of the Siege of Savannah, which was published by C. Smith, New York, without date (size about 8 x 8 inches).

St. Mémin returned to France in 1810, but came back again in 1812. His eyes were now too tired to engrave, and so he took up the painting of portraits and landscapes in oil.

In October, 1814, he again returned to France with his mother and sister, where, in 1817, Louis XVIII made him a lieutenant-colonel in the army. In July of this same year, he became Director of the Dijon Museum. In 1826, he perfected his "pantographe-perspectif," which traced from a plan elevations in perspective. He remained Director of the Museum until his death, January 23, 1852, at the age of 82.

Engraved, in 1912, by W. M. Aikman for the Society of Iconophiles.

Reproduction: Valentine's *Manual*, 1850, opp. p. 98.

Reference: Stauffer: 2736.

Plate 63

Custom House New York

Aquatint. 12⅜ x 8⅞ Date depicted: Probably about 1796.
Date issued: After May 1, 1799.

Engraver: Rollinson (William).
Owner: Down Town Association.
Other copies: The original drawing for this plate was bought by the N. Y. Hist. Society at the Edwin B. Holden sale, together with a proof before all letters. The only other known copy is in the collection of Edward W. C. Arnold, Esq.

Only known state, except as above. Rollinson changed his style from line to stipple, according to Stauffer, in 1795 or 1796, at about which time this view was probably made. At all events, it seems logical to suppose that it was drawn before the Milbourne View (Pl. 66), which bears the date 1797, as this latter view shows an additional dormer-window and other slight changes which evidently were later additions. It shows also a flagged pavement west of the approach to the Custom House, which pavement apparently did not exist at the time when the Rollinson View was made. It is interesting to note that the columns and pilasters are here unfluted; whether they ever existed in this condition or not, the author has been unable to determine.

The street seems to be in process of repaving, but no records have been found of any paving between August 12, 1791, when a warrant was issued for the Corporation's part of the cost of paving in front of the Government House (*M. C. C., MS.*, X: 147), and

June 5, 1809, when an ordinance was passed for paving the street opposite the Government House (*Ibid.*, XX: 149). It is possible that the plate was made at the time of this last paving, in which case it would be necessary to explain the omission of the dormer-window, etc., as due to carelessness or disregard of details, or to their removal after the Milbourne View was drawn. This theory, it must be admitted, is strengthened by the fact that the engraving is an aquatint, which process was very little used in this country until after 1800. The engraving was evidently not *issued* until after May 1, 1799, as it was not until that date that the Government House became the Custom House. It had, for a year prior to May 1, 1799, been leased as a tavern to John Avery (see Chronology).

The building seen to the right of the Custom House probably consisted of the three houses, Nos. 4, 5, and 6 State Street. According to the directories, No. 4 was first occupied in 1794, by D. Penfield. It was, therefore, probably built in that or the preceding year. No. 5 was first occupied in 1797. On March 20th of this year this house was sold by James Watson to Elkanah Watson of Albany, for £6,000 (*Liber Deeds*, LIV: 510). The deed recites that the lot with the dwelling-house or messuage was in the occupation of Philip Livingston. No. 6 was first occupied in 1794, by James Watson (see Pl. 56). This block of houses appears very distinctly in the St. Mémin View of 1796. The house at the extreme left, on the north-east corner of Whitehall and Stone Streets, was formerly the property of Frederick Phillipse; but as he espoused the British cause, it was confiscated after the Revolution and sold by the Commissioners of Forfeiture to Isaac Hubble.

Cf. Pl. 55-b; for history of Government House, see Chronology, 1790.

Engraved on copper, in 1906, by W. M. Aikman for the Society of Iconophiles, with title: The Custom House, New York, 1799–1815.

Plate 64

A New & Accurate Plan of the City of New York in the State of New York in North America. Published in 1797.

[The Taylor-Roberts Plan]

Engraved on copper.	Map: 36¾ x 22⅞	Date depicted: 1796.
	Inset View: 6¾ x 2⅜	Date issued: 1797.

Author: B. Taylor.

Engraver: J. Roberts.

Owner: I.N.P.S.

Other copies: N. Y. Public Library, No. 11892 in portfolio containing large views, plans, maps, etc., transferred from the bound volumes of the Emmet Collection; N. Y. Hist. Society. The three copies mentioned are the only ones known to the author, although Muller, in his 1875 Catalogue, *Books on America, Early Voyages*, Part III, item 2248, describes what is probably a fourth copy.

Only known state. One of the most accurate and beautiful engraved plans of the city, and particularly interesting on account of its tiny bird's-eye views of some of the most important buildings, as well as for the clear idea which it gives of the country estates lying along the East River in the vicinity of Crown Point.

Reproduction: Valentine's *Manual*, 1853, opp. p. 324.

Reference: Stauffer, 2702.

Plate 65
New York from Long Island

Water-colour drawing. 24⅝ x 17 Date depicted: Probably late in 1796 or in 1797.

Artist: Archibald Robertson.
Owner: Columbia University, the gift of the late J. Pierpont Morgan.

This drawing is on paper with water-mark 1794. The inscription in the lower right-hand corner, illegible in the reproduction, reads: "Drawn by Archibald Robertson, my father." A note, in brackets, "Washington's Headquarters in Foreground," was probably added by the same hand. The other pencil notes are doubtless modern additions.

From the fact that the roof of the Park Theatre (begun in May, 1795, and opened in January, 1798) appears just above St. Paul's Chapel, which roof we know, from a letter of Walter Rutherfurd's, dated October 2, 1796 (see Chronology), had then only just been completed, we may safely assume the view to have been made at a somewhat later date.

A comparison with the St. Mémin General View (Pl. 61), which is dated 1796, establishes the fact that they were drawn at about the same period; although, from the fact that in the latter the Park Theatre does not appear, we can assume that there was an interval, probably of some months, between them. The buildings which rise above the general sky-line are—beginning at the south—Nos. 4, 5, and 6 State Street, Government House, Trinity Church, The Wall Street Presbyterian Church, City Hall, City Hotel, Middle Dutch Church, St. Paul's Chapel, Park Theatre, North Dutch Church, Brick Church, St. George's Church, and the Jail.

Reproduced and described here for the first time.

Plate 66
(The Government House)

Water-colour drawing on paper. 20¼ x 14¾ Date depicted: 1797.
Artist: C. Milbourne.
Owner: N. Y. Hist. Society.

This water-colour sketch was reproduced in color-lithography by Wm. Ells, and copyrighted by H. R. Robinson in 1847. The lithograph, which measures 20¼ x 13¾ inches, bears the following title and imprint: "From the original drawing by W. J. Condit—Printed in colours by Wm. Ells / Entered according to Act of Congress, in the year 1847, by H. R. Robinson, in the Clerk's office of the District Court of the Southern dist. of New York./ From an original drawing in the possession of N. Campbell Esq.—Lith. & Pub. by H. R. Robinson 142 Nassau St. New-York./ THE GOVERNMENT HOUSE./ This edifice was erected 1790, at the foot of Broad Way facing the Bowling-Green. It was originally designed for the Residence of Genl. Washington (then President of the United States), but, the Capitol being removed, he never ocupied [*sic*] it. It then became the Govenors' [*sic*] House; and was the residence of Governors George Clinton and John Jay. The building was subsequently used for the Custom-House, from the year 1799 until 1815, when it was taken down."

The note in the lower left-hand margin, "From the original drawing by W. J. Condit," may refer to the drawing on the lithographic stone, as the original water-colour bears the signature of Milbourne; or it may indicate that Milbourne painted the picture from a sketch by Condit. Were it not for the signature, we should be disposed to attribute the view to Holland, as it bears a very marked resemblance to his work, especially to his water-colour sketch of Broad Street and Federal Hall (Pl. 67). Compare particularly the drawing of the pushcart and man in the two drawings.

Besides the first state referred to above, at least four different states of the lithograph from this view are known. In the second state, the word "occupied" is correctly spelled and "Thomas N. Campbell" takes the place of N. Campbell; the lines "Printed in colours by Wm. Ells" and "From the original drawing by W. J. Condit" have been redrawn.

In the third state, the line "Printed in colours by Wm. Ells" has been erased, and the line "Lith. and Pub. by H. R. Robinson 142 Nassau St. New-York" has been replaced by "Lith. & printed in colours by C. Currier, 33, Spruce St N. Y." The Valentine *Manual* imprint has been added in this state. The plate, however, was never issued with the *Manual*, although a small reduction is found opposite page 371 in the issue for 1848. In this state the sky, which perhaps had become worn from frequent printing, seems to have been redrawn.

It is possible that still other states exist, in addition to the modern re-strike from the stone, which is now in the possession of Mr. J. S. Bradley. In this last state the inscription reads: "From the original drawing by W. J. Condit / From an original drawing in the possession of Thomas N. Campbell Esq./ (Copyright line) / The Government House / This edifice was erected . . . . when it was taken down." It will be noted that in this last state the lines "Printed in colours by Wm. Ells" and "Lith. & printed in colours by C. Currier, 33, Spruce St N. Y.", as well as the Valentine imprint, have been erased on the stone, traces of all these erasures being plainly apparent.

There is also in general circulation a lithograph somewhat less careful in execution and colouring, but so closely resembling the first state of the print described above as to have been generally accepted by collectors as a second state. A minute comparison, however, with the view in its various states, shows conclusively that it was printed from a different stone. The most conspicuous variation is in the drawing of the upright stone in the base of the building at the left, No. 1 Broadway, occupied at this time by Daniel Boardman, merchant, which stone corresponds to seven horizontal courses of brickwork on both sides, whereas, in all other states of the lithograph, this stone corresponds to eight courses on the right and six on the left side. In this connection it is of interest to note that the original water-colour has a window in the basement, the right jamb of which has been erroneously reproduced in the lithograph as the upright stone above referred to. Other variations, all of which are very slight, occur in the drawing of the cobblestones, in the addition of sills under the windows of several houses on Marketfield Street, in the beginning of a second fence-post at the extreme right of the view, and in the drawing of the push-cart man's hat in relation to the guard behind it. Furthermore, in this state, the "t" of "Delint" after "Milbourne" is lacking, and in the inscription beneath, "Pus." is incorrectly printed for "Pub." in the line beginning "Lith & Pub." Otherwise, the inscription is identical with that of the first state described above. This lithograph is found in but one state. Whether this stone was broken, by accident or otherwise, and another made, which, as above stated, is still in existence, or whether the lithograph is an unusually clever and deceptive counterfeit, it is not possible to say. The author has never seen a more accurate hand-drawn copy of any view.

For a description of the Government House, see Pl. 55 and Chronology, 1790. The iron railing surrounding the Bowling Green, seen in the view, was built in 1771 to protect the statue of King George, which had been erected in the previous year. During the Revolution the small iron balls which adorned the fence at intervals were broken off by patriotic Americans and used as cannon balls, and the fence was partly broken down. It was repaired in 1786, and is still in existence.

The house on the south-east corner of Marketfield Street and Whitehall belonged, at the time when this view was drawn, to John Lasher, "Gentleman," one of the prominent figures in the history of the city. On May 28, 1806, his son, John Bender Lasher, ship-master, sold this corner house to Charles Duryee for $8,300.—*Liber Deeds*, CV: 348.

The house next to the corner, on Whitehall, was mortgaged February 15, 1775, by Matthias Bender, cooper, to the executors of Richard Waldron for £100.—*Liber Mortgages*, V: 240. It is described as "A Messuage, tenement, or dwelling house between the houses of John Lasher on the North and the heirs of John Waters on the South." This shows Lasher's house, as well as Bender's, to have been in existence prior to 1775, but the date of their erection is not known. It is possible that both of these early houses had been demolished by Captain John Lasher and replaced by the large dwellings shown in the view. Matthew *Bendor*, of Acquacanonck, in the County of Essex, State of New Jersey, cooper, by his will dated July 27, 1779, bequeaths his lot on the Broadway adjoining John Lasher's lot on one side and Daniel Evels's lot on the other side unto his "good friend James Boggs."—*Liber Wills*, XXXVII: 159. From the fact that there is no deed of record into either Bender or Lasher, and from the further fact that John Lasher named his son John Bender Lasher, it may be inferred that the property descended from an earlier Bender, the father of Matthew Bender and Mrs. John Lasher. The house bequeathed to James Boggs was conveyed by John Bender Lasher as a dwelling-house to Jacob Levy, Jr., "Gentleman," May 20, 1806, for $9,500 (*Liber Deeds*, LXXIII: 457).

Plate 67

(A View of the Federal Hall of the City of New York)

[Broad Street and Federal Hall]

Water-colour drawing on paper. 16¾ x 11½ Date depicted: 1797.
(This date is found on the lithographic reproductions issued, respectively, by H. R. Robinson and by C. Currier.)

Artist: George Holland.
Owner: I.N.P.S.

This very important and interesting drawing is the only contemporary view which we have of the upper end of Broad Street in the eighteenth century. The view is taken looking up Broad Street to the old Federal Hall, which occupied the site now covered by the Sub-Treasury Building, corner of Wall and Nassau Streets. (For description and history of Federal Hall, see Chronology, 1788–9; see also Frontispiece to Vol. II and Addenda.) The steeple on the left is that of St. Paul's. The cupola of the First Presbyterian Church on Wall Street is also seen, appearing above the gable of the tall house on the west side of Broad Street. The little street running out from Broad Street to the west is, of course, Garden Street, now Exchange Place.

The original water-colour from which our reproduction was made has been divided into squares by fine pencil lines, evidently to facilitate the making of the lithographic reproduction. These lines may still be seen on the margins. The lithograph measures 20 x 13⅝ inches and bears the following title and imprint: "From the original drawing by George Holland—Lith. & printed in colors by H. R. Robinson, 31, Park Row, N. Y. . . . . A VIEW OF THE FEDERAL HALL OF THE CITY OF NEW YORK, / as appeared in the year 1797; with the Adjacent building thereto / Drawn expressly for D. T. Valentine's Manual." Apparently, however, this view was never issued with the *Manual*.

A later state bears the same title and inscription, except that the publisher's line has been altered to "Lith. & printed in colors by C. Currier, 33 Spruce St. N. Y." Until a few years ago the original sketch was in the possession of Messrs. Currier & Ives, successors to the old firm of C. Currier. The lithographic stone is still in existence, in the possession of Mr. J. S. Bradley. The lines "Lith. & printed in colors by C. Currier, 33 Spruce St. N. Y." and "Drawn expressly for D. T. Valentine's Manual" have been erased on the stone. The lithograph does not include the three houses shown in the drawing south of the corner house on Exchange Place.

This lithograph has been reproduced in *Early New York Houses*, by William S. Pelletreau, under the title "Broad Street in 1796," and accompanied by a list of the owners of the buildings on both sides of Broad Street. It may be of interest to supplement this list by some further notes regarding the owners of the property and the occupants of the houses, compiled from the *Libers* of Deeds and Mortgages, etc., and from the city directories of the period.

Beginning at the south-west corner of Broad and Wall Streets, we find the following names of occupants, etc.:

No. 2 Broad Street, Mary Jaffries, widow. Owned by Nathaniel McKinley, tailor, who purchased it on July 24, 1759, from Wm. Peartree Smith, for 200 pounds.—*Liber Deeds*, CCLXXIV: 210. On May 19, 1796, the heirs of McKinley sold the property to the City of New York for 800 pounds (*Ibid.*, CCLXXIV: 212-16), and, on May 1, 1832, the city disposed of the small parcel to John Glover for $17,750.—*Ibid.*, CCLXXXV 512-14. The city had bought the property "for the purpose of widening Wall Street at the South West corner of the City Hall" (*M. C. C., MS.*, XI: 379); but this proposed work was never carried out, as is shown by the fact that when the corner was sold the same dimensions were given, as well as from tax maps, etc., in the office of the Title Guarantee & Trust Co.

This building is described by Grant Thorburn (*Fifty Years' Reminiscences of New York*, etc., 1845) as having been, in 1794, "an old Dutch frame-building, the gable-end fronting the street, with five or six steps to climb up to the stoop, having a broad board on each side of the door, forming a comfortable seat for eight persons. Here John Babb kept an iron cage manufactory, wherein to confine tame birds in a free country. It was from this stoop that General Hamilton addressed the sovereign people, assembled in front of the old City-hall, in 1795, to consider on, dispose of, and discuss the merits of the famous British treaty, whose fate was then pending before Congress. . . . A large buttonwood-tree stood at the corner of Broad and Wall-streets at that time."

No. 6 Broad Street, Garret Walgrove, cooper and culler of staves. Nos. 4 and 6 were owned by George Walgrove at this period. In 1822, the records show Garret Walgrove as the owner of the property.—*Liber Deeds*, CCLXXIV: 216; *Liber Mortgages*, LVI: 274. No. 8, Anthony Latour, tavern-keeper, who also owned the building (1792–1800).—*Liber Deeds*, LII: 335; LVIII: 16. Latour evidently combined or alternated the business of hair-dresser with that of tavern-keeper, as the directories for 1794 and 1799 give his occupation as "hairdresser." No. 10, John Borris, tavern-keeper. Owned by George Douglass (1794–1827).—*Ibid.*, C: 34; CCXCIV: 253. No. 12, Wm. I. Deverix, sea captain. Also owned by George Douglass. Nos. 10 and 12 were sold in 1791 by Thomas Barrow and wife to Dr. James Tillary, Robert Lenox, James Renwick, Rev. John Mason, D. D., and ten others—all of Scotch ancestry—for the occupation of the St. Andrew's Society, which had been organised in 1756. The deed recites that the property was purchased for this purpose, and was to be held for the use of the Society.—*Ibid.*, XLVII: 515–25. This scheme, however, proving impracticable, was abandoned, and, on March 14, 1794, the property was sold by the Society to Douglass. Nos. 10 and 12 are apparently represented in the view by the stepped gable Dutch house with a tall chimney, the fifth house south of Wall Street. It is difficult to understand why these lots, which we know from the records had a combined frontage of 44.8 feet, should appear so narrow.

No. 14 Broad Street, James Bisset, "taylor"; Mrs. Douglass, school mistress; Peter Shackerly, cabinet maker. Owned by David Coutant, 1783–1824.—*Liber Deeds*, XLIV: 74; CLXXXIII: 254. No. 16, James A. Stewart, ship chandler, who also owned the property, 1793–1816. His store was at No. 84 Wall Street.—*Ibid.*, LV: 196; CXVII: 77. No. 18, Lemountis (Lemontis or LeMontes) Noe, "Gentleman," who also owned the property, 1793–1833.—*Ibid.*, XLIX: 26; CCXCVI: 604. This is probably the large house with the four iron S stays on the side. The deed shows that Noe paid £1175, which is more than was paid for any other house in the neighbourhood, and is a further proof that the large house was his. No. 20, Wm. Franks, miniature painter; Wm. Gerrard, merchant. Owned by Peter Garretson, 1793–1810.—*Ibid.*, XLIX: 26; LVII: 411; *Liber Mortgages*, XXVII: 460.

No. 22 Broad Street, John Hoes, cabinet maker. Owned by Peter Wilson, 1798–1800.—*Liber Deeds*, LVI: 301; LVII: 411. Nos. 24 and 26, Aaron Pell, coachmaker. The directory for 1796 gives Pell's address as 22 and 26 Broad Street, but this is evidently an error and intended for 24 and 26, as his address in earlier directories is No. 24 Broad Street, while in 1798 he is at No. 26 Broad Street. In 1793 Pell owned the property which, by December 30, 1797, had passed into the possession of Samuel Boyd, who, on this date, sold it to Nicholas Evertson.—*Ibid.*, LII: 302. No. 28, Wm. Carsan, grocer; in 1784 this property was owned by Mary Fletcher and continued in the possession of her heirs until 1804, when it was purchased by Joseph Winter. In 1825, it came into the possession of Jacob Lorillard.—*Ibid.*, XLI: 261-3; LXX: 508; CLXXXIX: 348.

The corner of Broad and Garden Streets was occupied in 1797 by Archibald M'Dougal. As no number is mentioned, we have no way of determining whether M'Dougal lived on the north or south corner, or whether he was on the east or west side of the street. It is probable, however, that he occupied the large house on the south-west corner of Exchange Place and Broad Street, or No. 30 Broad Street, although the directory gives only Edward Moore and Carlisle Pollock, brokers, as occupants of No. 30 Broad Street, which was owned by Thomas Stevenson. No. 32, Hannah Boughen, widow. Owned by Jeremiah Wool.

On the opposite side of Broad Street, across Wall Street from the City Hall, although it does not appear in our view, stood the watch house, at No. 1 Broad Street. This was the headquarters of James Culbertson, high constable. The property was owned by the City of New York, 1789–1816.—*Liber Deeds,* CCLXXIV: 214; CXIV: 287. This corner is now covered by the offices of J. P. Morgan & Co., Bankers. No. 3, George P. Weissenfels, conveyancer, whose house was at 81 Barclay Street; Thomas Cooper, clerk in Chancery Office; W. Temple Browne, attorney at law; and Vincent Tillou, chairmaker, who was also the owner of the property.—*Ibid.*, LXII: 172. No street number is given for this house in the deeds until 1835, when it is called No. 3 Broad Street. No. 5, Henry Burtsell, marshall. Owned by Hester Roos. The heirs of Hester Roos sold the property in 1807.—*Liber Conveyances,* CCCI: 452. It was referred to in later deeds as No. 5 Broad Street. No. 7 was owned by James A. Stewart, 1796–1812, who purchased it of Abraham Willson as Nos. 7 and 9 Broad Street.—*Ibid.*, CCLXXXVIII: 599. It was also designated as Nos. 7 and 9 in 1819. No. 9, M. Carrahan. Owned by Dr. George Anthon, who purchased it, on April 25, 1789, from Alexander Hamilton.—*Ibid.*, XLV: 501. No street number was given, but later (1819) a part of the property was referred to as No. 11 Broad Street. No. 11, George Anthon, M. D., who was also the owner. No. 13, Wm. Willcocks, counsellor at law, who also owned the property, 1794–1816.—*Ibid.*, CIII: 599; CXV: 478. No. 17, Joshua Dyett, merchant. Owned by John Walker, 1790–1799.—*Ibid.*, CCCXXI: 548; LVII: 35. No. 19, John Abrams, merchant. Owned by Elcy Smith, who owned also Nos. 21 and 23 Broad Street.—*Ibid.*, LX: 357; CXIV: 201. She was the daughter of Charles Phillips, one of the executors of John Hendricks De Bruyn, who owned property here as early as 1691. Phillips may have inherited from De Bruyn, although the records do not show this.

No. 21 was occupied by James Bryson, merchant, and by Moses Smith. If this number is the house with the figures "1698" which, as will be shown hereafter, is altogether likely, it may very well have been built by De Bruyn. This house was still standing in 1830, when it was shown by A. J. Davis in his view of Broad Street, reproduced as No. 17 in the 1831 Peabody Collection of views. No. 23, John Ellsworth, hatter. No. 25, Thomas Hardie, silk dyer. Owned by Robert Watts, 1792–1801.—*Ibid.*, CXLII: 183; LX: 357.

No. 27 (n. e. corner of Garden Street, now Exchange Place), the Widow Curtis. The "Widow Curtis" was very probably engaged in the tailoring business, as a careful inspection of the original view shows that the sign hanging below the southernmost of the three windows on the second floor bears the representation of a woman's figure. In the directory for 1797–8, the "Widow Curtis" has disappeared from No. 27 Broad Street, and Margaret Curtis, tailoress, is given at No. 61 Gold Street. In 1800, the widow Margaret Curtis, "tailor," appears at No. 4 Courtlandt Street; and there can be very little doubt that this was the same "Widow Curtis" who, in 1796, lived at No. 27 Broad Street, on the north-east corner of Garden Street. The house was owned by John McClenahan or his heirs from about 1792 to 1828.—*Ibid.*, CCXLVIII: 17; CXLII: 183. No. 29, Samuel Abbott, grocer. The directory gives this as the "corner of Garden St.", and we know from the deeds that No. 29 was at this period on the south-west corner. The house was owned by Samuel Abbott in 1797, and until 1800.—*Ibid.*, LIX: 406–8.

Working backward toward Wall Street from the corner of Garden Street, which, as we have seen, may be safely assumed to have passed just south of the last house shown in the view (No. 27), it is clear that we were right in assigning No. 21 to the stepped gable house with the date 1698. A little view of Broad Street taken from about the same point, in 1825, and reproduced in Valentine's *Manual* for 1850, erroneously shows the eastern extension of Garden Street adjoining this last house, which has evidently been confused with No. 27, which it closely resembles. It is interesting to compare the City Hall, as here shown, with Du Simitière's sketch drawn after the third story was added. (See Vol. II, Addenda).

By comparing the view with the Taylor-Roberts Map (Pl. 64), it will be seen that the bend in Broad Street, which in reality occurs south of Garden Street, is here shown to the north. This is, no doubt, the result of the artist's effort to make the view more interesting by showing the façades of the houses on the east side, which would not otherwise have been visible.

The original water-colour is reproduced and described here for the first time.

Plate 68–a

[Trinity Church]

Water-colour drawing on paper. — $20\frac{1}{4} \times 15\frac{1}{4}$ — Date depicted: 1799.

Artist: J. J. H. (John Joseph Holland).
Owner: Trinity Corporation.

The authorship and date of this drawing are established by a placard on the building at the extreme right, which bears the inscription: "J. J. H. Pt. 1799." These letters evidently stand for John Joseph Holland, who also drew the companion picture of St. Paul's Chapel (Pl. 68–b), which bears his name. Although erroneously shown too far to the south, the building in the right foreground is evidently intended to represent the north-east corner of Broadway and Wall Street. Indeed, "Wall Street" is found inscribed on this corner house in a contemporary drawing made from the same point and owned by the N. Y. Hist. Society. A very similar drawing, ascribed to Robertson, is in the author's collection.

Prior to 1775, this prominent corner, which at the period of the view was known as No. 88 Broadway, had become vested in Collin van Gelder by an unrecorded deed. —*Liber Wills*, XXIX: 62. Van Gelder had five children, one of whom was the wife of William G. Forbes. Although not specifically mentioned, this piece of property evidently descended to Mrs. Forbes, in whose estate and that of her husband it remained until 1809, when it was sold to Najah Taylor and others as No. 88 Broadway, for $10,600.—*Liber Deeds*, C: 256. The description bounds it on the south by Wall Street, on the west by Broadway, on the north by No. 90 Broadway, and on the east by No. 2 Wall Street. Very curiously, *The New-York Directory* for 1786 gives William G. Forbes, goldsmith, at No. 88 Broadway, although we know that in 1794 the numbering throughout the city was changed. In 1799 he is at No. 90 Broadway, while No. 88 is given as the address of Peter Andrews "skinner," evidently a tenant of Forbes.

On the extreme left the large house with the pediment is that of John R. Livingston, who in 1791, acquired the two lots on which it stood, one from the heirs of Collin van Gelder, *Liber Deeds*, XLVII: 360, 363, and the other from Elliston and John Perot.—*Liber Deeds*, LVIII: 397. At the time of this purchase both lots had houses on them, so that it seems a fair presumption that Livingston had the old buildings demolished and the new double house built some time shortly after 1791.—See Pl. 56. In 1798, Dr. Hosack occupied the south half of the house, No. 65 Broadway, and Livingston the north half, No. 67.

The building No. 69 Broadway was a hotel, run at this time by John Lovett who, in 1802, became proprietor of the Tontine City Hotel, erected in 1792, and shown in the view on the north-west corner of Thames Street and Broadway. Just north of Lovett's hotel are the ruins of the old Lutheran Church, at this period used as a storehouse by David and Philipp Grim. As early as 1792 David Grim, who was treasurer of the Lutheran Church, had rented the old church building for a store, paying £28 per annum. In September, 1793, the lease was renewed at £16, "he to keep the same in repair." Mr. "Cambhel" (Campbell), a school-master, applied on January 5, 1795, for a lease of the old church, promising, if granted the use of the building, to lay out £200 in repairs in order to make it fit for an academy, and to allow the free use of the church to the Lutheran congregation for divine services on Sunday and one other day in the week. At about this period subscriptions were solicited to rebuild the church, but, although £880 was subscribed, the Board lacked the courage to proceed and decided, on January 19th, to rent the church to Mr. Campbell at £60 per annum for not more than five years, on condition that he "put the Church Yard in a good fence." When, however, it was found that Mr. Campbell's plans for alterations differed materially from those first proposed, the matter was dropped. Again, in 1800, Campbell attempted to secure a lease of the old church, but it was decided, in "order to Keep the peace of the Congregation and other obvious reasons," not to rent the church to him, but that "David and Philipp Grimm the present occupiers should have and occupy the said burnt Church as a Store only they puting (*sic*) the same in decent repair for that purpose at their own expences." They were to pay $100 per annum rent for its use.

The *Lutheran Minutes*, from which the above notes were taken, contain no further reference to the rental of the old church. In the church *Journal* of 1796–1821, p. 113, under date of May, 1805, we find a reference to the sale of the ground in Broadway to Trinity Church for £6000. The old church was torn down soon after this period and upon its site, in 1806–9, was erected Grace Church, an independent Episcopal organisation, although founded by Trinity Church.

North of Trinity Church is the old Van Cortlandt mansion, sold in 1791 to Cornelius Ray.—*Liber Deeds*, XLVI: 434, 436. In the directory for 1799, Cornelius Ray, State Loan Office, is given at No. 111 Broadway. The steeple appearing above the City Hotel must be intended for that of St. Paul's Chapel, although it is drawn much too far back from Broadway.

Cf. Pls. 54-a and 81-b.

Reproduction: Valentine's *Manual*, 1861, opp. p. 696.

Plate 68-b

[St. Paul's Chapel]

Water-colour drawing on paper. 22¼ x 17¼ Date depicted: 1798.
Artist: John Joseph Holland.
Owner: Trinity Corporation.

An old manuscript label, pasted on the back of the frame and evidently transferred from the sketch, is inscribed:

"Painted by John Jos. Holland, 1798
Corner stone laid May 14th 1764
Consecrated Oct. 30th 1766."

This drawing and that of Trinity Church (Pl. 68-a) hang in the Trustees' Room of the Trinity Corporation, 187 Fulton Street. They are by the same author as Plate 67. Plate 66, the Government House, shows a marked resemblance in style and workmanship to these drawings, and were it not for the signature which it bears, we should have no hesitancy in ascribing it to the same author.

The house shown in the view on the north-west corner of Vesey Street and Broadway was the residence of Walter Rutherfurd, Esq., No. 219 Broadway. No. 221 was in 1796 occupied by Lewis A. Scott, Secretary of the State of New York. The directory for the year ending May 1, 1799, gives this number as the address of Aaron Burr and John B. Prevost. The small wooden house on the opposite corner of Chatham Row (Park Row) and Broadway was occupied at this time by Andrew Hopper, merchant; while the large building at No. 209 Broadway, on the south-west corner of Fulton Street, was occupied, according to the directory for 1799, by Sylvester Buskirk and Fred Rausch.

William Alexander Duer, in his *Reminiscences of an Old Yorker*, 38-9, gives us the following interesting account of this locality:

> At the time referred to in my former numbers [1783 and later], Broadway terminated at St. Paul's church, above which were what were called "the Fields," which are now in part enclosed within, and with much less propriety called "the Park." There were then but two brick houses at the upper end of the street opposite to the church, both of which are still remaining, and are now among the oldest in the city, viz: that occupied by the Chemical Bank, and the one next to it. There were but two also above the church; one of which was situated on the opposite corner of Vesey Street, and the other adjoining it under the same roof. They formed together a uniform building of two stories, and were erected before the war—the one by Major Walter Rutherford, the other by Colonel Axtell, both half pay officers in the British army, who married and settled in New York. The former took part in the Revolution—and continued to reside in his house many years after the war. The conduct of the latter during that period was such as to induce the confiscation of his estate, upon which his house became the property of the state, and was the official residence of Lewis A. Scott, the Secretary of the State, until the seat of Government was removed to Albany. These houses were afterwards raised a story—and are now absorbed in the Astor House.
>
> When I first remember them, there was a board on that of Mr. Rutherford's, bearing the aristocratic inscription of "Great George street," which was succeeded by another inscribed, with more republican simplicity, and with greater regard to appearances, "Road to Albany," while the opposite corner, the house of old Andrew Hopper, where the American Museum now stands, bore a similar direction for Chatham row, as the "Road to Boston."

The following extract is taken from the *Manual of the Common Council* for 1865, p. 551:

> About this time [1794] the march of private improvement began by the erection of residences of the first class on the block between Vesey street and Barclay street, which were owned and occupied by leading citizens, among whom may be named Walter Rutherfurd, Rufus King, Cornelius Roosevelt, Richard Harrison, and Abijah Hammond. The premises (then No. 221) next to the corner of Vesey street was owned by the State of New York, and was occupied in 1802 by Aaron Burr [who removed the following year to Richmond Hill], as the official residence of the Vice-President of the United States. Edward Livingston, then Mayor of the city, occupied the adjoining premises (No. 223), which were owned by John Jacob Astor.

In the Bancker Collection in the N. Y. Public Library, there is an undated survey of the west side of Broadway between Vesey and Barclay Streets, showing the owners of the property to be as follows, beginning at Vesey Street: Rutherfurd, Axtell, King, Roosevelt, and Harrison (corner Barclay). As Axtell's property was confiscated after the Revolution, the survey must have been made some time prior to 1783.

The Diary; or, Evening Register, of April 9, 1794, refers to Broadway between Trinity Church and St. Paul's as "Jarvis's Parade." It suggests that a row of trees be planted which would "look very beautiful, and cause the said Parade to be cool and pleasant for a walk in the summer mornings." A "card" in *Greenleaf's N. Y. Journal, & Patriotic Register* of December 17th, of the same year, gives an interesting description of this locality:

> It is with admiration that strangers and with most agreeable sensations that the citizens of New York must view the daily improvements of this place:—the years 1791 and 92 have compleated one of the most pleasant walks and prospects in America (perhaps in the world) and this season has nearly finished an elegant steeple, and other ornaments to St. Paul's Church, which does honor to the designer and executors: But among all these improvements the city is without a chime of bells, and numbers are not without hopes that St. Paul's is destined as the repository of so great an acquisition: So great an expence ought not to be borne by one society, but should a subscription be set on foot for the express purpose, at the Tontine Coffee House, it would be filled in one month with an adequate sum for the accomplishment of it.

It may be of interest to note that in 1797 Trinity Church brought over a "Ring of Bells" from London.

The pump shown in the view is probably that referred to in the *Minutes of the Common Council* (V: 435) under date of January 15, 1754: "Ordered that Mr Mayor Issue his Warrant to the Treasurer of this City to pay to Alderman De Peyster or his Order the sum of Eight pounds in Order to Defray the Expence of Sinking a well Opposite to Spring Garden in the West Ward of this City." In 1806 all the wells in the middle of Broadway were removed and others established at the sidewalks. This well, in its new position, is shown on Pl. 81-a.

This view has never before been reproduced except in the *Trinity Church Bicentennial Celebration* book, published by the Rev. Dr. Morgan Dix, in 1897, in commemoration of the two hundredth anniversary of the founding of the Parish. A contemporary view of the original interior of St. Paul's, dated October 30, 1766, is reproduced in the same publication.

It is interesting to compare this view with Pls. 54-b and 81-a, and with Mr. Arnold's lithograph (Vol. III, Addenda).

Plate 69

[The Tontine Coffee House]

Oil painting on canvas. 65 x 43 Date depicted: 1796–1800?.

Artist: Francis Guy.

Owner: N. Y. Hist. Society, acquired in 1907 from Miss Margaret A. Ingram, who states in a letter addressed to the Society that the picture was originally the property of her grandfather, John Salmon, a New York builder, and was finished in 1797.

According to Stiles (*A History of the City of Brooklyn*, II: 102-4), Guy came to New York from London in September, 1795, and in November, 1796, entered into a partnership with John Harmer for carrying on the business of silk dyeing, scouring, and calendering. He failed, however, to receive expected funds from England, and the partnership was dissolved. Guy then removed to Philadelphia, where he painted the picture of the Tontine Coffee House, here reproduced, which is said to have won the admiration of

President John Adams and others. It remained unsold, however, and was finally disposed of at a raffle, where it "yielded barely sufficient to pay for paints and canvas." Stiles refers to a manuscript autobiography by Guy, but this has not been found, although inquiries have been made of all of the likely repositories.

Among other paintings by Guy is one entitled "Winter Scene in Brooklyn," owned by the N. Y. Public Library; the companion picture of Brooklyn in summer belongs to the L. I. Hist. Society. Another, entitled "Brooklyn in 1816," is in the Brooklyn Institute. In 1811, an exhibition of Guy's paintings was held in Baltimore, and in 1820 a similar exhibition was held in New York. Guy died on August 12, 1820.—*The N. Y. Eve. Post*, August 14, 1820.

The Tontine Coffee House was erected in 1792–3, on the north-west corner of Wall and Water Streets, occupying in part the site of the old Merchants' Coffee House, which had been built prior to 1738.—*The N. Y. Weekly Journal*, January 30, 1737 (8). For a summary of the history of this latter building, in which took place so many events connected with the history of our city, see Chronology, 1738 (prior to). The old Merchants' Coffee House was abandoned as a tavern in 1772 and demolished in 1792 to make room for the new Tontine building. The new coffee-house was projected by five merchants who had purchased the property under the title of the Tontine Association. The building was maintained under the rules of the Association until 1834, when the restrictions governing its use as a coffee-house were removed by the Court of Chancery, and the building was leased for general business purposes. It was torn down in May, 1855. For a summary of the history of the Tontine Coffee House, see Chronology, 1792.

The building at the extreme right, on the south-east corner of Wall and Water Streets, is the Merchants' Coffee House, opened in 1772 by Mrs. Ferrara (or Ferrari). The following account of this event appeared in *The New-York Gazette; and the Weekly Mercury*, of May 4, 1772: "On Monday last [April 27] Mrs. Ferrari, removed from the old [i. e. on the north-west corner of Wall and Water Streets], and open'd the spacious elegant new Coffee-House on the opposite cross corner, where the merchants and other gentlemen of this city her usual customers, assembled in a numerous company, and were unexpectedly and genteelly regalled with arrack, punch, wine, cold ham, tongue, &c., since that the gentlemen of the two Insurance Offices, which are likewise removed from the old to the new Coffee House, have each of them with equal liberality regaled the company present: The agreeable situation, the elegance of the house, &c. had occasioned a great resort of company ever since it was open'd." This coffee-house stood until 1804 when it burned in the great fire of December 18th.

The Phoenix Coffee House was erected on the same site in 1805. From the Peabody view of Coffee House Slip, drawn probably in 1830, we know that at this time the south-east corner of Wall and Water Streets was occupied by a five-story building, differing entirely from the one shown in Guy's painting. As it is not likely that the new Phoenix Coffee House, erected in 1805, would have been so soon replaced, the evidence seems pretty conclusive that our view shows the coffee-house erected in 1772 and destroyed by fire in 1804.

The two-story wooden house in the centre of the picture, on the north-east corner of Wall and Water Streets, was owned from 1765 to 1801 by A. Kennedy, who occupied at this time the fine mansion at No. 1 Broadway. It was evidently at this period used as a furniture shop, as numerous pieces of furniture, as well as trunks, are displayed in front of the store and in the store windows.

For an interesting account of the Tontine Association, see an article by Frederick de Peyster in Valentine's *Manual* for 1852, p. 458. The lithographic view accompanying this description bears the date 1797, which must be erroneous as it depicts a period evidently later than our view. Indeed it shows conditions very similar to those depicted in the Peabody view of Coffee House Slip (*c.* 1830), already referred to.

In the N. Y. Hist. Society are preserved two elevations by David Grim of the Tontine Coffee House, on the corner of Wall and Water Streets. In these drawings the building is shown four stories high, instead of three as depicted in the painting, and has a cupola with a weather-vane in the form of a ship.

Engraved, in 1910, by W. M. Aikman, for the Society of Iconophiles, with title: "The Tontine Coffee House, Wall & Water Streets, about 1797."

Plate 70

A Plan and Regulation of the City of New-York (etc.)
[The Goerck-Mangin Plan]

Engraved on copper. 40¼ x 35⅛, including border. Date depicted: 1799.
38⅛ x 33, inside border. Date issued: 1803, November.

Authors: Casimir Th. Goerck and Joseph Fr. Mangin.

Engraver: Peter Maverick, who, under date of December 5, 1803, was granted £69 "for printing copies of the City Map" (*M. C. C., MS.*, XIV: 226).

Owner: N. Y. Hist. Society.

Other copies: N. Y. Hist. Society (second copy); Library of Congress; Henry Goldsmith, Esq. (much restored); Office of Francis W. Ford, City Surveyor (imperfect); I.N.P.S. These are the only copies known, and all have the paster attached (see below).

On December 11, 1797, the city contracted with Messrs. Goerck and Mangin, City Surveyors, for a survey and plan of all the streets of the city (*M. C. C., MS.*, XII: 273; see also Chronology). Before December of the following year Goerck died and the work was brought to completion by Mangin. On July 15, 1799, the map was ordered engraved "by Mr. Maverick or other competent persons." In the *Minutes of the Common Council*, under date of November 28, 1803, appears the following entry: "The committee, to whom was referred certain reports of the Street Commissioner on the subject of a plan for the future streets in the vicinity of the City, reported that the Map of the City lately printed and ready for sale contains many inaccuracies and designates streets which have not been agreed to by the Corporation and which it would be improper to adopt, and which might tend to lead the proprietors of Land adjacent to such streets so laid down into error." The committee resolved, therefore, to return the money paid by subscribers and to recall the map. They also requested that the Street Commissioner report to the Board at its next meeting "what shall be proper to be printed and pasted on the face of such copies of the said Map as may hereafter be sold or distributed." The paster added by order of the Common Council is as follows:

> Plan of the City of New-York, Drawn from actual survey, by Casimir Th. Goerck and Joseph Fr. Mangin, City Surveyors. This Plan shews the Wards of the City as lately altered by the Legislature, and designates with accuracy, most of the Streets, Wharves, Slips, &c., lying

to the Southward of a line beginning on the North-River, at Water-Street, thence extending through said Street to Hudson-Street, thence to Leonard-Street, thence to Broadway, from thence in a line to Bayard-Street, through this Street to Bowery-Road, thence to Bullock Street, and through this street to the East-River. Except Brannon and Spring Streets, none of the Streets to the Northward of the line above mentioned have been ceded to the Corporation, or have been approved and opened under their authority; they are therefore to be considered subject to such future arrangements as the Corporation may deem best calculated to promote the health, introduce regularity, and conduce to the convenience of the City. New York Nov. 1803.

The N. Y. Hist. Society, as noted, has two copies of this map, from one of which (here reproduced) the paster above referred to has been removed, disclosing the original title, which reads: "A Plan and Regulation of the City of New-York, made from Actual Survey by Casimir Th. Gorrek [*sic*] and Joseph F[s] Mangin, City Surveyors by order of the Common Council, and protracted by Joseph F[s] Mangin, Anno Domini 1800."

On January 3, 1804, the Common Council resolved: "That application be made to Jos. F. Mangin for the field book which by his contract he was to furnish to the Common Council with the map of the city made by him, and that he be required to insert as far as is practicable on the large map made for and furnished to the Common Council the descriptions and specifications which he contracted to do by his agreement with the Mayor, Aldermen & Commonalty on the 11th of December 1797." This perhaps refers to the original manuscript map, a search for which in the various city departments has so far proved unavailing.

The coat of arms of the city, in the medallion in the lower right corner of the plan, was no doubt designed by Mangin. It is one of the most beautiful representations of the city arms which we have, although some liberty has been taken in the treatment.

For further information regarding Mangin, see Pl. 75 and Chronology, 1800, under City Hall.

Reproduction: Valentine's *Manual*, 1856, opp. p. 338.

Plate 71

State Prison, on the Bank of the North River, New York

Engraved on copper. 11½ x 8½ Date depicted: *c.* 1797?.
Owner: N. Y. Hist. Society, purchased at the Holden sale.
No other copy known.

The view depicts the Prison as it was described by Thomas Eddy, one of the Commissioners appointed for the erection of the Prison, in his *Account of the State Prison*, published in 1801. This description may be summarised as follows:

The State Prison was begun in the summer of 1796 and finished in 1797, and stood about two miles from the City Hall. At the time of its construction it faced Greenwich Street. The length of the main building was 204 feet; from each end of this building projected a wing extending towards the river, and from these sprang two other wings in the same direction but of less extent. The building, which was of the Doric order, was two stories high above the basement, and was surmounted by a cupola. It contained fifty-four rooms for prisoners and a large room with galleries which was used as a chapel. A stone wall, twenty-three feet high along the river and fourteen feet on the land side, surrounded the prison and grounds. Two watch-houses were constructed, on the north and south sides of the building, overlooking the grounds and workshops. The entire expense of the ground, buildings, and wharf was $208,846. Eddy's book contains a plan and an elevation of the Prison, both signed by Joseph Fr Mangin, who was probably the architect.

At the time depicted by our view, the Prison stood close to the water's edge. Washington Street, which later passed close to its eastern front, had not yet been opened. The primitive appearance of the shore-front in the foreground shows that no street had been laid out along the river-bank in the neighbourhood of the Prison. It is impossible to fix the exact date of the view, which was, however, probably made shortly after the completion of the Prison in 1797. It cannot be later than 1817, as Longworth's Map for that year shows the shore filled in in front of the Prison.

The first recorded suggestion regarding the opening of West Street is found in the *Minutes of the Common Council* for June 10, 1794, in which they accept a report of the committee appointed to confer with the Corporation of Trinity Church on the subject of their petition for a grant of rights "in the soil from High to Low water mark so far into the River as to extend to the East side of a Street of Fifty feet wide which said Street is to be one hundred and sixty feet from the west side of Washington street to be continued on Condition . . . " etc. These conditions were accepted by Trinity Corporation on June 16th.—See Chronology. The opening of West Street was, however, not begun until many years later. There is no trace of it on the Taylor-Roberts Plan of 1797 (Pl. 64). The Goerck-Mangin Plan of 1800 (Pl. 70) shows the street laid out as far north as Hetty Street, but this plan is known to be inaccurate, or rather anticipatory. The Commissioners' Plan of 1811 (Pl. 80) shows it laid out to the State Prison, but it, too, is not a representation of the city as it actually was, but a proposed plan. The Commissioners' Plan shows also Washington Street laid out to and beyond the Prison, although, in *Trinity Minutes* (*MS.*), for March 13, 1811, we find a memorial addressed to the city praying for opening and regulating Washington Street from Clarkson Street to the State Prison, and for permission to enclose the east side of Washington Street from Morton Street to Christopher Street. This shows that in 1811 Washington Street was not laid out so far north as it appears on the Commissioners' Map.

No further reference has been found in the *Minutes* of the Vestry of Trinity Church to the opening of West Street, and the *Minutes of the Common Council* contain nothing more until 1828, when that portion of the street from "its northerly termination to its intersection with a continuation of the Great Kill road [Gansevoort St.]" was designated as the permanent exterior street on the North River. We know, however, from the Longworth Map of 1817, which shows the city as it actually existed at the time, that West Street was then completed between Liberty and Chambers Streets, and between Clarkson and Leroy Streets. These portions must have been opened after 1808, as they do not appear on Longworth's Map of that year. In 1830, by a Law of the State, provision was made for laying out West Street from Albany Basin to Battery Place.

In 1828–9 the prisoners were removed to Sing Sing, and in the latter year the grounds, which had been purchased of the state by the corporation of the city for $100,000, were sold at auction, divided into one hundred lots, ninety-two of which brought collectively $117,000, or nearly $1,300 per lot. The remaining eight lots were reserved by the Corporation. The buildings were not sold.—See Chronology. One of them, according to Valentine's *Manual* for 1853, p. 461, was at that time used as a brewery by Nash, Beadleson, & Co.; and a portion of one of the old buildings is supposed to be incorporated in a building in Weehawken Street, still occupied by the brewery.

Among the Philip Schuyler papers in the N. Y. Public Library is a folder containing a ground-floor plan and an elevation of the New York State Prison, together with a number of descriptive notes and estimates, dated Philadelphia, April 19, 1796, and addressed by Caleb Lowndes, the "Institutor of the Penitentiary System of Prison Discipline," to Thomas Eddy; evidently written in answer to an inquiry for information regarding prison design and administration. The plan and elevation correspond closely to those reproduced in Mr. Eddy's book and were probably the architect drawings.

There are also, in the Bancker Collection in the N. Y. Public Library (folder marked "Greenwich Village"), several sketches of the State Prison Grounds, dated 1796 and 1797.

A charming little view, taken from the south-east, is found in *A View of the New-York State Prison in the City of New-York* (etc.), New-York, 1815. This view was drawn by I. (J.) R. Smith, and engraved by Hoogland in 1814.

Reproduced and described here for the first time.

Plate 72–a

St Paul's Church & New Presbyterian Meeting New York

Water-colour drawing on paper. 11⅜ x 8¼ Date depicted: Probably 1800.
Artist: (Archibald?) Robertson.
Owner: N. Y. Hist. Society.

The new Presbyterian Meeting, or the Brick Church, as it was more commonly called, occupied the triangle bounded by Chatham Row (present Park Row), Beekman, and Nassau Streets. It was originally a part of the "Governor's Garden," later known as the "Vineyard." A "Map of the Vineyard Property," drawn by Francis Maerschalck, and dated March 2, 1759, is preserved in the N. Y. Register's Office (filed May 1, 1830, No. 153). It shows that the south line of this property intersected Broadway at the obtuse angle of the St. Paul Building, south of Ann Street. The Vineyard fence joined the fence of the Spring Garden. Its east line was Nassau Street, its west line the Highway, and its north line at about Beekman Street. Governor Kieft granted this plot to Cornelis van Tienhoven, on March 27, 1646 (*Liber GG*, 142), although it was not confirmed to the creditors and heirs of Van Tienhoven when the rest of his property was so confirmed, on October 3, 1667.—*Patents* (Albany), II: 113. Governor Dongan granted the land to John Knight, Feb. 10, 1685.—*Patents* (Albany), V: 297. Knight re-conveyed to Dongan by deed of March 9, 1685—*Liber Deeds* (Albany), IX: 387. Thomas Dongan conveyed to Thomas White, July 13, 1762.—*Ibid.*, XVI: 207. Valentine (*Manual*, 1860, p. 543) says:

> Before Governor Dongan granted his charter to the city, in 1686, by which all the "waste, vacant and unpatented lands," on the island, were vested in the Corporation; he appropriated this piece to himself, built a cottage upon it, and laid out the ground in a handsome manner, as a garden, which was subsequently, for many years, called the Governor's Garden. It embraced about two acres of land. After the governor's departure to his native Ireland (where he afterwards became Earl of Limerick), his garden was a pleasure resort, commonly called the Vineyard. His kinsman, Thomas Dongan, of London, subsequently exercised control of this property, which, in 1762, was sold to Thomas White, a wealthy Englishman, then lately become a resident of this city. In 1773, a lot on the present line of Ann Street, where it comes into Broadway, 49 feet front, 81 feet on Ann street (a triangular piece), was sold by White to Hopper for £238.

Dongan had mortgaged this property, as well as Whitehall, in 1697, for £296. It is thus described in the mortgage (*Liber Deeds*, N. Y. Co., XXI: 290): "North side of ye said citty adjoining the Commons: of ye land called ye Vyneyard, for 14 years from May 1st next thence at 1 Pepper corn at ye feast of St. Michael the Archangel." This is a mortgage recorded in a liber of deeds. The date, April 22, 1697, is perhaps the first time that the name "Vineyard" is used. (The old form of mortgage was practically a deed in trust, subject to redemption.)

The church was built on this site in 1766–8, and the steeple was added in 1793. The building was torn down in 1856. A photograph, showing it in process of demolition, is in the author's collection. In 1858, the congregation removed to the present edifice on the north-west corner of Fifth Avenue and 37th Street. The date depicted is probably 1800, as this date can be definitely assigned to the companion picture by the same artist (Pl. 72-b). See also Chronology, 1766.

The steeple seen on the left is that of Trinity Church. The pediment of the Park Theatre can just be discerned to the right of the Brick Church. The large house across Vesey Street from St. Paul's was at this time the residence of Walter Rutherfurd (see Pl. 54-b).

There is in the Bancker Collection in the N. Y. Public Library, a "Plan of Mrs. Ann Whites Estate Known by the Name of the Vineyard," drawn by James Willson, January, 1795, and copied by "E. B." in 1797.

This view is reproduced in the *Manual* for 1856, opp. p. 109, where the drawing is erroneously ascribed to David Grim.

Plate 72–b

Two Banks & Insurance Office Wall Street, New York

Original water-colour drawing on paper. 11⅜ x 8¼ Date depicted: 1800.
Artist: (Archibald?) Robertson.
Owner: N. Y. Hist. Society.

The three buildings here shown are the New York and the United States Banks, and the New York Insurance Company, the first of which stood on the north-east corner of Wall and William Streets. In the directory for 1800 the three institutions appear for the first time together, at the following addresses:

Bank of New York, 32 Wall Street.
New York Insurance Co., 34 Wall Street.
Bank of United States, Branch, 38 Wall Street.

In the directory for 1801, No. 34 Wall Street is given as the residence of Chas. McEvers, Junr. Prior to 1799 it was occupied by John Lamb.

The Bancker papers in the N. Y. Public Library include certain information regarding the interior arrangements and dimensions of these buildings. The *Manual of the Common Council* for 1856, opp. p. 72, contains a lithographic reproduction of this view with the title: "New York & City Banks and the McEvers Mansion, Wall Street in 1800. The Residence of Gen. Knyphausen during the Revolution."

The N. Y. Hist. Society has an interesting water-colour drawing of "Wall St. & Old-Town Hall" by Robertson (1798), exactly similar in form, size, and execution to the drawing here reproduced, and much resembling the Tiebout View (Pl. 57), although evidently somewhat later.

Reproduction: Valentine's *Manual*, 1866, p. 549.

PLATE 73

NEW YORK FROM HOBUCK FERRY HOUSE NEW JERSEY

[The Robertson-Jukes View]

Aquatint, coloured. 17⅞ x 12⅞ Date depicted: June, 1796.
Date issued: 1800.

Artist: Alexander Robertson.

Engraver: Francis Jukes.

Published, London, March 31, 1800, by F. Jukes, No. 10 Howland Street, and by Al Robertson, Columbian Academy, Liberty Street, New York. This print was originally issued as one of a set of four American views. Only one complete set of these charming prints is known, and is in the author's collection. The other three views are of Mount Vernon, Passaic Falls, and Hudson River near West Point. In the New York view belonging to this set (not the one here reproduced), a number of houses have been added in the city, but only in water-colour, after the print was pulled.

Owner: I.N.P.S.

Other copies: N. Y. Public Library (Emmet Collection, No. 11169); N. Y. Hist. Society, etc.

Only known state. A rare and very beautiful view.

Miss Greatorex, in *Old New York from the Battery to Bloomingdale*, I: 24, reproduces the original sketch from which this view was made, which, as stated in the text written by M. Despard, was at the time (1875) in the possession of Dr. Thomas Addis Emmet—who still owns it. From M. Despard's description, it appears that the house in the left middle distance was the Van Boskerck farmhouse, which was probably the first summer home of Mr. Robertson after his arrival from England. A comparison of the print here reproduced with the original sketch shows the two to be different in several particulars. The house in the original bears the date 1772, and near it stands a coach or covered wagon. There is no tree on the right of the picture, no figures appear in the foreground, and the inscription reads: "New York from Hobuck N. Jersey shore. Archibald Robertson. June '96."

PLATE 74

NEW YORK FROM LONG ISLAND

[The Rollinson View]

Aquatint. 19⅞ x 13½ Date depicted: Probably 1800.
Date issued: February 14, 1801.

Artist: John Wood.

Engraver: W. Rollinson.

Owner: N. Y. Hist. Society.

Other copies: The only other copies known to the author are the Holden copy, now belonging to Mr. Robert Goelet, which is in colour, and bears a small collector's stamp with the initials "E. W. W." (Edward W. West); one in the collection of R. T. H. Halsey, Esq.; one belonging to Anos F. Eno, Esq.; one owned by Percy R. Pyne, 2d, Esq.; and one in the collection of Edward W. C.

Arnold, Esq. Mr. Goelet's copy is exquisitely coloured and in wonderful condition. It is one of the most beautiful prints of old New York.

Only known state. The original wash sketch by John Wood was purchased by the N. Y. Hist. Society at the Holden sale.

It is not generally known that Rollinson engraved a Plan of Washington, which was published, in 1795, by I. Reid, L. Wayland, and C. Smith.—Stauffer, II: 2724. This was probably the first plan of Washington engraved in New York.

Reference: Stauffer, II: 2723.

Plate 75

[Front Elevation, Cross Section, and Plan of the City Hall]

Pen and ink drawings on paper.	a–37 x 16½ b–25⅝ x 16½	Date depicted: 1802.
	c–36 x 22½	Probably 1803.

Provenance: From a collection of drawings left by John McComb, and inherited by his granddaughter, Mrs. Edward S. Wilde, from whom they passed into the possession of the N. Y. Hist. Society on March 1, 1898, together with McComb's Diary (dated March 10, 1803, to January 27, 1808), and his record book labelled "Orders for Marble, New City-Hall, [dated November 3, 1803, to July 10, 1807]."

There are one hundred and five drawings relating to the City Hall in this interesting collection. Ninety-five of these have been listed by Mr. Wilde in an incomplete "Index," to which should be added ten other drawings which have recently been removed from the miscellaneous McComb drawings and placed with those of the City Hall. The front elevation and cross-section here reproduced, and the rear elevation, are marked by Mr. Wilde as being the only drawings which were among the original prize designs. The others are additional drawings, made when the size of the building was reduced before the construction work began, drawings necessitated by changes in plan during construction, and large-scale working drawings and details made while the building was in course of erection. Fifteen of these City Hall drawings bear the signature of McComb, none the name of Mangin, or Mangin and McComb, who jointly won the premium offered in the competition for an acceptable design. There is, however, an erasure over McComb's signature on the drawing of the front elevation, which has been painted over, apparently with the water-colour used for the foreground, although this wash may have been a later addition. A similar erasure of the signature is found on the rear elevation and cross-section, although on these it is less evident.

In the McComb Collection there are many other drawings, which have not been indexed. Comparatively few of these are indorsed in such a way as to make it possible to identify them, either as to date or as to the location of the building; some of these, however, the author has been able to identify by careful inspection and comparison with other views or documents.

Among the most important of these miscellaneous identified drawings are:

1. *The Government House*

Plan, of which the outline corresponds exactly with the outline of the building as shown on a survey of the plot made in 1808 and now in the office of Francis W. Ford's Sons, Surveyors.

Another plan, quite different from the above.

An elevation, not at all like that of the building as executed and shown on plates 55-b and 66. These may be unsuccessful competitive drawings presented by McComb, or they may be studies that were made by him for the builders. It seems evident from the records (see Chronology, 1790) that McComb had no connection with the actual building of the Government House. The constantly reappearing statement that he was the architect is not substantiated by any record or reliable tradition known to the author. It is certain that the drawings in the McComb Collection are not the designs from which the Government House was built, although it is possible that they may have influenced the final design, especially as to plan (see description of Pl. 55-b).

2. *North Dutch Church*

Two sheets, apparently much older than most of the others in the collection.

A front elevation, indorsed "Front Elevation of the North dutch Church by John McComb."

Two drawings on one sheet, a side elevation and below it a plan, indorsed, "Plan & Side Elevation of North dutch Church by John McComb 1772." Below this date has been added "1769." These drawings were undoubtedly made by John McComb, Senior.

3. *Washington Hall*

A large collection of drawings, including a full set of plans, elevations, both "exhibition" and working drawings and details,—some loose and some bound in a folio volume.

4. *St. Paul's Chapel*

Drawing of the steeple, not by McComb.

A measured drawing of the Montgomery monument. This may have been drawn by McComb.

5. *Murray Street Church*

Ground plan, signed by McComb as architect.

Rendered elevation made in 1811. This is a careful, and in some respects an excellent example of architectural rendering. It is not signed and the building is not designated. The elevation, however, corresponds with the plan of the Murray Street Church in every particular, and the author feels no hesitancy in pronouncing it the "exhibition" drawing or original design for this church, which was completed in 1812.

Large scale details of capital and base for gallery columns.

Detail of pediment and first stage of tower.

Half of capital's for Ionic pilasters.

Details for mouldings.

Elevation of the building below pediment and plan of the front wall; two drawings on one sheet.

Another elevation; unfinished.

Still another do. do.

6. *Brick Presbyterian Church*

Plan, probably by John McComb senior or John Bessonte, who, as masons, built the church in 1767.

Plan "as altered in the year 1822 by John McComb arch. Dec. 14 1822."

A number of other drawings.

7. *St. John's Chapel*

A large collection of drawings, which, although unsigned and unnamed, evidently relate to St. John's Chapel. The collection consists of numerous studies, including many sketches and some drawings for the final design of the church as it stands to-day. Perhaps the most interesting is the set of competitive drawings, mentioned in the minutes of Trinity Church and reproduced in Vol. II, Addenda. These drawings correspond in all important points with the various early studies for the chapel and consist of a plan and three elevations, rather crudely drawn and grouped on a single sheet. It is interesting to note that, although this sheet of drawings is signed "John McComb jun Del" and was made when he was not less than forty years of age, some later hand has added, in the lower left-hand margin "Drawn by McComb when a boy, probably at age of 12 or 15." As an example of McComb's own draughtsmanship, this drawing should be compared with the beautifully executed drawings for the City Hall, which were made at approximately the same date (Pl. 75 a and b).

8. *Wall Street Presbyterian Church*
Elevation of a pseudo-Gothic church, indorsed "Wall Street."
Elevation of a pseudo-Gothic church, dated April, 1823; plan and elevation on one sheet signed by John McComb.
A letter to McComb regarding the Presbyterian Church in Wall Street, etc.

9. *Cedar Street Church*
Plan.
Elevation.
Another elevation, with steeple.

10. *Bleecker Street Presbyterian Church*
Plan.
Plan with variations from above.
Plan, "Approved on Jan. 19 1825 by the board of Trustees."
"Front View designed for the Bleecker st Church."
Sketch of ceiling.
Detail of door.

11. *St. Peter's Church*
"Front View of St. Peters Church with intended Steeple. J. McComb jun."

12. *Residence for John Coles.* State and Whitehall Streets.
Two plans on one sheet "Basement and First Story of house designed for John B. Coles Esquire. John McComb jun."
Second and third floor, with title as above; two plans on one sheet.

13. *Residence for Rufus King*
"Elevation of a House for Rufus King Esq. Stanton and McComb."
Numerous other elevations, evidently designs for city and county work, including residences, public buildings, churches, etc.

The authorship of the design of the City Hall, as presented in the prize design here shown, has been the subject of some controversy. From time to time since the laying of the corner-stone, and especially during recent years, exclusive credit as designer has been claimed sometimes for Mangin and sometimes for McComb. An effort has been made here to bring together all the available evidence of any real importance touching upon this question of authorship, and to point out a fair and just conclusion as to the amount of credit due to each.

A detailed account of the building of the City Hall is given in the Chronology, in two parts, the first (under 1800) covering the initial steps from the inception of the idea in 1800 to the laying of the corner-stone, in 1803, and the second (under 1803) covering the details of construction from the laying of corner-stone to the furnishing of the building, in 1813 and 1814. From this account the following information bearing upon this question of authorship is condensed:

On February 20, 1802, the following advertisement appeared in the *New York Daily Advertiser* and in the *American Citizen and General Advertiser:*

> The Corporation of the City of New York having it in contemplation to build a new Court House and City Hall, the undersigned, a Committee appointed for the purpose, hereby offer a premium of 350 dollars for such plan to be presented to either of the subscribers, prior to the first day of April next, as may afterwards be adopted by the board. The scite on which it is to be erected is insulated, covering an area of three hundred by two hundred feet. The plan must shew the elevation of the four facades. The interior arrangement of the building must comprize four court rooms, two large and two small, six rooms for jurors, eight for public offices, and for the common council, and appropriate rooms for the city-watch, the house-keeper in the vestibule or wings. Occasional purposes may require other apartments, which may also be designated. A calculation of the expense requisite for its construction, must accompany the plan.
>
> J. B. Prevost — Selah Strong
> J. B. Coles — Philip Brasher.
> Robt. Lenox

Besides Mangin and McComb, the names of only two of the twenty-six competitors who we know took part in the competition, have been found. In a "Communication" in the *Daily Advertiser* of October 25, 1802, the comment is made that "If originality of design has any merit, that delivered by Dr. Smith claims attention, and may be seen at the City Tavern, Lovet's Hotel," etc.; and Dunlap (*Arts of Design*, I: 403) states that Archibald Robertson, the miniature painter, "though never professionally such [an architect], has shown his skill on several occasions by plans for public buildings. He was among those who presented designs for the city hall of New York."

On October 4, 1802, "The board having proceeded to ballot for the plan of a Court House and that of Mr. Joseph F. Mangin and John McComb Junr having a large majority of votes was accordingly adopted. Ordered that the recorder be authorized to draw a Warrant on the Treasurer in favor of Mangin and McComb as a premium for their plan being the successful on [*sic*] for $350."

Announcement of the award, as published in various newspapers, states that "a variety of plans were submitted for their [the Corporation's] approbation"; that "the elevation is elegant, and does no less credit to the taste and talents of the architects, than it reflects honor on the judgement of the Corporation," and that the plans of "Messrs. Mangin and Macoube [*sic*] obtained the preference and we presume the *premium*." An advertisement in the *New-York Evening Post* for January 1, 1803, states, "A Transparancy of the Design that the Corporation have accepted for the new City Hall, painted by Messrs. Mangin & Macoube [*sic*] may be seen at the store of Aug. Lannuier, Confectioner, 100 Broadway."

On October 11, 1802, it was ordered that "a new City hall be erected conformable to the plan of Messieurs Mangin and Macomb lately adopted by this board," but on March 7th of the next year "several members of the Board . . . had a particular wish if possible that the plan of Messieurs Mangin and Macomb heretofore agreed on for the new City hall might in some degree be Curtailed in its size and form. The Committee therefrom [*sic*] in Order to satisfy themselves and the Board generally having consulted the Gentlemen who drew the said Plan . . . who gave it as their unanimous opinion the original plan and design may be carried into effect in something of a smaller scale than was at first contemplated." Among the changes proposed was one that "the projecting wings . . . may be curtailed near 20 feet and the order preserved." The committee was opposed, however, to "totally taking the said wings away" for the reason that doing so would "defeat the whole plan and would require almost an entire new one to be made and submitted for the adoption of the Common Council."

At this meeting McComb was appointed the committee's "particular agent"; neither architect nor builder, but simply to act for the committee in obtaining samples of the various materials to be used in the building and in securing estimates for its erection, etc. A week later this committee was discharged by the Common Council and a new one appointed. In spite of the wish expressed by the former committee that the Mangin and McComb plan be retained and used with slight modifications as a basis of construction, McComb, on March 16th, submitted to the new committee a "reduced Plan," embodying changes referred to at the last meeting of the former committee. It is evident that the name of Mangin did not appear on this drawing, as it had on the competitive set, McComb alone assuming responsibility for it.

At the meeting at which this drawing was presented, it was "Resolved, that the reduced Plan . . . presented by Mr. Jno McComb, Junr—be adopted," and on March

22d, McComb, quoting from the Minutes of the committee, entered in his Diary the following: "Res^d that an Architect be appointed to superintend the Building . . . Res^d That M^r Jno McComb Junr be appointed as Architect."

From the time of McComb's appointment and the adoption of his substitute drawings, the name of Mangin no longer appears in the records in any transaction relating to the City Hall. Instead, during the whole course of the work commencing at the time of the discharge of the first committee and the presentation of McComb's substitute plan, which followed, there is a very apparent indifference on the part of the Common Council, as well as by McComb, to whatever claim Mangin may have had as one of the original designers. As far as actual design is concerned, there was no evident reason for this new drawing. It seems, however, to indicate a desire on the part of McComb to put before the committee a substitute drawing, signed by himself alone, in place of the one that was identified in the *Minutes* as the "Mangin and Macomb" plan.

A second instance of this neglect is found in a resolution of the Building Committee, quoted in McComb's Diary on April 2, 1803, when it had been decided to build substantially along the lines of the Mangin and McComb plan, "That a report be made to the Corporation informing them that it would be proper to retain the length in front of the N. C. Hall agreeable to the Plan originally made by Mr J. McComb. Say 215 feet." In its report to the Common Council, however, the committee simply mentions "the original plans," without referring to McComb as their author, though it gives him credit earlier in the report for the "reduced Plan."

Again, on April 18th of the same year, when the Common Council prescribed the text for the inscription to be cut on the corner-stone, the name of Mangin was omitted and that of "John McComb Junr Architect" appeared alone. At the bottom of the page in the book of original *Minutes*, immediately following the text for the inscription (for which see Chronology), the following line has been added, evidently by a reader who resented the injustice: "*Jos. F. Mangin drew the plan which done credit to this superstructure."

The corner-stone was laid on May 26, 1803. Although it does not appear in the foundation at the present time, it is evident, from subsequent events and records, that it contained no mention of Mangin's name. In *The Daily Advertiser* of May 28, 1803, there is the following editorial, which seems to strengthen this supposition:

> A spectator of the Ceremonial of laying the foundation Stone of the New City Hall, expresses surprise and mortification at the absence of Mr. Mangin, whose plan of the Edifice was adopted in preference to every other offered to the Corporation; and asks whether it was owing to an oversight in the arrangements of the day . . ."

Again, on June 2, 1803, there appears in the *Evening Post*, at greater length, an even more significant article on the same subject, in the course of which the editor remarks, "It would be much to be lamented that in the erection of this magnificent edifice, any difference among the members of the Corporation, or any private partialities or prejudices should be permitted to obtain . . ." and suggests "that in an edifice of this magnitude and importance, it requires the constant superintendance of an architect of science." The subject is again mentioned in the same column as follows: "It is with extreme regret that we have to record a transaction so illiberal as the one which forms the subject of the following communication. We should have given it place sooner, but we wished first to make some inquiries into the correctness of the facts, and we should now have suppressed it, had we not satisfactory reasons to believe it is founded in too much truth."

The communication to which this refers, and which immediately succeeds these remarks is as follows:

For the Evening Post

Mr. Editor,

As one of the spectators of the procession of last Thursday, I had observed that the French architect, Mr. MANGIN, the real author of the plan of the New City-Hall, did not appear, and that Mr. Macomb, alone, was carrying it in ceremony. The embarrassment in his countenance, which indeed was not unbecoming, reminded me of that charming line of Virgil—

Miratur . . . novas frondes et non sua poma.

All this, however, I explained in my own way: The real author, said I, should be here; but he may be sick, or absent, and I thought no more of the matter. However, when afterwards on reading the Inscription on the corner-stone I saw that the name of the architect was not to be found among the large list of persons concerned in the planning and erection of the edifice, who are thus to be handed down to posterity, I grew a little out of humor—Now said I to myself, it is strange that the name of him who invented the plan should be the only one missing: surely this must be a mistake; the stone is large enough, and such an injustice to a man of talents can never have been designed. The modesty of Mr. Macomb himself must, I think, be put to a severe test, thus to be held up as the only projector of the edifice. Thus reasoning, I walked along, reflecting how this omission could be repaired. The stone was laid down. There was no altering the inscription. I then recollected the famous distich of Virgil, on an occasion somewhat similar, when Bathyllus, a very indifferent poet of that age, attributed to himself certain verses of the Mantuan Bard. I immediately went home and set to work, and on a strong sheet of brass I engraved the following lines, with some alterations, and contrived the next day to have it laid in the foundation of the building, not far from the corner-stone:

VII. ID. MAI. A.D. MDCCCIII.

Justis Nepotibus.

Hanc Œdem invenit Mangin, tulit alter honores.

Sic vos non vobis nidificatis aves
Sic vos non vobis mellificatis apes
Sic vos non vobis vellera fertis oves
Sic vos non vobis fertis aratra boves.

And when the resistless hand of time shall have laid low the immense fabric, our descendants, in finding the stone, will also find the brass, and thus render to the artist who planned it, the justice he had a right to expect from his contemporaries. An old Italian proverb says, *è meglio tardo chì [chè] mai.*

JUSTICE.

This communication, unsigned in any way by which its writer could be identified, would be worthless as evidence, were it not for the editor's statement that he would have suppressed it after making "some inquiries into the correctness of the facts . . . had we not satisfactory reasons to believe it is founded in too much truth."

To these direct criticisms of his conduct, and to the editorial suggestion of "private partialities or prejudices" McComb made no reply. In his Diary, under date of June 2d, he dismisses the subject without comment by an evasion of the actual point of discussion thus: "Another communication was published in the evening Post—about the Manner Mr. Mangin was treated in not having his name published as the Principal Architect." It is worth noting that the question was not that Mangin had not been given credit as "Principal Architect," but, according to "Justice," that he had been deprived of a share of the credit with McComb which he "had a right to expect from his contemporaries."

It seems perfectly clear from the records quoted that the Common Council had reason to believe Mangin was associated with McComb in the presentation of the original prize designs. It seems clear, also, that the newspapers were given to understand that the plans were by Mangin and McComb, and that upon investigation this understanding was verified by the editor of the *New-York Evening Post*, who stated that the facts contained in the "Justice" communication were "founded in too much truth." It is certain that they were still in partnership on March 7, 1803, from a statement in the *Minutes*, in which the plan of "Messieurs Mangin and McComb" is mentioned. We may infer that both were present at a meeting on this day, when certain changes in plan were discussed, from the fact that the "Gentlemen who drew the said plan" are mentioned.

In articles printed in *The American Architect* for August 12 and 19, 1908, Mr. Edward S. Wilde puts forth the claim that to McComb alone belongs exclusive credit as designer of the building, that Mangin was simply a draughtsman in his employ, that McComb's name alone appears on the prize drawings, and that "the original drawings were designed and draughted by McComb, just as the reduced ones were." In support of this he states, "It became well known at the time of the meetings of October 4 and 11, during McComb's absence, and in the absence of the Mayor, representations were made that McComb and Mangin were partners in the plan, but when it became apparent that the latter had been employed simply as a draughtsman, the Common Council very properly ignored the claim." No authority is given for this statement and a careful examination of the *Minutes of the Common Council* shows no authority for it. Neither does there appear before or after these meetings anything that could be taken to have been remotely suggestive of it.

That McComb did not *employ* Mangin as an expert draughtsman, which of course he was, is evident from the records quoted and from various newspaper accounts of the award. There is also other, though unofficial, evidence to substantiate further the author's belief that Mangin and McComb were associated as true partners in the plan.

J. Milbert, the distinguished French artist and traveller, referring to the City Hall, in 1828, wrote in his *Itineraire Pittoresque du Fleuve Hudson*, I: 27, "Mr. Mongin [*sic*] a French architect, is the author of the plan of this building, which has cost $500,000 and the erection of which was directed by an American Contractor."

When McComb died, an obituary notice in the *New York Herald* (May 27, 1853) stated, "He was also one of the architects for the City Hall and a contractor for the erection of that building." Thus we have an unbroken tradition, extending from before the laying of the corner-stone to the death of McComb, to add to the official sources of evidence, and all state most emphatically either that McComb had a partner in the design, or, like Milbert, that Mangin alone was responsible for it. From the fact that the name of Mangin in both the *Minutes* and newspapers is given priority in each instance, we may assume that he was the senior member in whatever partnership or collaboration may have existed. Whether this priority was because of Mangin's superior knowledge and experience as a designer, or from the fact that he was the original competitor and may have himself suggested the association, it is not possible to say. That the name apparently erased on the original drawing, as has already been mentioned, was before, or above that of McComb, also tends to establish Mangin's priority.

While it is not possible to assign with any amount of assurance the respective positions of the partners, it is comparatively easy to determine the part that each contributed to the design. A jury of architects, attempting to assign to each his proper share of credit, in the absence of direct documentary proof, would have to draw its conclusions from the presumptive evidence presented by all the facts involved. Most probably, in their collaboration upon the plans, Mangin and McComb each contributed that sort of advice and counsel which his talents, education, and experience best fitted him to give, and to a large extent these personal attributes of the two men are known, although much less is known of Mangin's life and work than of McComb's. It is of course possible that a further search may still reveal information bearing directly upon Mangin's part in the work, and especially in connection with the competition drawings. "Mangin Brothers, Architects, 68 Chambers Street," are mentioned in the city directories of 1796, 1797, and 1798. They were Frenchmen, and no doubt endowed with the idealism and imagination of their country. Their only known joint work was the Park Theatre (see Chronology, 1795). Joseph F. Mangin, alone, was the architect of the first St. Patrick's Cathedral (see Chronology, 1809) and of the State Prison (see Chronology, 1796–8), of which two of his early drawings, a plan and an elevation, are preserved in the Schuyler Collection in the N. Y. Public Library. He also collaborated in making, and finally finished alone, the Goerck-Mangin Plan (Pl. 70). His interest in practical problems and his ability as an engineer is shown by his interesting suggestion to the Common Council of a comprehensive and carefully worked out plan to build a "safe harbor for shipping" out of the Collect Pond, which plan the city, however, did not adopt.

A careful study and comparison of the designs and draughtsmanship of these two architects, and a close inspection of the City Hall plans, leaves little doubt that the competitive drawings for the City Hall embodied the ideas as well as the draughtsmanship of Mangin rather than of McComb. Their presentation is distinctly French; the shadows are cast in the conventional French "graded wash" manner, which was never used by McComb, and the drawing itself is superior to any drawing known to have been made by McComb. A comparison of the City Hall competitive drawings, both plan and elevation, with the sheet of drawings containing the original competitive designs for St. John's Chapel (Vol. III, Addenda), which McComb was willing to sign as "*John McComb, Jun Del*," will settle beyond a doubt the respective positions of Mangin and McComb, both as designers and as draughtsmen. To an architect, it appears self-evident that he who made the one (St. John's) could not have made the other (the City Hall).

Moreover, while it has never been questioned that the design of the City Hall is distinctly French, a study of the work known to have been designed by McComb, alone, shows that at this period he was practically unacquainted with any style of architecture other than the so-called late Colonial or Georgian in which all his work was designed.

All of the above facts make it clear, to the architectural reader at least, that Mangin deserves the greater share of credit in connection with the original designs. It is, undoubtedly, equally true, and the importance of this fact should not be minimized, that McComb collaborated in their preparation, perhaps contributing as much as Mangin to the *plans;* and that, as "architect of record," in actual charge during the entire period of construction, he developed the working drawings, made the details, and met acceptably every demand upon his artistic as well as upon his practical ability, thus establishing the right, already earned through much other important work, to be counted among the distinguished architects of our city. It is equally true that, as McComb's partner in the designing and planning of the building, though he had no connection with the actual work of construction, Mangin should be given at the present day that share of the credit which, as "Justice" wrote, "he had a right to expect from his contemporaries."

PLATE 76

THE CITY OF NEW YORK IN THE STATE OF NEW YORK NORTH AMERICA
[The Birch View with the White Horse]

Engraved on copper. 24 x 18¾ Date depicted: 1802.
Date issued: January 1, 1803.

Artist: William Birch.
Engraver: Samuel Seymour.
Published by W. Birch, Springland near Bristol, Pennsylvania.
Owner: I.N.P.S.
Other copies: Two other copies, only, of this print are known, one belonging to Robert Goelet, Esq., and one, slightly imperfect, from the Lossing Collection, sold by Anderson in 1912, and now belonging to Edward W. C. Arnold, Esq. A faithful reproduction of this view is painted on the inner surface of a large punch-bowl, presented in 1812 by General Jacob Morton to the Corporation of the City of New York. This bowl was for many years kept in the attic of the City Hall, but was removed to the "Governors' Room" after its restoration in 1908–9, and, in 1912, was deposited for safe-keeping in The Metropolitan Museum of Art.

Reference: Stauffer, II: 2884.

PLATE 77

THE CITY OF NEW YORK IN THE STATE OF NEW YORK NORTH AMERICA
[The Birch View with the Picnic Party]

Engraved on copper. 24 x 18¾ Date depicted: 1802.
Date issued: January 1, 1803.

Artist: William Birch.
Engraver: Samuel Seymour.
Published by W. Birch, Springland near Bristol, Pennsylvania.
Owner: I.N.P.S.
Other copies: N. Y. Public Library (Emmet Collection, No. 11924); N. Y. Hist. Society, etc.

Second state. This state of the print has the same title and date as the first state. It has, however, numerous variations and was probably issued some months later. The principal changes are the addition of three trees in the foreground and of a group of trees which conceal the dock on the Long Island shore, and the substitution of a picnic party of four persons for the white horse. There are also some changes in the city itself. The Middle Dutch Church in Nassau Street has been considerably raised, and the spire of St. George's Church in Beekman Street redrawn. A new tower appears above and beyond the roof of the Park Theatre. This may be the cupola of Columbia College, or more likely still, that of St. Peter's Roman Catholic Church on Barclay Street, which was built in 1785–6, and which in 1819 had a cupola, as we know from the Wall View of that date (Pl. 89), as well as from the two Wall Views of 1823 (Pls. 92 and 93). Just when this cupola, which does not appear in the views before 1800, was added, it has not proved possible to determine, but from the fact that it does not appear on the first state of the Birch View and does on the second, issued presumably later in the same year, it seems likely that it was built in 1803.

A third state exists, similar to the above, but with the imprint of Wm. H. Morgan, 100 Arch Street (Philadelphia). In this form the plate was reissued, probably about 1820. The three impressions are without doubt from the same plate. For names of the important buildings, see Pl. 80-a.

Plate 78

[The "Clermont" on the Hudson River]

Lithograph. 12⅝ x 8½ Date depicted: *c.* 1810.
Date issued: Probably about 1820.

Artist: Charles-Balthazar-Julien Févret de Saint-Mémin.
Publisher: F. Berthaux, Dijon.
Owner: R. T. H. Halsey, Esq.
Other copies: An impression similar to the one here reproduced except that it bears in the right lower corner the inscription, "Dessiné sur pierre de Dijon," is owned by the author. No other copy is known.

This interesting early lithograph probably represents the "Clermont" shortly after she was lengthened, in 1807-8, although this cannot be stated with positiveness; nor can it be definitely asserted that the drawing is by St. Mémin, although it bears his initials and was published at Dijon, St. Mémin's home in his later years. Both assumptions, however, seem reasonably certain. It will be noticed that the ship shows side, or lee-boards which, while prevalent in American waters, were very little if at all used in Europe at this period, no foreign prints of early steamships which the author has examined showing them. Furthermore, the flag on the foremast, although not entirely distinct, certainly suggests the stars and stripes. Mr. R. T. H. Halsey and the late Mr. Edwin B. Holden believed the lithograph to have been prepared from a drawing made in America by St. Mémin, and published in France.

It is possible that the hill seen in the background is the wooded knoll at the northern extremity of Manhattan Island, now known as Inwood, in which case the "Clermont" would be just emerging from the Harlem into the Hudson River, and the fort seen at the top of the hill would be Cock Hill Fort. *Cf.* Randel's Map of Farms (Pl. 86). It is, however, more likely that this hill is intended to represent West Point.[1]

It is strange that no authentic contemporary representation of the "Clermont," or, as the boat was first called, the "North River Steamboat of Clermont," is known to

[1] Since writing the above description, a copy of the print has come to light (now in Mr. Pyne's collection) with the following title: "A View of West-Point on the River Hudson, with the Steam-boat, invented by M. Fulton going up from New-York to Albany [Title also in French] Vue de West-Point sur la Rivière d'Hudson, et du Bateau-à-Vapeur, inventè par M. Fulton remontant de New-York à Albany." l. l.: "Lithographie de F. Berthaux à Dijon." l. r.: Dessiné sur pierre de Dijon."

From a comparison of this impression with the others, it seems clear that the copy here reproduced is an artist's trial proof in the earliest state, that the copy in the author's collection is a later trial proof, and that Mr. Pyne's copy is an impression from the completed plate. This last copy is in colours and, so far as known, is unique. The United States flag is very clearly drawn in Mr. Pyne's copy.

exist. That such a drawing was made by Fulton is almost certain. The boat was built by Charles Browne, whose ship-yard lay at Corlear's Hook, and was given a preliminary trial on Sunday, August 9, 1807. On August 17th, the public trial trip was made with about forty guests on board. In a letter written by Fulton to Joel Barlow (*The Livingstons of Callendar*, by E. B. Livingston), he describes the journey to Albany. It took thirty-two hours going, and thirty returning. In the winter of 1807–8 the "Clermont" was virtually rebuilt, and for several years was used as a regular passenger-boat on the Hudson. What disposition was finally made of the boat is unknown. For further information regarding the "Clermont," see Chronology, 1807, August 9.

The print here reproduced was consulted by the board having in charge the design for the replica of the "Clermont" built for the Hudson-Fulton Celebration. A steam-boat which may be the "Clermont," is shown in the membership certificate of the General Society of Mechanics and Tradesmen. This certificate, which also shows the Mechanics School and Apprentices' Library, erected in 1821, was drawn by Charles Canda, who received therefor from the Society the sum of $75, on December 4, 1822. It was engraved by B. Tanner, who, on January 14, 1822, received, on account, the sum of $200.

Reproduced and described here for the first time.

Plate 79

A Map of the City of New York by the Commissioners appointed by an act of the Legislature passed. April 3RD 1807

[The Randel Survey, or the Commissioners' Map]

Pen and ink drawing on paper. 106 x 30 7/8 Date depicted: 1811.

(The width is measured between the outer border lines. At the upper or northern end of the map this border has been cut away and the paper bound with pink tape. The measurement of the length has been taken to the edge of this binding.)

Author: John Randel, Jr.

Owner: City of New York, filed in office of the Commissioner of Public Works (Manhattan), Bureau of Design and Survey.

The original survey was made in accordance with the provisions of "An Act relative to Improvements, touching the laying out of Streets and Roads in the City of New-York, and for other purposes," passed April 3, 1807. The map here reproduced is one of three original manuscript drafts authorised by the Act, and was signed by the Commissioners, Governeur Morris, Simeon De Witt, and John Rutherford, on March 22, 1811; acknowledged by Morris and Rutherford before Ben Ledyard, Master in Chancery, on March 29th, and by De Witt before Mayor De Witt Clinton on May 4th. It was filed April 1, 1811, with J. Morton, clerk of the Common Council. The signature and seal of De Witt were witnessed by Archd. Campbell and John Randel, Jun.; and those of Morris and Rutherford by John Randel, Jun. One of the original manuscript maps was filed, as the Act required, in the office of the Secretary of State at Albany, where it still remains; one in the office of the Clerk of the City and County of New

York, now in the record-room of the Clerk of the County of New York (Room 3, 8th floor, of the Hall of Records); and the third (the one here reproduced), which the Act provided was to belong to the Mayor, Aldermen and Commonalty of the City of New York, is now preserved in the Bureau of Design and Survey, which forms a part of the Department of the Commissioner of Public Works, in the new Municipal Building. It is interesting to note that the certificate of filing inscribed on the map in the County Clerk's office bears the date of March 30th, two days prior to the filing of the one here reproduced. This certificate is as follows: "Filed by John Randel, Junior March 30, 1811." The map in the Secretary of State's office, on the other hand, was filed two days later than the one here reproduced, namely on April 2d. This certificate reads: "Filed by the Surveyor General April 2nd 1811 Anthony Lamb Dep. Secretary." Also, it is to be noted that, on the last named map, Simeon De Witt made his acknowledgment before De Witt Clinton on April 2d, instead of on April 4th, as on the other two.

The Commissioners' Plan and the accompanying report were duly approved, and all subsequent developments on the island have been carried out in substantial accord therewith so that this plan may be regarded as marking the end of Old New York and the beginning of the Modern City.

The original Act appointed Governeur Morris, Simeon De Witt, and John Rutherford Commissioners of Streets and Roads in the City of New York for a period of four years, with

> exclusive power to lay out streets, roads and public squares, of such width, extent, and direction, as to them shall seem most conducive to public good, and to shut up, or direct to be shut up, any streets or parts thereof which have been heretofore laid out, and not accepted by the Common Council of the said City, within that part of the said City of New-York to the northward of a line commencing at the wharf of George Clinton, on Hudson River, thence running through Fitzroy-road, Greenwich-lane and Art-street, to the Bowery-road; thence down the Bowery-road, to North-street; thence through North-street, in its present direction, to the East River: and no square or plot of ground, made by the intersection of any streets, to be laid out by the said Commissioners, shall ever, after the streets around the same shall be opened, be or remain divided by any public or open lane, alley, street or thoroughfare.

The Act further provided, in Section IX, that after the Commissioners had estimated the damage which owners would suffer by relinquishing their lands for the purposes of the Act, and had also considered the cases where the benefit would exceed the value of the land required, they should estimate and determine such damage or benefit and report the amount to the Supreme Court without delay; after which it was provided that the Mayor, Aldermen and Commonalty of the City of New York should proceed to assess the same in the manner directed by Section XI of the Act entitled "An Act for regulating the buildings, streets, wharves, and slips in the City of New-York," which had passed the Legislature on April 3, 1801. This provision of the Act was, however, considerably modified in 1812.

The Commissioners' remarks or report, in manuscript, also issued in triplicate, and accompanying each copy of the survey, throw much interesting light upon the motives which actuated them in determining upon the plan which was for all time to fix the general street system on the Island of Manhattan. This report together with the Act of April 3, 1807, and a list of references to the public buildings, churches, chapels, places of amusement, principal manufactories, etc., was printed (with some slight modifications), in 1811, in a fifty-four page pamphlet accompanying the so-called Bridges Map, which map is shown and described as Pl. 80 in the ICONOGRAPHY, Vol. III.

In this printed report (copy in N. Y. Public Library; N. Y. Hist. Society; I. N. P. S. Coll., etc.), the Commissioners state:

That one of the first objects which claimed their attention, was the form and manner in which the business should be conducted; that is to say, whether they should confine themselves to rectilinear and rectangular streets, or whether they should adopt some of those supposed improvements, by circles, ovals, and stars, which certainly embellish a plan, whatever may be their effects as to convenience and utility. In considering that subject, they could not but bear in mind that a city is to be composed principally of the habitations of men, and that strait sided, and right angled houses are the most cheap to build, and the most convenient to live in. The effect of these plain and simple reflections was decisive.

Having determined therefore, that the work should in general be rectangular, a second, and, in their opinion, an important consideration, was so to amalgamate it with the plans already adopted by individuals as not to make any important change in their dispositions. This, if it could have been effected, consistently with the public interest, was desirable, not only as it might render the work more generally acceptable, but also as it might be the means of avoiding the expense. It was therefore a favourite object with the Commissioners, and pursued until after various unfruitful attempts had proved the extreme difficulty; nor was it abandoned at last but from necessity. To show the obstacles which frustrated every effort, can be of no use. It will, perhaps, be more satisfactory to each person who may feel aggrieved, to ask himself, whether his sensations would not have been still more unpleasant, had his favourite plans been sacrificed to preserve those of a more fortunate neighbour?

If it should be asked, why was the present plan adopted in preference to any other? the answer is, because, after taking all circumstances into consideration, it appeared to be the best; or, in other and more proper terms, attended with the least inconvenience.

It may, to many, be matter of surprise, that so few vacant spaces have been left, and those so small, for the benefit of fresh air, and consequent preservation of health. Certainly, if the City of New-York were destined to stand on the side of a small stream, such as the Seine or the Thames, a great number of ample places might be needful; but those large arms of the sea which embrace Manhattan Island, render its situation, in regard to health and pleasure, as well as to convenience of commerce, peculiarly felicitous; when, therefore, from the same causes, the price of land is so uncommonly great, it seemed proper to admit the principles of economy to greater influence than might, under circumstances of a different kind, have consisted with the dictates of prudence and the sense of duty.

It appeared proper, nevertheless, to select and set apart, on an elevated position, a space sufficient for a large Reservoir, when it shall be found needful to furnish the City, by means of aqueducts, or by the aid of hydraulic machinery, with a copious supply of pure and wholesome *water*. In the meantime, and indeed afterwards, the same place may be consecrated to the purposes of science, when public spirit shall dictate the building of an Observatory.

It did not appear proper, only it was felt to be indispensable, that a much larger space should be set apart for Military Exercise, as also to assemble, in case of need, the force destined to defend the City. The question, therefore, was not, and could not be, whether there should be a *Grand Parade*, but where it should be placed, and what should be its size. And here again it is to be lamented, that in this late day the Parade could not be brought further south, and made larger than it is, without incurring a frightful expense.

The spot nearest to that part of the City already built, which could be selected with any regard to economy, is at the foot of those heights called Inklangberk, in the vicinity of Kip's Bay. That it is too remote and too small, shall not be denied; but it is presumed, that those who may be inclined to criticism on that score, may feel somewhat mollified, when the Collector shall call for their proportion of the large and immediate tax which even this small and remote Parade will require.

Another large space, almost as necessary as the last, is that, which in no distant period will be required for a *Public Market*. . . .

To some it may be matter of surprise, that the whole Island has not been laid out as a City; to others, it may be a subject of merriment, that the Commissioners have provided space for a greater population than is collected at any spot on this side of China. They have in this respect been governed by the shape of the ground. It is not improbable that considerable numbers may be collected at Haerlem, before the high hills to the southward of it shall be built upon as a City; and it is improbable, that (for centuries to come) the grounds north of Haerlem Flat will be covered with houses. To have come short of the extent laid out, might therefore have defeated just expectation, and to have gone further, might have furnished materials to the pernicious spirit of speculation.—See Chronology 1811, April 1.

The mile-stones—fourteen in number—are shown on this map (see also Randel's Map of the Farms, Pl. 86). The early mile-stones which started from the Federal Hall at the head of Broad Street are shown on Christopher Colles's Map of Broadway, the Bowery Road, Kingsbridge, etc., published in 1789 in *A Survey of the Roads of the United States of America*, which map also shows the principal public buildings and residences adjacent to this route.

It will be found interesting, in connection with the pamphlet issued with the Bridges Map, and quoted above, to refer to the report by John Randel, Jr., who acted as secretary, surveyor and chief engineer to the Commission of 1807, "superintending and aiding in the surveys and maps of the assistants employed by them," which report was printed in full in Valentine's *Manual* for 1864 (pp. 846–56), and is quoted in part in the Chronology under 1821.

In this latter year Randel published an interesting map, engraved by P. Maverick, of the territory now known as Greater New York. There is a copy of this map, which has become very scarce, in the N. Y. Hist. Society and one in the author's collection. A copy printed on satin was recently offered for sale in New York by a nephew of John Randel. A still more important map by Randel has hitherto been known only through an advertisement in the *New York Evening Post* for April 8, 1814, which announces: "Randel's Map of Manhattan Island, is now exhibited for inspection at the Bookstore of Messrs. Eastburn, Kirk & Co. Wall-street, . . . This Map will show the exact position of each dwelling house, and the size in feet and parts of a foot of every block north of North-street, and Greenwich-Lane, which are not contained in the Map published by Mr. Bridges—Also, the latitude, together with the longitude of places from the City Hall. It will be ready for delivery about December next." Recently, a copy of this map, which was published in 1814, has been found in the Collections of the N. Y. Hist. Society. It will be found reproduced in the Addenda, Vol. III. See also Pl. 86.

Reproduced here for the first time.

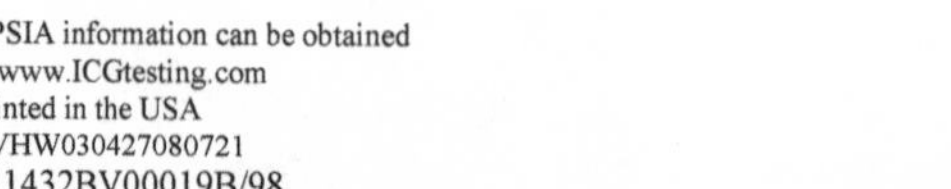

CPSIA information can be obtained
at www.ICGtesting.com
Printed in the USA
BVHW030427080721
611432BV00019B/98

9 789354 484582